An Introduction to German Law and Legal Culture

An Introduction to German Law and Legal Culture offers students, comparative law scholars, and practitioners an insightful and innovative survey of the German legal system. While recognizing the significant influence of the Civil Law tradition in German law, the book also considers the role of other legal traditions – Common Law, Socialist Law, Islamic Law, Adversarial Law, European Law – that are woven into the varied and colorful fabric of the German legal culture. The book provides an informed yet accessible introduction to the foundations of German law as well as to the theory and doctrine of some of the most relevant fields of law: Private Law, Constitutional Law, Administrative Law, Criminal Law, Procedural Law, and European Law. It is an engaging and pluralistic portrayal of one of the world's most interesting, important, and frequently modelled legal systems.

Russell A. Miller is the J. B. Stombock Professor of Law at Washington and Lee University. He was the Head of the Max Planck Law Network from 2020 to 2022. He is a respected scholar and teacher of comparative law, with an emphasis on German constitutional law. He is a two-time recipient of a Fulbright Senior Research Fellowship and, in 2021, he was awarded an Alexander von Humboldt Foundation Research Prize for his scholarly work on German law. He is the coauthor of *The Constitutional Jurisprudence of the Federal Republic of Germany* (Duke University Press, 3rd ed., 2012). In 2002 he graduated with a LL.M. from the University of Frankfurt. From 2000 to 2002 he was a judicial clerk (*wissenschaftlicher Mitarbeiter*) at the German Federal Constitutional Court. He is the cofounder and long-serving editor of the *German Law Journal*.

Law in Context

Series editors
Professor Kenneth Armstrong
University of Cambridge
Professor Maksymilian Del Mar
Queen Mary, University of London
Professor Sally Sheldon
University of Bristol and University of Technology Sydney

Editorial advisory board
Professor Bronwen Morgan
University of New South Wales
Emeritus Professor William Twining
University College London

Since 1970, the Law in Context series has been at the forefront of a movement to broaden the study of law. The series is a vehicle for the publication of innovative monographs and texts that treat law and legal phenomena critically in their cultural, social, political, technological, environmental and economic contexts. A contextual approach involves treating legal subjects broadly, using materials from other humanities and social sciences, and from any other discipline that helps to explain the operation in practice of the particular legal field or legal phenomena under investigation. It is intended that this orientation is at once more stimulating and more revealing than the bare exposition of legal rules. The series includes original research monographs, coursebooks and textbooks that foreground contextual approaches and methods. The series includes and welcomes books on the study of law in all its contexts, including domestic legal systems, European and international law, transnational and global legal processes, and comparative law.

Books in the Series
Acosta: *The National versus the Foreigner in South America: 200 Years of Migration and Citizenship Law*
Alaattinoğlu: *Grievance Formation, Rights and Remedies*
Ali: *Modern Challenges to Islamic Law*
Alyagon Darr: *Plausible Crime Stories: The Legal History of Sexual Offences in Mandate Palestine*
Anderson, Schum & Twining: *Analysis of Evidence, 2nd Edition*
Ashworth: *Sentencing and Criminal Justice, 6th Edition*
Barton & Douglas: *Law and Parenthood*
Baxi, McCrudden & Paliwala: *Law's Ethical, Global and Theoretical Contexts: Essays in Honour of William Twining*
Beecher-Monas: *Evaluating Scientific Evidence: An Interdisciplinary Framework for Intellectual Due Process*
Bell: *French Legal Cultures*
Bercusson: *European Labour Law, 2nd Edition*

Birkinshaw: *European Public Law*
Birkinshaw: *Freedom of Information: The Law, the Practice and the Ideal, 4th Edition*
Blick: *Electrified Democracy: The Internet and the United Kingdom Parliament in History*
Broderick & Ferri: *International and European Disability Law and Policy: Text, Cases and Materials*
Brownsword & Goodwin: *Law and the Technologies of the Twenty-First Century: Text and Materials*
Cane & Goudkamp: *Atiyah's Accidents, Compensation and the Law, 9th Edition*
Clarke: *Principles of Property Law*
Clarke & Kohler: *Property Law: Commentary and Materials*
Collins: *The Law of Contract, 4th Edition*
Collins, Ewing & McColgan: *Labour Law, 2nd Edition*
Cowan: *Housing Law and Policy*
Cranston: *Making Commercial Law Through Practice 1830–1970*
Cranston: *Legal Foundations of the Welfare State*
Darian-Smith: *Laws and Societies in Global Contexts: Contemporary Approaches*
Dauvergne: *Making People Illegal: What Globalisation Means for Immigration and Law*
David: *Kinship, Law and Politics: An Anatomy of Belonging*
Davies: *Perspectives on Labour Law, 2nd Edition*
Dembour: *Who Believes in Human Rights?: Reflections on the European Convention*
de Sousa Santos: *Toward a New Legal Common Sense: Law, Globalization, and Emancipation*
Diduck: *Law's Families*
Douglas-Scott: *Brexit, Union, and Disunion: The Evolution of British Constitutional Unsettlement*
Dowdle: *Transnational Law: A Framework for Analysis*
Dupret: *Positive Law from the Muslim World: Jurisprudence, History, Practices*
Emon: *Jurisdictional Exceptionalisms: Islamic Law, International Law, and Parental Child Abduction*
Estella: *Legal Foundations of EU Economic Governance*
Fortin: *Children's Rights and the Developing Law, 3rd Edition*
Garnsey: *The Justice of Visual Art: Creative State-Building in Times of Political Transition*
Garton, Probert & Bean: *Moffat's Trusts Law: Text and Materials, 7th Edition*
Ghai & Woodman: *Practising Self-Government: A Comparative Study of Autonomous Regions*
Glover-Thomas: *Reconstructing Mental Health Law and Policy*
Gobert & Punch: *Rethinking Corporate Crime*
Goldman: *Globalisation and the Western Legal Tradition: Recurring Patterns of Law and Authority*
Haack: *Evidence Matters: Science, Proof, and Truth in the Law*
Harlow & Rawlings: *Law and Administration, 4th Edition*
Harris: *An Introduction to Law, 8th Edition*
Harris, Campbell & Halson: *Remedies in Contract and Tort, 2nd Edition*
Harvey: *Seeking Asylum in the UK: Problems and Prospects*
Herring: *Law and the Relational Self*
Hervey & McHale: *European Union Health Law: Themes and Implications*
Hervey & McHale: *Health Law and the European Union*
Holder & Lee: *Environmental Protection, Law and Policy: Text and Materials, 2nd Edition*

Jackson & Summers: *The Internationalisation of Criminal Evidence: Beyond the Common Law and Civil Law Traditions*
Kostakopoulou: *The Future Governance of Citizenship*
Kreiczer-Levy: *Destabilized Property: Property Law in the Sharing Economy*
Kubal: *Immigration and Refugee Law in Russia: Socio-Legal Perspectives*
Lewis: *Choice and the Legal Order: Rising above Politics*
Likosky: *Law, Infrastructure and Human Rights*
Likosky: *Transnational Legal Processes: Globalisation and Power Disparities*
Lixinski: *Legalized Identities: Cultural Heritage Law and the Shaping of Transitional Justice*
Loughnan: *Self, Others and the State: Relations of Criminal Responsibility*
Lunney: *A History of Australian Tort Law 1901–1945: England's Obedient Servant?*
Maughan & Webb: *Lawyering Skills and the Legal Process, 2nd Edition*
McGaughey: *Principles of Enterprise Law*
McGlynn: *Families and the European Union: Law, Politics and Pluralism*
Mertens: *A Philosophical Introduction to Human Rights*
Miller: *An Introduction to German Law and Legal Culture: Text and Materials*
Moffat: *Trusts Law: Text and Materials*
Monti: *EC Competition Law*
Morgan: *Contract Law Minimalism: A Formalist Restatement of Commercial Contract Law*
Morgan & Yeung: *An Introduction to Law and Regulation: Text and Materials*
Nash: *British Islam and English Law: A Classical Pluralist Perspective*
Ng: *Political Censorship in British Hong Kong: Freedom of Expression and the Law (1842–1997)*
Nicola & Davies: *EU Law Stories: Contextual and Critical Histories of European Jurisprudence*
Norrie: *Crime, Reason and History: A Critical Introduction to Criminal Law, 3rd Edition*
O'Dair: *Legal Ethics: Text and Materials*
Oliver: *Common Values and the Public–Private Divide*
Oliver & Drewry: *The Law and Parliament*
Palmer & Roberts: *Dispute Processes: ADR and the Primary Forms of Decision-Making, 1st Edition*
Palmer & Roberts: *Dispute Processes: ADR and the Primary Forms of Decision-Making, 3rd Edition*
Picciotto: *International Business Taxation*
Pieraccini: *Regulating the Sea: A Socio-Legal Analysis of English Marine Protected Areas*
Probert: *The Changing Legal Regulation of Cohabitation, 1600–2010: From Fornicators to Family, 1600–2010*
Radi: *Rules and Practices of International Investment Law and Arbitration*
Reed: *Internet Law: Text and Materials*
Richardson: *Law, Process and Custody*
Roberts & Palmer: *Dispute Processes: ADR and the Primary Forms of Decision-Making, 2nd Edition*
Rowbottom: *Democracy Distorted: Wealth, Influence and Democratic Politics*
Sauter: *Public Services in EU Law*
Scott & Black: *Cranston's Consumers and the Law*
Seneviratne: *Ombudsmen: Public Services and Administrative Justice*
Seppänen: *Ideological Conflict and the Rule of Law in Contemporary China: Useful Paradoxes*
Siems: *Comparative Law, 3rd Edition*
Stapleton: *Product Liability*

Stewart: *Gender, Law and Justice in a Global Market*
Tamanaha: *Law as a Means to an End: Threat to the Rule of Law*
Taylor: *Fortin's Children's Rights and the Developing Law, 4th Edition*
Tuori: *Properties of Law: Modern Law and After*
Turpin & Tomkins: *British Government and the Constitution: Text and Materials, 7th Edition*
Twining: *General Jurisprudence: Understanding Law from a Global Perspective*
Twining: *Globalisation and Legal Theory*
Twining: *Human Rights, Southern Voices: Francis Deng, Abdullahi An-Na'im, Yash Ghai and Upendra Baxi*
Twining: *Jurist in Context: A Memoir*
Twining: *Karl Llewellyn and the Realist Movement, 2nd Edition*
Twining: *Rethinking Evidence: Exploratory Essays, 2nd Edition*
Twining & Miers: *How to Do Things with Rules, 5th Edition*
Wan: *Film and Constitutional Controversy: Visualizing Hong Kong Identity in the Age of 'One Country, Two Systems'*
Ward: *A Critical Introduction to European Law, 3rd Edition*
Ward: *Law, Text, Terror*
Ward: *Shakespeare and Legal Imagination*
Watt: *The Making Sense of Politics, Media, and Law: Rhetorical Performance as Invention, Creation, Production*
Wells & Quick: *Lacey, Wells and Quick: Reconstructing Criminal Law: Text and Materials, 4th Edition*
Woodhead: *Caring for Cultural Heritage: An Integrated Approach to Legal and Ethical Initiatives in the United Kingdom*
Young: *Turpin and Tomkins' British Government and the Constitution: Text and Materials, 8th Edition*
Zander: *Cases and Materials on the English Legal System, 10th Edition*
Zander: *The Law-Making Process, 6th Edition*

International Journal of Law in Context: A Global Forum for Interdisciplinary Legal Studies

The *International Journal of Law in Context* is the companion journal to the Law in Context book series and provides a forum for interdisciplinary legal studies and offers intellectual space for ground-breaking critical research. It publishes contextual work about law and its relationship with other disciplines including but not limited to science, literature, humanities, philosophy, sociology, psychology, ethics, history and geography. More information about the journal and how to submit an article can be found at http://journals.cambridge.org/ijc

German Law Journal

The *German Law Journal* is a leading forum for legal scholarship from a transnational perspective. The GLJ pioneered the online and open access format that has become a standard for legal scholarship. Drawing on the transnational law commitments of scholars in Germany, and around the world, the GLJ publishes on a wide range of topics from a diversity of perspectives and methods. The *German Law Journal* also publishes a number of externally-proposed special issues each year. More information about the GLJ can be found at www.cambridge.org/core/journals/german-law-journal

An Introduction to German Law and Legal Culture

Text and Materials

RUSSELL A. MILLER
Washington and Lee University

Shaftesbury Road, Cambridge CB2 8EA, United Kingdom

One Liberty Plaza, 20th Floor, New York, NY 10006, USA

477 Williamstown Road, Port Melbourne, VIC 3207, Australia

314–321, 3rd Floor, Plot 3, Splendor Forum, Jasola District Centre, New Delhi – 110025, India

103 Penang Road, #05–06/07, Visioncrest Commercial, Singapore 238467

Cambridge University Press is part of Cambridge University Press & Assessment, a department of the University of Cambridge.

We share the University's mission to contribute to society through the pursuit of education, learning and research at the highest international levels of excellence.

www.cambridge.org
Information on this title: www.cambridge.org/highereducation/isbn/9781107141131

DOI: 10.1017/9781316493342

© Cambridge University Press & Assessment 2024

This publication is in copyright. Subject to statutory exception and to the provisions of relevant collective licensing agreements, no reproduction of any part may take place without the written permission of Cambridge University Press & Assessment.

First published 2024

A catalogue record for this publication is available from the British Library

A Cataloging-in-Publication data record for this book is available from the Library of Congress

ISBN 978-1-107-14113-1 Hardback
ISBN 978-1-316-50637-0 Paperback

Additional resources for this publication at www.cambridge.org/russellamiller

Cambridge University Press & Assessment has no responsibility for the persistence or accuracy of URLs for external or third-party internet websites referred to in this publication and does not guarantee that any content on such websites is, or will remain, accurate or appropriate.

Contents

List of Figures		*page* xii
List of Tables		xiv
Acknowledgments		xv
Note on Translations and Citation Style		xix
Note on the Cover		xxi
Country Summary – Germany, *The World Factbook* (2021)		xxiii

1 Introduction: Encounters with Foreign Legal Cultures — 1
   1.1 Comparatively Modest — 8
   1.2 What We Compare — 10
   1.3 How We Compare — 17
      1.3.1 Difference or Similarity — 18
      1.3.2 Subjectivity or Science — 26
   1.4 Conclusion — 31

2 The Civil Law Tradition — 37
   2.1 The Civil Law Tradition: Historical Development — 39
   2.2 The Central Elements of the Civil Law Tradition — 44
   2.3 Scholars and Legal Science in the Civil Law Tradition — 57
   2.4 Conclusion — 63

3 Germany's Plural Legal Culture — 67
   3.1 Free Law — 71
   3.2 Pure Law — 76
   3.3 Moral Law — 79
   3.4 Objective Order of Values — 87
   3.5 Conclusion — 92

4 Foundations I: Legal History — 96
   4.1 Old German Legal History — 97
   4.2 New German Legal History — 106
   4.3 Alternative Histories of German Law — 117
   4.4 Conclusion — 119

5 Foundations II: Political and Legal Institutions — 123
  5.1 Federalism — 125
  5.2 Lawmaking Institutions — 130
  5.3 Executive Authority — 135
  5.4 Legal System and Courts — 140
  5.5 Conclusion — 149

6 Foundations III: Legal Education, Legal Method, Legal Actors — 154
  6.1 Legal Education — 155
  6.2 Legal Method — 164
  6.3 Legal Actors: Judges and Lawyers — 173
  6.4 Conclusion — 191

7 German Private Law: The Civil Code — 196
  7.1 The German Civil Code and the Civil Law Tradition — 199
  7.2 Values and Style: What Makes the *Bürgerliches Gesetzbuch* a *German* Civil Code? — 209
  7.3 The Regulatory Technique of the German Civil Code — 214
  7.4 Using the Code: A Suretyship Contract Dispute — 223
  7.5 Conclusion — 237

8 German Public Law: Constitutionalism — 242
  8.1 Constitutional Supremacy: The German Basic Law — 247
  8.2 Judicial Review: The Federal Constitutional Court — 256
  8.3 Horizontal Effect (*Drittwirkung*): The Encounter between Common Law and Civil Law — 272
  8.4 Application of *Drittwirkung* by the Constitutional Court: The *Suretyship Case* — 276
  8.5 Conclusion — 286

9 German Public Law: Administrative Law — 291
  9.1 The Common Law and Civil Law Qualities of German Administrative Law — 294
  9.2 German Administrative Law: Substance Not Process — 299
  9.3 Administering Islamic Law in Germany — 314
  9.4 Conclusion — 334

10 German Criminal Law — 340
  10.1 The Theory and Logic of German Criminal Law — 343
  10.2 An Example of German Criminal Law: The *Frankfurt Police Torture Case* — 359

		Contents	
	10.3	Criminal Law in German Popular Culture: *Terror*	369
	10.4	Conclusion	376
11	**German Procedural Law**		**380**
	11.1	German Procedure: Inquisitorial or Adversarial Justice	383
	11.2	German Civil Procedure	387
	11.3	German Criminal Procedure	400
	11.4	Conclusion	414
12	**The Europeanization of German Law**		**418**
	12.1	A European Legal Tradition: Supranational and Supreme	422
	12.2	A European Legal Tradition: Common Market and a Neoliberal Agenda	427
	12.3	Europeanization of German Law: The Example of Contract Law	432
	12.4	Limits to the Europeanization of German Law	448
	12.5	Conclusion	458
13	**Epilogue: Germany's German Law**		**461**
	Index		470

Figures

1.1	Glenn: From Legal Families to Legal Traditions: (a) Legal Families; (b) Legal Traditions	*page* 16
1.2	Frankenberg's "Distancing" and "Differencing": (a) Distancing; (b) Differencing	31
2.1	Enlightenment Painting: Joseph Wright of Derby, "A Philosopher Giving a Lecture on the Orrery" (1766)	52
2.2	Romantic Painting: Caspar David Friedrich, "Wanderer Above the Sea of Fog" (1817)	53
2.3	Legal Science and Commentaries: A Pillar of Justice	63
3.1	Germany's Plural Legal Culture: (a) Hermann Kantorowicz; (b) Hans Kelsen; (c) Gustav Radbruch	85
3.2	Veit Harlan's Films – The Foundation for Germany's "Objective Order of Values": (a) *Jud Süss* movie poster; (b) Veit Harlan movie protest	88
4.1	Old German Law – The *Sachsenspiegel*: (a) Prologue of the *Harffer Sachsenspiegel* 1295 CE; (b) *Sachsenspiegel* manuscript from 1385 CE	105
4.2	St. Paul's Church Constitution of 1849: (a) The Frankfurt St. Paul's Church; (b) Interior of the Frankfurt St. Paul's Church today	116
4.3	German-Jewish Jurists: Otto Dix, "Family of Attorney Dr. Fritz Glaser" (1925)	119
5.1	Germany's Federalist Tradition: Principalities of the Holy Roman Empire in the Late Eighteenth Century	128
5.2	Germany's Legislative and Executive Institutions: (a) *Bundestag* (Federal Parliament); (b) *Bundesrat* (Federal Council of States); (c) Federal Chancellery; (d) Federal President's Residence – *Schloss Bellevue*; (e) Federal Government of newly elected Chancellor Olaf Scholz (2021)	141
5.3	German Court System	147
5.4	Tradition Shapes Modern German Governance	150
6.1	The Path to Becoming an *Einheitsjurist*	162
6.2	(East) German Justice as a Foil for (West) German Professional Standards	184

List of Figures

7.1	The German Civil Code – "A Monument of Legal Learning": (a) Political cartoon from 1896; (b) Cover from a popular edition of the German Civil Code published in 1909	206
7.2	German Civil Code and Suretyship: An Example of the *Klammerprinzip*	225
7.3	The "Palandt" BGB Commentary Controversy	232
8.1	The Basic Rights	254
8.2	Federal Constitutional Court: Guardian of the Constitution	262
8.3	Decisions of the Federal Constitutional Court	284
9.1	Federal Administrative Court	308
9.2	Ritual Slaughter: The Intersection of German Administrative Law and Islamic Law	328
10.1	German Criminal Code: The *Straftatsystem*	356
10.2	*Frankfurt Police Torture Case*	361
11.1	Exceptional German Criminal Process – The Red Army Fraction (RAF) Trial: (a) RAF Terrorist Andreas Baader; (b) RAF Terrorism Trial	404
11.2	Mythological Depictions of Criminal Law Proceedings – Adversarial and Inquisitorial: (a) Defense lawyer Atticus Finch in the film *To Kill a Mockingbird* (1962); (b) Medieval Inquisitor Konrad of Marburg	406
12.1	Germany's Schreber Gardens and the European Union: (a) Leipzig Physician Daniel Gottlob Moritz Schreber; (b) German Garden Gnomes	420
12.2	The European Court of Justice	427
12.3	German Beer Purity Law and the European Union	431
12.4	European Anti-discrimination Law Applied in Germany: The *Minus "Ossi" Case*	448

Tables

8.1	Procedures before the Federal Constitutional Court	*page* 264
9.1	The German Administrative Law "Code"	297
11.1	German Procedural Law Framework	386

Acknowledgments

I received help from a large number of institutions and colleagues while writing this book. I fear that I will neglect or overlook someone in this brief expression of gratitude. The risk of that is even greater than usual because I have worked on this project for many years. I hope those whom I might fail to mention will accept these remarks as a general, but deeply felt, statement of my appreciation. I know very well that my work benefits from the generosity and support of many colleagues, mentors, and friends. That was especially true for this project.

First and foremost, I want to recognize the stimulation, support, and subvention I received from the community of scholars connected with the Max Planck Society. Since 2001, I have been a frequent visitor at the Max Planck Institute (MPI) for Comparative Public Law and International Law in Heidelberg. This has fostered contact with brilliant doctoral candidates and post-doctoral researchers based at the Institute. It has also given me the chance to work alongside, learn from, and marvel at the accomplishments of the Institute's Directors. I cherish Professor Anne Peters and Professor Armin von Bogdandy as scholarly mentors and long-standing friends. My affiliation with the MPI-Heidelberg has given me a home in Germany for my research on German law. In Heidelberg I have been surrounded by inspiring colleagues and I have had access to the best possible research resources, including one of the world's best library collections devoted to comparative law and international law. On several occasions the Institute organized funding for my work, including sponsoring my Fulbright Senior Research Fellowship in 2008 and providing a grant for my sabbatical visit in 2015. During the latter stay in Heidelberg I presented the proposal for this book and, as always, I received encouraging, insightful, and constructive feedback.

My debt to the Max Planck community deepened in the last years. From 2020 to 2022 I had the privilege of serving as the Head of the Max Planck Law Network. In addition to the administrative demands of that role, I was given the chance to continue my work on this book. The Chair of the Directors' Council that is charged with overseeing the Max Planck Law initiative is the Director of the MPI-Frankfurt, Professor Stefan Vogenauer. He masterfully supervised my efforts on behalf of Max Planck Law. He also was an encouraging colleague and scholarly role model. My two years with Max Planck Law vastly expanded the universe of Directors and researchers (now encompassing Max Planck Law's ten Institutes) who have provided inspiration and insight for my work on this project.

My debt to the University of Münster Law Faculty is no less substantial. Through the Schumann Centre for Advanced International Legal Studies the Münster Law Faculty supported my work with summer research grants (2018–2020). The Münster Law Faculty sponsored my Fulbright Senior Research Fellowship in 2020. I benefitted from conversations with Münster colleagues about this book. I spent my time in the quiet setting – and making use of the excellent collection – at the *Gemeinsame Bibliothek der Zivilrechtlichen* Institute in the Law Faculty Building. I also found a productive workspace (and much-needed coffee) at the Floyd Café on Münster's Domplatz. Münster is a singularly lovely German university town! The Münster Law Faculty lodged the nomination that led to my receipt of an Alexander von Humboldt Foundation Research Prize in 2021. That prize is one of the great honors of my career. It also provided much-needed funding for my residency in Germany and work on this book in the last years. In all of this, Professor Matthias Casper has been a friend and unwavering advocate. Christian Johannes Wahnschaffe, the former Manager of the Schumann Center, provided professional and reliably good-natured support that regularly went above and beyond the ordinary demands of his position. All of this excellent assistance and collaboration allowed me to convene an informal workshop with law students in Münster in the fall and winter of 2021/2022. I was able to test preliminary drafts of the book's chapters in the workshop while the students provided priceless feedback and additional research. The contributions of the Münster workshop students were impressively smart and substantive. The book was vastly improved by their efforts.

This work also was meaningfully facilitated by Washington and Lee University (W&L), my home law faculty in Virginia. The Law School has a generous research leave policy. Former Dean Brant Hellwig enthusiastically supported my leave requests and worked creatively to ensure that they were as productive and enriching as possible. This was representative of his thorough and thoughtful support for W&L's faculty. I have also had the chance to present preliminary drafts of the book's chapters in the Comparative Law seminar I offer at W&L. The student editors who work tirelessly to edit and publish the *German Law Journal* enroll in the seminar. It is meant to give them the opportunity to reflect on the practice of comparative legal studies and to gain some insight into the German legal system, which is often relevant to the scholarship the *Journal* publishes. I feel certain that I gained much more from the students in that seminar than they learned from me. For several years they have engaged with preliminary drafts of these materials, reacting with the energy, seriousness, and civility that characterizes W&L's excellent students. I hope the book is accessible and benefits from an open and engaging tone. If it does those things, then it will largely be due to the feedback I have received from my students in Virginia.

Several W&L colleagues have also supported the project: inspiring me with their impressive research, challenging me in our informal conversations, and extending to me the kind of friendship that fosters the confidence needed to tackle big projects like this one. The most important of these faculty compatriots is my dear friend Professor Mark Drumbl. His critical and playful intellect provides the standard toward which I strive in all my work. The W&L law library staff are invariably prompt and professional with their support, including the delivery of the far-flung resources I needed for this project. Finally, I am sustained daily at the Law School by the dedicated and warm-hearted support of the Law School's team of faculty assistants. This especially includes Jane McDonald and Wendy Rice, who are tireless, generous, and capable. They do excellent work for the faculty. But I am just as grateful for their care and concern. Finally, I want to express my gratitude to the Frances Lewis Law Center at W&L. The Center supports the scholarly activities of the Law Faculty by funding student research assistant positions and providing summer research grants. This project benefitted from both of these commitments.

Many students, research assistants, and readers supported my work on this book. Julia Ngoc Anh Nguyen (Münster) was a brilliant project manager in the end-stages of the effort, overseeing administrative tasks and providing substantive research and feedback. I wouldn't have finished the book without her contributions, which were admirably professional, patient, and persistent. I am deeply indebted to her. A number of other German-trained jurists and law students aided me with substantive research, editorial reviews, and insightful recommendations. Each of them also visited me in Virginia: Peggy Fiebig (W&L), Nicole Schreier (Gießen), Carmen Vetter (Gießen), Matthias Schmidt (MPI-Heidelberg), and Desirée Schmitt (Saarbrücken/MPI-Heidelberg). They have become cherished friends. Students at W&L helped with editing, citation-checking, and substantive research, including Ariel Brio (W&L 2022) and Rachel Silver (W&L 2024).

I am very grateful to the editorial team at Cambridge University Press, including the inestimable Finola O'Sullivan, with whom I had the pleasure of working on several occasions. But others at Cambridge University Press added a great deal to the project – Marta Walkowiak, Caitlin Lisle, Toby Ginsberg, and Laura Blake showed great confidence in the book, offered extensive editorial and administrative assistance, and applied creativity and vision to meeting the project's unique needs. Above all, they were very patient as professional detours and pandemics slowed my progress. It has been a pleasure and privilege to work with them.

I am also deeply indebted to the many authors and scholars whose work I have excerpted and collected here, as a way of illuminating and illustrating my commentary and insights. Many of the scholars represented in this collection have been personal colleagues or long-standing (albeit far-off) inspirations, informing and guiding my work on German law and comparative law across the last decades. Besides producing brilliant and informed research, they also form an informal, but for me, quite tangible scholarly community. The generosity and support of these scholars was once again confirmed in the process of publishing this book as many of them personally endorsed my request to republish excerpts of their work and offered to waive the royalties or license fees they might have been owed. This significantly streamlined the process of securing those rights and licenses from the respective publishers. The editorial teams I corresponded with at those publishing houses were invariably professional and well-intentioned.

I owe the last, but heartiest, word of thanks to my family. This book is an expression of my long professional affection for and immersion in the German law world. I'm afraid I dragged my family along on that odd journey. They accompanied me (sometimes happily and sometimes in bafflement) on many long stays in Germany. Those residencies disrupted the flow of their lives and, for that reason, involved significant sacrifices. But that wasn't the end of it. I also tried to make the German language and German culture a centerpiece of our lives back in the United States. They helped host German colleagues for German-language dinners. They watched an impressive catalogue of (more-or-less interesting) German films and television series. They endured my annual *Spargel* dinner and played along with the Americanized versions of the *Laternenfest* and *Niklolaustag* I organized. They tolerated countless references to the decisions of the Federal Constitutional Court during family dinners (even while I mostly failed to respect the embargo they tried to place on those references during our Thanksgiving dinners!). I know I can't take all of this for granted. How lucky I have been to be able to share my life's passion and work with such wonderful, willing, and wise souls. They enabled and facilitated and supported all of this. The book's achievements – and none of its failings – are theirs as much as they are mine.

Note on Translations and Citation Style

Any study of a foreign legal system involves a departure – a deviation – from the way in which that system is understood and presented by those for whom it is a primary or "national" juristic culture.

Often the most significant variation involved in the comparative study of a foreign legal system is linguistic. This book is written in English. I hope that will give it (and the German legal system surveyed here) a broader audience. But it should be obvious that German law is done in the German language. That makes this book a kind of false or nonnatural (re)presentation of German legal culture. I have tried to account for that problem in several ways. First, I have used excellent English-language translations of many primary and secondary German-language materials. Some of those translations come from respected sources, such as the translated statutes collected by the German Federal Ministry of Justice and the Federal Office of Justice (www.gesetze-im-internet.de/Teilliste_translations.html) and the English-language judgments prepared by the professional team of translators at the German Federal Constitutional Court (www.bundesverfassungsgericht.de/SiteGlobals/Forms/Suche/EN/Entscheidungensuche_Formular.html?language_=en). I have prepared other translations that are presented in this book. In my commentary, I tried to develop and maintain a systematic *transliteration* into English of the German legal concepts, terms, and principles discussed. For many concepts I provided the original German-language term in conjunction with an English-language *transliteration*. Thereafter, in most instances, I used only the English-language *term*. I refer to these efforts as "transliteration," as opposed to "translation," because I have aimed for explanatory presentations of the concepts – sometimes resorting to equivalent or parallel terms from American law – rather than literal, word-for-word translations. The idea was that, by taking this approach, I might help to orient readers as they encounter German legal concepts. But all of this underscores the traditional caveat in works like this one. Only the original German-language terms and texts are authoritative. The English-language material presented here is simply an approximation, a path-marker, to the German-language reality of German law and legal culture.

A second variation that emerges from a comparative study of a legal system involves the citation style used to document primary or secondary sources. Each legal system has its own citation system, even if in some cases there is no established system at all. Like so much else in the law, the citation rules reflect the system's priorities, values, and assumptions. For example, the refined approach to citing case law in the American system signals the priority the Common Law tradition places on case law. Similarly, the bewildering array of abbreviations the Germans have developed for the titles of law journals signals the priority the Civil Law tradition places on scholarly commentary. But the legal-cultural "reality" of one system's citation rules can raise a barrier to access for uninitiated foreigners. I used an adapted version of the citation system established by *The Bluebook: A Uniform System of Citation*. That is the orthodox citation system used in legal practice and scholarship in American law. This means the book involves a not-insignificant cultural departure from the way in which German jurists would cite sources. Pinpoint cites, for instance, refer to page numbers as opposed to paragraph numbers. Something is lost by this decision. But I hope that the loss is offset by the sense of familiarity and accessibility this decision might foster among the book's non-German readers. The goal, in any case, was to make it possible for readers to easily find – and find their own way into – the sources and materials that informed my work.

Note on the Cover

Gerhard Richter's work *Schwarz, Rot, Gold I* (Editions CR:107) (1989) is described by the artist as a "collage of three squares of white, lightweight cardboard, each painted in a single tone of oil paint." This smaller work was created in conjunction with Richter's monumental *Schwarz, Rot, Gold* (CR:856) (1999) – a glass and colored-enamel production 20 meters × 3 meters in size – that was commissioned for the luminous west entrance hall of the Reichstag building in Berlin. The larger work was installed as part of the renovation of the historic building as the home of the German Federal Parliament (*Bundestag*) after reunification. Both works – and others in the series – explicitly engage with the colors, shape, and meaning of post-war Germany's black, red, and gold flag.

Richter is regarded as one of the giants of post-war German high culture. As part of the excitement accompanying a major exhibition of his work at New York's Museum of Modern Art in 2002, the *New Yorker Magazine* called him "the good German." The *New York Times* has described Richter's artistic achievement as "colossal." It also happens to be the case that his last name (Richter) is the German word for "judge." Alone, these points might have recommended this work for an introduction to German law. But Richter's biography, and the painting's effects, make this a particularly profound image for the book's cover. The book tries to account for the diversity of influences and traditions relevant to German legal culture. It studiously refuses to accept that German law can be reduced to or adequately characterized by the core elements of any single legal tradition or "legal family."

Richter himself embodies a number of different Germanys. He built his artistic career in East Germany, painting murals for the socialist government. He emigrated to West Germany in the 1960s. Despite his growing success as an artist, Richter's work suggests that he struggled to adapt himself to West Germany's more individualistic and consumerist culture. Richter describes himself as an atheist who has developed a strong affinity for the Catholic Church. This, too, reflects Germany's complex mix of modernism and tradition, science and sectarianism.

In one celebrated mode of his artistic work, Richter paints in a realistic style that achieves an uncanny approximation of detailed photographs – except that these images are often rendered slightly out-of-focus or blurred. In these "abstract pictures," the subjects are often turned away from the artist and the viewer. Luke Smythe (*Gerhard Richter, Individualism, and Belonging in West Germany* [Routledge 2022]) explains that the images evoke a sense of unevenness and uncertainty. They express Richter's "critical but not confrontational" approach to German history: What do we know about the past? What do we not see accurately? Can we face the past and move toward the future? The painted cardboard tiles of which *Schwarz, Rot, Gold I* is composed participate in this symbolism. Their color is not sharply rendered. The edges of the tiles are roughly cut. The placement of the tiles is fragmented. All of this suggests uncertainty about Germany. It portrays the country's disrupted and disjointed history and creates the possibility for recognizing different values and movements that have shaped German society. The work obviously references the German flag, but it imposes new perspectives on our expectations, not least by arranging the image vertically rather than horizontally. This is a patchwork Germany, seen anew, that eludes attribution of a single fact about the country. To paraphrase Christian Lotz (*The Art of Gerhard Richter: Hermeneutics, Images, Meaning* [Bloomsbury 2017]), the painting follows its own "law of form" and realizes itself in its disconnection from any single tradition, any single expectation, any single genre. That's what this book aims to say about German law and legal culture.

Country Summary – Germany, The World Factbook (2021)

Washington, DC – Central Intelligence Agency, www.cia.gov/the-world-factbook/ (updated May 27, 2022)

Introduction

Background – As Europe's largest economy and second most populous nation (after Russia), Germany is a key member of the continent's economic, political, and defense organizations. European power struggles immersed Germany in two devastating world wars in the first half of the twentieth century and left the country occupied by the victorious Allied powers of the US, UK, France, and the Soviet Union in 1945. With the advent of the Cold War, two German states were formed in 1949: the western Federal Republic of Germany (FRG) and the eastern German Democratic Republic (GDR). The democratic FRG embedded itself in key western economic and security organizations, the EC (now the EU) and NATO, while the communist GDR was on the front line of the Soviet-led Warsaw Pact. The decline of the USSR and the end of the Cold War allowed for German reunification in 1990. Since then, Germany has expended considerable funds to bring eastern productivity and wages up to western standards. In January 1999, Germany and 10 other EU countries introduced a common European exchange currency, the euro.

People and Society

Population – 84,316,622 (2022 est.)

Ethnic groups – German 86.3%, Turkish 1.8%, Polish 1%, Syrian 1%, Romanian 1%, other/stateless/unspecified 8.9% (2020 est.)

Languages – German (official); note – Danish, Frisian, Sorbian, and Romani are official minority languages; Low German, Danish, North Frisian, Sater Frisian, Lower Sorbian, Upper Sorbian, and Romani are recognized as regional languages under the European Charter for Regional or Minority Languages

Religions – Roman Catholic 26.7%, Protestant 24.3%, Muslim 3.5%, other 4.8%, none 40.7% (2020 est.)
Population growth rate – –0.11% (2022 est.)

Government

Government type – federal parliamentary republic
Capital – name – Berlin
Executive branch – chief of state: President Frank-Walter Steinmeier (since 19 March 2017); **head of government**: Chancellor Olaf Scholz (since 8 December 2021)
Legislative branch – description: bicameral Parliament consists of: Federal Council or Bundesrat [...], Federal Diet or Bundestag [...]

Economy

Economic overview: leading EU services-based, export-driven economy; COVID-19 disrupted its modern manufacturing sector; highly skilled and educated labor force; positive current account balances; increasing public debt; low defense spending; second Russian gas pipeline
Real GDP (purchasing power parity) – $4,238,800,000,000 (2020 est.)
Real GDP per capita – $50,900 (2020 est.)
Agricultural products – milk, sugar beet, wheat, barley, potatoes, pork, maize, rye, rapeseed, triticale
Industries – among the world's largest and most technologically advanced producers of iron, steel, coal, cement, chemicals, machinery, vehicles, machine tools, electronics, automobiles, food and beverages, shipbuilding, textiles
Exports – $1,671,650,000,000 (2020 est.)
Exports – partners – United States 9%, France 8%, China 7%, Netherlands 6%, United Kingdom 6%, Italy 5%, Poland 5%, Austria 5% (2019)
Exports – commodities – cars and vehicle parts, packaged medicines, aircraft, medical cultures/vaccines, industrial machinery (2019)
Imports – $1,452,560,000,000 (2020 est.)
Imports – partners – Netherlands 9%, China 8%, France 7%, Belgium 6%, Poland 6%, Italy 6%, Czechia 5%, United States 5% (2019)
Imports – commodities – car and vehicle parts, packaged medicines, crude petroleum, refined petroleum, medical cultures/vaccines (2019)

Country Summary – Germany, *The World Factbook* (2021)

Map of the Federal Republic of Germany
Source: Shutterstock

1

Introduction

Encounters with Foreign Legal Cultures

Key Concepts

- **Comparative Legal Studies**: The study of similarities and differences between the law and legal culture of two or more legal systems.
- **Foreign Legal Studies**: The study of another legal system (usually thought of as a national jurisdiction) other than one's primary or "national" legal system.
- **Legal System**: The set of laws (substantive and procedural), legal institutions, legal actors, legal methods, and legal practices in one jurisdiction.
- **Legal Families**: The attempt by comparative law scholars to assign distinct legal systems to broad categories (families) based on common or shared characteristics in legal history, substantive law, procedural law, and legal method.
- **Legal Tradition**: A set of deeply rooted, historically conditioned attitudes about the nature of law, about the role of law in society and the polity, about the proper organization and operation of a legal system, and about the way law is or should be made, applied, studied, perfected, and taught.[1]

Study Tips

Throughout this textbook I will occasionally refer to a promotional brochure entitled *Law – Made in Germany*. The brochure was produced by major stakeholders in the German legal system, including the German Federal Bar Association, the German Bar Association, the German Association of Judges, and the German Chamber of Commerce. With each new edition of the brochure, the current Federal Minister of Justice has provided a foreword. The brochure is meant to favorably position German law and the German legal system in the global competition for legal services. That aim makes the brochure fairly patriotic and uncritical. Still, it provides unique insight into the way Germans see their legal culture. The brochure is available at www.brak.de/fileadmin/05_zur_rechtspolitik/international/140829-broschuere-law_en.pdf.

This textbook will introduce you to German law and legal culture.

There are good, practical reasons for setting off on this adventure. Germany's geopolitical significance hardly needs confirmation. This remains true despite the dramatic pivot in global affairs towards Asia generally, and China more specifically. Germany, after all, is the world's fourth largest economy. It is the unrivaled engine at the center of the European Union, which is the world's largest common market and most dramatic experiment in organizing state power at a supranational level. Germany famously punches well above its size as one of the world's leading exporters. It is an outpost for manufacturing in the West. This is partly attributable to the fact that Germany is one of the world's leading technology innovators, especially in the automotive sector, in fields related to precision industrial engineering, and in clean energy. And, in the face of the Russian war against Ukraine, Germany seems ready to put aside its reservations about muscular security policy in order to play a more robust (if still cautious) role in the collective security frameworks established by the North Atlantic Treaty Organization (NATO) and the European Union (EU). With a "mere" 80 million residents, Germany is nevertheless the world's third largest book market. It is home to three of the world's ten-best symphony orchestras. Germany has tradition-rich universities and it lavishly subsidizes research and development. In a global poll conducted annually by the BBC in the 2010s, Germany repeatedly scored as the world's most popular country.[2] That reflects an era during which Germany won the 2010 Eurovision Song Contest, claimed the 2014 men's football World Cup, welcomed nearly a million refugees in 2015 and 2016, and led the world with the development of the first-to-market COVID-19 vaccine in 2021.

Germany is exceptional, and so is German law. It is closely entwined with German achievement across many social and economic sectors. German law has served as an inspiration for legal innovation and reform in diverse legal systems around the world, from South Africa to China. Its immense influence on European and international law is indisputable. Even the American tradition of "legal science," which fostered the still-prevalent "case-method" used to teach law in American law schools, carries the DNA of German legal philosophy.[3] Germany competes neck and neck with the United Kingdom for the second largest share of the global market for legal services (behind the top-ranked United States). That explains why dozens of the world's leading law firms now have large offices in Frankfurt, Berlin, Dusseldorf, and Munich.

If you are going to take up the challenge of becoming familiar with a foreign legal system, Germany makes a powerful, pragmatic case for itself. Increasingly, the path to a full and meaningful appreciation of the way the law works in the world passes through Germany.

But there are less practical reasons to study a foreign legal system – whether Germany's or any other. That endeavor is a form of comparative law, and that field of study is sometimes justified in more philosophical terms. On the one hand, comparative legal studies can enrich your understanding of the law as an abstract or theoretical matter. Seeing what it is and how it works in different contexts might suggest some elemental truths about "the law" writ large. On the other hand, comparative legal studies can enliven your legal imagination. For example, encounters with other legal systems and traditions, such as the one that takes place in this book, expose you to the world's splendidly diverse normative landscape. That might give you reason to wonder what "the law" could be. For both of these reasons, this introduction to German law and legal culture is part of a cosmopolitan education for a generation of lawyers who are destined to encounter laws and legal actors from other legal cultures in our globalizing world and a globalizing legal profession. As former United States Supreme Court Justice Stephen Breyer concluded in his book *The Court and the World*: "[I]t has become clear that, even in ordinary matters, [legal] awareness can no longer stop at the border."[4] Perhaps this brave, first step toward Germany will lead to other encounters with other legal systems, other laws. The materials in this book should nurture your curiosity, bolster your confidence, and help you develop the skills you need to conscientiously search out and engage with the laws of new and foreign jurisdictions. There is, so it is said, a whole world (of laws) out there to discover.

The path to the broader vista of the law that this book opens up will take you across many borders. Obviously, it is a journey across the boundaries that still separate states and largely demarcate the jurisdictions in which those states' legal systems operate. You will be leaving the state – and legal system – of your primary or "national" legal identity to travel in the German "law-world."[5] Especially in the case of Germany, this adventure will also require you to move back and forth between state, supranational, international, and transnational legal realms. Those normative orders play a significant role in German law and legal culture. Naturally, a survey like this tries to succinctly account for the past while presenting the contemporary state of the law. That involves traveling across the border of legal history and contemporary legal doctrine and practice. You will also be asked to move between secular and sacred worlds in ways that may be unfamiliar to you. Germany is categorically a secular state. But sectarian legacies have a continuing resonance in society and the law in Germany. This includes an intensifying intersection with the normative values and commitments of Germany's rapidly growing Muslim population. The lines that have traditionally divided the public and private spheres of law will also be challenged. For example, you will learn that in Germany constitutionally guaranteed liberties can indirectly limit private conduct as well as impose the more traditional limits on state action.

The defiance of all these borders, in its own right, is one of the chief callings of comparative legal studies. This book should give you the experience of ignoring, surmounting, and skirting "conceptual boundaries [… and refuting] hard categories."[6] Let go of trusted classifications. Call into question well-worn assumptions. That is an essential and exhilarating part of the comparative law enterprise. It is a posture that pursues productive criticism and probing self-reflection. Those habits will serve you equally well in an exclusively domestic legal practice (if such a thing exists today).[7] After all, history's great advocates and jurists saw old doctrine in a new light or refused to yield to received legal truths.[8]

Fundamentally, this book will require you to disregard – even if only for the time you spend with these materials – one of law's most enduring boundaries. By wading into these pages you have already exhibited the courage and curiosity needed to question the hidebound notion that your legal education and training should be devoted to nothing more than mastering the prevailing substantive rules, legal procedure, and practice skills relevant to the jurisdiction where you will work as a lawyer, civil servant, business manager, civil society advocate, legal scholar, or judge. In spurning your primary or "national" legal system for this book's foreign affair, you will cultivate the habit of pursuing creative directions in your life in the law, and in your life more generally.

After your encounter with this new legal system and the conscious disregard of borders that is necessary to make the encounter possible, there is another hope for this book. It should cause you to reflect critically on your domestic legal system. Your outward journey into the German legal system should have an unsettling effect that will lead to an inward journey as well. You will discover that the way things are done in your primary or "national" legal system are by no means "given" or "ordained." There are other problems for the law to confront. And, where the problems appear to be familiar, you'll see that there are other ways of responding to them through law. Let these surprises stir you to question the way things are done in the legal system you call home. "Comparative law," the German scholar Günther Frankenberg implores, "might [...] inspire students to learn more about and rethink the biases of their own [legal system]."[9]

The more sublime aims of this project do not, however, detract from the book's prosaic and practical ambition. The chapters that follow this introduction provide a summary and subjective – albeit well-intentioned – survey of German law and legal culture.

It is a *summary effort* because it cannot provide the comprehensive and painstakingly detailed understanding of German law that you would need to be an effective jurist in Aachen or Zwickau. Similar to the years of intensive academic and practical training you receive in your primary or "national" legal system, a professional life in the law in Germany requires years of study at the university, years of apprenticeship under the supervision of experienced jurists, and success on two notoriously difficult state exams. It should go without saying that it would also require mastery of what the American humorist Mark Twain only half-jokingly called "the awful German language."[10] These materials can only introduce you to some of the most important concepts, terms, themes, subjects, values, mechanisms, and impulses in German law. The book aims to paint an impressionistic portrait. This is more about "legal culture" viewed from a broad panorama than it is about applied legal doctrine.

Introduction: Encounters with Foreign Legal Cultures

David Nelken tells us: "Legal culture, in its most general sense, is one way of describing relatively stable patterns of legally oriented social behaviour and attitudes [...]. Like culture itself, legal culture is about who we are not just what we do."[11] By adding "legal culture" to its title, I am signaling that the book is interested in "who German jurists are." The story the book tells focuses on the "rich tapestry of habits and heritages" and the "customs, traditions and manners" that color and shape German law.[12] I hope this survey will equip you to confidently wade further into the intricacies of German legal doctrine and practice. It should prepare you for the work of refining and deepening your understanding of *Rechtswissenschaft* (the scholarly study of the law), *Privatrecht* (private law), *Öffentliches Recht* (public law, including constitutional and administrative law), *Strafrecht* (criminal law), *Prozessrecht* (procedural law), the omnipresent *Europäisches Recht* (European law), and other normative frameworks operating in the German legal system.

It is a **subjective effort** because the concepts, terms, themes, subjects, values, and impulses presented in this book represent my unique answers to my distinct questions about German law and legal culture. There are many ways to "introduce German law" and none could be objectively "correct." You should seek out other treatments of the subject. They will enrich and expand your understanding of German law, which is an endlessly remarkable and remarkably rewarding object of study. To help you with that, I include in each of the following chapters a brief list of other books in English to which you could turn in order to deepen your engagement with German law. Ultimately, the choices that shape this book's presentation of German law and legal culture unavoidably bear the imprint of my particular (or peculiar) perspective. Perhaps the most distinct characteristic of this survey is that it has been prepared by an American legal scholar. I have decades of personal and professional experience in Germany. But there is no point in denying that this is a foreigner's – an American's, and simply *my* – portrayal of German law and legal culture. I agree with two of comparative law's very thoughtful commentators, who would remind you that the meaning I assign to German law and legal culture is unavoidably colored by the American legal culture to which I belong.[13] This book is one American's (well-informed, well-intentioned, and deeply admiring) depiction of German law and legal culture. It couldn't be anything other than that. It is surely not the introduction most German law scholars would have written. The foreignness of this survey, whatever defects it contains, at least holds out the promise that it is acutely aware of the thrilling but vertiginous feeling that comes when one stands – as a non-German with no formal training in German law – at the precipice, gazing down into the wonder of German legal culture for the first time. Not so long ago I stood where you stand now.

The book begins with this introductory chapter devoted to a consideration of the comparative law theory and method that informs the book's unifying approach, which is to take the German legal system as the meeting place for a diverse set of legal traditions. The concept of "legal tradition" might be unfamiliar to you. That's ok. It's a disputed concept in any case. My use of "legal tradition" will come into focus in this and the following chapters. The important thing to note at this point is that I'm convinced that no legal system (such as Germany's) can be exclusively and comprehensively defined by – or portrayed exclusively as an example of – a single legal tradition. I think that many legal traditions – some more prominently than others – are at play in any jurisdiction, including in the German legal system. This book pursues a pluralistic perspective of German law and legal culture.

Chapter 2 prepares you for that agenda by introducing you to the Civil Law tradition. This is the predominant legal tradition in the German legal system. Many other comparative studies of German law are content to treat the Civil Law tradition as the exclusive framework for understanding German law and legal culture. My introduction to the Civil Law tradition will be especially useful for readers whose primary legal identity has been developed in a legal system chiefly influenced by another legal tradition, such as the Common Law tradition that is prevalent in the Anglo-American legal systems. But Chapter 2 might be of interest to experienced "Civilian" jurists (admittedly consisting of most lawyers in the world) because it represents an American's distinct portrayal of the Civil Law's jurisprudential mentality and practice. That unique perspective is bound to stir self-reflection (but I hope not dubiousness towards this book).

By giving the Civil Law tradition such priority in this project I might seem to be conceding the notion that the most you need to know, as a comparativist encountering the German legal system, is that Germany is "just" another Civil Law country. To the contrary, the introduction to the Civil Law tradition in Chapter 2 is a necessary foundation for the argument I set out in Chapter 3, namely, that German legal culture is better understood as a pluralistic encounter amongst a number of diverse legal traditions – starting but by no means ending with the Civil Law tradition. I imagine German law as a tapestry consisting of many colorful threads (legal traditions) woven together. As this book progresses I will happily acknowledge that this undeniably includes the Civil Law tradition as the tapestry's most prominent thread. But I will suggest that it also includes other legal traditions, such as the Common Law tradition, echoes of Socialist Law, encounters with Islamic Law, the Inquisitorial tradition of procedural law, the Adversarial tradition of procedural law, and a dialogue with the *sui generis* tradition of European Law. I pave the way for that effort in Chapter 3 by pointing out that the Civil Law tradition's sway over German legal culture has been persistently challenged and disputed.

I provide introductions to foundational elements of the German legal system in Chapters 4–6. It was a challenge to develop that coverage because it is not possible to know what background or experience this book's readers will have with Germany in general, and with German law in particular. As a survey of German law and legal culture, this book cannot devote attention to the broader sweep of German history, or to a thorough study of German politics and culture. As important as all of that insight is for an understanding of German law, those topics are properly the subject of other surveys prepared for other courses at the university. Still, in order to open a wide and accessible path into German law, I provide a brief glimpse into German legal history (Chapter 4) as well as a sketch of contemporary Germany's most important political and legal institutions (Chapter 5). I continue this presentation of the foundations of the German legal system with an examination of German legal education, a primer on the unique legal method learned in German legal training, and a reflection on the roles played by German judges and lawyers as the system's chief legal actors (Chapter 6).

Having presented the book's thesis, and having sought to secure the reader's footing in the foundations of the German legal system, the remainder of the chapters introduce a range of discrete legal subjects. Maybe these are the most important fields of law in Germany, although others would certainly argue that I have overlooked some important subject. The coverage includes: Chapter 7 – Private Law, with an emphasis on the Civil Code; Chapter 8 – Public Law, focusing on constitutional law and the German Federal Constitutional Court; Chapter 9 – Public Law, treating administrative law; Chapter 10 – Criminal Law, with an emphasis on the Criminal Code; Chapter 11 – Procedural Law, briefly treating both private law procedure and criminal law procedure; and Chapter 12 – European Law, which considers the growing importance and influence of European Union law in the German legal system. As I suggested earlier, however, these are not exhaustive presentations or comprehensive treatments of the relevant doctrine in those fields. Instead, I hope to provide you with a sense of some of the concepts, terms, themes, subjects, values, mechanisms, and impulses relevant to the German approach to these legal subjects. And, as promised, I intend to use these fields as distinct vantage points for observing the diverse traditions – the unexpected threads of legal thinking – that wind and wend their way throughout the tapestry of German legal culture.

In Chapter 13, the book's coda, I encourage you to imagine in a more concrete way how it is that the Civil Law and Common Law traditions interact and interweave in the German legal system, using German constitutional law as a case study. I conclude there that the result is neither an exclusively "Civilian" nor particularly "Common Law" approach to constitutionalism. Instead, I hope you'll see what I call "Germany's German Constitutional Law." That's a way of characterizing this book's agenda. It is a story about the diversity and complexity of Germany's uniquely German legal culture.

This textbook will introduce you to German law and legal culture. But how should one go about studying a foreign legal system? That basic question of comparative law theory and method is considered in the remainder of this opening chapter.

1.1 Comparatively Modest

There are many reasons, and many ways, to study the laws of different jurisdictions, different peoples, and different cultures. The methods for comparing laws have been heavily, but still seemingly unsatisfactorily, theorized.[14] This book does not wade systematically into these teeming and treacherous waters; it is not a survey of the theories and methods of comparative law.[15] Still, it is important for you to be aware of the comparative law choices I have made in presenting this introduction to German law and legal culture.

To begin, it might be said that this book is not a work of comparative law at all. It draws you and your primary or "national" legal identity into dialogue with German law and legal culture. But there is no concerted effort to compare the familiar and the unfamiliar in the formal or systematic sense of examining "two or more items to establish similarities and dissimilarities."[16] Rather, this is a presentation of a single legal system – German law and legal culture – without an accompanying treatment of the law and legal culture of other legal systems. Some comparative law scholars disregard such monophonic efforts as the mere study of "foreign law," suggesting that it is not a properly comparative enterprise.[17]

There is more comparative law taking place here than those scholars dare to dream. After all, as you move through this book a natural and unavoidable juxtaposition will occur between your primary or "national" legal identity and the German law-world depicted here. You will encounter and assess this foreign legal system and tradition from the perspective and through the lens of the law and legal culture of your "home" jurisdiction.[18] In this sense, the book's objects of comparison (*comparata*) are the German law and legal culture presented in this book and always, even if only implicitly, each reader's "mother legal system."[19] That unavoidable dynamic, without more, constitutes an informal but profound kind of comparison (*tertium comparationis*).[20] In fact, mentioning that natural phenomenon here opens up the possibility that this will be more than a passive occurrence. Similarities and differences between German legal culture and your primary or "national" legal system will ceaselessly come into and out of focus in the course of your study of these materials, even if they are not systematically "established" and "assessed." You should try to be conscious of this implicit comparative experience. Document it in the margins of these pages – or keep a journal – jotting notes at those moments when you find yourself thinking things such as: "that's exactly the way my legal system would have approached this problem," or "that's the craziest thing I've ever heard." Thoughts like those are the seeds of worthwhile and productive comparative legal studies, even if the enterprise pursued in this book formally involves only one foreign legal system.

That kind of implicit and informal comparison is a planned consequence of the book's coverage and approach. But there is also quite a lot of explicit comparison conducted in these pages. As I acknowledged earlier in this chapter,

1.1 Comparatively Modest

I am an American-trained legal scholar. That means that I frequently contrast German norms, legal institutions, or legal practices, with parallel American norms, institutions, or practices. That is seldom a systematic effort. But it is unavoidably present. In fact, I may have felt liberated to do more of that in this book because I hoped that some of its readers would be American-trained jurists like me. American lawyers are notoriously parochial and typically preoccupied with domestic American law. Perhaps, by leaving American "breadcrumbs" along the trail, I'll lure American readers deeper into this comparative law adventure and away from their familiar paths. But more significantly, my comparative side-glances to American law represent the (sometimes instinctive and, I hope, always informed) implicit but conscious comparative encounters that inescapably take place between my primary legal system and German law. If you were trained in one of the world's nearly 200 other legal systems, then I hope that those references to American law won't alienate or discourage you. Instead, view them as a model for the self-reflective approach to this comparative law journey that I hope you'll also attempt.

Another important point to make is that I have modest goals for this book. First, I would like to survey German law and legal culture as a way of helping you expand your legal horizons and, thereby, encourage you to engage in some legal-cultural self-reflection. Second, I hope to nod towards a diverse range of legal traditions. If that's convincing here, maybe you'll begin to wonder about law's fundamental plurality, seeing it as a diversity of influences, contexts, and meanings.[21] Those modest ambitions allow me to be somewhat less theoretically and methodologically rigorous.

More than anything, this is an "intellectual adventure" and there are no rules for discovery except, perhaps, that one must be curious. The book draws its inspiration more from Raymond Grew, one of the leading scholars of comparative history, than from the leading theorists of comparative law:

> Efficacious comparison still seems to me to rest on a cast of mind. More than from any particular method, theory, or topic, comparison flourishes from an imaginative openness to discovery, from an ability to recognize when assumptions need to be challenged, from a willingness to probe expectations unmet, and from the capacity to move across established conceptual boundaries [...]. [C]omparison in itself is neither a theory nor a method.[22]

This book sets a course for discovery and embraces the many lessons that naturally accompany that process, including encounters with new worlds, the liberating experience of transcending boundaries, and a healthy measure of self-reflection. But even these loose goals merit some deeper explanation. That is the purpose of the following materials. They provide only the briefest treatment of some of the long-standing questions in comparative law. Your exposure to those questions here is meant to give you a glimpse of the old debates – and some of the answers – that have preoccupied comparative law scholars. It should also give you a better understanding of the particular approach this book takes to introducing German law and legal culture. There are, of course, many ways this could have been done. There are as many ways of doing comparative law as there are comparative lawyers.[23] You should seek out those other approaches to comparative law and – pun intended – compare them with the approach taken by this book. Make your own choices and reach your own conclusions about the right way to study foreign legal systems.

The following sections consider two elemental questions: **what should we compare** and **how should we compare**? The thinking prompted by those questions illuminates the distinct choices that have shaped this survey of German law and legal culture.

1.2 What We Compare

Comparative law scholars often imagine pursuing their work on two levels. On one level, "macro-comparison" involves the survey of the world's legal systems – usually aligned with national jurisdictions – in an attempt to classify them for assignment to manageable categories that are thought to be demarcated by shared or representative jurisprudential characteristics. As H. Patrick Glenn explained, "the number and diversity of our laws has led to an apparently irresistible process of aggregation or categorization."[24] This is the effort to draw a map, complete with pastel-colored spheres from a schoolhouse globe, of the world's legal systems.[25] On another level, "micro-comparison" involves the systematic juxtaposition of various systems' distinct norms or legal institutions. Especially when considering different systems' norms, it is common to start with a particular social problem in mind, such as when one person takes another person's life (is that murder?), or when a promise to do something for another person goes unfulfilled (is there a contractual duty invovled?). This is a side-by-side, functional comparison. Macro-comparison operates on a "broader" conceptual scale. Micro-comparison works on a "narrower" conceptual scale, even if it might involve scores of different legal systems (especially when employing quantitative methods).

This book's broad portrayal of German law and legal culture is more closely akin to the macro-comparative law project. It acts as though it is interested in understanding where the German legal system stands in relation to the world's other legal systems. But this is not a traditional macro-comparative law effort.

Typically, macro-comparison involves distilling a legal system to its supposed essence and assigning it to one of several "legal families" in the same way that biologists allocate living organisms, based on biological criteria, to different families, genera, and species. In macro-comparative law various jurisdictions are studied to determine their classification relative to a handful of globally relevant groups. A number of these classifications have been theorized and proposed. Perhaps the most prominent – and still exercising considerable influence on comparative lawyers – are the systems proposed by the French scholar René David and by the German scholars Konrad Zweigert and Hein Kötz. In 1950 David began a life's work seeking to arrange the world's various jurisdictions

1.2 What We Compare

into a set of "major systems."[26] His controversial but now entrenched classifications included: Western Law (including Romano-Germanic Civil Law and Anglo-Saxon Common Law), Socialist Law, Islamic Law, Hindu Law, and Chinese Law. Two decades later Zweigert and Kötz proposed their own, stubbornly influential set of global legal "families": the Romanistic Legal Family, Germanic Legal Family, Anglo-American Legal Family, Nordic (Scandinavian) Legal Family, Far Eastern Legal Family, Islamic Law, and Hindu Law.[27]

Despite the expansive list of legal groupings these and other scholars have proposed, comparative law has largely been fixated on two legal families, typically labeled "Civil Law" and "Common Law." Those categories have come to dominate research and teaching in the field of comparative legal studies. There are two reasons for this. First, it can be argued that these two families, taken together, encompass most of the world's population and most of the world's national jurisdictions.[28] Second, and more troubling, comparative law's focus on these two families reveals the discipline's deeply internalized Eurocentrism. After all, David clustered these two classifications under the single, rather telling, label "Western Law." Especially the latter explanation for the dominance of the Civil Law and Common Law families in the work of comparative law scholars demands new, critical approaches.[29] But, for the purposes of this book's survey of German law and legal culture, you only need to know that the German legal system is habitually, universally, and exclusively assigned to the Civil Law classification (David's "Western Law" or Zweigert's and Kötz's "Germanic Legal Family"). Don't worry if you aren't clear what that classification might mean for German law. As I promised earlier, Chapter 2 will introduce you to the Civil Law tradition, which is a predominant influence in German legal culture.

Disputes surrounding comparative law scholars' pursuit of broad, general categories of legal systems have largely centered on the criteria on which one relied to distinguish between different legal families. Does it make sense, for example, to group the Romano-Germanic and Anglo-Saxon categories together in a single "Western Law" legal classification as David proposed? Comparative law scholars have mostly adopted Zweigert's and Kötz's view, which recognizes a distinction between the European legal systems (whether Romanic or Germanic) and the Anglo-American legal systems. So, a major consequence of generations of work on macro-comparative law has been the confident, self-evident acceptance of at least two families: the Common Law and the Civil Law. Another consequence of the never-ending efforts to "perfect" the system for classifying legal systems has been the emergence of new and uniquely refined classifications, including impressive proposals for recognizing so-called "hybrid" or "mixed" legal systems.[30]

Few comparative law scholars have disputed the integrity of the macro-comparative law enterprise as a fundamental matter. That changed, however, when H. Patrick Glenn published his seminal work *Legal Traditions of the World: Sustainable Diversity in Law* in 2000.[31] Glenn offered two objections to macro-comparative law. First, he worried that legal families had come to serve as proxies, allowing comparativists to disregard a vast array of law-worlds altogether. Once one understands the characteristics of a broad grouping or legal family, for example, it is less necessary to become acquainted with any single legal system covered by that particular classification. It doesn't matter how distinct the particular system may be, or how enriching it would be to study it in greater detail. What matters is that it is a system of a particular type, belonging to a particular class or "family." Second, Glenn objected to the idea of making socially organic and evolving legal systems fit into particular classifications. He thought the effort involved crude and superficial generalizations about legal systems, which can't really be boxed up because they are dynamic and evolving. Especially the second of these two concerns animated Glenn's innovative departure from macro-comparative legal studies. Embracing the profound insight we have won from years of research and theorizing about legal families, Glenn proposed inverting the macro-comparative law project. It would no longer be interested in placing a particular legal system in a particular global classification. Instead, it would aim to study the way the world's "grand systems" or "legal families" – recast now as "traditions" – manifest themselves and interact within a single legal system.

The following is an excerpt from a book chapter in which Glenn summarized his innovative – and provocative – agenda.

H. Patrick Glenn
Comparative Legal Families and Comparative Legal Traditions
THE OXFORD HANDBOOK OF COMPARATIVE LAW 423, 426–428
(Mathias Reimann & Reinhard Zimmermann eds., 2nd ed. 2019)[*]

* * *

The Taxonomic Project

* * *

[…] [T]he concept of tradition is simply that of normative information and national [legal] systems may repose on different and varying amounts of (traditional) normative information. The concept of legal tradition thus suggests that one look for the *degrees* to which different traditions have been influential in the make-up of different national laws, and would be antithetical to exclusivist categorizations according to a limited range of criteria [of the kind that are necessary to identify national legal systems or construct legal families]. Legal traditions […] underlie and infiltrate national legal systems, which could no longer be taken as simple objects of classification and taxonomy.

It is true that one can still debate the manner of identification of legal traditions, and there could be perhaps as much disagreement on this question as there is on the definition of legal families. Moreover, many legal families […] reappear as legal traditions, such as those of the civil and common law. As normative information, however, legal traditions

---

[*] © The several contributors 2019. Reproduced with permission of the Licensor through PLSclear.

are largely self-identifying and need not answer to taxonomic requirements of providing the best means of understanding and structuring legal systems. The information of a legal tradition tells you that it is a common law tradition, or a Romano-Germanic tradition, or an Islamic tradition, and people and lawyers adhere to each tradition because of its content and identification. The boundaries of a legal tradition, moreover, are fuzzy. Since information is largely uncontrollable, the information at the core of every legal tradition will be complemented, in some measure and to some degree, by information drawn from other legal traditions. So legal traditions themselves are not exclusivist in character and debate as to their content and identity is essential and internal to them, not to be avoided through imposition of scientifically defined criteria. Debate is the normal state of things, and not an obstacle to scientific precision. If taxonomy and classification are effected through fixing the scientifically chosen boundaries of various classes, the nature and working of tradition is thus opposed to the fixing of boundaries and criteria for their fixation. Taxonomy and legal families have the task or objective of separation and distinguishing, whereas legal traditions have the task only of supporting their own forms of normativity. This usually involves more art than science, more attempting to do justice than attempting to build and classify systems.

* * *

Taxonomy and Stasis

* * *

How exactly is the concept of legal families a static one? Like all means of classification it is inherently static by fixing, at least temporarily, the objects of classification for purposes of their classification. Where the objects of classification are not physical objects, but large amounts of legal information, the classification attempts to freeze the contemporary flow of information in the world, for purposes of the present classification. The process parallels the contemporary concept of the national legal system, which would exist not in enduring form but rather as a succession of "momentary" legal systems, each one of which would represent the law in force at a given moment. Each of these "momentary" systems would be classified during the brief moment of its existence. Once the law is no longer in force by virtue of the present system, however, it is dead law, of no interest for purposes of the present system. More precisely, it becomes legal history, which thereby becomes the study of law which is no longer in force. So the process is inherently static because it has no means of assessing or appreciating what is often referred to as the "development" of law or its variation over time. […]

The taxonomic endeavor in the physical sciences rested in large measure on the physical stability of the objects of classification. There is, however, no such stability of legal systems, which exist not as "solid and sensible entities" but rather as "thought-objects, products of particular discourses rather than presuppositions of them." If we fix them at particular times, we lose the flow of the discourse, the variation of the system over time and any sense of direction this may provide. We are unable to assess the extent of change or the extent of resistance to change. There is an inevitable loss of normativity, and it is an inherent element of the teaching of positivist legal systems that they are unable to create an obligation to obey the law. They simply exist, at a given moment. The concept of legal families adds no normativity to this way of thinking, but would rather simply confirm the existence of these systems within the broader cadre of (descriptive) legal families.

In contrast to the inherently static character of legal systems and legal families, legal traditions exist as ongoing, normative information, and their normative force is drawn in large measure from their duration over time.

* * *

Questions/Comments

- According to Glenn, the fatal shortcoming in the old "legal families" approach to macro-comparative law is that classifications such as "grand systems" or "legal families" are necessarily exclusive and static. What does he regard as the negative implications of these facets of macro-comparative law's reliance on legal families? Do you share his concerns?
- Glenn argues that, on one hand, legal families are "exclusivist categorizations according to a limited range of criteria." On the other hand, he says that the concept of legal tradition is "simply [...] normative information," that is, information about what or how the law ought to be. Why isn't such information just as exclusive and static (temporally, territorially or theoretically) as legal families? Surely Glenn means to delimit *something* with the descriptor "traditions."
- Glenn's understanding of legal traditions has the great advantage of leaving open and, thereby, making vastly richer the objects of our comparative legal studies. All that would be lost through the process of defining and deploying legal families has been regained. In light of the stated aims for this book – discovery, the experience and practice of transcending borders, and self-reflection – it should be clear why I am persuaded by Glenn's critique of legal families. Yet, does Glenn's definition of legal tradition result in a concept of any practical use in comparative law? Are traditions *fixed* enough to at least allow us to distinguish one from another? Glenn's characterization of them might suggest the image of sand slipping through your fingers: tradition is self-identifying, fuzzy, ongoing, normative information – "more art than science." Glenn offers the following explanation for how "traditions" might be used in a comparative law study: "national systems may repose on different and varying amounts of (traditional) normative information. The concept of legal tradition thus suggests that one look for the degrees to which different traditions have been influential in the make-up of different national laws [...]. Legal traditions would thus underlie and infiltrate national legal systems [...]."[32] That is the thesis I pursue in this book: German law is shot-through with different traditions, which have been influential in the make-up of different (German) norms. Let's see if we can discover those threads, even if some will be rather faint and marginal.
- If you are still wondering what is meant by "legal tradition," maybe another definition provided by the scholars Merryman and Pérez-Perdomo will help. They explain that a legal tradition is "a set of deeply rooted, historically conditioned attitudes about the nature of law; about the role of law in the society and the polity; about the proper organization and operation of the legal system, and about the way law is or should be made, applied, studied, perfected, and taught."[33]
- Glenn accepts, as I noted earlier, that the most influential classification in comparative law refers to the Civil Law and the Common Law families. It is

1.2 What We Compare

important to note that Glenn does not reject these (or other) classifications as irrelevant to comparative law. Instead, he explains that "many legal families [...] reappear as legal traditions, such as those of the civil and common law." These venerable traditions are central to this book's study of German law and legal culture. Our study of German law will reveal the presence of these traditions. But I don't end my study of German legal culture with the Civil Law and Common Law traditions. I also consider the role (perhaps only remote or peripheral) of other legal traditions in the German legal system, including the residue of Socialist Law, the growing relevance of Islamic Law, the Inquisitorial approach to legal procedure, the Adversarial approach to legal procedure, and a still-coalescing tradition of European Law. The book uses these *legal traditions* in the manner that Glenn urges, and not as exclusive and static *legal families*. My examination of the German legal system considers the ways in which various legal traditions have influenced the makeup of law and legal culture in Germany. The Civil Law and Common Law traditions, for example, have greater or lesser sway in the German legal system. But neither of these traditions (or any other) can be said to conclusively and categorically characterize the German law-world. The materials in this book abundantly demonstrate that various legal traditions operate in combination in the German legal system – as they do in all legal systems. Figure 1.1a and 1.1b illustrate the two approaches: use of legal families to cluster and describe several, distinct legal systems; and Glenn's argument that different legal "traditions" are woven together to inform various norms in a distinct legal system.

- Ugo Mattei suggested a new catalogue of global legal families that he believed to be more open to normative pluralism and free of the Western bias evident in the legal families on which macro-comparative law has relied. Mattei explains that "[i]n my proposed classification, systems may belong to the *rule of professional law*, the *rule of political law*, or the *rule of traditional law*."[34] What might these classifications mean? What would Glenn's critique of them be? Or would Glenn simply refashion these new "families" as new expressions of legal tradition and then urge us to look for the ways that they appear as an influence in a particular legal system? Do you agree with Mattei that some form of classification or taxonomy is necessary in comparative law, that is, that comparative legal studies are a science (like the study of biology) and not an act of interpretation (like the study of literature).[35] Do you think Mattei's new families might provide a productive system for thinking about and engaging with the German legal system?
- Distinct factors justify a brief consideration of Islamic Law in this book's survey of German law and legal culture. I make a special effort in this regard in Chapter 9, which presents German administrative law. Germany is home to a large number of observant Muslims. After the arrival of hundreds of thousands of Muslim refugees in 2015 and 2016, there are now roughly 5.5 million Muslims in Germany, accounting for more than 6 percent of the

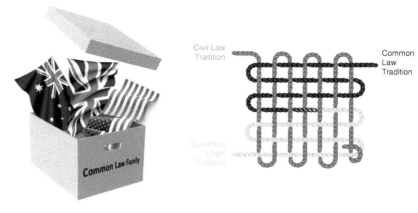

(a) Legal Families
The "legal families" approach to macro-comparative law seeks to classify (national) legal systems into broad, global legal families.

(b) Legal Traditions
Glenn's "legal traditions" approach to macro-comparative law seeks to identify the legal traditions present in the German (or any other) legal system.

Figure 1.1 Glenn: From Legal Families to Legal Traditions

country's population.[36] For many of these Muslims the doctrine and dictates of their faith have a normative force on their life that is every bit as relevant and resonant as Germany's secular state law. This touches fundamental facets of their lives, such as dietary concerns, family affairs, and financial matters.[37] Glenn points out that comparative law's reliance on legal families has generally neglected or marginalized the significance of Islamic Law (and other traditions). For Glenn, comparative law's Western bias is an inherent consequence – perhaps the most disturbing consequence – of the exclusion that is an essential feature of classification and taxonomy.

- Maybe comparative legal studies are so thoroughly tainted by the traditional Western bias, by the Western way of thinking, that the project is now irredeemably compromised, even when the comparative law project opens itself up for the consideration of non-Western legal systems and traditions. Upendra Baxi argues that we will have gained nothing by bringing Islamic Law into the practice and teaching of comparative legal studies if we do so only to ridicule it as "non-law" or as an understanding of law that has fallen short of Western standards.[38] Pluralism in comparative legal studies, as masterfully advocated by Werner Menski,[39] will not be enough. Baxi calls on us to acknowledge that at "the threshold of the edifice of comparative legal studies [...] lies the Althusserian logic of *indifference*, an order of knowledge/power relation in which all concrete differences are regarded as 'equally indifferent.'" The willful disregard of difference has been a core feature of macro-comparative law's traditional pursuit of the "legal families" agenda.

From Glenn you get a sense of *what* I hope we'll be "comparing" in this book. This project is not meant to confirm the German legal system's assignment to a particular "legal family." Instead, I want to take up Glenn's challenge, flip macro-comparative law's old script on its head, and examine the German legal system to try to identify the various legal traditions at play there. That promises a rich and textured portrayal of German law and legal culture.

1.3 How We Compare

There may be no more natural cognitive function than comparison. From the earliest phases of human development we have needed to be able to compare, even as a matter of survival: this plant is edible and that plant is poisonous; my clan offers me safety and sustenance while that clan is hostile and threatening. Comparison persists as a bedrock of the human capacity for thought and directed action, even if its most predominant role today is to help us distinguish products in a saturated consumer market, reduced now to the banal act of a left- or right-swipe on our smart phones. If each of us is a natural born, highly evolved, and extensively experienced comparing machine, then is it really necessary to consider *how* we should go about comparing laws? Can't we just get on with doing comparison the way we instinctively do it?

Generations of thoughtful, theoretical work on comparative law methodology demonstrates that there is a lot to be gained from reflecting on and refining our approach to comparative legal studies. Law, as a social construct, is infused with values and subjectivity in a way that distinctions amongst edible and inedible plants is not. There's nothing subjective about whether a plant is poisonous. But our view of one law or the other is much more normative, much more dependent on our view of things. There can't be an objective answer to the question: which law is better? As far as methodology goes, this means that comparative legal studies can be influenced (perhaps decisively) by the comparativist's normative perspectives, and by his or her motivations for embarking on the comparison in the first place. Our reason for comparing laws might condition the methods we apply. And naturally, the choice of method is likely to determine the outcome of the comparison. Unlike other areas of research, which depend on the essential components of the established scientific method (propose a hypothesis, experimentation to test the hypothesis, analyze the data produced by the experimentation, report the result), comparative law is a uniquely "teleological science."[40] That is, the approach one takes to comparative legal studies is largely determined by the aims and objectives motivating the comparative undertaking in the first place.

If the means are stipulated by the ends, then should we consider what the aims of comparative legal studies might be? Two broad themes have emerged to respond to that question. The first theme centers on whether comparative legal studies should emphasize the similarity of the objects of comparison, or whether comparison should focus on the differences. The second theme centers on whether comparison points us towards objective (scientific) legal truths, or whether it is an interpretive and critical enterprise. The plot points mapped by these concerns have jurisprudential and ethical implications. And different methods point the way to those ends. Maybe you can already imagine how your intentions regarding these themes (similarity/difference; objectivity/subjectivity) would require you to use altogether distinct methods for pursuing a comparison of laws.

The following materials highlight these themes and help to explain why this book has opted for an approach to comparative legal studies that emphasizes difference and subjectivity.

1.3.1 Difference or Similarity

It is possible to see Glenn as being engaged in a struggle on behalf of *difference* and against the impulse to prioritize *similarity* in comparative law. Glenn's condemnation of legal families essentially aims to salvage and validate all the difference that gets lost through the static and exclusive process of classification. In this sense, Glenn staked a position with respect to one of the most fundamental debates about how we should compare laws: should we compare in ways that serve *universalizing* or *particularizing* ends? Are we animated by abstract, generalizable claims that depend on finding similarity, or are we drawn to law's embeddedness in culture that comes into view when we prioritize difference?[41]

In the following three excerpts Pierre Legrand, comparative law's oracle of difference, makes a clamorous case for law's cultural contingency – for its inherent difference. I include the first excerpt, from the book chapter entitled "The Same and the Different," because it offers a breathless survey of the "orthodox" emphasis on similarity in comparative legal studies. In a second excerpt, from the article "The Impossibility of 'Legal Transplants,'" Legrand rejects comparative law's yearning for similarity because he insists that law has force only when it has meaning for those it is meant to govern. That meaning, he explains, derives as much from the contextualized understanding provided by the norm's interpreter as it does from the text of the norm itself. Finally, in the excerpt from the article "Negative Comparative Law," Legrand outlines the broad range of social factors that give law its meaning and ensure its fundamental, culturally embedded difference. This is difficult material. Legrand pursues his arguments from the perspective of legal philosophy and critical theory. The puzzled-together reconstruction of these arguments across various, excerpted texts also risks adding confusion to the presentation of Legrand's ideas. But, if you can push ahead with these ideas, you'll be treated to a shrewd and passionate explanation of the cultural and contextual sensitivity that informs my interest in the inherent difference – in the cultural uniqueness – of German law.

Pierre Legrand
The Same and the Different
COMPARATIVE LEGAL STUDIES: TRADITIONS AND TRANSITIONS 240, 245–248
(Pierre Legrand & Roderick Munday eds., 2003)*

* * *

In a very important sense, the recent history of comparative legal studies must be read as a persistent, albeit not always adroit, attempt to identify sameness across laws and to demote difference to a *modus deficiens* of sameness. As John Merryman observes, "[d]ifferences between legal systems have been regarded [...] as evils or inconveniences to be overcome." Not surprisingly, "[w]hen differences are discovered, gentility seems to require that [they] be dissolved." Indeed, as he engages with his (impossible) object of study, "the comparati[st] *presumes* similarities between different jurisdictions in the very act of searching for them" and assumes differentiating features to be largely indifferent. The desire for sameness breeds the expectation of sameness which, in turn, begets the finding of sameness. Even a posteriori re-presentations contradicting sameness appear not to prevent comparatists from "catch[ing] sight [...] of the grand similarities and so to deepen [their] belief in the existence of a unitary sense of justice." Illustrations of the reigning proleptical orthodoxy abound.

In his general report to the 1900 Paris Congress, Edouard Lambert claimed that "the comparatist, in order to fulfil his task, must select [as the object of his comparison] the most similar laws." For a French jurist, therefore, the study of English law ought to occur only "accessorily"; it must occupy no more than "a discreet place." However, "a comparison can be very usefully drawn between the Latin group and the Germanic group" – that is, among legal "systems" partaking in the Romanist legal tradition. For Ernst Rabel, "[comparative research] ascertains throughout the world the facts common to all, the common life problems, the common functions of the legal institutions." Konrad Zweigert and Hein Kötz indeed postulate a *"praesumptio similitudinis"* to the effect that "legal systems give the same or very similar solutions, even as to detail, to the same problems of life," so that a finding of difference should lead comparatists to start their investigation afresh. In these authors' words, "the comparatist can rest content if his researches through all the relevant material lead to the conclusion that the systems he has compared reach the same or similar practical results, but if he finds that there are great differences or indeed diametrically opposite results, he should be warned and go back to check again whether the terms in which he posed his original question were [...] purely functional, and whether he has spread the net of his researches quite wide enough." For Alan Watson, the circulation and reception of legal rules point to substantial sameness across laws. One of the numerous illustrations developed by this author over the years concerns the rules on transfer of ownership and risk in sale: "Before the *Code civil* the Roman rules were generally accepted in France [...]. This was also the law accepted by the first modern European code, the Prussian *Allgemeines Landrecht für die Preußischen Staaten* of 1794." According to Ugo Mattei, there exists, and there can be discovered, a "common core of efficient principles hidden in the different technicalities of [...] legal systems." Thus, "common core research is a very promising tool for unearthing deeper analogies hidden by formal differences." Rudolf Schlesinger's own "common-core" project, which concerned contract formation, was directed toward the

---

* © Cambridge University Press 2003. Reproduced with permission of the Licensor through PLSclear.

formulation of an area of agreement "in terms of precise and narrow rules." Various contemporary applications demonstrate the enduring attraction of Schlesinger's *esprit de simplification* and offer fully or partly mimetic variations on his coarse model. For his part, Basil Markesinis argues that "we must try to overcome obstacles of terminology and classification in order to show that foreign law is not very different from ours but only appears to be so." Elsewhere, Markesinis observes "how similar our laws on tort are or, more accurately, how similar they can be made to look with the help of some skilful (and well-meaning) *manipulation*." [...]

In sum, the picture painted by Tullio Ascarelli remains compelling: comparative legal studies is either concerned with unification of laws within substantive or geographical limits or is more philosophically inclined and aspires to a uniform law that would be universal. Under both approaches, the point is not to explain legal diversity, but to explain it away, to contain it in the name of an authoritative ideal of knowledge and truth somehow deemed to be above diversity, to be intrinsically diversity-free. [...] The frantic urge to eliminate difference as a valid analytical focus for comparative legal studies – without any apparent concern for what is being lost along the way – has even prompted James Gordley to write that "there is no such thing as a French law or German law or American law that is an independent object of study apart from the law of other countries." The outreach of the dominant and enveloping epistemological discourse that has operated an institutionalization of sameness and ensured the disqualification of difference – that has wanted to bring matters to a kind of degree zero of comparatism – is not in doubt. Through the development of a monistic framework, comparatists have made it their collective and coercive purpose to proscribe what they regard as disorder and to invalidate what they apprehend as dissonance. Difference, then, is in tension with the comparative project of wanting to get things right, to keep things straight. It is in tension with the self-control that purports to characterize comparative legal studies's totalizing, *hygienic* style. In fact, the forgetting of difference within comparative legal studies is so profound that even this forgetting is forgotten (which, I suppose, is a courteous way of saying that comparative legal studies denies difference and denies this denial). [...]

* * *

Pierre Legrand
The Impossibility of "Legal Transplants"
4 MAASTRICHT JOURNAL OF EUROPEAN AND COMPARATIVE LAW 111, 114–115 (1997).[*]

* * *

No form of words purporting to be a "rule" can be completely devoid of semantic content, for no rule can be without meaning. The meaning of the rule is an essential component of the rule; it partakes in the ruleness of the rule. The meaning of a rule, however, is not entirely supplied by the rule itself; a rule is never completely self-explanatory. To be sure, meaning emerges from the rule so that it must be assumed to exist, if virtually, within the rule itself even before the interpreter's interpretive apparatus is engaged. To this extent, the meaning of a rule is acontextual. But, meaning is also – and perhaps mostly – a function of the application of the rule by its interpreter, of the concretization or instantiation in the events the rule is meant to govern. This ascription of meaning is predisposed by the

---

[*] Excerpt reprinted with permission of SAGE Publications Inc.

way the interpreter understands the context within which the rule arises and by the manner in which she frames her questions, this process being largely determined by who and where the interpreter is and, therefore, to an extent at least, by what she, in advance, wants and expects (unwittingly?) the answers to be. The meaning of the rule is, accordingly, a function of the interpreter's epistemological assumptions which are themselves historically and culturally conditioned.

These pre-judices (I use the term in its etymological, not in its negative, or acquired, sense) are actively forged, for example, through the schooling process in which law students are immersed and through which they learn the values, beliefs, dispositions, justifications and the practical consciousness that allows them to consolidate a cultural code, to crystallize their identities, and to become professionally socialized. Indeed, even before they reach law school students will have assimilated a cultural profile (let us say the Gadamerian "*Vorverständnis*") – whether English or Italian or German – which will colour in a most relevant way their legal education experience and their internalization of the narrative and mythology in which they will share. Each English child, for example, is a common-law-lawyer-in-being long before she even contemplates going to law school. Inevitably, therefore, a significant part of the very real emotional and intellectual investment that presides over the formulation of the meaning of a rule lies beneath consciousness because the act of interpretation is embedded, in a way that the interpreter is often unable to appreciate empirically, in a language and in a tradition, in sum, in a whole cultural ambience.

An interpretation, then, is always a subjective product and that subjective product is necessarily, in part at least, a cultural product: the interpretation is, in other words, the result of a particular understanding of the rule that is conditioned by a series of factors (many of them intangible) which would be different if the interpretation had occurred in another place or in another era (for, then, different cultural claims would be made on interpreters). [...]

* * *

Pierre Legrand
Negative Comparative Law
10 JOURNAL OF COMPARATIVE LAW 405, 420–421, 429–430, 431–432 (2015)[*]

* * *

[...] A text is indeed a fabric (consider the word "textile"). A law-text thus exists as an interface where an array of discursive threads have come together to be absorbed and transformed in order to be made to *speak legally*. These threads operate to colligate or fasten or bind or band *as the law-text* as they amalgamate to constitute it. A thread leaves a discernible *trace* within the law-text entailing that the text exists as "a fabric of traces," that it is knotty. For example, traces of historical configurations enmeshed with traces of political rationalities intertwined with traces of social logics interwoven with traces of philosophical postulates plaited with traces of linguistic orders darned with traces of economic prescriptions interlaced with traces of epistemic assumptions morph into a foreign statute, that is, they become *jurimorphs*. Crucially, the discourses therefore assembling to constitute a law-text, thus being gathered consciously or not by the author of the text (say, the legislator drafting a statute or the judge writing an opinion), are not

---

[*] Excerpt reprinted with permission of the author.

to be regarded as external to the law-text or contextual vis-à-vis it or as some sort of par-ergon pertaining to the realm of non-law. Rather, these discourses concern the very texture of the law-text: they inform the making or fabrication of it, and they remain of it, as survivancies, once the law-text has emerged as law-text. Again, they leave a *trace* within the law-text that reveals how the text is marked, from its very inception, *ipso facto*, as the instantiation of a historical configuration, a political rationality, a social logic, a philosophical postulate, a linguistic order, an economic prescription, an epistemic assumption and so forth. On account of these ascertainable traces, a law-text thus conceals remains or vestigial presences [...].

* * *

[...] Indeed, on account of its traces, every foreign law-text always already exists as a singularly plural entity [of traces]. It exists, to borrow from Jean-Luc Nancy's, as a plural singularity. What orthodox "comparative law" has classically understood as other-than-law (history, politics, society, philosophy, language, economics, epistemology and so forth... culture!) is, through the law-text's structuring spectral principle, revealed to be very much present *as* the law-text: the selfness of the law-text exists as an assemblage of "othernesses" (history, politics and so forth... culture!) – a situation that implies, in Derrida's more challenging philosophical language, that "the same is the same only in affecting itself of the other, by becoming the other of the same." Once again, Derrida's claim is that the foreign law-text exists as the foreign law-text that it exists as on account of its being imbued or infused by otherness – specifically, by other discourses such as history, politics and so forth (... culture!). In other words, the foreign law-text's authentic self exists as something other than a pure self. It is a more complicated self than the pure self that it has been said to be by orthodox comparatists, who continue to envisage legal knowledge and other disciplinary knowledges as so many silos. [...]

* * *

So, what difference do "culture" and "tracing" *effectively* make to work on foreign law and to comparative analysis? [...] For a culturalist [studying French law, for example] the law-text proves traceable, by way of supplement to judicial decisions, textbooks and law-review articles – and much more rewardingly, if one is in search of *explication* – to constitutive ideas (all of them manifestations of French culture and, in particular, of French legal culture), such as a strongly assertive state, a well-honed social demand for state interventionism, the deep distrust into which the individual is readily held, a time-honoured aversion for the unfettered play of the market and the related assumption that only the state can bring to bear the appropriate dose of *solidarité* that must feature within a French contractual relationship.

A view of law-as-culture indicates these various aspects of the law-text as being relevant features of [a French norm, such as the civil-code provision] compelling the need for judicial authorization before a contract can be "terminated" rather than allowing a party unilaterally to declare the contract at an end subject to the payment of damages in case of subsequent retaliatory litigation – which is, in a nutshell, the position obtaining in the common-law tradition [...]. But in order to generate the sort of interpretive yield that, alone, can permit a deep or thick understanding of the law-text, a comparatist must be prepared to approach law *as culture* (i.e., to treat law as law-as-culture) and to trace the law-text to its constitutive features on the understanding that the traces deemed relevant are an integral part of the text, that these traces exist *as* the text [...], that they exist *as* the text that therefore exists *as* culture. In other terms, the comparatist-at-law writing [about the French civil code, for example] must be disposed to be *writing culture*. [...] [But, because] there is no algorithm to determine the vectors of cultural extension, the quality of "legality" (if this be the apt word) is thus conferred to the *interpretandum* on the basis of the heterogeneous elements that the comparatist-at-law himself connects or assembles, that he understands as pertaining to the "legal" and that he names ["the French law"] [...].

* * *

Questions/Comments

- Revisit the excerpt from the book chapter "The Same and the Different." What does Legrand say motivates comparative law's "frantic urge" towards sameness? The starkest example of this urge, also highlighted by Legrand in his compact survey of the history of comparative legal studies, must be Zweigert's and Kötz's proposed "*praesumptio similitudinis*" – a presumption of similarity. Those scholars argued that we can presume that "developed nations answer the needs of legal business in the same or in a very similar way."[42] This presumption is an extension of another, more fundamental contribution that Zweigert and Kötz made to comparative law methodology. Their "principle of functionality" holds that the purpose of comparative legal studies is to identify the legal solutions different systems offer to "essentially similar problems" facing societies. Theirs is a regime of sameness: similar problems, they say, have produced similar legal responses. Functionalism is the most common approach taken to micro-comparative studies.
- In "The Same and the Different," Legrand suggests that comparative law's "totalizing, hygienic style" takes two forms: it is part of a political act of unification, or it is part of the scientific pursuit of law's uniformity. Can you think of examples of these two agendas?
- In documenting comparative law's "orthodoxy" of sameness in "The Same and the Different," Legrand tells us that James Gordely concluded that there is no such thing as French, German, or American law. Gordley cannot mean that literally. What fundamental point – emphasizing law's sameness – might he be making?
- In the second excerpt in the series, Legrand further develops his case against sameness by arguing that law is better characterized by difference. In "The Impossibility of 'Legal Transplants,'" Legrand explains that the very purpose of a law – that its meaning might shape human conduct – makes comparative law research an effort to discover a foreign norm's meaning. "The meaning of the rule," he explains, "is an essential component of the rule." But meaning can't be deduced by merely translating and reading the text of the law, as if it exists in a vacuum or a sterile laboratory. Legrand insists that meaning is culturally determined. It is conditioned by the context within which the rule is meant to operate. That context shapes the character of the norm's addressees and its interpreters. A law's cultural context *differentiates* it for its *particular* legal system. Legrand argues that meaning is drawn from the law's "cultural ambience," that is, the cultural framework in which understanding of the

law forms and operates. Legrand even argues that the "cultural framework" of law's meaning is being fashioned even before aspiring jurists undertake their formal legal training. That's why he says that every English child "is a common law lawyer in waiting." Legrand approvingly quotes the German philosopher Walter Benjamin, who reasoned that "the word *Brot* [bread in German] means something different to a German than the word *pain* [bread in French] to a Frenchman." Can you imagine what those different, culturally determined meanings of bread are for Germans and the French? Can you think of a legal norm or principle – the same word, albeit in translation – that might mean something altogether different in two legal systems?

- Legrand's complex, multi-step argument (meaning is central to the essence of a rule; but meaning is culturally determined) is leveled against Alan Watson who developed the theory of "legal transplants." Watson argued that most law possesses common roots as a result of the movement or migration of rules from one society to another. Watson believed that the process of "legal transplantation" goes back to shared sources from the earliest periods of recorded history. That led him to conclude that "the history of a system of law is largely a history of borrowings of legal materials from other legal systems."[43] A consequence of the legal transplants theory, according to Watson, is that systems have rules that show similarities of "formulation and substance."[44] It seems indisputable that norms and legal institutions have moved from system to system as Watson describes. Can you think of an example? What, then, does Legrand mean when he says that "legal transplants are impossible"?

- What does Legrand's insistence on the cultural framing of law – its essential distinctiveness – mean for the methodology of comparative legal studies? The excerpt from his article "Negative Comparative Law" tells us that the comparativist must try to account for the "cultural ambience" that forms a rule's meaning. This is an effort that takes the comparative law scholar away from the narrow, positive law itself (statutes, judicial decisions, law textbooks, law review articles) and into other disciplines, into other frameworks for understanding a society and its laws. But Legrand insists that, because those external or extracurricular "traces" shape the rule's meaning, they are themselves a part of the rule. For Legrand, the exploration of these other disciplines, these other sources of meaning, also count as legal research. Legrand identifies several of these "traces" of cultural meaning in law: history, politics, sociology, philosophy, language, economics, and epistemology (a particular way of knowing). Do you agree that understanding something about some or all of these frameworks is necessary for your engagement with the law? Do you possess this insight in relation to the law of our primary or "national" legal system? Can you think of a rule or legal institution that would be essentially unintelligible without the benefit of a fuller understanding of history or politics? Would you guess that one of these cultural "traces" is more relevant to law's meaning in Germany?

1.3 How We Compare

- Has Legrand neglected any important "traces" or cultural influences on law's meaning? I might add religion to his list, especially considering the formal and informal power religious institutions have wielded, and continue to wield, in most societies. Even in the absence of that direct political influence, religion contributes significantly to shaping a society's morality and values, which are often expressed or reinforced by law. Can you imagine a way that religion has impacted law in your primary or "national" legal system? Can you imagine a way that religion has impacted law in Germany?
- Legrand's program is intimidating and imposing. He urges us to develop a "deep" or "thick" understanding of the laws we compare. While you're doing the hard work of acquainting yourself with a new legal system, he piles on the demand that you also account for many other dimensions of the society in which that legal system operates. But be reassured. For Legrand, even a stumbling effort in this direction is nobler than the stubborn refusal to acknowledge law's essential, cultural moorings. Elsewhere, Legrand concedes that comparative law scholars are likely to fail at this big and complex task. Still, he urges us to "fail better."[45] Legrand's culturally rooted comparative legal studies might call on you to get help from specialists in other academic disciplines, or at least tap into your own interest in a field typically thought of as being "outside" the law. Legrand's comparative law is interdisciplinary.
- Chapters 4–6 of this book provide some of the external, cultural framing for German law that Legrand calls for. They aren't comprehensive treatments of each of the "traces" Legrand identifies. But they provide some foundational or contextual depth about German law and society so that you have a better chance at grasping the culturally determined meaning of the German law presented in later chapters. I hope, with those and other cultural materials, this book "fails better."
- Can Glenn's critique of boundaries be rationalized with Legrand's embrace of the boundaries that are necessary for marking out legal-cultural difference between legal systems? Legrand defends his reliance on legal culture (as the basis for his insistence on and respect for difference) by noting that "[f]or a culturalist [...] the law-text, much more rewardingly, is seen to conceal constitutive ideas, which inform it and have indeed generated it – all of them manifestations of long-standing ways of living and working together, which one can helpfully style as 'French culture' and specifically as 'French legal culture.'"[46] Do you agree that national communities are a fair demarcation of distinct ways of doing things? Is there *French* cuisine? Is there *English* humor? Is there *Spanish* soccer? Are there long-standing *German* ways of living and working together in the law? Legrand acknowledges the strong opposition to the assertion of national culture, especially among legal universalists. Does all of this difference, for example, erode claims for a regime of universal human rights? Does Legrand adequately recognize the proximity of his claims about cultural identity to brutish traditions of nationalism

and nativism? Can one share Legrand's sentiments and, at the same time, aspire to universalism and oppose national chauvinism?

- Legrand agonizes over comparative law's preoccupation with similarity and he pleads for comparativists to "resign themselves to the fact that law is a cultural phenomenon and that, therefore, differences across legal cultures can only ever be overcome imperfectly. [... They] must purposefully privilege the identification of differences across the laws they compare lest they fail to address singularity with scrupulous authenticity. They must make themselves into difference engineers." What does he mean by "difference engineers"?

At least two strains in Legrand's approach suggest that it has a normative gravity of its own. Legrand is interested in more than just deconstructing (or, as some might see it, destroying) the traditional approach to comparative law.

First, with his comparative law of difference, Legrand advocates a particular vision of the human condition by recognizing the significance of the "self" and "other" in human experience. This has particular resonance in all comparative undertakings, which presuppose the comparativist's legal identity and the difference presented by the foreign legal system. Legrand remarks:

> Difference, of course, suggests a dimension unknown to the self, something like *das Unheimliche* [the uncanny]. Difference belongs to thought's unthought realm. Perhaps it even partakes in what thought cannot think. Difference lies beyond the self. It is vexatious, at times maddening. It threatens the death of the self even.

With remarks like these, it is clear that Legrand's prioritization of difference is indebted to the work of the French philosopher Jacques Derrida.[47] Second, with his comparative law of difference, Legrand advocates a particular political vision that seeks to protect the individual "as the expression of the human capacity for choice and self-creation" against totalitarian and totalizing impulses. In this way, Legrand's prioritization of difference builds upon the liberal, individualizing political philosophy of John Locke.[48] Combining these strains allows Legrand to speak of his approach to comparative law as an ethical endeavor that shows respect for the integrity of the other (and the self) as it resists totalizing tendencies. Legrand's approach embraces and celebrates diversity and sees comparative law as an ethical endeavor. We might sum up those ethics with the one word: Respect. Assuming a posture of respect (even bemused respect) will vastly enrich your encounter with the many differences you are bound to encounter during this journey into German law and legal culture.

1.3.2 Subjectivity or Science

The comparative law advocates of similarity want to have science on their side. They imagine that foreign laws can be studied in the abstract by neutral, lab-coat-wearing comparative law scholars. And don't be surprised if, despite your exposure to Legrand's teaching about difference, you discover similarities between the German legal culture and your primary or "national" legal system. There is, after all, a strong human tendency to see the "self" in the "other." But there is a risk that what you recognize as similar is merely the familiar forcing its way back into your thinking. Whether that dynamic can be avoided (or at least mitigated) is questionable. Maybe the best we can do is to recognize the risk and avoid dignifying our comparative claims with an assertion of objectivity. It is a particularly problematic trap for the comparativist to imagine that he or she has achieved scientific neutrality.

How can this trap be avoided? An important step is to adopt a self-reflective posture that casts light on your subjectivity. Rudolf Schlesinger, one of the major figures in comparative legal studies, urged us to be wary of "taking it for granted that the concepts and precepts of [your] law will be duplicated in other legal systems [...]."[49] An embrace of comparative law's inherent subjectivity and its related potential for fostering critical self-reflection was brilliantly described in Günter Frankenberg's masterful article "Critical Comparisons: Re-thinking Comparative Law."

Günter Frankenberg
Critical Comparisons: Re-thinking Comparative Law
26 HARVARD INTERNATIONAL LAW JOURNAL 411, 413–416, 441–443 (1985)[*]

* * *

Distance and Difference

* * *

Learning [...] demands a change in a person's cognitive status quo. Basic prerequisites for a cognitive transformation are that one (1) become aware of her assumptions, (2) no longer project characteristics of her own way onto the objects of her scholarly attention, and (3) decenter the personal point of view so that through the vantage the new allows her she can consider not only the new, but the truthfulness of her own assumptions. In other words, it is crucial how we select the information we are exposed to and how we relate new knowledge to settled knowledge. Unless we assimilate what we get to know to what we know already and accommodate what we know to what we get to know, we merely accumulate information. The new information has to be processed, that is, to be integrated and contextualized with the known to make sense to us. And what we already know has to be connected with what we get to know in order for the latter to make a difference. The risks are that in integrating knowledges we will level the new in the hard-worn categories of the old or that in looking too hard for the new we will abandon the stability and prudence embodied in the old's normative vision or keep the new and old separate and not allow ourselves to learn the lessons of each. Metaphorically speaking, new and old knowledge enter into a dialogue with each other, in which their respective claims to completeness, authenticity and truth are mutually questioned and tested.

---

[*] Excerpt reprinted with permission of the author.

Learning does not require us to sell out what we know to any novelty or just to enlarge the quantity of the knowledge we store, but to review and transcend both.

A dialogue between the settled and the new knowledge or, for that matter, a dialectical exchange between the self and the other may sound right in theory. Yet, how does it work in practice? I suggest that the dialectic of learning requires at least two operations that prevent the old categories and way from being merely projected onto the world and that allow the new to speak for itself. These operations I call "distancing" and "differencing." Distance is needed to gain a vantage on who we are and what we are doing and thinking. Distancing can be described as an attempt to break away from firmly held beliefs and settled knowledge and as an attempt to resist the power of prejudice and ignorance. From a distance old knowledge can be reviewed and new knowledge can be distinguished as it is in its own right. Distance de-centers our world-view and thus establishes what might be called objectivity.

Mere distance, however, neither opens our eyes nor makes us see clearly. As long as foreign places only look like or unlike home, as long as foreign legal cultures only appear to be un-common or un-civil, and as long as they are treated as same or other, they do not speak for themselves. In order to break the unconscious spell that holds us to see others by the measure of ourselves without abandoning the benefits of criticism, traveling as well as comparison has to be an exercise in difference. By differencing we not only develop and practice a sharp sense for diversity and heterogeneity but, more importantly, we make a conscious effort to establish subjectivity, that is, the impact of the self, the observer's perspective and experience, is scrupulously taken into account. Differencing calls into question the neutrality and universality of all criteria; it rejects the notion (entertained by many comparatists and travelers alike) that the categories and concepts with which new experiences are grasped, classified, and compared have nothing whatsoever to do with the socio-cultural context of those who see in terms of them. Differencing is necessary to prevent the observer-comparatist from confusing the present content of (Western) ideas and concepts with the criteria of a universal truth and logic. By the same token, however, recognition of subjectivity threatens the objectivity of any observation, analysis or comparison. Differencing can thereby prevent the traveler-comparatist from regarding the world only in terms of the language of security and self-understanding and from leveling others with old concepts, imagery, and experience.

* * *

[…] I suggest we abandon the notion of cultures or laws as objects whose reality can be grasped, represented wholly and classified systematically, for what appears to be "objective reality" is an intricate tangle in which the comparatist's cultural, historical, and personal preconceptions inevitably shape the way she perceives and compares. Therefore critical comparisons, instead of dichotomizing new against old knowledge, would have to recognize that new always and inescapably reveals old. To transcend old orders and to understand new ones as different and same the comparatist has to become aware, first and foremost, of the limitations the domestic legal regime imposes on any comparative approach. […]

* * *

Re-imaging Comparative Legal Studies

* * *

For Comparative Legal Studies to become a learning experience, much more critical work has to be done. Stated in very broad terms, critical comparisons require a greater sensitivity to the relationship between the self and the other rather than merely intellectual sophistication. Instead of continuing the endless search for a neutral stance and objective status, comparatists have to recognize that they are participant observers, therefore their studies have to be self-reflective and self-critical. Instead of presupposing the necessity, functionality, and universality of law, critical comparisons have to question "legocentrism," the religion guiding and pervading legal education and practice. Instead of "getting straight" the histories and diversities of laws, critical comparisons must call for a rigorous analysis of and tolerance for ambiguity.

* * *

Yet, despite all these claims that the comparatist be open-minded and think supranationally, the civil and common law still rule over the comparatists' world. And the individual as an abstract legal entity bestowed with rights and duties has been transplanted from the Western to almost every other legal culture. The law that "We" have dominates the law that "Others" have. Our schema dictate to a degree what we find in others and classify them as relevant or marginal, familiar or exotic, and so on.

Perspective is not only a cognitive or emotional defect or disposition that can be manipulated or cured by a "right" ethic, attitude or reasoning. It is an integral aspect of every person's history of learning. Being socialized into a particular culture – or simply: growing up – means to become familiar with, to gain a particular perspective on and be biased toward that environment. Are we therefore victims to our culture? Can a Western head only think in Western terms? I do not think so. We can transcend perspective, we can learn about, understand and empathize with what we find "strange" or "foreign" or "exotic," provided that we always recognize that we are participants of one culture and observers of any other. To transcend perspective means to realize that we use our language, which is culture-based, to grasp what is new and seemingly other than us. While the self, our cognitive history and its baggage of assumptions and perspective, cannot be disposed of at will, we can still try to honestly and consciously account for it, exposing it to self-critical re-examination. Though using our language is necessary, there is no a priori truth or universal logic to how we use it. That is why comparative work could be enlightened by a skeptical attitude toward allegedly authentic interpretations and universal categories.

Comparison has to be self-reflective. The comparatist has to reflect upon herself as a subject of and to law. Instead of pretending to the posture of a neutral, objective, and disinterested observer, the comparatist has to regard herself as being involved: involved in an ongoing, particular social practice constituted and pervaded by law; involved in a given legal tradition (a peculiar story of law); and involved in a specific mode of thinking and talking about law. Once the comparatist asks herself how she came to be what she is in terms of the law (an "individual" with "rights" and "duties," a "tenant," "taxpayer," "parent," "consumer," etc.) and how she came to think as a "legal scholar" about her own law and the other laws the way she does, notions of normality and universality begin to blur. It becomes clearer then that any vision of the foreign laws is derived from and shaped by domestic assumptions and bias.

* * *

Questions/Comments

- Frankenberg concedes that the critical self-reflection and subjectivity he advocates – the distancing and differencing – "does not come naturally." But in a bit of circular reasoning he also acknowledges that the comparativist, perhaps even the uncritical traditionalist, "is in a privileged-position [by virtue of] the very fact that she is confronted with different legal forms and categories, with alternative legal and non-legal strategies all of which may be more or less realistic, adequate, mystifying, reifying, alienating, and so forth." This might be the basic hope for what this survey of German law and legal culture can achieve: that you acquire the information presented here about German law as a necessary (albeit, not sufficient) precondition for reflecting critically on your primary or "national" legal system. You should make use of this information to engage in the kind of self-conscious learning Frankenberg describes: "(1) become aware of [your] assumptions, (2) no longer project characteristics of [your] way onto the objects of [your study], and (3) decenter the personal point of view so that through the vantage the new allows [you] can consider not only the new, but the truthfulness of [your] assumptions."

- To achieve the critical self-reflection and subjectivity in comparative legal studies that Frankenberg proposes, he urges us to embrace "distance" and "difference." Which of the two moves has the most to do with breaking the "unconscious spell that holds us to see others by the measure of ourselves [...]."?
- According to Frankenberg, critical comparative law consists of a "conscious effort to establish subjectivity, that is, [to scrupulously take account of] the impact of the self, the observer's perspective and experience [...]." But how is this accomplished? A fundamental starting point in recognizing that you are a "participant observer" of the German legal system surveyed in this book is to reflect on the fact that you are being or have been trained as a legal professional. For what kinds of "normative preferences and emotional reactions" does this precondition you? A layperson or a trained sociologist, for example, might expect and encounter a different depiction of German law and legal culture. At a next level of self-reflection, you should recognize that you are a particular kind of legal professional, trained in a distinct national legal system and perhaps specialized in a particular field of law. How do those factors shape your expectations about law? Subsequent layers of self-reflection would require you to ask similar questions about your broader cultural or national identity, your gender, your socioeconomic standing, or your experience of race. The hope is that you will come to appreciate, perhaps only vaguely and imperfectly, how your cultural grounding and legal training condition your perspective on the social and legal issues presented in this book.
- Figure 1.2a and 1.2b illustrate Frankenberg's call for "distancing" and "differencing." The former requires you to examine your assumptions and position. The latter requires you to see the other on its own terms and not only as a reassertion of what is familiar to you.
- George Fletcher endorsed the critically self-reflective potential of comparative legal studies in these terms:

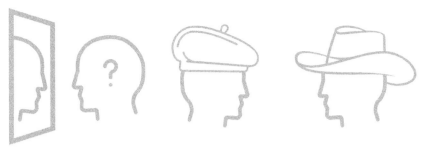

(a) Distancing
Looking in a mirror - "Distancing" calls on us to strive to become aware of our position - our assumptions, expectations, and biases - as they shape our understanding of the law.

(b) Differencing
It's a "hat," but not my kind of "hat" - "Differencing" calls on us to avoid overlaying our understanding of the law onto foreign legal systems. Instead, we should strive to allow differences in other legal systems to present themselves to us on their own terms.

Figure 1.2 Frankenberg's "Distancing" and "Differencing"

> "The great challenge for comparative lawyers is to probe our legal culture for its sources of resistance, for its implicit judgments about the normal way of doing things, for the way in which our identity is bound up with our practices."
>
> * * *
>
> "By becoming aware of […] differences, we can generate a sense of our historical contingency. We could have evolved in a different way. The way things are is the way they must be. And if we can understand the roots of our resistance to change, perhaps reforms become thinkable. This is the subversive potential of comparative law."[50]

- Try to develop the discipline of Frankenberg's "distancing" and "differencing" as you progress in this project. As you encounter features of German law and legal culture ask yourself tough questions about how your background shapes your experience of these encounters, and press hard to assess the elements of German law and legal culture on their own terms rather than as reflections of all that is already familiar to you.

1.4 Conclusion

This book will introduce you to German law and legal culture. Unavoidably, it pursues that project in a summary and subjective manner. But it is a passionate effort, resulting from my deep admiration of German law and my years of study and immersion in the German legal culture. I'm glad you'll join me for this adventure, which will lead through a treatment of the foundations of the German legal system into encounters with several doctrinal fields of German law. Throughout all of this, I will highlight the predominant influence of the Civil Law tradition in German law while urging you to consider the other legal traditions woven into the tapestry of German legal culture. That agenda, as I have explained in this introductory chapter, represents a rejection of the traditional, "legal families" approach to macro-comparative law. Instead it acknowledges law's rich cultural difference and our enriching interpretive subjectivity.

Alongside all of this, maybe a project such as the one I propose for this book will help us draw nearer to the dream of justice. Through encounters with new law-worlds, through the conscious disregard of world-worn boundaries, and through the practice of studied self-reflection – we can imagine law in new and noble ways. Vivian Grosswald Curran believed that "[t]he successful comparativist's immersion must be a journey from the realm of the unimaginable to the imagined to the known, a process which alters the comparativist's own mentality as the different, the other, becomes imagined and, finally, albeit imperfectly, known."[51]

That's my hope for this book's journey into German law and legal culture.

Further Reading

- Pierre Legrand, *Comparative Law and the Task of Negative Critique* (Routledge) (2023)
- Mathias Siems, *Comparative Law* (Cambridge University Press) (3rd ed. 2022)
- Uwe Kischel, *Comparative Law* (Andrew Hammel trans.) (Oxford University Press) (2019)
- H. Patrick Glenn, *Legal Traditions of the World* (Oxford University Press) (5th ed. 2014)
- Konrad Zweigert & Hein Kötz, *An Introduction to Comparative Law* (Tony Weir trans.) (Oxford University Press) (3rd ed. 1998)

NOTES

1 *See* JOHN MERRYMAN & ROGELIO PÉREZ-PERDOMO, THE CIVIL LAW TRADITION 2 (4th ed. 2018).

2 A similar *U.S. News and World Report* poll routinely places Germany among the top-five "best countries" in the world. *U.S. News Best Countries 2021*, U.S. NEWS AND WORLD REPORT, www.usnews.com/news/best-countries/rankings.

3 *See* Edwin W. Patterson, *The Case Method in American Legal Education: Its Origins and Objectives*, 4 J. LEGAL EDUC. 1 (1951); Max Rheinstein, *Law Faculties and Law Schools: A Comparison of Legal Education in the United States and Germany*, 18 WIS. L. REV. 5 (1938).

4 STEPHEN BREYER, THE COURT AND THE WORLD 4 (2015).

5 I borrow the concept of "law-world" from Pierre Legrand, who defines it as "a process of differentiation leading to the gradual appearance of an idiosyncratic construction [...] based on a combination of pre-reflexive faith and reflexive thought in the value of that construction." Pierre Legrand, *Paradoxically, Derrida: For a Comparative Legal Studies*, 27 CARDOZO L. REV. 631 (2005–2006). Legrand often uses the concept to differentiate between the "civil law world" and the "common law world." *See, e.g.*, Pierre Legrand, *John Henry Merryman and*

Comparative Legal Studies: A Dialogue, 47 Am. J. Compar. L. 3 (1999). Legrand makes his debt to Jürgen Habermas explicit in his book chapter "The Same and the Different" by using the German term *"Lebenswelt"* in conjunction with his discussion of distinct "law-worlds." Pierre Legrand, *The Same and the Different*, in Comparative Legal Studies: Traditions and Transitions 240, 244, 254 (Pierre Legrand and Roderick Munday eds., 2003); *See* Jürgen Habermas, Legitimation Crisis (Thomas McCarthy trans., 1975).

6 Aram A. Yengoyan, *Introduction – On the Issue of Comparison*, in Modes of Comparison 1, 19 (Aram A. Yengoyan ed., 2006).

7 Vivian Grosswald Curran, *Dealing in Difference: Comparative Law's Potential for Broadening Legal Perspectives*, 46 Am. J. Compar. L. 657, 660 (1998); Vivian Grosswald Curran, *Cultural Immersion, Difference and Categories in U.S. Comparative Law*, 46 Am. J. Compar. L. 43, 45 (1998).

8 There are many examples of revolutionaries in law who, having rejected the *status quo*, left enduring impressions on the world. This is an eclectic (and necessarily incomplete) slate of my inspirations in the law – you should consider preparing your own list: John Adams, Abraham Lincoln, Arabella Mansfield, Karl Marx, Mahatma Gandhi, Elisabeth Selbert, Thurgood Marshall, Paul Robeson, Fritz Bauer, Nelson Mandela, Ruth Bader Ginsburg, Shirin Ebadi, Stephen Bright, Barack Obama, Michelle Obama, and Susanne Baer. *See* James E. Moliterno, *The Lawyer as Catalyst of Social Change*, 77 Fordham L. Rev. 1559 (2009).

9 Günter Frankenberg, *Critical Comparisons: Re-thinking Comparative Law*, 26 Harv. Int'l L. J. 411, 412 (1985).

10 Mark Twain, *The Awful German Language*, in A Tramp Abroad 299 (Dover Publications 2002) (1880).

11 David Nelken, *Using the Concept of Legal Culture*, 29 Austl. J. Legal Phil. 1 (2004).

12 Terry Eagleton, Culture 60 (2016).

13 *See* Simone Glanert & Pierre Legrand, *Law, Comparatism, Epistemic Governance: There Is Critique and Critique*, 18 Ger. L. J. 701, 711 (2017).

14 A persistent malaise hangs over the field. *See, e.g.*, Ralf Michaels, *Im Westen nichts Neues? [Nothing New in the West?]*, 66 Rabels Zeitschrift 97 (2002); Mathias Reiman, *The Progress and Failure of Comparative Law in the Second Half of the Twentieth Century*, 50 Am. J. Compar. L. 671 (2002); M. M. Siems, *The End of Comparative Law*, 2 Am. J. Compar. L. 133 (2007).

15 For this I can recommend two excellent books. *See* Mathias Siems, Comparative Law (3rd ed. 2022); Uwe Kischel, Comparative Law (Andrew Hammel trans., 2019).

16 Merriam-Webster's Online Dictionary, www.merriam-webster.com/dictionary/comparison.

17 *See* Konrad Zweigert & Hein Kötz, Introduction to Comparative Law 6 (Tony Weir trans., 3rd ed. 1998) ("As has often been observed, the mere study of foreign law falls short of being comparative law."); Alan Watson, Legal Transplants 4 (2nd ed. 1993) ("To begin with, Comparative Law is not the study of one foreign legal system or of part of one foreign system.").

18 *See* WATSON, *supra* note 17, at 4 ("No doubt it is impossible to follow such a course [in the study of a single foreign legal system] without reflecting on, and making comparisons with, one's own law [...].").

19 "In the literature on the methodology of comparative law, comparatists often distinguish research in foreign law from true comparative law research, which for them begins only with at least two different legal systems. I always found this approach rather narrow-minded. Researching and writing about another legal system always has a comparative dimension. A look from the outside from a lawyer with a different training and culture brings new approaches and new insights to the foreign law that would not have been available to somebody on the inside." Brun-Otto Bryde, *In Praise of Transnationalism*, 10 GER. L. J. 1291, 1292 (2009), www.germanlawjournal.com/pdfs/Vol10-No10/PDF_Vol_10_No_10_1291-1294_Articles_Bryde.pdf.

20 *But see* Zweigert & Kötz, *supra* note 17, at 43 ("But merely to juxtapose without comment the law of various jurisdictions is not comparative law: it is just a preliminary step.").

21 *See* BRIAN Z. TAMANAHA, LEGAL PLURALISM EXPLAINED: HISTORY, THEORY, CONSEQUENCES (2021); THE OXFORD HANDBOOK OF GLOBAL LEGAL PLURALISM (Paul Schiff Berman ed., 2020).

22 Raymond Grew, *On Rereading an Earlier Essay*, in MODES OF COMPARISON 118, 131 (Aram A. Yengoyan ed., 2006); *see* Grosswald Curran, *Cultural Immersion, Difference and Categories in U.S. Comparative Law*, *supra* note 7, at 64 ("[... The] leap into a foreign mentality necessarily involves a leap of imagination, [...].").

23 Mathias Siems has published a useful survey of the various approaches to comparative law. *See* Siems, *supra* note 15.

24 H. Patrick Glenn, *Comparative Legal Families and Comparative Legal Traditions*, in THE OXFORD HANDBOOK OF COMPARATIVE LAW 421, 422 (Mathias Reimann & Reinhard Zimmermann eds., 2nd ed., 2019).

25 *See, e.g.*, JURIGLOBE – WORLD LEGAL SYSTEMS (University of Ottawa), www.juriglobe.ca/eng/.

26 *See* RENÉ DAVID, TRAITÉ ÉLÉMENTAIRE DE DROIT CIVIL COMPARÉ: INTRODUCTION À L'ÉTUDE DES DROITS ÉTRANGERS ET À LA MÉTHODE COMPARATIVE (1950); RENÉ DAVID, LES GRANDS SYSTÈMES DE DROIT CONTEMPORAINS (1964). David's work was published in English in a book coauthored with the French-Canadian scholar John E. C. Brierley. *See* RENÉ DAVID & JOHN E. C. BRIERLEY, MAJOR LEGAL SYSTEMS IN THE WORLD TODAY (3rd ed. 1985).

27 *See* KONRAD ZWEIGERT & HEIN KÖTZ, I EINFÜHRUNG IN DIE RECHTSVERGLEICHUNG AUF DEM GEBIETE DES PRIVATRECHTS (1971). Zweigert's and Kötz's book became a standard work in the field of comparative law. The German-language version, with a shortened title, entered a third edition in 1996. KONRAD ZWEIGERT & HEIN KÖTZ, EINFÜHRUNG IN DIE RECHTSVERGLEICHUNG (3rd ed. 1996). The English-language translation is now also in its third edition. *See* ZWEIGERT & KÖTZ, *supra* note 17.

28 *Percentage of World Population, Civil Law and Common Law Systems*, JURIGLOBE – WORLD LEGAL SYSTEMS, www.juriglobe.ca/eng/syst-demo/tableau-dcivil-claw.php.

29 *See* Lena Salaymeh & Ralf Michaels, *Decolonial Comparative Law: A Conceptual Beginning*, 86 RABELSZEITSCHRIFT 166 (2022); *see also* Upendra Baxi, The Colonialist Heritage, in COMPARATIVE LEGAL STUDIES: TRADITIONS AND TRANSITIONS 46 (Pierre Legrand and Roderick Munday eds., 2003).
30 *See* VERNON VALENTINE PALMER & MOHAMED Y. MATTAR, MIXED LEGAL SYSTEMS, EAST AND WEST (2015); Jacques Du Plessis, *Comparative Law and the Study of Mixed Legal Systems*, in THE OXFORD HANDBOOK OF COMPARATIVE LAW 474 (Mathias Reimann & Reinhard Zimmermann eds., 2nd ed. 2019).
31 *See* H. PATRICK GLENN, LEGAL TRADITIONS OF THE WORLD (5th ed. 2014).
32 Glenn, *supra* note 24, at 426.
33 MERRYMAN & PÉREZ-PERDOMO, *supra* note 1.
34 Ugo Mattei, *Three Patterns in Law: Taxonomy and Change in the World's Legal Systems*, 45 AM. J. COMPAR. L. 5, 16 (1997).
35 *See* Grosswald Curran, *Cultural Immersion, Difference and Categories in U.S. Comparative Law*, *supra* note 7, at 62–64.
36 Katrin Pfündel et al., *Executive Summary of the Study "Muslim Life in Germany 2020" – Study Commissioned by the German Islam Conference*, GERMAN FEDERAL OFFICE FOR MIGRATION AND REFUGEES (Sept. 2021), www.bamf .de/SharedDocs/Anlagen/EN/Forschung/Forschungsberichte/Kurzberichte/ fb38-muslimisches-leben-kurzfassung.pdf?__blob=publicationFile&v=14 #:~:text=The%20data%20of%20the%20MLD,million%20and%205.6%20 million%20persons.
37 *See* MATHIAS ROHE, DER ISLAM IN DEUTSCHLAND: EINE BESTANDSAUFNAHME (2016); ISLAM AND MUSLIMS IN GERMANY (Ala Al-Hamarneh & Jörn Thielmann eds., 2014); MATHIAS ROHE, DAS ISLAMISCHE RECHT – GESCHICHTE UND GEGENWART (3rd ed. 2011).
38 Baxi, *supra* note 29, at 59.
39 WERNER MENSKI, COMPARATIVE LAW IN A GLOBAL CONTEXT (2nd ed. 2006).
40 Teology means "an explanation by reference to some purpose, end, goal, or function." The Editors of the Encyclopedia, *"Teleology,"* ENCYCLOPEDIA BRITANNICA, www.britannica.com/topic/teleology (last visited May 16, 2022).
41 In his article "In Westen nichts Neues?" [Nothing New in the West?] Ralf Michaels describes the problem as the "classical tension between potential universal reason – or natural law, on one side, and national positive law, on the other side […]." Michaels, *supra* note 14, at 98 (Russell A. Miller trans.).
42 ZWEIGERT & KÖTZ, *supra* note 17, at 40.
43 WATSON, *supra* note 17, at 22.
44 *Id.* at 24.
45 Pierre Legrand, *Antivonbar*, 1 J. COMPAR. L. 13, 25 (2006).
46 Pierre Legrand, *Jameses at Play: A Tractation on the Comparison of Laws*, 65 AM. J. COMPAR. L. 1 (2017).
47 *See* JACQUES DERRIDA, WRITING AND DIFFERENCE (Alan Bass trans.) (1978); JACQUES DERRIDA, MARGINS OF PHILOSOPHY (Alan Bass trans.) (1982). *See also* Legrand, *Paradoxically, Derrida: For a Comparative Legal Studies*, *supra* note 5.

48 *See* JOHN LOCKE, TWO TREATISES OF GOVERNMENT (Peter Laslett ed., 3rd ed. 1988).
49 RUDOLF B. SCHLESINGER *ET AL.*, COMPARATIVE LAW 46 (6th ed. 1998).
50 George P. Fletcher, *Comparative Law as a Subversive Discipline*, 46 AM. J. COMPAR. L. 683, 696–97, 700 (1998).
51 Grosswald Curran, *Cultural Immersion, Difference and Categories in U.S. Comparative Law*, *supra* note 7, at 65.

2

The Civil Law Tradition

Key Concepts

- **Civil Law Tradition**: Drawn largely from Roman Law heritage, the Civil Law tradition gives precedence to statutory law, particularly in the form of systematic codification.[1]
- **Common Law Tradition**: Drawn largely from English Common Law heritage, the Common Law tradition involves concepts and legal organizational methods that assign a preeminent position to case law.[2]
- **Roman Law**: The body of law developed by the ancient Romans, codified by Emperor Justinian around 530 CE in the *Corpus Juris Civilis*, which forms a basis of many modern codes in Civil Law systems.[3]
- **Inductive Reasoning**: Reasoning that draws conclusions from the inferences that can be derived from the specific circumstances of a case. It is a form of logic that moves from the specific to the general.
- **Deductive Reasoning**: Reasoning that draws conclusions from the application of broad or general principles to the specific circumstances of a case. It is a form of logic that moves from the general to the specific.
- **Rechtswissenschaft (Legal Science)**: Primarily the creation of German legal scholars, *Rechtswissenschaft* (Legal Science) calls for the development of law (in the process of codification or in the interpretation of codes and statutes) through a systematic and logical study of norms with the aim of arranging them in a coherent system.[4]

Study Tips

Rooted as it is in the Roman Law, your understanding of the Civil Law tradition might be enhanced by independent study of Roman Law resources collected by Professor Ernest Metzger (University of Glasgow School of Law) at an online clearinghouse entitled "Iuscivile.com" (https://iuscivile.com/). Metzger explains: "This site provides information on Roman law sources and literature, the teaching of Roman law, and the persons who study Roman law. The site is available in English and German. Users are invited to submit to this site any materials or information which might interest other users."

Not long ago a number of the leading legal institutions and organizations in Germany formed the *Bündnis für das deutsche Recht* (Alliance for German Law). The Alliance's goal is to "engage more strongly in the international competition between legal systems," including the "external presentation of the continental legal position of Germany."[5] The Alliance's charter members should be well-positioned to pursue these aims. They include the Federal Ministry of Justice, the German Bar Association, the German Judges Association, and the German Federal Bar Association. Among the Alliance's first efforts was the production of a glossy, lushly illustrated promotional brochure – in German, English, and several other languages – presenting the many virtues of German law.

The brochure, entitled *Law – Made in Germany*, is a revealing document.[6] It embraces the most common generalization about the German legal system. Thus, we learn in the brochure's introduction (penned by the Federal Minister of Justice), that "German law is part of the codified legal system that has developed across the European continent."[7] The brochure repeatedly emphasizes Germany's membership in "the long-standing legal family of continental legal systems," which is "characterized by its codified system of legal provisions."[8]

This is consistent with the view of most comparative law scholars, who present German law as an example of the Civil Law tradition – what René David originally referred to as "Western Law" before refining the classification and labeling it the "Romano-Germanic" system.[9] The best-known English-language introductions to the German legal system unfailingly – and exclusively – treat German law as representative of the Civil Law tradition. Two well-regarded English-language introductions to German law underscore this point in their opening sentences:

> The distinctive features of the German legal system arise in large part from the relatively comprehensive and rapid assimilation of Roman principles of law in the middle ages, the codification of the nineteenth century, in part influenced by codification in France [...]. The German legal system belongs to the central European family of legal systems, broadly classified as civil law countries.[10]

> The idea of codifying the law, which grew out of the European Enlightenment of the 17th and 18th centuries, together with 19th century political efforts to achieve unification, led to the creation of comprehensive statutes for a series of important areas of law. These give German law the characteristics of a codified legal system, in other words, one whose rules are laid down in legislation which covers all aspects of the law. This characteristic is not the least of the factors which identify German law as Continental European.[11]

You can see that commentators on Germany's legal culture make use of the "legal families" approach to macro-comparative law that was described, and repudiated by H. Patrick Glenn, in Chapter 1. This book, however, aims to heed Glenn's critique of that approach to comparative legal studies. Recall that Glenn urged us to convert the old, static "legal families" into dynamic "legal traditions" that operate in varying degrees of relevance to give a particular legal system its distinct spectrum of color, contour, and contingency. That means we are not going to shoe-horn Germany into the Civil Law family. Instead, I hope you'll become aware of the many legal traditions that are woven together to form the tapestry of German legal culture.

Still, that effort requires us to pay special attention to the Civil Law tradition. There can be no doubt. The codified (continental) way of doing law has shaped German "attitudes about the nature of law, about the role of law in [...] society and [the] polity, about the proper organization and operation of the legal system, and about the way law is or should be made, applied, studied, perfected and taught."[12] In fact, it is fair to view the Civil Law as the predominant legal tradition in the German legal culture. The Civil Law tradition is the background operating system of German law. For that reason we will start our journey into the German legal culture with an examination of the Civil Law tradition.

But don't lose sight of the fact that the Civil Law tradition is not the end of the story I want to tell about German law and legal culture. Glenn's point – and my point in this book – is that there are some ghosts in the system representing other legal traditions. Throughout this book, I will illuminate various legal traditions that may have influenced and informed German law. That will include a predominant role for the Civil Law tradition examined in this chapter. But it will involve other legal traditions as well. This chapter's introduction gives you a chance to spend some time with the Civil Law tradition so you can become familiar with what a legal tradition is and how to spot one.

There is another reason to offer this chapter's introduction to the Civil Law tradition at such an early stage of our journey. Many readers, especially those whose primary or "national" legal identity was formed in a system heavily influenced by the Common Law tradition, will be altogether unfamiliar with the essential qualities and perspectives of the Civil Law tradition. This chapter should help orient these readers to an utterly new and different way of imaging what the law is and how it works. In fact, many comparativists define the Civil Law tradition *against* the Common Law tradition. They view the Common Law as the Civil Law's essential opposite. Seizing on those claims, this introduction to the Civil Law tradition presents a double opportunity. It will involve a comparative reflection on both of these legal traditions – Civil Law and Common Law – posing the question: How do these traditions differ from one another?

The following materials present a history of the Civil Law tradition; seek to highlight its fundamental characteristics; and consider more closely the unique and important role played by legal scholars in the Civil Law tradition.

2.1 The Civil Law Tradition: Historical Development

This much is clear: The Civil Law tradition has ancient roots that reverberate even in its modern iterations. That history begins in Rome.

H. Patrick Glenn
Legal Traditions of the World 132, 137–143 (5th ed. 2014)[*]

* * *

Substantive, Secular Law

Roman law [...] found its origins in advice given [...] by jurisconsults, with respect to particular cases or disputes. The law which emerged looks very much like life [...]. There is a law of persons, or the family, which reflects Roman family life, with the paterfamilias, the wife and children, and the slaves. Marriage is constituted by present intent to live as man and wife, though became the object of various forms of celebration. It was rigorously monogamous; concubinage existed but its offspring was not legitimate, following the maternal line and not entering the family of the father. Legitimation was possible, notably through subsequent marriage. Adoption too was possible and various forms of tutelage or guardianship existed. Since marriage was consensual so, in general, was divorce, on the part of husband or wife.

[... Things] could be owned, and we now see multiplication of criteria for organizing the world of things. They could be patrimonial things or extra-patrimonial things; common things or sacred things; principal things or accessorial things; corporeal things or incorporeal things. The categorizations went on and on, a dedicated application of Plato's principle of division as a means of knowledge. Ownership was essentially private, though there were things that looked like trusts, in which someone had to look after the property of another. Many forms of ius existed short of ownership, notably the hypothec, the civilian equivalent of the mortgage. Deposit existed, and has given its content to the common law of bailment. Contracts, again, were contracts (in the plural) and there was no general, consensual concept. So there are real contracts (requiring transfer of the thing); verbal contracts (solemn words); literal contracts (in writing); and, in certain instances, consensual contracts (sale, lease, partnership, mandate (agency)). Delictual conduct is sanctioned, though there is no general principle of liability, whether of fault or negligence or some stricter form. Liability exists when the conditions of liability are met, according to the objective descriptions of how damage is caused (burning, breaking or rendering property, disabling a limb, etc). Liability can only be described as objective. There is also a law of quasi-contract, recognized as such, and this more than two millennia ago.

So roman law became an object of admiration, because the jurisconsults were able, so convincingly, to state conditions for governance of complex personal relationships. There were highs and lows in roman legal history; the period of the classical jurists, those whose opinions have lasted longest, ran from the first century BC to the middle of the third century AD. Gaius wrote his famous Institutes, or hornbook, near the end of this time. From then on things ran down; by the middle of the fifth century AD there was such a mass of opinion that a law of citations was passed (to *create* order): Papinian, Paul, Gaius, Ulpian and Modestinus were to be treated as authoritative; in case of conflict the majority would prevail; Papinian would prevail in the event of a tie. Later in the century Rome had fallen; Justinian, presiding in the eastern remains a half-century later, ordered a compilation of laws. It was pulled together in three or four years, finishing in 533 AD, paralleling in time the Babylonian Talmud. This main compilation of Justinian was called the Digest or the Pandects (from Greek, meaning all is included), yet it left out a lot. If it consisted only of opinions of jurists, gathered together with no systematic design, it also represented a choice of opinions. There was inclusion, and also much exclusion. When it was finished, it was very finished. Justinian prohibited all further comment on it [...].

---

[*] © Patrick Glenn 2014. Reproduced with permission of the Licensor through PLSclear.

Roman Law and Law in Europe

The Romans took their law with them, all over Europe, as far north as what we now know as Germany and as far west as the British Isles. So a lot of people knew about roman law in Europe, but it was the law of the conqueror and not always loved as such. When the Romans were eventually driven out they essentially took their law with them, and the old [customary law], which everyone still remembered, became once again the law of the lands. So there is here a re-assertion of a different tradition in law, taken with full knowledge of the alternatives. The re-assertion was not a fleeting thing; it largely drove roman law off the European territorial map for centuries, except for some rudimentary versions of it in Italy and the south of France. Even when roman law was "re-discovered" in the eleventh century, the opposition went on for more centuries and has not disappeared today.

We already know a lot about the [customary law] that prevailed over roman law at this time. It was mostly unwritten; it didn't say much about contracts or obligations; its family and succession law kept large families together, since many members were necessary for many tasks; its property law looked mostly to communal use rather than any formal or individual concept of ownership. The legal notion was seisin (saisine, gewehr) and this was often joint or collective in nature ("*le foin à l'un, le regain a l'autre, ou les arbres à l'un, l'herbe à l'autre*"). The Allmend of contemporary Swiss law was a kind of general, European model. Feudalism bound the [customary] law, and its people, to the soil; it also allowed elites to develop and social inequality to become flagrant. Christianity had spread throughout Europe by now; Augustine in the fifth century had begun to teach the necessity of inner reflection and spirituality; Aquinas in the thirteenth was to allow for a certain measure of human flowering and creation, linking Christianity to Greek philosophy.

Roman law came crashing back in the tumultuous events of the eleventh to thirteenth centuries in Europe. In a very short space of time, a certain distance between state and church was formalized, universities begun, legal professions created, legal proof radically reformed, roman law revitalized and Greek philosophy unearthed; the common law began its own, particular, uncommon history. Maimonides also wrote his reforming version of the Talmud. Why this all happened so fast had much to do with the Arabs, who were already occupying a large part of the Mediterranean basin, including Spain. They too had certain (influential) ideas about law. Whatever the ultimate reasons, this first European renaissance marked a further challenge to the primacy of chthonic law and very interesting things then took place, a rare combination of different traditions.

[The] legal procedures of [customary law] were essentially open ones; there were no barriers such as the praetor of roman law or (later) the chancellor (keeper of the writs) of the common law. Recall also that roman law had abandoned such barriers with the adoption of the so-called extraordinary procedure nearing the end of its reign (third and fourth centuries AD). Both traditions therefore had notions of what could be called substantive law; whether written or unwritten it addressed substantive obligations, and perhaps even rights. And since substantive law existed, there was general agreement that judges had to get the facts right, so the substantive law would be applied where it was meant to be applied. Procedure had to be investigative (which is not what the common lawyers call it). There also had to be courts of appeal, since a substantively erroneous decision was illegal, according to criteria external to the decision itself. It *had* to be quashed. So there was a certain underlying harmony in continental Europe in the eleventh century. If the time had come to engage in a major debate on the type of law to have, everyone agreed that the debate should be about the type of *substantive* law to have, given that procedures or courts or institutions should be open. In common law language, there was never any real question of a closed writ system. In modern language, nobody could raise issues of alleged incommensurability between European chthonic and roman law. In the absence of conceptual or institutional barriers, and under immediate external challenge by a highly civilized Arab world, Europe had to get its legal act together. Christianity no longer appeared as a major obstacle to this; since the fourth century it had been developing its own canon law and by the twelfth century major legal works were being written by canonists, notably Gratian. Canon law was to take its place beside roman law (as "the two laws," or, better, the one and the other law, the utrumque ius), exercising great influence in the slow overturning of the chthonic tradition in Europe.

This did, however, take a long time, since if roman law could be looked at as a base of legal learning, much of it had a peculiarly Roman look, requiring recasting for the modern Europe. So the great, new universities, with law and theology as their primary disciplines, took on the tasks of adapting roman law to the new ways. This process took centuries, and there is much intellectual ambiguity in the process. For centuries, those who wrote the glosses on roman law seemed more talmudic than civilian. They were more interested in questions (quaestiones) than answers; more interested in accumulating opinions than choosing among them; more interested in debate than action. They may have seen themselves as reviving a more ancient tradition, that of rhetoric. Their intellectual leader, in Italy, was Bartolus, and for centuries it could be said "siamo tutti Bartolisti" ["we are all Bartolists"]. A new substantive law was being created, however, in general language which could be applied anywhere in Europe. It became known as a common law or ius commune (there have been many of them in Europe, all distinctive, this one based on "the two laws"); it slowly began to exercise influence in a persuasive manner, in the different parts of Europe. The Christian Church played a major, unifying role in the process. This process of reception, like that of the concept of the state later in the world, varied according to the locale. It was most influential in Germanic countries, understanding themselves as descendants of the first Roman empire and the (differently inspired) Holy Roman empire (that of Charlemagne). It met resistance from the kings of France, who didn't quite see themselves in the same new empire as the German princes. There was resistance too in Scandinavia, the enlightenment idea losing some of its allure on entering "the cooler climate of the North." Resistance was often in the name of the old law, the chthonic law, itself often seen as inspired by God. "*Juristen, böse Christen*" ["lawyers, evil Christians"] went the Germanic, religious, and customary denigration of the new, rationalizing, roman lawyers. In seeking to take the church back to its roots, a revolving, Luther also attacked the lawyers. "The real reason you want to be lawyers," he said, "is money. You want to be rich." This theme too is still with us.

Constructing National Law

The tradition of rationality in law, however, was on a roll. There was so much good thinking going on, such a "chaos of clear ideas," that more had to be begotten. Those exercising political power were not insensitive to certain features of the new thought. The royal ordonnances of Louis XIV in the seventeenth century were the first indications of a centrally directed, national law on the continent. The notion of teaching French law, as French law, had emerged already in the sixteenth century, and in the same century legislation was used to create French as a national language in France, even though it was then spoken by only a minority of the population. France's codification of private law, under Napoleon in 1804, was the world's first national, systemic and rational codification of law. It was seen as bringing together the state of France as it came into force, by virtue of its own article 1, on successive days in a series of concentric circles radiating out from Paris, each a day's ride further than the last. The civil code of Germany, of 1900, advanced systemic legal thought still further. Then all of Europe, including eastern Europe and Russia, had to have their codes. It was an idea whose time had come, the culmination of a long struggle, a long tradition.

2.1 The Civil Law Tradition: Historical Development

Questions/Comments

- By "Civil Law tradition" this book means a distinct normative approach that has influenced the content of law and the nature of legal institutions in a large number of countries. It is a way of thinking about the law that is distinguished by "certain learned features that are shared more extensively" by some peoples than by others.[13] The character of the Civil Law tradition will be clearer after you read the rest of the material in this chapter. But this book's passion for pluralism requires the following qualification: "there is no such thing as *the* civil law system […]."[14] The Civil Law tradition manifests itself differently in particular legal systems. It is probably more appropriate to think of "Civil Law traditions."

- It also must be said that the label "Civil Law" is itself a bit misleading. As a broad, cultural understanding of the law, the Civil Law's influence has not been limited only to the subjects traditionally covered by the Roman *ius civile*, including the law of Persons, Things, and Obligations (today's contract law, tort law, property law, and family law) – the areas of substantive law traditionally concerned with regulating private interactions between individuals. Alongside the term "Civil," these subjects today are often classified as "private law." Rather, the characteristics of the Civil Law tradition can be more or less evident throughout a legal system, even in public law fields such as constitutional law and administrative law – the areas of substantive law traditionally concerned with regulating the state and its interactions with its citizens. As you will see in Chapter 9, for example, Germany's administrative law has a distinct Civil Law feel even though that is decidedly a public law field. Even when approaching German constitutional law, the archetypal subject of public law, one should keep the Civil Law's thoroughgoing imprint on German legal culture in mind. This means that you have to be aware that the phrase "Civil Law" as we use it here means more than just "private law." Ironically, the phrase "Civil Law" is given its narrower meaning in most of the legal systems where the Civil Law tradition has had its greatest influence.[15] In Germany, for example, *Zivilrecht* (civil law) comprises the substantive field of private law. This apparent misnomer has taken hold largely because the Civil Law tradition is so closely identified with the two great codifications described by Glenn – in France in 1804 and Germany in 1900. Both of these historic codifications were chiefly concerned with the "private" law, that is to say, the "civil" law. The alternative label for this particular legal tradition is no less problematic. Considering the Civil Law tradition's influence in legal systems around the world, referring to it as the "Continental" or "European" legal tradition hardly seems appropriate, even if, as Glenn explains, its origins are distinctly continental and European.

- John Merryman and Rogelio Pérez-Perdomo have said that "the civil law tradition is older, more widely distributed, and more influential than the common law tradition."[16] But Glenn made clear that its arrival as a modern legal tradition is not the result of an unbroken progression from Justinian to the German Civil Code and beyond. First, he explained that the Roman Law was a reaction against the customary law that operated across Europe 3,000 years ago. Customary law refers to the systems of social order that were prevalent amongst those peoples that "live in or in close harmony with the earth."[17] These were oral legal systems developed by clannish societies with uncomplicated institutions and informal methods of dispute resolution. Glenn suggests that the Civil Law tradition, beginning with Roman Law, constituted a radical break with the customary past. The new ordering system was written, depended on sophisticated institutions, and had formal dispute settlement mechanisms. Above all, it was rational and systematic. Glenn explains, however, that customary law made a comeback across Europe in the period roughly between the fifth and twelfth centuries, which, incidentally, are sometimes referred to as the "Dark Ages." In keeping with that pejorative tone, the accepted narrative celebrates the ultimate triumph of Roman Law's rationalism over the barbarians' customary order in the European Renaissance. Is it the legacy of this "modernizing" break with European customary law, or simply its antiquity, that leads "many people to believe that the civil law is culturally superior [...]"?[18] Might the claimed "modernizing" essence of the Civil Law tradition have played a role in, or might it have been a reflection of, the spirit that fueled European colonialism? Does that complicate your feelings about the continued predominance of the Civil Law tradition in many former colonies?

- How does Glenn's claim that the Roman Law "looked like life" relate to his characterization of the Roman Law (and, thus, the Civil Law tradition) as "rational" and "systematic"?
- Besides the influence of the Roman Law, what other social or political developments featured significantly in the historical emergence of today's Civil Law tradition? In answering this question, it may be helpful to look backward and forward. Looking backward, you should keep in mind the characteristics of the customary law from which the Civil Law is seen as a fundamental departure. Customary law was oral, tribal and informal. Looking forward, what kind of society did the French and German Civil Law codifications help fashion or help secure when they were finally achieved?

To this point there have been repeated references to codes and codification as emblematic of the Civil Law tradition. Let's turn now to the idea of codification and other characteristics that form central elements of the Civil Law tradition.

2.2 The Central Elements of the Civil Law Tradition

More than any other legal tradition, the Common Law tradition has been viewed, to paraphrase Pierre Legrand, as "the civil law's other, the difference of its identity."[19] Thus, it may be helpful to introduce the central elements of the Civil Law tradition by way of a juxtaposition of the contemporary world's "two most influential legal traditions."[20] That is what Vivian Grosswald Curran does in the following excerpt. This is an effort to understand the Civil Law tradition better by understanding what its opposite – the Common Law tradition – is thought to be. To aid her effort, Grosswald Curran argues that the Civil Law tradition is reflective of the frame of mind characteristic of the Enlightenment while the Common Law tradition is reflective of the frame of mind characteristic of Romanticism. As you read Grosswald Curran's article, try to identify what typifies these divergent intellectual and cultural traditions and consider what they might say about the Civil Law and Common Law traditions.

Vivian Grosswald Curran
Romantic Common Law, Enlightened Civil Law: Legal Uniformity and the Homogenization of the European Union
7 COLUMBIA JOURNAL OF EUROPEAN LAW 62, 70–71, 75–77, 81–82, 85–89, 91–97, 99–100, 103, 107–108 (2001)*

* * *

The influences of the Enlightenment and Romanticism in Europe are the subject of countless commentaries, and have been amply documented. […]

Romanticism is kindred to the common-law mentality in many ways, and […] the Enlightenment is kindred to the civil-law mentality in many ways […].

* * *

[There are] critical differences between the common and civil-law legal systems. […]

* * *

The common law is a law defined in terms of past judicial decisions. The resulting methodology is such that the common-law perpetually is in flux, always in a process of further becoming, developing, and transforming, as it cloaks itself with the habits of past decisions, tailored to the lines of the pending situation. The common-law evolves with the ongoing derivation of legal standards from prior judicial decisions, but it is defined by continuous motion. This means that the common-law is that which cannot be crystallized, frozen or ever entirely captured. It is fluid, with a suppleness that resides in its inseparability from each discrete, concrete set of facts, the facts of the lived experiences which formed the basis of the litigation that led to the prior relevant court adjudications.

The common law is the analysis of the particular because common-law legal rules derive from a series of unique life experiences, by definition not amenable to exact repetition. The common-law signifies by way of the courts' assessments of the legal significance attributable to unique events, to facts in the unicity of their particular life contexts. By virtue of their inextricable connection to the factual life scenarios that lead to litigation, common-law legal issues also must be unique. It is thus clear that reasoning by analogy from a prior adjudicated case to a pending case never can attain scientific precision. The comparison must at best remain simile; it never can reach the exact equivalence of metaphor.

The common law's analogical reasoning is defined in terms of the pending case's outcome – in other words, common-law legal reasoning consists of arguments, some of which succeed in practice, and others of which fail. Those arguments destined for success join the ranks of a hierarchy of legal axioms, the springboard for future analogies to meet the needs of future arguably similar cases. Thus, each legal standard is linked irreducibly

---

* Reproduced with permission of the Columbia Journal of European Law.

to the factual context from which it emerged, rendering both legal standard and legal argument inextricably bound to factual context.

* * *

Facts [...] are central to the very meaning and concept of law in the common-law legal [tradition]. This centrality of the particular facts to the common-law legal [tradition] is conveyed to United States law students through the casebook method of education. From their first day of studies, law students read series of cases that provide the data from which they are to deduce governing legal norms. The task of formulating legal principles by extracting them from individual cases is a task never wholly achievable to the extent that the factual baggage is a constant and necessary companion to common-law legal principles.

* * *

This [...] implies an absence a priori of any single correct result in an absolute sense. It implies substantive law's flexibility and dependence on argumentation. Thus, at the heart of the common-law lies an exaltation of methodology, of argumentation that not only rivals, but also determines, substantive law. Justice Scalia has written that "[t]he rule of law is *about form*." Indeed, according to H.L.A. Hart, in the United States, there is "a concentration, almost to the point of obsession, on the judicial *process* ...."

* * *

By way of contrast [...], [civil-law] legal culture traditionally has focused on a less flexible hierarchy of legal authority, on what Professor Thomas Fleiner refers to as a "hierarchical order of legal norms." According to Professor Fleiner, civil-law legal culture de-emphasizes procedure: "It is not the procedure which guaranties legitimacy, good law and justice, but ... the higher instance which is close to the roots of justice." The civil-law focus on that "higher instance" of authority, once a king who ruled by divine right, and more recently a legislature empowered by the State's most organic law, its Constitution, to pass laws, has had as a consequence, according to Professor Fleiner, that civil-law states have "a different understanding of democracy as legitimacy of the legislature and not as legitimacy of the courts."

Perhaps the most frequently expressed complaint on the part of beginning law students in the United States is that their professors don't tell them what the law is. This discomfort stems from their not yet having "un-learned" their still civil-law mentality, imported from the domain of their prior life experience and prior intellectual training, from their still equating law with immutable governing principles that, once learned, should, they believe, serve to solve and resolve all questions of law. They enter law school committed to the concept that law school will teach them the discrete guiding principles that resolve all legal disputes. This conception of law [has its reflection in the civil-law, but] does not tally with the common law [...]. Common-law legal education in the United States thus begins a process of teaching law students to "un-learn" this approach when thinking of legal issues, to re-conceptualize law as a process of argumentation, as a body of cases which form a point of departure for reasoning by analogy and distinction.

* * *

The common-law is a law of almost boundless potential for both judge and lawyer, but the measure of its potential, the measure of the opportunities for ingenious creativity, is also the measure of its inherent uncertainty, fluidity and capacity for transformation. In these attributes, the common-law corresponds to the ethos of Romanticism.

* * *

Describing the young Goethe in his early Romantic period, [Isaiah] Berlin cites Hamann as a major influence on Goethe's Romantic reaction [against ...] the tendency on the part of the French [Enlightenment] to generalise, to classify, to pin down, to arrange in albums, try to produce some kind of rational ordering of human experience, leaving out the *élan vital*, the flow, the individuality, the desire to create, the desire, even, to struggle, that element in human beings which produced a creative clash of opinion between people of different views, instead of that dead harmony and peace which, according to Hamann and his followers, the French were after.

[...] [Herder had the] view that the particular is significant as the expression of the general. In this we see an important attribute that Romanticism shares with the common-law. As we noted above, it is from the particular case, from each decision of each court, that the common-law is derived. The common-law's focus on the particular tallies with Romanticism's focus on "the irreducible variety of human self-expression ...." and its rejection of purely scientific aspirations and methodology: "We have recourse to purely scientific methods of displacement only when communication breaks down ...."

The common-law espouses Vico's method of "imaginative insight," and Herder's idea of empathy through immersion in the "other's" world and standards, what he called "*sich einfühlen,*" for common-law courts assess legal issues in the context of the parties, the parties' lives, and of the parties' experiences as situated in the particular society in which they live. Accordingly, Von Mehren describes United States case law as "a vast collection of human experience." By contrast, he views German case law, and describes its self-understanding, "less as a collection of human experience and judicial experimentation than ... *judicial applications of the written law.*"

In her recent book, Jutta Limbach, a former law professor who [later served as the President of] Germany's Federal Constitutional Court, describes the German judicial decision's failure to attend to the concrete facts of cases, noting specifically that the first pages of German judicial decisions refer neither to the defendants nor to their particular offenses, and that the remainder of court opinions, although generally lengthy, pays scant attention to the particulars that transpired. According to Limbach, German judicial decisions' references to the concrete particulars of cases consist of no more than "isolated/scattered indications" ("*eingestreuten Hinweise*").

The civil-law judicial tradition of neglecting facts in court decisions traditionally has been still more pronounced in French court decisions than in German ones, although the French judiciary also is sparing in its discussion of law, leaving much of the significance of its decisions to be explained by *la doctrine*, scholarly commentary. Dawson aptly described the French judicial opinion as noteworthy for "extreme parsimony" in its references to facts. The great paradox embedded in French judicial discourse is that, on the one hand, it must include the court's reasoning or motivations, in order to enable the public to prevent the judiciary from sliding into any semblance of the pre-Revolutionary corruption, arrogance and arbitrariness that had aroused the public's antipathy against France's judges. On the other hand, however, the very humility that France's judiciary adopted after 1789, in its zeal to demonstrate its republican loyalty, also acts as a restraint against judicial engagement in lengthy discussion of any kind, for fear that such a practice might look discomfitingly similar to a judicial usurpation of a formative role in law, rather than a passive application of legislative intent.

The Italian tradition of *massime* perhaps represents the epitome of the civil-law tradition of inattention to facts. According to Professors Taruffo and La Torre, decisions of Italy's Court of Cassation generally are not published in full. Rather, the published versions of Italian supreme court cases recast the cases as abstract propositions of law.

* * *

[… The] common-law remains focused on concrete, temporal facts, and this is in contrast to the isolated, timeless, acontextual abstraction of rules that civil-law societies apply to govern the lived experiences of parties. The common-law is a formalized undertaking to institute Herder's idea of understanding the general by listening to the particular, by listening to the individual, and by trying to feel as the "other" does in the environment in which the "other" dwells. A civil code, on the other hand, in the words of Portalis, the chief drafter of France's Civil Code, "governs everyone; it considers men *en masse*, never as individuals … Were the situation otherwise, … [i]ndividual interests would besiege legislative power; at each instant, they would divert its attention from society's general interests."

* * *

In contrast to this ahistoricity embedded in the civil-law mentality, Romanticism and the common-law share a profoundly historical nature. The common-law is historical inasmuch as it privileges the present – the particular set of facts surrounding the case at bar, in the context of the present, the actual (in both French and German, "*actuel*" and "*aktuell*," respectively, connote both of these concepts), what Llewellyn so aptly calls "*living facts*," connected to the current situation of the people who are the parties, with differences in facts sufficient to allow the court to determine that a prior case is not a valid "precedent" if it is distinguishable on *its facts*. But what are the "facts" if not historically bound, if not part of the life context of the parties who arrive in court from an evolving, ever-changing society? By contrast, as Zippelius put it, in his *Introduction to [German] Legal Methodology*, "[t]he [civil-law] legal order is … a structure/compilation ["*ein Gefüge*"] of ought-norms. The purpose of their articulation is not to describe facts, but, rather, to prescribe behavior."

* * *

[…] The common-law legal rule or standard, then, derives from the scrutiny of particulars. Its rule cannot be absolute, however, because its formation is inductive in nature, rather than deductive. The crafting of the common-law legal standard inductively; that is, reasoning *from* the accumulated body of precedents *to* a legal norm, is a method that dictates a contestable nature to the outcome.

* * *

Conversely, the civil-law court begins with the general, universal legal norm that applies to the particulars, such that a case is defined as "a particular state of affairs falling under a rule …." By positing legal norms that govern particular cases, the civil law offers the possibility of absolute truth to the extent that its axioms are valid. While both [traditions] observe particular humans in the context of their problems, the common law exalts the particulars, which, as the court encodes them in its narrative, become a set of givens, enabling the formation of the legal standard or proposition for which the pending case will stand in the future, for others to claim as legal precedent.

The civil-law, on the other hand, scrutinizes that which is above the factual context. It embodies the Enlightenment perspective of truth as univocal and absolute. This view does not suppose that every judge will identify the correct resolution to every case, or will [arrive] at the right solution to the legal issues and dilemmas presented. In other words, Enlightenment ideology would not suggest that judicial decisions necessarily are correct. Enlightenment ideology suggests, rather, a concept also embedded in civil-law mentality: namely, that a correct answer exists if only the judge is clever enough to find it, and that it is in principle deducible from the applicable legal authority, whether that authority is the Code or another governing textual source of law: "The Germans will, of course, admit

2.2 The Central Elements of the Civil Law Tradition

the occurrence of the 'hard' case; in such instances opinions may differ over which is the right solution, *but in theory one exists.*"

[...] Civil-law legal systems nevertheless emanate from, and are structured in accordance with, an underlying principle of the possibility of correct judicial decisions. The civil-law legal structure corresponds to the Enlightenment tenet that, in Berlin's words, "a true answer must be discoverable in *principle*, though I may not happen to know it ...."

The Enlightenment sought to universalize the scientific methods that had furthered knowledge greatly in the seventeenth century. Thus, according to Enlightenment philosophy, just as to the underlying civilian conception of law,

> [t]o every genuine question there were many false answers, and only one true one, once discovered it was final – it remained forever true; all that was needed was a reliable method of discovery. A method which answered to this description had been employed by "the incomparable Mr. Newton"; his emulators in the realm of the human mind would reap a harvest no less rich if they followed similar precepts. If the laws were correct, the observations upon which they were based authentic, and the inferences sound, true and impregnable conclusions would provide knowledge of hitherto unexplored realms, and transform the present welter of ignorance and idle conjecture into a clear and coherent system of logically interrelated elements – the theoretical copy or analogue of the divine harmony of nature ....

* * *

The other great bedrock of Enlightenment thinking that Berlin attributes to western thought from the time of classical antiquity until the advent of Romanticism is the belief that all truths are mutually reconcilable, that no two truths can be contradictory. So entrenched is this assumption that Berlin calls it a *"philosophia perennis."* The civil-law mentality also mirrors this view inasmuch as it presents its Code as a coherent and complete representation of law, all of its parts mutually reconcilable. As Kant has argued, to the extent that we view "[t]he unity of nature under a principle of the thoroughgoing connection of everything contained in th[e] sum of all appearances ... [t]o this extent we are to regard experience in general as a system under transcendental laws ... and not as a mere aggregate." Along these lines, what codes lack in specificity they provide in spirit. The codified embodiment of the national law is of a piece, whole and harmonious. As a mathematician put it in analyzing the nature and multifaceted functions of the concept of zero, "[n]ature abhors a vacuum and so do we."

The traditional conception of the completeness of the civil-law codes has given way in recent times to a recognition that they contain or may contain gaps. These gaps are to be filled in by judges in accordance with the spirit of the codes, a directive often found explicitly within the code itself, or, as Saleilles put it, "[b]eyond the Civil Code *but by means of the Civil Code*" (*"Au-delà du Code civil, mais par le Code civil"*). [...]

* * *

Code *lacunae* in civil-law legal cultures represent imperfections in the legislative attempt to create a complete and coherent body of law. Still more importantly, the judges who purport to fill in the gaps are to do so under the guidance of the Code itself – that is, in keeping with the nation's legal spirit as expressed both explicitly and implicitly in the text. While code lacunae necessitate active judges, the decisions reached by those judges do not attain either a binding precedential value, or a legal authority comparable to that of the Code's provisions, nor are they the norm [...].

* * *

Thus, the traditional French theory of judicial conduct incorporates the idea that judges will fill the code's gaps by case decisions, yet conceives of that conduct more as law application than as law creation. Portalis suggested room for judicial creativity, intelligence and analytical acuity, but only within the realm of remaining within the spirit of enacted legislation, in order to apply what the legislators may not have had the foresight to ordain, but which the texts they have enacted suggest through the filter of the judiciary's understanding of their implicit import. As Olivier Moreteau, a French law professor, has put it, "[t]he judge *contributes* to the law, but does not *create* it."

This outlook has remained current in France, at least inasmuch as Professor Moreteau states "it has remained heretical to admit openly that judges can be lawmakers or that they may have some normative powers." Moreover, Portalis' idea that judges should have more than a merely mechanical role in applying the law *predated* the view that later came to dominate in France; namely, that the judiciary should be restricted to rote application of legislative enactments.

By contrast, in common-law legal cultures, judicial creation of law traditionally has been the norm, not the exception, and statutes "are conceded [by common-law judges] to be applicable to certain cases ... but are not conceived of as entering into the legal system as an organic whole." Still more importantly, the idea of an "organic whole" does not underlie the common-law conception of law. However much progress statutes may have made in winning judicial deference, statutes themselves purport to remedy particular problems at particular times, rather than to proceed from an overweening, cohesive legal schema.

Unlike the common-law judge, the task of the civil-law judge who searches for the correct resolution to pending legal issues seeks an expression of that consistent body of law that is the Code, a manifestation of the "organic whole," one that confirms, strengthens and represents its harmony, eschewing any interpretation that might undermine its cohesive, all-inclusive spirit. Romanticism represents the converse. It suggests pluralism, the concept that there are many truths. Romanticist value pluralism also is an attribute of common-law legal culture inasmuch as the common-law court's vision is primed on the mosaic of facts and circumstances presented in their unicity with each case.

By contrast, the civil-law focuses on codes, written texts designed to govern throughout time, designed to embody the immutably true, to embody principles so reliable that they supersede and can withstand the vicissitudes of the particular, of the temporal, of the myriad contextual elements that connect human beings to the legal issues they ask courts to adjudicate. The civil-law poses as a "superstructure of theory valid for any time or place."

* * *

The Romantic de-emphasis of rational justification and universal objectivity is not compatible with the stated objective of most civil-law scholars. Justice Holmes' famous statement that the life of the law has been experience rather than logic is illustrative of the common-law's perspective, just as the reaction of the eminent French legal scholar André Tunc is illustrative of the civil-law's perspective. Commenting that the Holmesian point is anathema to the civil-law lawyer, Tunc makes clear that this is not because of Holmes' emphasis on the importance of experience. [...] According to Tunc, the civilian's problem resides not in Holmes' emphasis of experience, but rather in his disdain for logic. Tunc takes the position that logic, albeit wedded to experience, is the very heart of the civilian's understanding of law.

* * *

[...] As Learned Hand put it,

2.2 The Central Elements of the Civil Law Tradition

[common-law] precedents will not have the force of instances of a general principle, but of precedents upon precisely the questions which were decided. While there is perhaps nothing inherently or inevitably necessary in such a result, since a court might extend the logical consequences of a decision beyond the precise question which it decided, yet, in fact, the result has been otherwise, as may be shown by the decisions themselves.

Not only is the rule created by each common-law judicial decision a function of the case's facts, an effort of "divin[ing] the underlying principles [from] the morass of particulars," but also, as Edward Levi demonstrated, the rules of prior cases change with each new application. Rules change as they are applied for various reasons, including the evolution of social values that is the focus of Levi's attention, but they also change with application of necessity because they are applied to new facts, by virtue of the inevitable factual disparity between the pending case and each precedent. Each case is thus like a new square in a mosaic, or a sculptor's stroke, changing the face of the whole, altering its meaning through the addition of facts in its trajectory through time.

The civil-law norm, by contrast, is loosened from factual specificity by virtue of its generality of expression and anonymity of origin. Although arguably no norm can be so general as to be completely free of factual baggage, at least implicitly, nevertheless one sees the disconnectedness between civil-law norm and fact in, for example, the five articles of the French Civil Code whose link to the entire field of French tort law they spawned is at best highly elusive if not utterly mysterious and elliptical. By contrast, the common-law rule that emerges from each case may be conceivable only in terms of numerous facts from the parties' lived experience, and the narrower the rule, the more numerous those facts will be.

* * *

Questions/Comments

- Resorting to a tired and not-very-illuminating cliché, it is tempting to say that the Civil Law tradition is from Mars and the Common Law tradition is from Venus. Or would you reverse that mythological alignment? After reading the excerpt from Grosswald Curran (and the many scholars, poets, philosophers, and artists on whom she relies), could you draft a list of the opposing terms, concepts, and qualities that exemplify the Civil Law and Common Law traditions? Typical questions that help illuminate the nature of a legal tradition include: what are the sources of law; what role does legislation play; what is the role of the judiciary; how central are facts, as opposed to logic, to the articulation of rules?
- Is Grosswald Curran's use of the Enlightenment and Romanticism helpful for understanding what characterizes and differentiates the Civil Law tradition and the Common Law tradition? Were you familiar with those schools of thought before reading Grosswald Curran's text? The Enlightenment describes the commitment to reason that reemerged in the seventeenth and eighteenth centuries. Romanticism refers to the turn towards individualism and emotionalism in the nineteenth century. Grosswald Curran largely relies on the work of philosopher Isaiah Berlin for her understanding of the two world views. Berlin steadfastly refused to define them, although he deigned

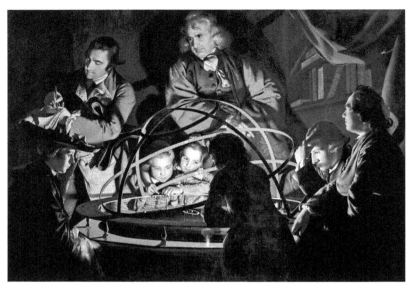

Joseph Wright of Derby
"A Philosopher Giving a Lecture on the Orrery" (1766)
Derby Museum and Art Gallery

"A key idea of the Age of Enlightenment—that empirical observation grounded in science and reason could best advance society—is expressed by the faces of the individuals in Joseph Wright of Derby's *A Philosopher Lecturing on the Orrery*."[22]

How are the characteristics and values of the Civil Law tradition captured by Wright's painting?

Figure 2.1 Enlightenment Painting

to describe Romanticism's opposite (the Enlightenment) as the "notion that there is somewhere a perfect vision, and that it needs only a certain kind of severe discipline, or a certain kind of method, to attain to this truth, which is analogous, at any rate, to the cold and isolated truths of mathematics – [… the belief that it is] possible to attain to some kind of, if not absolute, at any rate nearly absolute knowledge, and in terms of this to tidy the world up, to create some kind of rational order […]."[21] With the benefit of that clarification, what does it mean, when trying to understand the nature of the two legal traditions, to say that the Civil Law is Enlightened and the Common Law is Romantic? What do the works of art in Figures 2.1 and 2.2, widely regarded as exemplary of the Enlightenment and Romantic periods, suggest about the qualities of the Civil Law and Common Law traditions?

- The Civil Law tradition prioritizes statutes and the "law as text." The Civil Law takes an "anti-organic" and "anti-atomic" approach to normativity. Law is promulgated in advance as propositional legislation. Law is a preplanned, plotted, overarching, interrelated, coherent, concrete whole. In the Civil Law tradition there are right and wrong answers. What is the Common Law's priority?

2.2 The Central Elements of the Civil Law Tradition

Caspar David Friedrich
"Wanderer Above the Sea of Fog" (1817)
Hamburg Kunsthalle

"*The Hiker Above the Sea of Fog* is the quintessential Romantic artwork. The aesthetic began as a reaction against the Enlightenment values (logic, rationality, order) that partially contributed to the bloody, monarch-toppling French Revolution of 1789. Throughout Europe, writers, artists, and musicians turned to emotion, imagination, and the sublime for inspiration. [. . .] In particular, the period exalted individuals and their strong emotions. Friedrich exemplified these qualities as he placed one man, gazing at a vast and unknowable territory, in the middle of his canvas."[23]

How are the characteristics and values of the Common Law tradition captured by Friedrich's painting?

Figure 2.2 Romantic Painting

- Do you agree with Grosswald Curran that, before entering law school, law students' mentality is more closely aligned with a Civil Law understanding of the law? Do you think so-called "modern" or "Western" thinking involves an innate "Civil Law mentality" that yearns for immutable governing principles like those that operate in mathematics, physics, or economics? The Civil Law tradition has had a significant influence on how people think about the law in much of the world. If that's not the case for you and your primary or "national" legal system, would you like to live and practice law in a system that insists on the existence (usually located in statutes or codes) of single, correct legal resolutions to all problems? Gosswald Curran seems to contradict Pierre Legrand who, in the excerpt from "The Impossibility of 'Legal Transplants'" in Chapter 1, claimed that everyone is preconditioned in the law by the society in which they grow up and live. He said that growing up in a country influenced by the Common Law tradition conditions those people to be Common Law lawyers "in waiting." But here Grosswald Curran says that her American law students arrive at law school as Civil Law lawyers "in waiting." Who has the better case?

- What does it mean to say that the Civil Law tradition relies on deductive reasoning and that the Common Law tradition relies on inductive reasoning?
- A working, shorthand definition of the Civil Law tradition might conclude that the Civil Law prioritizes statutes (in the form of codes), embraces positivism and formalism, yearns for scientific and systematic objectivity, and seeks to limit judicial discretion. Can you find support for each of the elements of this summary depiction in the excerpt from Grosswald Curran? In particular, how does she characterize the role of judges in the Civil Law tradition? Are there other facets of the Civil Law tradition illuminated by Grosswald Curran that are neglected by this shorthand description?
- The Common Law tradition approaches normative progress and development through discrete judicial decisions, reacting to discrete factual scenarios. The Civil Law tradition aspires to science, system, and certainty. By comparison the Common Law appears "relativist," with each judge empowered to (potentially) create the law anew, by mixing principles, policy, and precedent pursuant to the judge's individual vision. Civil Law trained lawyers suspect that this process of legal development is arbitrary, unsystematic, subjective, and prejudicial. Grosswald Curran quotes Thomas Lundmark who explained that Civil Law jurists' "insistence [...] that judge-made law is not real law does not mean that judge-made norms do not exist. Rather, it means that judge-made norms should not exist." This might be another characteristic of the Civil Law tradition: it imagines itself to be superior to other traditions, and especially superior to the Common Law tradition. A part of this attitude is the Civil Law's historical, Roman pedigree. Do you think it makes sense to say that one legal tradition is better than other legal traditions – like saying that soccer is better than basketball, or that pasta is better than sushi? What standards or criteria should we use to make that assessment? That was precisely the agenda undertaken by the "legal origins" school of comparative law, which argued, much to the shock of Civil Law jurists, that the Common Law tradition more effectively promotes economic growth than the Civil Law tradition does.[24] Considering what you now know about the two traditions, would you be willing to guess what qualities of the Common Law tradition seem to have produced that outcome? In any case, the "legal origins" research has attracted strong criticism.[25]

2.2 The Central Elements of the Civil Law Tradition

Grosswald Curran quotes Friedrich Kubler as saying that, for the Civil Law jurist, codification represents the ideal understanding of the law. In Chapter 7, when you encounter German private law and the German Civil Code, we'll consider in greater depth what a "code" is and how it differs from other kinds of legislation. For now, it will be enough to remark that Kubler (a German-trained – and convinced Civil Law – jurist) criticized the Common Law's lack of elegance, symmetry, comprehensiveness, systematization, and fitted ordering. His point was: The Common Law is not codified! Grosswald Curran's article explains that codification is part of the Civil Law tradition's preference for legislative enactments, as opposed to judge-made law. But in their *elegance, symmetry, comprehensiveness, systematization, and fitted ordering*, codes are not ordinary legislation. Other characteristics of codification bear this out. Usually, codification is meant to *supersede* all existing law; codes are *revolutionary*. In many cases, including with respect to the most highly regarded codifications (the French Code Civil [1804] and the German Civil Code [1900]), the revolutionary effect of codification also contributed to efforts to forge *new nations* or *national identities*. But once enacted, and having achieved their revolutionary agenda, codes establish long-standing legal regimes that *endure*, in some cases for centuries. Both Grosswald Curran and Glenn (whose understanding of legal traditions was discussed in Chapter 1) emphasize that codes are viewed as *complete* and *absolute* normative frameworks. In their completeness, and in their national resonance, codes are often seen as directly *accessible* to and *understandable* by the citizens they regulate. Codes are *clear* so that lawyers and judges cannot manipulate the law enacted by the people's representatives. Codes are *democratically legitimate* because, in ideal circumstances, they are enacted by republican legislatures and they limit counter-majoritarian judicial arbitrariness. To achieve all of this, codes rely extensively on *logic* and *abstraction* in identifying prescribed solutions to human dilemmas. Codes are *propositional* and, therefore, *rational*. Codes are *scientific*. Pierre Legrand explains that

> [t]he importance of a civil code for a jurisdiction adopting that form of legal ordering can hardly be exaggerated. […] A code is as fundamental to human life as, say, weights and measures. […] A civil code is a form of governmentality. As it emphatically prioritises positivism and formalism, a civil code (and its accompanying "codification effect") excludes other approaches to legal knowledge. Once there is a code, hermeneutical, as distinguished from grammatical, perspectives on law find themselves de-legitimised. […] Because a civil code is a totalizing technocratic form, once there is a civil code there is very little "outside space" left […]. A civil code, then, is much more than a way of dealing with culture. It *is* culture.[26]

John Henry Merryman and Rogelio Pérez-Perdomo made the essential point that "[t]he distinction between legislative and judicial production of law can be misleading. There is probably at least as much legislation in force in a typical American [Common Law] state as there is in a typical European or Latin American [Civil Law] nation."[27] The distinct codified quality of legislation in the Civil Law tradition marks the difference between American statutes and Germany's major codes. Merryman and Pérez-Perdomo made another essential point, explaining that "the existence of something called a code [is not the] distinguishing criterion" of the degree to which a legal system has been influenced by the Civil Law tradition.[28] "Codes do not exist in most civil law systems," they pointed out, while "bodies of systematic legislation covering broad areas of law and indistinguishable from European or Latin American codes [may] exist in a number of common law nations."[29] The important thing to grasp is that, with or without a prominent codification, a legal system influenced by the Civil Law tradition will show signs of what Legrand called the "codification effect," a culture of law that prioritizes legislation, limits the discretion of the judiciary, and aspires to scientific systematization in the law.

Much comparative law scholarship has attempted to minimize the differences between the Civil Law and Common Law traditions. Grosswald Curran's article also argues that lawyers in the Western, developed world have been hardwired in equal parts with Enlightenment and Romantic mentalities, giving them a reservoir of familiarity that can be tapped when called upon to engage with norms that have been significantly influenced by either the Civil Law tradition or the Common Law tradition. Her thesis is that no matter how different the two may be, the gulf between them surely can be bridged. This book embraces that possibility, believing that you can cross into other legal traditions and gain some sense of their logic, aims, and qualities. The Civil Law has had a predominant influence on German law and legal culture. That fundamental feature will surface again and again. But you know from the introductory material in Chapter 1 that I will urge you to consider whether other legal traditions also have influenced parts of German law. The Common Law tradition will be prominent among those "alternative" threads in the tapestry of German legal culture.

Still, I reject a homogeneity thesis. Contact and confluence amongst legal traditions – perhaps especially the Civil Law and the Common Law – has not had the effect of reductively blending the traditions into an indistinct sameness. Joseph Dainow explained that some comparative law scholars believe that "there no longer exists any real difference between the civil and the common law by reason of parallel developments that have taken place in order to satisfy the same societal needs in general conditions which are similar – the differences which remain being only matters of degree than nature."[30] This sounds like more of the "frantic urge towards sameness" about which Legrand agonized in the excerpt from "The Same and the Different" presented in Chapter 1. Elsewhere, Legrand pleads that we must not

> [l]ose sight of basic, historically-shaped, politically-delineated, and sociologically-sensitive epistemological pointers, the common law is fact-based adjudication rather than propositional language, rhetoric rather than logic – the open hand rather than the closed fist [...].[31]

Another central feature of the Civil Law tradition is the prominent role played by legal scholars in promulgating, interpreting, and developing the law. That characteristic has an exaggerated profile in Germany's version of the Civil Law tradition. The scholarly study of the law in Germany is a prestigious and powerful professional undertaking referred to as *Rechtswissenschaft* (legal science). That is the subject of the next section of this chapter.

2.3 Scholars and Legal Science in the Civil Law Tradition

Of course, the Civil Law tradition cannot achieve a perfectly resolved, static, preordained normative order. The confounding, intricate facts of life would bring such a system to its knees. The churn of history would also eventually overwhelm such a system as it struggled to make a nineteenth-century code relevant to problems arising in the twenty-first century. In the Common Law tradition, the lawmaking judge ensures that the law responds to the facts of the case and reflects the social-historical reality. In the Civil Law tradition this role is largely assumed by legal scholars who, pursuing legal science, carefully scrutinize the details of legislation, including codes. They make claims about the broad principles and values that underlie legislation, on the one hand, and the detailed governing doctrine of the legislation, on the other hand. In turn, judges and legislators in the Civil Law tradition consult the conclusions of these scholar scientists – set out in vast, systematic, multivolume commentaries – to learn how to resolve a case at bar or develop new regulation without disturbing the existing normative architecture. It is not an exaggeration to depict the legal scholar in the Civil Law tradition as wearing a white lab-coat in his or her jurisprudential laboratory carefully dissecting normative subjects. The legal science undertaken by these scientist-scholars is viewed as logical and technical. It is not political, or at least only a little more political than a physicist's conclusions about the governing laws of the subatomic universe. In the following excerpt, Merryman and Pérez-Perdomo describe the unique role played by legal scholars in the Civil Law tradition. As you read it, ask yourself: Are the legal scholars who bear so much authority in the Civil Law tradition really so impartial, dispassionate, and neutral?

John Henry Merryman & Rogelio Pérez-Perdomo
THE CIVIL LAW TRADITION: AN INTRODUCTION TO THE LEGAL SYSTEMS OF EUROPE AND LATIN AMERICA 57, 60–69 (4th ed. 2018)[*]

* * *

We have seen that the role of the civil law judge is generally thought to be much more restricted and modest than that of the common law judge. It is reasonable to speak of

---

[*] © 1969, 1985, 2007, 2019 by the Board of Trustees of the Leland Stanford Jr. University. All rights reserved. Used by permission of the publisher, Stanford University Press, www.sup.org.

the common law as a law of the judges, but no one would think of using such terms in speaking of the civil law even if the world is changing. The alleged abuses perpetrated by judges under the old regime, and the conception of the role of judges that emerged in France during the revolution converge to limit what judges are supposed to do. Legislative positivism, the dogma of the separation of powers, the ideology of codification, the attitude toward interpretation of statutes, the peculiar emphasis on certainty, the denial of inherent equitable power in the judge, and the rejection of the doctrine of stare decisis – all these tend to diminish the judge and to glorify the legislator.

From this, one might suppose that the protagonist of the legal process in the civil law tradition is the legislator. Indeed, it was hoped for a time that the legislature would produce bodies of law that were complete, coherent, and clear, so that interpretation would be unnecessary. The retreat from the dogma of legislative infallibility has been a slow, grudging one. Although it is now admitted that civil law courts have an interpretive function, the fiction is still maintained that in performing that function, the judge does not create law but merely seeks and follows the expressed or implied intent of the legislator. All this suggests that the civil law legislator occupies the dominant position held in the common law tradition by the judge. For brief periods in the history of the civil law tradition this may have been true, but the legislators soon found themselves again in the shadow of the people who were primarily responsible for the theory of the modern nation-state; for the doctrines of legislative positivism and the separation of powers; for the form, style, and content of codification and for the dominant view of the nature of the judicial function. The teacher-scholar is the real protagonist of the civil law tradition. The civil law is a law of the professors.

* * *

We begin to understand the true importance of the civil law scholar when we look at how lawyers are educated, the role of law professors in explicating the law and the nature of their scholarly publications. Historically, civil lawyers were educated at the university by law professors, and from the eighteenth century onward, the method was the professors' lectures. The systematic treatises of the school of natural and international law do not leave room for the discussion of cases or for discussion at all. They just have to be explained. The same happened when the law was codified and the codes occupied the center of teaching in the nineteenth century. The authority of the professor-lecturer (and frequently book author) is supreme. The legal science, originally a German innovation that was later adopted by other civil law jurisdictions, accentuated the systematic character of law and legal scholarship. In the twentieth century, shorter books (précis or manuals) gave systematic treatment to specific branches of the law and gradually replaced the old treatises. Across these changing forms, the literature produced by the professor-scholars tends to give the image of law as a well-organized system of norms.

A typical book on Continental legal history illustrates the important role of the civil law scholar. Much of what is called legal history in the civil law tradition is baffling to common lawyers who first approach it. They are used to thinking of legal history as an account of legal rules and institutions in their historical, economic, and social contexts. The legal history they read is full of great cases, occasional statutes, and historical events. But when they pick up a book on legal history in the civil law tradition, they are likely to find the bulk of it devoted to a discussion of schools of legal thought and of disputes between legal scholars and their followers. They will read about the glossators, the commentators, the humanists, about the differences among the French scholars of the eighteenth century; and about the debate between Savigny and Anton Thibaut on codification

2.3 Scholars and Legal Science in the Civil Law Tradition

in Germany. All in all, it is a peculiar form of intellectual history, almost entirely divorced from socioeconomic history on the one hand, and from discussion of the origin and development of specific legal institutions on the other. The protagonist of this form of legal history is the legal scholar, and its subject matter is currents of thought about the structure and operation of the legal order.

This is what we mean when we say that legal scholars are the dominant actors of the civil law. Legislators, executives, administrators, judges, and lawyers all come under the scholars' influence. Scholars mold the civil law tradition and the formal materials of the law into a model of the legal system. They teach this model to law students and write about it in books and articles. Legislators and judges accept their ideas of what law is, and when legislators and judges make or apply law, they use concepts the scholars have developed. Thus, although legal scholarship is not a formal source of law, the doctrine carries immense authority.

In the United States, where the legislature is also theoretically supreme, there is a well-known saying (originated by a judge) that the law is what the judges say it is. This is, properly understood, a realistic statement of fact. Judges have to decide how to characterize legal problems presented to them, which principles of law to apply to the problems, and how to apply them in order to arrive at a result. Whether the principles they choose are embodied in legislation or in prior decisions, they achieve substantive meaning only in the context of a specific problem, and the meaning attributed to them in that context is necessarily the meaning supplied by the judges. In a similar sense it is reasonably accurate to say that the law in a civil law jurisdiction is what the scholars say it is.

* * *

[…] The contemporary civil law world is still under the sway of one of the most powerful and coherent schools of thought in the history of the civil law tradition. We will call it legal science. […]

* * *

The concept of legal science rests on the assumption that the materials of the law (e.g., statutes, regulations, customary rules) can be seen as naturally occurring phenomena, or data, from whose study the legal scientist can discover inherent principles and relationships, just as the physical scientist discovers natural laws from the study of physical data. As a leading German scholar of the time, Rudolph Sohm, put it: "The scientific process, by means of which principles are discovered that are not immediately contained in the sources of law, may be compared to the analytical methods of chemistry." Under the influence of this kind of thinking, legal scholars deliberately and conscientiously sought to emulate natural scientists. They intended to employ the scientific method, and they sought admission to the community of scientists. (It should be added that similar assumptions, but with less emphasis on science and the scientific method, underlay some of the work of legal scholars in the United States in the late nineteenth century and constituted one source of justification for the famous case method of teaching in American law schools.)

Like the natural sciences, legal science is highly systematic. Principles derived from a scientific study of legal data are made to fit together in a very intricate way. As new principles are discovered, they must be fully integrated into the system. If new data do not fit, either the system must be modified to accommodate them, or they must be modified to fit the system. In this way the preservation of systematic values becomes an important consideration in criticizing and reforming the law.

This emphasis on systematic values tends to produce a great deal of interest in definitions and classifications. Much scholarly effort has gone into the development and refinement of definitions of concepts and classes, which are then taught in a fairly mechanical, uncritical way. The assumption of legal science that it scientifically derives concepts and classes from the study of natural legal data on the one hand, and the generally authoritarian and uncritical nature of the process of legal education on the other, tend to produce the attitude that definitions of concepts and classes express scientific truth. A definition is not seen as something conventional, valid only so long as it is useful; it becomes a truth, the embodiment of reality. Serious arguments are conducted about the "autonomy" of certain fields of law, such as commercial law or agrarian law, or about the "true" nature of specific legal institutions. Law is divided into clearly delimited fields. Public law and private law [...] are treated as inherently different and clearly distinguishable. There is a precisely defined legal vocabulary and an accepted classification of law that are reflected in the curricula of the law schools, in the professorial chairs in the faculties of law, in the arrangement of books in law libraries, in the subject matter of works written by legal scholars, and in the approach of legislators to lawmaking.

**

Because the components of this systematic restatement of the law, although theoretically inherent in the existing positive legal order, did not exist there in identified, articulated form, and because the legal order was a universe of data within which inherent principles were to be identified, new concepts had to be invented to express these components and principles. The novelty of these concepts and their prominence in the work of scholars committed to legal science eventually led critics to call this kind of doctrine conceptual jurisprudence. Because communication without concepts is difficult, it hardly seems fair to criticize legal science for using them. What was peculiar to legal science was that its concepts were new (or were given a new emphasis), that the accent was on their "validity" rather than their functional utility, that their proper arrangement and manipulation were thought to be the province of scholars, and that they tended to be highly abstract.

This high level of abstraction – this tendency to make the facts recede – is one of the most striking characteristics of legal science to a lawyer from the United States or England. The principles developed by legal scientists have been taken out of their factual and historical context, and are consequently lacking in concreteness. Legal scientists are more interested in developing and elaborating a theoretical scientific structure than they are in solving concrete problems. They are on a quest for the ever more pervasive legal truth, and in the process of making statements more abstract, "accidental" details are dropped. The ultimate objective is a general theory of law from which all but the essential elements have been removed.

The work of legal science is carried on according to the methods of traditional formal logic. The scholar takes the raw materials of the law and, by an inductive process sometimes called logical expansion, reasons to higher levels and broader principles. These principles themselves reveal on further study the even broader principles of which they are only specific representations, and so on up the scale. The principles derived by logical expansion are, at one level, the "provisions that regulate similar cases or analogous matters" and, at a higher level, the "general principles of the legal order of the state" that judges should employ in dealing with the problem of lacunae in the interpretation of statutes [...]. Intuition and the subconscious, despite their powerful influence on human affairs, are excluded from this process. The result is something that Max Weber called "logically formal rationality."

Finally, legal science attempts to be pure. Legal scientists deliberately focus their attention on pure legal phenomena and values, such as the "legal" value of certainty in the law, and exclude all others. Hence the data, insights, and theories of the social sciences, for example, are excluded as nonlegal. Even history is excluded as nonlegal – and this seems peculiarly inconsistent in view of the fact that Savigny and his disciples are called the historical school. It is of interest to historians (including legal historians) but not to legal science. Nor is the legal scientist interested in the ends of law, in such ultimate values as justice. These may properly be the concern of philosophers, including legal philosophers, but the legal scientist is concerned only with the law and with purely legal values. The result is a highly artificial body of doctrine that is deliberately insulated from what is going on outside, in the rest of the culture.

* * *

The special attitudes and assumptions about law that characterized the work of the Pandectists [German law scholars in the nineteenth century who studied and taught the Roman Law] and that make up what is here called legal science can thus be summarized in the following terms: "scientism," "system-building," "conceptualism," "abstraction," "formalism," and "purism." These characteristics of legal science are apparent to many civil lawyers, and there have been many reactions against it in the civil law world. These reactions have taken a variety of forms, and they seem to have been gathering force in the period since World War II; but legal science is far from dead. In all except the most advanced civil law jurisdictions it reigns practically undisturbed. It dominates the faculties of law, permeates the law books, and thus is self-perpetuating. Most law students are indoctrinated early in their careers and never think to question it: its characteristics, and the model of the legal system that it perpetuates, are all they know. Legal science has been subjected to direct attack and to subversion from many sides. Its critics have tried to introduce consideration of concrete problems, to see that the existence of a subconscious and of intuition are taken into account, to bring nonlegal materials to bear on the legal consideration of social problems, and to involve legal scholars in the conscious pursuit of socio-economic objectives. Nevertheless, most civil lawyers still form their own ideas of the law according to the teachings of legal science. [...]

* * *

The basic difference [between the Common Law's and the Civil Law's scholarly scientism] is epitomized in another quotation from the German legal scientist Rudolph Sohm, in the *Institutes of Roman Law*: "A rule of law may be worked out either by developing the consequences that it involves, or by developing the wider principles that it presupposes. [...] The more important of these two methods of procedure is the second, i.e., the method by which, from given rules of law, we ascertain the major premises they presuppose.... The law is thus enriched, and enriched by a purely scientific method." An American legal realist would resist the implication that rules of law should be the principal objects of study or the suggestion that there are only these two ways of studying them. But if pushed to Sohm's choice, most law professors, judges, and lawyers in the United States would easily and quickly choose the first of his two methods. Most civil lawyers would still choose the second.

Questions/Comments

- What are the elements of legal science? Is there something about the Civil Law tradition that predisposes it to giving legal scholars such prominence? Is there something inherent to the Common Law tradition that de-emphasizes the role of legal scholars? Merryman and Pérez-Perdomo conclude, while "the influence of law professors and legal scholarship may be growing in the United States, judges still exercise the most important influence in shaping the growth and development of the American legal system. [...] The common law is still a law of the judges."[32] In fact, Merryman and Pérez-Perdomo may be wrong about the growing influence of American legal scholars. In 2007 the *New York Times* reported, under the glaring headline "When Rendering Decisions, Judges Are Finding Law Reviews Irrelevant," that there had been a precipitous decline in federal court citations to law review articles written by scholars over the last decades. The *New York Times* article opened with this line: "In a cheerfully dismissive presentation, Judge Jacobs and six of his colleagues on the United States Court of Appeals for the Second Circuit said in a lecture hall jammed with law professors at the Benjamin N. Cardozo School of Law this month that their scholarship no longer had any impact on the courts."[33] According to the report, federal court citations to the *Harvard Law Review* were down by more than half from the 1970s to the 1990s.

- Legal scholars have star roles in each of the pivotal periods in the development of the Civil Law tradition. Merryman and Pérez-Perdomo explain that "both Justinian and Napoleon called on prominent jurists to carry out the very complicated task of drafting far-reaching legal reforms [...]."[34] The Glossators at the University of Bologna revived interest in Roman Law and, through their teaching and commentary, aided its informal reception across Europe during the Renaissance. But Merryman and Pérez-Perdomo conclude that "legal science is primarily the creation of German legal scholars of the middle and late nineteenth century, [evolving] naturally out of the ideas of Savigny."[35] Savigny and German legal science played an especially prominent part in the drafting and enactment of Germany's prized Civil Code from 1900. That history will be dealt with in greater depth in Chapter 4, which presents German legal history, and Chapter 7, which considers German private law and the German Civil Code.

- Although some contemporary German legal scholars will no doubt contribute to paradigmatic jurisprudential shifts,[36] the run-of-the-mill "legal scientists" have their impact in the scrupulously detailed commentaries they write or edit about codes and statutory regimes. It seems there can be no limit to the number of these commentaries, with each generation of scholars seeking to make its mark. Figure 2.3 offers a glimpse of the prominence and pervasiveness of scholarly commentaries in the German legal culture. The work of art depicted features a stack – forming a pillar – of these commentaries. For an example of what they look like and how they read, a brief sample of a commentary on the German Civil Code is presented in Chapter 7.

2.4 Conclusion

Legal Commentaries

Stacks of German legal commentaries forming a "pillar of justice" in an exhibition at the Historical Museum Bielefeld. There are commentaries from eighteen separate code/statutory regimes represented in this clever and ironic work of art. The codes and statutes are identified by commonly-used abbreviations, including some of the most prominent codifications or regimes: GG (*Grundgesetz* / Basic Law or Constitution), BGB (*Bürgerliches Gesetzbuch* / Civil Code), StGB (*Strafgesetzbuch* / Criminal Code), StPO (*Strafprozeßordnung* / Code of Criminal Procedure), SGB (*Sozialgesetzbuch* / Social Code), HGB (*Handelsgesetzbuch* / Commercial Code). C.H. Beck, a prominent publisher in the legal field, lists more than 125 commentaries—covering fifteen different legal subjects—in its digital series. Hundreds more are offered in print.

Figure 2.3 Legal Science and Commentaries: A Pillar of Justice

2.4 Conclusion

The *Dictionary of International and Comparative Law* defines "Civil Law" as the "system of law based on Roman Law as codified in the Napoleonic Code."[37] This chapter has sought to provide a broader and more textured understanding of the Civil Law tradition. It is an approach to law that prioritizes statutory law, embraces positivism and formalism, seeks to limit judicial discretion in the interpretation and application of statutes, and aspires to scientific systematization and objectivity. Peter de Cruz adds additional depth with his conclusion that legal systems strongly influenced by the Civil Law "share a tradition of devising systematic, authoritative and comprehensive codifications as their law-making style, working from general concepts and providing solutions to problems. [...] The primacy of legislation is [...] common to [the civil law tradition]."[38] Yet, these affirmative depictions exclude or neglect too much. Thus, the *Dictionary of International and Comparative Law* and de Cruz also resort to a blunt technique, defining the Civil Law tradition by what it is not: The Common Law tradition. This book does much the same. The excerpts I have presented – from Glenn, Grosswald Curran, and Merryman and Pérez-Perdomo – rely explicitly and extensively on a comparative understanding of the Civil Law tradition, which is defined in juxtaposition with the Common Law tradition.

Especially for those unfamiliar with "Civilian" or "Continental" law, this chapter should give you a foundational understanding of the rhythm, logic, values, and assumptions of the Civil Law tradition. That already tells you a great deal about the life of the law in Germany, where the Civil Law tradition is the most prominent thread in the fabric of German legal culture. Yet, the next chapter and the rest of this book demonstrate that the Civil Law tradition has never enjoyed a wholly uncontested status in German law and it is by no means the whole story of German law and legal culture today.

Further Reading

- *Common Law – Civil Law: The Great Divide?* (Christoph Bezemek, Frederick F. Schauer & Nicoletta Bersier eds.) (Springer) (2021)
- John Heny Merryman & Rogelio Pérez-Perdomo, *The Civil Law Tradition* (Stanford University Press) (4th ed. 2018)
- H. Patrick Glenn, *Legal Traditions of the World* (Oxford University Press) (5th ed. 2014)
- George Mousourakis, *Roman Law and the Origins of the Civil Law Tradition* (Springer) (2014)
- Thomas Lundmark, *Charting the Divide between Common and Civil Law* (Oxford University Press) (2012)

NOTES

1 *See Civil Law Systems and Mixed Systems with a Civil Law Tradition*, JURIGLOBE – WORLD LEGAL SYSTEMS (University of Ottawa), www.juriglobe.ca/eng/sys-juri/class-poli/droit-civil.php.
2 *See Common Law Systems and Mixed Systems with a Common Law Tradition*, JURIGLOBE – WORLD LEGAL SYSTEMS (University of Ottawa), www.juriglobe.ca/eng/sys-juri/class-poli/common-law.php.
3 Roman Law, in Australian Law Dictionary (Trischa Mann & Audrey Blunden eds., 2010).

4 *See* JOHN HENRY MERRYMAN & ROGELIO PÉREZ-PERDOMO, THE CIVIL LAW TRADITION 63 (4th ed. 2018).
5 *Bündnis für das deutsche Recht*, BUNDESMINISTERIUM DER JUSTIZ (2020), www.bmj.de/DE/Themen/EuropaUndInternationaleZusammenarbeit/BuendnisDeutschesRecht/BuendnisDeutschesRecht_node.html.
6 LAW – MADE IN GERMANY (2009), www.lawmadeingermany.de/Law-Made_in_Germany.pdf.
7 *Id*. at 3.
8 *Id*. at 7.
9 RENE DAVID & JOHN E.C. BRIERLY, MAJOR LEGAL SYSTEMS IN THE WORLD TODAY (2nd ed. 1978).
10 NIGEL FOSTER & SATISH SULE, GERMAN LEGAL SYSTEM AND LAWS 3 (4th ed. 2010).
11 GERHARD ROBBERS, AN INTRODUCTION TO GERMAN LAW 15 (7th ed. 2019).
12 MERRYMAN & PÉREZ-PERDOMO, *supra* note 4 at 2.
13 Pierre Legrand, *Antivonbar*, 1 J. COMPAR. L. 13, 17 (2006).
14 MERRYMAN & PÉREZ-PERDOMO, *supra* note 4 at 2.
15 *Id*. at 6.
16 *Id*. at 3.
17 H. PATRICK GLENN, LEGAL TRADITIONS OF THE WORLD 60 (5th ed. 2014).
18 MERRYMAN & PÉREZ-PERDOMO, *supra* note 4, at 3.
19 Legrand, *supra* note 13, at 23.
20 MERRYMAN & PÉREZ-PERDOMO, *supra* note 4, at 1.
21 Isaiah Berlin, *In Search of a Definition*, in THE ROOTS OF ROMANTICISM (Henry Hardy ed., 1999).
22 Abram Fox, *Wright of Derby, A Philosopher Lecturing on the Orrery*, KAHN ACADEMY, available at www.khanacademy.org/humanities/ap-art-history/later-europe-and-americas/enlightenment-revolution/a/wright-of-derby-a-philosopher-lecturing-on-the-orrery.
23 Alina Cohen, *Unraveling the Mysteries behind Caspar David Friedrich's "Wanderer,"* ARTSY (Aug. 6, 2018, 5:32 PM), available at www.artsy.net/article/artsy-editorial-unraveling-mysteries-caspar-david-friedrichs-wanderer.
24 *See* Rafael La Porta, Florencio Lopez de Silanes, Andrei Shleifer, & Robert W. Vishny, *Legal Determinants of External Finance*, 52 J. FIN. 1131 (1997); Rafael La Porta, Florencio Lopez de Silanes, Andrei Shleifer, & Robert W. Vishny, *Law and Finance*, 106 J. POL. ECON. 1113 (1998).
25 *See* Mathias M. Siems, *Legal Origins: Reconciling Law & Finance and Comparative Law*, 52 MCGILL L. J. 55 (2007).
26 Legrand, *supra* note 13, at 16.
27 MERRYMAN & PÉREZ-PERDOMO, *supra* note 4, at 27.
28 *Id*.
29 *Id*.
30 Joseph Dainow, *The Civil Law and the Common Law: Some Points of Comparison*, 15 AM. J. COMPAR. L. 419, 420 (1966–1967).
31 Legrand, *supra* note 13, at 20.
32 MERRYMAN & PÉREZ-PERDOMO, *supra* note 4, at 58.

33 Adam Liptak, *When Rendering Decisions, Judges Are Finding Law Reviews Irrelevant*, N.Y. TIMES (Mar. 19, 2007) http://select.nytimes.com/2007/03/19/us/19bar.html?scp=1&sq=liptak+rendering+decisions&st=nyt.
34 MERRYMAN & PÉREZ-PERDOMO, *supra* note 4, at 60.
35 *Id.* at 61.
36 At the risk of excluding obvious additional candidates, the following scholars (some of whom come to jurisprudence via other disciplines, like sociology) are surely some of the recent heavyweights in German legal philosophy: Niklas Luhmann, Jürgen Habermas, Gunther Teubner, and Robert Alexy.
37 JAMES R. FOX, DICTIONARY OF INTERNATIONAL AND COMPARATIVE LAW 55 (3rd ed. 2003).
38 PETER DE CRUZ, COMPARATIVE LAW IN A CHANGING WORLD 27–28 (4th ed. 2018).

3

Germany's Plural Legal Culture

Key Concepts

- *Legal Positivism*: The theory that legal issues can be solved based only on appropriately enacted law – a social fact – without reference to value judgments or consideration of the norm's merits.[1]
- *Legal Formalism*: The use of deductive logic to derive the outcome of a case from premises accepted as authoritative. Formalism enables a commentator to pronounce the outcome of the case as being correct or incorrect, in approximately the same way that the solution to a mathematical problem can be pronounced correct or incorrect.[2]
- *Natural Law*: The theory that there is an ideal, immutable body of law that is thought to be superior to positive law because it would consist of the highest principles of human morality. Natural law is absolute because it does not result from conventions but is discoverable by the exercise of human reason.[3]
- *Free Law Movement*: Early twentieth-century anti-formalist legal theory advocated by Hermann Kantorowicz, who argued that judges should be free to fill gaps in the law by resorting to their legal system's or society's values. Kantorowicz insisted that judges already exercised this discretion despite the positivist and formalist ideal of Civil Law jurisprudence.
- *Pure Theory of Law*: A strict positivist theory of law. Hans Kelsen argued that all that matters in law is the discovery and application of appropriately enacted norms without regard for – and wholly separate from – any moral considerations.
- *Radbruch's Formula*: Mid-twentieth-century anti-positivist, natural law legal theory articulated by Gustav Radbruch after World War II. Radbruch's Formula urged the application of "nonstatutory law" (natural law) in circumstances in which the character of the relevant statutory (positive) law was so immoral or unjust as to qualify as "statutory non-law."
- *Objective Order of Values*: Doctrine announced by the German Federal Constitutional Court that held that the fundamental rights secured by the post-war German Constitution (*Grundgesetz* or Basic Law) established the controlling values for all of German law and society. The omnipresence of these values led the Court to conclude that all law, including private law, must be interpreted and applied in a manner that ensures the realization of the constitution's fundamental rights. This involves the *Drittwirkung* (indirect horizontal effect) of the Basic Law's values.

Study Tips

On a website entitled "Famous Scholars from Kiel: A Selection," the University of Kiel has published brief English-language biographies of some of the university's most prominent researchers and teachers, including two of the scholars discussed in this chapter: Hermann Kantorowicz and Gustav Radbruch. These short biographies are available at www.uni-kiel.de/grosse-forscher/index.php?lang=e.

The *Lex Animata* Series presents animated videos explaining central topics of international law, including a video on the theory of "Positivism: Nature of International Law" (www.youtube.com/watch?v=WtX_uku1Zd8). The video provides a helpful introduction to positivism, which is understood to be a key characteristic of the Civil Law tradition.

In Chapter 1, I suggested that we approach this introduction to German law and legal culture by considering how different legal traditions are woven together to influence and inform the way Germans "do law." In Chapter 2, I offered a deeper introduction to the Civil Law tradition (and, seemingly by necessity, the Common Law tradition as the Civil Law's foil). That is a productive progression because it gave you a better sense of what I mean by "legal tradition." Armed with the exposure you gained in Chapter 2, you can begin to ask questions about a range of assumptions and priorities that distinguish one legal tradition from another: what are the sources of law; who are the main actors in the process of developing and interpreting the law; what logic informs legal reasoning; what values does the law promote. This should equip you to unearth the presence of various legal traditions, some prominent and some less readily observable, as we examine the substance of German law. The aim of all of this is to allow us to paint a more richly textured and pluralistic portrait of German legal culture.

The focus in Chapter 2 on the Civil Law tradition was also justified by the fact that the Civil Law tradition – some call it the Continental Legal tradition or the Roman-Germanic legal tradition – exercises immense gravitational power over German law, bending the entire legal culture in the direction of that tradition's striving for systematic, authoritative, and comprehensive statutory law. Even as I expect us to cast a searching eye across the German legal landscape, hoping to catch fleeting glimpses of different legal traditions at play there, it cannot be disputed that the Civil Law tradition shines the brightest light in German legal culture. It is important that you come to appreciate how the Civil Law shapes Germans' way of thinking about and practicing law. This should be less challenging for those readers whose primary or "national" legal system is also significantly influenced by the Civil Law tradition. But the Civil Law "operating system" that conditions much of the life of the law in Germany will present a new and confounding framework for other readers. For the uninitiated or those unfamiliar with the Civil Law tradition, let me offer these reassuring words: Comprehending the Civil Law tradition's significance for German legal culture must be a process, deepened by the coverage in Chapter 2 and continuing throughout this book.

As I noted at the start of Chapter 2, the role of the Civil Law tradition in German legal culture is so predominant that, when assigning the German legal system to a classification or "legal family" (as part of the traditional macro-comparative law project), most comparative law scholars categorically and exclusively assign Germany to the Civil Law family. These are just a few examples of that convention:

- "[T]he civilian tradition [...] still provides a fair idea of what may be dubbed German legal culture."[4]
- "The German legal system belongs to the central European family of legal systems, broadly classified as civil law countries."[5]
- "The German legal system remains, generally speaking, a system of (positive) norms that is, traditional German legal thinking revolves, in the vast majority of cases, around the twin immutable 'pillars' of an established system and norms regarded as authoritative."[6]
- "German law is a member of a family of laws, which one might well call the European Continental laws, [...]. Notwithstanding many and striking differences between the branches and members of this family, the basic structure [...] is very similar."[7]
- "German law [has] the characteristics of a codified legal system, in other words, one whose rules are laid down in legislation which cover all aspects of the law. This characteristic is not the least of the factors which identify German law as Continental European."[8]

According to these scholars, the introduction to the Civil Law tradition you gained from Chapter 2 is the most consequential step in your journey to understanding German legal culture. The Civil Law tradition is German law. German Law is the Civil Law tradition.

To say it again: This book is determined to distance itself from the notion of "legal families." The risk in that approach is evident in the passages quoted above. The idea of legal families allows scholars to sum up Germany's legal culture in a few words *and* account for most other European legal systems, all of which are shorn of any distinct character, including even the names of the relevant national jurisdictions. The promise inherent in this taxonomic approach is that, if you have a grasp of the Civil Law character of the German legal system, then you simultaneously will have gained fundamental insight into the law of most European jurisdictions. This would apply by extension to legal systems around the world that also are part of the so-called "Civil Law family." After all, as comparative law is frequently taught and as comparative legal research is often conducted, the Civil Law family accounts for the legal systems of Europe, Latin America, and East Asia.

It is true that Germany shares with many other legal systems, in Europe and elsewhere, "a set of deeply rooted, historically conditioned attitudes about the nature of law; about the role of law in the society and the polity; about the proper organization and operation of the legal system, and about the way law is or should be made, applied, studied, perfected, and taught."[9] The shared heritage of the Civil Law tradition tells us important things about the legal culture of these systems. Yet, the Civil Law orientation of a legal system should not obscure the more nuanced and complex life of the law in any particular system. Let me offer just two examples of this more nuanced perspective.

In many Muslim-majority countries the Civil Law tradition operates in tandem – in discourse – with the Islamic Law tradition to distinctly characterize the legal systems of "most North African states as well as [...] many Near and Middle Eastern countries."[10] With that in mind, it would be a profound omission to insist on exclusively classifying these legal systems as belonging to either the Islamic Law family or the Civil Law family. As the material on German administrative law in Chapter 9 of this book suggests, the Islamic Law tradition is of some relevance in Germany, too.

Another example of all that can be lost by overstating a system's Civil Law alignment is as confounding as it is exhilarating. The one thing traditional macro-comparative law might have allowed you to count on is that the United Kingdom's legal system (typically presented as exemplary of the Common Law family) and Germany's legal system (typically presented as exemplary of the Civil Law family) are plainly and cleanly differentiated. Yet, for all their differences (and the differences are many and tangible), features of the Common Law tradition can be seen contending for influence in the German legal system. I will hint at this later in this chapter. We will explore that dynamic more thoroughly in Chapter 8, when we consider the emergence of German constitutionalism and its accompanying, judge-empowering emphasis on an "objective order of values."

All of this means that an understanding of the Civil Law tradition offers a broad and essential – but still only partial – understanding of the German law-world. Contrary to the tidy use to which conventional comparative legal studies puts legal families as a system of classification, life in the law is (delightfully) messier than that. Classifying Germany as *merely* a member of the Civil Law family excludes too much that is textured and paradoxical and interesting about German legal culture.

Yes, the Civil Law tradition is a predominant – even the principal – framework for the German legal system. But there are other jurisprudential forces at work in German legal culture, and with far greater relevance than is typically ascribed to them by comparative law scholars. This chapter advances the case for this plural understanding of German law and legal culture by tracing the persistent resistance to the Civil Law tradition's dominance over the German legal system. The Civil Law tradition – especially its emphasis on codified law and its embrace of notions of positivism and formalism in statutory interpretation – never has enjoyed unchallenged primacy in the German law-world. That is true, no matter how most comparative law scholars might like to have the story told. A latent, counter-Civilian tendency has long been an irritant in German legal culture. The following sample of developments in German jurisprudence in the twentieth century demonstrates that law in Germany was never tidily and singularly "Civilian."

3.1 Free Law

The first exhibit in this survey of German dissents, departures, and dissidents from the Civil Law tradition is an excerpt from Hermann Kantorowicz's revolutionary pamphlet *Der Kampf um die Rechtswissenschaft* (*The Battle for Legal Science*).[11] In his 1906 text, Kantorowicz objected to the Civil Law tradition's positivism and formalism and appealed for a *Freirechtsschule* (Free Law Movement) that would liberate judges from the Civil Law's dogged focus on the four corners of the statute and the German (scholarly) tradition of interpreting the law through the blinkered, doctrinal method known as "logical expansion." Resembling American legal realism,[12] the Free Law Movement "stressed three points about adjudication: first, that it is inherently free and creative, involving a significant amount of discretionary lawmaking by judges; second, that written law, from codes to case precedent, is unavoidably incomplete and incapable of providing answers to all legal questions; and third, that all rules of legal construction, including those aimed at limiting the freedom of judges, involve implicit value judgments and the application of extralegal principles."[13] Kantorowicz's response to all of this was to "free" judges to fill in the gaps in the law through the discretionary application of values. Considering the Civil Law tradition's veneration of the statutory text – and the accompanying constraint that imposes on the judiciary – Kantorowicz hardly could have proposed something more provocative.

Gnaeus Flavius [Hermann Kantorowicz]
The Battle for Legal Science (1906)

[Translated from the German by Cory Merrill]

12 GERMAN LAW JOURNAL 2005, 2006–2011, 2017, 2019–2020, 2024–2025, 2028 (2011)

* * *

A new movement has come to legal science [...].

* * *

The reigning ideal image of the jurist is as follows: a higher civil servant with academic training, he sits in his cell, armed only with a thinking machine, certainly one of the finest kinds. The cell's only furnishing is a green table on which the State Code lies before him. Present him with any kind of situation, real or imaginary, and with the help of pure logical operations and a secret technique understood only by him, he is, as is demanded by his duty, able to deduce the decision in the legal code predetermined by the legislature [...].
 [...] Continental Europe [...] not only made this ideal its own, but also moved it straight to the heart of its political beliefs and buttressed it with that most intense security of quasi-religious consecration. [...] But only in the last few years has the situation

fundamentally changed [...]. This new movement [...] aims at removing no less than the entire previous ideal and erecting in all respects the exact opposite [...].

* * *

The new conception of law presents itself as a resurrection of natural law in renewed form. The positivism of the nineteenth century, which had emerged triumphant over natural law, dogmatized its conviction that there is no other kind of law than that recognized by the state. Natural law was pursued right down to its last hiding place, fed by the belief that the teachings of natural law were to be condemned because it dreamed of a universally valid law, unconditioned by the statute [...] natural law [...] claimed to be valid independently from state power. [...] [We] indicate every such law to be a *free law* [...].

[Free law justifies deposing the reigning ideal image of the jurist because] propositions will always be determined that are certain to assess, complete, develop, or overthrow statutory law. Propositions that as a result of this function, cannot be statutory law nonetheless must be law, and therefore must be free law. [...]

* * *

The civil code must at last be completed by free law; its gaps must be filled. And here we encounter the dogma of statutory law's completeness [...].

[...] Even the widespread theory that admits there are gaps in the statutory code and so demands and anticipates their filling by means of dogmatism is a concession to our view. But we should not take satisfaction from this concession. For it is not the case that gaps in the code are found here and there – no, we can confidently say that there are no fewer gaps than there are words. Not a single concept is dismantled into its smallest units, only a few are defined, these being defined only by other concepts which are themselves undefined. Only an unlikely fate could henceforth make a legal case so widespread that it was represented by all applicable legal concepts down to their sound conceptual cores, instead of only being recognized by their swimming contours. In this situation, the solution to fill in the gaps by means of legal interpretation would be an unnavigable task, even if this means were not as unfit as it will soon show itself to be. Faced with an individual case, only free law, with the spontaneity of its decisions and the emotional clarity of its content, can bring about this filling in, and has, in fact, brought it about. [...]

* * *

And all other arts of interpretation are as little good for employing logical means to fill in the fragments of the legal code, for merging the appropriate legal system with all cases of life [...]. Nevertheless, jurisprudence has always advanced confidently in its impossible task, has sought again and again to undo all the locks with its few keys; so it cannot help but sometimes resort to [...] breaking the locks; erecting constructions so violent that their incompatibility with the text of the legal code was obvious even to the dullest eye; or, conversely, clinging to the code in order to achieve results that stood in blatant contradiction to the necessities of life [...]. However, underlying [dogma's resort to interpretation] was the idealistic assumption that it was only necessary to fit a few missing tiles here and there to complete the great mosaic of legal concepts. In truth, the task is just the opposite. Because the elements from which the undefined elements ought to be ascertained are in large part also in need of definition by others, from which the same is needed – or worse, by those first elements sought, so that we either must turn eternally in vicious circles or be endlessly carried away. The few air-tight elements we have do not even remotely aid in deciding [...] the only permissible outcome from the myriad possible combinations. An entire animal can be constructed from as little as a single bone – despite Cuvier. Indeed, dogmatic jurisprudence [...] makes cursory references to the famous "Spirit of the Law."

3.1 Free Law

But as we've seen, it would likely be easy to ascertain very many spirits, but quite impossible to establish a single one. And what will be passed off as it [...] is nothing but the spirit that one would gladly see prevail in the law according to one's highest personal taste.

* * *

[...] So then no legislator, no power, no will, not that mystical "will of the legal code," and certainly no reality will stick [...] [to these] universal propositions [...]. [They are] the hollow sound of words and the ink of printed paper. Therefore, repulsive is the individual who fails to examine an individual case freshly and independently out of fealty to a rashly binding moral-legal imperative, and deplorable is the judge who, "in the name of the king," believes it necessary to declare law to be only what that paper authority commands.

[...] [Our] movement rejects this paper jurisprudence, [...] [for] the law that we live and feel living in us [...].

* * *

[...] If legal science recognizes free law, then judicature will no longer be able to be based on statutory law! If it is creative, then judicature will no longer be merely the servant of the code! If the science constantly has gaps to fill, the practice will not be able to correctly decide every case! If theory makes room for emotional values, an exactly-reasoned verdict will no longer be necessary! If theory's individual factor were acknowledged, the practice would lose its quality of predictability, uniformity! Should the theory itself become anti-dogmatic, judicature could no longer be scientific! If the will is predominant in judicature, then it can no longer remain affectless! In short, the ideals of legality, passivity, merit, scientific nature, legal certainty, and objectivity appear to be irreconcilable with the new movement. But – fortunately – it can be shown that these postulates in part still haven't been realized, and some do not deserve to be realized.

[...] Perhaps one might also say that the judge would judge solely according to the code, even if our code contained only a paragraph: the judge decides according to reasonable discretion.

[...] We therefore demand that the judge, bound by his oath, decide a case as much as a case can be decided according to the clear wording of the code. He may and should abandon this [mandate on the following terms:] first, the moment the code appears to him not to offer an undisputed decision; and second, if it, according to his free and conscientious conviction, it is not likely that the state authority in power at the time of the decision would have come to the decision as required by law. In both of these cases he ought to arrive at the decision that, according to his conviction, the present state power would have arrived at had it had the individual case in mind. Should he be unable to produce such conviction, he should then decide according to free law. Finally, in desperately involved or only quantitatively questionable cases such as indemnity for emotional damages, he should – and he must – decide according to free will. [...]

* * *

We believe [with this] that we give no more to the judge than what he has already – necessarily – taken himself, and much less than what we Germans in earlier times – to say nothing of the Roman prator – allowed, as well as what the English still allow today. [...]

* * *

[...] [T]he movement strives with all its might towards a goal that contains [...] the highest goal of all legal action: justice. Only where the narrow canon of a few paragraphs is burst open and free law's abundance imparts the opportunity to provide every case with its appropriate ruling, is there justice. Only where there is freedom is there justice. Only where, instead of a barren thistle, a creative will gives rise to new thought, only where there is personality, is there justice. Only where a forward-directed glance from the book to life measures an action's distant consequences and requirements, only where there is wisdom, is there justice.

* * *

Questions/Comments

- Kantorowicz's son, in a moving and insightful tribute to his father's work, noted that the manifesto "had an immediate impact, arousing heated debate and bitter controversy [...]."[14] Gustav Radbruch, Kantorowicz's friend and collaborator on the Free Law project (about whom we will hear more later), wrote after the book's publication: "The people are in revolt, the storm is breaking."[15] Apparently, Kantorowicz used the pseudonym "Gnaeus Flavius" for two reasons. First, he feared the work wouldn't be taken seriously if it was discovered that it had been written by a lowly post-doctoral researcher. Second, he feared that the controversial pamphlet might doom his chances of becoming a professor in Germany, especially in light of the legal academy's thoroughly Civilian orthodoxy. Kantorowicz's concerns were well-founded. The eventual revelation of his authorship cost him the prospects of further post-doctoral work at the University of Heidelberg. And, upon resumption of his post-doctoral research at the University of Freiburg, he was "required to address [his highly suspect] Legal Methodology in his 'Trial Lecture' [...]."[16] Famously provocative, Kantorowicz also would have reveled in the symbolism of his chosen pen name. Gnaeus Flavius was the son of a freed slave whose rise as a civil servant and renowned legal expert scandalized fourth-century Roman society.
- Maybe there is no sharper or more biting depiction of the "ideal image" of the Civil Law jurist than the one Kantorowicz penned for the opening of *The Battle for Legal Science*. Do you recognize in that description, and in the rest of the excerpt, the central characteristics of the Civil Law tradition? How does this differ from your ideal image of a life in the law? Try to write a corresponding one-paragraph description of the "ideal image" of the jurist in your primary or "national" legal culture. What are the inherent benefits of a legal culture that finds its expression in a system like the one Kantorowicz satirized? Kantorowicz says that the Free Law Movement aims to replace "paper jurisprudence" with the "law that we live and feel living in us." Does that sound something like the Common Law tradition? Why?
- Would you have joined the Free Law Movement, even if subscribing to its tenets would place your career at risk? What is the "high goal" that Kantorowicz says the Free Law Movement was striving towards? Do you see a parallel – in critical and controversial postures, as well as in aims – between the challenge posed by the Free Law Movement at the turn of the

twentieth century and the present-day jurisprudential demands of Critical Race Theory?[17]

- The Free Law Movement fashioned itself as a revival of natural law philosophy, which is positioned by Kantorowicz in opposition to the positivism and formalism of the Civil Law tradition. Natural law theory has a long and rich history. For the purpose it plays as a contrast to the Civil Law tradition, it is enough to use Brian Bix's definition:

  > Within legal theory, there are two well-known groupings which cover most (but not all) of the writing that has carried the label "natural law": (1) "traditional natural law theory" sets out a moral theory (or an approach to moral theory) in which one can better analyze how to think about and act on legal matters; and (2) "modern natural law theory" argues that one cannot properly understand or describe the law without moral evaluation.

  To which of these schools does the revived natural law envisioned by Kantorowicz belong?

- According to Kantorowicz, what problems made the Free Law Movement necessary? How had the Civilian "ideal" sought to solve those problems? Kantorowicz says that one tool the dogmatic (Civil Law) jurists found for filling in gaps in the code was to refer to the "famous 'Spirit of the Law.'" This builds on Montesquieu's canonical treatise *The Spirit of the Law* (1748), which argued that a society's political and legal institutions were informed by the social (and even geographical) reality of the community. It was suggested that *lacunae* (gaps) could be resolved, without formally straying from the positive law text, by insisting that applications of the law promote or align with this spirit. A version of Montesquieu's claims found expression in the work of the German legal theorist Friedrich Carl von Savigny, who argued that the law is an expression of the *Volksgeist* (spirit of the people).[18] What is Kantorowicz's criticism of this approach to interpretation and legal practice? Why isn't it an acceptable solution to the problem of gaps in the positive law?

- Can you identify the concrete test or standard that Kantorowicz articulates for the implementation of the Free Law program? Why do some scholars argue that the Free Law Movement, expressed by that standard, wasn't so "free" after all? If there is some truth to that critique, then it might say something about just how powerful the force of the Civil Law tradition is in the German legal culture. Even while writing his revolutionary manifesto, there were limits to how far Kantorowicz was willing (or able) to go. For a sense of what those limits were, one only need consider Kantorowicz's criticism of American Legal Realism. Many scholars believe that American realist jurisprudence drew inspiration from the Free Law Movement.[19] Legal Realism, however, isn't at all interested in the formal or written law. It focuses instead on empirical evidence of the law found in its actual application and practice.[20] Legal Realists draw their understanding of the law from the sociology and psychology that conditions decision-makers (especially judges) and determines the decisions they make.[21] This extreme anti-formalism was simply too much for Kantorowicz. In a 1934 *Yale Law Journal* article (which was based on a lecture he delivered at Columbia University) Kantorowicz announced his intention to criticize the "exaggerated" sociological and empirical claims of the "realist movement in American jurisprudence."[22] Kantorowicz insisted that his Free Law Movement should not be held responsible for the Realists' exaggerations. He growled: "It is disagreeable enough for a man to have to pay alimony for his own illegitimate issue; but he cannot be expected to pay for other men's bastards, and like it."[23]

3.2 Pure Law

The Free Law Movement stirred trouble, especially for Kantorowicz. But it did not change much in German legal culture. By contrast, Legal Realism swept through and reshaped American jurisprudence.[24] Positivism and formalism, and the Civil Law tradition with which they are indissolubly linked, maintained their primacy in German law and legal thinking in the first decades of the twentieth century even as so much else was changing. Germany was a latecomer to industrialization and colonialism. Both of those forces gained strength in the early 1900s. The disastrous outcome of World War I for Germany culminated in the abdication of the Kaiser and the declaration of the country's first republic. Street fighting between conservatives and communists ensued. The debilitating Treaty of Versailles that settled World War I crippled the German economy. A feverish wave of liberalism swept the country, especially in roaring and rowdy 1920s Berlin. None of that seemed to dislodge the primacy of the Civil Law tradition in Germany. Thus, it was natural that the eminent Austrian legal scholar Hans Kelsen would eventually settle into a position with the Law Faculty of the University of Cologne. Kelsen is regarded as one of the twentieth century's leading legal theorists and, among the other positions he championed, Kelsen is seen as a clarion theorist and defender of positivism. In fact, he advocated a "pure" theory of the law that rigidly distinguished between law, on one hand, and politics and morality, on the other hand. Positivism and formalism, perspectives that are central to the Civil Law tradition, were means to that end. Kelsen was not bothered if those approaches to applying the law deny to judges the fuller and more subjective spectrum of considerations that the Free Law Movement regarded as the inescapable elements of the judicial function – and of the pursuit of justice. The following excerpt from Kelsen's 1929 article "Judicial Formalism and Pure Jurisprudence" suggests the distance between Kelsen, who represented the prevailing Civilian ideal of the law in Germany, and the Free Law Movement's failed challenge to that paradigm.

Hans Kelsen
Juristischer Formalismus und reine Rechtslehre

[Translated by Belinda Cooper and republished]

58 JURISTISCHE WOCHENSCHRIFT 1723 (1929)
WEIMAR – A JURISPRUDENCE OF CRISIS 76, 76–78, 81, 83
(Arthur J. Jacobson & Bernhard Schlink eds., 2000)*

The Pure Theory of Law is nothing other than a *theory of positive law* and pretends to be nothing else. It refuses to respond to the question of the correct law, without judging the dignity of this question. It wants to discover only what *is* in the law; not what *ought* to be. [...]

[...] Like all cognition, cognition of law must formalize its object. No one can reproach it for *this* "formalism." For precisely in this formalism lies that which is held up as a virtue, in contrast to the "formalism" frowned upon as a vice: its *objectivity*. "Only the formal is objective; the more formal a methodology, the more objective it can become. And the more objectively a problem is formulated in all the depths of the issue, the more formally it must be grounded." [...] Those who do not understand this do not know what is essential to scientific knowledge. [...]

Therein lies the essence of its "purity": that it wants only to cognize, not to want; only to be scholarship, not politics. [...] It is one of the characteristic signs of our times that there are scholars who find the questionable courage to make a virtue of [...] denying the professional ethos of all scholarly work, abandoning the ideal of objective knowledge free of subjective interests – that is, free of political tendencies – and defending the right of methodological syncretism by proclaiming the inseparable link between legal scholarship and politics. [...]

* * *

[...] By far the largest part of what is brought forward against legal formalism in the literature, with varying degrees of passion, is a dispute over the methods of statutory interpretation. But when is an interpretation "formalistic"? It is telling that most lawyers who rush to make the charge of formalism are at a loss when asked for a more precise definition of this characteristic. And an analysis of the exceedingly frequent use of this word in the critical literature would hardly reveal anything even approaching agreement on its meaning. However, here it is enough to state that of the various methods of interpretation, so-called plain meaning is for the most part described as "formalistic." And even this is not without exception. If one can give reasons for a decision considered to be expedient or desirable only by showing that it can be subsumed under the language of a legislative text, without coinciding with the provable intent of the legislator, one will be highly unlikely to reject the decision as "formalistic." But if such a decision conflicts with interests one considers worthy of protection, then and only then will one call it a formalistic interpretation. [...] And then it is simply the opposing interests that would like to gain recognition through criticism of prevailing interpretive methods by using the argument of formalism. Nothing is more easily understandable than the fact that the strict application of a statute that takes little consideration of the interests of a particular group will be combated as "formalistic" by that group's legal ideologues. In today's jurisprudence it is self-evident that the interests that use this critique will present themselves as the better interpretive method with higher "scholarly" standards.

* * *

---

* © 2000 by the Regents of the University of California.

[...] Because the Pure Theory of Law is only cognition of existing positive law, not a prescription for its correct production, it neither provides directions on how to make good laws nor gives advice on how to make good decisions and take good administrative action on the basis or within the frame of statutes. Therefore it takes only minor account of the problem of interpretation. [...]

[...] [Formalist approaches will face the criticism] that legal scholarship must serve "life" or even "pulsating life!" This is certainly an incontrovertible phrase. But one can serve life through scholarship by attempting with incorruptible objectivity to *understand* the nature of things, and thus the essence of state and law, and one can serve life through *politics* by *willingly* and *actively* implementing values, especially enacting and applying laws. Those for whom scholarship is not doing enough by serving objective knowledge actually expect it – through the demand that it "serve life" – to serve interests that, as cognition shows, can be none other than individual and group interests, even if they pretend to be objective values. It is not scholarship but politics that rails against the Pure Theory of Law with the accusation of formalism. And with this argument, the Pure Theory of Law cannot be refuted by scholarship, by a differing scholarly position; it can only be shouted down by politics with this slogan. But the Pure Theory of Law does not fear. For the history of the human spirit shows that scholarship, and thus also the scholarship of state and law, has always freed itself from the bondage in which politics has always attempted to keep it, because the innermost nature of science forces it to be, if not something *more*, then at least something *other* than an instrument in the struggle for power. If there is any point at all upon which one can stand outside the arena of power, then it is science and scholarship. Even the science of power; which is then a pure theory of state and law.

Questions/Comments

- Kelsen argues that the very features of the Civil Law tradition that attract criticism – positivism and formalism – are its most redemptive qualities. He tells us that formalism is a "virtue" because it engenders "objectivity" and permits the assessment of law beyond power and politics. Indeed, he seeks to expose the ideological subjectivity inherent in criticism leveled against formalism in the law. According to Kelsen, what motivates such objections?
- Why might Kelsen's particularly rigorous form of positivism be characterized as the "separation thesis"? What is Kelsen seeking to separate?
- Both Kantorowicz and Kelsen are concerned with legal science. You might substitute the word "science" for "scholarship" throughout the translated excerpt. Recall from the discussion in Chapter 2 that legal scholars and their scholarship play a fundamental role in the Civil Law tradition. Kelsen doesn't have to worry that German legal scientists (legal scholars) will wield undesirable discretion and subjectivity because they are constrained by a well-established tradition and methodology that strives for objectivity and neutrality. That tradition, the focus of Kantorowicz's scorn and Kelsen's confidence, is often portrayed as dogmatic. In a lecture delivered at the University of Frankfurt, Pierre Legrand remarked that it had been a decade since he last made a scholarly presentation in Germany, "the land of *Rechtswissenschaft*, of seemingly relentless legal conceptualism and

systematization, of apparently incessant categorical thinking, the country where one appreciates being told one is a good dogmatician."[25]

- Kelsen's jurisprudence has been derided as "law on the page and not in the heart." Do you agree with that description? Can you see the contrast between Kelsen's theory of "Pure Law" and Kantorowicz's embrace of "the law living in us"? Do you agree with the criticism that Kelsen's approach lacks human and emotional qualities? Would Kelsen have seen that as a discredit to his approach to law? Throughout this book's treatment of substantive German law one repeated theme will be the effort – clearly informed by the Civil Law tradition's positivism and formalism – to elevate the law's scientific objectivity and to minimize subjectivity, discretion, and emotion in the law. This is especially true of German criminal law, which will be explored in Chapter 10.

3.3 Moral Law

Kelsen's position, though theoretically distinct, ultimately was rooted in the Civilian understanding of the law. He shared this posture with nearly all other legal theorists in Germany in the first half of the twentieth century, including Gustav Radbruch. This is a remarkable testament to the pull of the Civil Law tradition in Germany, with its preference for codes and its embrace of positivism and formalism. After all, as I noted earlier, Radbruch had been Kantorowicz's close collaborator in the revolutionary Free Law Movement. By the 1930s, however, Radbruch had been brought back onside. This is how one scholar portrayed Radbruch's views:

> Judges have the professional duty to be "subservient to the law without regard to justice." The criterion of legal certainty [for Radbruch] legitimizes this strict loyalty to the law: By enforcing positive law, whatever its content, the judges guarantee the protection of safety and order as the "most immediate task of the law." In line with this argument, Radbruch states: "We despise the person who preaches in a sense contrary to his conviction, but we respect the judge who does not permit himself to be diverted from his loyalty to the law by his conflicting sense of right."[26]

Although a very careful reading of Radbruch's scholarship might suggest very little difference between his prewar and post-war thinking,[27] most scholars accept that the trauma of Hitler's tyranny and terror – and the Nazi's distinct instrumentalization of the law – left Radbruch deeply skeptical of the Civil Law's fundamental assumptions, particularly its insistence on positivism and formalism. As the following excerpt from his renowned essay "*Gesetzliches Unrecht und übergesetzliches Recht*" ("*Statutory Lawlessness and Supra-Statutory Law*") demonstrates, after the war Radbruch prayed for a different, less Civilian jurisprudence. For clarity's sake it may be helpful to note that this excerpt from Radbruch itself contains several lengthy excerpts drawn from reports about a post-war criminal trial that raised the question: Must immoral positive law be formalistically respected and enforced?

Gustav Radbruch
Gesetzliches Unrecht und übergesetzliches Recht

[Translated by Bonnie Litschewski Paulson & Stanley L. Paulson]

1 Süddeutsche Juristen-Zeitung 105 (1946)
Bonnie Litschewski Paulson & Stanley L. Paulson
Statutory Lawlessness and Supra-Statutory Law
26 Oxford Journal of Legal Studies 1, 1–4, 6–8 (2006)[*]

* * *

By means of two maxims, "An order is an order" and "a law is a law," National Socialism contrived to bind its followers to itself, soldiers and jurists respectively. The former tenet was always restricted in its applicability; soldiers had no obligation to obey orders serving criminal purposes. "A law is a law," on the other hand, knew no restriction whatever. It expressed the positivistic legal thinking that, almost unchallenged, held sway over German jurists for many decades. "Statutory lawlessness" was, accordingly, a contradiction in terms, just as "supra-statutory law" was. Today, both problems confront legal practice time and time again. Recently, for example, the *Süddeutsche Juristen-Zeitung* published and commented on a decision of the Wiesbaden Municipal Court [handed down in November of 1945], according to which the "statutes that declared the property of the Jews to be forfeited to the State were in conflict with natural law, and null and void the moment they were enacted."

In the criminal law, the same problem has been raised [...].

A justice department clerk named Puttfarken was tried and sentenced to life imprisonment by the Thuringian Criminal Court in Nordhausen for having brought about the conviction and execution of the merchant Göttig by informing on him. Puttfarken had denounced Göttig for writing on the wall of a WC that "Hitler is a mass murderer and to blame for the war." Göttig had been condemned not only because of this inscription, but also because he had listened to foreign radio broadcasts. The argument made at Puttfarken's trial by the Thuringian Chief Public Prosecutor, Dr. Friedrich Kuschnitzki, was reported in detail in the press. Prosecutor Kuschnitzki first takes up the question: Was Puttfarken's act a violation of law?

> The defendant's contention that his belief in National Socialism had led him to inform on Göttig is legally insignificant. Whatever one's own political convictions, there is no legal obligation to denounce anyone. Even during the Hitler years, no such legal obligation existed. The decisive question is whether the defendant acted in the interests of the administration of justice, a question presupposing that the judicial system is in a position to administer justice. *Fidelity to statutes, a striving toward justness, legal certainty – these are the requirements of a judicial system.* And all three are lacking in the politicized criminal justice system of the Hitler regime.
>
> Anyone who informed on another during those years had to know – and did in fact know – that he was delivering up the accused to arbitrary power, not consigning him to a lawful judicial procedure with legal guarantees for determining the truth and arriving at a just decision.
>
> With respect to this question, I subscribe fully to the opinion given by Professor Richard Lange, Dean of the Law Faculty of the University of Jena. So well known was the situation in the Third Reich that one could say with certainty: Any person called to account in the third year of the war for writing "Hitler is a mass murderer and to blame for this war" would never come out alive. Someone like Puttfarken

---

[*] Permission granted by Oxford University Press.

certainly could not have had a clear view of just *how* the judiciary would pervert the law, but he could have been sure *that* it would.

No legal obligation to inform on anyone can be drawn from section 139 of the Criminal Code either. It is true that, according to this provision, a person who obtains reliable information of a plan to commit high treason and fails to give timely notice of this plan to the authorities is subject to punishment. It is also true that Göttig had been condemned to death by the Appeal Court at Kassel for *preparing to commit high treason*. In a legal sense, however, there had certainly been no such preparation to commit high treason. After all, Göttig's brave declaration that "Hitler is a mass murderer and to blame for the war" was simply the naked truth. Anyone declaring and spreading this truth threatened neither the *Reich* nor its security, but sought only to help rid the *Reich* of its destroyer and thus to rescue it – in other words, the opposite of high treason. Scruples of legal form must not be allowed to obfuscate this plain fact. Furthermore, it is at least questionable whether the so-called *Führer* and Chancellor of the *Reich* should ever have been regarded as the legal head of state at all, and therefore questionable whether he was protected by the provisions on high treason. In any event, the defendant had not reflected at all on the legal implications of informing on Göttig, and, given his limited understanding, he could not have done so. Puttfarken himself has never declared that he informed on Göttig because he saw Göttig's inscription as an act of high treason and felt obliged to report it to the authorities.

The Chief Public Prosecutor then addresses the question: Did Puttfarken's act render him culpable?

Puttfarken essentially admits that he intended to send Göttig to the gallows, and a series of witnesses have confirmed his intention. *This is premeditated murder, according to* section 211 *of the Criminal Code*. That it was a court of the Third Reich that actually condemned Göttig to death does not argue against Puttfarken's having committed the crime. *He is an indirect perpetrator*. Granted, the concept of the indirect commission of a crime, as it has been developed in Supreme Court adjudication, usually looks to other cases, chiefly those in which the indirect perpetrator makes use of instruments lacking in will or the capacity for accountability. No one ever dreamed that a German court could be the instrument of a criminal. Yet today we face just such cases. The Puttfarken case *will not be the only one*. That the Court observed legal *form* in declaring its pernicious decision cannot argue against Puttfarken's indirect commission of the crime. Any lingering hesitancy on this score is cleared away by article 2 of the Thuringian Supplementary Law of 8 February 1946. Article 2, in order to dispel doubts, offers the following rendition of section 47, paragraph 1, of the Criminal Code: "Whoever is guilty of carrying out a criminal act, either by himself or through another person, even if that other person acted lawfully, shall be punished as perpetrator." This does not establish new, retroactively effective substantive law; it is simply an authentic interpretation of criminal law in force since 1871.

After a careful weighing of the pros and cons, I myself am of the opinion that there can be *no* doubt that this is a case of murder committed indirectly. But let us suppose – and we must take this contingency into account – that the Court were to arrive at a different opinion. What would come into question then? If one rejects the view that this is a case of murder committed indirectly, then one can hardly escape the conclusion that the *judges who condemned Göttig to death, contrary to law and statute, are themselves to be regarded as murderers*. The accused would then be an *accomplice to murder* and punishable as such. Should this view, too, raise serious misgivings – and I am not unmindful of them – there remains the Allied Control Council Law No. 10 [of 20 December 1945]. According to article 2, paragraph 1(c), the accused would be guilty of a crime against humanity. Within the framework of this statute, the question is no longer whether the national law of the land is violated. Inhuman acts and persecution for political, racial, or religious reasons are, without qualification, subject to punishment. According to article 2, paragraph 3, the criminal is to be sentenced to such punishment as the court deems just. Even capital punishment.

I might add that as a jurist I am accustomed to confining myself to a purely legal evaluation. But one is always well advised to stand, as it were, *outside* the situation and view it in the light of ordinary common sense. Legal technique is, without exception, merely the instrument the responsible jurist uses in order to arrive at a legally defensible decision.

Puttfarken was condemned by the Thuringian Criminal Court not as an indirect perpetrator of the crime, but as an accomplice to murder. Accordingly, the judges who condemned Göttig to death, contrary to law and statute, had to be guilty of murder.

* * *

With statutory lawlessness and supra-statutory law serving, then, as points of reference, the struggle against positivism is being taken up everywhere.

Positivism, with its principle that "a law is a law," has in fact rendered the German legal profession defenceless against statutes that are arbitrary and criminal. Positivism is, moreover, in and of itself wholly incapable of establishing the validity of statutes. It claims to have proved the validity of a statute simply by showing that the statute had sufficient power behind it to prevail. But while power may indeed serve as a basis for the "must" of compulsion, it never serves as a basis for the "ought" of obligation or for legal validity. Obligation and legal validity must be based, rather, on a value inherent in the statute. To be sure, one value comes with every positive-law statute without reference to its content: Any statute is always better than no statute at all, since it at least creates legal certainty. But legal certainty is not the only value that law must effectuate, nor is it the decisive value. Alongside legal certainty, there are two other values: purposiveness and justice. In ranking these values, we assign to last place the purposiveness of the law in serving the public benefit. By no means is law anything and everything that "benefits the people." Rather, what benefits the people is, in the long run, only that which law is, namely, that which creates legal certainty and strives toward justice. Legal certainty (which is characteristic of every positive-law statute simply in virtue of the statute's having been enacted) takes a curious middle place between the other two values, purposiveness and justice, because it is required not only for the public benefit but also for justice. That the law be certain and sure, that it not be interpreted and applied one way here and now, another way elsewhere and tomorrow, is also a requirement of justice. Where there arises a conflict between legal certainty and justice, between an objectionable but duly enacted statute and a just law that has not been cast in statutory form, there is in truth a conflict of justice with itself, a conflict between apparent and real justice. This conflict is perfectly expressed in the Gospel, in the command to "obey them that have the rule over you, and submit yourselves," and in the dictate, on the other hand, to "obey God rather than men."

The conflict between justice and legal certainty may well be resolved in this way: The positive law, secured by legislation and power, takes precedence even when its content is unjust and fails to benefit the people, unless the conflict between statute and justice reaches such an intolerable degree that the statute, as "flawed law," must yield to justice. It is impossible to draw a sharper line between cases of statutory lawlessness and statutes that are valid despite their flaws. One line of distinction, however, can be drawn with utmost clarity: Where there is not even an attempt at justice, where equality, the core of justice, is deliberately betrayed in the issuance of positive law, then the statute is not merely "flawed law," it lacks completely the very nature of law. For law, including positive law, cannot be otherwise defined than as a system and an institution whose very meaning is to serve justice. Measured by this standard, whole portions of National Socialist law never attained the dignity of valid law.

* * *

We must not fail to recognize – especially in light of the events of those twelve years – what frightful dangers for legal certainty there can be in the notion of "statutory lawlessness," in duly enacted statutes that are denied the very nature of law. We must hope that such lawlessness will remain an isolated aberration of the German people, a never-to-be-repeated madness. We must prepare, however, for every eventuality. We must arm ourselves against the recurrence of an outlaw state like Hitler's by fundamentally overcoming positivism, which rendered impotent every possible defence against the abuses of National Socialist legislation.

* * *

Questions/Comments

- This excerpt from Radbruch's article might benefit from additional clarification. Radbruch reports on a post-war criminal trial as an example of a dilemma that plagues the Civil Law tradition's emphasis on positivism and formalism. That trial featured charges brought against Puttfarken after the war. During the Nazi era, Puttfarken informed on the subversive, anti-Nazi activities of Göttig. Puttfarken's denunciation led to Göttig's arrest and execution. The long excerpts presented by Radbruch come from the closing statement of the prosecutor at Puttfarken's post-war trial. The prosecutor first argued that the court should dismiss the defense offered by Puttfarken, namely, that he was obligated by the (Nazi era) criminal law of treason to inform on Göttig. Second, the prosecutor argued that, by informing on Göttig in a context that would almost certainly lead to his execution, Puttfarken was guilty of murder as an "indirect perpetrator." Third, the prosecutor sought to reassure the court that convicting Puttfarken is the right thing to do, even if Puttfarken's actions might not be perfectly aligned with the relevant provisions of the criminal code. The prosecutor urged the court to rise above a "purely legal evaluation" and to assess the case from the perspective of "common sense." Especially in the first and second parts of his argument, the prosecutor condemned the formalism that conditions legal practice in German law. He pleaded that the "scruples of legal form" should not obscure plain facts. And he argued that Puttfarken should not be allowed to hide behind the Nazi era court's "observance of legal form" when it convicted and condemned Göttig. It is against the backdrop of this case, and the prosecutor's remarkable "nonstatutory" arguments, that Radbruch raises his critique of positivism and formalism.

- Radbruch condemns positivism because he finds that it played a particular role in German legal culture under Hitler's barbarous and tyrannical regime. This legacy underscores positivism's "separation thesis" – the idea that law and morality should be separated. Richard Miller explained that "Nazis argued that law is neutral, a tool that can be used for any purpose."[28] While no moral, credible commentator can defend the administration of the law under Hitler as anything resembling justice, not everyone agrees that Nazi law was distinctly positivist. Stanley Paulson argued that, in their fervent pursuit of Nazi ideology, German jurists arbitrarily strayed from the law on the books when necessary:

  > Legal positivism meant that the judge was bound by the statute come what may, and so, owing to legal positivism, judges in Nazi Germany had no choice, no discretion, bound as they were by the letter of the law. The falsehood reflected in apologetics along these lines has been well documented, for example, by Ingo Müller in his book *Hitler's Justice. The Courts of the Third Reich*, [...]. "Nazi law," with its emphasis on the "concrete, *völkische* situation" championed by Schmitt, Welzel, and many others, marked a wholesale departure from the letter of the law and, by the same token, from "positivism." [...] Indeed, as Müller points out, the President of the Reich High Court [...] let the cat out of the bag when, in 1938, he wrote: "The judiciary [...] can fulfill the task imposed on it by the Third Reich only if it does not remain glued to the letter of the law, but rather penetrates to its innermost spirit; the judiciary must do its part to see that the goals of the lawmakers are achieved."[29]

Indeed, some insist that the Nazi order was so perversely and pervasively unjust that it does not make sense to conceptualize any part of the system as "law." Radbruch seems to come close to this position when he concludes that "whole portions of National Socialist law never attained the dignity of valid law."

- Radbruch's critique of positivism – treating some statutory law as nonlaw, and some nonstatutory norms as law – has come to be called "Radbruch's Formula." Can you distill his formula into a discrete, workable rule? When, according to Radbruch, is it appropriate to stray from the clear terms of statutory law? Why might some argue that, in fact, Radbruch's Formula is too narrow? Much like Kantorowicz's equivocal attempt at a break from Civil Law's positivism and formalism, Radbruch's revolutionary thesis still seems anchored to the priority the Civil Law tradition gives to statutory law.

- Radbruch's Formula again played a prominent role in German law after East Germany and West Germany were reunited in the early 1990s. The question arose: Could the East German soldiers who shot and killed East Germans while they were trying to flee over the Berlin wall be tried for murder? The border guards justified their actions by claiming "the law was the law." East German law, and the orders of their superiors, obliged them to prevent the westward escapes, using deadly force if necessary. The German courts in these *Mauerschützen* (Wall Shooting) cases invoked Radbruch's Formula to justify the convictions. Peter Quint explained the courts' reasoning this way:

3.3 Moral Law

(a) Hermann Kantorowicz
Kantorowicz's "Free Law" Movement urged German jurisprudence to abandon positivism and formalism when necessary to fill gaps in the statutory law, and in recognition of the discretion that judges already, unavoidably exercised.

(b) Hans Kelsen
Kelsen's "Pure Theory of Law" doubled-down on positivism and formalism in the law, crediting as law only positively enacted norms. This, in turn, limited the work of jurists to merely identifying the applicable norms. Kelsen argued for a strict separation between the positive law (as the only enforceable law) and morality.

(c) Gustav Radbruch
Disillusioned by the way Nazis sought to hide behind a positivist and formalist approach to the law, "Radbruch's Formula" urged the disregard of positive statutory law if it would produce immoral results. Instead, Radbruch called for the application of "non-statutory law" to achieve justice. But what is the source of these non-statutory norms?

Figure 3.1 Germany's Plural Legal Culture
Sources: (a) Schleswig-Holsteinische Landesbibliothek; (b) and (c) Getty Images

"Even if the action was legal at the time it was committed, the action was so reprehensible that justice allows (or requires) us to penalize that action now."[30]

- Radbruch, like Kantorowicz before him, offers a version of natural law as the opposite of the positivism of the Civil Law tradition that was championed by Kelsen. Figure 3.1 contains portraits of these three monumental German thinkers whose work embodied both the predominance, but also challenges to, the Civil Law tradition in Germany.

The excerpt from Radbruch draws attention to the fact that an appreciation of contemporary German law and legal culture necessarily requires an engagement with the National Socialist regime and its horrors. Gerhard Robbers concluded that:

[t]he current shape of German law cannot be understood without bearing in mind the catastrophe of the National Socialist dictatorship from 1933 to 1945. Up to the present day the formulation and application of laws is influenced in significant ways by the desire to avoid a repetition of such injustice.[31]

This troubling facet of contemporary German law and legal culture is recognized here and, where relevant, in the subsequent chapters. But I do not frame my entire presentation of German law through that particular lens, not the least because German legal history is deeper and more complex than that. You will get a sense of that complex history in Chapter 4. In the case discussed by Radbruch, for example, both Puttfarken and the prosecutor resort to and offer interpretations of the controlling provisions of the German Criminal Code, which was enacted in 1871 and is still in force today. The legacy and function of that enduring regime is examined in Chapter 10 of this book. It was impacted by the Nazi regime, but also has an historical momentum that transcends that blot.

Still, there are excellent and important works that thoroughly consider the meaning of the Nazi era for German law and legal culture.[32] One point about that heritage, made by Gerhard Robbers, is that the legacy of the National Socialist regime has fostered and fueled persistent critiques of the Civil Law tradition in German legal culture. Robbers explained:

> The catastrophe of National-Socialism also runs through the ongoing debate between legal Positivism and anti-positivist legal thinking. This discussion is about the question, from whence the law receives its binding force. Typical of legal Positivism is the currently dominant view that positively given law and morality are strictly separate issues. In this view even extremely immoral laws can claim to be legally binding, although not morally binding. The only prerequisite is that the provisions in question should have been declared to be law by the appropriate authorities. The positive effects of this view are that it leads to dependability, constancy and certainty of legal orientation, negative effects can be that it leads to unacceptable contents of the legal order. Anti-positivist theories, on the other hand, insist that it is an essential requirement for a valid law that it should be in accordance with ethical principles. In this view law loses its binding force whenever it comes into conflict with fundamental moral principles.[33]

Straining for an approach to law that would counter the Civil Law tradition's positivism and formalism, both Kantorowicz (at the turn of the last century) and Radbruch (midway through the last century) appealed for a notion of the law in Germany that would be free (and especially would free judges) to pursue justice beyond the letter of the law. This bears repeating. Kantorowicz and Radbruch sought to invest the law's interpreter with considerably more discretion than the Civil Law tradition typically affords. Thus, the empowerment of the judiciary seems to be a central feature of alternative approaches that have struggled for relevance against the Civil Law's predominance in the German legal system. Kantorowicz failed with this aspiration. And, despite Radbruch's convincing documentation of the appalling use to which positivism had been put during the National Socialist period, there was little chance that the Civil Law would be supplanted as the principal legal tradition in Germany. Robbers concluded that "[b]oth the positivist and the anti-positivist schools of thought are of approximately equal strength [in Germany]." But he conceded that "in practice a cautious positivism is perhaps the predominant view again."[34]

3.4 Objective Order of Values

As Radbruch suggested, the traumatic experience of the Nazi era pried open the door to the German legal culture, until then largely held shut by the Civil Law tradition. A distinct form of natural law – or at least an anti-positivist approach to the law – crept through that opening to gain a substantial foothold in the German legal system. Robbers explained that this was chiefly accomplished by the values commitments of the new, post-war West German Constitution known as the *Grundgesetz* (Basic Law), which we will study in greater depth in Chapter 8. The Basic Law's values permeate all other areas of the law, leading Robbers to conclude that, despite the prevalence of the Civil Law tradition, "[t]oday the key characteristics of the German legal system are the central role of the Bill of Fundamental Rights (*Grundrechte*) and the principle that Germany is a constitutional state under the rule of law (*Rechtsstaatsprinzip*). They give the entire legal system, down into its smallest details, structure and direction."[35]

This means that the Basic Law's open-textured and generally framed values would supersede *mere* legislation. This remarkable maneuver was both perpetrated *by* judges, and it had the effect of bestowing considerable discretionary authority *on* (at least a sub-set of) judges.

After your exposure to Radbruch's essay, it might not surprise you that the case responsible for the dramatic arrival of judge-made "values jurisprudence" in Germany involved one of many examples of Germany's post-war reckoning with the Nazi past. As you have seen, that legal agenda was peculiarly ill-served by the Civil Law's inherent positivism and formalism. After all, in that approach to the normative order, it is often enough to say that "the law is the law."

The case that opened up this new, decidedly un-Civilian jurisprudence involved Veit Harlan, a popular film director under the Nazi regime and the producer of the notorious, grotesquely anti-Semitic film *Jud Süss* (1940). In 1950, several years after he was acquitted of having committed Nazi war crimes for producing hate-filled propaganda films, Harlan directed a new movie entitled *Unsterbliche Geliebte* (*Immortal Beloved*). Erich Lüth, Hamburg's director of information and an active member of a group seeking to heal the wounds between Christians and Jews, was outraged by Harlan's post-war reemergence as a film director. Speaking before an audience of motion picture producers and distributors Lüth urged his listeners and the German public to boycott *Immortal Beloved*. Harlan's rehabilitation, in Lüth's view, would damage the nation's reputation in the eyes of the world and warrant the moral condemnation he thought the film's showing would bring down on Germany's film industry. The obscenely anti-Semitic poster from Harlan's film *Jud Süss*, and a protest outside a screening of Harlan's film *Unsterbliche Geliebte*, are presented in the images in Figure 3.2.

The distributor of Harlan's new film secured an injunction from the Hamburg Regional Court restraining Lüth from continuing his call for a boycott. The

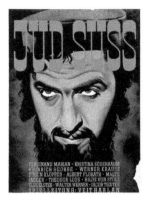 

(a) *Jud Süss* movie poster

(b) Veit Harlan movie protest
After the war Veit Harlan was charged with war crimes for his role in the Nazi propaganda machinery, including his work directing the film *Jud Süss*. He could return to the movie business only after he was acquitted of those charges in 1950. The release of Harlan's 1951 film *Unsterbliche Geliebte* (*Immortal Beloved*) prompted Erik Lüth to call for a boycott, like this one that took place in Frankfurt in 1953. The ordinary courts, relying on the Civil Code, prohibited Lüth from urging the boycott of Harlan's film.

Figure 3.2 Veit Harlan's Films – The Foundation for Germany's "Objective Order of Values"
Source: Getty Images

court regarded Lüth's conduct as actionable within the meaning of § 826 of the Civil Code.[36] As if to fulfill Radbruch's concerns about the Civil Law tradition's ability to secure justice, the Hamburg Higher Regional Court affirmed the lower court's positivistic and formalistic approach to the case and upheld the injunction. Lüth then filed a complaint with the Federal Constitutional Court (*Bundesverfassungsgericht*), the German court exclusively responsible for interpreting and enforcing the Basic Law. Lüth asserted a violation of his basic right to freedom of opinion under Article 5(1).

In one of its most famous and influential rulings, the Federal Constitutional Court sustained Lüth's complaint. The Court articulated, for the first time, the doctrine of an "objective order of [constitutional] values" that recalibrated the relationship between imprecise, judicially defined constitutional rights, on the one hand, and the old Civil Code (the embodiment of the Civil Law tradition in Germany), on the other hand.

The Court began by conceding that the protections secured by the Basic Law are primarily defensive rights enjoyed by individuals protecting them against state intrusions on their freedom. But the Court held that the basic rights also articulate an "objective order of values." At the center of that objective order of values is respect for human dignity, which is announced as inviolable in

3.4 Objective Order of Values

Article 1 of the Basic Law. The objective order of values, the Court explained, informs all law, including the private law that governed the film distributor's case against Lüth. "Every provision of private law," the Court said, "must be compatible with this system of values, and every such provision must be interpreted in its spirit." Private relations are still governed exclusively by private law norms. Yet, the Court insisted that the interpretation and application of private norms by the ordinary courts must take the constitution's objective order of values into consideration. This is especially true, the Court explained, of the Civil Code's general provisions, which permit consideration of broader social and human interests in the application of the detailed and systematic rules of the Civil Code. The general provisions, the Court said, are the windows through which "constitutional rights enter the domain of private law." We will give these "general provisions" closer consideration in Chapter 7 when we examine German private law and the Civil Code. In the *Lüth Case* the Constitutional Court demanded that the ordinary courts ensure that the interpretation and application of the private law take account of the Basic Law's values. And the Constitutional Court threatened to review and constitutionally condemn the private law decisions of those courts if they failed to adequately carry forward those values.

The Federal Constitutional Court found just such an interpretive failure in Lüth's case. The ordinary courts had not adequately accounted for the Basic Law's essential value commitment to the freedom of opinion in their interpretation and application of § 826 of the Civil Code. The ordinary courts' understanding of the relevant Civil Code provision, the Constitutional Court concluded, cut too sharply against the Basic Law's general, objective commitment to the freedom of opinion. The Federal Constitutional Court explained that the ordinary courts should have weighed the harms in the case. On the one hand, § 826 of the Civil Code would prevent the real – but less compelling – harm the boycott might have caused to the film distributor's economic interests. On the other hand, by considering the impact of the case on Lüth's free-speech rights under Article 5, the court could have prevented a diminishment of Lüth's freedom of opinion. The Constitutional Court described the latter interest as one of "the most immediate expressions of the human personality living in society [...] one of the noblest of human rights [... it is a right that is] absolutely basic to a liberal-democratic constitutional order because it alone makes possible the constant intellectual exchange and the contest among opinions that form the lifeblood of such an order."

With that reasoning, the Constitutional Court freed German jurisprudence from the restrictive positivism and formalism of the Civil Law tradition. After the *Lüth Case*, German judges wouldn't just mechanically apply the intricate, systematic functions of code law. They would be required to give force to higher, more fundamental values that are expressed in the Basic Law and given life by the interpretations of the Federal Constitutional Court.

German Civil Code

Section 826
Intentional Damage Contrary to Public Policy

A person who, in a manner contrary to public policy, intentionally inflicts damage on another person is liable to the other person to make compensation for the damage.

[Translated by Russell A. Miller]

German Basic Law of 1949

Article 5
Freedom of Expression, Arts and Sciences

(1) Every person shall have the right freely to express and disseminate his opinions in speech, writing, and pictures and to inform himself without hindrance from generally accessible sources. Freedom of the press and freedom of reporting by means of broadcasts and films shall be guaranteed. There shall be no censorship.

(2) These rights shall find their limits in the provisions of general laws, in provisions for the protection of young persons, and in the right to personal honor.

(3) Art and scholarship, research, and teaching shall be free. The freedom of teaching shall not release any person from allegiance to the constitution.

[Translated by Russell A. Miller]

Federal Constitutional Court
Lüth Case
BVerfGE 7, 198 (1958)

[Translation from]

Donald Kommers & Russell Miller
The Constitutional Jurisprudence of the Federal Republic of Germany 441, 444–445, 448 (3rd ed. 2012)[*]

* * *

Judgment of the First Senate....

* * *

[...] [T]he Basic Law is not a value-neutral document. Its section on basic rights establishes an objective order of values, and this order strongly reinforces the effective power of basic rights. This value system, which centers upon dignity of the human personality developing freely within the social community, must be looked upon as a fundamental constitutional decision affecting all spheres of law, both public and private. It serves as a

---

[*] Excerpt reprinted with permission of Duke University Press.

yardstick for measuring and assessing all actions in the areas of legislation, public administration, and adjudication. Thus, it is clear that basic rights influence [the interpretation of] private law as well. Every provision of private law must be compatible with this system of values, and every such provision must be interpreted in its spirit.

The legal content of basic rights as objective norms informs the content of private law by means of the legal provisions directly applicable to this area of the law. Newly enacted statutes must conform to the value system incorporated into the basic rights. The content of existing law must also be brought into harmony with this system of values. This system infuses specific constitutional content into private law, which from that point on determines its interpretation. A dispute between private individuals concerning rights and duties emanating from provisions of private law – provisions influenced by the basic rights – remains substantively and procedurally a private-law dispute. Courts apply and interpret private law, but the interpretation must conform to the Constitution.

The influence of the value system informing basic rights is particularly relevant to certain mandatory rules of private law that form part of the public order – in the broad sense – that is, rules that in the interest of the general welfare apply to private legal relationships, whether the parties so choose or not. These provisions, complementing as they do the public legal order, are substantially exposed to the influence of constitutional law. This influence may be brought to bear on general laws such as § 826 of the Civil Code, pursuant to which standards such as "good morals" (gute Sitten) are applied to human conduct. To determine what is required by social norms such as these one must first consider the totality of value concepts developed by the nation at a certain point in its intellectual and cultural history and laid down in its constitution. That is why the general clauses have rightly been described as the points where constitutional rights enter the domain of private law.

[…] The Constitution requires the ordinary court judge to determine whether basic rights have influenced the substantive rules of private law in the manner described. If this influence is present, the judge must then, in interpreting and applying these provisions, modify accordingly the interpretation of private law. This follows from Article 1 (3) of the Basic Law requiring the legislature, judiciary, and executive to enforce basic rights "as directly applicable law." If the judge does not apply these standards and ignores the influence of constitutional law on the rules of private law, he or she violates objective constitutional law by failing to recognize the content of the basic right (as an objective norm); as a public official, he or she also violates the basic right whose observance by the courts the citizen can demand on constitutional grounds. Apart from remedies available under private law, citizens can bring such a judicial decision before the Federal Constitutional Court by means of a constitutional complaint.

The Constitutional Court must ascertain whether an ordinary court has properly evaluated the scope and impact of the basic rights in the field of private law. But this task is strictly limited: It is not up to the Constitutional Court to examine decisions of the private-law judge for any legal error that he or she might have committed. Rather, the Constitutional Court must confine its inquiry to the "radiating effect" of the basic rights on private law and make sure that the ordinary court judge has correctly understood the constitutional principle involved in the area of law under review […].

* * *

On the basis of these considerations, the Federal Constitutional Court holds that the regional court, in assessing the behavior of the complainant, has misjudged the special significance of the basic right to freedom of opinion. Courts must consider [the significance of this right] when it comes into conflict with the private interests of others. The ordinary court's decision is thus based on an incorrect application of the standards applying to basic rights and violates the basic right of the complainant under Article 5 (1) of the Basic Law. It must, therefore, be quashed.

* * *

Questions/Comments

- Recall Grosswald Curran's depiction of the Civil Law tradition (Enlightenment) and the Common Law tradition (Romanticism) in the excerpt presented in Chapter 2. Does the Constitutional Court's objective order of values, superimposed on the ordinary courts' interpretation and application of statutory law, feel like Enlightenment (Civil Law) or Romantic (Common Law) jurisprudence?
- The Federal Constitutional Court is a remarkable institution. Some regard it as the most striking feature of the post-war German polity. That statement alone, considering how it elevates a judicial organ, indicates an important cultural shift away from the priority the Civil Law tradition gives to statutes. The Basic Law and the Constitutional Court are more fully considered in Chapter 8.

In *Lüth* the Constitutional Court held that the Basic Law's objective order of values has a radiating effect on all areas of law, including private law. This is a theoretically complex doctrine in German law (referred to as *Drittwirkung* – literally the "third-effect"). That principle is also treated more fully in Chapter 8. For present purposes it is sufficient to know that the Constitutional Court held that the Basic Law's objective order of values has an *indirect* or horizontal effect on private law disputes between individuals. Thus, general laws must be interpreted against the backdrop of the Basic Law and in the light of its values. The ordinary courts' fatal error in *Lüth* was their failure to consider the Basic Law's commitment to freedom of opinion when interpreting and applying the Civil Code. Their exclusive focus on Harlan's private interests, secured by the explicit terms of the Civil Code, are an archetypal example of the positivistic and formalistic character of the Civil Law tradition. But those approaches to the law, the Constitutional Court concluded, should have been overridden by weightier constitutional values.[37]

With its decision in the *Lüth Case*, the Constitutional Court freed German judges from their formalist fealty to positivistic statutes, perhaps even in the way that Kantorowicz and Radbruch hoped they might someday be liberated. Yet, even if judicial power and values have been given new gravity in post-war Germany, it is important to remember the lesson of Kantorowicz's and Radbruch's attempts to extricate German law from the predominance of the Civil Law tradition. For all their revolutionary fervor, neither could (or even really wanted to) break completely clear of the Civil Law's positivism and formalism. The impulse expressed by the *Lüth* jurisprudence is an important – but subtle and subaltern – thread in the tapestry of German legal culture that nevertheless remains predominantly characterized by the Civil Law tradition.

3.5 Conclusion

I hope this chapter does enough to justify some skepticism towards the narrow view that German legal culture is best – or perhaps fully – understood as a manifestation of the Civil Law tradition. It is absolutely essential that we pay attention to the Civilian facets of German legal culture. But the Civil Law has never been the sole and singular jurisprudential force in the German law-world. Many of this book's remaining chapters will return to the anti-positivist approach to law that has long sought – and after the *Lüth Case*, finally achieved – a measure of relevance in German law. A deeper and richer experience of German legal culture requires that we push past the Civil Law tradition's prioritization of statutes, and its embrace of positivism and formalism, to recognize the role that the Common Law tradition – and other traditions – play in German legal culture.

Further Reading

- Robert Alexy, *Law's Ideal Dimension* (Oxford University Press) (2021)
- *The Cambridge Companion to Legal Positivism* (Patricia Mindus & Torben Spaak eds.) (Cambridge University Press) (2021)
- *Modern German Non-positivism from Radbruch to Alexy* (Martin Borowski ed.) (Mohr Siebeck) (2020)
- *Hans Kelsen and the Natural Law Tradition*, (Ian Bryan *et al.* eds.) (Brill) (2019)
- *Kelsen Revisited – New Essays on the Pure Theory of Law* (Luís Duarte d'Almedia *et al.* eds.) (Bloomsbury) (2014)
- Frank Kantorowicz Carter, "Gustav Radbruch and Hermann Kantorowicz: Two Friends and a Book – Reflections on Gnaeus Flavius' 'Der Kampf um die Rechtswissenschaft' (1906)," 7 *German Law Journal* 657 (2006)
- Hans Kelsen, *Pure Theory of Law* (Max Knight trans.) (The Lawbook Exchange) (2005)
- Vivian Grosswald Curran, "Rethinking Hermann Kantorowicz : Free Law, American Legal Realism, and the Legacy of Anti-Formalism," in *Rethinking the Masters of Comparative Law* 66 (Annelise Riles ed.) (Hart Publishing) (2001)
- *Weimar: A Jurisprudence of Crisis* (Arthur Jacobson & Bernhard Schlink eds.) (Belinda Cooper trans.) (University of California Press) (2000)

NOTES

1 *See* Leslie Green & Thomas Adams, *Legal Positivism*, in The Stanford Encyclopedia of Philosophy (Edward N. Zalta ed., 2019), https://plato.stanford.edu/archives/win2019/entries/legal-positivism/.
2 *See* Richard A. Posner, *Legal Formalism, Legal Realism, and the Interpretation of Statutes and the Constitution*, 37 Case Western L. Rev. 179, 181 (1986).
3 *See* A. G. Chloros, *What Is Natural Law?*, 21 Mod. L. Rev. 609 (1958).
4 Reinhard Zimmermann, *Characteristic Aspects of German Legal Culture*, in Introduction to German Law 1, 9 (Mathias Reimann and Joachim Zekoll eds., 2005).
5 Nigel Foster & Satish Sule, German Legal System and Laws 3 (4th ed. 2010).

6 Howard D. Fisher, The German Legal system and Legal Language xxvii (6th ed. 2015).
7 Ernest Joseph Cohn & W. Zdzieblo, 1 Manual of German Law 3 (2nd ed. 1968).
8 Gerhard Robbers, An Introduction to German Law 15 (7th ed. 2019).
9 John Henry Merryman & Rogelio Pérez-Perdomo, The Civil Law Tradition 2 (4th ed. 2018).
10 Mary Ann Glendon, Michael W. Gordon & Paolo G. Carozza, Comparative Legal Traditions (in a Nutshell) 48 (4th ed. 2014).
11 Gnaeus Flavius, *The Battle for Legal Science (1906)*, 12 Ger. L. J. 2005 (Cory Merrill trans., 2011).
12 *See* American legal Realism (William W. Fisher *et al.* eds., 1993).
13 *Free Law Movement*, in The Philosophy of Law – An Encyclopedia (2013), www.bookrags.com/tandf/free-law-movement-tf/.
14 Frank Kantorowicz Carter, *Gustav Radbruch and Hermann Kantorowicz: Two Friends and a Book – Reflections on Gnaeus Flavius' Der Kampf um dir Rechtswissenschaft (1906)*, 7 Ger. L. J. 657, 658 (2006).
15 *Id*. at 687.
16 *Id*. at 689.
17 *See, e.g.*, Derrick A. Bell, *Who's Afraid of Critical Race Theory*, 1995(4) Univ. Ill. L. Rev. 893 (1995); Kimberle Williams Crenshaw, *Twenty Years of Critical Race Theory: Looking Back to Move Forward*, 43 Conn. L. Rev. 117 (2011); Anneke Dunbar-Gronke, *The Mandate for Critical Race Theory in This Time*, 69 UCLA L. Rev. Discourse 4 (2022).
18 *See* Frederick Charles Von Savigny, The Vocation of Our Age for Legislation and Jurisprudence (Abraham Hayward trans., 1831). *See also* Frederick C. Beiser, The German Historicist Tradition (2011).
19 James E. Herget & Stephen Wallace, *The German Free Law Movement as the Source of American Legal Realism*, 73 Va. L. Rev. 399 (1987).
20 Joseph M. Pellicciotti, *American Legal Realism*, 12 J. Legal Stud. Educ. 335, 336–338 (1994).
21 *Id.*
22 Hermann Kantorowicz, *Some Rationalism about Realism*, 43 Yale L. J. 1240 (1934).
23 *Id*. at 1242.
24 Neil Duxbury, Patterns of American Jurisprudence 158–159 (1995).
25 Pierre Legrand, *Negative Comparative Law*, 10 J. Compar. L. 405 (2015).
26 Frank Haldemann, *Gustav Radbruch vs. Hans Kelsen: A Debate on Nazi Law*, 18 Ratio Juris 162, 164 (2005) (*quoting* Gustav Radbruch, *Legal Philosophy*, in 4 The Legal Philosophy of Lask, Radbruch, and Dabin 43–244 (Kurt Wilk trans. & ed., 1950)).
27 *See* Stanley L. Paulson, *Statutory Positivism*, 1 Legisprudence 1 (2007).
28 Richard Lawrence Miller, Nazi Justice 2 (1995).
29 Stanley L. Paulson, *On the Background and Significance of Gustav Radbruch's Post-War Papers*, 26 Oxford J. Legal Stud. 17, 33–34 (2006) (*quoting* Ingo Müller, Hitler's Justice 221 (Deborah Lucas Schneider trans., 1991)).

30 Peter E. Quint, *The Border Guard Trials and the East German Past-Seven Arguments*, 48 AM. J. COMPAR. L. 54, 543 (2000).
31 ROBBERS, *supra* note 8, at 15.
32 *See, e.g.,* THE LAW IN NAZI GERMANY: IDEOLOGY, OPPORTUNISM, AND THE PERVERSION OF JUSTICE (Alan E. Steinweis & Robert D. Rachlin eds., 2013); MICHAEL STOLLEIS, THE LAW UNDER THE SWASTIKA (Thomas Dunlap trans., 1998); RICHARD LAWRENCE MILLER, NAZI JUSTICE (1995); INGO MÜLLER, HITLER'S JUSTICE (Deborah Lucas Schneider trans., 1991).
33 ROBBERS, *supra* note 8, at 16.
34 *Id.*
35 *Id.*
36 Bürgerliches Gesetzbuch [BGB] [Civil Code], § 826, translation at www.gesetze-im-internet.de/englisch_bgb/index.html ("Whoever causes damage to another person intentionally and in a manner offensive to good morals is obligated to compensate the other person for the damage.").
37 There are a number of excellent commentaries on the *Lüth Case* in German. *See* GERHARD CASPER, REDEFREIHEIT UND EHRENSCHUTZ 30 (1971); Günter Dürig, *Zum "Lüth Urteil" des Bundesverfassungsgerichts vom 15.1.1958* DIE ÖFFENTLICHE VERWALTUNG 184 (1958); Peter Lerche, *Zur verfassungsgerichtlichen Deutung der Meinungsfreiheit*, in FESTSCHRIFT FÜR GEBHARD MÜLLER 197 (1970). There is excellent critical analysis of *Lüth* in English. *See* Peter Quint, *Free Speech and Private Law in German Constitutional Theory*, 48 MD. L. REV. 252–265 (1989).

4

Foundations I
Legal History

Key Concepts

- **Germanic Customary Law**: The law of the various Germanic peoples from the time of their initial contact with the Romans until the change from tribal to national territorial law. This change occurred at different times for different parts of the Germanic world.[1]
- **Blood Feud** or **Vendetta**: A right acquired in customary law by injured parties that permitted them to avail themselves of violent self-help in revenging or remedying their harms. This often involved extreme violence. The blood feud has been portrayed as a distinctively Germanic custom. That claim seeks to affirm and perpetuate stereotypes about the uniquely violent nature of the German character and Germanic societies.
- **Roman Law**: The body of law developed by the ancient Romans, codified by Emperor Justinian around 530 CE in the *Corpus Juris Civilis*, which forms the basis of many modern codes in the Civil Law systems.[2]
- **Canon Law**: A body of laws made within certain Christian churches (Roman Catholic, Eastern Orthodox, independent churches of Eastern Christianity, and the Anglican Communion) by lawful ecclesiastical authority for the government both of the whole church as well as the behavior and actions of individual Christians.[3]
- **Codification**: The process of reducing and reframing law (primarily private law) to a comprehensive and systematically arranged framework of positive, statutory law. Many view the codifications of private law in France (1804) and Germany (1900) as the two "great codifications." A code should be differentiated from more discrete or narrowly focused legislation, on the one hand, and a collection or compendium of laws or legal practices, on the other hand.
- **Constitutionalization**: The process of reducing and reframing law (primarily public law) to a written, static, and superior regime. This process will encompass structural concerns, such as the foundation of the state, and the establishment and regulation of the institutions of government. It can also involve the articulation of enforceable rights.

Study Tips

Professor Marco Staake at the University of Wuppertal posted an excellent lecture on YouTube in which he introduces the German legal system. The first seven minutes of the lecture cover German legal history (www.youtube.com/watch?v=vVpy0ewz0RE)

Before we begin to consider some of the prominent areas of law in the German legal system – always with an eye towards the various legal traditions at play in German legal culture – I want to acknowledge that many of you will know little about the basic features of the German political and legal systems. For that matter, you may be only vaguely familiar with German history generally, let alone the specifics of German legal history. If that is the case, then you are bound to face some difficulty in pursuing this book's introduction to German law and legal culture. After all, "legal rules and decisions must be understood in context […] law is not autonomous, standing outside of the social world, but is deeply embedded within society."[4] Much of what we will discuss across the rest of this book necessarily refers to, reacts to, and confirms features of German history, politics, economics, society, and culture.

I cannot provide anything like a comprehensive survey of those varied and deeply interesting subjects – at least not if we hope to get on with our more focused encounter with the German legal system. Fortunately, there are many excellent English-language resources offering a broad and general overview of Germany.[5] In the next three chapters, however, I hope to familiarize you with some of the basics:

- Chapter 4 provides a survey of German legal history ("old" and "new").
- Chapter 5 provides a survey of German political and legal institutions (federalism, law-making institutions, executive authority, and judicial institutions).
- Chapter 6 provides a survey of the essentials of German legal practice (legal education, legal method, and legal actors).

It is an incomplete tour of these rich and fascinating topics. Still, I hope it will give you sound footing for the journey ahead.

Let's start this tour of the foundations of German legal culture with some history.

4.1 Old German Legal History

Where else, except at the "beginning," should you start your exposure to the foundations of German law? The following excerpt from Felix Schorling's essay provides a mad-dash through a millennium and a half of ancient and medieval German legal history. Naturally, these few pages provide only a partial picture of remote times and distant legal developments. Yet, exposure to a "Deeper History of German Law" is important because it touches upon vital features of German legal culture, many of which still resonate in contemporary German law.

Felix Schorling
A Deeper History of German Law
SSRN (July 5, 2022)
https://ssrn.com/abstract=4154541[*]

* * *

This essay aims to achieve the impossible: to give a brief overview of two millennia of German legal history, even considering the law of the Germanic peoples before there was a Germany. In pursuing that grand, sweeping assignment, the essay will give special attention to law in the Medieval age (roughly from the fall of the Western Roman Empire to the fall of the Byzantine Empire).

Where does the history of German law start? The Germanic tribes, the first known inhabitants of the region in central Europe north of the Alps and east of the Rhine River, did not leave us with anything in writing. We have only their burial grounds and the goods placed with them in their graves. That record gives us very little that is definitive, except that we know that they esteemed their warriors.

[...] [It] is assumed that some of [the Roman historian Tacitus'] claims have a basis in the reality of the life and culture of the Germanic tribes the Romans encountered. For example, Tacitus likely provided some credible insight with his description of the Germanic tradition of the "feud" or vendetta. This institution permitted the victim to demand compensation, either by revenge or payment in livestock, when he or his family was harmed. [...]

One major column of German legal history starts in the Sixth Century in the flourishing city called Constantinople, known today as Istanbul. The Byzantine Emperor Justinian wanted to collect and structure the law of the Roman Empire and ordered his *quaestor sacri palatii* Tribonian to do exactly that. You might think of Tribonian as something like a Minister of Justice. Compilers working under his supervision went through the texts of jurists and collected them, adapted them, and added new rules. They gathered these texts into a volume known as the *Digest*. It was expanded to include a collection of imperial edicts (*Codex/Novellae*) and a textbook (*Institutiones*). Much later the resulting book came to be called the *Corpus Iuris Civilis*. It was used as applicable law in the remnants of the Roman Empire. But, as the Byzantian Empire's influence on the Italian peninsula declined, Roman Law was nearly forgotten in Central Europe, which was ruled by the tribes.

The only legal texts we have from the time of the tribes are referred to as the *Leges Barbarorum* [laws of the barbarians], written in Latin. [...] Latin was not the language of the tribes, which explains the Germanic terms sprinkled throughout the *Leges*, terms such as *Malbergo*, which referred to the hill where the *Thing* – a court-like institution – took place. We know that the *Leges* were the tribes' customs codified in writing. What we don't know is whether these laws were applied in practice, or if they were only used by the clan chiefs to legitimize their rule [...]. Although the *Leges* were written as a compilation, they lacked what you would expect in a modern codification, such as systematization, structure, and certainty. One of the most prominent of the *Leges* was the *Lex Salica*. This law was promulgated around the Fifth Century. The *Lex Salica* contained a compilation of customary rules that still reflected a pagan world view, for example referring to the *Strigae*, a demon like creature. The substantive rules largely reflected the customary norms of the tribes, including the practice of the "feud" or vendetta to which Tacitus referred: If you committed a crime, such as killing a person, the family of the victim had

---

[*] Excerpt reprinted with permission of the author.

the right of revenge or the right of compensation (*Wehrgeld*). And the ruler also was entitled to a payment. The Church tried to increase the role of compensation in the law by providing loans for those who needed money to pay compensation. The *Lex Salica's* roots in tribal custom remind us that customary rules have played a significant role in German legal history, with echoes even up to the present day.

[...] Pope Leo III made Charlemagne the "Roman Emperor" in 800 AD.

Charlemagne passed the imperial title to his son, Ludwig the Pious. After Ludwig's death the empire was divided. The part consisting of the Germanic lands ruled by the heirs of Charlemagne came to be called the Holy Roman Empire. The emperor gave territories to his bannermen as fiefdoms, which fell back to the emperor after their death. If nothing lasts forever, then it is no surprise that the powerful rule of the Carolingian emperors weakened over time, especially because the heirs of the bannermen resented having to surrender their lands with the passing of each generation. Eventually, the fiefdoms transformed into hereditary principalities. The relationship between these princes and their vassals was determined by Feudal Law. [...]

At times the empire consisted of more than one thousand principalities. The power of the princes grew and they tried to diminish the role of the Germanic "feud" or vendetta – still functioning as a legal institution – with the so called *Kompositionensystem* (a monetary system for atoning for a crime). This legal system, exemplified by the *Lex Salica*, listed what the defendant should pay as compensation for every crime. The princes started to enforce this system instead of allowing private revenge. This process of transforming the "feud" into an enforced *Kompositionensystem* continued over time. The prince served as a mediator and guarantor to ensure that the payment would be delivered and that there would be no resort to the tradition of the Germanic "feud." The compensation system survived in some rural areas of Germany until the penal code of 1871 was implemented.

The law of the medieval Holy Roman Empire was fractured. There was quite a lot of variation in the law from one principality to the other. There also was: feudal law, guild law, merchant law, and many other legal traditions. In this jurisdictional mix two legal systems were predominant: The Roman Law and the Canon Law.

Some of the *Leges Barbarorum* exhibited the influence of the Roman legal tradition. But in the main, Roman Law had been forgotten until the Eleventh Century when it was rediscovered and revived by scholars. The chances for a new era of Roman Law were good. Medieval scholars viewed the *Digest* as a major achievement. The study of the *Digest* even led to the establishment of the first university in Bologna. But several provisions in the *Digest* were contradictory and the jurists needed to deal with this problem. The so-called Legists, scholars of Roman Law, and the Canonists, scholars of Canon Law (the Law of the Catholic Church), developed a scholastic method on the basis of theological study. This is why the jurists are also called Scholastics. It dealt with conflicts by comparing documents, relying on authority, and inferring principles from the texts. The jurists of this epoch are called "glossators" in the sense that, through their method, they were "putting a gloss" on the legal materials. A glossator carefully studied texts and tried to harmonize the contradictions in a dialectical process. The glossators' work, a so-called *glossa*, was written by adding commentary and explanations beside or between the lines of the *Digest*. [...]

The glossators thought the newly rediscovered and revamped Roman Law was generally admissible and binding. But they were stuck in their academic ivory towers. In reality, Roman Law wasn't observed in the daily life of medieval society. [...]

[...] [Another] legal tradition [...] enjoyed priority in this era because it was seen as modern in comparison to Roman Law. This tradition is called Canon Law. Canon Law gained favor because the secular jurisdiction was seen as merely customary. This regime, observed and enforced by the local nobility, came to be seen as arbitrary and self-interested. The Church courts looked better by comparison because they were staffed by educated professionals working within institutions that were seen as fair and rational. Most importantly, Canon Law judgements were enforceable throughout the empire. The Canonical process, also known as the inquisitorial process, had a number of merits. It was codified in the Canon Law and thoroughly recorded, it relied on the public prosecution of crimes as opposed to private prosecution in the Germanic tradition. And it was more rational than the old process. This Canon Law process was influenced by Roman Law and it evolved into the Roman-Canon process. The main aim of this inquisitorial system was the discovery of the truth. This led to the abandonment of oath-taking and trial by combat as an assurance of truthfulness. The confession emerged in their place. But how to get the reluctant and recalcitrant to admit their guilt? Judicial torture, which has given the infamous Inquisitor his bad reputation, was seen as a reasonable – and necessary means to a greater good. The implementation of this process helped to distinguish between private law and criminal law, a classification that still has meaning in law today.

The second part of Roman-Canon law, as the name suggests, was the Canon Law. It was – and still is – the law for administering and governing the Catholic Church and the lives of its adherents. [...] Besides the holy scripture, Canon Law also drew from the rulings of the early Church councils and from the teachings of the Church fathers (such as Augustine of Hippo or Ambrose of Milan). A final source for Canon Law were the decrees of the Bishop of Rome (also known as the pope) whose authority derived from his status as the successor of Saint Peter. Canon Law aimed to provide a legal framework for dealing with all problems and situations that could arise in a Christian life. [...]

The influence of papal jurisprudence grew. This prompted the popes to issue more decrees. That, in turn, led to the creation of more compilations of Canon Law. [...] The scope of Canon Law was expansive, dealing, for example, with ecclesiastical offices, procedure in contentious litigation, property issues, marriage, inheritance, and criminal law. In 1220 the *Confoederatio cum principibus ecclesiastics* recognized the judgements of Church courts as enforceable and that excommunication would automatically result in a declaration of outlawry issued by the emperor as the secular authority. The Canonists made many major contributions to German law and legal procedure. For example, the Canon Law system developed the modern *ne bis in idem* principle, which prohibits a second prosecution based on a single set of facts. And the Canonists theorized the difference between negligence and intent.

* * *

Charlemagne's empire was based on custom. Nevertheless, both Roman Law and Canon Law saw their influence increase. The *glossa ordinaria* of Accursius was given the force of law in some jurisdictions and Roman Law was assessed through his *glossa*. Roman Law's application faced some difficulties. As expressed in the Digest, Roman Law is formulated as answers to specific cases. And even if they were resolved by making use of underlying principles, its case-specific character made Roman Law less practical. The next school of jurists, known as the Commentators, tried to solve this problem. They combined the legal insights of the *glossa ordinaria* with the more contemporaneous Canon Law. With this mix, the Commentators tried to create a practice-oriented legal regime that accounted for the problems of the present-day. They succeeded in extracting abstract rules from these sources and that, beside the use of Roman-Canon Law in the ecclesiastical courts, fostered the relevance and eventual reception of Roman-Canon Law throughout Europe. This hybrid system of Roman-Canon law, benefiting from Canon Law being universal in nature, came to be known as the *ius commune*. This led to the "scientization" of jurists because work with the system required highly specialized training. The fact that Canon Law already was universal in nature facilitated the wide-ranging adoption of the *ius commune*.

In 1220–1235 the *Sachsenspiegel* was published. In German the word "*Spiegel*" means "mirror" and the *Sachsenspiegel* was meant to be just a mirror (collection) of the customary norms of the Saxons. The Saxons were a Germanic ethnic group that dominated northern and eastern Germany. Their *Sachsenspiegel* incorporated many of the old Germanic customs, such as trial by combat. These Germanic customary rules, preserved and perpetuated in other codes, were formalistic and austere. The system worked largely on the basis of confirming the fulfillment of formal criteria, such as the correct words of an oath before God. This meant that an oath was regarded as effective only if it was ritualistically recited every time in the same exact way. Even a minor misspelling or mispronunciation was seen as a sign from God of a person's guilt. The Church, through its Canon Law, antagonized the oaths and trial by combat and sought to supplant these old ways.

It is amazing to think of it, but the *Sachsenspiegel* was in effect in some German jurisdictions until 1900. In some instances, contemporary German courts still refer to it. Parts of present-day German procedural law and inheritance law have their origins in the *Sachsenspiegel*. But in its day, the *Sachsenspiegel* could have an effect beside the Roman-Canon law because the emperor granted its princes evocation privileges, which they could use, *inter alia*, to preclude appeals from their courts to the imperial tribunals. This insulated local law from the harmonizing and cosmopolitan forces of the empire. [...]

Still, the empire managed to implement some norms across the realm. There were the organizational (proto-constitutional) *Reichsgrundgesetze*, which included the Golden Bull (1356) and the Concordat of Worms (1122). The empire also promulgated a common criminal law, the *Constitutio Criminalis Carolina* of 1532. This law established general rules for criminal procedure that ultimately facilitated a transition to the rules of the Roman-Canon Law. The empire's princes could substitute this system with their own, but few did so. With its Canon Law DNA, the *Constitutio Criminalis Carolina* furthered the shift to inquisitorial procedure. But the *Carolina* allowed departures from the provisions of Canon Law in the case of *crimen exceptum* (abominable crime). The loophole was used to permit torture and murder in the Sixteenth and Seventeenth Centuries. It was the basis for arbitrary and grotesque "witch" trials involving more than 100,000 people, most of whom were women. These trials were conducted in the secular and not in the Church courts.

A central project of the Church was to oppose and replace irrational customary law, which drew its authority from history and habit, not the scripture. [...]

The Church had a dominant position in the empire. [...] [The] most important influence of the Church was the legal institution known as the *forum internum* – the sacrament of confession, and the threat of excommunication. The latter stripped individuals of the right to enforce contracts. Almost everyone regularly confessed their sins. Priests then instructed the faithful to redeem themselves, oftentimes by obliging them to pay their debts or honor their contracts. This semi-formal but very effective regime for the interpretation and enforcement of the law drew on Catholic natural law, which held that a good Christian would keep his or her word. The practice of confession acquired this "juridical nature," with accompanying books of redemption (*libri poenetentiales*). All of this may sound unremarkable but it was a major development. Roman Law provided for *pacta*, certain contracts that were not binding on their own. The Church corrected this arrangement with the principle *pacta sunt servanda* (contracts are inherently binding). This principle underpins the idea of contract law in the Western world and it is one of the foundational pillars of International Law.

The year of 1495 can be seen as a turning point in the legal history of the German lands. First, that was the year of the *Ewiger Landfriede* (Perpetual Public Peace) issued by the

Emperor Maximillian I. This *Landfriede* brought an end to the two-century long development of temporary and limited *Landfrieden*. The *Ewiger Landfriede* prohibited every "feud" and the use of violence for every private person. The state acquired a monopoly on the use of force. This notion is often associated with the birth of the modern state. Second, the *Reichskammergericht* (Imperial Chamber Court) was established as a court for all of the Holy Roman Empire. The Court changed the application of Roman-Canon Law dramatically, especially since it had been staffed with legal scholars. [...] The Roman-Canon Law was not the official law of the realm. But the Court recognized it as the *ius commune*. The regime was applied by the Court and, subsequently, by more and more institutions.

* * *

The Sixteenth Century was dominated by the tectonic shift known as the Reformation. Martin Luther changed the religious landscape of Europe when he posted his Ninety-Five Theses on the door of the Wittenberg Castle Church. But considering the close entwinement of the Church and the law, his demands for reform also prompted new legal approaches. Even before Luther's movement the authority of papal decrees and Church teachings was contested to some degree. Still, they were found to be universally binding. But once the Catholic Church's monolithic status and power was cast in doubt by the emergence of the Protestant confessions, the very idea of a united European system influenced and backed by the Catholic Church, began to decay. That process was accelerated by the challenges posed by the era of European exploration and settlement in the "new world."

Now several different traditions existed and they began to overlap.

One tradition can be characterized as "juristic humanism." It should be clear that this humanism was rooted in Christian thought. But as a legal system it operated on the basis of reason that was formally independent of Christian theology. This school criticized the Scholastics for not paying enough attention to the historical dimension of the text, and for neglecting the Greek authors. They also complained that academic jurists relied too formalistically on scholarly authorities. The humanists took a legal text as it was, accepting it as an historical document and not as divinely authoritative. Despite the doubts sown by the humanists, some elements of the *ius commune*, such as its procedural provisions, went unchallenged, even in Protestant jurisdictions.

* * *

The most significant legal development of this era might have been the "subjective turn" in criminal law, which is concerned with the personal guilt of the accused rather than being preoccupied with an assessment of whether the formal, objective elements of a crime had been met. Another impactful contribution was the notion that a contract could be rescinded rather than being automatically nullified. The Roman Law and the *ius commune* had imagined only the nullification of a contract. Finally, the era saw a modest but important strengthening of the status of women in the law.

The idea that natural law was universal, and not just European or Christian, was the achievement of the next influential legal movement. It was advanced by scholars such as Grotius and Pufendorf. For centuries Catholics could rely on the universal authority of the pope to support their legal frameworks. Unable to continue in that mode as a basis for the general principles of law, jurists tried to reason from things like tradition, the experiences made during the devastating Thirty Years War, or a perceived "consensus of the nations." This was a secular turn in the understanding of law, a development that sought to move beyond the major role attributed to religion in jurisprudence and legal theory. This impulse was dogged by the entrenched understanding that legal traditions were thought to be supported by "God's revelation." Some of Grotius' ideas are reflected in the modern law of error.

4.1 Old German Legal History

The humanists changed the way of thinking about the law. But their ideas had little influence amongst the Germans who rejected their critique. Instead, the *glossa* and the *ius commune* were used and implemented in the *usus modernus pandectarum*, which was named after the work of the German scholar Samuel Stryk. This visionary school sought to account for and connect all the threads of law: Roman-Canon Law, natural law theories, humanism, the insights of the School of Salamanca, local customary norms, and national laws. The traditional legitimation of Roman-Canon Law through *translatio imperii* and the universality of the Catholic Church was no longer in effect. New grounds for law's legitimacy had to be found. Hermann Conring, for example, argued that Roman-Canon Law had achieved customary law status through its reception in the law faculties. This led to the suggestion that the *Reichskammergericht* should rely on the common law. Yet, the *usus modernus* differentiated between received rules and rules that had not been received. Rules that were used by academics and courts as part of the *ius commune* were legitimate. But rules not included in that reception were not accepted as applicable law. The *usus modernus* served as the basis for a number of specific rules of law. The method of law in this time period laid the foundations for the legal principles expressed in the General Part of Germany's present-day Criminal Code.

The French Revolution of 1789 altered the power monopoly of the monarchs. It also dramatically changed Europe's legal landscape. Prussia had already legislated with its 1794 codification known as the *Allgemeines Landrecht für die Preußischen Staaten*. But Napoleon's *cinq codes* (Civil Code [1804], Code of Civil Procedure [1806]; Commercial Code [1807]; Code of Criminal Procedure [1808]; and Criminal Code [1810]) are regarded as the first major codifications of the Roman-Canon law and customary law. They started the era of enlightenment and codification and modernized the Roman-Canon law procedure with the principles of public access and orality. These developments made the work of lawyers more important and attractive. They also led to the creation of the prosecutor as an institution separate from the judge. The *Policeyordnungen* (mixing administrative, police, private and criminal law concerns) regulated almost all spheres of life in the Nineteenth Century, at least until a Prussian court changed the role of the police. Then the revolutions of 1848/49 led to reforms of the absolutist monarchies that inched towards constitutionalism (and especially the separation of powers) in German law. The *Reichsjustizgesetze* (Imperial Courts Acts) of 1877/79 deepened the principle of orality and changed the jury system that had functioned in Germany for centuries. Juries would now be allowed only in certain procedures while *Schöffengerichte*, consisting of lay-judges and professional-judges, were implemented in first instance proceedings.

Napoleon brought the one-thousand-year-old Holy Roman Empire to a close, even if its last decades had been more shambling and habitual than deliberate. With this came the end of the reign of the bishopric, and the termination of the special privileges of the so-called "free cities," the knights, and the guilds. But these were all the old imperial institutions through which the *ius commune* was passed from one generation to the next. Bonaparte conquered some portions of modern Germany and French law was in effect in those regions as the Rhine Law even after Napoleon lost the territories. In fact, they used French law until the unification of the German state under Prussia and the promulgation of the German Civil Code and Imperial Courts Acts. After the fall of the French Empire, the German Confederation was created by the Congress of Vienna. The Confederation's chief legal concern was trade law. There was room for innovation and unification here because the Canon Law had always permitted freedom of form in the matters of trade and commercial affairs. The Confederation's Commercial Law Code of 1861 preceded Germany's criminal and civil codes.

Across all of the years of the Nineteenth Century, Germans were debating the need for and the possibility of their own codifications. […]

As things go, the Nineteenth Century gave way to Germany's tumultuous Twentieth Century, with all its hope and chaos, terror and division, and reunification and renewal. The law accompanied these events – sometimes prompting them and other times reacting to them. But that's the more familiar history of the failed Weimar Constitution with its "emergency measures" provision (Article 48); Hitler's *Reichstag* Emergency Decree and the Nuremberg Race Laws; West Germany's post-war *Grundgesetz*, and the Two-Plus-Four Unification Treaty. This survey only hints at a deeper and older history of German law, a history that stretches back before the time of Charlemagne's empire into the mists of central Europe's tribal peoples. All of that law is part of German law today. The echoes may be faint. But they are there to be heard if one knows what to listen for.

* * *

Questions/Comments

- A major theme in Schorling's "deep" history of German law is the struggle to move past Germanic customary norms towards a more rational system of law and justice. Exemplary of the old way of doing law is the tribal tradition of the "feud." As Schorling explains, this custom entitled those who felt themselves to have been treated unfairly to exact justice through violent vengeance. The prevalence of these vendettas in the medieval Germanic realms can't be overstated. One scholar explained: "One of the striking features of late medieval and early modern Germany was the pervasiveness of feuds by noblemen. Foreign observers found it difficult to explain. A Roman cardinal, overcome with indignation, exclaimed 'all Germany is a gang of bandits and, among the nobles, the more grasping the more glorious.'"[6] As long as the customary "feud" provided the nobility with a ready and legitimate resort to violence rooted in tribal and clan traditions, it would be hard to establish the more reliable public order that was needed to develop infrastructure or foster trade. This means that the modernization of German law involved two processes. On one hand, rational law and procedure supplanted traditional customary norms, as with the *Sachsenspiegel* described by Schorling and depicted in Figure 4.1. On the other hand, authority – especially the monopoly on violence – had to be centralized in a way that disadvantaged the German feudal princes. A series of successive movements and developments was needed to make these transitions: the revival of Roman Law; the ascension of Canon (Church) Law; Napoleon's destruction of the *Ancien Régime*; the liberal revolution of 1848–1849; and ultimately the process of codification. The consequence of these rationalizing and centripetal developments was the emergence of what Germans refer to as the *Rechtsstaat* (a state governed by law) and a definitive turning away from the customary "feud." As you work through the remaining chapters of this book you might ask yourself: Was codification of the private law the final triumph of the *Rechtsstaat*? Is there something of the customary way of doing law (diffuse, arbitrary, and vengeful) still percolating in contemporary German law and legal culture?

4.1 Old German Legal History

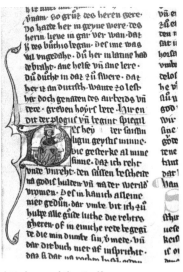

(a) Prologue of the *Harffer Sachsenspiegel* 1295 CE

(b) *Sachsenspiegel* manuscript from 1385 CE

Figure 4.1 Old German Law – The *Sachsenspiegel*

- Schorling highlights the fractured and mixed nature of law in the Germanic world. Scores of principalities constituted numerous territorial jurisdictions, often still embracing customary law. In the next chapter you will learn about the modern federalist manifestation of this old pluralistic tradition in Germany. But, alongside these territorial divisions, there also were cross-cutting jurisdictions based on confession, trading rights, feudal status, and vocational "guild" privileges. Meanwhile, influential legal scholars were promoting the revived Roman Law from their ivory towers. What a confounding cacophony of laws! Overcoming that muddle with a coherent, unified legal system is another of the major themes in German legal history. Are codification and the objective, scientific character of the Civil Law tradition particularly well-suited to that ambition?
- One of the enduring legacies of the Canon Law as described by Schorling is the tradition of inquisitorial procedure. As you will learn in Chapter 11, comparative law scholars today still describe German procedural law as "inquisitorial." Other legal systems have what is referred to as an "adversarial" procedural tradition. Based on your brief encounter with the inquisitorial tradition in Schorling's essay, can you say what the basic features of "inquisitorial" justice are?
- A key lesson from Schorling's essay is that the Roman Law casts a long shadow over German law. There was evidence of this in Chapter 2, which confirmed Roman Law's essential contribution to the Civil Law tradition generally. The significance of this heritage should come into clearer focus with this book's introduction to the German Civil Code in Chapter 7. But

independent of that seemingly direct link to the Roman past, Germans hold the general impression that their law and legal culture are expressions of the ancient but noble Roman Law. German law schools offer courses on Roman Law.[7] Among the respected academic institutes and centers focusing on legal history in Germany, many are involved in researching Roman Law.[8] After reading the excerpt of Schorling's essay, do you think the German preoccupation with Roman Law is justified? What other deep historical legal frameworks and systems played a role in shaping German law? Can you define and distinguish these various historical legal frameworks and systems?

- How does Schorling's presentation of "deeper" German legal history differ from the way you would tell that story for your primary or "national" legal system?

I excluded from this excerpt Schorling's reference to the German *Kodifikationsstreit* (codification dispute), which took place in the nineteenth century. The lead protagonists in that academic dispute, which concerned the need for a civil code in Germany, were the scholars Friedrich Carl von Savigny and Anton Thibaut.[9] The *Kodifikationsstreit* will be discussed briefly in the following section of this chapter, and again in Chapter 7 as part of the introduction to Germany's beloved Civil Code. The main dividing line in the dispute was whether a German civil code could be imposed, primarily by relying on Roman Law principles, or whether a civil code must emerge from the German people as a systematized compilation of their customary norms and practices (which themselves had been influenced by Roman Law). In some ways, it was a dispute between theoretical and applied approaches to the law.

As with any effort to frame epochs or periods in history, it is somewhat arbitrary for me to suggest that the long-running *Kodifikationsstreit* in the nineteenth century marks the beginning of a "new" era in German legal history. Impulses and movements from a previous era continue to unfurl or only gradually wind down. At the same time, there might be only faint evidence in the nineteenth century of some of the important developments of "modern" German law. Yet, as it turns out, the nineteenth century was pivotal for both German private law and constitutional law. That justifies treating that era as a functional point of demarcation as we turn to a consideration of "new" German legal history.

4.2 New German Legal History

The march of modern German legal history was strikingly different in the fields of private law and constitutional law. On the one hand, German private law's path seems steady and ordained for progress. That process culminated in the Civil Code's entry into force on January 1, 1900. On the other hand, the path of German constitutional law in the modern era was stumbling and vexed. In this section, I present these different trajectories, both of which emanate from developments that took place in the nineteenth century. I begin with the history of modern private law (with an excerpt from David Gerber), followed by the history of modern constitutional law (relying on an excerpt from Werner Heun).

David J. Gerber
Review Essay – Idea-Systems in Law: Images of Nineteenth Century Germany
10 LAW AND HISTORY REVIEW 153, 154–157, 159–163 (1992)*

* * *

- James Q. Whitman, *The Legacy of Roman Law in the German Romantic Era: Historical Vision and Legal Change*, Princeton University Press, 1990. Pp. xi, 281 $39.50 (ISBN: 0-691-05560-2).
- Michael John, *Politics and the Law in Late Nineteenth-Century Germany: The Origin of the Civil Code*, Oxford: Clarendon Press, 1989. Pp. 227 $64.00 (ISBN: 0-19-822748-5).

* * *

In nineteenth-century Germany, legal idea-systems achieved an importance perhaps unparalleled in modern legal history, and thus this period affords particularly valuable insights into the roles of idea-systems in law. During the first part of the century the idea-system of Roman law dominated German legal culture, providing much of its vocabulary as well as many of its central values and defining the roles of important institutions. During the last quarter of the century, a new civil code was created that was to provide much of the language of law until the present day. To understand these two idea-systems is to understand much about the development of law in modern Germany.

James Whitman and the Roman Law Tradition in Post-Reformation Germany

James Whitman's book is far broader in scope than the title suggests. It focuses on Roman law not primarily as a "legacy" of the past, but as an active agent in German legal, intellectual, and political life. Moreover, the book's temporal scope is not limited to the German Romantic period. It portrays the evolution of an intellectual-institutional tradition from the Protestant Reformation through the 1860s. [...]

Professor Whitman tells the story of how Roman law influenced legal and political developments for more than three centuries. During this period Roman law was a source of authority, an interpretive construct, and a lever of power. It structured thought, guided the interpretation of events, generated and supported powerful institutions, and mediated the relationship between political power and legal culture.

Whitman traces the beginnings of this tradition to Philip Melanchthon, the Reformation leader who began using Roman law as a tool for resolving conflicts in the strife-ridden German territories of the sixteenth century. Roman law had, of course, played important roles in medieval Europe, but in the German Protestant context its political uses changed. Roman law's influence continued to be anchored in the glory of the "cultural idea of Rome" and in the traditions of medieval Roman law scholarship. In the new context, however, its political success derived from its practical value as a source of neutral and, it was thought, objectively ascertainable solutions to social conflicts, and from its capacity to legitimate institutions competing for power in a newly fragmented political world.

* * *

The pressures of Enlightenment thought and absolutist institutions almost crushed Roman law during the eighteenth century. The rationalism of the Enlightenment focused on the creation of law through Reason, leaving little room for Roman law and its weighty centuries of scholarly accretions. The belief that Reason was the only proper basis of

---

* Excerpt reprinted with permission of the author.

law undercut the claims that Roman law was authoritative because it represented time-sanctioned principles of conduct.

* * *

During the German Romantic period (roughly the first half of the nineteenth century), Roman law and its associated institutions managed to recover from these setbacks and to reemerge at the center of the legal world. As the Napoleonic wars were eroding confidence in princely absolutism, the new forces of liberalism were challenging the moral and intellectual foundations of the eighteenth-century state, and Roman law provided support for those efforts.

German reformers were attempting to develop a law-based state (*Rechtstaat*) in which even the supreme power of princes would be constrained by law. This goal required a neutral set of substantive principles and reasonably objective and independent institutions to apply them. The Roman law tradition promised both. It represented a time-honored and well-developed idea-system known for the balance of its conceptual scheme. Moreover, its institutional base was in the universities, which were among the few institutions in post-Napoleonic Germany that could serve as reasonably autonomous power bases.

Roman law thus returned to its central position within German legal culture. Roman law's emphasis on private property rights and contractual autonomy fit well with liberalism's economic and political doctrines without unduly threatening the existing political system. […]

* * *

But the revival was only temporary. A reputation for objectivity was increasingly difficult to maintain amid the growing social and political unrest of the years before the 1848 revolutions. Law professors were induced to take sides, and as they did, they lost their claim to confidence as neutral arbiters of legal disputes. […]

Although the relatively tranquil years that followed the 1848 revolutions witnessed a brief resurgence of Roman law and its institutions, the movement toward national unification, which became increasingly powerful during the 1860s and culminated in the founding of the German Reich in 1871, changed the political context of Roman law. A unified German state operating in an atmosphere of legal positivism did not need Roman law; it would, and did, create its own laws and legal institutions.

Yet Roman law remained an important intellectual force, and it is in this narrower context that one might more appropriately speak of the "legacy" of Roman law. Indeed, the conceptual foundations of the new German Civil Code derived from Roman law scholarship. The vocabulary as well as the structure of the code were based on Roman law.

* * *

Michael John and the Creation of the Civil Code

Michael John's story is the creation of the German Civil Code (*Bürgerliches Gesetzbuch*) – the idea-system that replaced Roman law at the center of German legal culture and has remained in that position. John picks up, therefore, roughly where Whitman leaves off. While Whitman analyzes the roles of an existing idea-system, John's objective is to elucidate the creation of such a system.

* * *

In contrast to James Whitman's situation, Michael John's basic storyline is well known. The creation of the German Empire in 1871 produced powerful political and economic incentives to draft a civil code that would apply throughout Germany. The process of codification was thus begun in 1874, and in 1888 an initial draft was completed. This draft was widely criticized, but it was approved in 1896 with comparatively few modifications and entered into force on January 1, 1900.

John's book does not, therefore, reconstruct an unknown or little-understood story. It is valuable because it provides a comprehensive and integrated account of a process that is immensely significant for understanding not only German law and German history, but also the development of modern Western legal systems. In addition, it generates many new insights into the political aspects of that process.

* * *

The creation of the German Civil Code was part of the process of national unification, and John effectively portrays the constellation of political forces that led to demands for national unity. The author may understate the role of liberalism as a political force during the early nineteenth century, but the damage is minor.

He also provides sufficient background for understanding why codification of private law was politically important. Focusing on the famous controversy between Friedrich Carl von Savigny and Anton Thibaut, both leading German law professors, he traces the arguments concerning the desirability of a national legal code and elucidates the main political and intellectual factors that influenced treatment of that issue.

Yet equally important as the question of whether there should be a code was the issue of what the code should be like – how it should be structured and what sort of legal mechanism it should entail. It is here that problems arise. The code's drafters were creatures of the legal culture of the period and had to fashion the code out of materials at hand – the ideas, structures, and values of that culture. These ideas defined the options open to the code's drafters and generated the standards for assessing those options.

[…] Roman law provided the conceptual language in which the code was written, but […] [John's] book contains little discussion of Roman law's roles, and the author does not provide the insights necessary to appreciate their influence. Thus, while John prepares the reader for the issue of whether to create a code, he is less effective in providing a basis for understanding subsequent decisions about the content, structure, and methods of the code.

* * *

Procedural and personnel decisions determined the basic shape of the code, and John's description of the political struggles that surrounded these decisions is enlightening. He ferrets out the relevant interests and conflicts and demonstrates the extent to which the bureaucracy was able to use the process to achieve its own goals. He pays particular attention to the often underrated role of the preparatory commission (*Vorkommission*) that organized the drafting process and established its basic objectives. It was here, for example, that the critical decision was made that the code should integrate the existing legal principles of the separate states.

The drafting commission itself also made immensely important procedural decisions. It decided, for example, to divide the substantive material into five parts and to assign primary responsibility for each to one of five members of the eleven-person commission. Not unexpectedly, each of the principal drafters was a bureaucrat with known conservative proclivities. Similarly, the decision to allow the principal drafters to work for years without outside input or influence created an internal dynamic that greatly augmented their power. No meetings of the entire commission were held until 1881, and by then the individual drafts already had taken shape. Given a jurisprudential ethos that demanded deductive coherence and precision, this made significant changes difficult.

Bureaucratic control of the drafting process meant that the code would serve bureaucratic interests. There was no attempt to make the code accessible to "everyman" in the manner of the French *Code Civil*. Early decisions concerning personnel and procedures assured that it would be a technical document accessible only to professionals. These decisions strongly influenced the subsequent development of German legal culture, defining the roles of legal professionals and structuring their education, their language, and their thought.

Political considerations were also critical in establishing the objectives of the drafting process. When political unity was finally achieved in Germany in 1871, many believed that a comprehensive national legal code was an important, even necessary symbol of that unity. The bureaucrats and politicians of the *Reich* as well as the nation's businessmen generally saw a national code as a means of tying the newly created nation together. Such a code also served their own interests, enhancing the power of the bureaucrats and politicians and promising greater profits to business as a result of a more uniform market.

This national unity goal was closely associated with the object of achieving *Rechtssicherheit* (roughly, legal security through an objective and neutral legal system). At least at its outset, the codification process had to promise this to overcome political resistance from the smaller states who feared that their interests would not be protected in the Prussian-dominated *Reich*.

* * *

When the draft code was presented in 1888, it met two types of criticism. Progressive critics focused on its high level of abstraction and on its lack of protection for the weaker members of society. It allowed, they said, the strong to exploit the weak. Conservative critics challenged what they regarded as an atomistic conception of society that emphasized individualism, undermined social cohesion, and failed to protect the agrarians and artisans who represented the core of their communitarian image of society. Both criticisms sprang from deep distrust of liberal values and skepticism about the society those values were creating.

* * *

Questions/Comments

- Gerber's review of the two books (authored by Whitman and John) claims that each book documents and elucidates a particular "idea system" that played a role in shaping German private law (and the broader German legal culture) during the nineteenth century. What are these two idea systems? What are their central features? Do you have the impression that the two idea systems worked against one another and that progress in German private law was a product of that tension? Or, do you think that the two idea systems built upon one another to shape modern German law?
- According to Gerber, Whitman points to the influence of the "Enlightenment" and the "German-Romantic movement" on German law. Is Whitman's reference to these schools of thought similar to the use to which Grosswald Curran puts them in the excerpt presented in Chapter 2? What is Whitman saying about the essential character of modern German private law as it was

formed in the nineteenth century? It must be noted that Yale Law Professor James Q. Whitman is one of the most profound and prominent scholars examining German law from a historical and comparative perspective. Besides the book Gerber reviews in this excerpt, Whitman has published prize-winning research on the roots of the criminal trial,[10] the difference in approaches to criminal punishment in the United States and Europe,[11] the difference between American and European notions of privacy,[12] and the influence of American racist and segregationist policy and law on the Nazi's genocidal agenda.[13]

In Gerber's account – relying on Whitman's and John's books – German private law underwent a process in the nineteenth century that wove together the legacy of the Roman Law and the logic of codification "to provide much of the language of law until the present day." Needless to say, the resulting "language" is largely attuned to the Civil Law tradition. The process was crowned by the enactment of the German *Bürgerliches Gesetzbuch* (Civil Code), which is still controlling for most private law issues in Germany today. Considering German law's history of fragmentation and the grudging surrender of the old, customary ways, the highly rational and systematic Civil Code is a major achievement. Gerber's portrayal of an almost divine, manifest destiny leading to modern German private law is not uncommon. I will revisit that theme when we make a closer study of the Civil Code in Chapter 7.[14]

That account of the progress of German private law contrasts pointedly with the story that must be told about modern constitutional law in Germany. In the following excerpt, Werner Heun describes constitutionalism's troubled German path.

That story can begin in Germany's deeper history with the proto-constitutional features of the Holy Roman Empire, eventually including an assembly of the princes (*Reichstag*) and an Imperial Court (*Reichskammergericht*). But those features never approximated the elements we now expect from a liberal constitutional order.[15] It was a regime of privileged noble estates with few limits on the princes' power. That "constitutional" system buckled under the forces unleashed by the Reformation and European colonial conquest, but it nevertheless managed to stagger into the nineteenth century. Napoleon delivered the knock-out blow.[16] After *le Petit Corporal* was banished to St. Helena, the restored nobility only managed to cobble together a German Confederation (*Deutscher Bund*) out of a handful of principalities.[17] That regime also had some quasi-constitutional institutions, such as a deliberative assembly known as the *Bundestag*. But the 1815 Confederation was "by and large only a defensive alliance, directed against foreign attacks but even more against the new liberal and national movement at home."[18] The Confederation's inevitable demise in the middle of the nineteenth century is a good place to start the tumultuous history of modern German constitutionalism.

Werner Heun
THE CONSTITUTION OF GERMANY – A CONTEXTUAL ANALYSIS 5–20 (2011)[*]

* * *

Within the framework of the German Confederation [of 1815] the monarchs had formally agreed to establish constitutions in their states. [...] The monarchs only reluctantly adopted constitutions that included the establishment of parliaments. The monarchical principle, which maintained the sovereignty of the monarchs as opposed to the dreaded popular sovereignty, had to be preserved. Therefore, the monarchs enacted constitutions by their free sovereign will. Once enacted, the constitutions were also binding for the monarchs so that they were not fully sovereign any more. This contradicted the theory of monarchical sovereignty and in the long run weakened the position of the monarchs. The constitutions spread over Germany in three waves (after 1815, 1830, 1848) from southwest to northeast, each following a revolutionary transformation in France. The model for all these pre-March constitutions was mostly the French Charte Constitutionelle of 1814, which was also based on the monarchical principle.

The Revolution of 1848, also spilling over from France, initiated [...] [another] wave of constitutions. After three broken promises to enact a constitution between 1806 and 1820 the Prussian King finally accepted a constitution. The Revolution forced the monarchs to agree to the election of a national assembly within the framework of the German Confederation to promulgate a constitution for the entire nation. The Bundestag of the Confederation of 1815 enacted the electoral law that for the first time in Germany provided general and equal voting rights for adult men. The resulting *Paulskirchenverfassung* of 1849 – named after the church in Frankfurt/Main where the constituent assembly met – in its structure mainly followed the model of the pre-revolutionary constitutions but included a few important modifications. The political system was designed as a constitutional monarchy. The monarch appointed and dismissed the cabinet but had only a suspensive veto in legislative matters which could be overruled by a qualified majority of both houses. Like all the state constitutions, the *Paulskirchenverfassung* included an extensive Bill of Rights that was enforceable by a constitutional court. The constitution did not provide for judicial review of legislation, however. Most important was the different principle of legitimation. The constitution could not be based on the monarchical principle but only on the sovereignty of the nation which was a disguise for the principle of popular sovereignty, a concept feared by the monarchs and their followers. This in the end was reason enough for the Prussian King to deny the emperorship offered to him by the National Assembly. Therefore this first attempt to unify the nation and introduce a liberal political system in Germany at the same time failed and the Constitution of 1849 was never put into force. [...]

The Imperial Constitution of 1871 after the political unification of Germany was almost identical with the 1867 Constitution of the North German Federation, which relied on a draft by Bismarck. The constitution contained progressive and reactionary elements. It was not based on the monarchical principle any more but neither was it based on popular sovereignty. Its legitimacy was founded instead on a combination of the ideas of unitary nationalism, a federation of monarchs and national caesarism embodied by the emperor. Its democratic elements were strengthened. The Parliament which was called *Reichstag* like the former Imperial Diet was elected by a general and equal vote of men excluding women and the monarch had no legislative or budgetary veto power at all. The Federal Council (*Bundesrat*) never gained much power. On the other hand the process of parliamentarisation was blocked until the end of the First World War. [...] [In addition,

---

[*] © Werner Heun, November 30, 2010. Hart Publishing (an imprint of Bloomsbury Publishing plc).

judicial review of legislation] was not provided for and did not develop either, since the Imperial Court (*Reichsgericht*) rejected it.

[...] [Germany's] military defeat [in World War I] instigated a revolution that made the establishment of a parliamentary government by constitutional amendment in the last days of the war obsolete. The revolution of 1918–19 dissolved the old system. The power was transferred to a revolutionary government mainly formed by Social Democrats under the leadership of Fredrich Ebert. The government soon channeled the revolutionary movement by promoting the election of a constituent national assembly.

The first completely democratic and liberal constitution was finally the Constitution of the Weimar Republic. It was based on popular sovereignty and promulgated by the popularly elected constituent assembly, which convened in Weimar because revolution and street fighting kept it away from Berlin. The Weimar Republic was a federal state although the centralisation of powers was remarkable. [...] The constitution created a parliamentary government but also a strong presidency. The Imperial President (*Reichspräsident*) appointed and discharged the government that could also be ousted by Parliament (*Reichstag*), he had extensive emergency powers and was elected by popular vote. This dual dependency [President and Parliament] made government inherently unstable. The governmental system was very similar to that of the Gaullist Fifth French Republic. The constitution also contained a Bill of Rights including several social rights imposing affirmative duties on the state. The constitution refrained from assigning judicial review of legislation to the courts. Judicial review developed slowly since the Supreme Court (*Reichsgericht*) which also kept its name cautiously affirmed the practice in some respects.

From the beginning the Weimar Constitution and Republic was under strain. The revolution had left the conservative military, bureaucracy, and judiciary more or less intact. The adoption of the Weimar Constitution followed the ratification of the hated Treaty of Versailles within weeks and was always connected with it in the minds of the people. The beginning and the end of the Republic were crippled by economic catastrophes, extreme inflation, burdensome reparations, and the world economic crisis triggered by Black Friday in 1929. In hindsight, several weaknesses of the Weimar Constitution were identified and blamed for supporting the demise of the Republic. Unalloyed proportional representation that was supposed to eliminate the injustices of the absolute majority voting system of the Empire was made responsible for splintering the Parliament, although the number of parties did not rise substantially in comparison to the time before 1918. The Reichstag never saw stable majorities. Within fourteen years twenty governments ruled the Republic and seven parliaments sat in these years. The parliament could be dissolved almost at will by the President and no parliament survived for its whole legislative period. The Cabinet could be voted out of office without agreeing on its successor. But this played a minor role because only three of the twenty governments were ousted in this way; mostly they resigned because of internal conflicts between the different parties of the coalitions. Yet the basic difficulty was not so much the constitution itself but the people whose majority did not fully accept the Republic and voted accordingly for opponents of the democratic and republican constitutional system. [...] In the end, the extreme parties of the left and the right, the Communists and the National Socialists, gained the majority of the votes and formed so called negative majorities, which opposed democratic governmental measures but could not agree on what to do positively. [...] Even more problematic and dangerous was the accepted practice that simply by passing an unconstitutional law by the requisite two-thirds vote, the legislature could depart from the Constitution without explicitly amending it. This so-called breaking-through of the constitution (*Verfassungsdurchbrechung*) was often – deliberately – practiced and allowed for the adoption of the infamous

Ermächtigungsgesetz of March 1933 which transferred practically all legislative powers of Parliament to the government under the new chancellor Adolf Hitler. Finally the transfer of power to Hitler was facilitated by the comprehensive powers of the President [...]. The President not only could more or less determine the acting government, he also had far-reaching and broadly interpreted emergency powers (Art. 48 WRV). [...]

All these features of the Weimar Constitution which were perceived as weaknesses were countered by explicitly contrary provisions in the Basic Law. [...]

* * *

[...] The German Basic Law of 1949 is [...] the result of a [...] "constitutional moment" that has successfully seized. At the time, the Basic Law constituted a new political order after the catastrophe of the Third Reich and its total defeat in the Second World War. Its genesis therefore can be called irregular because it had to be created under the occupation of the Western Allied Powers and because it was territorially reduced to the western part of the whole nation, while East Germany was under Soviet control. These circumstances were the motivation for the prime ministers of the Länder to call the new document not a full constitution but only a "Basic Law" (*Grundgesetz*). This means fundamental law in the German legal tradition and has therefore deeper historical roots. In order to preserve the possibility of reunification the Basic Law was declared to be only a provisional constitution. This provisionality has been often overstated until today. [...]

The making of the Constitution was initiated and influenced by the Allied Powers. [...]. The Americans in particular also wanted a self-supporting and responsible Germany as an essential condition for the restoration of stability on the federal level. The West could only be defended against the communist Soviet Union if a strong democratic government were established in Western Germany. On 1 July 1948, following a six-power conference in London, the Western Allies presented the three so-called Frankfurt Documents to the prime ministers of the eleven [western] German states setting forth a framework for the establishment of a German federal state. They required as essential conditions for the eventual allied approval democracy, federalism and the protection of fundamental rights. [The Parliamentary Council (Parlamentarischer Rat) – serving as a constitutional convention] [...] was convened in Bonn, predetermining the seat of the Capital of the Federal Republic. The Allies followed the work of the Parliamentary Council closely and intervened several times mostly in favour of more decentralisation [...]. Eventually a compromise was reached that was also acceptable to the German side. The draft of the Basic Law was finally passed by the Council on the symbolic date of 8 May 1948, exactly four years after the surrender [to end World War II]. All of the Länder except for Bavaria approved the Constitution. It took effect on 23 May 1949. [...]

Questions/Comments

- Gerber tells a story of progressive development and perpetuity about German private law. The story Heun tells about German constitutionalism is punctuated and punctured. The history of German constitutionalism features fits, starts, failures, reboots, and a fragile post-war experiment breathed into life and initially sustained by the Allied occupying powers. I am reminded of a complaint raised by Fritz Stern, the celebrated scholar of German history, who once wondered: "Why do German democracies have to be identified, limited as it were, by associating them with the names of cities: Weimar, Bonn, Berlin.

All this does is to emphasize unwelcome discontinuity."[19] In any case, the post-war experiment in constitutionalism – the Bonn Republic – has taken root and grown into the sturdy constitutional tradition of the present-day, reunified Berlin Republic. Germany now possesses one of the world's most successful, admired, and emulated constitutional regimes. We will engage in a more focused study of German constitutional law and the 1949 *Grundgesetz* (Basic Law) in Chapter 8.

- Why did the two fields – private law and constitutional law – have such different trajectories in German history? Why did private law more seamlessly and enduringly flourish while constitutionalism struggled to gain a foothold in Germany? Can you think of any contemporary examples in the world today where you might say that the development of liberal private law is running several steps ahead of liberal constitutionalism?
- Recall that Gerber credited private law with providing "the language of [German] law until the present day." Is he suggesting that private law's relative stability and pedigree have made it the foundation of all law in the German legal system, if not by constitutional fiat then as the definitive model? That would certainly be true with respect to the predominance of the Civil Law tradition in German legal culture, which has obvious ties to Germany's evolution towards codification. But doesn't that flip things on their head? Shouldn't the constitution "constitute" the state and thereby set the terms and tone for all law in a polity? What does it mean that a lot of law and state authority in Germany (especially including private law) seemed to be chugging along even as constitutions rose and fell? This arrangement seems to confirm the old German adage: Constitutions come and go, but the state administration remains. You could add to this: The private law and criminal law also remain, despite all the constitutional trials and tribulations. You might guess from these circumstances that, in order to succeed as it has, the post-war constitution had to assert its supremacy over long-established and much-esteemed legal regimes, especially including the revered Civil Code. You already had a glimpse of that struggle in the discussion of the German Constitutional Court's *Lüth Case* in Chapter 3. The tension (some might prefer to call it a "dialogue") between German private law and German constitutional law is a central theme in the survey of German constitutional law that I present in Chapter 8. In keeping with this book's thesis, I suggest that this dynamic can be regarded as an encounter between different legal traditions in the German legal culture. Without getting too far ahead of ourselves, can you guess which two legal traditions the Civil Code and German constitutionalism represent in my thesis?
- How many German constitutions does Heun identify in this excerpt, just covering the period from the nineteenth century to the present? One of them is the extraordinary *Paulskirchenverfassung* (St. Paul's Church Constitution) of 1849. The Frankfurt am Main church where the constitution was drafted, debated, and adopted, is depicted in Figure 4.2. Was a single culprit

(a) The Frankfurt St. Paul's Church
Jean Nicolas Ventadour
The Frankfurt St. Paul's Church in 1848 (1848)
Historical Museum Frankfurt

(b) Interior of the Frankfurt St. Paul's Church today

Seizing on revolutionary fervor, a liberal parliamentary assembly gathered at the Frankfurt St. Paul's Church throughout 1948 to debate and enact democratic reforms for the German nation. A catalogue of individual basic rights was announced in December 1848. In March 1849 the delegates adopted an Imperial Constitution that established the *Reichstag* (Imperial Parliament), "which was to comprise a House of States and a democratically elected House of the People, [empowered to promulgate] legislation, enact the budget, and [exercise] scrutiny [over] the executive." The Prussian King refused to recognize the new regime and the liberal revolutionaries were crushed by the summer of 1849.

Figure 4.2 St. Paul's Church Constitution of 1849

responsible for the serial failure of the constitutional systems? Heun traces the emergence in German constitutional law of several features of a liberal constitution: popular sovereignty; parliamentary democracy; separation of powers; difficulty in changing the constitution; and judicial review. Which of these emerged earlier in modern German constitutionalism? Which elements were established later in the process? Even as the Basic Law reaches its 75th Anniversary in 2024, it would be a mistake to regard that as a rigidly static constitutional regime. The German Federal Constitutional Court has reimagined and reinterpreted the Basic Law, sometimes responding to social and political change, in an impressive corpus of decisions filling 160 volumes. The Basic Law has also been amended more than sixty times since 1949. "Among these amendments were the constitutional provisions for rearmament in 1956, and emergency legislation in 1968. Major constitutional reforms were enacted in 1994 following reunification and in 2006 and 2009 in order to reorganize the federalist competences and financial structures of Germany."[20] The textual and jurisprudential evolution has continued as Germany participates in the ongoing process of ever-closer cooperation, coexistence, and convergence in the European Union. It seems that, even in the stability achieved by the post-war Basic Law, change is a key feature of German constitutionalism.

4.3 Alternative Histories of German Law

The history of German law – old and new – that I have presented is rather conventional: tribal customs, Roman Law, Canon Law, codification, and constitutionalism. But there are many ways to tell the story of the past. What perspectives and priorities do I perpetuate with the history offered here? Who or what draws the spotlight, and which stories are left untold, awkwardly or unjustly awaiting their turn on the stage? I hope you have considered these critical questions as you made your impression of German legal history. As a sign of the earnestness with which I raise this concern, let me at least hint at one alternative history of German law.

Like many other parts of German society, the German legal community has pursued a wide-ranging and extensive accounting of the role the law and legal actors played in the Nazi regime and the Holocaust.[21] That's a different, less comfortable history of modern German law. One of the many insights that work yields is a painful paradox: The persecuted community of Jewish jurists and legal scholars made immense contributions to German constitutionalism.

Those contributions begin, at least, with the work of the Hamburg lawyer Gabriel Riesser at the Frankfurt National Assembly where he played a leading role in entrenching a right to religious freedom in the ill-fated 1849 *Paulskirchenverfassung*.[22] Later, Riesser would become Germany's first Jewish judge. Seventy years later Hugo Preuß, a Jewish law professor and politician from Berlin, was asked to prepare a draft constitution for the Weimar National Assembly to consider and debate.[23] The resulting Weimar Imperial Constitution, largely based on Preuß's proposal, can be celebrated in theory even if it was a catastrophe in practice. As Heun pointed out, the post-war Basic Law explicitly rejected many of the provisions of the *Weimarer Reichsverfassung*. But that paints an incomplete picture. The Basic Law also incorporated a significant number of the Weimar Constitution's policies and principles, including some verbatim or wholesale borrowings. That extends Preuß's influence on German constitutional law right into the present day.

Many characteristic elements of the constitutional order established by the Basic Law drew on theories advanced by Jewish scholars. For example, the Basic Law's muscular protection of liberal democracy, sometimes achieved through illiberal measures such as bans of political parties, was heavily influenced by the thinking of the exiled German-Jewish legal scholar Karl Loewenstein. Loewenstein published groundbreaking articles on "militant democracy" in the United States.[24] Another example involves Hans Kelsen, the Austrian-Jewish legal scholar you encountered in Chapter 3. Many regard Kelsen as the "jurist of the twentieth century." He conceptualized and instituted the special jurisdiction of a constitutional court in Austria in the interwar years.[25] That, in turn, served as the model for the Federal Constitutional Court established by the Basic Law. Around the world, Germany's Constitutional Court is now seen as the leading example of the "Kelsenian model" of constitutional adjudication. Yet another example involves Hermann Heller, whose interwar study of the rule of law and dictatorships advocated for two principles that became foundational, unalterable commitments of the constitutional order created by the Basic Law: the social state (*Sozialstaat*) and the rule of law (*Rechtsstaat*).[26]

All three of these prominent Jewish public law theorists (Loewenstein, Kelsen, and Heller) were forced into exile by the Nazi regime.

Their immense influence on modern German constitutional law should inspire us to wonder what a broader "Jewish history of German law" would look like.[27] There is a long and cruel history of European anti-Semitism, Jewish integration, and Jewish self-governance – each of which involved the law in distinct ways. Jewish scholars and lawyers were prominent in every field of German law prior to the Holocaust. This is captured by Otto Dix's family portrait of the German-Jewish lawyer Fritz Glasser in Figure 4.3. Glasser was one of Dix's wealthy, fully integrated, bourgeois patrons. By pursuing that history, we might even detect the Jewish Legal tradition as one of the threads woven into the richly varied tapestry of German law.[28] How enriching and productive, but also sorrowful, it would be to consider the ways in which a distinctly Jewish approach to the law may have filtered into German legal culture – perhaps through the work of scholars, practitioners and jurists such as Loewenstein, Kelsen, Heller, and many others.

4.4 Conclusion

Otto Dix
"Family of Attorney Dr. Fritz Glaser" (1925)
Staatliche Kunstsammlungen (Dresden, Germany)

Otto Dix captured his patron's family in this portrait that served as a "landmark in his mature style" and "secured his position as one of the most sought-after portraitists in Germany during the Weimar period."[29] Glaser was a wealthy German-Jewish lawyer in Dresden who was excluded from practicing law, first by the Nazis in 1933 and again by the East German Communists after the war.[30] The portrait allows us to easily imagine the extent of German-Jewish lawyers' assimilation and professional success in Germany prior to the Nazis' rise to power. The weighty history of the persecution – and murder – of many German-Jewish jurists is brilliantly documented in the book *Lawyers Without Rights* (2018).[31]

Figure 4.3 German-Jewish Jurists
Source: bpk Bildagentur / Art Resource, NY Dix, Otto (1891–1969). © ARS, NY Photo: Jürgen Karpinski. Location: Galerie Neue Meister

4.4 Conclusion

As we move on from German legal history to the next chapters' presentation of other foundational elements of German legal culture, it is worth recalling that this chapter has not only been summary and incomplete but it also has made choices – no matter how orthodox – that excluded many other compelling histories of German law and legal culture.

Further Reading

- Michael Stolleis, *Public Law in Germany: A Historical Introduction from the 16th to the 21st Century* (Thomas Dunlap trans.) (Oxford University Press) (2017)
- Rebekka Habermas, *Thieves in Court: The Making of the German Legal System in the Nineteenth Century* (Kathleen Mitchell Dell'Orto trans.) (Cambridge University Press) (2016)
- James Q. Whitman, *The Legacy of Roman Law in the German Romantic Era* (Princeton University Press) (2016)
- Werner Heun, *The Constitution of Germany – A Contextual Analysis* (Hart Publishing) (2011)
- Peter Stein, *Roman Law in European History* (Cambridge University Press) (1999)
- R. H. Helmholz, *The Spirit of Classical Canon Law* (University of Georgia Press) (1996)

NOTES

1 Mary Ann Glendon & Peter G. Stein, *Germanic Law*, in Encyclopedia Britannica (Apr. 9, 2013), www.britannica.com/topic/Germanic-law.
2 *Roman Law*, in Australian Law Dictionary (Trischa Mann & Audrey Blunden eds., 2010).
3 Peter J. Huizing & Ladislas M. Örsy, *Canon Law*, in Encyclopedia Britannica (Feb. 19, 2021), www.britannica.com/topic/canon-law.
4 Lynn Mather, *Law and Society*, in The Oxford Handbook of Political Science (Robert Goodwin ed., 2011).
5 *See* Nigel G. Foster, German Legal System and Laws (4th ed., 2010); Gerhard Robbers, An Introduction to German Law (7th ed. 2019); The Oxford Handbook of Modern German History (Helmut Walser Smith ed., 2011).
6 Hillay Zmora, The Feud in Early Modern Germany 1 (2011) (quoting Johann Kamann, Die Fehde des Götz von Berlichingen mit der Reichstadt Nürnberg und dem Hochstift Bamber 1512–1514 103 n. 2 (1893)).
7 Thomas Duve, *German Legal History: National Traditions and Transnational Perspective*, 22 Rechtsgeschichte – Legal History 2 (2014).
8 *See, e.g.*, *The Institute for Roman Law*, University of Cologne (May 28, 2018), https://roemrecht.jura.uni-koeln.de/; *The Institute for Roman Law and Comparative Legal History*, Universität Bonn, www.jura.uni-bonn.de/institute-und-lehrstuehle/institut-fuer-roemisches-recht-und-vergleichende-rechtsgeschichte; *The Institute*, Max Planck Institute for European Legal History, www.lhlt.mpg.de/the_institute;
9 Felix Schorling, *A Deeper History of German Law*, SSRN (July 5, 2022), http://dx.doi.org/10.2139/ssrn.4154541.
10 James Q. Whitman, The Verdict of Battle: The Law of Victory and the Making of Modern War (2012).
11 James Q. Whitman, Harsh Justice: Criminal Punishment and the Widening Divide between America and Europe (2005).

4.4 Conclusion

12 James Q. Whitman, *The Two Western Cultures of Privacy: Dignity versus Liberty*, 113 YALE L. J. 1153 (2004).
13 JAMES Q. WHITMAN, HITLER'S AMERICAN MODEL: THE UNITED STATES AND THE MAKING OF NAZI RACE LAW (2017).
14 *See* JOHN HENRY MERRYMAN & ROGELIO PÉREZ-PERDOMO, THE CIVIL LAW TRADITION 3 (4th ed. 2018).
15 *See* DIETER GRIMM, *Types of Constitutions*, in THE OXFORD HANDBOOK OF COMPARATIVE CONSTITUTIONAL LAW 98 (Michel Rosenfeld & András Sajó eds., 2012); JOSEPH RAZ, BETWEEN AUTHORITY AND INTERPRETATION 323–329 (2009).
16 WERNER HEUN, THE CONSTITUTION OF GERMANY – A CONTEXTUAL ANALYSIS 14 (2011).
17 *Id.*
18 *Id.*
19 *Verleihung des Friedenspreises an Fritz Stern: "Was blühen kann in der Berliner Republik" – Auszüge aus der Rede des amerikanischen Historikers*, DER TAGESSPIEGLE (Oct. 18, 1999), www2.tagesspiegel.de/archiv/1999/10/17/ak-ku-de-16569.html.
20 *Constitution of the Federal Republic of Germany*, FEDERAL MINISTRY OF THE INTERIOR AND COMMUNITY, www.bmi.bund.de/EN/topics/constitution/constitutional-issues/constitutional-issues.html.
21 *See* MICHAEL BAZYLER, HOLOCAUST, GENOCIDE, AND THE LAW (2017); THE LAW IN NAZI GERMANY: IDEOLOGY, OPPORTUNISM, AND THE PERVERSION OF JUSTICE (Alan E. Steinweis & Robert D. Rachlin eds., 2013); *The Thousand Year Reich's over One Thousand Anti-Jewish Laws*, in THE ROUTLEDGE HISTORY OF THE HOLOCAUST (Jonathan C. Friedman ed., 2010).
22 *Gabriel Riesser*, JEWISH VIRTUAL LIBRARY, www.jewishvirtuallibrary.org/gabriel-riesser
23 *Hugo Preuß*, in THE OXFORD COMPANION TO GERMAN LITERATURE (Henry Garland & Mary Garland eds., 1997).
24 *See* Karl Loewenstein, *Militant Democracy and Fundamental Rights*, 31 AM. POLITICAL SCIENCE REV. 417 (1937).
25 Sara Lagi, *Hans Kelsen and the Austrian Constitutional Court (1918–1929)*, 9 REVISTA CO-HERENCIA (2012), https://go.gale.com/ps/i.do?p=AONE&u=googlescholar&id=GALE|A362853535&v=2.1&it=r&sid=AONE&asid=0f610636.
26 *See* HERMANN HELLER, SOZIALISMUS UND NATION (jungeuropa Verlag ed., 2019); HERMANN HELLER, DIE SOUVERÄNITÄT (Verlag Classic ed. 2010); HERMANN HELLER, EUROPA UND DER FASCHISMUS (Esther von Krosigk ed., 2007).
27 Throughout this book I have tried to provide English-language sources in support of my commentary, largely due to my understanding that many readers will not speak or read German. In this instance, however, I must point towards German-language materials that take up the question of German-Jewish legal history. There is an emerging concentration of significant material on this topic, especially as public institutions and private legal organizations seek to account for their role in the persecution and murder of Jewish jurists during the Holocaust. These are only a few examples. *See, e.g.*, ARNOLD PAUCKER,

DEUTSCHE JUDEN IM KAMPF UM RECHT UND FREIHEIT (2003); JUDEN IM RECHT (Sonderausgabe), 39 ZEITSCHRFIT FÜR HISTORISCHE FORSCHUNG (Andreas Gotzmann & Stephan Wendehorst eds., 2007); DEUTSCHE JURISTEN JÜDISCHER HERKUNFT (Helmut Heinrichs et al. eds., 1993); EMANZIPATION UND RECHT (Till van Rahden & Michale Stolleis eds., 2021).

28 Chaim Perelman described Jewish law as an "extreme example of law without a legislator" that relies on textual interpretation for its evolution. *See* Chaim Perelman, *Legal Ontology and Legal Reasoning*, 16 ISRAEL L. J. 356 (1981).

29 *Otto Dix (1891–1969) – Familie Glaser – Karton zum Gemälde (Lot Essay)*, CHRISTIE'S (Nov. 2007), available at www.christies.com/en/lot/lot-4983627.

30 SIMONE LAWIG-WINTERS, LAWYERS WITHOUT RIGHTS 220 (2018).

31 *Id.*

5

Foundations II

Political and Legal Institutions

Key Concepts

- **Federalism**: The division of government powers between member units and common institutions. Unlike in a unitary state, sovereignty in federal political orders is noncentralized, often constitutionally, between at least two levels so that units at each level have final authority and can be self-governing in some issue areas. Citizens thus have political obligations to, or have their rights secured by, two authorities.[1] German federalism involves the centralized authority of the *Bund* (federation), and the authority of the *Länder* (federal states) and *Gemeinden* (municipalities) as political subunits.
- **Dual Sovereignty Federalism** and **Cooperative Federalism**: Two common federalism frameworks include the "Dual Sovereignty" model and the "Cooperative Federalism" model. In the former, typically attributed to the American scheme, there is a strict separation between the central authority and the subunits. They do not share responsibility for exercising public authority in their respective jurisdictions. In the latter, more representative of the German scheme, the central authority and the subunits cooperate in the exercise of shared public authority in their respective jurisdictions.
- **Bundestag**: Germany's Federal Parliament in which first-past-the-post and party-proportional members sit to elect the chancellor and enact legislation, mostly along strict party lines.
- **Bundesrat**: Germany's Federal Council of the States in which members designated by and representing the state governments may exercise a veto over federal legislation and policy in which the states are particularly interested. Because of Germany's "administrative federalism," pursuant to which the states administer most federal law, the *Bundesrat* is extensively involved in lawmaking.
- **Bundesregierung**: The German Federal Government is headed by the chancellor, who selects the federal cabinet ministers. Policy is developed across the relevant ministries and draft legislation can be proposed to the *Bundestag* upon agreement of the federal government.
- **Bundeskanzler**: The Federal Chancellor is elected every four years by the majority of a newly elected *Bundestag*. The chancellor exercises so much authority in German politics that the system is often referred to as a

Kanzlerdemokratie (chancellor's democracy). The chancellor selects and can freely dismiss the cabinet ministers. He or she also dictates the federal government's policy agenda and can enforce that prerogative with his or her *Richtlinienkompetenz*. It is difficult for the *Bundestag* to discipline the chancellor because the principle of a "constructive vote of no confidence" requires the parliament to simultaneously dismiss a sitting chancellor and elect a replacement. At the same time, the chancellor can call for a vote of confidence as a means of disciplining his or her majority in the parliament.

- *Parteiendemokratie*: The principle of a "party democracy" gives political parties, as opposed to individual representatives or civil society, priority for forming, channeling, and actualizing Germans' free democratic will.
- **Administrative Federalism**: The principle that the lawmaking and law-executing functions are split between two or more units in a federal system. In Germany administrative federalism takes the form of state-level or municipal institutions realizing or implementing law enacted by the federation.
- **Decentralized Judicial System**: The principle that a federal state's judicial competence is shared among courts administered by the central authority and the subunits.
- **Specialized Judicial System:** The principle that the courts of a legal system are specialized and exercise their authority only with respect to their strictly defined subject matter jurisdiction.

Study Tips

The Bertelsman Foundation, a nonpartisan think tank based in Washington, DC, promotes strong transatlantic relations. It has produced several fun, short, and accessible animated videos introducing German politics and government. The videos cover topics such as "Germany's Basic Law," "How the German Government Works," and "How Laws Are Made in Germany" (scroll through the videos available under the "Democracy" category at www.bfna.org/updates/).

The Oxford University Department of Politics and International Relations produced a series of podcasts entitled "German Politics: An Introduction" (2007). Those episodes are freely available at iTunes or wherever you access podcasts.

The Deutsche Welle news agency published an insightful survey of Germany's political parties prior to the 2021 federal election (www.dw.com/en/cdu-csu-spd-afd-fdp-left-greens/a-38085900).

The previous chapter looked backward to German law's distant, and not-so-distant, past. We now consider present-day Germany's political and legal institutions. The following materials introduce you to parts of the contemporary framework for government that are relevant to the function of the German legal system. Even if they had precedents in German history, most of these governmental, political, and judicial institutions were formally established (or acknowledged) by the new, post-war constitution known as the *Grundgesetz* (Basic Law).

As with the previous chapter's treatment of German legal history, this presentation must be selective and summary. I make extensive use of Eric Langenbacher's essential English-language study of *The German Polity*.[2] That excellent book is among the best resources available for a more thorough and thoughtful English-language examination of German politics, government, and society.

5.1 Federalism

The previous chapter's discussion of German legal history often referred to the large number of principalities that were stitched together to form various historical manifestations of "Germany," such as the Holy Roman Empire of the German Nation and the German Confederation. But even when dwelling under an imperial or confederal roof, those fiefdoms jealously clung to their autonomy. The German principalities continued to resonate – as centers of regional culture and local identity after Prussia's unification of Germany in 1871. With that in mind, it may not be surprising that one of the most important features of contemporary German politics and law is its system of federalism. That scheme, eternally and inalterably enshrined in the Basic Law, provides for the *Bund* (Federation), the *Länder* (states), and the *Gemeinden* (municipalities) as the country's functional governing units. As Langenbacher explains, the Basic Law's federalism acknowledges and instrumentalizes Germany's tradition of regionalism to aid in organizing social and political life in the *Federal* Republic of Germany.

Eric Langenbacher
THE GERMAN POLITY, 305–307 (12th ed. 2021)[*]

* * *

The Development of German Federalism

The German *Reich* that was founded in 1871 was composed of twenty-five historic German states, which "voluntarily" entered into a federation. These entities, however, were grossly unequal in size and population. Seventeen of them combined made up less than 1 percent of the total area of the *Reich* and less than 10 percent of the total population. The Duchy of Braunschweig, for instance, had fewer than 500,000 people in 1910 (the principality of Reuss, elder line had about 70,000), whereas Prussia, which had absorbed many other states over the course of its history (including Hanover in 1866), was by far the largest unit in the federation, accounting for two-thirds of its area and populations and 40 million

---

[*] © 2022 by the Rowman & Littlefield Publishing Group, Inc. Reproduced by arrangement with the Rowman & Littlefield Publishing Group.

people on the eve of World War I. Many Germans were attached to their state, region, or even city–their *Heimat* (homeland). Indeed, "particularism" – exacerbated by regional dialects and confessional differences – was one of the defining features of Germany history and had long hindered the formation of a nation-state. After the Peace of Westphalia in 1648, there were over two hundred territorial units in the Holy Roman Empire and the rationalized post-1815 German Confederation had thirty-eight states, including Austria.

The unity of [the *Reich* formed in 1871] was tenuous. Some of the member states had, in fact, been forced into the federation by a combination of military defeat at the hands of Prussia and the power politics practiced with consummate skill by Bismarck. Religion was a major cleavage during this period, with the predominantly Catholic areas like Bavaria, Baden, or Alsace-Lorraine resenting the dominance of Prussia, which was about two-thirds Protestant. But the remarkable industrial and economic growth that followed unification temporarily stilled opposition to Prussian dominance and reduced particularistic sentiment. Germany's defeat in World War I, coupled with the political, social, and economic unrest that plagued the post-war Weimar Republic, brought forth a variety of individuals and groups in areas such as Bavaria and the Rhineland who demanded the end of the more centralized *Reich* and the restoration of full sovereignty to the constituent states. The Nazis, who ironically in their early years found common ground with such separatists in their opposition to the Republic, abolished state government in 1934 and imposed a centralized administration on the Third Reich along with thirty-four subdivisions called "*Gaue*." Bavaria, for instance, was divided into five *Gaue*. The leaders of these divisions, the "*Gauleiter*" were some of the most important figures during the Nazi period.

The destruction of the Nazi system and post-war military occupation returned the forces of decentralization to a dominant position. All of Germany's conquerors wanted a decentralized post-war Germany in some form. The French would have preferred a completely dismantled *Reich* composed of several independent states, none of which would be powerful enough ever to threaten France again. The American occupiers, having considerable experience with federal structures, urged an American-type system. The British, although more supportive of centralized power than the Americans or French, also envisioned a decentralized post-war Germany. Among the Germans, opposition to a strong federal system was mostly limited to the SPD and those Christian Democrats in the Soviet zone, which incorporated much of what remained of post-war Prussia before that entity was officially abolished in 1947 after four hundred years of existence.

With the emerging Cold War and division of Germany, the influence of centralizing proponents waned still further, and by 1949, there was little significant West German opposition to plans for a decentralized state. Indeed, western occupiers could count on German support for federalism in their occupation zones because the zones included the historically most particularistic and anti-Prussian segments of the former *Reich*: Bavaria, the Rhineland, the province of Hanover, and the Hanseatic cities of Hamburg and Bremen. The framers of the Basic Law were also largely *Länder* [state] or former Weimar politicians, who since 1946 renewed their political careers at the state level. Thus, the delegates to the Parliamentary Council [charged with drafting West Germany's post-war constitution] were a very states' rights-oriented group.

The Basic Law [Germany's post-war constitution] ensures the states' substantial influence in three ways:

1. Through powers reserved to them (education, police and internal security, administration of justice, supervision of the mass communications media)
2. Through their responsibility for the administration of federal law, including the collection of most taxes and, since 2006, their power to adopt their own regulations for the implementation of some federal law
3. Through their direct representation in the parliament (the *Bundesrat*)

5.1 Federalism

* * *

State Level Politics – Unity and Diversity among German States

[Germany's] sixteen states differ in tradition, size, population, and socioeconomic resources. In the "old" Federal Republic (i.e., before unification), only three of the states – Bavaria and the two city-states of Hamburg and Bremen – existed as separate political entities before 1945. The remaining *Länder* were created by the Allied occupiers, in many cases to the consternation of tradition-conscious Germans. That said, many of the newly formed states corresponded loosely to older entities. Lower Saxony, for instance, mirrored the old kingdom and then the Prussian province of Hanover. In the American zone, two new states, Hesse and Baden-Württemberg, were formed. In the French zone, on the left bank of the Rhine, another new state, Rhineland-Palatinate, was created from territories that had earlier been provinces of Prussia, Bavaria, and Hesse. In the north, some previously independent areas and still more Prussian provinces were rearranged by the British to make the two new states of Schleswig-Holstein and Lower Saxony. In 1957, the Saar region, which had been under French control since 1945, returned to Germany after a plebiscite and became the tenth *Land*. Finally, West Berlin, whose status as a *Land* was disputed by the GDR [East Germany or German Democratic Republic] and the Federal Republic [West Germany], as well as the western powers and the former Soviet Union until the 1990 unification, existed *de facto* as a state after 1949. On October 3, 1990, Berlin's division ended and the city, East and West, is now a full-fledged member of the federation.

The five new eastern states have also had a checkered post-war history. Several of the states – Mecklenburg, Saxony, and Thuringia – had existed as political entities before World War II. The Soviet occupation authorities created a new state, Saxony-Anhalt, predominantly from the old Prussian province of Saxony. The state of Brandenburg, which surrounds Berlin, was formed from the remains of the prewar Prussia, which was dissolved after World War II, and has a long history as a Mark and Electorate. But in 1952, only three years after formation of the German Democratic Republic and five years after the reconstruction of the states, all five were abolished and replaced with fifteen administrative districts (including East Berlin). East Germany's first (and last) freely elected government reestablished the five states prior to the October 1990 unification.

Questions/Comments

- A map of contemporary Germany is provided in the Country Summary section in the book's front materials. It indicates the sixteen *Länder* (federal states), several of which are mere "city-states," such as Hamburg, Bremen, and Berlin. There had been eleven states in the former West Germany. Berlin's status as a state was settled by reunification, which saw four other "new" states from the former East Germany join the Federal Republic.
- There are many reasons why a polity might adopt a federalist system of government. The historical relevance and momentum enjoyed by political subunits might leave little choice in the matter. For example, there could have been no United States without a role for the established communities (and governments) in the several colonies, which, in turn, became the first states in the new union. The same is true of the German tradition of principalities and regionalism, which is colorfully depicted in Figure 5.1. This is a map of the constituent parts of the Holy Roman Empire of the German Nation

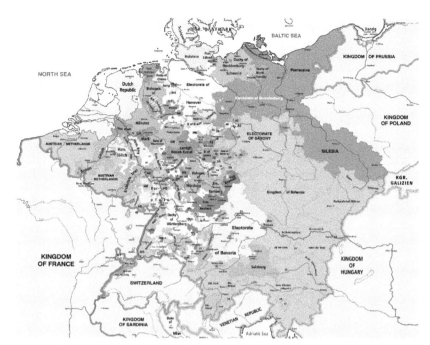

Map of the Holy Roman Empire, 1789. Wikimedia Commons

Schorling made brief references to the Holy Roman Empire of the German Nation in the excerpt provided in Chapter 4. The Holy Roman Empire provided modernizing and centralizing impulses to the development of German law. But, as this map reveals, even at the dawn of the Nineteenth Century the German realm still consisted of dozens of fiercely autonomous principalities of various sizes and strengths, all jumbled together in central Europe. Some estimates place the total number of these principalities at close to 1,800. However miniscule, sometimes even bordering on the absurd, these principalities retained their regional significance—involving culture, dialect, religion, and politics—in a way that made contemporary German federalism a historical necessity. One example of these historical entities, which nevertheless managed to elude the Prussian-fueled forces of unification and retain its autonomy up to the present day, is the Principality of Liechtenstein. Marked with the abbreviation "FL" (*Fürstenturm* (Duchy) of Liechtenstein), this microstate is just a fleck on the map above, nestled between Switzerland and the Tirol region of the Kingdom of Bohemia. Today it consists of a mere 62 square miles and around 40,000 residents. But it is a proud, independent nation with membership in the United Nations. That's a curious throwback to the old German tradition of autonomous principalities.

Figure 5.1 Germany's Federalist Tradition: Principalities of the Holy Roman Empire in the Late Eighteenth Century

at the end of the eighteenth century, just prior to the French Revolution and the rise of Napoleon. Across the sweep of German history, only the tyrannical Nazi regime imagined a completely centralized Germany without a role for some local autonomy or federalist arrangement.

- Another, more instrumental justification for federalism was famously expressed by US Supreme Court Justice Louis Brandeis. He explained that local governments can experiment with different policies and, in that way, serve as "laboratories of democracy" for the development of new national law and programs.³ In fact, over the centuries the sometimes-benign and sometimes-belligerent competition among the German princes produced an intense version of Justice Brandeis' "laboratories" dynamic. Some argue that the princes' efforts to outdo one another as "potentates and patrons" was a unique source of the "German genius." It is true that the competition among the princes too often dissolved into bloody conflict. The devastating Thirty Years War, which desolated the Germanic lands and reduced the population by nearly 20 percent, is a bitter example of one of these bellicose "competitions." But there were more peaceable and progressive versions of the Germanic rivalries. The princes competed "for buildings, orchestras, festivals and gargantuan meals."⁴ You could add a long list of other sectors that enjoyed profound achievement in the German-speaking territories due in part to competition among the princes: founding and funding universities, recruiting and patronizing composers, pursuing reforms to promote administrative efficiency, martial innovation, religious identity and reform, and industrial prowess. Even the timid emergence of constitutionalism in Germany was partly fostered by competition among the princes as they experimented with ways to accommodate growing liberal ambitions in the nineteenth century.

- Modern German federalism is no longer characterized by competition. Instead, in the scheme established by the Basic Law, the competences of the federation, the sixteen federal states, and the municipalities are interwoven and intermingled to create a thick form of cooperative federalism. This framework is particularly meaningful in legal affairs. For example, the Basic Law grants the states the priority to legislate "insofar as this Basic Law does not confer legislative power on the Federation."⁵ It turns out, however, that the constitution assigns exclusive legislative competence to the Federation in a wide range of important areas. That is why the federal codes for civil law and criminal law are the governing law of the land. But the states are not completely sidelined by this arrangement because they share responsibility for implementing and interpreting federal law. That merits emphasis. The states "execute federal laws in their own right."⁶ And, as will be discussed later in this chapter, the judicial authority to interpret and apply federal law is shared between "the federal courts provided for in [the] Basic Law and by the courts of the [states]."⁷ In many other ways, the federation and the states mutually exercise what is understood to be a single source of public authority. Like several cooks gathered around one pot, this sometimes creates conflicts and deadlocks that stall or stymie policymaking, leading to calls for a revival of *Wettbewerbsföderalismus* (competitive federalism).⁸ With respect to making, administering, and interpreting the law, what are the benefits of Germany's cooperative federalism? What are the disadvantages of cooperative federalism in legal affairs? Highlighting some of the problems with such an arrangement, the US Supreme Court has ruled that closely integrated

cooperative federalism is unconstitutional in America's "dual sovereigns" federalism framework.[9]
- Some federal systems are justified by the massive territorial scale of the polity. After all, it might be hard for a remote central government to maintain authority and attract loyalty in far-flung provinces stretching across an entire continent. That is the case in Australia, Brazil, Canada, or the United States. Other federal systems are justified by diverse identity groups with distinct, deeply entrenched languages or religions. Examples of this kind of federalism can be found in Belgium, Bosnia and Herzegovina, Canada, Iraq, or India. Are either of these factors – territorial scope or cultural diversity – part of the explanation for German federalism?
- Why did the Allies insist on a decentralized system of government in post-war Germany? Langenbacher explains that in the post-war era, during which the Basic Law was negotiated and debated, only the Social Democratic Party of Germany (the country's oldest active political party, which won respect for its staunch opposition to the Nazis) expressed skepticism for a federal system. Why would a social democratic party favor centralized power?

5.2 Lawmaking Institutions

For those subjects over which the states retain legislative competence (education, cultural policy, police affairs), law is enacted by state-level parliaments. But as you now know, the federation has a sweeping legislative mandate. Federal law is made on the recommendation of the *Bundesregierung* (the Federal Government – consisting of the chancellor and his or her cabinet) and on the basis of a vote of the *Bundestag* (Federal Parliament). The states can veto some federal legislation in the *Bundesrat* (Federal Council of States).

The *Bundestag* consists of parliamentarians with two kinds of mandates. Half the members of the *Bundestag* are first-past-the-post winners of balloting held in electoral districts. The other half of the seats in the *Bundestag* are awarded to candidates who are named by their parties. The parties fill these seats according to the proportion of their share of the federal vote. On the basis of both mandates – direct-district vote and party-proportional vote – the *Bundestag* is the German federation's only popularly elected institution.

By contrast, the *Bundesrat* consists of delegations selected by the state governments. The members of the *Bundesrat* are not directly and popularly elected to serve in that institution, as is now the case for the United States Senate. The *Bundesrat* ensures that the significance and interests of the states are reflected in federal lawmaking. It also provides the states with a role in the federal lawmaking process not least because, due to Germany's cooperative federalism, the states will play a significant role in administering most federal laws.

Langenbacher describes these institutions – *Bundestag* and *Bundesrat* – in the following excerpt.

Eric Langenbacher
THE GERMAN POLITY, 225–277, 228–229, 232, 236–239 (12th ed. 2021)*

The Bundestag: The Main Political Battleground

In theory, the center of the policy-making process in the German political system is the Bundestag, or parliament. The Basic Law assigns to it the primary functions of legislation, the election and control of the federal government (chancellor and cabinet), the election of half of the membership of the Federal Constitutional Court, and special responsibilities for supervision of the bureaucracy and military. Its [roughly 700] members are elected at least every four years and are the only directly elected officials in the constitutional structure. In practice, however, the parliament, like its predecessors – the Reichstag of the empire (1871–1918) and the Weimar Republic (1919–1933) – has had a long uphill struggle to realize the lofty authority assigned to it in the constitutional documents. Prior to 1949, parliamentary government had both a weak tradition and a poor record of performance in the German political experience.

* * *

The Bundestag, established in 1949, inherited this tragic parliamentary tradition. Unlike earlier parliaments, however, in theory, at least it no longer had to compete with an executive over which it had no direct control. For the first time in German constitutional history, the Basic Law assigned sole control over government and bureaucracy to parliament. Although this control function of parliament was undercut by the strong leadership of Adenauer during the early years of the Federal Republic, the Bundestag since the mid-1960s had begun to assume a role in the policy-making process more congruent with its formal and legal position.

* * *

Structure and Organization

The key organizing agents of the Bundestag are the parliamentary groups of the political parties, or Fraktionen (caucuses). A *Fraktion* is a group of parliamentary members all belonging to the same party. From an organizational and operational standpoint, the parliament is composed of these *Fraktionen* and not individual deputies. The size of a party's Fraktion determines the size of its representation on committees, the number of committee chairpersons it can name, and the amount of office space and clerical staff it receives [...].

The importance of the political parties in organizing the work of the chamber also extends to the relationship between the leadership of the parties and the individual deputy. As in the UK, party discipline, and hence party-line voting, is high in parliament: Approximately 85–90 percent of all votes are straight party votes, with all deputies following the instructions of the Fraktion leadership or the results of a caucus vote on an upcoming bill. Free votes or votes of conscience, when the party gives no binding instructions to its deputies, are rare, but important and have included votes on abortion laws and same-sex marriage in 2017. The constitution guarantees that a deputy who cannot support his or her party can leave its Fraktion and join another without having to resign, at least for the duration of the legislative period.

---

* © 2022 by the Rowman & Littlefield Publishing Group, Inc. Excerpt reproduced by arrangement with the Rowman & Littlefield Publishing Group.

***

Electing and Controlling the Government

The Bundestag elects the federal chancellor. Unlike the procedures under the Weimar Constitution, the chamber does not elect specific ministers but only the chancellor, who then appoints the cabinet ministers. Although this election is by secret ballot, it follows strict party lines and has, with the exception of the CDU's/CSU's unsuccessful attempt to bring down the Brandt government in 1972, provided few surprises.

***

The Bundesrat: The "Quiet" Second Chamber

Located close to the Bundestag in Berlin is Germany's second legislative body, the Bundesrat or Federal Council. Few non-Germans are aware of its existence, much less importance, and even many Germans do not know how powerful this institution can be in the legislative process. [...]

***

The purpose of the Bundesrat is to represent the interests of the states (Länder) of the federation in the national legislative process. It is the continuation of a tradition that extends back to the Bundesrat of the empire [...]. The framers of the Basic Law, many of whom were state officials themselves with strong Allied and especially American encouragement, returned to the federal structure of the empire and Weimar Republic and in some ways gave the Länder, now without Prussia, more influence than had either of the two earlier regimes.

Each state has three to six votes in the Bundesrat, depending on size, for a total of sixty-nine. [...] The degree of malapportionment in the Bundesrat ranges from one vote for every 227,000 inhabitants of Bremen to one vote for just under three million citizens of North-Rhine Westphalia. Thus, although the Bundesrat does not represent the states as equal units (as the U.S. Senate does), the smaller states are still clearly favored in the distribution of votes.

There are no dedicated representatives elected from each state. Rather, the delegation from each state, usually headed by the state's chief executive or premier (Ministerpräsident), must cast the state's votes as a unit, based on the decision of the state's government. [...]

[...] [The] composition and thus partisan voting blocs in the Bundesrat change periodically whenever there is an election at the Land level. Partially because many states have five-year terms, these elections are not aligned with those for the Bundestag. [...] [This can make] Bundesrat majorities quite unpredictable. Indeed, most chancellors have had to deal with lack of support in the Bundesrat, usually divided into government, opposition, and neutral blocs. The almost constant stream of elections at the Land level is frequently seen as plebiscites of the national coalition's performance.

Functions

According to the Basic Law, the Bundesrat can initiate legislation, and it must approve all laws directly related to the states' responsibilities, such as education, police matters, state and local finance questions, land use, most transportation issues, and emergency public health orders as during the COVID-19 pandemic during 2020–21. In addition, any legislation affecting state boundaries, national emergencies, and proposed constitutional amendments requires Bundesrat approval.

***

Expansion of Veto Power

The framers of the Basic Law anticipated that only about 10 percent of all federal legislation would require Bundesrat approval and hence be subject to the chamber's veto. In practice, however, through bargaining in the legal committees of each house and judicial interpretation, the scope of the Bundesrat's absolute veto power was enlarged to the point at which by the early 1970s, it could veto roughly 60 percent of all federal legislation. This unforeseen development occurred largely because many federal laws that refer to matters not subject to Bundesrat veto nonetheless contain provisions that set forth how the states are to administer and implement the legislation. Citing Article 84 of the Basic Law, the states have argued that because they are instructed as to how the federal legislation is to be administered, the legislation requires Bundesrat approval in both its substantive and procedural aspects. The courts have generally supported this coresponsibility theory. [...]

This enlargement of Bundesrat power was a major factor in the Federalism Reform package [...] passed in 2006 by Merkel's first Grand Coalition government. The changes have reduced the veto power of the states via the Bundesrat to only 38 percent of laws between 2006 and 2017. In exchange, the states received more power to administer federal laws as they see fit and greater independence in establishing education and regulatory policies. [...]

Questions/Comments

- Five forces shape the relevance and effect of the *Bundestag*. The first is the power of the chancellor. The second is the power of the political parties. The third is the power of the states. The fourth is the popular will of the people. A fifth, rather attenuated but important power, is wielded by the *Bundesverfassungsgericht* (Federal Constitutional Court). This tribunal can demand the revision of federal law so that it conforms with the Basic Law. In rare cases, the Constitutional Court declares a law null and void. The Court has not been shy in exercising its power of judicial review. The first four of these forces are discussed in the following comments. You'll learn more about the powerful Federal Constitutional Court in Chapter 8.
- The federal election for the *Bundestag* is held every four years. A major function of each newly empaneled parliament is to elect the chancellor. That means that *Bundestag* campaigns are dominated by the question: Which party (or coalition of parties) will emerge with the parliamentary majority needed to name the chancellor. The appeal of the parties' *Spitzenkandidaten* (lead candidates for the chancellorship) is as important to the parliamentary election as the parties' (or any individual parliamentary candidate's) policy platform. This indicates the relatively weak profile of the *Bundestag*, despite the fact that it enjoys Germany's only national, direct, and popularly confirmed legitimacy. In a significant sense the *Bundestag* is *just* the organ that ordains the powerful chancellor. Later in this chapter we will discuss the

chancellor's prominence in the German system, which also involves significant influence over lawmaking.
- Political parties play a decisive role in German governance. The constitution calls on the parties to participate in "the formation of the political will of the people."[10] They have constitutional entitlements and they receive public funding for their election campaigns and to support their policy development activities. As you read in the Langenbacher excerpt, the *Bundestag* chiefly serves as a framework for actions taken by the parties, which operate as cohesive and highly disciplined blocks. These disciplined blocks elect the chancellor and vote on legislation or other initiatives presented to the *Bundestag* by the government. This means that, because he or she is a product of a parliamentary majority, the chancellor can expect the same parliamentary majority to endorse the government's legislative agenda. The members of the *Bundestag* usually vote as instructed by their party, despite the fact that the Basic Law guarantees parliamentarians' autonomy.[11] The parliament is seldom the scene of decisive political debates, negotiations, or compromises aimed at winning over a handful of undecided legislators.
- The centrality of the political parties in this framework is expressed by the term *Parteiendemokratie* (party democracy). Why do you think the German lawmaking scheme prioritizes parties, as opposed to individual parliamentarians who may have their own political agenda based on their local mandate or their national prominence?
- There are six established political parties in Germany: the center-right *Christian Democratic Union* (CDU), which partners with its independent "sister" party in the state of Bavaria known as the *Christian Social Union* (CSU); Germany's oldest political party is the center-left *Social Democratic Party of Germany* (SPD); the *Bündnis 90/Die Grünen* (Greens) began as an eco-pacifist protest movement in the late 1970s but the group has evolved into a broadly popular eco-bourgeois party that has twice joined a coalition government; the liberal *Free Democratic Party* (FDP), which was the kingmaking coalition partner in the Federal Republic's first half-century; the far-left *Left Party* (*Die Linke*), which splintered into distinct party blocks after the 2021 federal election, had its roots in the disbanded East German *Socialist Unity Party of Germany* (SED); and the appalling, right-wing *Alternative for Germany Party* (AfD). Only the Christian Democrats (five times) and the Social Democrats (four times) have ever succeeded in having their *Spitzenkandidat* elected chancellor. For a long time those parties had such a broad base of support they were often referred to as the *Volksparteien* (people's parties). They usually achieved their parliamentary majority by forming a coalition with one of the smaller parties (the FDP or the Greens) or with one another (creating what is known as a Grand Coalition). But the German electorate is beginning to atomize, shrinking the profile of the *Volksparteien* while the smaller parties have gained voters and clout. For the first time in

the history of the Federal Republic, the 2021 federal election led to a three-party coalition (SPD, Greens, and FDP).
- If the *Bundestag's* legislative role is more or less perfunctory – with the content of legislation dictated by the government and the outcomes settled along strict party-block votes – then what other functions does the parliament serve? The *Bundestag* is meant to oversee the government, but Langenbacher qualifies this arrangement as "theoretical." Why? An important means for asserting parliamentary control over a government is a no-confidence vote. Why is that a limited instrument in the German scheme?
- The cohabitation and codependence of the parliamentary majority and the chancellor's government means that the *Bundestag* is sometimes viewed chiefly as a platform for the parties that are not part of the government. The opposition parties are entitled to participate in committees and can call for parliamentary investigations. They can even raise their concerns – or the interests of the *Bundestag* as a whole – in proceedings before the *Bundesverfassungsgericht* (Federal Constitutional Court).
- You have learned that the states, acting through their veto authority in the *Bundesrat*, can influence federal lawmaking. You should note, however, that Langenbacher refers to the *Bundesrat* as Germany's "second legislative body." It is a subtle but important point. Germany does not have a bicameral legislature with two chambers fully participating in the enactment of legislation. The *Bundestag* is the unitary and primary legislative organ. The *Bundesrat*, as a separate body, can only exercise its veto over a select range of legislative matters.
- The public's political sentiment is channeled and constrained in Germany's policymaking processes, including at the *Bundestag*. Direct democracy actions were common in the Weimar Republic, the tumultuous political system in Germany between the wars. But the Basic Law anticipates federal referenda in only two very discrete and rare circumstances (reorganizing the territory of states or enacting a new constitution). Why does the system established by the Basic Law rely so robustly on representative democracy and seek to diminish the role of popular politics? Despite this framework, there have been dramatic episodes during which the "street" shook up German politics. This was especially true of the *Sitzblockaden* that took place in the late 1970s and early 1980s. During these large and persistent civil-disobedience demonstrations, tens of thousands of Germans protested against nuclear energy and NATO's nuclear weapons stationed in Germany by occupying and disrupting facilities and transport systems around West Germany.[12]

5.3 Executive Authority

The discussion of Germany's lawmaking institutions suggested that the parliament is relatively weak because it is caught between the power wielded by the chancellor, by the political parties, and by the states. In fact, that portrayal might be overly generous towards the parties and the states. The political system largely revolves around the chancellor and his or her government. The chancellor is so prominent in the Federal Republic that many regard the system as a *Kanzlerdemokratie* (chancellor's democracy). This view regards Germany's executive as something between a presidential system (such as in the United States or France) and the traditional parliamentary system (such as in the United Kingdom).[13]

Yet, the chancellor and the federal government are only two components of a diversified executive branch in Germany. A *Bundespräsident* (Federal President) is elected every five years by a specially convened Federal Convention to serve as Head of State. That, however, is a mostly symbolic and ceremonial position.[14] The state-level *Ministerpräsidenten* (governors) and their governments also exercise executive authority, including the states' role in administering federal law. Finally, there is an old and well-established public administration that is staffed by the historical and constitutionally endorsed civil service.[15] The following discussion of German executive power focuses on the powerful chancellorship and the entrenched administration.

Russell A. Miller
Executive Extremes: German Lessons for Our Authoritarian Era
69 Jahrbuch des Öffentlichen Rechts der Gegenwart 311, 314–318
(Oliver Lepsius et al. eds., 2021)[*]

***

Executive Power in Germany

Germany's post-war executive, the *Bundeskanzler* (Federal Chancellor), possess considerable power. The Basic Law prescribes this. The chancellorship has strengthened its position through the tradition and practice of the country's eight post-war chancellors. Germany's strong executive also finds support in accepted constitutional theory.

The Basic Law's Strong Executive

The Basic Law envisions a *Bundesregierung* (Federal Government) consisting of the Federal Chancellor and the Federal Ministers. But this is no "working cabinet" in which the chancellor is the greater among equals. The chancellor possesses the power to determine the number and competence of the federal ministries. The chancellor appoints and dismisses the ministers. And the constitution gives the chancellor exclusive responsibility for determining the "general guidelines" of federal policy. The chancellor's authority over the government's policy is enforced with the so-called *Richtlinienkompetenz* – a peremptory and hierarchical red-line the chancellor can invoke in order to prevail in disagreements with her ministers. The Federal Government's Rules of Procedure confirm this power in their first paragraph: "The Federal Chancellor determines the guidelines of domestic and foreign policy. These decisions are binding on the Federal

---

[*] Excerpt reproduced with permission of Mohr Siebeck (Tübingen, Germany).

Ministers, [...] In the event of a dispute, the Chancellor shall take the decision." The ministers only exercise independent control over their departments within the scope of the chancellor's agenda and authority. This, however, also serves to empower the chancellor by insulating him or her from the political fallout resulting from misdeeds or mistakes occurring within a ministry. Langenbacher and Conradt explain that the cabinet has a "relatively low profile," serving as a "loose board of managers" that approves the chancellor's decisions rather than debating and deciding on policy. The chancellor's authority over the cabinet is enhanced by the functions and capacity of the *Bundeskanzleramt* (Chancellor's Office), which doles out to and can demand information from the ministries. The Chancellor's Office operates as an "institutional watchdog over the various ministries to ensure that the chancellor's guidelines and cabinet decisions are indeed being carried out." The Government's Rules of Procedure provide that the "Federal Chancellor has the right and duty to ensure the implementation of [her] policy guidelines."

Nor is the chancellor's power materially constrained by the fact that he or she is elected by a majority of the *Bundestag* (Federal Parliament). Several interrelated factors minimize the parliament's capacity to control the chancellor.

The first is post-war Germany's traditional concentration of electoral power in two *Volksparteien* (people's parties or large, big-tent political movements open to all classes, ages, and generations). Even if this landscape is shifting today, it has been the privilege of the center-right Christian Democrats and the center-left Social Democrats to put forward the relevant and realistic candidates for the chancellorship. It also is the case that the chancellor wields considerable power over his or her party. On the one hand, he or she often serves as the party's chairperson. On the other hand, the German parties are characterized by strict discipline. This discipline is partially a product of electoral design. Germany's system of "personalized proportional" voting awards half the seats in parliament to lists of candidates assembled by the party itself. That is, half of all parliamentarians are beholden to the party, as much as to the electorate, for their seats in the *Bundestag*. The result is a disciplined party-line vote for the chancellor (and most other policies) that provides few surprises and few departures from the chancellor's agenda.

Parliament's ability to control and constrain the chancellor also is limited by the two institutions' cohabitation and codependence. In that relationship the Basic Law privileges the chancellor by permitting a parliamentary vote-of-no-confidence to topple the chancellor only if the parliament is able, at the same time, to "elect a successor by the vote of a majority of its members." [It is practically impossible to simultaneously deconstruct and reconstruct] a government – especially within Germany's tradition of stable and disciplined party politics [...]. At the same time, the constitution grants the chancellor an easy and blunt mechanism for enforcing discipline in his or her parliamentary majority. The chancellor can call for a vote-of-confidence (risking the dissolution of the parliament) "to strengthen his or her position by [...] compelling dissidents in his or her party and/or the coalition partners to support the government or risk new elections."

* * *

All that remains for the parliament to constrain Germany's powerful chancellor are, on the one hand, the formalities of oral and written questions posed to the government for answers, and, on the other hand, parliamentary investigations. [...]

* * *

Questions/Comments

- Formally, Germany's chancellorship is a traditional parliamentary executive. In practice, however, the chancellor sometimes seems to wield the power of a president. What are the key features of these two arrangements for executive power (presidential and parliamentary)? What are their advantages and disadvantages?
- What are the means for checking the chancellor in the German system? Do you think they are adequate to protect against abusive or excessive exercises of executive power? Despite the limited checks on the chancellor, post-war Germany has not slipped towards a domineering or repressive executive. Why? The German system also gives the chancellor a tool for disciplining his or her majority in parliament. What is that tool?
- One source of the chancellor's strength comes from the long terms in office several of them have enjoyed. This allows the chancellor to take a commanding role in his or her party, to impose his or her will on the parliament and cabinet ministries, and to engender personal support in the electorate that is independent of the parliament. Konrad Adenauer, the Federal Republic's first chancellor, served for fourteen years. He developed a highly personal and strong-willed leadership style in the Republic's founding era that continues to shape the character and authority of the chancellorship. Helmut Kohl occupied the office for sixteen years, from the early 1980s to the late 1990s. During that time Chancellor Kohl navigated the precarious process of German reunification. Angela Merkel, the first woman to hold the chancellorship, enjoyed a sixteen-year tenure that ended in 2021. Merkel managed a number of crises (economic convulsions and a wave of refugees) and steered Germany towards deeper integration in the European Union. These three Christian Democratic chancellors presided for forty-six of the Federal Republic's seventy years. The long terms these chancellors served – and the power they unavoidably accumulated – seems to align with one observer's claim that, "in their political tradition there is little […] which could cause [Germans] to mistrust the strong state, *i.e.*, the strong and capable executive. The National Socialist *Führer* state was for them not a break in tradition, only its exaggeration and perversion. […] If, therefore, democracy is to be made acceptable and impressive for the Germans it can only be in the form of democracy in which a strong executive rules and provides not only for prosperity but also for law and order."[16] Are those sentiments – and German chancellors' long terms in office – compatible with democracy or the cherished German *Rechtsstaat* (a state governed by the rule of law)?

The chancellor wields considerable power over the cabinet ministers. Still, it wouldn't be accurate to portray the ministers as mere puppets. They oversee large and powerful ministries that are profoundly involved in administration and policymaking. Although the chancellor unilaterally names, and can dismiss his or

5.3 Executive Authority

her ministers, the constitution ensures that ministers manage "the affairs of [the] department independently and under [the minister's] own responsibility."[17] The cabinet ministries include traditional briefs, such as foreign affairs, internal affairs, justice affairs, financial affairs, social affairs, and defense. As noted earlier in this chapter, Chancellor Olaf Schulz was elected in 2021 at the head of a coalition that includes his Social Democrats, the Greens, and the Free Democrats. His government also features ministries for economics and climate protection, family affairs, health matters, education affairs, digitalization and transportation, food and agriculture, and housing and urban development.

The ministers forming the chancellor's federal government are significant political figures. But neither they, nor the chancellor for that matter, preside over the largest and most impactful segment of Germany's vast administration. The German federal executive "is significantly small in size."[18] The state-level administration is much larger.

> This special feature of the country's administrative system [...] is based on the division of responsibilities. The central (federal) level develops and adopts most of the public programmes and laws, and the state level (together with the local level) implements them. The administration at the federal level comprises the ministries, some subordinated agencies for special issues (*e.g.,* the application of drugs, information security and the registration of refugees) and selected operational tasks in single administrative sectors (*e.g.,* foreign affairs, the armed forces, the federal police and the supreme courts). [...] According to the Basic Law, the states are, in principle, responsible for public administration, regardless of whether state or federal law is being enforced.[19]

Germany's executive power is exercised by an army of civil servants and other public employees. Most of these administrators are employed by the states and municipalities. Despite the diversity that results from having seventeen separate administrations (the limited federal administration and the administrations of the sixteen federal states), the work of Germany's public authorities is largely harmonized across the country. First, federal law has imposed a significant measure of uniformity and accountability on the administration. For example, as you will learn in Chapter 9 of this book, German administrative law provides for extensive judicial scrutiny of administrative actions based on federal standards, including constitutional basic rights. Second, federal and state civil servants "share a common background and training, and they work within a similarly structured bureaucratic framework."[20] The editors of a big English-language study of Germany's public administration explained that within the "varying structures, administration seems to be relatively homogeneous, not least because of the very similar staffing structures, career patterns and administrative cultures."[21]

Germany's administrative culture draws on an old and sophisticated bureaucratic tradition that derives from Prussia. That powerful German principality (and eventual kingdom) developed refined systems for its administration and military in the nineteenth century. The advantages those systems brought helped Prussia to dominate and ultimately unite the Germanic realms in 1871. It then transposed its administrative model to the rest of a newly unified Germany. At the same time, the widely admired Prussian bureaucracy served as a model for administrative reforms in far-flung corners of the world. The Prussian administrative tradition "cultivated a catalog of values for civil servants and the military, including punctuality, frugality, a sense of duty, and diligence [...]."[22] One of the central characteristics of the German administrative culture is that it is strictly rule-bound. The administration can only act on the basis of – and within the parameters established by – law. There is little room for discretion. Details of these principles will be discussed in Chapter 9.

Max Weber, the definitive theorist of modern bureaucracy (and, unsurprisingly, a German) extolled the German bureaucracy in these terms: "The fully developed bureaucratic apparatus compares with other organisations exactly as does the machine with the non-mechanical modes of production."[23] This reference to the "machinery" of governance recalls Kantorowicz's depiction of the German juristic method, presented in Chapter 3. Kantorowicz claimed that German legal practice was similar to the operation of a "logic machine." In the administration, as well as the judicial function, Germans seem to yearn for a mechanistic exercise of public power: reliable, predictable, objective, and intricately systematic. Even if that instinct contributes to the common stereotype that Germany is suffocatingly bureaucratic, it also helps to explain why "Germany rates as one of the best-governed countries in the world."[24]

The physical architecture of the lawmaking and governmental institutions discussed in this chapter are depicted in the photographs presented in Figure 5.2, including the *Bundestag*, the *Bundesrat*, the Chancellery, and the federal president's residence. Figure 5.2(e) is a photograph of newly elected Chancellor Olaf Scholz being inducted into office by Federal President Frank-Walter Steinmeier. These two central figures are surrounded by the chancellor's hand-picked federal ministers who form the Federal Government.

5.4 Legal System and Courts

Another set of institutions with great relevance for Germany's legal culture – perhaps the greatest relevance – are the courts. After all, the judiciary is responsible for interpreting and applying the law.

Germany's judiciary has a tradition that preceded the new, post-war constitutional order. That tradition is stamped on the judicial branch, even if there has been some change and innovation since the establishment of the Federal Republic. Similar to the legislative and administrative branches, the competence over judicial power is shared between the federation and the states in Germany's cooperative federalism.

5.4 Legal System and Courts

(a) *Bundestag* (Federal Parliament)   (b) *Bundesrat* (Federal Council of States)

(c) Federal Chancellery   (d) Federal President's Residence – *Schloss Bellevue*

(e) Federal Government of newly elected Chancellor Olaf Scholz (2021)

Figure 5.2 Germany's Legislative and Executive Institutions
Source: (a), (b), (c) Shutterstock; (d) Aliaksandr Mazurkevich/Alamy Stock Photo; (e) Getty Images

The judicial branch is large. Counting both federal and state courts, it includes around 22,000 judgeships, or one judge for every 3,800 Germans. By contrast, the United States has only 32,000 judges staffing its federal and state courts. That is one judge for every 10,000 Americans.

The Basic Law assigns the judicial power to the judges themselves, and not to the judicial branch as an institution. The established traditions for staffing and operating courts largely continue. Having passed through the tumultuous first-half of the twentieth century, they are now codified in the *Gerichtsverfassungsgesetz* (Courts Constitution Act) from 1950. Central to the judicial power anticipated by the Basic Law and the Courts Constitution Act is the independence of the judiciary.[25]

The following excerpt describes the contemporary judicial scheme, and it refers to the *Bundesgerichtshof* (Federal Court of Justice) as representative of Germany's judiciary. Following the excerpted text, the diagram in Figure 5.3 depicts Germany's complex, decentralized and specialized, judicial framework.

Russell A. Miller
German Legal System and Courts
OXFORD HANDBOOK OF GERMAN POLITICS 196, 199–205
(Klaus Larres *et al.* eds., 2022)[*]

***

Contemporary Judicial Authority and Courts

Many of the central features of the contemporary German judicial system are products of evolution from its long-ago roots in the wilds of Germania; from the institutions and norms of conflict resolution in the era of medieval European feudalism; and from European Enlightenment and Romanticism, which served as the duel impetuses for German modernization, liberalization, unification, and codification.

Two of the most important of these inherited and evolved features are the contemporary judicial power's *decentralization* and *specialization*.

Decentralization

As the country's name – Federal Republic of Germany – establishes, Germany consists of a federalist political structure. There are sixteen *Länder* (states) exercising a spectrum of public authority in *cooperation* with the public authority exercised by the *Bund* (federation). I emphasize the word "cooperation" because German federalism largely imagines that there is a single source of state authority that happens to be shared and – collegially and complementarily – implemented by the Republic's two political entities: the federation and the states. This model of cooperative federalism differs from the American "dual sovereignty" approach, which, at least in theory, claims to have "split the atom of sovereignty" between the U.S. government and the governments of the fifty states so that both political entities separately exercise their own autonomous and exclusive spectrum of state sovereignty.

The distinction between the two models of federalism can be overstated, especially as there is evidence of both paradigms in both systems. But the essence of the distinction can be seen in the structures the two countries have established for the exercise of judicial power. In the American dual sovereignty model each sovereign – the federation or one of the states – enjoys its own exclusive jurisdiction and autonomously administers all the judicial infrastructure needed for that role. That's why there is a federal court system charged with interpreting and implementing federal law, while, at the same time, each American state has its own court system charged with interpreting and implementing its law. It is said that American judicial power is *centralized* because these sovereigns'

---

[*] © Oxford University Press 2022. Reproduced with permission of the Licensor through PLSclear.

independent legal systems host the full complement of courts and judicial actors, from first-instance courts up to a last-instance supreme court. The entirety of the judicial function is centralized in the hands of a single sovereign. A startling example of this separation and autonomy is the long-recognized possibility that, despite the U.S. Constitution's prohibition on double jeopardy, a person can be accused of and tried for a crime in one of the jurisdictions (the federal courts, for example) even if he or she has been acquitted of the same criminal conduct in one of the other jurisdictions (a state's courts, for example). One sovereign's crimes and judicial processes have nothing to do with another sovereign's criminal regime. That's true even if the two systems are responding to the same set of facts and events.

The German model of cooperative federalism, however, permits a *decentralized* judicial structure. The administration of the state's single expression of judicial power is shared between the German *Bund* and the *Länder* so that there is only one court system over which the two sovereigns share responsibility by operating distinct parts. In the German system this means that the sixteen states largely are responsible for providing the infrastructure and personnel for the system's *Amtsgerichte* and *Landgerichte* (first-instance courts) and *Oberlandesgerichte* (intermediate appellate courts). For its part, the federation largely is responsible for providing the infrastructure and personnel for the system's *Bundesgerichte* (last-instance or supreme federal courts). If one imagines the trajectory of a court case as a vertical ascent from a first-instance trial court and perhaps involving a stop at an intermediate appeals court before ending at a last-instance court of appeals, then in the German system the first and second rungs on the ladder take place in state courts. If the case proceeds to the highest appellate court, then it is handed over to the federation for proceedings in a federal supreme court. In this way the German state's unified judicial authority is said to be decentralized because the exercise of that power is shared among separate sovereigns.

The decentralization of the justice system in Germany accommodates two prominent frames in German history and politics. On the one hand, it reflects the deeply federalist character of state power in Germany, including the old principalities but also the local states that the Western Allies rapidly reconstituted and empowered after World War II. On the other hand, decentralization of the judicial function reflects the German imperial tradition, whether of the Holy Roman or Prussian variety, which involved a powerful overarching authority as the seat of the last-instance of justice. Those historical influences are important. But decentralization of the justice system also can be justified on functional terms. The states' administration of justice at the level closest to the citizens lends the system legitimacy and, at least in theory, permits some variation in the exercise of judicial authority out of respect for the character and culture of a particular locality. These gains in the integrity of the judicial function should reinforce respect for the law and the courts. For its part, the federal jurisdiction, consisting of last-instance appellate courts, helps to ensure the quality and uniformity of the interpretation and application of the law across the whole of the Federal Republic.

Specialization

The decentralization of the German judicial system calls on us to imagine the judicial process as if it is arranged vertically, with the lower rungs of the ladder administered locally by the states and the highest rung of the ladder administered by the federation.

The specialization of the German judicial system involves a horizontal perspective that represents the division of the German judiciary into six distinct, specialized subject matter jurisdictions. From this vantage point it is as if there were six separate ladders lined up next to each other. The courts in Germany, different to most courts in the American legal system, are not courts of general jurisdiction that are charged with interpreting the law and resolving disputes across the full spectrum of possible legal issues. Instead, German courts are highly specialized and exercise jurisdiction over a discrete set of legal issues. The relevant jurisdictions in Germany's system of specialized courts include: constitutional law jurisdiction; ordinary jurisdiction (civil law and criminal law), labor law jurisdiction, administrative law jurisdiction, tax and finance law jurisdiction, and social law jurisdiction. Each of these jurisdictions has competence – jurisdiction – to adjudicate disputes arising under a particular legal code. These codes are understood to provide a highly-complex and intricate – but also comprehensive – normative resolution of all possible legal concerns in the related realm of society. For example, the *ordentliche Gerichtsbarkeit* (ordinary courts jurisdiction) is responsible for interpreting and adjudicating disputes arising under the *Bürgerliche Gesetzbuch* (German Civil Code) and the *Strafgesetzbuch* (German Criminal Code). As civil law (contracts, torts, property, family law, and succession) and criminal law involve a big swath of the law's nexus with life, the ordinary courts charged with hearing cases under those codes are the most prominent and present of Germany's specialized jurisdictions. That is not to say that the other five specialized jurisdictions are unimportant. Especially in Germany's heavily bureaucratized political-economy and in light of its extensive, cradle-to-grave social welfare system, the administrative and social courts also feature prominently in ordinary Germans' lives.

Germany's courts are tethered to distinct substantive codes. Each also is accompanied by a distinct set of procedures. Staying with the example of the Civil Code and Criminal Code as adjudicated by the ordinary courts, the relevant procedure in civil and criminal matters is established by the *Zivilprozessordnung* (Code of Civil Procedure) and the *Strafprozeßordnung* (Code of Criminal Procedure). Finally, each jurisdiction is constituted and coordinated by a seperate legislative grant. The ordinary courts, for example, are formed and regulated by the *Gerichtsverfassungsgesetz* (Courts Constitution Act).

The positive law elements of Germany's specialized judiciary – substantive, procedural, and constitutive – are reproduced for each of the systems' six specialized jurisdictions.

This hermetic horizontal framework and its positive law predisposition present some interesting points for reflection, especially in relation to the German system's decentralization. There is a blending, or sharing, of administrative responsibility for justice between the federation and the states. But the subject matter authority of the German judiciary is highly compartmentalized. One justification for this is that the quality of justice produced by the complex and sophisticated codes benefits from judicial specialization. Here one picks up the echoes of Kant's influence on German jurisprudence. In rejecting the classical notion of natural law as a product of human reason, Kant inspired hopes for *Rechtswissenschaft* (science of law), which would focus exclusively on the positive law and rely on empirical and systematizing approaches. The German codes drafted under the influence of these ambitions, and the judicial method developed to help realize them, suggest something like the delicate inner-works of a carefully calibrated watch. Just like you wouldn't hand your Breitling Aviator timepiece over for repairs to a mall kiosk selling sunglasses and watch batteries, the function and interpretation of the German codes call for master technicians. The early Twentieth Century German legal scholar Hermann Kantorowicz described this phenomenon in terms that do not mask his sarcasm: [...]

Another point meriting reflection is that the entire positive law framework for each of these jurisdictional ladders is formed by federal statutes. The specialized substantive codes, the specialized procedural codes, and the specialized acts constituting the six specialized jurisdictions – all of this law is a product of federal legislative authority. This further complicates the cooperative federalism exemplified by the German judicial system's decentralization because it means that in the states' portion of the process (first-instance proceedings and intermediate appeals on the lower rungs of the ladder) the state administered courts are nevertheless interpreting and implementing substantive federal law, while conforming to federal procedural rules, by way of state-run judicial institutions constituted according to federal standards. That's an intricate web of sources and systems that even might have confounded Tacitus' barbarian Germans.

Federal Court of Justice as a Representative Court

The last, or "highest," rung on the ladders of the vertically decentralized judicial framework operating within each specialized subject matter jurisdiction in the German legal system is occupied by a federal court. These courts sit atop their respective jurisdictions. This is not the forum for a detailed accounting of all of these supreme federal courts. Instead, I will sketch the structure, personnel, function, and praxis of the *Bundesgerichtshof* (Federal Court of Justice), which serves as the supreme court for the *ordentliche Gerichtsbarket* (ordinary courts). It is one of the most important courts in the German legal system. In its structure and practice, it also is representative of the other federal supreme courts.

* * *

The Federal Court of Justice (FCJ) was established under the supervision of the Federal Republic's Ministry of Justice in 1950 (in fulfillment of the constitutional mandate from Article 95 of the Basic Law). But the founding of the FCJ did not take place without the benefit of some precedent. From 1879 up to the collapse of Hitler's Third Reich and the subsequent Allied occupation, the *Reichsgericht* (Imperial Court) served as Germany's apex court. For much of this tenure there was little judicial specialization so the Imperial Court, with its seat in Leipzig, was Germany's truly supreme court. But after the turn of the Twentieth Century the trend was towards specialization. In that process the Imperial Court ceded some of its jurisdiction. On the one hand, new Imperial courts concerned with tax and financial matters were established. On the other hand, a separate administrative law jurisdiction emerged.

The November Revolution in 1918 led to the creation of the Weimar Republic under a new liberal-democratic constitution. The Imperial Court continued in its traditional role but it also came to host the newly ordained *Staatsgerichtshof* (State Court), which exercised limited jurisdiction over constitutional issues involving the organization of the state (competence, separation of powers, or federalism issues). Significantly, the Imperial Court sought to use the basic rights secured by the Weimar Constitution as the basis for a cautious exercise of judicial review. In a legal culture such as Germany's, which prioritizes the positive law promulgated by the legislature, the idea that the judiciary might overturn legislation it finds to be unconstitutional (a jurisprudential innovation famously justified by Chief Justice John Marshall in the U.S. Supreme Court decision *Marbury v. Madison* [1803]) was revolutionary. Like many revolutions, however, the Imperial Court's foray into judicial review proved to be short-lived and ineffectual. The court was hemmed-in by the novelty of the practice. The absence of a citizens' constitutional complaint for adjudicating basic rights violations was a choke-point. When issues under the basic rights were presented to the Court it struggled to make much out of social rights guarantees that lacked a broad political consensus. Traditional liberal rights of freedom were too broadly framed to significantly constrain the state's institutions. Hitler and the Nazis made the Weimar Constitution's basic rights – and many other provisions – a cynical front for their horrific regime. In that era the Imperial Court served as the institutional base for Hitler's *Volksgerichtshof* (People's Court).

Today the Federal Court of Justice sits in Karlsruhe and Leipzig with a presiding President of the Court and another 150 judges serving in collegial fashion in six criminal law Senates and thirteen civil law Senates. Each Senate is assigned from six to eight judges. But a Senate seldom acts with its full complement of judges. Instead, it usually hears cases as a *Sitzgruppe* (panel) of five judges. The FCJ is responsible for last-instance appeals in civil law and criminal law matters. In that role it hears *Revisionen* (appeals) from decisions of the lower, state-administered *Amtsgerichte*, *Landgerichte* and *Oberlandesgerichte*. It is the keeper and definitive interpreter of Germany's esteemed Civil and Criminal codes. It is a widely-respected tribunal, both inside and outside Germany, even if its jurisprudence remains of greatest interest to sitting German judges and practicing German lawyers. The Federal Court of Justice is widely thought to engage in a rather traditional and dogmatic jurisprudence that seems well-suited to its Karlsruhe residence – the Neo-Baroque palace once occupied by the Grand Dukes of Baden. The limits on the FCJ's progressive potential is reinforced by two conservative factors. First, the Court's judges are successful career jurists who often are promoted from the state-administered courts. Appointment to the FCJ with life-tenure follows vetting and election by the Judicial Selection Committee, which is convened by the Federal Ministry of Justice and consists of the 16 state-level ministers of justice and 16 members of parliament. This is a conservative talent pool selected by a conservative institution. Second, civil law appeals can be brought before the FCJ only by specially qualified lawyers who gain admission to this practice upon approval of the Federal Minister of Justice. The small, insular, and elite Federal Court of Justice Bar currently numbers fewer than forty lawyers all of whom have offices in provincial Karlsruhe. There is little diversity or dynamism in this group.

* * *

Questions/Comments

- What does it mean to say that the German judicial system is "decentralized"? What are the benefits of this arrangement?
- The Free State of Bavaria provides a charged example of the way in which decentralization can "localize" justice, supposedly as a way to enhance the legitimacy of the judicial function. Bavaria is "just" one of the Federal Republic's sixteen *Länder* (federal states). But even beyond FC Bayern Munich's dominance of German professional soccer, Bavaria is special. The one-time kingdom clings to its traditional identity, which consists of a strong local dialect, staunch Catholicism, *Altbayern Lederhosen* suits and *Dirndl* dresses, alpine folk music featuring accordions and yodeling, and sausage-heavy cuisine washed down with beer sloshing out from one-liter (or larger!) *Steins*. Munich, the state's capital city, is home to the annual *Oktoberfest*, an exaggerated and excessive enjoyment of these expressions of the local culture. Bavaria proudly exercises the maximum degree of residual autonomy held by the states in Germany's federalist system. After all, it is the only West German territory that did not ratify the new post-war Basic Law.[26] And, Bavaria's center-right conservatives (which have unvaryingly held power in the state) operate as an independent and local political party, the Christian Social Union, that nevertheless reliably partners with the national Christian Democratic Union. One expression of Bavarian identity involves the tradition of hanging a crucifix in public buildings, including in courtrooms. That

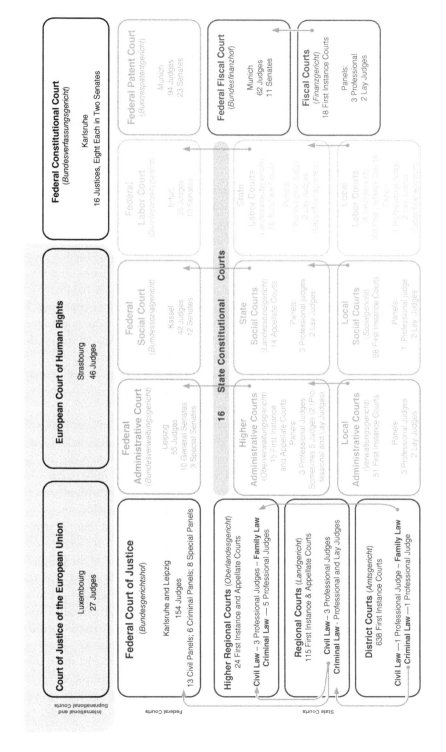

Figure 5.3 German Court System

is not the practice elsewhere in Germany. The public display of crucifixes in Bavaria has been the subject of extensive and rather complex court rulings, such as the canonical *Crucifix Case* (1995) from the Federal Constitutional Court, which found the crucifixes hanging in Bavarian classrooms to be unconstitutional.[27] Still, a controversial order requiring the display of a crucifix in the reception area of state offices was recently upheld by the Bavaria Administrative Court.[28] The Bavarian justice ministry insists that the presence of the crucifix in courtrooms "expresses the Christian tradition of our polity."[29] How is the decentralization of the judicial system, which tolerates this and other local practices or peculiarities, helpful for the administration of justice?

- The excerpted text describes the German judicial system as "specialized" and explains that each jurisdiction is associated with a discrete regime of positive law, likely involving a particular codification. When they are confronted with this framework, American law students – who are accustomed to their system's courts of general jurisdiction – invariably worry: How does a lawyer know which specialized jurisdiction to invoke, and what happens if the lawyer files his or her action in the courts of the "wrong" subject matter jurisdiction? Are the courts in your primary or "national" legal system also specialized? How would you put these American law students at ease? Does the specialization of the German courts relate to the predominance of the Civil Law tradition in the German legal culture?

- Can you name the six specialized jurisdictions in the German judicial framework? Does that list strike you as complete, or has some area of law – some segment of life – fallen through the cracks?

- In the next chapter you will learn about German legal education and the legal professions. But, describing the German judiciary, Langenbacher concluded: "The socioeconomic background, recruitment, and professional socialization of judges would seem to make for a rather conservative group oriented toward the status quo."[30] Does the worldview of a judge matter in a system heavily influenced by the Civil Law tradition?

- One respected German judge was concerned that the demographics of the judiciary presented risks for the legitimacy of German courts. He argued that, if courts are meant to rule "in the name of the people," then the "judiciary stands and falls with the question of whether a plurality of society is reflected in the judiciary."[31] He saw reassuring signs of progress in the growing number of women serving as judges. One detailed study showed that, by 2015, the "number of women judges [had] risen to 46% (out of 20,500)" and that "more than 50% are taken in annually, which means that their numbers will keep on rising."[32] In 2022, nine of the sixteen judges at the revered Federal Constitutional Court were women. Nevertheless, there is problematic evidence that women do not enjoy the same career success in the German judiciary as men do. "They move up the ladder slower than their male colleagues and we can notice glass ceiling effects. The bulk of women are gathered in the local courts of first instance [...]. In all jurisdictions, their share in positions in the appeal courts is too low compared to their overall number, age and time of service."[33] Ulrike Schultz has researched the status and effect of women in the German legal profession for decades. One of her large studies (concerned with women in the judiciary in the state North Rhine-Westphalia) identified a number of barriers to women's advancement as judges. Most troubling was the finding that gender stereotypes still play a role. Schultz reported: "Men and women in the judiciary are unable to free themselves from stereotypical perceptions. [...] This has a direct impact on the leadership structure which follows a male model. 'Leadership posts are a man's game' said one of our female interviewees. From the start, women are expected to have lower career ambitions than men, they are regarded as less suited for a career due to 'typically female qualities' [...]. They are 'the Other' that might endanger the traditional institutional image."[34]

- The Federal Court of Justice has more than 150 judges. Why so many? Does such a large number of judges say something about the way Germans think about the law?
- The judges at the Federal Court of Justice usually sit in panels. That is typical throughout the German judicial system, with a few notable exceptions. First, in private law matters the "ground level" first-instance courts (known as the *Amtsgerichte* or local district courts) conduct much of their business with a single judge. Second, in criminal law matters, the mid-level first-instance courts (known as the *Landgerichte* or regional courts) sit as a bench of three professional judges and two lay judges. The lay judges (*Schöffen*) should not be confused with jurors in the Anglo-American tradition. Still, their presence helps to legitimize the work of the criminal courts in part by ensuring that the perspective of nonprofessional jurists is included in the courts' deliberations.

5.5 Conclusion

Germans can be proud of their public institutions and system of governance, including the elements presented in this chapter: federalism, the legislative branch, the executive branch, and the judicial branch.

In terms that might be equally attributable to the other branches, the promotional brochure *Law – Made in Germany* praises German courts for being "independent, fast, and cost-effective."[35] These qualities have been confirmed by a number of global and regional studies. In part, the strengths of the Germany judiciary and other governing structures are the fruit of deep traditions that are still relevant and help to shape the contours and character of these institutions.

Perhaps, as an example of this, one court's architecture can be used to represent the present-day power of tradition in the Germany judiciary. A commentator, describing the Moabit Court Complex in Berlin (see Figure 5.4), explained that:

Foyer With Steps of the Criminal Court in Berlin-Moabit, 2018. Wikimedia Commons

Figure 5.4 Tradition Shapes Modern German Governance

today [it] houses both a division of the [local district court] and a division of the [regional court], and all criminal matters in the City of Berlin are decided here. The court building with its surrounding structures is one of the largest complexes of its kind in all of Germany, with almost two hundred judges working in the local court division alone. Built in 1906, this impressive Neo-baroque structure, considered one of the finest examples of architecture from the reign of Emperor Wilhelm II, has survived almost intact throughout the course of the tumultuous twentieth century, avoiding even the bombs of World War II. When members of the public enter through the main portal, they are greeted by a twenty-nine-meter-high vestibule containing an impressive and ornate staircase.[36]

For more than a century, generations of judges, advocates, defendants, prosecutors, and claimants have passed through the grandiose entryway at the Moabit Court, as if court proceedings in Germany continue in an unbroken stream of justice across the years. Much of what passes for judicial proceedings in the Moabit Court today would look familiar to the jurists who worked in its courtrooms 100 years ago. Much the same could be said of Germany's administration, which draws on Prussian tradition for its contemporary structures and practices. The most significant modern change in governance has been the post-war emergence of a settled and thriving democratic culture animating effective, representative lawmaking institutions and an impressive executive tradition embodied by the Federal Republic's powerful chancellors.

Further Reading

- Eric Langenbacher, *The German Polity* (Rowan & Littlefield) (12th ed. 2021)
- *The Oxford Handbook of German Politics* (Klaus Larres *et al.* eds.) (Oxford University Press) (2022)

- *Public Administration in Germany* (Sabine Kuhlmann *et al.* eds.) (Palgrave-Macmillan) (2021)
- Hugh Ridley, *Law in West German Democracy: Seventy Years of History as Seen through German Courts* (Brill) (2020)
- Geoffrey Roberts, *German Politics Today* (Manchester University Press) (3rd ed. 2016)
- *The Routledge Handbook of German Politics & Culture* (Sarah Colvin ed.) (Routledge) (2015)
- Arthur Gunlicks, *The Länder and German Federalism* (Manchester University Press) (2013)
- Donald P. Kommers & Russell A. Miller, *The Constitutional Jurisprudence of the Federal Republic of Germany* (Duke University Press) (3rd ed. 2012)
- Geoffrey K. Roberts, *German Electoral Politics* (Manchester University Press) (2006)
- *German Political Party System* (Christopher S. Allen ed.) (Berghahn Books) (1999)
- Gerard Bruanthal, *Parties and Politics in Modern Germany* (Routledge) (1996)

NOTES

1. Andreas Follesdal, *Federalism*, in THE STANFORD ENCYCLOPEDIA OF PHILOSOPHY (Edward N. Zalta ed., Summer 2018), https://plato.stanford.edu/archives/sum2018/entries/federalism/.
2. ERIC LANGENBACHER, THE GERMAN POLITY (12th ed. 2022).
3. New State Ice Co. v. Liebmann, 285 U.S. 262, 311 (1932) (Brandeis, J., dissenting).
4. RODERICK CAVALIERO, GENIUS, POWER AND MAGIC 103 (2013).
5. GRUNDGESETZ FÜR DIE BUNDESREPUBLIK DEUTSCHLAND [GG] [Basic Law], art. 70(1).
6. *Id.* at art. 83.
7. *Id.* at art. 92.
8. *See, e.g.,* Katrin Auel, *Between Reformstau and Länder Strangulation? German Co-operative Federalism Re-considered*, 20 REGIONAL & FEDERAL STUDIES 229 (2010).
9. *See* Printz v. United States, 521 U.S. 898 (1997); New York v. United States, 505 U.S. 144 (1992).
10. GRUNDGESETZ FÜR DIE BUNDESREPUBLIK DEUTSCHLAND [GG] [Basic Law], art. 21(1).
11. "Members of the German Bundestag shall be elected in general, direct, free, equal and secret elections. They shall be representatives of the whole people, not bound by orders or instructions and responsible only to their conscience." *Id.* at art. 38(1).
12. *See* PETER QUINT, CIVIL DISOBEDIENCE AND THE GERMAN COURTS: THE PERSHING MISSILE PROTESTS IN COMPARATIVE PERSPECTIVE (2008).
13. *See* JOSE ANTONIO CHEIBUB, PRESIDENTIALISM, PARLIAMENTARISM, AND DEMOCRACY (2007).

14 The Federal President takes the following oath when assuming his or her office: "I swear that I will dedicate my efforts to the well-being of the German people, promote their welfare, protect them from harm, uphold and defend the Basic Law and the laws of the Federation, […]." Grundgesetz für die Bundesrepublik Deutschland [GG] [Basic Law], art. 56. Among his or her duties are: the authority to convene a session of the parliament; the representation of Germany in international law as the head of state; formal certification of appointed ministers, civil servants, judges, and military officers; formal nomination of the chancellor to be elected by his or her majority in the parliament; formal appointment of the chancellor following his or her election by the parliament; approval of the rules of procedure for the function of the federal government; dismissal of the chancellor should he or she lose a vote-of-no-confidence called by the parliament; dissolution of parliament in the event the chancellor loses a vote-of-confidence called by the chancellor; declaration of a state of emergency permitting deviations from ordinary governing processes; counter-signing legislation as the final step in the promulgation of law; and declaring the initiation or termination of a state of military defense.

15 *Id.* at art. 33.

16 KURT SONTHEIMER, THE GOVERNMENT AND POLITICS OF WEST GERMANY 135 (1972).

17 GRUNDGESETZ FÜR DIE BUNDESREPUBLIK DEUTSCHLAND [GG] [Basic Law], art. 65.

18 Sabine Kuhlmann *et al.*, *German Public Administration: Background and Key Issues*, in PUBLIC ADMINISTRATION IN GERMANY 1, 5 (Sabine Kuhlmann *et al.* eds, 2021).

19 *Id.*

20 LANGENBACHER, *supra* note 2, at 273.

21 Kuhlmann *et al.*, *supra* note 18.

22 *See* Cristina Burack, *German Efficiency: The Roots of a Stereotype*, DEUTSCHE WELLE (Mar. 28, 2021), https://p.dw.com/p/3r47W.

23 MAX WEBER, ECONOMY AND SOCIETY: AN OUTLINE OF INTERPRETIVE SOCIOLOGY (Volume 3) 973 (Guenther Roth & Claus Wittich eds., Ephraim Fischoff *et al.* trans., 1968).

24 LANGERNBACHER, *supra* note 2, at 278.

25 *See* GRUNDGESETZ FÜR DIE BUNDESREPUBLIK DEUTSCHLAND [GG] [Basic Law], art. 97(1); Gerichtsverfassungsgesetz [GVG] [Courts Constitution Act], May 9, 1975, BGBl. I at 1077, last amended by Act, June 25, 2021, BGBl. I at 2099, art. 4, § 1.

26 The charter entered into force, also against Bavaria, because a requisite supermajority of the other states ratified the Basic Law.

27 Crucifix Case, BVerfGE 93, 1 (1995).

28 Thomas Balbierer, *Richter weisen Klagen gegen Söders Kreuzerlass zurück*, SÜDDEUTSCHE ZEITUNG (June 2, 2022), www.sueddeutsche.de/bayern/bayern-kreuzerlass-verwaltungsgerichtshof-klagen-1.5596617. It seems that it is only tradition that keeps crucifixes in Bavarian courtrooms, even while the law now prohibits court personnel from wearing openly religious symbols. *See* Henning Ernst Müller, *Bayerischer Verfassungsgerichtshof verbietet Kreuze in*

Gerichtssälen! Oder?, BECK-COMMUNITY (Mar. 20, 2019), https://community.beck.de/2019/03/20/bayerischer-verfassungsgerichtshof-verbietet-kreuze-in-gerichtssaelen-oder.

29 *Richter entfernt Kruzifix dauerhaft aus seinem Gerichtssaal,* WELT (Jan. 23, 2018), www.welt.de/politik/deutschland/article172745863/Bayern-Richter-entfernt-Kruzifix-fuer-immer-aus-seinem-Gerichtssaal.html.
30 LANGENBACHER, *supra* note 2, at 291.
31 Hans-Ernst Böttcher, *The Role of the Judiciary in Germany*, 5 GER. L. J. 1317, 1323 (2004).
32 Ulrike Schultz, *Judiciary and Gender Topics – German Experience and International Perspectives*, 24 E-CADERNOS CES (Dec. 15, 2015), https://journals.openedition.org/eces/1998#text.
33 *Id.*
34 Ulrike Schultz, *"I was noticed and I was asked …," Women's Careers in the Judiciary. Results of an Empirical Study for the Ministry of Justice in North Rhine-Westphalia, German*, in GENDER AND JUDGING 145, 161 (Ulrike Schultz & Gisela Shaw eds., 2013).
35 LAW – MADE IN GERMANY (2009), www.lawmadeingermany.de/Law-Made_in_Germany.pdf.
36 Stephen Ross Levitt, *The Life and Times of a Local Court Judge in Berlin*, 10 GER. L. J. 170, 176 (2009).

6

Foundations III

Legal Education, Legal Method, Legal Actors

Key Concepts

- **Richter**: The German word for "judge."
- **Staatsanwalt**: The German word for "public prosecutor."
- **Rechtsanwalt**: The German word for "attorney."
- **Einheitsjurist**: The goal of German legal education is the development and training of "complete" or "full" jurists competent to serve as members of the judiciary. These *Einheitsjuristen* have completed a university education, two intensive state exams, and a lengthy practical training program. Even if the training is oriented to service on the bench, this status grants access to the broader legal profession, including work as a prosecutor or a lawyer. The qualification is general and does not permit a legal professional to develop much in the way of specialization until the beginning of one's professional career.
- **Referendariat**: Two-year period of practical legal training during which aspiring German jurists gain exposure to the work of several traditional legal roles: civil court judge, criminal court judge, public prosecutor, civil servant, and attorney. One commences the *Referendariat* after completing the full program of legal studies at a university and passing the first state exam. During the *Referendariat* the trainees are supervised and given instruction by assigned practitioners. These years also are used to prepare for the intensive second state exam.
- **Claim Relationship**: The all-important first step in the method used to address private law cases in Germany. In this step it is determined who might have a claim against whom. This is necessary in order to proceed with an analysis because these relationships will frame and delimit the possible legal causes of action.
- **Hypothetical Cause of Action**: The second step in the method used to address private law cases in Germany. In this step, based on identified claim relationships, a potential cause of action is identified, including the relevant legal elements (often conceived of as a syllogism – if x, then y).
- **Private Law**: Norms governing interactions among persons (natural or artificial). In its paradigmatic Lockean incarnation, private law provides the means of enforcing whatever bargained-for agreement competent individuals freely conclude.[1]

- *Public Law*: Norms pertaining to allocation and exercise of public authority or to the vertical relation between public authority and persons to the extent that public authority imposes an obligation on persons or directly confers a right or entitlement on persons.[2]
- *Lustration*: Processes used by governments in Central and Eastern Europe to purge public officials whose communist backgrounds or political sympathies were thought to disqualify them for service in post-communist societies.

Study Tips

The Ministry of Justice and Federal Office of Justice provide English-language translations of a number of important German codes and statutes at the website "Gesetze im Internet" (www.gesetze-im-internet.de/). This includes the *Deutsches Richtergesetz* (DRiG – German Judiciary Act) and the *Bundesrechtsanwaltsordnung* (BRAO – Federal Lawyer's Act).

This book's survey of the foundations of the German legal system continues – and concludes – here with glimpses into how legal professionals are trained (legal education), how they pursue their work (legal method), and the various roles they can assume (focusing particularly on judges and attorneys).

The principal actors in the German legal system are judges (*Richter*), public prosecutors (*Staatsanwälte*), lawyers (*Rechtsanwälte*), and legal scholars (*Rechtswissenschaftler*). Their functions and roles are specialized. But all of them receive the same foundational training – the same professional socialization – through Germany's unique system of legal education.[3] The goal of this program of education and training is the development of *Einheitsjuristen*, which roughly translates into something like a "complete jurist." For more than a century, modern German legal education and training has succeeded in minting highly skilled legal practitioners who have found great success at home and around the world. One reason for this success is the efficiency, efficacy, and surprising portability, of the distinctly formalistic and systematic legal method Germans learn at law school and continue to refine in their careers on the bench and at the bar. By now you will expect that these professional roles differ from their counterparts in other legal systems. That is especially true of those legal systems in which the Common Law tradition is predominant. But, as you will see in this chapter, it also applies to the character and function of judges and lawyers in the former East Germany, which was largely aligned with the Socialist Legal tradition.

6.1 Legal Education

Despite the highly skilled legal professionals it produces, German legal education is one segment of the German legal system that has not won admirers around the world. Of the top-100 global law faculties in the *Times Higher Education* "World University Rankings," only three are based in Germany.[4] Language dims German law schools' international standing. Dominating these global rankings, Anglo-American law faculties clearly enjoy the windfall of the English language's status as the world's *lingua franca*.

German legal education also has its skeptics at home. The eighteenth-century poet, playwright, and philosopher, Johann Wolfgang von Goethe, is the most important literary figure in the German language. His vast body of work helped shape the spirit of the Enlightenment, defined literary Romanticism, and conditioned the German language. Maybe his most important work is the dramatic poem *Faust*, which retells the legend of the student (Faust) who promises his soul to the devil (Mephistopheles) in exchange for human enlightenment and wisdom.[5] I mention the epic poem here because Goethe was a jurist by training, having studied law (at his father's insistence) in Leipzig and Strasbourg. He hated his law studies and was a famously petulant and, ultimately, unexceptional student.[6] One senses a bit of autobiography in the disdain Faust and Mephistopheles heap on the study of law in Germany as the two discuss Faust's academic plans.

Student [Faust]:	I respectfully solicit your favor and protection. I come with the best inclination, A good disposition and coin in moderation. My mother with reluctance gave me leave to roam, But something good I'd like to learn away from home.
Mephistopheles:	To the right place you happen to have come,
Student [Faust]:	Indeed if I the truth must say, I'd like to go again away, Nor any longer here to stay. All is confin'd within these halls— Naught to be seen by dingy walls— Nothing that the eye can please— Neither green grass nor lofty trees; And in these rooms, and on these benches, I lose my hearing, sight, and sober senses.

* * *

Mephistopheles:	Tell me now which faculty would suit you best!
Student [Faust]:	For the law I think I have no taste.
Mephistopheles:	To that I cannot blame much your aversion. I know the ins and outs of that profession. In succession right and law descend, Like a hereditary disease that comes never to an end.

> They glide from race to race,
> And softly steal from place to place.
> Reason then becomes nonsense,
> And a plague benevolence.
> But woe to you, should you a grandchild be!
> The sense of right with which all are created,
> Will in your case be quite obliterated.
>
> *Student [Faust]:* You make me dislike the law exceedingly.

Based on Stefan Korioth's description of legal studies in Germany, excerpted below, it is fair to wonder if Goethe would be any more enthusiastic about studying law today. In any case, the system Korioth presents changed little in more than a century,[7] and it has stubbornly resisted major reform in the decades since he published the article.[8]

Stefan Korioth
Legal Education in Germany Today
24 WISCONSIN INTERNATIONAL LAW JOURNAL 85, 85–86, 90–94, 96–99, 103–106 (2006)[*]

* * *

German legal education has four main characteristics. First, legal education is separated into two stages. The first stage consists of legal studies at university law faculties in a program of at least four years. This first stage is followed by a compulsory practical training (*Referendarzeit*, or apprenticeship) of two years. [...]

Second, both stages end with a state examination covering the entire scope of the law. Students do not specialize in training for specific legal professions. Only the last reform of 2002 introduced a certain degree of specialization during legal study; this is examined by the law faculty but counts for the state examination.

Third, after successfully passing both state examinations, the young lawyer, at this stage called an *Assessor*, is theoretically qualified to adopt any legal profession, including that of a judge. The second examination provides a uniform qualification for all legal professions. German legal education produces the so-called *Einheitsjurist*. Only a few young lawyers, however, become civil servants, judges, or public prosecutors. Most of them practice as *Rechtsanwälte* (attorneys at law), as only a formal admission to the bar is required for *Assessoren*.

Fourth, legal education in Germany is strongly regulated by federal and state law. Its focus lies on the judiciary. Law faculties and lawyers traditionally have had very little impact on the frame of legal education. Only recently has their influence grown; the 2002 reform has strengthened their position.

Each of these characteristics has been in question since the 1950s, with the debate about the necessity of reforms, and the direction they should take, peaking during the late 1960s and again in the 1990s. In the end, only a few details have changed. Apart from these small alterations, legal education has remained unamended, despite social and economic changes. [...]

* * *

---

[*] Excerpt reprinted with permission of the author and the *Wisconsin International Law Journal*.

Unlike students in other countries, German law students begin legal studies without an undergraduate degree. At the age of nineteen or twenty, after thirteen years of school (nine years in the *Gymnasium* with the uniform final examination/graduation *Abitur*), most students go directly to a university. There is no admission test for law students. Students can choose the law faculty they want to attend. Only in cases of overcrowded law faculties can students be refused, and those not accepted are guaranteed a place at another university. Studies are free of charge. Law faculties are not allowed to establish admission exams.

This easy access to the university system results in a high number of students. Some students soon find out that they have chosen the wrong subject. About 20 percent or more change their subject or leave the university before taking the First State Examination, but the number of college dropouts is regressive.

* * *

Today, universities struggle with cuts in state contributions. While the number of students has doubled in the last thirty years, neither the number of teaching staff nor the amount of funding has increased. As one example of the student-teacher ratio, the law faculty of the Ludwig-Maximilians-Universität Munich has thirty full professors and about fifty-five full time assistants (who teach and do research under the supervision of a professor) for four thousand law students. [...]

According to section 5a, subsection 1 of the [German Judiciary Act], legal studies at university normally take four years. The average duration is, in fact, about five years at the moment, including six months for the first examination. Since the reform of 2002, this examination is no longer called the state examination because 30 percent of it is now organized by the law faculties. The remaining 70 percent is still organized by the ministry of justice of the states (*Bundesländer*). The board of examiners is made up of practitioners and university professors. As the frame of the legal education system is set by federal law, legal education is almost completely standardized throughout the country. The reputation of a law faculty plays a minor role in the students' choice of university compared to Anglo-Saxon countries, especially the United States.

* * *

During the four years at university, all law students have to cover a wide range of compulsory subjects (*Pflichtfächer*) and an elective subject (called *Wahlfach* until 2002 and now called *Schwerpunktbereich*). In addition, universities require students to learn a foreign language, either in a lecture or in a language class. Students also must complete a practical stage of at least three months during the breaks.

This frame, binding upon the legislation of the states, is set by the [German Judiciary Act] in Section 5a. It also prescribes the compulsory subjects: the main elements of civil law, criminal law, public law, procedural law, and the law of the European Union; legal methodology; and the philosophical, historical, and social foundations of the law. The optional subjects are not set by federal law. [...]

To a great extent, law education at university still consists of formal lectures, a one-way presentation by the professor or the assistants. [...] In addition, besides the lectures there are seminars and study groups in which lecturers and students work together on the subjects. The standards for the students are high.

As the system deals primarily in abstract, theoretical concepts and is formed systematically rather than through the influence of case law, students must learn to evaluate concrete situations in light of abstract norms. [...]

The "great lectures" in civil, criminal, and public law are attended by two hundred to six hundred students at the larger law schools. Thus, students and professors have little personal contact, about which both groups complain. The lectures in civil, criminal, and public law are accompanied by compulsory tests during the term (*Übungen*). In written examinations and papers, the students must give legal opinions for a set of hypothetical facts, applying statutes, legal doctrines, and cases to draw up a proper legal report. Students are required to render impartial opinions for the facts presented. They are taught to deal with the facts and the law from a judge's point of view.

Because the focus is on rendering impartial decisions, in general, students are not trained to take adversarial positions during their studies at university. [...]

* * *

Between 50 and 90 percent of the students, depending on local customs, rely on the expensive services of private repetition classes, where they are taught the required knowledge during the preparation period for the state examination. The reason for this is, first of all, a psychological one: as students have to pay for and attend these classes regularly, they show a certain discipline which cannot be ensured at a law faculty. Moreover, students often think that professors are unable to teach them in a manner that is suitable for the preparation of the First State Examination. Law faculties are trying to keep up with the private repetition classes by offering special preparation classes which, of course, are free of charge. Most faculties are more and more successful with these programs.

First Examination

The First Examination is a comprehensive final examination. It covers all the knowledge acquired during all semesters at the university. It consists of a written and an oral part. Students take between seven and eleven written exams in which they have to give legal opinions on hypotheticals related to civil, criminal, and public law. Each exam is evaluated by a professor and a practitioner. The oral part, which composes about 30 percent of the examination, takes four to six hours. Two professors and two practitioners, usually judges, form the board of examiners and examine four students.

Most students think the State Examination is very demanding. They are right. It is a great challenge to have complete command of the entire law in force at the time of the examination. In addition, the students do not know in advance which professors and practitioners are going to examine them. Thirty percent of the candidates fail to pass the First Examination successfully, and only 10 percent reach a level above average. The examination period is about six months, mainly because the exams have to be evaluated and a date for the oral examination has to be set. The examination may only be re-taken once, unless the student made use of the possibility of a "free shot," which is granted if the exam is taken before the ninth semester.

Practical Training and the Second Exam

Practical Training

The First Examination marks the end of legal study at the university and opens the way to the second and practical stage of legal education. All successful students, now called *Referendare*, obtain a practical training, the *Vorbereitungsdienst* (preparatory service). Section 5b of the [German Judiciary Act] sets the legal framework for practical training, which is filled out by the requirements imposed by state legislation. During the two years of this preparatory service, the *Referendare* have the special status of civil servants and receive a salary [...]. The aim of the preparatory service is to train the *Referendare* in the practical work of jurists in the main legal professions. Practical instruction takes place in several compulsory stages (civil court, criminal court, public prosecutor's office, administrative agency, and the law firm). In an additional, optional stage, the *Referendar* can choose any legal profession, training again at court, but also in parliaments, ministries, companies, international organizations, churches, and elsewhere.

During each stage, the *Referendar*, to whom a supervisor is assigned, has to draft legal documents of the respective profession. *Referendare* mainly learn to write a court decision.

Prior to the reform of 2002, the practical training had little focus on lawyering skills like negotiation, advocacy, and legal advice, but now more emphasis is placed on these skills. [...]

Second Examination

The Second, or Great State, Examination marks the end of legal education. As in the first examination, the candidates take from eight to twelve written tests and have to pass an oral examination. In contrast with the First Examination, the Second Examination aims at testing practical skills, and the board of examiners consists exclusively of practitioners. Again, the examination is very demanding. Only 15 percent reach a level above average. The results of this examination are very important for a lawyer's career, especially in the beginning. After passing the Second State Examination, the *Referendar* becomes an *Assessor*. He or she has spent at least six or seven years, and in most cases, eight or nine years, undertaking the study of the law. The *Assessor* is qualified for any legal profession, including that of a judge.

* * *

Legal Education Reform: An Unending Story

The reform debate is as old as the legal education system itself. Some aspects have been criticized again and again, and some reproaches are new, due to the challenges of European integration and globalization. For every change in legal education, the [German Judiciary Act] and the state legislation have to be amended; this makes it difficult to introduce major changes. Some reforms took place during the last few decades; the most recent one, implemented in 2002, was intended to emphasize the lawyering skills most students would need in their career. Also, elective parts of the study became more important. However, the two-stage approach with accompanying state examinations remained unchanged.

It is the long duration of the legal education for which today's system is most often criticized. [...]

A second complaint about the current system concerns its broad educational content. The system of the *Einheitsjurist* requires that all students have broad knowledge in all fields of law until they have passed the Second State Exam. It is often doubted whether it is sensible for a company lawyer to be experienced in criminal law, planning law, and family law, or whether a public prosecutor needs to learn property law in detail. [...]

The third complaint is closely connected with the second one. The examination is very demanding and has colossal dimensions. The eight or eleven written examinations and the oral examination cover years of university study. However, though the system is hard, it proves again to be fair and a suitable way to find the best candidates.

In my view, the main problem of legal education in Germany today is the great number of students who face the general problem of overcrowded classes. [...]

* * *

6.1 Legal Education

Last but not least, it will be necessary to question the division of theoretical education at university and practical training during the second stage of legal education. [...]

* * *

The decision to keep the *Einheitsjurist* as the product of the legal education system [has been] the right one. The *Einheitsjurist* is qualified to work in any legal profession – as a lawyer in a law firm, in the public administration, and as a judge – after having successfully completed the study, the practical training, and the examinations. Even if the scope of the law tends to widen and becomes more diversified and complicated, holding on to the ideal of a broad legal education prevents loss of the overall view of the law.

* * *

Questions/Comments

- Korioth characterized the work of judges as "impartial" and notes that German legal education is keyed to developing that demeanor, as opposed to the demeanor of an advocate. What assumptions about the law and judging does this claim reveal? How does this claim point to the broad influence of the Civil Law tradition on legal education in Germany?
- With a bit of sharp irony, Karl von Lewinsky drew a direct line between the university facet of German legal education and the predominance of the Roman Law and the Civil Law tradition in the German legal system:

    [University] lectures are like a map, showing the student all the different ways, high roads and side trips which he will have to take not only during his university course but through his entire life as a lawyer. At the same time, he is guided to the main street entering the Kingdom of European Continental Jurisprudence by two courses of lectures – one in the history of Roman law and one on the fundamental principles of Roman law. He comes to know and to admire, in these lectures the most striking and – at least for the European continent – the most important creation which mankind has ever produced in the province of Jurisprudence. The admirable system of Roman law and the clear everlasting truth of its general principles are the good sharp tools with which the German student has to erect and to work out the building of his knowledge, and which help him to understand, to revive and to systematize the seemingly dead letters of codes and statutes. [...] The second and third half year are devoted almost entirely to the exact study of the new German civil code. [...] All these lectures are presented in a merely theoretical, scientific way, without reading cases and without question and answer. [...][9]

- How might the period of practical training (*Referendariat*) that follows university studies and the first state exam help perpetuate the "ideal image" of the civilian jurist that Kantorowicz painted in the excerpt in Chapter 3?
- The German program for legal training is depicted in Figure 6.1. It consists of university education, first state exam, *Referendariat*, and concludes with the

Figure 6.1 The Path to Becoming an *Einheitsjurist*

second state exam. Those who complete these steps are fully eligible to take a position in the German judiciary. What does the fact that newly qualified jurists can become judges – in their late twenties or early thirties – say about the role of judging in a system influenced by the Civil Law tradition? Are your conclusions in reaction to that question affected by the reality that German jurists embark on their training directly after completing the *Abitur* (secondary education certificate or high school diploma), a fact that means that they do not generally have the benefit of studying another discipline before their legal education (as American law students must do in order to earn a Bachelor's degree and, thereby, qualify to enroll in law school)?

- Describe an *Einheitsjurist*.[10] As the goal of German legal education, how is an *Einheitsjurist* different – in competence, skill, and jurisprudential vision – to someone who has completed his or her basic legal education and training in your primary or "national" legal system?
- Korioth identified a number of problems that plague legal training in Germany: (1) it takes too long (typically nine to eleven years); (2) there is an overwhelming number of courses piled into the core curriculum in the university program; (3) the examination system is time consuming, repetitive and unrealistic; and (4) students are chiefly trained for service as judges despite the fact that very few *Einheitsjuristen* are hired as judges. Korioth concluded that there is consensus among policymakers and the profession that these issues must be answered with comprehensive reform. Are there similar calls for reform of legal education and training in your primary or "national" legal system? At least in the United States, there is constant demand for reform of legal education. A decade ago, there was great pressure for American law schools to add practical value by ensuring that graduates were "practice-ready."[11] This led to dramatic overhauls of the curriculum to include skills-based courses and clinical programs.

Today there are demands that legal education actively combat entrenched racism, in part as a way of preparing a new generation of anti-racist leaders for American law, business, and politics.[12] To account for these concerns, law schools are adapting traditional courses, adding new courses, hiring new administrators, and establishing new programs. What do these evolving reform agendas say about the understanding of the law and legal education in the American system? What values inform the critiques of the German system identified by Korioth? Why do you think American legal education might be so amenable to change while the German program seems to resist it?

Another criticism of German legal education is that it has not adapted to fulfill Germany's obligations under the European Community's mandate to lower barriers to a European-wide market in legal services. This development has gained ever-greater meaning in the years since Korioth published his article. As part of European integration, the Bologna Process was initiated in 1999 with the aim of creating a common European higher education framework in which standards and programs are harmonized and credentials become more widely accepted and transportable within the EU. In pursuit of these objectives Germany's proud and ancient university tradition passed through a convulsive period of reform, the chief components of which were the creation of: (1) the "Bachelor's" degree awarded following an initial three- or four-year program of study focused on a required curriculum of courses; and (2) the "Master's" degree awarded following a one- or two-year program of study focused on research. This was a radical departure from the traditional, less structured course of study that led to the *Diplom* at German universities for the last centuries. Under the pre-Bologna system many university students took six or seven years to earn the *Diplom*, a leisurely pace cited as a problem by Korioth and a phenomenon not in the least discouraged by the fact that there are no, or only very minimal, fees charged for attending university in Germany.[13] The powerful faculties of law and medicine at most of Germany's universities secured exemptions from the broader Bologna reform process that imposed dramatic changes on all other faculties in Germany's universities. The pressure to accommodate these European reforms has not quieted. Germany's private law faculties now offer programs leading to a Bachelor of Laws (LL.B.) after three years of university study.[14] But standing alone, this degree does not entitle a student to enter the traditional legal professions as an *Einheitsjurist*. That coveted professional status requires the student to pursue additional university studies, sit for the first state exam, participate in the lengthy program of practical training, and sit for the second state exam. One argument offered in favor of the grudging emergence of a law-based Bachelor's degree is that it leaves students with some marketable academic credential even if they stumble out of the rigorous program that is meant to lead to full professional qualification.

6.2 Legal Method

Matthias Reimann argued, in a prominent lecture delivered at the prestigious Max Planck Institute for Private International Law in Hamburg, that "American-trained jurists enjoy an advantage in global lawyering because their conception of law fits the contemporary global legal order better than the continental European (and more broadly, civil law) understanding."[15] In particular, Reimann insisted, "the American conception of law is inherently more pluralistic, pragmatic, and political."[16] If there's any truth to that critique, then the distinct legal method drilled into German law students during their time at the university and in their practical training – and almost unfailingly deployed by German judges and lawyers long after they leave the university – must bear some of the blame. That method, sometimes referred to as the "step method" of legal analysis, is described in the following excerpt from Lutz-Christian Wolff.

Lutz-Christian Wolff
Structured Problem Solving: German Methodology from a Comparative Perspective
14 LEGAL EDUCATION REVIEW 19, 22–29, 33–34, 51 (2003)[*]

* * *

[…] German legal education and also, consequently, Germany's legal profession, is dominated by a certain methodological approach when it comes to the structuring of private law problem solving. Historically, this methodology has been developed since the 1950s and has been acknowledged and "picked up" in a more substantial way by academics during the 1980s. The major textbook introducing this approach was written by Dieter Medicus and first published in 1968. However, to date there has hardly been any deeper scholarly discussion of this approach and its scientific justification. Further, it is interesting to note that such a methodological approach seems to have one of its main origins not in academic writings, but in the training provided by private lecturers (so-called "Repetitoren") who act outside the (public) German universities. The up to two-year-long courses offered by these private lecturers are designed especially to prepare students for the state examinations and are attended by the major proportion of German law students.

The Step-by-Step Method

Generally speaking, according to the aforementioned methodological approach, private law problems in Germany are to be solved on a step-by-step basis as follows:
   Step 1 Analysis of the facts of a problem in order to determine and identify claim relationships between different parties;
   Step 2 Identification of a legal rule as the hypothetical basis of a specific claim;
   Step 3 Identification of the preconditions for the application of such a legal rule and examination that these preconditions have been fulfilled, that is that the claim has been established;
   Step 4 Verification that the original claim is still with the claimant;
   Step 5 Examination of the enforceability of the claim.

---

[*] Excerpt reprinted with permission of the author.

Following is a more detailed discussion of these different steps, in particular their significance for the problem-solving process.

Step 1: Obtaining Control over the Facts

In order to be able to identify the legal questions that are to be answered as an initial step, the facts of a given problem/dispute must be analysed. For this purpose, claim relationships, that is actual or potential claimants and defendants, must be identified. In other words, "Who Wants What from Whom?"

For the sake of transparency and in order to avoid confusion, it is necessary in this context that relationships between different parties ("Who from Whom") must be "broken down" to two-party relationships. Only the analysis of claim relationships between two parties guarantees the possibility of a clear distinction between the (potentially different) legal situations of different claim relationships. [...] If more than one claim relationship can be identified, then all of them have to be analysed on a separate basis, as further explained below.

The same applies with regard to the object of the claim (the "What"). If different objects of potential claims are to be discussed, then for the sake of transparency a separate analysis for each object is required. [...] Again, this is due to the fact that [...] joint examination may cause confusion.

Step 2: Identification of a Hypothetical Legal Basis of the Claim

The next step in the legal analysis of a problem is the identification of a hypothetical legal basis for a specific claim of each party against another party. A claim only exists if it is acknowledged by the law, that is, if it can be based on a legal rule. Consequently, it is necessary to start out with the identification of such a rule as the basis of a claim. This identification can at this stage only be accomplished on a hypothetical basis since the final decision requires verification as to whether or not all claim-related preconditions have been fulfilled, that is if such rule can really serve as a legal basis for the related claim. Nevertheless, it is necessary to start out with the identification of such a hypothetical legal basis of a claim in order to be able to determine the direction of any further analysis, that is, in order to decide which preconditions must be fulfilled for the establishment of the claim. Consequently, it is regarded as methodologically incorrect if the analysis of a claim relationship starts with a specific, but abstract, legal question, even if such a question were the main problem.

Which rules can serve as the basis of a claim? Only legal rules may function as the basis of a claim [...]. These rules can either be found in the law itself or in contractual provisions on the basis of which one party (the claimant) has the right to request the other (the defendant) to do something, or not to do something. The question as to which legal rule can serve as the basis of a claim is determined by two aspects. First, the related rule must, as a matter of fact, stipulate the legal consequence that one party (the potential claimant) has a claim against the other (the potential defendant). Related rules always take a conditional approach as follows: "If ... [=identification of pre-conditions], then ... [= legal consequence: claim of claimant against defendant]."

The second aspect that needs to be considered for the identification of a legal rule as basis of a claim (only) comes into play where the claimant requires a specific legal consequence. In such a case the potential basis of the claim must lead to exactly such a consequence.

In a particular situation it may be possible to base a claim on different legal rules. In this case, a comprehensive legal analysis would have to deal with all of the rules which support the claim in order to be able to assess all existing alternatives. But, again, the examination must distinguish between different legal rules, claim relationships and the object of such claims for the sake of precision, transparency and in order to avoid confusion. In the event that more than one hypothetical basis of a claim has to be analysed, it is generally assumed that a special order of examination should be observed. [...].

Step 3: Analysis of the Preconditions of the Claim

[...] The identified hypothetical basis of the claim [...] determines the sequence of further legal analysis.

For the purpose of examining (in step 3) whether or not the preconditions for the application of a certain rule that shall serve as the basis of a claim have been fulfilled, again a two-step examination is necessary. First, the related preconditions need to be identified on an abstract basis. Having identified the preconditions (on an abstract basis) one must examine if, in the current situation, these preconditions have been fulfilled. If the preconditions have been fulfilled, then it can be concluded that the claim has been established. Otherwise, the examination of this particular claim basis must be stopped here for the value of efficiency. The final conclusion would then be that the respective legal rule cannot serve as a basis for the claim.

Step 4: Verification that the Original Claim is Still with the Claimant

If the examination in Step 3 has led to the result that the claim has been established, then further legal analysis is necessary. This is because the fact that the claim has (once) been established does not necessarily mean that the claimant is still holding this claim. There are basically three reasons why this may no longer be the case: (i) the claim could have been transferred to another party (e.g., by way of assignment agreement); (ii) the claim could have been extinguished (e.g., by way of fulfilment or termination); or (iii) the claim could have been amended (e.g., through conclusion of an amendment agreement). It is logical to analyse these questions only after the examination of Steps 2 and 3 above, because only the establishment of the claim allows for its transfer, extinction or amendment.

The examination should only be continued if it can be concluded at this stage that the claim is still with the claimant. If the claimant has lost the claim for whatever reason, then the analysis must be stopped here in order to avoid superfluous work.

Step 5: Examination of the Enforceability of the Claim

Even if – as a result of the examination in Steps 2 to 4 – the claimant still holds the original claim, it must finally be analysed if the claim is enforceable. A claim is only enforceable if it is not permanently or temporarily blocked by defences. The unenforceability of a claim would not affect its existence as such, but would block its realisation for reasons set forth by substantive law.

Reasons for the (permanent or temporary) lack of enforceability could, for example, be that the (statutory or contractual) time limit for bringing in a suit has expired (permanent obstacle to enforceability) or that the claimant has failed to fulfil corresponding obligations (temporary obstacle to enforceability), which enables the defendant to refuse performance. The enforceability of a claim must be examined at this final stage because only if a claim has been validly established and is still (unchanged) held by the claimant can its enforceability be questioned.

Language

Legal language should always correspond with the contents discussed. As suggested by the above step-by-step method, the legal analysis of a problem can never start out with the final result. On the contrary, the final result must be developed step-by-step. German legal education emphasises that the language used by law students should reflect such step-by-step verification of an initial hypothesis by using the conditional form. Such language is supposed to correctly reflect the real sequence of examination in order to provide the reader with an understandable, comprehensive and thus convincing answer of the related legal questions. This style is called "*Gutachtenstil*" ("legal opinion style").

It must be noted at this point that in German legal practice documents are often not drafted in this cumbersome and time-consuming way. In particular, language used by German courts for their judgments does not follow the above order, but states the conclusion first and then argues why such a result is correct. Consequently, this style is called "*Urteilsstil*" ("judgment style"). It needs to be kept in mind also, however, that German judges do not know the outcome of their legal examination of a dispute from the beginning and therefore have to carry out their examination on the basis of a hypothetical assumption of the outcome. The wording of German judgments does not reflect correctly such a work order.

* * *

Justification of the Step-by-Step Method

* * *

[…] [The] sole criterion which allows for the assessment of different methodological approaches is the criterion of efficiency. Efficient problem-solving stands for methodological optimised problem solving by way of the application of a logical, precise and clear work order. If one legal method is more efficient than another then the more efficient method must be regarded as superior. In other words, the most efficient problem-solving method should prevail over others.

* * *

The step-by-step method, as it was introduced above, complies with the requirement of efficiency, in fact it embodies efficiency. The predominant objective and result of its application is to identify and solve legal problems as early as possible and to deal with those questions first which are predetermining for others. No more efficient way of structured problem solving is available. Because efficient problem-solving is inherent in the step-by-step method, this may be regarded as its major advantage.

* * *

Summary and Kiss of Death

German legal education and consequently also German legal practice is dominated by this step-by-step approach.

The late Karl N. Llewellyn once advised a young colleague never to identify an idea as being based on foreign law because such a revelation would be "the kiss of death." Accordingly, it is not the intention of this article to suggest that any German methodology should be applied also in other jurisdictions. As it was demonstrated in this article, however, the above step-by-step method is neither a product of any specific country or culture nor is its application limited to any single jurisdiction. It rather gives expression to the logical sequence a lawyer would always follow when analysing claim relationships in the most efficient way. The step-by-step method is therefore a logical result of efficient problem solving and applicable and inherent (sometimes as tacit knowledge) in any private law system. Acknowledging the significance of the step-by-step method facilitates the utilisation of this methodological tool, which guarantees efficient problem solving. Ignoring this significance means to neglect the impact of efficiency on successful legal work.

Questions/Comments

- Is Reimann correct to conclude that the German legal method described by Wolff is not adequately pluralistic, pragmatic, and political? At least as Wolff understands it, the step-by-step method has an immense and inherent pragmatic quality: it is more efficient than any other legal method. Do you agree that the method described by Wolff is not "a product of a specific country or culture"?
- Christian Boulanger defines "legal doctrine" as the institutionally legitimized practices of making statements on what the law is."[17] Isn't he referring to "legal method," such as the German step-by-step system outlined by Wolff? The aim of that method is to efficiently and definitively discover what the law says about a particular dispute. Boulanger explains that Germans use the words "*Dogmatik*" or "*Rechtsdogmatik*" when speaking about their legal method. What other fields of study – what other professions – are concerned with "dogma" or "dogmatics"? Are you surprised to find that label used to describe a jurist's analytical work in the law?
- Wolff reduces Step 1 in his five-part analysis to the question: "Who Wants What from Whom?" This might be expanded – and reformulated – by adding Steps 2 and 3 (hypothetical legal basis and preconditions of a claim), so that the applicable phrase becomes: "Who Wants What from Whom on Which Basis?" In fact, this is the condensed version of the analysis German law students learn.
- Steps 2 and 3 in the analysis described by Wolff are concerned with identifying the rule applicable to the case, including its controlling elements. Does the method permit the German jurist to argue for the existence, or about the content, of the rule to be applied? Or, is the law already settled, requiring merely that the applicable rule be identified? Wolff explains: "The rules can either be found in the law itself or in contractual provisions." With respect to this question, which of the theorists discussed in Chapter 3 seems to have prevailed: Kantorowicz, Kelsen, or Radbruch? In a legal system influenced by the Common Law tradition advocating for the existence or distinct content of a rule would be part of a jurist's analysis because the court itself can be the author of the rule to be applied to the case. Analogizing to or distinguishing existing precedent, or perhaps making an argument about justice based on social science, a Common Law lawyer makes a claim about what the law in his or her case should be. The different approach to identifying the applicable law in the methodology of these traditions says almost everything you need to know about the distinction between the Civil Law and Common Law traditions. Why?
- Bernhard Großfeld wondered whether the application of Germany's highly formalistic and systematic legal method might hinder creativity.[18] This seems to be a part of Reimann's claim as well. In response to this critique Wolff argued: "This argument can only be correct if the step-by-step method

is regarded or used as a legal instrument which replaces substantive law as such or if it is used as a mere checklist without reflecting about the rationale behind it. However, methodology can never replace substantive law and should also not be applied for its own sake. On the contrary, methodology is only the tool used to apply and implement substantive law efficiently. If this methodological functioning is kept in mind then the claim approach and the step-by-step method do not at all hinder legal creativity but can provide major input for a disciplined and structured jurisprudence." Does Wolff claim that there is room for creativity in the step-by-step method he has described? Or, does he claim that creativity in the law is to be achieved elsewhere?

- In any case, Wolff seems satisfied that, if the German method discourages creativity, then it compensates for that weakness by delivering considerable efficiency. But why is efficiency so important? What other values, as the basis for a legal order (and its prevailing legal method), would you prioritize?
- Could you reduce the problem-solving approach or method in your primary or "national" legal system to an invariable five-step checklist (adding or subtracting a few steps if necessary)?
- Many German law students who come to the United States for a Master of Laws (LL.M.) program find the absence of a prevailing and clearly articulated legal method a supreme frustration. It is hard to know where to begin when trying to solve a legal problem without the benefit of a step-by-step checklist. That makes the outcome of cases – and thereby, the law itself – less determinate: The law is harder to identify and apply. Maybe the root of the Germans' frustration lies in the fact that they have internalized the idea that a jurist's task is to "solve" a legal problem. The German word for "solve" is *lösen*. When trying to orient these students to their new legal habitat I explain that American lawyers don't imagine themselves to be "solving" a legal problem, in the supposedly objective, nearly mathematical manner that the German method implies. Instead, they understand that they are advocating for their client's eventual triumph in the dispute. The equivalent word in German is *verfechten* (a variation on the word for fencing or dueling). American lawyers aren't working to "solve" a case, they're trying to "win" it. That mandate calls on the jurist to grasp for any resources or tools that might help his or her client prevail. An effective and professional interpretation and application of the law (i.e., the deployment of the acceptable legal method) is just one of those tools. What other resources might a lawyer reasonably resort to when advocating for his or her client? And what about those frustrated German law students in America? They often fall back on the logic and structure of the German legal method when writing their American law school exams – and they regularly get excellent grades. Why is that?
- James Maxeiner summarized the lack of a systematic method in American law, and the resulting indeterminacy, in this way: "Legal indeterminacy is a perennial issue in American law. In the first half of the twentieth century

American legal realists developed it to challenge formalism. In the second half, proponents of Critical Legal Studies used it to attack the rule of law itself. In this century, Professor Frank Upham concluded that notwithstanding American proselytizing for the rule of law, the structure of the United States legal system makes its realization 'literally impossible.'"[19] Do you agree that Germany's formalistic legal method is an essential assurance of the rule of law and the achievement of justice?

Wolff narrows the application of the method he describes to the private law. Different methods operate in public law and criminal law cases. Before I summarize the different methods used in other fields, however, I should comment on the distinction between private and public law that these different approaches take for granted. The distinction between private law and public law is a central means of framing the law in Germany. This begins with the obligation that law schools mandate courses in these *Pflichtfächer* (mandatory subjects), including private law, public law, and criminal law (but now also extending to procedural law and European law).

Like so much you have and will encounter in this book's survey of German law, the division between private law and public law is, in part, a legacy of the Roman Law.[20] Roman Law recognized a distinction between the *ius civile* (civil law) and the *ius publicum* (public law). On the one hand, private law regulates relations between individuals (including natural or artificial persons) and typically extends to the subjects with which Roman civil law was concerned: property law, the law of obligations (contract and tort), family law, and the law of succession. Private law facilitates and fosters the cherished notion of *Privatautonomie* (private autonomy), which is a general expression of individual freedom. The free and equal autonomy promoted by private law is thought to be essential for a "functioning social order at the 'grassroots level' because it expresses trust in and makes legal institutions available for the initiating power and market engagement of civil society."[21] On the other hand, public law was concerned with the more remote interests of the Roman state. Today, it is understood that public law regulates the exercise of public authority, including those instances in which state actions touch the interests of an individual. Public law establishes and manages sovereign power as opposed to individual autonomy. It does this primarily through constitutional law and administrative law. With its uniquely profound impact on citizens' lives (victims and criminals) and its highly specialized aims, criminal law represents a special subset of public law. It is the law concerned with the "*strafende Staat*" (punishing state).[22]

The private/public dichotomy retains significant power in German legal culture. As I mentioned earlier, the curriculum at German law schools is built on this framework. In fact, law scholars are categorically classified along these strict lines, with some professors exclusively teaching and researching private law subjects while other professors teach and research public law or criminal law.

When I was studying at the University of Frankfurt the professors of private law and public law used different elevators to reach their separate wings of the old *Juridicum* (law faculty building) on the Bockenheim Campus! The private/public distinction also informs the foundational codification of law in Germany and the resulting, specialized jurisdictions that I described in Chapter 5.

Not everyone is convinced by the classification of separate fields of private and public law. Marx suspected that the dichotomy was part of a capitalist ideology that advantaged the property-holding bourgeoisie, who were treated as the workers' equals by the private law (despite their immense advantages in wealth, power, and access) and who were insulated from democratic or popular intrusions on their power by the notion of private autonomy.[23] More recent critiques condemn the distinction between private law and public law with claims of "collapsing" incoherence and irrelevance. Duncan Kennedy, for example, noted that both fields of law consist of rights, privileges, and obligations that are created, assigned, adjudicated, and enforced by public power.[24] This suggests that all law is an extension or delegation of public authority and are rightfully subjects of public law. It is easy to see, for example, that the private law field of family law touches upon significant public policy concerns that might be regulated by public law. The imposition of the constitutionally ordained "objective order of values" on the private law (described briefly in Chapter 3 and again more fully in Chapter 8) embraces some measure of this critique in German law.

Not every legal system insists on a strict conceptual dichotomy between private law and public law. In Germany the distinction is entrenched and it leads to different private law and public law methods. When compared with the multistep method Wolff describes for the private law, the method applied in public law and criminal law cases is less systematic and intricate.

Public law, encompassing constitutional law and administrative law (presented in Chapters 8 and 9), involves just two overarching questions: *Zulässigkeit* (Is the case admissible?) and *Begründetheit* (Are the merits of the case well-founded?).[25]

First, the issue of admissibility is addressed. Out of respect for the democratic mandate given to the state, admissibility of a claim against an act of public authority is strictly defined and delimited. Public law causes of action are specified by the *Bundesverfassungsgerichtsgesetz* (Federal Constitutional Court Act) and the *Verwaltungsgerichtsordnung* (Code of Administrative Court Procedure). There are specific admissibility requirements for each discrete cause of action, but they typically involve the issue of standing, the question whether the subject matter is covered by public law, formal requirements for pleading and filing, and an assessment of the need for judicial intervention (similar to questions about ripeness or mootness in the American legal tradition).

Second, it must be determined if the merits of the claim are well-founded. The method asks whether the state's action conforms with the relevant constitutional law or administrative law provisions. This part of the analysis is less susceptible to a systematic method because it is dependent on the distinct elements of the relevant substantive law. Only in the context of complaints brought by individuals asserting a violation of basic rights do we find a prescribed and elaborate method in the substantive part of a public law case analysis. In those cases, the courts are required to enforce the constitutionally mandated *Verhältnismäßigkeitsgrundsatz* (proportionality principle), which tolerates intrusions on constitutional rights only if they are found to be proportional.[26] That determination involves a carefully crafted assessment with several highly formalized and extensively theorized steps: (1) determining whether the state's objective, and the means chosen to accomplish it, are *legitimate* (pursuing public interests as ordained by law); (2) determining whether the means chosen are *suitable* to achieving the state's objective (with considerable deference given to the state, so long as the means can support the realization of the objective); (3) determining whether the means chosen are *necessary* to achieve the state's objective (there is no less-intrusive option available); and (4) determining whether the means chosen are *reasonable* ("proportional" in the narrow sense), which requires the conclusion that the benefits of the policy or state action outweigh the harm done by the state's infringement of a basic right. This proportionality analysis is so habitually deployed by practitioners and courts, and in such a disciplined manner, that it is possible to say that this four-step assessment – as much as the material rights protections themselves – has become the essence of the constitutional guarantee of basic rights in Germany.

The **criminal law** method will be presented in greater depth in Chapter 10, not the least because some parts of the analysis represent very distinct features of German criminal law. For this summary, however, the following points are insightful.

First, in contrast to the method applied in public law cases, a criminal case analysis requires a careful mapping of the actors and facts so that a closed and complete legal frame is created for each actor and each potential criminal law violation. This is similar to the establishment of discrete "claim relationships" in Step 1 of the private law method described by Wolff. But rather than the "Who Wants What from Whom" inquiry in the private law method, in the criminal law analysis this assessment should establish "Who Did What to Whom."

With those issues preliminarily resolved, several questions remain in a criminal law analysis. It must be determined whether the facts proven in the case align with the specific elements of a statutorily established crime (*Tatbestandsmäßigkeit*). Any statutory limits on prosecution for the relevant crime must be addressed. It must be determined whether the defendant acted wrongfully (*Rechtswidrigkeit*), or whether he or she had an objective justification for the criminal conduct. It must be determined whether the defendant was culpable (*Schuld*), or whether he or she had a subjective excuse for the criminal conduct. In some cases, it is possible to proceed with a prosecution only if the victim files a complaint pressing for criminal charges. In those cases, it is necessary to show that a *Strafantrag* was filed, or to make a showing, absent a complaint, that a "special public interest in prosecution calls for *ex officio* intervention."[27] Finally, if a defendant is found guilty after these determinations, the court must settle on the punishment within a range of fines or a term of imprisonment proscribed by the specific criminal law provision in question. Here, too, it is possible to assess the defendant's "guilt" as part of a consideration of aggravating and mitigating circumstances.

Whether private, public, or criminal – all fields of law nevertheless use a common and well-established method of statutory interpretation that involves four key approaches in the following order of priority:[28]

- *Plain-meaning*: Interpretation of the provision's exact wording and syntax, involving the question: What do the discrete terms and requirements mean?
- *System*: Interpretation looks to the location of a provision within a legal act (under what heading; in what chapter, section or book) and considers what meaning can be derived fom surrounding provisions.
- *History*: Interpretation considers what led to the enactment and current form of the provision, especially assessing how the law developed over time. You might ask, for example, whether the legislator deliberately departed from a previous rule when last changing the provision.
- *Teleology*: Interpretation strives to determine what the provision wanted to achieve and seeks to advance that aim. But determining the law's purpose is a matter of assessing its history and its context. It is not a subjective assessment aligned with one's policy ambitions.

6.3 Legal Actors: Judges and Lawyers

German lawyers and judges benefit from folklore surrounding these two professions, a folklore that is largely reflective of the significant influence of the Civil Law tradition in Germany.[29]

Two points receive special attention with respect to German judges: judicial independence and the judiciary's active control over and management of legal proceedings. For example, the promotional brochure *Law – Made in Germany* declares that German judges are "[…] independent in their rulings [… everyone] litigating in Germany can rely on the independence of German courts."[30] The brochure then praises the dominant role played by German judges in shaping and managing legal proceedings: "[a]s early as the first hearing, the matter at hand is discussed with the parties and their lawyers, with the judge providing guidance as to the issues that he or she considers relevant. This enables the parties to adapt their litigation strategies, saving both time and money […]"[31] You will learn more about the priority placed on German judge's independence and the control they exercise over their proceedings in Chapter 11's presentation of German procedural law.

The promotional brochure *Law – Made in Germany* also describes lawyers as independent. But their competence is given greater weight:

> In Germany, you have access to highly qualified legal experts, who are proficient in several languages and have a good understanding of other legal systems, gained during the course of extended stays in the relevant countries. You can therefore rest assured that your concern or request will be treated with the highest level of competence and professionalism and that you will be given thorough and qualified legal advice by lawyers [… who] are independent and work as self-employed professionals. They provide comprehensive legal advice and are entitled to act on your behalf before all courts and in relation to all government authorities. [...] Lawyers represent the interests of their clients and assert and enforce their claims.[32]

I want to conclude my presentation of the foundations of German law with an examination of the folklore surrounding these key actors in the German legal system. Before moving on, however, it is necessary to note that there are a number of other important legal actors that will receive no treatment here.[33] Among these, Germany's respected and powerful legal scholars might be the most important. After all, John Merryman and Rogelio Pérez-Perdomo claimed that "[t]he teacher-scholar is the real protagonist of the civil law tradition. The civil law is the law of professors."[34] Indeed, it would be a grievous omission to neglect the central role scholars play in the life of German law, which is so strongly influenced by the Civil Law tradition. I tried to give them their due in Chapter 2, in which the Civil Law tradition is introduced in general terms.

Up to this point in the book I have rather loosely referred to "Germany," "German law and legal culture," or to the "German legal system." This portrayal of Germany isn't completely accurate, even if it might have been fair for me to assume that you understood that I mean the Federal Republic of Germany and the legal system in operation there today. But, in light of this book's self-professed objective to identify the diverse threads that make up the tapestry of German law and legal culture, it must be said that my reference to the unified, contemporary German legal system crudely glosses over a dramatic and profound source of diversity.

It has only been a few short decades since East Germany (the German Democratic Republic or GDR) and West Germany (the Federal Republic of Germany or FRG) achieved their wholly unexpected reunification after almost a half-century of Cold War dismemberment. The two Germanys sometimes seemed to be caricatured proxies in the struggle between two determined ideologies. That meant that their respective legal systems, although sharing important German traditions and operating in some instances only the width of the wall apart from one another, were self-consciously dedicated to contradictory values and sought to advance conflicting principles. Most respectable surveys of postwar German law at least try to acknowledge this schizophrenic situation. But East German law is usually relegated to asides or footnotes or cursory paragraphs. And why not? The result of unification was the accession of the East German

6.3 Legal Actors: Judges and Lawyers

territory to the Federal Republic of Germany, including the extension of West Germany's legal system to those "new federal states." Law in Germany today, in the former East and former West, means the law of *West Germany*. Moreover, East Germany's reputation as one of the most relentlessly repressive of the East bloc's socialist dictatorships serves to heavily discount, if not altogether dismiss, its jurisprudential traditions and contributions. Radbruch, who you read in Chapter 3, might have reminded us that it is "law" we are talking about here, not the "statutory lawlessness" of the East German Communist Party.

At this point, however, I'd like to briefly break from this book's habit of neglecting the East German legal system. I want to consider the values and practices of East German judges and lawyers as a foil – as a comparative irritant – for emphasizing the prevailing expectations for those roles in the West German (now unified Germany's) legal culture.

There are several reasons for choosing this framework. First, and most importantly, my determination to embrace legal pluralism as this book's guiding mandate cautions against a reactionary rejection of legal systems (such as East Germany's) on the basis that they do not look and work like "ours." The examination of the character and role of East German judges and lawyers I undertake here should give you the chance to try out your critical flexibility (Frankenberg's "distancing"?) and comparative law open-mindedness (Frankenberg's "differencing"?) on a *repudiated and retired socialist legal system*. A second reason to devote some attention to the East German legal system at this point is that doing so marks the historic development of reunification, which was a thoroughly legal process,[35] while at the same time noting that, by many measures, the process of unifying East and West Germany is far from complete. The festivities marking the twentieth anniversary of reunification in 2010 were clouded by evidence of the lack of integration by former Easterners. That challenge doesn't seem to have abated in the succeeding decades, as we approach the fortieth anniversary of reunification. Germans talk of a *Mauer im Kopf* (wall in the mind) that continues to divide the country roughly along the lines of the Berlin Wall. One common response has been the conclusion that unification was achieved without unity. This glance at the East German legal system, then, might serve as a modest acknowledgment of the presence of the quiet millions of former East Germans who (at least for another generation or two), when they think of "German law" or the "German legal system," bear an awareness of two Germanys and two legal cultures.

There is a final justification for this brief consideration of the character and role of East German judges and lawyers as a lens for thinking about the character and role of (West) German lawyers and judges. As I suggested above, it is valuable because it presents a contrast – a counterfactual – to the prevailing folklore surrounding German judges and lawyers today. That is not just a clever academic trick. As Inga Markovits describes, the newly unified German authorities, dominated by Westerners, overlaid their vision of these legal actors on the East German past in making momentous decisions about whether East

German judges and lawyers had the right to continue their legal careers in unified Germany. Where an East German judge or lawyer was disqualified in that lustration process, the West German understanding of those professions served as the underlying standard.

Inga Markovits
Children of a Lesser God: GDR Lawyers in Post-Socialist Germany
94 MICHIGAN LAW REVIEW 2270, 2271, 2275–2276, 2278–2280, 2282, 2284, 2292–2295, 2298–2299, 2303, 2305 (1996)[*]

* * *

In this essay, I want to investigate German vetting policies by looking at one particular subgroup of examinees: GDR lawyers. In Germany, no other former socialist elite has been submitted to so thorough an ideological cleansing process as the legal profession. After reunification, all GDR judges and prosecutors hoping to remain in office had to undergo investigations that by March 1994 had left only 9.2% of their former numbers in permanent positions. Virtually all East German law professors were removed from their university posts. More than 5000 attorneys in Germany's eastern half are currently being examined for former contacts with the State Security apparatus *(Stasi)* and other transgressions. And of all prosecutions for "government crimes" committed by socialist officials, between 75% and 80% are directed at former judges and prosecutors accused of miscarriages of justice.

* * *

[... Our] first question should be: who *were* these East German lawyers?

Unlike Western lawyers, who are jacks-of-all-trades and are present wherever power and influence is wielded in capitalist countries, East German lawyers (like those of other East European states) were not generalists, but trained to be specialists. After a common start, East German law students were divided into two subgroups: future judges, attorneys and prosecutors followed the "justice" curriculum, while those meant to serve as legal counsel to the state-owned economy *(Justiziare)* followed the "economics" curriculum. [...]

[...] All in all, the [East German legal education] system was geared to produce reliable, cooperative, unselfish technocrats, trained in the application of state rules to that particular area of public endeavor for which they had specialized. Unlike capitalist lawyers, East German lawyers were not preoccupied with processes but with state-defined outcomes.

* * *

How useful were socialist lawyers to the state or their clients? Let us begin with the judges. From its earliest days, adjudication in the GDR was seen as an exercise in political authority. Judges were functionaries rather than watchmen, aligned with and dependent upon the state rather than charged to supervise its activities. Clashes between individual and government were not considered proper subjects for judicial inquiry. The law should not stand between the socialist state and its citizens. [...]

* * *

[...] East German civil litigation [...] concerned itself with social and interpersonal relationships. Accordingly, East German judges would focus not so much on the efficient

---

[*] Excerpt reprinted with permission of the author.

6.3 Legal Actors: Judges and Lawyers

processing of private claims as on education and peacekeeping. They were expected to investigate thoroughly the social context of disputes and could do so at their own initiative. Even hearings in minor civil cases, by West German standards, took very long: between one-half and one-and-one-half hours. Criminal cases might take even longer. "We started out with the primordial swamp," a judge once told me, by which she meant: we investigated a defendant's entire social career beginning from childhood. [...] East German judges primarily seem to have seen themselves as educators and social workers.

[...] Uwe-Jens Heuer, formerly a member of the GDR Academy of Sciences [...], once called the East German political system "*eine Erziehungsdiktatur*" ("a pedagogic dictatorship"), and GDR judges were very much the products of that system: authoritarian, didactic, strict towards the obstinate and willful, lenient towards the repentant and submissive, and, by Western standards, remarkably willing to assist the court's clients in their day-to-day troubles. Every Tuesday, during the court's "legal consultation" hours, judges gave free advice to countless citizens. They mediated between warring spouses or neighbors, helped track down debtors of alimony or support obligations and saw to it that they paid, made sure victims of crimes received compensation from their attackers, and always were available to collectives or social organizations in need of a speaker. [...] Unlike our judges, whom we think of as detached umpires between competing individual interests, socialist judges were political functionaries committed to asserting the parental authority of the state.

* * *

Attorneys [were] outsiders. [...]

* * *

Even once in court, East Germans would rarely use the services of an attorney. Under GDR procedure, representation by counsel was mandatory only in first-instance criminal trials before a regional court or in cases before the Supreme Court, that is, primarily in murder or treason cases. All other cases could be tried without a lawyer. There are no national figures on how many citizens chose representation anyway. Official GDR statistics, although very thorough on other issues, apparently considered the participation of legal counsel too insignificant to warrant registration. According to my own data, in 1979, 15.3% of all civil litigants and 5.6% of all criminal defendants in Lüritz [the invented name Markovits attributes to the former East German town where she concentrated her research] had hired a lawyer to represent them. Unlike Westerners, who would consider legal help most indispensable in confrontations with as powerful an opponent as the state, East Germans apparently found lawyers more useful in areas removed from state authority. Towards the end of the GDR, growing disaffection with the system seems to have led its citizens to a greater appreciation of attorneys: by 1988, in Lüritz 21.1% of all civil parties and 16% of all criminal defendants were represented in court. [...]

* * *

[... It] was a far more ambiguous and contradictory system of judicial control than Westerners usually will allow. East German legal doctrine never renounced the concept of "judicial independence" proclaimed in the GDR Constitution. Judges were not to be told how to decide individual cases, and if they were, it was possible to resist that kind of crude and unveiled interference, at least in later years. But they were meant to get their answers "right": not to find fair solutions by impartially applying formal rules to some private dispute of concern only to the participants, but to find the politically correct solutions to social ills whose diagnosis and remedy usually had already been prescribed by the Party.

Only a legal system that does not claim to know all the answers (and therefore does not favor one prospective outcome over another) can place its faith in procedural justice.

Socialist law believed in substantive justice: it knew the answers (even if those answers changed over time) and therefore had to make sure that each individual judge would find them. Hence the innumerable instructions, analyses, inspections and consultations constantly keeping judges abreast of the current political line. The Party, in this scheme of things, was the medical authority on all social ills. The judge was the local practitioner treating the patient. The responsibility – according to the official claim – remained his or hers in each individual case. The GDR Ministry of Justice's official catalogue of the qualities required in future judges thus listed both "political steadfastness and an unfaltering commitment towards the Party" and a character trait likely to undermine that commitment: "*Zivilcourage*" – the courage to speak up in the face of authority.

* * *

[… The East German legal system was distinctly positivist]: East German judges liked to stick closely to the letter of the law since it could be trusted to reflect authoritative Party positions and, at the same time, provided shelter against interferences from the outside. […]

What follows for the attitudes of East German lawyers toward that central element of our legal faith: our respect for legal forms and procedures? Leaving aside the "antiformalism" and "antineutralism" of its earlier years, the East German legal system, throughout most of its history, stressed the importance of legal order and discipline. Law was the Party's blueprint for building socialist society and had to be carried out religiously. "Socialist legality" was defined as the "strict observance of the law combined with Party spirit" (again, the attempt to square the circle), and while the "Party spirit" introduced uncertainty and manipulability into the equation, the "strict observance of the law" was something socialist legal officials could hold onto. East German judges and prosecutors were taught to work in an orderly manner and with care, to investigate each case thoroughly and to follow exactly prescribed procedures. If local courts occasionally got their signals wrong and slipped (no wonder, given the fundamental inconsistency of the official demands for both precision and partisanship), regional courts (who, as a Lüritz judge put it, could be "real sticklers for form") would usually call them to order. Regular court inspections from above made sure that everyone at the trial court level followed the rules. Reports of such inspections provide detailed, even finicky, accounts of the inspected judges' compliance, or lack thereof, with whatever provisions governed their work.

But the East German regard for rules lacked jurisprudential conviction. […]

* * *

It is this different attitude toward form which lies at the heart of most cognitive dissonances now clouding East-West German interactions. I have had difficulties, for example, explaining to East German lawyers why that popular GDR practice of judges regularly giving legal advice to citizens whom they might later encounter as plaintiffs or defendants in the courtroom might conflict with judicial impartiality; why trials conducted before an "invited public" to drive home a particular moral lesson must have favored a particular outcome of the case and therefore could not be called unprejudiced; or why in reunited Germany neofascists cannot more easily be locked up. Even if East German judges observed what to us looks like demands of procedural fairness, they often would do so for motives quite different from our own. […]

* * *

To sum up, East German legal professionals were not generalists but specialists, with relatively brief and narrow training, much lower status than Western jurists, little professional cohesiveness, accustomed to close supervision and control, unaggressive, supportive rather than critical, inexperienced in the free-for-all of Western litigation, and probably without much respect for, or even understanding of, the significance of legal forms. No doubt about it – they were different. As the second man in the Berlin Administration of Justice, Detlef Borrmann, once told me: "They don't fit." For Undersecretary Borrmann, it was this lack of fit rather than any individual guilt that justified the Berlin policy of excluding all but 15% of East Berlin's judges and prosecutors from the united city's administration of justice.

But then, how could they "fit"? East German jurists are the products of their society, and it would be miraculous if they were not. Their entire country, one might argue, "does not fit," emerging, as it is, from a confining, coddling, and manipulating system of government in which law that needs freedom, contention, private property, money, and a market to flourish played only a minor role. East German citizens, in this sense, "do not fit": used to withdrawing from an overbearing state into their private lives, inexperienced in the interactions of civil society, unaccustomed to being left out in the cold, afraid of the competitiveness of the market, unfamiliar with its laws. As Gregor Gysi once said: East German citizens lived "as in a monarchy." Rules did not always hold, connections counted more than entitlements, decisions were never final, law just as easily could give way to leniency as to oppression.

* * *

I have drawn a contradictory picture of East German jurists: different from ourselves, yet also similar; both in line and at odds with the society they come from; not quite socialist fish nor capitalist fowl. […]

* * *

In the event, West German reconstruction policies excluded no other East German professional group from participating in the remaking of their own country as thoroughly as legal professionals. Today, those former judges and prosecutors who passed the vetting process are, as a rule, too young, too inexperienced, and too preoccupied with learning the ropes to be able or willing to push for reform. East German lawyers presently in private practice – most of whom are not former attorneys but ex-judges, - prosecutors, -jurisconsults, and newly admitted *Diplomjuristen* – are struggling to survive in the new market and also are unlikely to peddle reform proposals with the smell of socialism. Former socialist academics have disappeared from East German law faculties. As a result, the legal debate in the Federal Republic is dominated by Westerners. When in 1991 the German Association of Administrative and Constitutional Law Teachers convened to discuss East Germany's integration into the rule of law, not a single East German law teacher spoke up and, for all I know, was even invited. When a year later the first post-reunification Convention of German Lawyers took place in Hannover, of the roughly 2600 participants, only about twenty-five had come from the new East German states. East German jurists do not appear at national meetings, have no real voice other than the PDS [Democratic Socialist Party, the successor to communist East Germany's Socialist Unity Party of Germany. The latter has now morphed into The Left Party] and the journal *Neue Justiz* (the first considered disreputable, the second ignored by most Westerners), and are unlikely to leave a mark on the profession. The rule of law in Germany's Eastern half – conceived by Westerners, built by Westerners, staffed with Westerners, and, by all signs, efficiently and smoothly run by Westerners – is likely to remain for some time a largely Western enterprise.

* * *

Questions/Comments

- If today's German judges and lawyers are independent and competent, then what terms would you use to describe judges and lawyers in East Germany? How do the two images differ? Do you see any similarities?
- One difference Markovits emphasized is the fact that East German jurists were specialized, which contrasts with generalist training of the West German *Einheitsjuristen*. Interestingly, greater specialization has been one of the suggestions for reform of the system of legal education in (West) Germany.
- Does Markovit's description of East German lawyers align in any way with the "ideal image" of the Civil Law jurist painted by Kantorowicz in the excerpt in Chapter 3?
- One of the East Germans who gained prominence in unified Germany (alongside former Chancellor Angela Merkel; former Federal President Joachim Gauck; and Michael Ballack, former captain of the German men's national soccer team) was the lawyer Gregor Gysi. Gysi was the last chairman of the East German Socialist Unity Party, ascending to that short-lived role after the collapse of the East German system had become inevitable. He led the party through reunification and various restructurings and rebranding efforts thereafter. Ultimately, Gysi served as chairman of The Left Party's parliamentary group in the *Bundestag*. He deserves much of the credit for repositioning the former communists as a credible, post-reunification political party with constituents even in the former West German states. Besides his political activities, Gysi was one of only a few independent lawyers in East Germany. In that capacity he occasionally represented critics of the East German regime. After reunification, Gysi represented prominent clients, including some of the heirs of Richard Wagner, Germany's most celebrated and characteristic opera composer. Does Gysi's career and important public standing following reunification blunt Markovits' criticism of the way in which East German jurists (and East Germans generally) fared in the revolutionary process of reunification?
- Does Markovits' portrayal of East German justice, as administered by judges and lawyers, seem keyed to the statutory positivism and formalism that characterizes the Civil Law tradition? East German jurists, we are told, sought to realize the socialist state's values. Did they have the "freedom" and discretion advocated by Kantorowicz and Radbruch? Can you reconcile the values orientation of East German jurists with Markovits' claim that "the East German legal system was distinctly positivist"? This question might be made more problematic by the fact that the East German legal system was also predominantly influenced by the Civil Law tradition.
- What did Markovits mean when she characterized East German jurists as "educators"? How does that differ from the role legal professionals play in your primary or "national" legal system?
- Markovits regarded the East German judges and lawyers who were excluded from the legal profession following reunification with a measure of sympathy. She barely acknowledges their contribution to "outrageous socialist

perversions of justice."[36] Is it proper – or even possible – to look past the role these jurists played in sustaining and supporting the brutal and suffocating East German dictatorship?

The newly unified German authorities (dominated, as Markovits notes, by Westerners) saw a clear and fundamental difference between the values and practices of East German justice and West German legal culture – as embodied and championed by the judges and lawyers of the Federal Republic. Is the West German image of the judge and lawyer clearly articulated in the following cases? They involve constitutional challenges to the disqualification of East German judges and lawyers following reunification.

In the *East German Disbarment Case* (1995), three East German lawyers complained to the Federal Constitutional Court about the revocation of their certificates to practice law in the newly unified Federal Republic of Germany. Two of the complainants were husband and wife, both of whom practiced law in East Germany starting in the early 1970s. In 1982 the couple agreed to collaborate with the repressive Ministry for State Security (*Stasi*), which had infiltrated and sought to monitor nearly all of private life in East Germany. The *Stasi* used brutal and intrusive means, including surveillance, torture, arbitrary detentions, and killings, to enforce the will of the Communist Party and government. After reunification, and the opening of the *Stasi* files, it was discovered that the husband and wife had reported a range of personal details about their clients and friends to the *Stasi*, including information about marital problems and political attitudes. In its summary of the facts in the wife's case, the Constitutional Court stated that "the most serious incident" involved her reports in 1985 about an acquaintance who eventually was arrested and sentenced to prison for attempting to flee East Germany. In a revolting turn of events that is only possible in an invasive, arbitrary dictatorship, the acquaintance who had been plotting an escape to the West relied on the husband as his defense counsel after being arrested. This merits a clear reiteration. The man hauled before the East German criminal justice system, at least in part on the basis of information reported by the wife-lawyer-collaborator, put his trust in the husband-lawyer-collaborator to serve as his defense counsel. To complete the betrayal, the husband dutifully disclosed his defense strategy, hammered out in pretrial meetings with his client, to the *Stasi*.

Federal Constitutional Court
East German Disbarment Case

[Translation by Russell A. Miller]

BVerfGE 93, 213 (1995)[*]

* * *

---

[*] Permission granted by the Federal Constitutional Court.

The legal profession in the German Democratic Republic was very small in comparison to the legal profession in the Federal Republic of Germany (approximately 600 lawyers). This can be explained not least by the fact that – according to the philosophical principles upon which the German Democratic Republic's social system was based – there was no objective difference between the interests of an individual and the interests of the state. Accordingly, there was considerably less legislation than in the Federal Republic of Germany and comparatively less recourse to the courts was available. In addition, the majority of court proceedings could be conducted without lawyers. The courts acted at the same time as sources of legal advice.

[…] [Most] lawyers were members of law firms; the East German Ministry of Justice gave the law firms directions and supervision. Lawyers were expected to take account of the philosophical foundations of the German Democratic Republic while practicing their profession. One of their tasks was to strengthen socialist legality, which was intended to be different from the law in a state governed by the rule of law where civil law applies. They were expected to help ensure that the subjective interest of citizens did not diverge from the objective interest of the state. Their work was aimed simultaneously at looking after the rights of the individual and supporting the politics of the Socialist Unity Party of Germany. […] The independence of lawyers existed only within this framework […].

A laywer's independence and duty of confidentiality to his or her clients were limited by the control exercised by the review commissions. Lawyers were obliged to provide comprehensive information and to submit documents to the review commissions. […] Furthermore, a lawyer's duty of confidentiality to his or her clients did not release him or her from the duty to report […], which also applied to serious cases of illegal border crossings. […]

There was no institutional connection between the legal profession and the Ministry for State Security. In spite of the legal profession's general obligation to cooperate with the representative body of the people and its organs and in spite of diverse cooperation between the Ministry for State Security and the Supreme Court of the German Democratic Republic, the Chief Public Prosecutor's office and the Ministry of Justice […] and in spite of the Ministry for State Security's role as the investigating authority in the so-called "state protection" offences, the tasks of the legal profession and the Ministry for State Security were clearly divided. In particular, lawyers were not obliged to make themselves available to the Ministry for State Security as unofficial collaborators. […]

The [law providing for the disqualification of East German lawyers from the bar in the newly unified Germany] serves to protect a community interest of paramount importance. It was intended by Parliament to ensure that the lawyers who were admitted to practice in the German Democratic Republic also were able to satisfy the requirements of personal integrity and reliability. This serves the general public's interest in the sound administration of justice. It is consistent with the ideas prevailing in a state governed by the rule of law and beneficial to the administration of justice if, simply for the sake of allowing a citizen a fair chance of defending himself or herself, a person learned in the law is available to the citizen whom the citizen is able to trust and who the citizen can expect will represent his or her interests independently of the influence of the state. For the administration of justice to function properly, the public's relationship with the legal profession must be based on a foundation of trust; minimum requirements for such trust include the personal integrity and reliability of individual members of the profession. If it can be shown that a lawyer violated the principles of humanity or of the rule of law, this will endanger such foundation of trust.

In the wake of German reunification, the danger of such trust being lost increased in a particular way. Under the Unification Treaty practicing certificates granted prior to the Treaty's entry into force remain valid. Therefore, lawyers who had previously worked

6.3 Legal Actors: Judges and Lawyers

in the German Democratic Republic could continue to practice their profession in the [newly united] Federal Republic of Germany; this is true in spite of their being untrustworthy due to their involvement in flagrant acts of wrongdoing by the Socialist Unity Party and, thus, posing a threat to the administration of justice in a state governed by the rule of law. The challenged law is intended to counteract this.

The legal consequence provided for in the law is [...] not disproportionate. If a lawyer proves himself or herself to be unsuitable to be a member of the legal profession as the result of a serious breach of duty, he or she may be excluded from the legal profession. However, the revocation of a practicing certificate may only be considered if it is suitable and necessary for the protection of the legal interests stated and if, after weighing all of the interests, the conclusion is reached that the constitutionally guaranteed interests of the person concerned must give way to the predominant interests of the public good. [...]

[...] [Violations] of humanity or the principles of the rule of law will disqualify a lawyer from the task of championing the legal cause of individual citizens. By specifically naming "activity for the Ministry of State Security" as one of the elements constituting an offence under the law, the law includes one of the elements that is especially well-suited to undermine people's trust in lawyers. [... The] removal of such lawyers can counteract the dwindling trust in the legal profession that was caused by their activities in the German Democratic Republic; it can also contribute to protecting the administration of justice from damage.

No less burdensome means for achieving this goal is apparent. [...] Whoever violated the principles of humanity or of the rule of law by acting as an unofficial collaborator does not deserve the trust of the people. If it can be shown that he or she personally was guilty of culpable conduct of some significance, it must be possible for Parliament to remove the lawyer from the profession – depending on the seriousness of the accusation and the lapse of time – at least for a period of time. Every other measure would permit the lawyer to continue practicing his or her profession and thus fail to achieve the statute's purpose [...] namely to preserve the integrity and absolute trustworthiness of the legal profession. [...]

Questions/Comments

- It is not clear from the excerpt but the Court ultimately concluded that the wife's disqualification was unconstitutional and that the husband's was constitutional. In rough terms, then, is it possible to suggest that the wife's behavior more closely aligned with the West German image of a lawyer? But what did the husband do that caused him to run afoul of that standard? Which facets of the description of German lawyers in the brochure *Law – Made in Germany* did the Federal Constitutional Court reinforce by upholding the husband's disqualification from the practice of law? Would you know, based on this ruling, what kinds of compromises you could be forgiven for making as an East German lawyer trying to make a career and life in a repressive system, and which concessions to the power of the Communist Party would be regarded as unacceptable?
- The Constitutional Court explained that the disqualification of former East German judges and lawyers might be justified in some cases in order to protect and promote a "community interest of paramount importance." What is that interest? What characteristics of respectable lawyering promote that interest?

Proceedings before the East German Supreme Court

This case before the East German Supreme Court in 1957 involved accusations of treason leveled against the editors (left in the photo) of the *Aufbau Verlag*, the leading East German publishing house. Convinced socialists, the editors nevertheless fell out of favor with the Communist Party by promoting literature sympathetic to moderation, reform, and reunification. These appellate proceedings were part of a heavily publicized "show trial" orchestrated by the Communist Party leadership. The editors were given prison sentences. Gregor Gysi, the East German lawyer and politician mentioned earlier in this chapter, is linked to this unseemly episode. His father was installed to lead the *Aufbau Verlag's* return to a posture more faithful to the Communist Party.

Figure 6.2 (East) German Justice as a Foil for (West) German Professional Standards
Source: Photo by AND-Bildarchiv/ullstein bild via Getty images

- You might note that the last five paragraphs in the case-excerpt constitute the proportionality assessment I described above. Recall that this is the fine-tuned, multistep analysis used to determine whether an act of public authority has unconstitutionally intruded upon a basic right. What does the Court say about the legitimacy of the lustration law? What does the Court say about the suitability and necessity of the lustration law? What is the result of the Court's cost–benefit analysis in the final stage of the proportionality assessment?
- Does the examination of the lawyers' conduct in East Germany involve a consideration of their competence or effectiveness? Is there an indication in the case that they produced unacceptable outcomes for their clients? Is it possible that their cooperation with the *Stasi* actually positioned them to obtain better results for their clients?
- Figure 6.2 depicts an infamous political trial in East Germany. Is there anything in that photograph that suggests the underlying injustice – including deceptive and collaborating lawyers like the husband and wife in this

case – that plagued the East German legal system? Or, does the image seem to capture a rational and professional legal proceeding? What about the image hints at the problems identified by the Constitutional Court in the *East German Disbarment Case*? Does the scene look more or less like a trial in your primary or "national" legal system?

In the *GDR Criminal Court Judge II Case* (2000) a former East German judge complained to the Federal Constitutional Court about her disqualification from service as a notary. Fully qualified lawyers, notaries are certified to provide some semi-public documentary services such as executing notarial deeds.[37] The complainant, as a judge and eventually the director of a Lower District Court in East Germany, had been involved in numerous prosecutions of East Germans for "attempting an illegal border crossing" and "impairment of state activity." These East German crimes were the ambiguous and ideological statutory basis for the state's persecution of its opponents. They were viewed by West German authorities as "political trials" involving an extreme abuse of judicial power. One of the appeals courts that heard the complainant's case explained that these criminal provisions were used to "relentlessly discipline and oppress citizens wishing to leave" East Germany. The administrative agency responsible for imposing the complainant's disqualification cited the fact that she participated in these proceedings and, on nine occasions, imposed prison sentences of greater than one year. "As the director of a Lower District Court," the agency explained, "it was [the complainant's] task to ensure that the value system embodied in socialist legislation was upheld. In doing so, she had violated the principles of humanity and the principles of the rule of law." A three-justice panel of the Federal Constitutional Court agreed that these principles frame the Western understanding of judicial power. But the Court was not satisfied that the complainant's conduct constituted a violation of those standards.

Federal Constitutional Court
GDR Criminal Court Judge II Case

[Translation by Russell A. Miller]

File No.: 1 BvR 514/97 (2000)[*]

* * *

Merely being part of the system does not constitute a violation in connection with being a full-time employee or unofficial collaborator of the State Security Service, although Parliament expressly included these circumstances as an indication for such violations in the statute. In contrast to its treatment of the plain fact that a person conspired and cooperated with the Ministry for State Security, Parliament did not make a person's involvement in the GDR's criminal justice system's handling of political crimes an indication that he or she was unworthy to practice as a lawyer or that he or she lacked aptitude for

---

[*] Permission granted by the Federal Constitutional Court.

being a notary. This is not an unintentional omission. At the time Parliament enacted the [challenged law] it was preparing the Law for Relieving Injustice Perpetrated by the Socialist Unity Party of Germany. This law, as regards rehabilitation, refers to what Westerners considered to be the objective injustice of certain clearly identified GDR criminal provisions. However, the decision-makers who applied these unjust provisions were not called to account. This was true despite the fact that, when viewed from the Western perspective, the application of the elements of those crimes did not correspond to the punishments permissible in a state governed by the rule of law. Therefore, according to the wording and drafting history of the challenged provision, violations of the principles of humanity and other principles of the rule of law shall only be found to have occurred in cases where, within the hierarchically structured criminal justice system in the German Democratic Republic, overzealous followers or obsequious servants of internal party directions acted to the accused person's disadvantage or used the criminal law in secret or sham trials to eliminate fellow citizens who were inconvenient.

A violation of the principles of humanity or of the principles of the rule of law by a judge applying the criminal law of the German Democratic Republic in a political trial can only be assumed if there are additional special circumstances and the judge's culpable conduct led him or her to personally injure protected fundamental interests, or if it was foreseeable that such injuries would result from his or her acts.

Therefore, if it is sought to be established that the principles of humanity or the principles of the rule of law have been violated, then the conduct of a judge must be carefully examined in each case. A finding of serious personal guilt will only be justified if the acts qualify as systemic acts of persecution and the fundamental rights of the person as well as the essence of a state governed by the rule of law have been violated. Whether the system required the act to be done, whether it was necessary for the person's own safety, or whether it was based on loyalty to socialist legality must always be considered.

If one considers the way the constitution was interpreted in the German Democratic Republic and the way criminal law in the German Democratic Republic was developed and continually tightened, there can be no doubt that the complainant passed light sentences. The opinions obtained [...] confirmed the information found in the reference material on customary criminal practice in the German Democratic Republic; the complainant was in fact one of the most lenient judges both in regard to the total length of the sentences she imposed as well as in regard to her generous suspension of sentences. Her conduct was characterized by her desire to retain her position as a judge hence she demonstrated the loyalty necessary and common for this goal. This does not give rise to serious accusations of personal guilt on her part. The standards imposed by the Federal Court of Justice place expectations on judges that they could not meet under the conditions of the GDR judicial system and in respect of which they could not avail themselves of any of the formal safeguards that safeguard the independent administration of justice in the Federal Republic of Germany.

In the written law of the German Democratic Republic there was no possibility of a restricted interpretation or application. Criminal Law was continually tightened, the range of penalties increased, the commencement of the offence brought forward to include preparatory acts. The complainant was trained in this legal system. As the court's director she was responsible for ensuring that these maxims were adhered to and she was accountable pursuant to [GDR law]. She was not acquainted with other standards. After all, since 1933 there had not at any time been a state governed by the principles of the rule of law on East German soil even though the political situation had changed dramatically within that time.

Moreover, the judges in the German Democratic Republic had no institutionally protected room for maneuver as far as applying the country's laws in accordance with human rights principles was concerned. [...] Judges in the German Democratic Republic were not independent, but instead highly dependent on being in favor with the party leadership due to their need to be re-elected, the continual control and the possibility of being removed at any time. [...] Besides they had almost no other opportunities to switch to other professions, in particular, because the right to freely choose to set up a legal office was excluded.

[...] [The] complainant's guilt cannot be measured according to how much or how little resistance she showed to the judicial system in the German Democratic Republic, but rather according to the events for which she was responsible – measured by fundamental rules of humanity and by the rules prevailing in a state governed by the rule of law. The punishments the complainant imposed must be seen in relation to the motives behind them and in relation to fundamental principles of humanity and the rule of law. [...]

Questions/Comments

- How important is the principle of judicial independence in the Federal Constitutional Court's characterization of the proper role of a judge? Does the Federal Constitutional Court seem to think that the East German judge possessed – and exercised – the requisite judicial independence? Or, does the Federal Constitutional Court suggest that the judge failed to act independently while nevertheless excusing her conduct in light of her immersion in the corrupted and compromised East German legal system?
- Is the following a simpler way to summarize the Constitutional Court's ruling in the cases involving the East German lawyers and judge: Collaboration with the *Stasi* is bad while participation in the system's "ordinary" criminalization of political dissent is excusable?
- The preceding materials hint at the priority the German legal system gives to judicial independence. But, should there be any doubt, Article 97(1) of the Basic Law enshrines the principle in ten unambiguous words: "Judges shall be independent and subject only to the law." This is echoed in Section 25 of the *Deutsches Richtergesetz* (German Judiciary Act). One constitutional commentator explained that "Article 97 guarantees [...] one of, if not the central foundation stone in the architecture of a state governed by the rule of law. [...] Article 97 directs itself against all attempts by state authorities (especially executive and parliamentary authorities) to directly or indirectly influence judicial decisions in concrete cases, including attempts to make such influence possible, or to influence the legal views of a judge by a measure greater than is otherwise unavoidable."[38] Does this help clarify the difference between Eastern and Western judges?
- You may be aware of the intense criticism of sweeping judicial reforms that have been implemented by the populist and semi-authoritarian governments in Hungary and Poland. Those developments have persisted and escalated, leading many European leaders and figures in the European Union to openly charge those countries with violations of the rule of law. Kim Lane

Scheppele, a deeply informed scholar and a critic of the Hungarian and Polish governments' democratic backsliding, described these developments as a form of partisan "capture" of the judiciary. For example, referring to the Polish reforms, Scheppele said that the governing Law and Justice Party (PiS) "attacked the judiciary in particular, packing the constitutional court with illegally elected judges, firing court leaders up and down the system to replace them with their own hand-picked judges, creating a new disciplinary chamber to punish judges who rule against what PiS wants [...]."[39] Blind fealty to a political party or particular leader, of the kind that has emerged in Hungary and Poland, represents one way in which a judge might lack the independence the German legal system demands from its judges. Was that the problem with the East German judiciary? What other commitments or orientations might undermine a judge's independence?

Maybe all of this noise about judicial independence overstates the case for the German judiciary. To what end is their celebrated judicial independence put if, as Wolff describes it, the German legal method calls for little judicial creativity? The Constitutional Court's portrayal suggests that East German judges had limited discretion and largely operated within the confines of the socialist state's positive law regime. But isn't that a fair description of the role played by a judge in the Civil Law tradition, which is the very culture of judging about which Kantorowicz and Radbruch complained (in the excerpts presented in Chapter 3)? After all, John Merryman and Rogelio Pérez-Perdomo speak of the judge in the Civil Law tradition in rather deflating terms. They explain that judges are "civil servants, functionaries."[40] Civil Law judges are supposed to decide their cases on the statute and nothing more – not by analogizing to other courts' decisions and certainly not by considering sociological or policy implications. Merryman and Pérez-Perdomo concluded that:

> [t]he picture of the judicial process that emerges is one of fairly routine activity; the judge becomes a kind of expert clerk. Presented with fact situations to which a ready legislative response will be readily found in all except the extraordinary case, the judge's function is merely to find the right legislative provision, couple it with the fact situation, and bless the solution that is more or less automatically produced from the union. The whole process of judicial decision is made to fit into the formal syllogism of scholastic logic. The major premise is in the statute, the facts of the case furnish the minor premise, and the conclusion inevitably follows. In the uncommon case in which some more sophisticated intellectual work is demanded of the judge, he or she is expected to follow carefully drawn directions about the limits of interpretation.
>
> The net image is of judges as operators of a machine designed and built by legislators.[41]

- Is it fair, based on this characterization of a Civil Law judge, to say that the difference between an East German and West German judge is not fundamentally different? In both cases, it seems, the judge is not viewed as a fully empowered agent but, rather, as a medium for the expression and application of state power and values declared by some other organ (the legislature or the Communist Party). In West Germany – and in Germany today – judges apply the law as set out by the parliament and as interpreted by scholars. In East Germany judges applied the will of the Socialist Unity Party of Germany. What is the core of the difference between acceptable (West) German judges' passivity and unacceptable (East) German judges' passivity?

One possibility opened up by my decision to rely on the provocative example of East German judging and lawyering as a way of thinking about the character of contemporary German legal professionals, is that we now might consider whether the lingering residue of East German legality in reunified Germany constitutes another (faint and fading) tradition woven in the tapestry of German legal culture. At the very least, East Germany's Socialist Legal tradition must occupy some territory in the jurisprudential subconscious of the former residents of GDR. What are the characteristics of that particular approach to law?

One interesting insight is that Socialist Law has almost always been paired with the Civil Law tradition. René David pointed out that this was especially true of its manifestation in the old Roman-Germanic legal systems of eastern and central Europe. Socialist Law, he explained, "has an undoubted affinity with Romanist laws; it has to a large extent retained the terminology of these laws and, in appearances at least, their structure; it has a concept of the legal rule which seems no different from that of French or German jurists."[42] David also highlighted the revolutionary nature of Socialist Law, which contrasted with the historical stability and longevity promoted by the Civil Law tradition. Socialist Law was part of the revolutionary political program – or super structure – that aimed to end the dominance of the bourgeois classes. The end game of the revolution was the disappearance of the state and its laws. That is surely a unique quality of the Socialist Law tradition. Another characteristic of socialist legality would be the near eradication of private law as the collectivization of property and the insistence that other traditional institutions be subjected to the will of the proletariat, as expressed by the Communist Party. This constituted the ascendance and predominance of public law. To achieve all of this it was necessary that law be regarded as materially determinate and not at all open-textured in the manner typical of the Common Law tradition. This quality had both positivistic and quasi-natural law consequences. Described in this summary fashion, do you see any "genetic" affinities between the Civil Law tradition and the Socialist Law tradition? What forms might the thread of the Socialist Law tradition take in the contemporary German legal culture? Are the German system's extensive social welfare commitments – and the legal regime built up to administer them – a window through which the Socialist Law impulses of the East German legal system might find renewed resonance? Germany's "objective order of values" (which I briefly described in Chapter 3 and will address again in Chapter 8) was ordained by the new post-war constitution. The Federal Constitutional Court concluded that it is meant to impact all law in Germany. Is that a liberal, humanist, dignity-oriented parallel for the socialist reality towards which East Germany's legal system was pointed? Both systems could be said to be "substantive" (with clear notions of "right and wrong" law) rather than "procedural" (providing fair rules for invoking and engaging the law without committing to particular outcomes).

In one respect, German judges are more active and German lawyers are less active when compared with their counterparts in legal systems influenced by the Common Law tradition. German judges exercise considerable control over the cases on their docket. They have wide-ranging authority to structure the proceedings and dictate the presentation of law and evidence. This more-involved role encompasses an "inquisitorial responsibility for determining the truth of the case at hand,"[43] perhaps by demanding the appearance of witnesses, posing questions to witnesses, or ordering evidence from a neutral, judicially named expert. It also includes the subtle and challenging obligation to "give hints and feedback to the parties to avoid surprise and promote the fair and just determination of the suit."[44] You will learn more about this spectrum of German court processes in Chapter 11's presentation of German procedural law.

Review the following provisions of the *Bundesrechtsanwaltsordnung* (Federal Lawyer's Act). That is the statute governing admission to and establishing the standards for the practice of law in Germany. What are the qualities and values demanded from lawyers? How are those qualities and values expressed in the East German lustration cases?

Federal Lawyer's Act

Section 43
General Professional Duties

A *Rechtsanwalt* [attorney] must practise his/her profession conscientiously. A *Rechtsanwalt* must show that he/she is worthy of the respect and the trust that his/her status as a *Rechtsanwalt* demands, both when practicing and when not practising his/her profession.

Federal Lawyer's Act

Section 43a
The Basic Duties of a *Rechtsanwalt*

(1) A *Rechtsanwalt* may not enter into any ties that pose a threat to his/her professional independence.
(2) A *Rechtsanwalt* has a duty to observe professional secrecy. This duty relates to everything that has become known to the *Rechtsanwalt* in professional practice. This does not apply to facts that are obvious or which do not need to be kept secret from the point of view of their significance.

(3) A *Rechtsanwalt* must not behave with lack of objectivity in professional practice. Conduct that lacks objectivity is particularly understood as conduct that involves the conscious dissemination of untruths or making denigrating statements when other parties involved or the course of the proceedings have given no cause for such statements.
(4) A *Rechtsanwalt* may not represent conflicting interests.
(5) A *Rechtsanwalt* must exercise the requisite care in handling any assets entrusted to him/her. Monies belonging to third parties must be immediately forwarded to the entitled recipient or paid into a fiduciary account.
(6) A *Rechtsanwalt* has a duty to engage in continuing professional development.

One issue attracting increasing concern about the German bench and bar is not focused on judicial independence and lawyerly competence. The worry is that there is a woeful "diversity-deficit" in the legal profession that poses a "serious problem for the legal system."[45] The authors of a recent, headline-grabbing study of this issue, faced a classic problem confronting discussions of minority status and discrimination in Germany. In part due to the murderous consequences of the Nazis' documentation of identity (including race, ethnicity, and religion), German public authorities maintain almost no record of demographic characteristics. Another, less acceptable justification for this willful disinterest in the status and experience of minorities, is the prevailing, ambiguous sentiment expressed by the phrase "*das haben wir nicht.*"[46] This can mean two troubling things: "we don't have minority groups in Germany," or "we don't have discrimination in Germany." Neither of these things are true. Despite the challenge of documenting the problem, the authors scoured available sources, reports, and studies in order to reach the "informed assumption that [in Germany] people of color do not have the same access to careers in the legal academy or the practice of law."[47] This diversity deficit, they explained, implicates violations of legal protections against discrimination. It also jeopardizes the acceptance and legitimacy of the legal system. The authors noted that "law firms and academic institutions not only miss out on talent as a result of a lack of diversity, but they also lose the benefit of additional perspectives."[48] Their work makes a compelling case for insisting on additional criteria for assessing the integrity of the German judiciary and practicing bar: representation, inclusion, and equity. It is not clear, however, whether the predominant, dogmatic Civil Law character of judging and lawyering in Germany leaves a path open for progress on this front.

6.4 Conclusion

Jutta Limbach was the first female president, or chief justice, of Germany's Federal Constitutional Court. We will consider that powerful and unique tribunal more fully in Chapter 8. For present purposes, however, it is sufficient to explain that her service as the Constitutional Court's president lends immense weight to Limbach's characterization of and conclusions about German judges and lawyers. In 1999 Limbach explained that:

> The times are long past – perhaps they never existed – when it was still believed that judges obtained their decisions from the logical operation of a statutory definition. Not only general clauses, but also a large number of more-or-less undefined legal concepts delegate the practical application of the law to the judge. At the least, these ambiguities create a semantic margin of discretion that permit more than one, correct decision. Judging is not just knowledge of the law, but always the *production* of the law. In the process of applying the law the judge also secures justice. This is truer when one considers that the code is now aged and the legislature may not address today's regulatory necessities.[49]

The materials in this chapter suggest that there is more than some truth to Limbach's claim, even if Kantorowicz's portrayal of technocratic German legal actors (presented in Chapter 3) still resonates. These different realities certainly reflect the distinct demands made of judges and lawyers by the diverse legal traditions woven together to form the German legal system. Just as there is no single, undifferentiated German legal culture, there is no single, undifferentiated way to portray the life and work of German judges and lawyers. But a foreigner, guided by an understanding of the Civil Law tradition – and the working sketches of the function and role of judges and lawyers presented in these materials – could find a way to understand the work of these jurists.

With the benefit of the foundation we developed here and in the previous chapters, I hope you can be confident as we wander deeper into our study of German law and legal culture. The next steps will lead you into encounters with the German legal system's distinct treatment of a number of specific fields of law.

Further Reading

- Bryant G. Garth & Gregory Shaffer, *The Globalization of Legal Education: A Critical Perspective* (Oxford University Press) (2022)
- Richard J. Wilson, *The Global Evolution of Clinical Legal Education* (Cambridge University Press) (2018)
- *Legal Education in the Global Context* (Christopher Gane & Robin Hui Huang eds.) (Routledge) (2016)
- Carel Stolker, *Rethinking the Law School* (Cambridge University Press) (2015)
- Reinhold Zippelius, *Introduction to German Legal Methods* (Kirk W. Junker & P. Matthew Roy trans.) (Carolina Academic Press) (2008)
- Ulrike Schultz, "Germany – Regulated Deregulation: The Case of the German Legal Profession," in *Reorganisation and Resistance: Legal Professions Confront a Changing World* (William Felstiner ed.) (Bloomsbury) (2005)

- James McAdams, *Judging the Past in Unified Germany* (Cambridge University Press) (2001)
- Erhard Blankenburg & Ulrike Schultz, "German Advocates: A Highly Regulated Profession," in *Lawyers in Society: The Civil Law World* (Richard L. Abel & Philip S.C. Lewis eds.) (University of California Press) (1988)

NOTES

1 Michel Rosenfeld, *Rethinking the Boundaries between Public Law and Private Law for the Twenty-First Century: An Introduction*, 11 INTL. J. CONST. L. 125 (2013).
2 *Id.*
3 *See, e.g.*, Duncan Kennedy, *Legal Education and the Reproduction of Hierarchy*, 32 J. LEGAL EDUC. 591 (1982).
4 *World University Rankings by Subject: Law*, TIMES HIGHER EDUCATION (2022), www.timeshighereducation.com/world-university-rankings/2022/subject-ranking/law#!/page/0/length/25/sort_by/rank/sort_order/asc/cols/stats.
5 JOHANN WOLFGANG VON GOETHE, 60, 62–63 (John Wynniatt Grant trans., 1867).
6 *See* Richard Friedenthal, GOETHE – HIS LIFE AND TIMES (2010); Peter Boerner, GOETHE (LIFE AND TIMES) (2006); John R. Williams, THE LIFE OF GOETHE – A CRITICAL BIOGRAPHY (2001);
7 *See* Karl von Lewinski, *The Education of the German Lawyer*, 20 GREEN BAG 516 (1908).
8 Annette Keilmann, *The Einheitsjurist: A German Phenomenon*, 7 GER. L. J. 293 (2006).
9 Von Lewinski, *supra* note 7, at 518.
10 *See* Keilmann, *supra* note 8.
11 *See* WILLIAM M. SULLIVAN ET AL., EDUCATING LAWYERS: PREPARATION FOR THE PROFESSION OF LAW (2007). For an executive summary of this Carnegie Foundation sponsored report, go to www.carnegiefoundation.org/sites/default/files/publications/elibrary_pdf_632.pdf; *see also* the American Bar Association's "MacCrate Report" from 1992, www.abanet.org/legaled/publications/onlinepubs/maccrate.html.
12 *See* Keeshea Turner Roberts, *Law Schools Push to Require Anti-Racism Training and Courses*, 46 ABA HUMAN RIGHTS MAGAZINE (Dec. 13, 2020), www.americanbar.org/groups/crsj/publications/human_rights_magazine_home/rbgs-impact-on-civil-rights/law-schools-push/; Letter from 150 Law Deans to the American Bar Association's Council of the Section of Legal Education and Admissions to the Bar (June 2020), https://taxprof.typepad.com/files/aba-bias-cultural-awareness-and-anti-racist-practices-education-and-training-letter-7.30.20-final.pdf.
13 *See* von Lewinski, *supra* note 7, at 517 ("Many [law students] prefer to live a really happy and lazy student's life – drinking, singing, fencing and amusing themselves, careless and free as only a German student can be. He is enabled to do this because of the almost entire want of control, due to recognition of the principle of students' freedom in Germany.").

14 There are very few private law faculties in Germany, not the least because fee-paying programs struggle to compete with the no-cost public university programs. Nevertheless, three private law schools have secured a place in German legal education: Bucerius Law School (Hamburg); EBS University of Economics and Law (Wiesbaden); and BSP University for Management and Law (Berlin).

15 Mathias Reimann, *The American Advantage in Global Lawyering*, 78 RABELS ZEITSCHRIFT FÜR AUSLÄNDISCHES UND INTERNATIONALES PRIVATRECHT 1 (2014).

16 *Id.*

17 Christian Boulanger, *The Comparative Sociology of Legal Doctrine: Thoughts on a Research Program*, 21 GER L. J. 1362 (2020).

18 Bernhard Großfeld, *Examensvorbereitung und Jurisprudenz (Preparations for Examinations and Jurisprudence)*, 41 JURISTEN ZEITUNG 22, 25 (1992).

19 James R. Maxeiner, *Legal Indeterminacy Made in America: U.S. Legal Methods and the Rule of Law*, 41 VALPARAISO UNIV. L. REV. 517 (2007).

20 Hermann Reichold, *Allgemeine Einführung*, in EINFÜHRUNG IN DIE RECHTSWISSENSCHAFT 1, 56 (Kristian Kühl et al. eds., 3rd ed. 2019).

21 *Id.* (Miller trans.).

22 *Id.*

23 *See* Gerald Turkel, *The Public/Private Distinction: Approaches to the Critique of Legal Ideology*, 22 L. & SOCIETY REV. 801, 805 (1988).

24 Duncan Kennedy, *The Stages of the Decline of the Public/Private Distinction*, 130 UNIV. PENNSYLVANIA L. REV. 1349, 1352 (1982).

25 Reichold, *supra* note 21, at 45.

26 *See* Russell A. Miller, *Proportionality Paradigm or Paradox? The Proportionality Principle in American and German Security Law Jurisprudence*, in PROPORTIONALITY IN CRIME CONTROL AND CRIMINAL JUSTICE 181–205 (Emmanouil Billis et al. eds., 2021).

27 *See, e.g.,* Strafgesetzbuch [StGB] [Criminal Code], Nov. 13, 1998, BGBl. I at 3322, last amended by Act, June 19, 2019, BGBl. I at 844, art. 2, § 303c.

28 *See* Olaf Muthorst, *Auslegung: Eine Einführung*, 45 JURISTISCHE ARBEITSBLÄTTER 721 (2013).

29 John Henry Merryman, *How Others Do It: The French and German Judiciaries*, 61 S. CAL. L. REV. 1865 1867 (1988) (using the term "folklore" to describe the traditional popular image of a particular society's judicial process and actors).

30 LAW – MADE IN GERMANY 19–20 (2009), www.lawmadeingermany.de/Law-Made_in_Germany.pdf.

31 *Id.*

32 *Id.* at 29.

33 *See* NIGEL FOSTER & SATISH SULE, GERMAN LEGAL SYSTEM AND LAWS 100–103 (4th ed. 2010).

34 JOHN HENRY MERRYMAN & ROGELIO PÉREZ-PERDOMO, THE CIVIL LAW TRADITION 57 (4th ed. 2018).

35 *See* A. JAMES MCADAMS, JUDGING THE PAST IN UNIFIED GERMANY (2001); PETER E. QUINT, THE IMPERFECT UNION – CONSTITUTIONAL STRUCTURES OF GERMAN UNIFICATION (1997); DONALD P. KOMMERS & RUSSELL A. MILLER, THE CONSTITUTIONAL JURISPRUDENCE OF THE FEDERAL REPUBLIC OF GERMANY (3rd ed. 2012).

6.4 Conclusion

36 Inga Markovits, *Children of a Lesser God: GDR Lawyers in Post-Socialist Germany*, 94 MICH. L. REV. 2270, 2275 (1996).
37 GERHARD ROBBERS, AN INTRODUCTION TO GERMAN LAW 34 (7th ed. 2019).
38 Helmuth Schulz-Fielitz, *Art. 97*, in III GRUNDGESETZ KOMMENTAR 567, 575–576 (Horst Drier ed., 2nd ed. 2008) (Russell A. Miller trans.).
39 Interview with Kim Lane Scheppele, *European Union's Top Court Rules Against Hungary and Poland in Rule of Law Showdown*, WORLD JUSTICE PROJECT (Feb. 16, 2022), https://worldjusticeproject.org/news/european-union%E2%80%99s-top-court-rules-against-hungary-and-poland-rule-law-showdown.
40 MERRYMAN & PÉREZ-PERDOMO, *supra* note 34, at 35.
41 *Id.* at 36.
42 RENÉ DAVID & JOHN C. BRIERLEY, MAJOR LEGAL SYSTEMS IN THE WORLD TODAY 156 (3rd ed. 1985).
43 PETER L. MURRAY & ROLF STÜRNER, GERMAN CIVIL JUSTICE 167 (2004).
44 *Id.* at 166.
45 MICHAEL GRÜNBERGER ET AL., DIVERSITÄT IN RECHTSWISSENSCHAFT UND RECHTSPRAXIS 86 (2021) (Russell A. Miller trans.).
46 Russell A. Miller, *We Don't Have That*, FAZ-EINSPRUCH MAGAZIN (June 16, 2021), www.faz.net/-irf-acsgq.
47 GRÜNBERGER, *supra* note 45, at 47 (Russell A. Miller trans.).
48 *Id.* at 86 (Russell A. Miller trans.).
49 JUTTA LIMBACH, "IM NAMEN DES VOLKES" 96–97 (1999) (Russell A. Miller trans.).

7

German Private Law

The Civil Code

Key Concepts

- **Bürgerliches Gesetzbuch**: The BGB or German Civil Code was enacted in 1896 and entered into force on January 1, 1900. The BGB codifies the traditional fields of private law, including obligations, property, family law, and the law of succession. Other private law concerns, such as commercial law or labor/employment law, are covered by separate statutory regimes. The Civil Code is thought of as one of the world's "great codifications" and one of the greatest jurisprudential achievements in German history. It is prized for its complex use of concepts and intricate systematic design. The drafting process took three decades and ultimately involved a mix of Roman Law principles and German customary law. The Civil Code made a significant contribution to German unity and has served as a major foundation for German law and legal culture.
- **Kodifikationsstreit**: The long-running nineteenth-century debate, associated with the legal scholars von Savigny and Thibaut, that was concerned with the wisdom and feasibility of codifying German private law. Von Savigny opposed codification, urging that the German peoples hadn't yet achieved the necessary measure of community cohesion and cultural coherence. Thibaut advocated for codification, suggesting that Roman Law principles could be used as a framework for a German Civil Code.
- **Privatautonomie**: Private autonomy is the principle that individuals should be empowered to act upon their free will in their relationships with others and society. *Privatautonomie* is an expression of liberalism and the Enlightenment ideal of human rationality. This is a central value of the German Civil Code, especially as the Code promotes freedom of contract, property rights, and freedom of association.
- **Rechtsgeschäft**: The fundamental basis for the Civil Code's normative regime, a *Rechtsgeschäft* (an act with legal significance or a legal transaction) involves one or more person's declared intention that a legal obligation should be formed.
- **Klammerprinzip**: A method for structuring a statutory framework so that general principles are identified in a "general part" followed by more detailed

or specific provisions in a "special part." This structure makes it possible to resolve a legal claim by first considering the broader or more general principles before treating the relevant specific rules.
- **Herrschende Meinung**: Prevailing opinion amongst scholars – and perhaps in court judgments – regarding the scope or meaning of a legal concept, provision, or principle. The *herrschende Meinung* isn't formed only on the basis of the quantity of scholars endorsing the viewpoint, but also is understood to be the qualitatively correct interpretation.

Study Tips

The Ministry of Justice and Federal Office of Justice provide English-language translations of a number of important German codes and statutes at the website "Gesetze im Internet" (www.gesetze-im-internet.de/). This includes the *Bürgerliches Gesetzbuch* (BGB – German Civil Code).

There is an old joke that circulates among German lawyers:

Question: What is the difference between the Bible and the German Civil Code?

Answer: Luther had to translate the Bible. But God gave us the Civil Code in his native language – German!

The joke is perhaps more revealing than it is funny. It highlights the fact that the *Bürgerliches Gesetzbuch* (BGB or German Civil Code) has been an intense point of pride for Germans. The Civil Code, after all, was a source of political and cultural unity for a long-fragmented German people. The BGB is regarded as an exceptionally well-designed and finely tuned work. In that way, it also says something about the quality of German thinking, design, and production. As you've learned in our engagement with the foundations of German law, more than any other legal regime, the Civil Code has long been law's basis and defining framework in Germany.

We might doubt the joke's suggested origin for the BGB. But, for our examination of German legal culture, the Civil Code is immensely important. Let me suggest just two (of many) reasons why.

First, the *Bürgerliches Gesetzbuch* serves as the strongest and clearest expression of the Civil Law tradition in the German legal system. By now you know that this means that it carries the DNA of a jurisprudential approach that draws on Roman Law, that prioritizes statutes in the form of comprehensive codifications, and that aspires to an objective formalism in the law by relying on systematization and intricately defined legal concepts. The promotional brochure *Law – Made in Germany* confirms the fact that the Civil Code is Germany's very present, very prominent link to the Civil Law tradition. The brochure boasts that:

[i]n Germany, all important legal issues and matters are governed by comprehensive legislation in the form of statutes, codes and regulations. The most important legislation in the area of business law includes [...] the Civil Code (*Bürgerliches Gesetzbuch*, abbreviated as BGB) [...].

Codification [is] an outstanding cultural achievement with economic benefits. Codification, i.e., the systematic development and regulation of a particular field of law, is a time-honored tradition. While the legislator provides the basic structures, contract drafters and courts focus on the essential details on a case-by-case basis.[1]

Law – Made in Germany doesn't stop there. The brochure emphasizes that German law, because it is codified, "is both predictable and reliable," that it "provides legal certainty," and that it produces contracts that are "more concise [...] more cost-effective and reliable than contractual agreements under English or US law."[2] The brochure concludes with the claim that "codification enables swift and straightforward access to the law."[3]

All of this triumphalism about the Civil Code sheds some light on the joke's ironic edge. Something so grand must have divine origins! It is important to note, however, that these claims are also German expressions of the view many lawyers around the world take towards the Civil Law tradition and the many civil codes it has fostered. As Merryman and Pérez-Perdomo tell us, "many people believe the civil law to be culturally superior to the common law [...]. That attitude itself has become part of the civil law tradition."[4] That is no different for the German Civil Code, which is revered in Germany, and which has almost achieved biblical significance in the German legal culture.

Second, as *Law – Made in Germany* suggests, the Civil Code is the most important private law regime in the German legal system. On its own, it merits all the attention I can give it in this survey. But, considering the limits (and hard choices) involved in a project like this, I will also have to use the Civil Code as the tentpole for my presentation of German private law generally. There are numerous other codifications and statutes that supplement and modify the Civil Code. The **Handelsgesetzbuch (HGB or Commercial Code)** acts as the Civil Code for merchants.[5] Its special rules supersede those of the BGB for commercial actors and are largely focused on facilitating transactions and making them more efficient. For example, merchants are required to immediately examine received goods if they want to make non-conformity claims. If they fail to do so, they lose their respective rights.[6] The **Gesetz betreffend die Gesellschaften mit beschränkter Haftung (GmbHG or Law on Private Limited Liability Companies)** sets out the rules regarding private limited liability companies, including their establishment, their operation, and their dissolution.[7] Similarly, the **Aktiengesetz (AktG or Public Limited Liability Companies Act)** regulates the establishment, operation, and dissolution of public limited companies.[8] Beyond that, there are codifications and supplemental statutes addressing labor issues,[9] insurance law,[10] and intellectual property matters.[11] Whatever private law issue one can imagine, the German legal system likely provides a set of legislated rules to address them. I hope my presentation of the history, values, and function of the Civil Code will encourage you – and equip you – to engage with these other very important private law regimes.

The first sections of this chapter present the background of the BGB's development and implementation over one hundred years ago in order to highlight the manner in which it served German unity and national identity and to illuminate some of the characteristics that make the BGB a distinctly *German* Civil Code. Some of that material will be familiar from discussions in earlier chapters, especially the general introduction to the Civil Law tradition (Chapter 2), and the brief encounter you had with the Civil Code in the treatment of "modern German legal history" (Chapter 4). Thereafter, the BGB's structure and regulatory technique are presented through the consideration of materials relevant to solving a suretyship contract dispute. Suretyship is by no means a particularly important or distinctive part of the Civil Code. But in its unexceptional character it might serve as a sound example of the "ordinary" life and logic of the BGB. More importantly, I've chosen suretyship law under the Civil Code because it sometimes has served as a bridge between private law and German constitutional law, the area of law that will be presented in the next chapter. That bridging function allows me to use suretyship law to foreshadow the presence of constitutionalism's Common Law impulses in the German legal culture, even amidst this presentation of Germany's most thorough manifestation of the Civil Law tradition. That possibility serves the book's broader agenda, which is to highlight the variety of intermingled legal traditions shaping German legal culture.

7.1 The German Civil Code and the Civil Law Tradition

Ernest J. Schuster's article was published at the end of the nineteenth century shortly after the Civil Code was enacted into law and only a few years prior to the BGB entering into force on January 1, 1900. Schuster, a contemporary observer of the Code's drafting process, underscores several elements that establish the BGB's relationship to the Civil Law tradition.

Ernest J. Schuster
The German Civil Code
12 Law Quarterly Review 17, 26–32 (1896)[*]

* * *

[…] Speaking broadly, it may be stated that out of a population of forty-two and a half millions, eighteen millions are governed by the Prussian Code, fourteen millions by the German common law, which remains the modernized law of Justinian, seven and a half millions by French law, two and a half millions by Saxon law, and half a million

---

[*] Excerpt reprinted with permission of the *Law Quarterly Review*.

by Scandinavian law. There are therefore six general systems of law, but only two out of these, the system of the French and that of the Saxon Code, are exclusive systems; the other systems are broken into by the manifold local laws and customs which have been referred to in my historical sketch. These local rules relate more especially to the laws of inheritance and the law relating to the effect of marriage on property. The number of variations and subdivisions is sometimes almost comical. It may happen that a boundary line runs through a house, or that even two boundary lines divide one building into three parts, and a story is told of a town in Bavaria in which the several estates of three persons respectively dying in different rooms of one house may have to be administered according to three separate systems; moreover the line of separation is not always geographical only, it also separates the various strata of the social edifice; thus in the towns of Mecklenburg-Strelitz the effect of marriage on property is different in the case of a shopkeeper and in the case of a government official. In several German States the nobility are under a law of their own. In the city of Brunswick the wives of traders being creditors to their husbands are postponed to creditors, whilst the wives of other persons have a privileged claim for their dowry. In addition to this, the geographical divisions separating the systems of law as a general rule do not coincide with the political divisions, and even, the State legislation is sometimes affected by this anomaly; thus the Prussian Code is in force in some parts of Bavaria, but it is not in force in four out of the eleven provinces of Prussia, and within the provinces there are frequent exceptions to the general rule. Again, some of the special legislation refers to the whole of a State, whilst other legislation refers to parts only; thus the Prussian law as to guardianship governs the whole of the Prussian monarchy, on the other hand the legislation referring to land registers differs for the several provinces. The result is that in every case which arises in Germany, the following questions must be asked: Is there any imperial statute? Is there any local modern statute? Is the subject affected by older legislation? What local law governs it? The confusion which arises from this state of things may easily be imagined, and it will not surprise anybody that the unification of German law was one of the things which was most eagerly asked for on the formation of the German empire. Attempts at codification of the whole of the general law had been made at various times during the century. An elaborate draft code had been prepared for Bavaria in 1858, and fragments of the same were published in 1860 and 1864. The arrangement of that draft and the division of the subject into five parts is the one adopted by the authors of the first draft German Code, which is the principal subject of this paper. Another draft was prepared for the Grand Duchy of Hesse between 1841 and 1853; the code for the kingdom of Saxony of 1862, which represents the only one of these attempts that was carried to a successful issue, has already been mentioned by me. As regards the whole of Germany, the codification of the law of obligations had been decided on by the Assembly of Delegates representing the German confederation in 1862. The preface to the draft, prepared by a commission in accordance with this resolution and known as the Dresden draft, was dated June 13, 1866; but on June 14 of that year the confederation was dissolved, and the draft was then thought to be a piece of waste paper. By a strange combination of facts the same draft now forms the basis of the law of obligations in the new code.

There were therefore the two old codes, the Prussian Code and the French Code, one new code, viz. the Saxon Code, and several carefully considered drafts which could be used as a guidance by the persons entrusted with the new work. But there was something more than that, the common law of Germany, which, as I have explained, is a modernized system of Roman law; this is not only administered as the law of one-third of the German population, but it is also the basis of all the codes, and it is the main subject of legal education throughout Germany. It is not taught in divisions or branches only, but as an organized system, each part being considered not only in itself, but also in its relations to the other part and to the whole. This conception of the system of private law as a whole, and the perfection of the classifications and definitions brought about by the successive work of generations of eminent men, is a preparation for the work of codification which cannot be overvalued. It is, in my opinion, a condition precedent to the success of any codification on a large scale.

On July 2, 1874, a commission was appointed for the purpose of preparing a draft Civil Code for the German empire. [...] The work was divided into five parts, which were apportioned among five members of the commission, who were respectively to prepare drafts relating to the parts entrusted to them. Each of these five draftsmen was provided with an experienced assistant taken from outside the commission. The business of the draftsmen was to collect materials as to the existing law, to consider how far they could be used, and each, besides drafting his part, was to furnish a summarized statement of the materials and of his manner of dealing with the same. The draftsmen were to hold regular meetings, in which they were to discuss the form and language of the code as well as such matters of principle which were relevant to the whole, or at least to several parts, and also all questions as to the systematic arrangements and the determination of conflicts of jurisdiction between the several parts. The commission was to meet when required for the purpose of determining all points involving important matters of principle, and also such conflicts of jurisdiction as the draftsmen could not agree upon.

Four out of the five parts were completed in this manner in the course of seven years; the parts dealing with the law of obligations were at first delayed owing to the illness of the draftsman, and on his subsequent death were abandoned altogether, the Dresden draft of 1866, which I have already mentioned, having been substituted as a basis of discussion. During the years from 1874 to 1880, the draftsmen held weekly meetings for the purposes I have mentioned, and the commission had altogether seventy-eight meetings. From December, 1880, to October, 1881, the meetings were interrupted so as to give all members time to study the proposed drafts. At the last-mentioned date the second stage of the work began, during which the draft was gone through section by section, and an elaborate procedure was adopted for the purpose of securing the proper drafting of the amendments; the whole draft as amended was then again submitted to the commission for discussion, and finally settled at the end of 1887. Thus the work of the commission had taken thirteen years, out of which seven were used for the first drafting and six for the revision. [...]

[An] invitation [for public comment] was responded to in the amplest manner. The floods of pamphlets, magazine articles, speeches, debates, newspaper leaders and paragraphs, and literary productions of all sorts and sizes, which deluged Germany soon after the publication of the draft, cannot be adequately described. Most of the criticism was fair, and some of it was sensible and useful. [...] As far as I have ascertained, only one of the critics, Mr. Bähr, a member of the imperial court at Leipzig, a very eminent but somewhat crotchety jurist, objected to the code on the ground of his general disapproval of codification. Several distinguished men were of opinion that the draft was so hopelessly bad that it could not be mended; others agreed as to the defective quality, but thought that the unity of law was so valuable to Germany that a bad code was better than no code. The great majority among practical as well as theoretical lawyers recommended a certain number of alterations, but approved of the draft as a whole. On December 15, 1890, another commission was appointed for the purpose of preparing a second draft on the basis of the first, but with due regard to the expressions of opinion, to which I have referred. [...] As in the last commission, one draftsman was appointed for each part, but one member was appointed as general draftsman. The second draft was completed and published during the current year, and it is generally thought that it will be submitted to the Reichstag during the now approaching session. A prolonged discussion is not expected. Either the draft will be accepted as it stands or with a few minor amendments, or it will be rejected. In the latter event several decades will probably elapse before another Sisyphus will roll the heavy stone up the steep hill. The general Congress of German lawyers which met in the course of the year 1895 has, by a large majority, expressed a strong hope that the present draft will be accepted. The most important Chambers of Commerce are successively passing similar resolutions; among practical lawyers and business men the opinion in favour of the code is almost unanimous. The irreconcilables may be divided into two classes; the members of the first class (whom in my introductory remarks I have called the pompous pedants) say the code is not German, and that it represents only a slightly Germanized system of Roman law. It is vain to tell them that the influence of Germanic law has been very marked throughout all the parts of the code; that, in their opinion, is not sufficient. They say that Roman law is constructed on a principle differing altogether from the principle of German law, and that the German law ought to abandon that principle. They do not heed, or perhaps they regret, that the thought of the educated classes in Germany has now for four centuries been under the influence of classical culture, of which the Roman law is by no means the worst product; that the Roman law itself is, by a large number of persons, looked upon with familiarity and fondness; that there never was any common Germanic law, and that neither they nor their Germanistic predecessors have succeeded in reducing the Germanic law into a scientific system. What these learned men would like is a return to the time when status was everything and contract was nothing. But they know quite well, or at least they ought to know, that whether the code be accepted or not, the great elemental forces which determine the economical life of nations are not diverted from their course by the affected and artificial aspirations of a retrogressive romanticism.

If they were alone, they would hardly be a danger to the prospects of the code; but the factious fanatics, whom I have mentioned as a second class of opponents, use the support of men of learning and distinction, about whose good faith and honourable feeling there can be no doubt, for their own sinister purposes. These violent politicians object to the code on various grounds. There is one section who takes up the German cry. They are the people who wish to re-introduce race-distinctions into modern life, and who affect to look upon the code as made in the interest of those whom they wish to treat as intruders. Their argument is rhetoric and most of their facts are fiction, but unfortunately, they are not a *quantité négligeable* in German public life. The Ultramontanes stand on more solid ground; to them obligatory civil marriage and the possibility of divorce *a vinculo* are abominations, and some of them will not sanction any code which affirms these institutions. The fact that civil marriage is now compulsory throughout the empire, that divorce is in most parts of Germany allowed by the existing law, and that there is no prospect of any change in that respect, whether the code be passed or not, has no influence on these politicians, and it is only a question whether they be numerous enough to outvote the supporters of the code.

Another section opposes the code on the ground that it is not sufficiently socialistic in its tendencies, and that in manifold ways it withholds the protection to which the weak are entitled in their struggle with the strong. In answer to these opponents it can be proved that in several respects the draft code goes further in the direction of socialism than any previous legislation, and also that whatever views may be held as to the ultimate prospects of socialistic doctrine, it is quite clear that at the present day a large majority among the educated portions of the German nation is opposed to them, and that a code which would disregard the view of that majority would have absolutely no chance of being accepted.

The same may be said of the opposition which proceeds on the ground that married women ought to have been treated in a manner more in accordance with modern ideas. It is quite true that married women in England are at the present moment in a much more satisfactory position than their German sisters are, or will be after the introduction of the code, but an attempt to imitate English legislation in that respect would have met with irreconcilable opposition. The general opinion, as I have mentioned before, is that all practical and substantial objections to the contents and arrangement of the first drafts have been recognized and removed by the authors of the second. It has in fact been said by competent men that the second draft is not the work either of the first or of the second commission, but of all lawyers in Germany. [...]

Questions/Comments

- Schuster points to several distinctly "Civilian" qualities in the BGB. It is, after all, a codification that aims to operate as an organized system. He explained that each part of the Code (e.g., its provisions on tort, contract, property, or family law) is to be considered in relation to the other parts, and to the whole of the Code, which is understood to be a comprehensive system of private law. Schuster praised the BGB's "perfection of classification and definitions." And, of course, he also lauded the BGB's Roman pedigree.
- The Roman influence on the BGB is one of the Civil Code's most contested attributes. Roman Law lay at the center of the intense intellectual debate – often referred to as the *Kodifikationsstreit* (codification dispute) – that swirled around the nearly century-long discussion over codification in Germany. Early in the nineteenth century the Heidelberg law professor Anton Friedrich Justus Thibaut called for the codification of private law in the German realm. Among his many arguments was the claim that unifying the law would nudge the divided German people towards social, cultural, and political unity. Thibaut proposed assembling a code through the logical extrapolation of received Roman Law. The Berlin law professor Friedrich Carl von Savigny strenuously objected to Thibaut's rush to codification, insisting that the Germans had not yet achieved the necessary level of legal sophistication. Central to von Savigny's position was his view that law should be reflective of the spirit of the people it sought to govern, a concept he labeled the *Volksgeist*. Thibaut's call for codification failed von Savigny's standards for at least two reasons. First, Germany's divided people still lacked a collective *Volksgeist*. Thibaut had it out of order, von Savigny argued. Codification could not precede, and be used to propel a people to, unity. Rather, codification was only possible as a derivative of a culturally and politically unified community. Second, Thibaut's proposed reliance on received Roman Law in his call for codification was an abandonment of the essential "Germanness" that should necessarily give life to a new German code. And lacking that German authenticity and legitimacy, von Savigny doubted a German code's chances for successfully regulating the Germans. The eventual enactment of the BGB (albeit almost a century after the *Kodifikationsstreit*) might suggest that Thibaut won the dispute. But von Savigny's historicism and sociological jurisprudence nonetheless prevailed as the means by which German

private law was eventually codified. The Civil Code involved a mix of Roman influences and a restatement and systematization of German customary law (which, itself, had been influenced by Roman Law).

- It was not until the many German principalities had been unified in 1871 under the iron, martial grip of Prussian King Wilhelm I and his chancellor Otto von Bismarck that a comprehensive German codification was possible. The opening lines of Schuster's article hint at the legal consequences of the atomization of the Germans into many local tribes, fiefdoms, and principalities, as had been the case in Germania for more than a millennium. Ernst Freund called the legal mélange operating at the dawn of the *Deutsches Reich* (German Empire) in 1871 "a perfect chaos of legal systems."[12] William Smithers provided a painstaking accounting of the "startling [legal] anomalies" that existed prior to the enactment of the German Civil Code. He noted, for example, that:

   > [w]ithin a few miles one could find the law of inheritance so different as to give a female no rights in one town, equal rights with other heirs in the next, with heirs of the full- and half-blood dividing the inheritance in a third town. Here the law of primogeniture was ancient and unyielding, there it had never existed. Some cities alone had two distinct bodies of private law, one for the ancient precincts within the walls and the other for the newer parts without.[13]

   In the succeeding pages of his article, Smithers documented the twenty-four jurisdictions into which the Empire was carved prior to German unification and identified their respective principal sources of private law.[14]

- The Prussian drive to unify Germany clearly motivated and facilitated the drafting of the BGB.[15] As noted in Chapter 2, codification has often served as part-and-parcel of nation building, if not crass nationalism. The BGB's entry into force at the dawn of a new century was seen as marking the end of the long process of the consolidation of the Germans and, at last, the emergence of a unified German state.

- What codes already existed as models and inspirations for the drafters of the BGB? What characteristics or qualities of those previous codes found their way into the BGB?

- What about the codification process, as described by Schuster, supports claims that the German Civil Code – as an example of the Civil Law tradition – is uniquely "scientific" and "systematic"? What developments does Schuster identify that contradict that claim?

- One of the values persistently attributed to codification and the Civil Law tradition is its superior legitimacy, at least when compared to the judge-made law in the Common Law tradition. By emphasizing legislation (whether codes or statutes), the Civil Law tradition depends on (hopefully) democratically elected legislatures for the generation of norms. Based on Schuster's description of the process of its drafting and enactment, how democratically legitimate is the BGB? Emphasizing the immense role played by drafting commissions and other unelected experts in the preparation of the BGB, what do you make of Schuster's claim that "[a] prolonged discussion [of the draft BGB was] not expected" in the Imperial Parliament? Does the BGB benefit from other sources of legitimacy?

- At the time of its enactment and entry into force the BGB was described in nearly breathless terms:

  "The greatest among [Germany's] exploits is a Civil Code."[16]

  "[The Civil Code is] a monument of legal learning and ... one of the ripest expressions of the aims and methods of modern civil jurisprudence."[17]

  "[The Civil Code] works an almost unprecedented revolution in the jural life of the German Empire. It may well be questioned whether an upheaval of like extent has ever taken place anywhere."[18]

  "[The Civil Code] is the most carefully considered statement of a nation's laws that the world has ever seen."[19]

  More than a century after its enactment the Civil Code remains in force, in much the same form as when it was adopted. One commentary summed up the wonder of the BGB's endurance in these terms: "The fact that the BGB has lasted so long, providing legal solutions to a variety of social and economic problems arising under imperial, social democratic, totalitarian and liberal social state political regimes, provides a lasting tribute to the wisdom and foresight of its drafters. The BGB has served Germany well."[20] The images in Figure 7.1 hint at the (biblical) reverence in which the BGB is held in Germany.

- Is it good or bad that a law or legal regime enjoys so much reverence? Is there a legal regime in your primary or "national" legal system that is so thoroughly embraced, appreciated, and celebrated? If so, why has it attracted so much acceptance and respect? Do those claims of exceptionalism preclude constructive criticism of the regime and hinder useful legal reform?

- The BGB's longevity should not be taken to mean that it has gone unchanged across the century of its operation. Mathias Reimann noted that "[m]assive changes were [enacted to] family law" where "post-World War II constitutional commands of gender equality and children's rights as well as changing social conditions required the replacement of the original patriarchal model with a modern regime."[21] Yet, other changes to the BGB were on the level of "detail." This led Reimann to conclude that "the BGB's provisions in the core areas of private law [...] stood by and large at the end of the twentieth century as they had stood at its beginning."[22] So, while it has evolved, the *Bürgerliches Gesetzbuch* has mostly remained the same. That is true even if it barely survived the Nazis, who planned to rewrite the Civil Code.[23] The Nazis' BGB reform initiative was never implemented and it died with Hitler.[24] Half a century later, prompted in part by a European Community directive requiring the harmonization of consumer sales law amongst the member states of the European Community, "the German legislature undertook a massive

(a) Political cartoon from 1896, the year the Civil Code was enacted

(b) Cover from a popular edition of the German Civil Code published in 1909

Figure 7.1 The German Civil Code – "A Monument of Legal Learning"

reform of the centerpiece of the German Civil Code [...]."[25] The changes rippling across the German legal system as a result of its membership in the European Union will be considered in this book's penultimate chapter.

- The BGB has strongly influenced Civil Law codifications around the world, including in China. Indeed, the first English-language translation of the BGB was prepared by the Chinese scholar Chung Hui Wang.[26]

The Civil Code was heralded as a modern platform for the launch of a modern Germany in the new century. Or, was the BGB a reactionary regime that entrenched the advantages held by the aristocracy and business elites? This question informed the critiques of the Civil Code that were raised by what Schuster called the "pompous pedants" and the "fractious fanatics." On one hand, the "pompous pedants" worried that the BGB would undo the privileges entrenched in the old system of private law. On the other hand, some of the "fractious fanatics" worried that the BGB did too little to advance progressive aims. The "pompous pedants" were rebuked by the Code, which rejected their view "that status was everything and contract was nothing." The new century for which the BGB had been drafted saw a dramatic embrace of the "liberal-contractual" social model. But the ink was barely dry on the new code before progressive impulses began to reorient German society towards a social welfare model in which the state would play a prominent role as a regulator, and a as redistributor of wealth. These were the aims of some of the "fractious fanatics." Soon after entering into force the BGB had to meet the "challenges of the altered economic and social conditions (influenced by corporate entities, emerging mass media and mass consumption)" even while it was largely "characterized by the bourgeois '*Leitbild*' of contracting parties being formally free and equal [and operating in] a social order consisting of mainly craftsmen, provincial and rural citizens."[27] Wary of its liberal essence, Berlin law professor Otto von Gierke criticized the new Civil Code for failing to adequately protect the weak in their contractual relations with more powerful commercial actors. The BGB, von Gierke pleaded, required a "drop of social oil":

> [I]t is a fatal error committed by the draft of the German Civil Code to think the social work can be left to special legislation so that the general private law can be shaped, without regard to the task that has thus been shifted, in a purely individualistic manner. There thus exist two systems ruled by completely different spirits: a system of the general civil law that contains the "pure" private law, and a mass of special laws in which a private law, tarnished by and blended with public law, governs. On the one side a living, popular, socially coloured law full of inner stimulus, on the other an abstract mould, romanistic, individualistic, ossified in dead dogmatics. The real and true private law can now develop in all its logical splendor oblivious of the heretical special laws [...]. But the general law is the native soil out of which the special laws also grow. By contact with the general law our youth learn legal thinking. The judges take their nourishment from it. What a fatal abyss opens before us! What a schism between the spirit of the normal administration of justice and the administrative jurisdiction that is being extended further and further! What a [...] danger of stagnation and degeneration of jurisprudence. [...][28]

Von Gierke's concern was not that German lawmakers would altogether neglect pressing social issues. He worried that relegating those policies to "special legislation" *outside* the Civil Code would have several troubling effects. First, there would be the great temptation to give special legislation less weight – even if it was formally the equal of the Code – merely because it operated outside the Code's (idealized) comprehensive system. Second, because special legislation would operate in tandem with the BGB, there was a risk that its implementation would be greatly complicated, not the least by potential conflicts with the Code. Third, the Code's centrality to German jurisprudential self-understanding ensured that German jurists would be socialized by and oriented to the BGB's liberalism, with *sub silentio* disregard for the social concerns addressed in supplementary statutes. I pointed to this complex arrangement in this chapter's introduction when I noted that the BGB functions as the gravitational core of German private law around which other codes and supplementary statutes orbit. We will get a concrete example of this structure – and the chance to consider von Gierke's concerns – in Chapter 12 of this book.

Perhaps in response to concerns like those voiced by von Gierke, at least two BGB provisions "have been applied with great effect to adapt the more formalistic clauses of the code to suit the circumstances of the situation."[29] In particular, these flexible provisions have permitted consideration of social justice concerns where the Code otherwise seems to neglect them. Section

German Civil Code

Section 138
Legal transaction contrary to public policy; usury

(1) A legal transaction which is contrary to public policy is void.
(2) In particular, a legal transaction is void by which a person, by exploiting the predicament, inexperience, lack of sound judgment or considerable weakness of will of another, causes himself or a third party, in exchange for an act of performance, to be promised or granted pecuniary advantages which are clearly disproportionate to the performance.

[Translation by Russell A. Miller]

German Civil Code

Section 242
Performance in good faith

An obligor has a duty to perform according to the requirements of good faith, taking customary practice into consideration.

[Translation by Russell A. Miller]

138 in the BGB's General Provisions (Book One), and Section 242 (one of the general provisions framing the Law of Obligations covered by Book Two), impose vague standards of "public policy" and "good faith" in private and contractual relations.

German courts have seized on these provisions to protect the weak in private relations that, in the courts' view, offend broadly defined public interests or expansive notions of good faith. Importantly, these provisions open up an interpretive space for German courts that appears to contradict the mechanical and formalistic function typically attributed to the judicial role in the Civil Law tradition.[30] Is this a small measure of the "Free Law" that Kantorowicz called for in the text we considered in Chapter 3? Not surprisingly, it is this judicial flexibility that gives §§ 138 and 242 (sometimes referred to as the "general clauses") an important role in the next chapter's examination of the dialogue taking place in the German legal system between the Civil Law tradition (embodied by the BGB) and the Common Law tradition (embodied by Germany's post-war constitutionalism). It is important to underscore, however, that §§ 138 and 242 are exceptions in the BGB, which otherwise strives to provide German judges and lawyers with a comprehensive, conceptually rigorous, and highly systematized regulatory regime of norms that merely await their (more or less) straightforward application to the infinite range of circumstances that can arise in life. That portrayal of the Civil Code might be just another way of saying that German private law is a classic expression of the Civil Law tradition.

7.2 Values and Style: What Makes the *Bürgerliches Gesetzbuch* a *German* Civil Code?

Sections 138 and 242 – the BGB's general clauses – also serve as an invitation to consider the significant differences between the BGB and other civil codes, such as the *Code Napoléon*. The French *Code civil* of 1804 is widely regarded as the world's other (and first!) great codification.[31] Like § 242 of the BGB, the French Code also has provisions calling for "good faith" in contractual relations. For example, Article 1134 of the French Code provides: "Agreements lawfully entered into [...] must be performed in good faith." The French Civil Code's demand for good faith could be permissively interpreted by the courts as a requirement for justice or equity. But similar to the BGB's general clauses, the French principle of good faith has not become a dominant feature of contract law. Article 1134, one commentator noted, is "difficult, not to say impossible," to apply.[32]

Are the similarities around the concept of good faith just one example – out of many – of a fundamental uniformity or convergence amongst civil codes, which might be seen as little more than localized expressions of the globally disseminated Civil Law tradition? In the following excerpt Catherine Valcke reminds us that, beyond God's decision to write it in German (as the joke suggests), other characteristics distinguish the *Bürgerliches Gesetzbuch* as uniquely German.

Catherine Valcke
Comparative History and the Internal View of French, German, and English Private Law
19 CANADIAN JOURNAL OF LAW & JURISPRUDENCE 133, 144, 148–150 (2006)[*]

* * *

It is well-known that German law shares the *ius commune* heritage of French law and indeed resembles it in many ways. But German and French legal histories differ in one fundamental respect: whereas the French legal system was a child of the French revolution, the German legal system did not congeal until a century later. And the intervening century happened to be particularly rife with political and intellectual transitions. [...] I will, here again, outline only those historical moments that are particularly useful for the purpose of understanding German private law from the inside.

The first such moment is the abrupt post-revolution decline of the reign of Reason triggered in large part by Kant's teachings, in particular his theory of knowledge. [...]

* * *

[...] One should therefore not be surprised to find that the idea/fact tension that ran through Kant, Hegel, and Savigny, while it manifested itself too late to impact in any

---

[*] © *Canadian Journal of Law and Jurisprudence* 2006. Reproduced with permission of the Licensor through PLSclear.

serious way upon the formation of French law, is palpable in many different aspects of German private law.

Within the BGB, this tension perhaps is most strongly reflected through the coexistence of the individualistic ideal of *Privatautonomie*, on the one hand, with the "socialist oil" of the general clauses of § 138 and § 242, on the other. Like the French principle of the autonomy of the will, the German notion of *Privatautonomie* celebrates the subjective – the freedom of each individual to govern himself through his own will. But unlike the French principle, its German counterpart is immediately tempered, within the BGB, by the imposition of constraints upon the way in which this freedom can be exercised. Sections 138 and 242 indeed insure that only those acts of will that are deemed acceptable in the larger context of the German juridical order ever materialize as legal facts. It has also been noted that some parts of the BGB are Germanic in tone, whereas others are unmistakably Romanistic. This suggests that the drafters of the BGB were concerned to preserve both the facts of German history and the written Reason of Roman law. Neither of the subjective or the objective is portrayed as overtaking the other in the BGB. In true Hegelian fashion, subjective and objective elements appear to be involved in a dialectic interplay, whereby each simultaneously limits and reinforces the other. As one German commentator aptly suggested, the BGB stands as an attempt "to reconcile several different value-systems which nineteenth-century German society had allowed to co-exist without coalescing."

The same subjective/objective tension can arguably be said to inform other institutional features of the German legal system beside the BGB, moreover. Legal historians have often noted, for example, that the German codification process was much longer than the French, and that it was conducted with greater concern for historical continuity. They have also commented on the BGB being more academic and exhaustive than the Napoleonic code, and German judicial decisions being less cryptic, more readily indexed, and generally more accessible than French ones. In addition, judges would be more active and the boundary between private and public law more elusive at German law than at French law. These features arguably all are consistent with German law being grounded in a conception of the subjective and the objective as dialectically interactive and French law being instead rooted in a conception of the subjective and the objective as hierarchically ordered, with the subjective coming first.

The German codifiers' greater concern for historical continuity is entirely consistent with the objective being considered as significant as the subjective. Moreover, the construction of an internally coherent system of rules based upon two theoretical opposites – the subjective and the objective – is bound to be a more difficult and protracted process than that of a system centered upon a single axle – the subjective only. That the German codification process lasted twenty years, whereas the French took only four, is not all that surprising from this perspective. That its final product was more academic similarly should have been expected, for a system that aspires to embody two theoretical opposites cannot but be more complex, less easily digestible, than a system whose components all are derived from a single first idea. That the German code was more comprehensive, finally, can also be explained in those terms. The construction of a system by way of logical deduction from a single idea is a linear process that need not be stopped at any particular level of abstraction. It may be that the French codifiers did not worry about their code being exhaustive because they considered that those who would be applying the rules, viz., the judges, or any other minimally intelligent French citizen, could, if needed, easily pick up the deductive process where the codifiers had left off and pursue it further. In contrast, the construction of a system grounded in equal and interacting parts of subjective and objective necessarily is itself a circular feedback process that combines deduction and induction

7.2 BGB: Values and Style

in proportions that cannot be determined *a priori*, through formal logic alone. The German codifiers thus would naturally have been concerned to provide judges with as much direction as could be given without reaching intolerable levels of complexity. They would have considered such levels to be quite high, furthermore, as those in charge of applying the code – the judges, and only the judges – were to be learned experts with levels of academic training comparable to their own.

***

Questions/Comments

- Valcke identifies six or seven ways in which the German Civil Code (its drafting, values, and style) are different to the French Civil Code. Can you identify them?
- The theoretical dialectic that Valcke attributes to the BGB and, by contrast, finds lacking in the French Civil Code, merits an explanation. According to Valcke, the French legal tradition is characterized by a single conceptual framework, namely the revolutionary force of rationality, including the new focus on the interests and power of the individual. After all, only rationality could explain the violent rupture with the historical inertia of tradition and caste according to which French society was organized prior to the Revolution. "Centuries of history were to be erased," Valcke explained, "and a whole new nation rebuilt out of ideas."[33] As its complex, systematic structure demonstrates, rationality also has its place in the BGB. But Valcke's point is that the German Civil Code also makes room for "facts" and "history." After all, von Savigny's historicism played a fundamental role in the German codification process. This ensured that elements of the fact of applied law in the Germanic realm – the "irrational" customary law that historically prevailed or operated alongside Roman Law – is evidence of the BGB's split personality. In no small part, the BGB is seen as a codification of the historical fact of (customary) German law, and not as a clean, revolutionary break with the jurisprudential past. One consequence of this, as Valcke sees it, is that the rational assertion of individuality (the subjective) so central to the revolutionary Napoleonic Code is tempered in the German Civil Code by communitarian interests that were carried into the present by traditional or customary law. Maybe this is a long-winded way of saying that the French Code more profoundly affirms individual will, while the German code makes a slightly less rigorous commitment to individual will.
- Valcke says there is a distinctly German "tone" to the BGB. What would that be?

Confirming much of the preceding discussion – both as regards the BGB's debt to the Civil Law tradition and as regards its distinctive German character – Mathias Reimann has identified four distinguishing "hallmarks" of the BGB's style.

Mathias Reimann
The Good, the Bad, and the Ugly: The Reform of the German Law of Obligations
83 Tulane Law Review 877, 879–881 (2008–2009)[*]

* * *

[...] [The] BGB's original hallmarks [include]: the BGB was the result of a thorough drafting process; it was the fruit of a highly developed legal science (*Rechtswissenschaft*); it was designed to contain elementary rules with a long shelf life; and it was the child of (German) nationalism.

To begin with, the BGB was the result of a lengthy and almost excessively thorough drafting process and debate. Over more than two decades, three successive commissions staffed by academics, government lawyers, judges, members of the bar, and even nonlawyers produced drafts which were widely discussed among experts, interest groups, and even among the public before being presented to the legislature. The Imperial Parliament (*Reichstag*) then thoroughly debated the draft and made substantial changes before enacting the final version in 1896. Even then, the legal profession was given four years to adjust to the new regime before the Code eventually entered into force. As a German saying goes, "good things take time" ("*Gut' Ding will Weile haben*"), and in making the BGB, both jurists and politicians took it to produce a quality product.

The BGB was also the fruit of nineteenth-century German legal science and especially shaped, in its style and structure, by its Romanist branch (*Pandectism*). As a result, the BGB was not only based on fundamental principles but also rigorously (although not flawlessly) systematic in its organization. It was highly integrated through the complex interplay of its five main books and its many chapters, sections, etc. And it was terse as well as precise in its formulations which required very close reading and great care in application. On the whole, the Code was like a complex and finely-tuned machine, built by highly trained experts for highly trained experts; in the hands of a layperson, it was virtually useless.

The Code was designed for a long shelf life. Especially in its law of obligations, it by and large limited itself to principles and rules considered so proven by pedigree and so warranted by rationality that they were essentially timeless. Of course, the BGB was not politically neutral, neither in its fundamentals nor in many of its individual provisions; most contemporary jurists fully recognized that, and the *Reichstag* debated the draft in openly political terms. But the BGB was apolitical in the sense that it sought to transcend the political battles and preferences of the day and that it did not compromise its fundamental principles for the benefit of particular interests. Thus, when the legislature decided to provide heightened protection for certain consumers or accident victims, it implemented these policies by separate statute, that is, outside of the BGB. The Code itself was to remain aloof.

Finally, the BGB was an ostensibly *national* Code. Like the French *Code civil* of 1804, the Italian *Codice civile* of 1865, and the Swiss codification(s) of 1907 and 1911, the BGB's very purpose was the unification of national law. The codification project began as soon as Germany had achieved political unity under Bismarck (1871) and the federation was granted the requisite legislative jurisdiction over all of private law (1873). The Code eventually replaced both the (theoretically residual but in fact often dominant) Roman law and the multitude of more particularized and local regimes. It gave the German nation a truly unified private law for the first time in its almost thousand year history. It was quite appropriate, then, that the Code was celebrated in strongly nationalist terms when it entered into force on January 1, 1900.

[*] Excerpt reprinted with permission from the author.

7.2 BGB: Values and Style

Questions/Comments

- Reimann seems to praise the BGB's reliance on abstract but enduring general principles. Besides facilitating the Civil Code's longevity, Reimann says this feature of the BGB also might have been a reaction to the excessive detail of the 1794 Prussian Civil Code, which was one of the BGB's Germanic predecessors. The Prussian Code was intended to be a truly comprehensive *ex ante* statutory regime addressing all of life's contingencies. The Prussian Code, it was hoped, might dispense with lawyers altogether. Judges were expected to exercise little or no interpretive discretion in their mechanical implementation of the Code, which had more than 17,000 sections.[34] By contrast, the BGB contains only 2,385 sections. This kind of reductionism in a civil code is possible only if it relies on impressive feats of abstraction and logical systemization. Not everyone sees the BGB's generality in positive terms. Robert Riegert criticized the Civil Code for its excessive abstraction. As an example, Riegert pointed to the broad application of the concept *Rechtsgeschäft* (an act having legal significance) across the BGB.[35] He questioned whether "all actions falling within [that] theoretical classification [should] be treated identically despite their differences? Should a person be able to rescind a transfer of property or a marriage as easily as he can an unexecuted purchase contract? No, the demands of real life will not permit the law to apply the same rules of rescission to all the diverse situations in which [*Rechtsgeschäften*] play a part."[36] For Riegert, another glaring example of the BGB's bewildering degree of abstraction is that it lumps together "the law of obligations" in a single "second book," including 133 generally applicable sections governing contracts, unjust enrichment, and torts. Riegert complained that "these areas have [little] in common: they are different forms of obligations. The relationships and facts leading up to tort and contract obligations differ completely."[37] Riegert also concluded that the BGB's abstraction makes it inaccessible to the layperson. Non-German jurists fare even worse. "The American lawyer trying for the first time to solve a contract problem under the BGB," Riegert said, "is like a hypothetical purchaser of a General Electric stove who discovers that the instruction manual covers all appliances General Electric manufactures and that he must work his way through six levels of abstraction in order to learn how to operate his stove."[38] What are the tools a German jurist has at his or her disposal when approaching the Civil Code's abstraction?
- As Reimann points out, despite its widely recognized importance in the history of a unified Germany, the working content of the BGB does not hold a place in the popular German imagination. It is a technician's instrument that is cherished, if at all, by scholarly experts. As a result of its graceful, literary quality, however, the French Code speaks directly to the French people. Konrad Zweigert and Hein Kötz confirm this view of the BGB:

The BGB is not addressed to the citizen at all but to the professional lawyer. It deliberately eschews easy comprehensibility and waives all claims to educate its reader; instead of dealing with particular cases in a clear and concrete manner it adopts throughout an abstract conceptual language which the layman, and often enough the foreign lawyer as well, finds largely incomprehensible, but which the trained expert, after many years of familiarity, cannot help admiring for its precision and rigor of thought.

The concepts used by the draftsman – "Verfügung," "Vollmacht," "Einwilligung," "unverzüglich," "in gutem Glauben," and many others – are always used in exactly the same sense. Sentence construction indicates where burden of proof lies, and repetitions are avoided by means of cross-references to amplifying sections. But the BGB has none of the elegance and rich compactness of the French Code Civil, none of its epigrammatical pith and suppressed passion; instead, in deference to accuracy, clarity, and completeness it often goes in for a prim Chancery style, complex syntax, and rather Gothic cumbrousness, even where it would have been easy enough to hit upon more lively and clearer words.

The BGB, then, is no work of literature, but "the legal calculating machine par excellence." [...] In France, Austria, and Switzerland ordinary citizens may have a feeling of warm affection, of closeness to their Code; in Germany not even the lawyer does; instead, the undeniable technical merits of the BGB exact a cool, even grudging, admiration.[39]

If we stay with the joke that opened this chapter, then all of this means that God meant to give the German people a perfect Civil Code in their native language, but then produced a text so obscured by its complexity and abstraction that it would need to be interpreted – and presented to ordinary Germans – by trained specialists. Not priests, in this case, but jurists.

Whatever advantage the French *Code civil* has over the German *Bürgerliches Gesetzbuch* regarding popular appeal, literary grace, and accessibility, it falls short of the intricacy and inner logic of the BGB's systematic organization. The French Code, we are reminded, "is hardly a model of ideal organization."[40] But a particular characteristic of the German Civil Code is its almost mechanistic complexity, like the intricate workings of a fine, German-made watch. It depends on logically constructed and carefully defined concepts from which the rule of decision in a case must be deduced. The following material is meant to give you a glimpse of the BGB's "rigorous system."

7.3 The Regulatory Technique of the German Civil Code

Generations of German jurists have been trained according to the "regulatory technique" of the BGB. This section offers a cursory sketch of the BGB's content, structure, and operation.

The BGB is arranged in five parts or "books" that roughly reflect the Pandects' division of the Roman Law into its relevant fields (recall Schorling's

7.3 The Regulatory Technique of the German Civil Code

mention of the Pandects in his text excerpted in Chapter 4). The Civil Code includes: Book One – General Provisions (*Allgemeiner Teil* – §§ 1–240); Book Two – Law of Obligations (*Recht der Schuldverhältnisse* – §§ 241–853); Book Three – Possession and Property Obligations (*Sachenrecht* – §§ 854–1296); Book Four – Family Law (*Familienrecht* – §§ 1297–1921); and Book Five – Law of Succession (*Erbrecht* – §§ 1922–2385).

Ernst Freund summarized the BGB's five books and its general character in an essay published prior to the Code's enactment and entry into force.

Ernst Freund
The Proposed German Civil Code
24 AMERICAN LAW REVIEW 237, 244–249 (1890)

* * *

[…] The establishment of fundamental divisions is only one and the less important part of the work of systematic jurisprudence; its great function is within each of those divisions, the grouping of rights and obligations, of rules and principles, according to their economic end and legal nature, the classification of contracts and estates, the formation and construction of legal conceptions and institutions of more or less comprehensive scope. In a large measure, this process is spontaneous, following the natural operation of legal thought upon the transactions with which it deals. A body of rules relating to a certain group of interests grows, coalesces and separates itself from rules relating to other groups by the mere force of logical discrimination incident to legal reasoning. This constructive work in jurisprudence is done for immediately practical purposes, and becomes part of the mental equipment of the legal profession […].

Upon these principles the plan of the code has been laid out. It is divided into five books, as follows:

A general part, which from a systematic point of view is perhaps the weakest. As the code states no elementary principles, this part contains all matters for which a place could not be found elsewhere. It treats of the law of persons, as far as the same could not be arranged under family law, and of corporations; of the effect of acts and declarations, of the requirement of form, of agency and ratification. It also contains miscellaneous provisions on negligence, error, computation of time, limitations, self-help, *res adjudicata*, evidence, and security.

The Law of Obligations. The first part treats of obligations in general: their subject-matter, their incidents, their extinction and transfer, and of joint and several parties. Obligations arise either from contracts or torts, or from other *quasi*-contractual relations. The subdivision on contracts likewise contains a general part, and then takes up the several classes in succession.

The Law of Things, or of Property Rights, treats of all rights *in rem*. Besides general provisions, especially on rights in real property, it contains the following subdivisions: possession, ownership, perpetual leases, easements and servitudes, and mortgages and pledges. By far the larger part of this book treats of the law of real property.

Family Law, divided as follows: Marriage, including its solemnization, its effect, especially upon the property of husband and wife, and its dissolution; consanguinity, including the relation of parent and child, and adoption, and guardianship.

Law of Succession, *mortis causa*, regulates the mode of transmission and its effect upon the estate. The first part naturally falls into three subdivisions, according to the titles of succession: By will, by contract and by descent. The distinction of succession to real and personal property is unknown to the German law.

In the limitation and classification of their material the codifiers derived valuable aid from the theory and principles established by scientific and practical jurisprudence: there remained another task relating to the formal part of the code, in which the example of former codes and their own judgment could alone afford them any guidance. This was the problem, with what degree of particularity the law should be stated, a problem involving the technical work of putting the material into paragraphs and sections, and the character and scope of every individual rule. The dangers to be avoided were the extremes of generality and of detail.

There are many principles that pervade our ideas of law, which need no expression, or are incapable of formal statement. [...] "All definition in civil law is dangerous;" therefore definitions have been avoided, and a statement of the principal attributes of some relation, in contract, for example, of the essential rights and obligations of both parties, substituted in their place. For this reason, the most general abstractions, such as law, right, or person, are not defined, since their legal effects are not capable of being stated in concise form. The principle of the code is to leave to the development of science all questions that deal with the nature of legal conceptions and cannot be answered by a directly practical rule. [...]

* * *

Instances of omissions of this kind might easily be multiplied, but the general policy of the code amply appears from these illustrations. The reason of the policy is doubtless this: principles of such general scope express only what may be gathered from the specific provisions of law; in so far as these bear out the general principle, it is maintained without express declaration; in so far as they modify or restrict it, the general principle will not be saved by its declaration, but will have to yield to the special rule, not being protected by a superior sanction.

Admitting that this policy is sound, and that an ideal standard of codification demands that the code should contain nothing superfluous or theoretical, yet it is certain that such perfection can be attained only in an advanced condition of legal science. The greatest conciseness and economy in statement is possible only where a scientific system of jurisprudence has become the foundation of legal education and knowledge, for only then the relation of every rule to more general principles, and its bearing upon other parts of the law, can be completely and quickly grasped. [...] This, it must be supposed, is the substance of the argument against codification in [the United States], which insists upon "the absence of those particular habits of thought and expression which are requisite to the task of putting into systematic and accurate form the unwritten rules of our common law."

* * *

To the absence of generalities corresponds a restriction of detail, of special provisions which would either be clearly embraced by principles of larger scope, or which would represent some peculiar combination of circumstances with no application beyond it. The preliminary commission had recommended that there should be no exegetical exposition, but merely a regulation of leading principles with their most important consequences and exceptions. Accordingly, the code was framed as a systematic statement of rules and principles, not as a compilation of precedents or a digest of case law.

If logical abstraction could be carried to perfection, and the law actually attain the standard of certainty towards which it is continually tending, we might indeed expect a code to furnish a plain rule of decision for every conceivable case. As a matter of fact, however well the law may be expressed, there is plenty of room for doubt in its application to particular facts. The question then arises whether the legislator should decide directly as many doubtful cases as may have previously occurred or as he may think of as possible, or whether he shall refuse altogether to enter upon this task as hopeless of satisfactory results. The Prussian *Landrecht* has vainly attempted the former plan, while the present code has repudiated it distinctly. Only where the great importance and frequent recurrence of disputed questions made some authoritative decision desirable, the codifiers have departed from their general policy, and to a certain extent, therefore, the code contains case law, in a number of special rules of construction.

Otherwise, whenever the commissioners foresee exceptional complications of principles, or difficulties in their application, they refer for further direction and development to "practice and science." The operation of practical jurisprudence will be easily understood without further comment. But the constant reference to science may strike us as peculiar, for in the countries of the common law a code would have no science to fall back upon, and the authority of writers would be measured exclusively by their more or less perfect accordance with the decisions of the courts. In Germany legal science claims equal rank with practice, although of course it must always lack the final sanction which belongs to the decision of a court of last resort; but the commissioners have evidently not intended to deny to science the place which it may claim by virtue of its historical position. [...]

* * *

Questions/Comments

- According to Freund, the greatest challenge facing Germany's codifiers was the need to strike the correct balance between abstraction and detail – finding the tolerable degree of generality and the minimally functional degree of specificity. On the one hand, if the code were to be overly general, then it would become a statement of grand theory that isn't useful in solving concrete cases. On the other hand, the code should not succumb to the futile ambition of devising an *ex ante* resolution for every possible conflict that might arise – down to the last detail – by offering discrete, narrow, and highly specific provisions. But this challenge suggests that there is a desirable quantum of abstraction and imprecision in the law. What value do those characteristics lend to a system of norms? Between the two – generality and specificity – where would you place an emphasis? In any case, as noted earlier in this chapter, Riegert believes the Code's drafters got this balance wrong.
- Freund tells us that the Civil Code responded to the generality/specificity challenge in two ways. First, the BGB avoids proclaiming overly abstract concepts by leaving many important or fundamental issues unaddressed. The Civil Code gets away with this, Freund concludes, because those concepts do not need definition, cannot be satisfactorily defined, or are expressed in the values of the Civil Code as a whole. Second, the BGB avoids rigid and overly detailed provisions by relying on a system that calls for

issues to be resolved at a higher level of abstraction – on the basis of broader principles – if possible. This system is referred to as the *Klammerprinzip* (brackets principle). Pursuant to this technique the law is structured to permit as many possible situations to be covered by a general rule – at a higher level of the normative hierarchy – with special circumstances regulated by subordinate provisions. Benefitting from the *Klammerprinzip*, except for a few sensational examples, the Civil Code does not devolve into a collection of thickly detailed provisions that try to respond to narrow and singular circumstances.[41]

- But what is to be done about the Civil Code's undefined broad principles or the gaps in the normative details that might be needed to resolve a case when higher-level general principles will not do the job? Freund suggests that both of these problems are to be addressed by scholarly research (what the Germans call "legal science"). At one end of the spectrum, legal scholars will define the Civil Code's unarticulated, broad principles by resorting to general reason, legal logic, or ethical commitments. At the other end of the spectrum, Freund acknowledges that the *lacunae* (gaps) resulting from the Civil Code's occasional lack of specific details might be resolved by the legislature through the enactment of new laws or the addition of more precise elements. But he worries that the legislature is not well-positioned to rationally and systematically respond to the gaps in the BGB's finely tuned inner workings. The legislature can be useful here, he explains, only if the issue is very important or persistently reoccurs. Otherwise, Freund says that the gaps in the Civil Code's provisions must be filled in by reference to the decisions of other courts and, above all, by the insights provided by legal science. Does this solution align with the passive posture judges are expected to hold in a system influenced by the Civil Law tradition?

- Freund very confidently points to the contribution legal scholars make to the function of the Civil Code. It is acceptable that the BGB fails to clearly articulate all the principles or rules needed to resolve a case because it is accepted that legal scholars will map the uncharted theoretical and doctrinal terrain. Freund concedes that the significant role anticipated for legal scholars in the function of the Civil Code would not be possible except that in Germany legal science has attained an "advanced condition" that serves as the basis for all legal education and legal knowledge. Freund even suggests that the absence of a tradition of sophisticated legal science is one reason why countries like the United States still remain mired in the unsophisticated Common Law tradition. On several occasions I have mentioned the importance of scholars in legal systems influenced by the Civil Law tradition. Thanks to Freund, I hope you now see just how central legal scholars are to the function and practice of German private law. How do you feel about the position of legal scholars in this system? How is their contribution legitimated? What perspectives does the significant role

7.3 The Regulatory Technique of the German Civil Code

of legal scholars prioritize or perpetuate? What are the advantages of the system's reliance on legal scholars?
- From Freund's excerpt it is possible to chart the key features of the BGB's regulatory technique. First, issues should be resolved at the highest level of generality possible, resorting to a deeper degree of specificity only when necessary and only when the code provides a more detailed provision. Second, gaps with respect to both broader principles or the details needed to address a particular case are to be resolved through a consideration of the commentary of legal scholars.

Freund's excerpt usefully summarizes the manner in which most private law is assigned to the BGB's five books. As difficult as that effort must have been, it was not the hardest task faced by the German codifiers. An even greater challenge lay in accounting for and conceptually classifying the innumerable legal interests arising within the broad fields of private law covered by each of those books.

The BGB's General Provisions in Book One, for example, are arranged in seven Divisions addressing what Freund described as "all matters for which a place could not be found elsewhere." A more generous characterization of the General Provisions might explain that it covers foundational concepts applicable to all private law issues, including the conceptualization and definition of: Persons; Things and animals; Legal transactions; Periods of time and fixed dates relevant to legal acts; Statutes of limitation; The manner in which rights are exercised, including self-help and self-defense; and The provision of security for transactions. Very loosely applying the system we gleaned from Freund's description of the BGB, you understand that the Civil Code invites you to first seek to resolve a case at the level of these most-general issues. That would be a first step, taken before moving more deeply into the particulars of the case by determining which of the subject matter books is implicated by the dispute. For example, applying the General Provisions of Book One, you should consider whether all parties to the dispute qualify as a "person" in the law.[42] Or, you should consider whether the object in dispute qualifies as a "thing" or "animal" susceptible to the Code's regime.[43] Or, you should consider whether the statute of limitations for a particular action has lapsed.[44]

If you move past the General Provisions of Book One and determine that the issue involved in your case touches on an obligation owed (perhaps through a contract, due to tortious conduct, or as a result of unjust enrichment), then you would move on to the BGB's Second Book on the Law of Obligations. Book Two is divided into eight Divisions that are thought by Germans to address all facets and the full spectrum of legally meaningful obligations, including contracts, torts, and unjust enrichment. To give you a sense of the intricate systematization of that legal terrain – what Reimann described as "a complex and finely-tuned machine" for addressing private law – nothing will do as well as simply reproducing the table of contents for Book Two.

German Civil Code – Book Two

Law of Obligations

Section 1 Content of the obligations
  Title 1 Obligation to perform
  Title 2 Default of the creditor

Section 2 Shaping legal obligation relations through terms and conditions

Section 3 Contractual obligations
  Title 1 Formation, content and termination
    Subtitle 1 Formation
    Subtitle 2 Principles in consumer contracts and special forms of distribution
      Chapter 1 Scope and principles in consumer contracts
      Chapter 2 Contracts entered outside of business premises and distance contracts
      Chapter 3 Contracts in electronic commerce; online-marketplaces
      Chapter 4 Deviating agreements and burden of proof
    Subtitle 3 Adjustment and termination of contracts
    Subtitle 4 One-sided right to determine performance
  Title 2 Reciprocal contract
  Title 2a Contracts on digital products
    Subtitle 1 Consumer contracts on digital products
    Subtitle 2 Special Provisions on contracts regarding digital products between businesses
  Title 3 Promise to perform to a third party
  Title 4 Paydown, contractual penalty
  Title 5 Rescission; right of withdrawal in consumer contracts
    Subtitle 1 Rescission
    Subtitle 2 Right of withdrawal in consumer contracts

Section 4 Expiration of obligations
  Title 1 Performance
  Title 2 Payment into court
  Title 3 Set-off
  Title 4 Debt forgiveness

Section 5 Transfer of a claim

Section 6 Assumption of debt

Section 7 Plurality of debtors and creditors

Section 8 Specific obligations
  Title 1 Purchase, exchange
    Subtitle 1 General Provisions
    Subtitle 2 Specific types of purchase

Chapter 1 purchase on approval
Chapter 2 Repurchase
Chapter 3 Preemption
Subtitle 3 Purchase of consumer goods
Subtitle 4 Exchange
Title 2 Contracts on part-time residence, contracts on long-term vacation products, agency contracts and exchange system contracts
Title 3 Loan agreement; financial aid and instalment supply contracts between a business and a consumer
Subtitle 1 Loan Agreement
Chapter 1 General Provisions
Chapter 2 Special Provisions on consumer loan agreements
Subtitle 2 Financial aid between a business and a consumer
Subtitle 3 Instalment supply contracts between a business and a consumer
Subtitle 4 Consulting services relating to property loan agreements for consumers
Subtitle 5 Imperative nature, application to entrepreneurs
Subtitle 6 Gratuitous loan agreements and gratuitous financial aid between a business and a consumer
Title 4 Gift
Title 5 Rental contract, lease contract
Subtitle 1 General provisions for rent
Subtitle 2 Rental agreements relating to housing
Chapter 1 General Provisions
Chapter 1a Maintenance and measures of modernization
Chapter 2 Rent
Subchapter 1 Agreements relating to rent
Subchapter 1a Agreements relating to the rent at the beginning of the lease in areas with a tense housing market
Subchapter 2 Provisions on rent amount
Chapter 3 Right of lien of the landlord
Chapter 4 Exchange of parties to the contract
Chapter 5 Termination of the lease
Subchapter 1 General Provisions
Subchapter 2 Rental agreements for an indefinite period
Subchapter 3 Rental agreements for a definite period
Subchapter 4 Company dwellings
Chapter 6 Specifics on the establishment of ownership of rented out apartments
Subtitle 3 Lease agreements on other things and digital products
Subtitle 4 Agreement on the right to a usufruct
Subtitle 5 Agreement on the right to a usufruct of a property

Title 6 Loan
Title 7 Contract for the loan of a thing
Title 8 Service contracts and similar contracts
    Subtitle 1 Service contract
    Subtitle 2 Treatment contract
Title 9 Contract to produce a work and similar contracts
    Subtitle 1 Contract to produce a work
        Chapter 1 General Provisions
        Chapter 2 Construction contract
        Chapter 3 Consumer construction contract
        Chapter 4 Mandatory nature of the provisions
    Subtitle 2 Architect contract and engineer contract
    Subtitle 3 Property developer contract
    Subtitle 4 Package travel contract, travel agency and arranging relevant travel services
Title 10 Brokerage contracts
    Subtitle 1 General Provisions
    Subtitle 2 Arrangement of consumer loan agreements and financial aid in return for permanent
    Subtitle 3 Marriage agency
    Subtitle 4 Arrangement on purchase agreements relating to apartments or single-family homes
Title 11 Offer of a reward
Title 12 Mandate, agency agreements and payment services
    Subtitle 1 Mandate
    Subtitle 2 Agency agreement
    Subtitle 3 Payment services
        Chapter 1 General Provisions
        Chapter 2 Payment service contracts
        Chapter 3 Delivery and usage of payment services
            Subchapter 1 Authorization of payment transactions; payment instruments; Refusal of access to payment account
            Subchapter 2 Execution of payment transactions
            Subchapter 3 Liability
Title 13 Agency without specific authorization
Title 14 Safekeeping
Title 15 Movement of things to the grounds of an innkeeper
Title 16 Corporation
Title 17 Collective corporation
Title 18 Life annuity
Title 19 Unenforceable obligations
Title 20 Suretyship

Title 21 Settlement
Title 22 Promise to pay, acknowledgement of debt
Title 23 Command
Title 24 Bond to the bearer
Title 25 Presentation of things
Title 26 Unjust enrichment
Title 27 Torts

[Translation by Russell A. Miller]

Questions/Comments

- Does the content of Book Two seem logical? Does it encompass the subjects and concerns you would have expected from a purportedly comprehensive regime addressing the Law of Obligations (including contract law and tort law)? What is missing? What is included that seems unfamiliar or out of place?
- Does the table of contents, as a starting point for solving contract or tort disputes, have a natural appeal to you? Is that because you also were socialized and trained in a system predominantly influenced by the Civil Law tradition? Maybe you expect law to be systematized and conceptually structured (that is to say: "codified") in the manner that Book Two approaches the Law of Obligations. Or, maybe your primary or "national" civil code is organized differently. The question is challenging for different reasons for those who were trained in a system predominantly influenced by the Common Law tradition. Are you drawn to or skeptical about Book Two's systematic architecture because it seems so different to the Common Law's reliance on often-opaque, frequently plural, and sometimes conflicting judicial decisions to establish a "regime" for contract law and tort law?
- The table of contents helps illustrate the *Klammerprinzip*. For example, analysis of a contract case begins with the relevant General Provisions in Book One. Application of the provisions generally relevant to obligations are set out in the first seven Divisions of Book Two. These sections address various common contractual issues like formation, extinction, transfer, and standing. Only if the case cannot be resolved with the guidance of the general rules does the analysis turn to the provisions addressing twenty-seven particular obligations identified in Division 8 of Book Two. Among these specific obligations are suretyship agreements.

7.4 Using the Code: A Suretyship Contract Dispute

Let's now consider an actual private law dispute in order to observe in practice some of the elements and functions of the Civil Code that we've discussed. I've chosen a suretyship case, not because it provides extraordinary insight into the character or technique of the Civil Code. To the contrary, one value of the following materials is that they involve a very basic, even ordinary engagement with the BGB. Instead, I chose a suretyship dispute because, like some other private law issues, suretyship has sometimes raised concerns that open up a bridge between the Civil Code (embodying the Civil Law tradition) and constitutional law (embodying the Common Law tradition). The resulting intersection of the two regimes allows me to touch on this book's overarching thesis. Recall that I hoped to convince you that it is not adequate or sufficient to characterize German law and legal culture as merely representative of the Civil Law tradition. As the suretyship materials in this chapter and the next chapter demonstrate, even in a thoroughly "civilian" context such as the codified world of private law covered by the BGB, there is evidence that other traditions are woven into the fabric of German law.

I present a sample of some of the materials relevant to solving a suretyship dispute, including the text of several BGB sections, an excerpt from a scholarly commentary, and a court judgment.

Before engaging with the following suretyship dispute, however, let me start by noting that the English-language term "suretyship" is used as a translation of the German concept of *Bürgschaft*.[45] Yet, in keeping with my view that the best comparative law remains sensitive to social and cultural difference, I do not mean to suggest that German *Bürgschaften* and Anglo-American suretyships are interchangeable equivalents. Contextual and self-reflective comparative work must be done on the subject before any conclusion about the comparative nature of the two institutions can be reached.[46] But, while acknowledging the many, rich challenges translation raises for thoughtful and effective comparison, the English term "suretyship" has been adopted as a usefully related concept that permits the chief work of this chapter to go forward.

With that caveat out of the way, you might be helped by knowing how a respected commentary in US law defines "suretyship":

> [A suretyship is a] contractual relationship resulting from an agreement whereby one person, the surety, engages to be answerable for the debt, default, or miscarriage of another, the principal. [...] In other words, a surety promises to assume responsibility for payment of a debt incurred by another should he or she fail to repay the creditor. [...] The surety's obligation is not an original and direct one for the performance of his [or her] own act, but rather accessory or collateral to the original obligation contracted by the principal and it is of the essence of the surety's contract that there be a valid obligation owed by the principal. [...] In other words, the surety is directly and equally bound with his [or her] principal.[47]

The BGB sections relevant to the suretyship dispute studied here are suggestive of the *Klammerprinzip* discussed above. The applicable regime consists of: the relevant General Provisions of private law from Book One; the relevant general provisions relating to the Law of Obligations in Book Two;

7.4 Using the Code: A Suretyship Contract Dispute

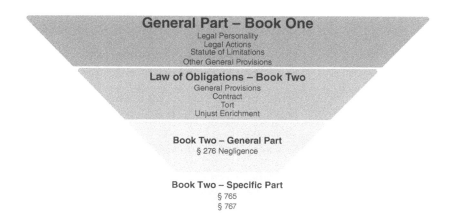

Figure 7.2 German Civil Code and Suretyship: An Example of the *Klammerprinzip*

and, finally, the specific provisions provided by Title 20 of Division 8 in Book Two (§§ 765–778). Only the provisions from the Civil Code's Second Book – the Law of Obligations – are highlighted below because the court judgment I reproduce in this section did not formally address the General Provisions covered by Book One. That is, the dispute could not be resolved on the basis of the legal personality of the parties (Book One, Division 1), doubts about whether a justiciable *Rechtsgeschäft* was at issue (Book One, Division 3), or the possible application of a statute of limitations barring the claim (Book One, Division 5). Instead, the governing rules were drawn from the general provisions of Book Two (§ 276 defining negligence) and the specific provisions dealing with suretyship contracts (§§ 765 and 767). The scheme follows a pattern something like the one shown in Figure 7.2. The text of §§ 276, 765 and 767 are provided below.

German Civil Code

Section 276
Responsibility of the obligor

(1) The obligor is responsible for intention and negligence, if a higher or lower degree of liability is neither laid down nor to be inferred from the other subject matter of the obligation, including but not limited to the giving of a guarantee or the assumption of a procurement risk. The provisions of sections 827 and 828 apply with the necessary modifications.

(2) A person acts negligently if he fails to exercise reasonable care.

(3) The obligor may not be released in advance from liability for intention.

[Translation by Russell A. Miller]

German Civil Code

Section 765
Typical contractual duties in suretyship

(1) By a contract of suretyship the surety puts himself under a duty to the creditor of a third party to be responsible for discharging that third party's obligation.

(2) Suretyship may also be assumed for a future or contingent obligation.

[Translation by Russell A. Miller]

German Civil Code

Section 767
Extent of the suretyship debt

(1) The currently applicable amount of the principal obligation determines the duty of the surety. This applies in particular, without limitation, if the principal obligation has been changed through no fault of or default by the principal debtor. The duty of the surety is not extended by a legal transaction that the principal debtor undertakes after assumption of the suretyship.

(2) The surety is liable for the costs of termination and prosecution of rights that are reimbursable by the principal debtor to the creditor.

[Translation by Russell A. Miller]

Questions/Comments

- What does § 276 accomplish as a provision generally applicable to legal obligations (including suretyship)? How does § 276 serve the dialectic between the objective and the subjective that Valcke attributes to the BGB? Where does § 276 fit in the balance between generality and particularity that Freund said is central to the BGB?
- Section 765 creates the possibility of suretyship and defines the general conditions under which they may come into existence and the purpose they serve. Section 767 provides the answer to the question "what is the scope of a surety's obligation?" This, as you might imagine, becomes a point of considerable significance because it is precisely this question that is likely to be raised when a surety refuses to fulfill a creditor's demand for payment on the credit guarantee. That is, the surety is likely to complain that the demand made by the creditor is not within the scope of the promised guarantee. What general rule does § 767 provide as a resolution for such a dispute?

- Would you have reservations about resolving a suretyship dispute exclusively on the basis of these provisions?

The following excerpt from a BGB commentary demonstrates the important contribution scholars make to the suretyship scheme (and to the rest of the Civil Code). As Freund explained, the relevant BGB provisions are terse and do not seem to provide a ready textual solution to a multitude of issues that might arise from a suretyship dispute. Those gaps are resolved by legal scholars through the application of their highly logical, dogmatic study of the Civil Code. Scholars often publish their analyses in large, painstakingly detailed commentaries that serve as the primary tools for legal practice in Germany. That is true for the private law, such as disputes arising under the BGB, as well as most other fields of law. The exegesis produced by scholars enables a more effective application of the code sections to various circumstances.

The *German Civil Code Volume I – Bürgerliches Gesetzbuch (BGB)* excerpted here is the first English-language commentary to the BGB.[48] Typical of a German legal commentary, it is a massive tome. It consists of two volumes, encompassing nearly 4,000 pages, and discussing – in great detail – each of the Civil Code's 2,385 sections.

Sörren Kiene and Nils Wigginghaus,
Title 20. Suretyships (§§ 765–778)
German Civil Code Volume I – Bürgerliches Gesetzbuch (BGB)
(Gerhard Dannemann et al. eds., 2020)[*]

* * *

§ 765
Function
Underlying Principle

[Margin No. 1] Suretyships are a form of security for obligations and are strictly bound to these obligations by the principle of "accessoriness" (*Akzessorietät*), whereby the suretyship is contingent of secured obligation. Suretyships enable persons with poor creditworthiness to obtain contracts, by making third parties, who are deemed reliable and solvent, liable for their obligations without those third parties entering the respective contracts as a party.

Position within the BGB

[Margin No. 2] Suretyships belong to the so-called personal securities (*Personalsicherheiten*). Consequently, the value of the suretyship depends on the financial standing of the surety. The suretyship has in itself a certain level of risk. The surety cannot directly control if or to which extent the principal debtor fulfils his obligation. This aleatoric element is reflected in the positioning of the suretyship in the BGB, namely after the provisions on gaming and betting.

---

[*] Excerpt reproduced with permission of C.H. Beck Verlag.

Scope of Application

[Margin No. 3] Unlike mortgages or pledges the security of the suretyship is not limited to an object *in rem*. Instead, the original obligation is secured by adding another legally independent obligation of a different party such as the independent guarantee contract (*Garantievertrag*) or the assumed joint liability (*Schuldbeitritt*). [...]

* * *

Context

* * *

Contrary to Public Policy

[Margin No. 8] There is extensive case law concerning the question of the suretyship contracts that are contrary to public policy and therefore void according to § 138(1). Such cases especially concern suretyships by close relatives of the principal debtor. In such instances there is a presumption of unconscionable exploitation by the creditor where the suretyship results in blatant financial burdens, for example, if the surety is not even able to cover the continuously accruing interest of the obligation. The test must be made at the time of the formation of the suretyship contract; later changes to the situation are not to be regarded. Furthermore, circumstances in the individual case must prove that the surety has entered into the surety under emotional pressure and that the creditor may have down-played the risk. The courts have devised several further factors that may be relevant, for example, a surety's lack of experience, though the creditor needs to be aware of such circumstances. The presumption of unconscionable exploitation is rebuttable. The creditor may prove that the suretyship is in fact not contrary to public policy, such as by showing that the surety himself has a commercial interest in the secured contract. The creditor could also demonstrate a lack of knowledge of the financial burden; however, the courts hold creditors responsible for checking the surety's financial standing beforehand. Suretyships that aim to prevent damages due to the transfer of assets to close relatives are usually not contrary to public policy where their use is limited by their purpose and this is expressly stated in the contract.

* * *

§ 767
Function

[Margin No. 1] The 1st Sentence of this provision expresses the scope of the basic principle of accessoriness (*Akzessorietätsgrundsatz*). Whilst § 765 sets the rule that a suretyship may not be created without the existence of a main obligation, § 767 limits the scope of the suretyship with regard to the amount of the surety's obligation. As a general rule, the amount of the surety's obligation may not exceed the amount of the principal debtor's obligation. This general rule has exceptions which each serve to protect the surety's or the creditor's interest. Accessoriness is the core component of any suretyship and is not open to amendment by the parties. Without accessoriness the basis for the third party's liability can never be a suretyship, instead it is a guarantee contract or similar. The 3rd Sentence aims to limit the accessoriness regarding unpredictable additional obligations or extensions of obligations to which the principal debtor agrees after the surety agrees to the suretyship. Restrictions imposed by German law on standard business terms (§§ 305 etc.) when deviating from the law to the detriment of the surety need to be strictly observed and will render most such changes in preformed terms and conditions unenforceable against the surety.

7.4 Using the Code: A Suretyship Contract Dispute

* * *

Explanation
Effects of Accessoriness

[Margin No. 3] Due to the principle of accessoriness (*Akzessorietätsgrundsatz*) of suretyships the currently applicable amount of the principal debtor's obligation is decisive. If the principal obligation was never effective, for example, due to a void contract, there can be no obligation of the surety. The surety's obligation will expire or becomes void if the principal obligation expires or becomes void. The same applies if the main obligation is validly challenged by grounds for avoidance (§§ 116 et seq.). This includes, inter alia, extinction of the main obligation through performance (§ 362), acceptance by the creditor of something else in lieu of performance of the original obligation (§ 364), the exercise of a valid right to set-off (§ 389), or if the debt ceases to exist by virtue of a settlement (§ 779). The suretyship may expire partially if these instruments only apply to a part of the principal's obligation. The suretyship will no longer exist if the principal debtor dies without a successor, though it is often the case that the parties agree that the suretyship should also secure this risk. The suretyship even ends if the main obligation ceases through the fault of the surety; the creditor may however have a claim against the former surety arising out of general principles (i.e., § 280).

Secondary Obligations

[Margin No. 4] If the parties to a suretyship have not agreed otherwise, the surety is also liable for secondary obligations of the principal debtor. Secondary obligations are created by law but have their basis in a contractual relationship and are typically associated with this relationship, such as claims regarding the breach of contractual obligations (cf. §§ 280 et seq.). Subparagraph 1, 2nd Sentence makes express reference to claims regarding damages due to default of the principal debtor (§§ 280(1), (2), 286) as an example only, the list is not exhaustive. Further examples concerning damages are damages in lieu of performance for non-performance or failure to render performance as owed (§ 281), damages in lieu of performance for breach of a duty under § 241(2), (§ 282), damages in lieu of performance where the duty of performance is excluded (§ 283). Secondary obligations within the meaning of Subparagraph 1, 2nd Sentence also include, amongst many others, claims regarding return of reimbursement (§ 285) or claims following a revocation (§§ 346 et seq.). In these cases the original obligation of the principal debtor is transformed into a different obligation. For example, after revocation the original obligation is changed into the obligation to return the performances received (§ 346(1)). Any suretyship for such a contractual relationship would then also secure the obligation to return the performances received.

Avoidance

[Margin No. 5] Claims regarding unjust enrichment (§ 812(1)) often arise where the contract is avoided. These claims are not changed obligations within the meaning of § 767. Whether and to what extent the suretyship secures these obligations, is subject to interpretation of the suretyship agreement alone. The surety will not be liable for those claims associated with the principal debtor's failure to fulfil his obligations, in particular contractual penalty clause, unless there is an express agreement in the contract of suretyship.

Extension

[Margin No. 6] There are several exceptions to the principle of accessoriness (*Akzessorietätsgrundsatz*) to the detriment of the surety, in particular in situations where the interest of the creditor on maintaining a security for his claim is superior to the interest of the surety (i.e., insolvency discharge pursuant to §§ 254, 301 of the *Insolvenzordnung* [InsO or Insolvency Code]). However, Subparagraph 1, 3rd Sentence expresses only one such exception: the liability of the surety cannot be extended unilaterally by a legal transaction (*Rechtsgeschäft*) undertaken by the principal debtor after formation of the suretyship. The wording extended (*erweitert*) shows that this provision does not apply if the legal transaction lessens the duty. The surety's duty may only be extended by legal transaction with his approval, whereby the written form requirement applies in order to protect the surety against an unforeseen and increased risk exposure by a unilateral act of the principal debtor. It does not protect the surety against greater liability, especially in cases where the surety agreed to pay an obligation of the principal debtor which is higher than when the suretyship was formed.

[Margin No. 7] In some instances it is difficult to ascertain whether modifications to a secured contract are in fact extensions or merely equivalent changes, and to which extent the surety has given his implied) approval. The [*Bundesgerichtshof* or Federal Court of Justice] has applied Subparagraph 1, 3rd Sentence to amendments regarding additional orders which led to a significant increase in the value of the principal debtor's performances. In this case, the liability of the surety remains unchanged; it is not increased nor does it expire due to the amendments. However, the liability of the surety does not remain if the amendments are extensive to such a degree that the original obligation has been replaced by a completely new obligation.

* * *

Questions/Comments

- You'll see that I added "margin numbers" in brackets to the Commentary's paragraphs. In fact, the original (and nearly all other German commentaries) simply enumerate the paragraphs (e.g., "1," "2," and "3") without adding the term "margin no." These margin numbers, and not page numbers, are used as the pinpoint citation for the commentary's text. A citation for the excerpt provided here would look like this: Kiene/Wigginghaus, *German Civil Code* (Dannemann, Schulze, Watson eds.), § 765 BGB mn. 1.
- "Margin No. 1" in the material on § 765 provides a simple restatement of the scope of a surety obligation established by the Civil Code, "which does not exceed the principal debt it secures." But the Commentary goes on to portray this rule as the "principle of 'accessoriness' (*Akzessorietiät*)." Where does that concept come from? How does it add to an understanding of the seemingly straightforward rule announced by § 765? Is this an example of the theoretical work Freund expected legal science to do where the Civil Code leaves broad principles unarticulated? Recall that the scholars pursue this task by resorting to general reason, legal logic, or ethical commitments. Do those scholarly tools and methods explain why, as it turns out, the *Akzessorietät* principle roughly aligns with parts of the *American Jurisprudence* definition of suretyship that I quoted earlier: "[a suretyship is] *accessory* or collateral to the original obligation contracted by the principal […]."

- "Margin No. 2" in the material on § 765 reveals the systematic and conceptual logic the scholars attribute to the Civil Code. The Commentary provides insight into the inherent riskiness of a suretyship by noting that the rule is located in the same part of the BGB as the sections relating to gambling.
- For an example of the way in which the Commentary also fills-in the gaps in the provisions' details, consider the depth and detail the scholars add to the terse terms of § 767. In "Margin No. 3," describing the "effects of accessoriness," the Commentary provides concrete rules for at least ten particular scenarios that are not mentioned by the minimal text of § 767. Where do the scholars find these more specific solutions? Other sections of the Civil Code are often cited as the basis for these rules. You should notice that many of the cited Civil Code provisions are found in the general provisions of the Law of Obligations found in Book Two. The Commentary is reminding you of the *Klammerprinzip*: a case should be solved by a more general norm whenever possible.
- I have deleted the small number of footnotes that accompany the excerpted passages from the Commentary. Those citations reveal that, in some instances, the Commentary cites other commentaries as the basis for the conclusions it reaches. Only three cases are cited. That is a typical approach to producing a commentary: extensive reference is made to other scholars' conclusions with an occasional nod to results reached by courts. Agreement among scholars across several commentaries can congeal into a *herrschende Meinung* (controlling opinion), which is a nearly definitive argument in German legal analysis.
- Maybe you can see, even from the brief portions of the Commentary presented here, why it is accepted practice among German lawyers and judges to begin – and often end – their legal research by grabbing a respected commentary and flipping to the pages devoted to the applicable Civil Code sections in order to discover the controlling rule (perhaps in extensive detail) for a case. How does that practice compare with the effort that must be made in your primary or "national" legal system to identify and more fully elaborate the applicable law? What does a German lawyer do if, after resorting to one or several commentaries, he or she finds that the *herrschende Meinung* suggests that his or her client has no prospects for winning the case?
- For eighty years the most prominent and trusted BGB commentary was known as the *Palandt*. It was named after Otto Palandt, a prominent mid-twentieth-century German judge and the work's original editor. Palandt presided over the Commentary's first thirteen editions. It is cherished for its succinct treatment of the Civil Code's thousands of complex sections. The *Palandt* managed to publish a thorough and conceptually sound survey of the BGB in a single volume, in part by deploying a nearly cryptographic system of abbreviation for the many long terms used in German legalese. Most German jurists regarded the *Palandt's* portrayal of a section of the Civil Code as an articulation of the *herrschende Meinung*. In 2021, after eighty years as the *Palandt*, the commentary was renamed for Judge Christian Grüneberg of the Federal Court of Justice. Following activism by students,

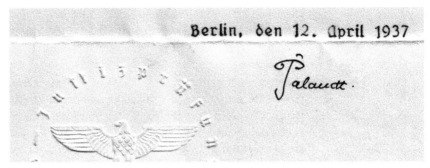

Palandt BGB Commentary
Professor Otto Palandt's signature on Nazi-era documents. Palandt served as the president of the *Reichsjustizprüfungsamt* (Imperial Justice-Examination Office), which was established by the National Socialists in order to centralize the administration of state exams for legal trainees. Previously, the state exams had been administered by state-level justice ministries.

Figure 7.3 The "Palandt" BGB Commentary Controversy

and eventually parliamentarians and powerful jurists, it became indefensible that one of the standard works of German legal culture was named after Palandt, who had been a convinced, prominent, and active National Socialist judge. In Figure 7.3 you can see Palandt's proud signature on a National Socialist-era document.

- Pay attention to "Margin No. 8" in the material on § 765. It mentions the not-infrequent role the Civil Code's general clauses play in the suretyship context. You know that the general clauses – § 138 (public policy) and § 242 (good faith) – serve as the flexible joints ("drops of social oil") in the rigid, liberal mechanics of the BGB. Their "extensive" application in suretyship disputes serves as the bridge to German constitutionalism (and the Common Law tradition) to which I have repeatedly hinted. How all of that functions will become clearer in Chapter 8.

Finally, I present the following excerpt from a judgment in a suretyship dispute. The opinion from the Hamburg Regional Court is an example of the way a German court applies the Civil Code – with help from commentaries and a few published cases. The point isn't that, through your exposure to all of these materials, you should become deeply informed about German suretyship law. Instead, this is a chance for you to see Germany's revered BGB in action, and to have an encounter with an "ordinary" German private law judgment. Read the case with those cultural and stylistic points in mind, without worrying too much about the substantive rules for suretyship involved.

The case featured a suretyship that was concluded in order to secure a building firm against the risk of liability that might result from defects in construction. Of course, there would be no case if no defects had been discovered. There were a large number of deficiencies in the building firm's work on a big new

7.4 Using the Code: A Suretyship Contract Dispute

Berlin apartment block. The building firm was the principal debtor for the resulting liability. It couldn't cover the damages because it had been dissolved as an entity under German corporate law. Due to the absence of the principal debtor, the plaintiff turned to the surety (the defendant in this case) for payment. In fact, the defendant made a series of payments in conformity with the suretyship agreement up to the date of the principal debtor's corporate dissolution. At that time, however, the defendant disclaimed any further obligations. The plaintiff argued that the defendant, as the surety, was liable for the cost of correcting the defects. The plaintiff insisted that the principal debtor's dissolution did not preclude the suretyship claim against the defendant. For its part, the defendant argued that the principal debt and, as a consequence, also the suretyship triggering the *Akzessorietät* principle, expired with the complete dissolution of the principal debtor. The defendant further argued that no exception to the *Akzessorietät* principle is justified because the dissolution of the principal debtor was not the risk the suretyship was intended to secure. The Court ruled for the plaintiff and ordered the defendant to pay damages plus interest.

Regional Court of Hamburg, 17th Civil Chamber
File Number 317 O 347/07; Date: July 2008

[Translation by Russell A. Miller]

12 Zeitschrift für Immobilienrecht 636 (2008)

Principal Contents:

1. Whether a suretyship, which provides security for liability arising from defects, endures after the liquidation and expiration of the principal debtor (a construction company with limited liability) is a question that must be resolved by examining the securitizing purpose of the suretyship and the interests of the parties at the time the suretyship contract was concluded.
2. An exception to the *Akzessorietät* principle may be recognized if the dissolution of the principal debt is the result of precisely the risk against which the suretyship was intended to secure the creditor. Such a case occurs if the liquidation of the principal debtor is caused by a decline in its assets leading to the principal debtor's removal from the Registrar of Companies due to insolvency.
3. In this case, a suretyship that also is intended to secure the money interest of the creditor relating to the fulfillment of liability claims against the principal debtor, nevertheless endures independently.

Tenor:
The defendant is ordered to pay to the plaintiff €10,554.07 plus interest of four percent since 1 February 2008.

* * *

Grounds for the Decision

* * *

[23] Pursuant to § 765 BGB in conjunction with §§ 634, 635 BGB old version, which in the present proceedings pursuant to Art. 229 § 5 S. 1 of the Introduction Act to the BGB,

the defendant owes the plaintiff damages amounting to €10,554.07. There is no dispute that this amount is equal to the maximum amount of the suretyship concluded [...] and for which there already has not been satisfaction.

[24] A suretyship contract has been concluded between the parties.

[25] There is no dispute that a suretyship obligation for the defendant has been created. The only dispute between the parties concerns the issue whether the dissolution or liquidation of the principal debtor discharged the suretyship made by the defendant and whether the defendant can assert this discharge in general and in the present case.

* * *

[28] b. The defendant's obligation has not been satisfied. [...]

[30] bb. The suretyship also has not been discharged due to the dissolution of the principal debtor. It is correct that, in the beginning, the suretyship is dependent upon the continuity and amount of the principal debt. This is the *Akzessorietät* principle, which typically leads to the result that the surety is set free with the termination of the principal debt. This also is true in the case that the principal debt ceases to exist due to the dissolution of the principal debtor (compare BGHZ 82, 323; BGHZ 153, 337; Higher Regional Court of Saarbrücken, OLGR 2007, 533; Higher Regional Court of Berlin, NJW-RR 1999, 25; KGR 2002, 294).

[31] (1) Yet, the continuity of the suretyship does not depend on the continuing existence of the principal debtor. The surety might still be in force, for example, where the principal debtor has been dissolved but has left behind assets. In these circumstances the principal debtor – a company – does not cease to exist merely because it has been removed from the Registrar of Companies (Higher Regional Court of Schleswig, NJW-RR 1993, 754; Higher Regional Court of Cologne, *GmbHR* 2004, 1020; Scholz-K. Schmidt, *GmbHG-Commentary*, Supplement to § 60, margin no. 18; Baumbach/Hueck, *GmbHG-Commentary*, § 60, margin no. 7, margin no. 67 each with further references; Hachenberg, *GmbHG-Commentary*, § 74, margin no. 34). This is not the case here. The plaintiff has not explicitly claimed that the principal debtor still has possession of the company's assets. In any event, this is not conceivable: the company's assets still include a claim against the insolvency administrator under § 73(3) GmbHG. Such a claim requires that the insolvency administrator distribute company assets despite the fact that there are still creditors' claims against the company or that such claims still could be asserted. In this case the insolvency administrator is obliged to satisfy creditors' claims from the dissolved company's assets or to secure them (Baumbach-Hueck, *GmbHG-Commentary*, § 73, margin nos. 9, 12). It cannot be concluded that the principal debtor's insolvency administrator was aware of the plaintiff's warranty claims. In particular, in the independent procedure for the preservation of evidence brought before the Regional Court of Berlin, the plaintiff did not sue the principal debtor. There is no disputing the fact that the company **** Service Ltd., which the plaintiff sued in the Berlin proceedings, is not identical with the principal debtor. It cannot be deduced from the extracts of the Registrar of Companies relating to the principal debtor (Appendixes Beklagter [Defendant] #3, Kläger [Plaintiff] #9) and the company **** Service Ltd. (Appendix Beklagter [Defendant] #4) that the organs possessing power of attorney are identical. It also has not been proven – despite the particular attention the Court paid to the matter during the oral proceedings that took place on 07 May 2008 – that the principal debtor knew about the plaintiff's warranty claims before the termination or dissolution of the principal debtor. If, however, the principal debtor's obligation only becomes known after the completion of the asset distribution in the insolvency process, then the creditor cannot bring forward claims against the company (Baumbach-Hueck, *ibid.* margin no. 9 with further references) with

the consequence that a claim of the company against the insolvency administrator does not arise under § 73(3) GmbHG.

[32] (2) In the present case, however, the suretyship continues in force as an independent obligation despite the complete termination and dissolution of the principal debtor. The *Akzessorietät* principle implicated by the suretyship is subject to exceptions. If this principle collides with the securitizing purposes for which the suretyship contract was concluded, then the suretyship may continue to exist as an independent obligation in its full amount (BGHZ 82, 323; Higher Regional Court of Saarbrücken, OLGR 2007, 533, Higher Regional Court of Berlin, KGR 2002, 294). This is especially true if the liquidation of the principal debtor is precisely the risk against which the suretyship was intended to secure the creditor. Such a case is recognizably present if the liquidation is the result of bankruptcy and the principal debtor – a limited liability company – is erased from the Registrar of Companies due to lack of assets (BGH 82, 323; BGHZ 153, 337; Higher Regional Court of Saarbrücken, OLGR 2007, 533; Higher Regional Court of Berlin, NJW-RR 1999, 25). This initially applies to cases in which the reasons for liquidation provided by § 60(1) Nos. 4, 5, 7 GmbHG are present. [...] That is not the case here. There is no dispute that the principal debtor has been liquidated pursuant to § 60(1) No. 2 GmbHG by way of the decision of the sole shareholder with effect on 29 December 2000. It has not been demonstrated that bankruptcy was the cause of the principal debtor's dissolution.

[33] Nonetheless, the suretyship endures in the present case. The liquidation of the limited liability company was necessarily a reaction to the company's complete lack of assets because this is, as explained, a requirement for the complete termination and dissolution of the GmbH as a legal subject. In other words, a limited liability company can only cease to exist as a legal person if there is, in fact, a complete lack of assets. And the suretyship was intended to apply precisely in the event of the principal debtor's complete lack of assets.

[34] It need not be decided whether this correlation always, or at least in principle, leads to the independent continuity of the suretyship, that is, when the dissolution of the principal debtor is not based on bankruptcy [...] (in that sense Higher Regional Court of Cologne, *GmbHR* 2004, 1020; Roth/Altmeppen, *GmbHG-Commentary*, § 74, margin no. 24; comp. also Baumbach/Hueck/Schulze-Osterloh, *GmbHG-Commentary*, § 74, margin no. 16; Scholz-K. Schmidt, *GmbHG-Commentary*, § 74, margin no. 16; dissenting opinion Higher Regional Court of Lübeck, *GmbHR* 92, 539).

[35] This is due to the fact that the present suretyship endures independently because it also was intended to secure the plaintiff's liability interests relating to the satisfaction of the warranty claims against the principal debtor. The Court follows the plaintiff's arguments. In principle, § 73 (1) 2 GmbHG protects the creditor against the risks of loss that result from the dissolution of the limited liability company. Therefore, the assets of the company may only be distributed after the lapse of a retention period of one year and redemption or indemnification of the registered or otherwise known obligations of the partners. In contrast, the unique nature of a suretyship against liability resulting from defects is such that the liability secured by the suretyship is of an accidental nature or, at least, will likely not be recognizable by the creditor beforehand. The practical assertion of legally existing warranty claims is dependent on the date on which the defects are discovered. Depending on the kind of defect, this can be the case after a long period of time, so long as it is still covered by the warranty, and also if, as is the case here, the plaintiff has already transferred the construction work. In such a case there is a recognizably high risk that the creditor cannot rely on the protection provided by § 73(1)[2] GmbHG. If the creditor is not aware of the defects until the beginning or within the retention period, and if the

creditor can thus assume that there has been a due completion by the principal debtor, then the existing warranty claims that result from hidden defects do not impair the rightful asset distribution of the liquidated company. With the rightful end of the liquidation and termination of the principal debtor, the plaintiff endures the loss of warranty claims against the principal debtor that were brought forward afterwards because these obligations cease to exist.

[36] This abstract, looming risk of the loss of the warranty claims was identifiable by the parties when they concluded the suretyship contract. The insurance against this risk of lost warranty claims was, therefore, served by the present unlimited directly liable suretyship for defects liability. Here, it is not relevant whether the plaintiff knew of the warranty claims relevant for this dispute in the concrete case. Whether the warranty suretyship endures in the case of liquidation and termination of the principal debtor is a matter that has to be judged with regard to the securitizing purpose of the warranty and the interests of the parties at the time they concluded the suretyship contract. This does not depend on the developments that arise after the conclusion of the suretyship contract, especially if the parties, as in the present case, have explicitly agreed on a directly liable suretyship upon first demand and the plaintiff was permitted to directly exercise rights against the defendant without limitation.

***

Questions/Comments

- How does the Hamburg Regional Court's judgment differ from a trial court judgment in your primary or "national" legal system?
- Did the Court implement the BGB's regulatory technique, as it has been described in this chapter? Did the Court rely on the private law method I described in Chapter 6, which involves the question: "Who Wants What from Whom on Which Basis?"
- Does the Court's judgment deliver the Civil Code's promised efficiency, predictability, reliability, and certainty? Does the judgment fulfill your expectations for legal practice that is heavily influenced by the Civil Law tradition?
- Based on what you learned about the *Akzessorietätsgrundsatz*, were you surprised that the Court ruled for the plaintiff? The Court seemed to go out of its way to enforce the suretyship despite the dissolution of the principal debtor. The suretyship obligation continued in force, the Court found, largely because none of the codified exceptions to the *Akzessorietätsgrundsatz* applied. The suretyship remained valid despite the fact that the principal debtor was not liquidated in a bankruptcy proceeding but, instead, at the request of the building firm's single shareholder. Are you able to summarize the reason why the Court insisted on enforcing the defendant's suretyship obligation? What is the basis for the Court's reasoning?
- Would you say that the outcome in the case lives up to the BGB's reputation as a strictly liberal normative regime?
- Exactly as Freund suggested, the Court cites other court judgments and scholarly commentaries as it frames a solution for the case. Can you distinguish

between the two kinds of citations? Which is a more prominent source – cases or commentaries?

7.5 Conclusion

From the beginning, the BGB was criticized for failing to include what von Gierke called "drops of social oil." The criticism of the Civil Code intensified during times of upheaval. In 1919, following the German Empire's defeat in World War I, Justus Wilhelm Hedemann pointed to the BGB's lack of character: "It is timid and dull; it displays no vigorous spirit, no characteristic personality."[49] Like von Gierke before him, Hedemann especially lamented the BGB's liberal orientation towards the prosperous citizen. This orientation also found disfavor with the Nazis who disapproved of what they saw as the Civil Code's exaggerated liberal individualism. Conflicting with their totalizing, authoritarian, and collectivist ideology, the Nazis regarded the BGB as "un-German." In post-war West Germany the leftist student uprisings of 1968 revived the aversion to the Civil Code. It was of no use, they said, for regulating the "social processes of our time."[50] Across the Wall in East Germany, the BGB stumbled along as the applicable private law in that communist regime despite attacks from officials and jurists who regarded it as a "bourgeois civil code."[51] A new, socialist civil code was enacted in East Germany in 1975. German reunification in 1990, following the collapse of the Soviet communist model in central and eastern Europe, was viewed by many as the definitive ratification (and triumph) of the liberalism inherent in the Civil Code. Old critiques of the BGB persisted just the same.

Through all of this, the German Civil Code – drawing on and distinctively embodying elements of the Civil Law tradition – has survived as a thick and brightly colored thread in the tapestry of German legal culture. The Civil Code contains the entwined DNA of the Roman Law and German customary law. It was the signal legal achievement of elusive German unity. It has continued to function under the Kaiser, the Fuhrer, the Occupying Powers, and (so far) nine post-war chancellors. It has inspired and informed codifiers across the globe. For these reasons, the praise lavished on the BGB is not unfounded. And, although it may not be a gift from God (as the joke would have it), the BGB is a distinctly German legal creation in more ways than just the fact that it was written in the German language. It leads this book's survey of the substance of German law because the Civil Code is distinctively and definitively German. And because it has distinctively and definitively shaped German legal culture.

Yet, the following chapters reveal that in the German legal system the Civil Law tradition (embodied by the Civil Code) has had to make room for other legal traditions. Perhaps none has asserted itself more strongly than the Common Law tradition (embodied by post-war German constitutionalism). That is the topic we turn to next.

Further Reading

- *German Civil Code – Article-by-Article Commentary (Volumes I & II)* (Gerhard Dannemann, Reiner Schulze & Jonathon Watson eds.) (C.H. Beck Verlag) (2020 and 2022)
- Dieter Schwab, Peter Gottwald & Saskia Lettmaier, *Family and Succession Law in Germany* (Wolters Kluwer) (3rd ed. 2017)
- Jean J. Plessis et al., *German Corporate Governance in International and European Context* (Springer) (2nd ed. 2012)
- Martin Schulz & Oliver Wasmeier, *The Law of Business Organizations: A Concise Overview of German Corporate Law* (Springer) (2012)
- Gerhard Dannemann, *The German Law of Unjustified Enrichment and Restitution: A Comparative Introduction* (Oxford University Press) (2009)
- *Key Aspects of German Business Law: A Practical Manual* (Michael Wendler, Bernd Tremml & Bernard Buecker eds.) (Springer) (2008)
- Basil S. Markesinis, Hannes Unberath & Angus C. Johnston, *The German Law of Contract* (Hart Publishing) (2nd ed. 2006)
- Reinhard Zimmermann, *The New German Law of Obligations* (Oxford University Press) (2005)
- Basil S. Markesinis & Hannes Unberath, *The German Law of Torts* (Hart Publishing) (4th ed. 2002)

NOTES

1 LAW – MADE IN GERMANY 7 (2009), www.lawmadeingermany.de/Law-Made_in_Germany.pdf. A comparative law movement known as "law and finance" or "legal origins" disputed the claim that the civil law tradition is somehow economically superior to its chief rival, the common law tradition. See Rafael La Porta et al., *Law and Finance*, 106 J. POL. ECON. 1113 (1998); Rafael La Porta et al., *The Quality of Government*, 15 J. L., ECON. & ORG. 222 (1999); Rafeal La Porta et al., *Government Ownership of Banks*, 57 J. FIN. 265 (2002); Thorsten Beck et al., *Law and Finance. Why Does Legal Origin Matter?*, 31 J. COMPAR. ECON. 653 (2003); Edward Glaeser & Andrei Shleifer, *Legal Origins*, 117 QUARTERLY J. ECON. 1193 (2002); Simeon Djankov et al., *The New Comparative Economics*, 31 J. COMPAR. ECON. 595, 605–6 (2003); Rafael La Porta et al., *What Works in Securities Law?*, 61 J. FIN. 1 (2006). Needless to say, I have little interest in a comparative method that seeks to superficially *quantify* legal culture while relying on the *old taxonomies* of legal families. See Ralf Michaels, *Comparative Law by Numbers? Legal Origins Thesis, Doing Business Reports, and the Silence of Traditional Comparative Law*, 57 AM. J. COMPAR. L. 765 (2009); Bénédicte Fauvarque-Cosson & Anne-Jule Kerhuel, *Is Law and Economic Contest? French Reactions to the Doing Business World Bank Reports and Economic Analysis of Law*, 57 AM. J. COMPAR. L. 811 (2009); Curtis J. Milhaupt, *Beyond Legal Origin: Rethinking Law's Relationship to the Economy – Implications for Policy*, 57 AM. J. COMPAR. L. 831 (2009); John Reitz, *Legal*

Origins, Comparative Law, and Political Economy, 57 AM. J. COMPAR. L. 847 (2009); Vivian Grosswald Curran, *Comparative Law and the Legal Origins Thesis: "[N]on scholae sed vitae discimus"*, 57 AM. J. COMPAR. L. 863 (2009); Ralf Michaels, *The Second Wave of Comparative Law and Economics*, 59 UNIV. TORONTO L. J. 197 (2009). It should be noted that the *Law – Made in Germany* brochure, to which I regularly refer in this book, can be viewed as a German response to the claim, raised by "legal origins" advocates and practitioners, that the common law tradition is (economically) superior to the civil law tradition.

2 LAW – MADE IN GERMANY *supra* note 1, at 7.
3 *Id.*
4 JOHN HENRY MERRYMAN & ROGELIO PÉREZ-PERDOMO, THE CIVIL LAW TRADITION 3 (4th ed. 2019).
5 Handelsgesetzbuch [HGB] [Commercial Code], BGBl. III at 4100-1, last amended by Act, July 15, 2022, BGBl. I at 1146, art. 1.
6 *Id.*
7 Gesetz betreffend die Gesellschaften mit beschränkter Haftung [GmbHG] [Limited Liability Companies Acts], Nov. 1, 2008, BGBl. I at 2446, last amended by Act, July 17, 2017, BGBl. I at 2446, art. 9.
8 Aktiengesetz [AktG] [Stock Corporation Act], Sept. 6, 1965, BGBl. I at 10809, last amended by Act, July 17, 2017, BGBl. I at 2446, art. 9.
9 *See, e.g.,* Allgemeine Gleichbehandlungsgesetz [AGG] [General Act on Equal Treatment], Aug. 14, 2003, BGBl. I at 1897, last amended by Act, Apr. 3, 2013, BGBl. I at 610, art. 8; Arbeitszeitgesetz [ArbZG] [Working Hours Act], June 6, 1994, BGBl. I at 1170, 1171, last amended by Act, Dec. 22, 2020, BGBl. I at 3334, art. 6.
10 *See* Versicherungsvertragsgesetz [VVG] [Insurance Contract Act], Nov. 23, 2007, BGBl I at 2631, last amended by Act, July 11, 2022, BGBl. I at 2754, art. 4.
11 *See* Urheberrechtsgesetz [UrhG] [Copyright Act], Sept. 9, 1965, BGBl. I at 1273, last amended by Act, June 23, 2021, BGBl. I at 1858, art. 25; Arbeitnehmererfindungen [ArbnErfG] [Employee Inventions Act], July 25, 1957, BGBl. I at 2521, last amended by Act, July 7, 2021, BGBl. I at 2363, art. 25.
12 Ernst Freund, *The New German Civil Code*, 13 HARV. L. REV. 627 (1899–1900).
13 William W. Smithers, *The German Civil Code*, 50 AM. L. REGIS. 685, 712 (Jan.–Dec. 1902).
14 *Id.* at 713.
15 *See* Ernst von Wildenbruch, *Das deutsche Recht*, 5 DEUTSCHE JURISTENZEITUNG 1 (1900) (*reprinted* HANS HATTENHAUER & ARNO BUSCHMANN, TEXTBUCH ZUR PRIVATRECHTSGESCHICHTE DER NEUZEIT 288–89 (1967)).
16 Frederic William Maitland, *The Making of the German Civil Code*, in 3 THE COLLECTED PAPERS OF FREDERIC WILLIAM MAITLAND 474, 476 (H. A. L. Fisher ed., 1911).
17 Ernst Freund, *The Proposed German Civil Code*, 24 AM. L. REV. 237, 254 (1890).
18 Arthur Ameisen, *The New Civil Code of the German Empire*, 33 AM. L. REV. 396, 407 (1899).
19 LAW AND JUSTICE IN A MULTISTATE WORLD 801 (Arthur Taylor Von Mehren & Symeon Symeonides eds., 2002) (*quoting* OTTO FRIEDRICH VON GIERKE, POLITICAL THEORIES OF THE MIDDLE AGE xvii (Frederick William Maitland trans., 1900)).

20 Joseph J. Darby, *The Influence of the German Civil Code on Law in the United States*, 1999 J. S. AFRICAN L. 84 (1999).
21 Mathias Reimann, *The Good, The Bad, and the Ugly: The Reform of the German Law of Obligations*, 83 TULANE L. REV. 877, 882 (2008–2009).
22 *Id.* at 883.
23 Robert A. Riegert, *The West German Civil Code, Its Origin and Its Contract Provisions*, 45 TULANE L. REV. 48, 66 (1970–1971).
24 *Id.*
25 Reimann, *supra* note 21, at 878.
26 *See* CHUNG HUI WANG, THE GERMAN CIVIL CODE – TRANSLATED AND ANNOTATED WITH AN HISTORICAL INTRODUCTION AND APPENDICIES (1907). *Compare* Ernest J. Schuster, *A Chinese Commentary on the German Civil Code*, 8 J. SOC. COMPAR. LEGIS. 247 (1907)
27 Hannes Rösler, *Harmonizing the German Civil Code of the Nineteenth Century with a Modern Constitution – The Lüth Revolution 50 Years Ago in Comparative Perspective*, 23 TULANE EUR. & CIV. L. FORUM 1 (2008).
28 OTTO VON GIERKE, DIE SOZIALE AUFGABE DES PRIVATRECHTS 16–18 (1889) (*translated in* B. S. MARKESINIS, HANNES UNBERATH, AND ANGUS JOHNSTON, THE GERMAN LAW OF CONTRACT 10 (2nd ed. 2006)).
29 NIGEL G. FOSTER & SATISH SULE, GERMAN LEGAL SYSTEM & LAWS 364 (4th ed. 2010).
30 *See* MERRYMAN & PÉREZ-PERDOMO, *supra* note 4, at 34–38.
31 *Id.* at 28–30.
32 *The Notion of Contractual Good Faith: Perspectives from Comparative Law*, SQUIRE PATTON BOGGS (May 31, 2006), https://larevue.squirepattonboggs.com/the-notion-of-contractual-good-faith-perspectives-from-comparative-law_a1010.html.
33 Catherine Valcke, *Comparative History and the Internal View of French, German, and English Private Law*, 19 CANADIAN J. L. & JURIS. 133, 139 (2006).
34 *See, e.g.*, P. A. J. VAN DEN BERG, THE POLITICS OF EUROPEAN CODIFICATION: A HISTORY OF THE UNIFICATION OF LAW IN FRANCE, PRUSSIA, THE AUSTRIAN MONARCHY AND THE NETHERLANDS (2007).
35 Robert A. Riegert, *The West German Civil Code, Its Origin and Its Contract Provisions*, 45 TULANE L. REV. 58–65 (1970–1971).
36 *Id.* at 48, 60.
37 *Id.* at 61.
38 *Id.* at 62.
39 KONRAD ZWEIGERT & HEIN KÖTZ, AN INTRODUCTION TO COMPARATIVE LAW 143 (Tony Weir trans., 3rd ed. 1998).
40 Riegert, *supra* note 35, at 52.
41 Maybe the most famous, hyper-specific provision of the BGB is the section addressing property interests in a bee-swarm than moves from an owner's hive to another person's property. *See* Bürgerliches Gesetzbuch [BGB] [Civil Code], Jan. 2, 2002, BGBl. I at 42, 2909; corrected in 2003, BGBl. I at 738, last amended by Act, Oct. 1, 2013, BGBl. I at 3719, art. 4 para. 5, §§ 961–964.
42 The Civil Code defines "natural" and "legal" persons and identifies their fundamental rights and duties. *See* Bürgerliches Gesetzbuch [BGB] [Civil Code], Jan.

2, 2002, BGBl. I at 42, 2909; corrected in 2003, BGBl. I at 738, last amended by Act, Oct. 1, 2013, BGBl. I at 3719, art. 4 para. 5, §§ 1–14; 21–89.

43 The Civil Code defines "animals" and "things" as possible subject of law. *See* Bürgerliches Gesetzbuch [BGB] [Civil Code], Jan. 2, 2002, BGBl. I at 42, 2909; corrected in 2003, BGBl. I at 738, last amended by Act, Oct. 1, 2013, BGBl. I at 3719, art. 4 para. 5, §§ 90–103.

44 The Civil Code provides a general regime that statutorily limits the time in which a person has "the right to demand that another person does or refrains from an act (claim)." *See* Bürgerliches Gesetzbuch [BGB] [Civil Code], Jan. 2, 2002, BGBl. I at 42, 2909; corrected in 2003, BGBl. I at 738, last amended by Act, Oct. 1, 2013, BGBl. I at 3719, art. 4 para. 5, §§ 194–218.

45 ALFRED ROMAIN, B. SHARON BYRD & CAROLA THIELECKE, DICTIONARY OF LEGAL AND COMMERCIAL TERMS – PART II GERMAN-ENGLISH 201 (4th ed. 2002); CLARA-ERIKA DIETL, DICTIONARY OF LEGAL, COMMERCIAL AND POLITICAL TERMS – PART II GERMAN-ENGLISH 172 (1983).

46 *See* CHRISTIAN FÖRSTER, DIE FUSION VON BÜRGSCHAFT UND GARANTIE (2010).

47 74 AM. JUR. 2d *Suretyship* § 1 (2010).

48 GERMAN CIVIL CODE COMMENTARY VOLUMES I AND II – BÜRGERLICHES GESETZBUCH (BGB) (Gerhard Dannemann, Reiner Schulze & Jonathon Watson eds., 2020 & 2022). The publisher's promotional material for this remarkable English-language commentary is revealing. It proclaims that "The *Bürgerliches Gesetzbuch* in the version as from 2 January 2002 is the very backbone of German civil law. Its institutions and principles are essential for the understanding of the law of Europe's major legal systems."

49 *Quoted in* Reinhard Zimmermann, *The German Civil Code and the Development of Private Law in Germany*, 1 OXFORD UNIV. COMPAR. L. FORUM (2006), http://ouclf.iuscomp.org/articles/zimmermann.shtml#fn148sym.

50 *Quoted in id.*

51 Inga S. Markovits, *Civil Law in East Germany – Its Development and Relation to Soviet Legal History and Ideology*, 78 YALE L. J. 1 (1968).

8

German Public Law
Constitutionalism

Key Concepts

- **Constitutionalism**: A system of law and governance centered on a constitution. In a "thin" sense, every polity has organizing principles that settle the rules and define the institutions for governance. Constitutionalism, however, refers to the existence of a "thick" constitution, which possesses most of the following features: a written constitutive text that is hard to change, that is superior to ordinary law, and that is enforced by judicial review. Some attribute liberal and democratic values to constitutionalism. Many, but not all, constitutions contain a catalogue of basic rights.
- **Grundgesetz**: West Germany's post-war constitution enacted in 1949. It is referred to as the *Grundgesetz* (Basic Law) because the West German framers viewed the regime as provisional until a reunified, all-German state could debate and enact a proper constitution. The Basic Law has endured, assimilating the new eastern states after reunification in 1990, and it is now accepted as the constitution (*Verfassung*) of the Federal Republic of Germany and for the "entire German people." The Basic Law establishes the principles and organs of governance, and it provides an extensive catalogue of basic rights. All of this is crowned by the inviolable commitment to human dignity secured in Article 1(1), by a slate of unamendable principles (democratic state, social state, federal state, rule of law, and proportional state action), and a mandate for European integration. The Basic Law has been amended more than sixty times in its first seventy-five years.
- **Human Dignity**: In Article 1(1) the Basic Law declares that human dignity is inviolable. This commitment sets the tone and terms for the entire constitution. It is animated by Germans' accountability for the atrocities perpetrated by the National Socialists. The content and meaning of "human dignity" is filled out by all the other basic rights secured by the constitution, beginning with broad principles such as personal freedom (Article 2(1)) and equality (Article 3), but also extending to the core of more specific rights such as

freedom of opinion and freedom of religion (Articles 4 and 5). In interpreting the mandate for human dignity, the Federal Constitutional Court has considered Christian and natural law principles. More prominently, however, the Court has relied on the theory and insights of Immanuel Kant in establishing the "*Objektformel.*" According to this doctrine, human dignity requires that humans must be treated as ends in themselves and may not be treated as mere objects or as means to an end.

- ***Bundesverfassungsgericht***: The German Federal Constitutional Court possesses exclusive and specialized jurisdiction for the interpretation and application of the Basic Law. It is not a court of last resort or supreme court providing definitive interpretation of ordinary law. The Court sits in Karlsruhe, Germany. The sixteen justices occupy two eight-justice Senates that have discrete areas of responsibility. The justices are appointed with super-majority votes by the *Bundestag* and *Bundesrat* to single, non-renewable twelve-year terms (with mandatory retirement at sixty-eight). The Court hears matters pursuant to a wide range of procedures that ensure its significant involvement in German politics and life.

- ***Rechtsstaatsprinzip***: The Basic Law's commitment to the *Rechtsstaat* is enforced as a guarantee that the state acts pursuant to law and justice. Above all, the *Rechtsstaatsprinzip* ensures that the state does not act arbitrarily. The *Rechtsstaatsprinzip* is realized through a number of doctrines, including the principle of the separation of powers, the proportionality principle, the principle of equality, and the legality principle.

- ***Verhältnismäßigkeitsprüfung***: The proportionality analysis used to interpret and apply constitutionally protected basic rights. An infringement of a right will be motivated by some state interest, perhaps even the advancement or realization of another constitutional norm. The proportionality analysis resolves this conflict in a way that seeks to maximize the state's policy interest *and* the rights protection promised by the constitution. The analysis ascertains whether an infringement is legitimate, suitable, necessary, and proportional. The last of these assessments involves balancing the interests involved in the conflict: how important is the state's policy, how important is the basic right, and how grave is the infringement on the basic right. The German Federal Constitutional Court has developed and perfected the proportionality analysis, which is now used for the interpretation of rights around the world.

- ***Objective Order of Values***: Doctrine announced by the German Federal Constitutional Court that holds that the fundamental rights secured by the post-war German Constitution (Basic Law) established the controlling values for all of German law and society. The omnipresence of these values led the Court to conclude that all law, including private law, must be interpreted and applied in a manner that ensures the realization of the constitution's fundamental rights (*Drittwirkung* or indirect horizontal effect).

Study Tips

The Ministry of Justice and Federal Office of Justice provide English-language translations of a number of important German codes and statutes at the website "Gesetze im Internet" (www.gesetze-im-internet.de/). This includes the *Grundgesetz* (GG – Basic Law) and the *Bundesverfassungsgerichtsgesetz* (BVerfGG – Federal Constitutional Court Act).

The Federal Constitutional Court provides a number of English-language resources at its website (www.bundesverfassungsgericht.de/EN/Homepage/home_node.html), including a searchable database of its judgments translated into English and an English-language newsletter service. The Court also has produced an English-language introductory video entitled "Key Facts on the Federal Constitutional Court" (www.youtube.com/watch?v=1UJ7YVT-CqA).

The Civil Code is the clearest and most prominent manifestation of the Civil Law tradition's far-reaching influence in the German legal system. At the same time, after an uneasy and halting history (sketched for you in Chapter 4), Germany has become a thriving and well-settled constitutional democracy. The post-war German *Grundgesetz* (Basic Law or constitution) is much admired and much emulated, making it an influential force in its own right – both in Germany and abroad. "Germany and Canada," it has been said, "are America's principal competitors in the export of constitutional norms."[1] German constitutionalism now serves as a fundamental legal regime that is superior to the private law of the Civil Code. The emergence of a robust constitutional regime in Germany has woven a new thread – a new legal tradition – into the tapestry of German legal culture. Just as codification is an expression of the Civil Law tradition, constitutionalism involves elements of law and legal practice that are closely attuned to the Common Law tradition.

This chapter introduces Germany's Basic Law and the *Bundesverfassungsgericht* (Federal Constitutional Court). The latter is the tribunal in Germany's system of specialized courts that has exclusive responsibility for interpreting and giving force to the constitution. The materials in this chapter will highlight two elements that often recur wherever constitutionalism operates as more than a formality or pretext: constitutional supremacy and judicial review. These characteristics shift a legal system (even if only subtly) towards the Common Law tradition, especially as they diminish the authority of statutes and codes while empowering (at least some) judges. In turn, this tilt towards the Common Law tradition can be an irritant in a system in which the Civil Law tradition has been the predominant influence. The German legal system has sought to manage the resulting dialogue between these traditions (Glenn called it a "difficult marriage"[2]) with a doctrine known as *Drittwirkung* (indirect horizontal effect). That doctrine makes German constitutional law relevant in the German private law regime. I present an example of the doctrine of *Drittwirkung* through a suretyship dispute at the end of this chapter. That fulfills my promise from Chapter 7 that I would use German suretyship law to highlight the bridge that exists between the Civil Code (embodying the Civil Law tradition) and German constitutionalism (embodying the Common Law tradition). All of this, as H. Patrick Glenn insisted, is evidence that "[t]he state and its legal system [are] a place of meeting and potential reconciliation of different [legal traditions]."[3]

It will help to orient this chapter's presentation of German constitutional law if I offer some explanation of what I mean by "constitutionalism." The legal theorist Joseph Raz identified seven fundamental characteristics of a "thick" constitutional regime: the charter establishes and defines the society's governing powers and organs; the charter is meant to operate for a long time, providing an enduring and stable framework for law and governance; the charter is often written as a canonical text; the charter articulates superior law that must render conflicting "ordinary law" inapplicable; the charter's regime is subject to review by the judiciary, which enforces the charter's superior status; the charter must be more difficult to amend or change than "ordinary" legislation; and the charter expresses or reinforces the identity and values of the society it governs.[4] Paul Craig, building on Raz's list, identified several uses for the term "constitutionalism":

> A second sense of constitutionalism is more descriptive in nature. The inquiry is as to the extent to which a particular legal system does or does not possess the features associated with a constitution set out [by Raz]. On this view constitutionalisation expresses the movement towards attainment of those features.
>
> We find a third sense of constitutionalism used to describe the juridical shift that has occurred in many continental legal systems post-1945. Here the term captures the following features of a polity. State institutions are established by, and derive their authority from, a written constitution; the constitution assigns ultimate power to the people by way of elections; power is only lawful if it conforms with precepts of the constitution; and these will be policed by a specialist constitutional court.[5]

That is what I mean by "constitutionalism" in this chapter. I am interested in the spectrum of German law that involves many of the features of a thick constitution, particularly constitutional supremacy and judicial review. But German constitutionalism also aligns with Craig's third definition. Germany is a post-war continental system committed to popular sovereignty, democracy, and the rule of law. As part of that framework, Germany relies on a specialist constitutional court to administer and sustain the constitutional system.

Another conceptual point requires attention in this chapter's opening. I have suggested that Germany's constitutionalism (expressed by the Basic Law) embodies the Common Law tradition. That claim, however, begs (at least) two questions. First, what is the Common Law tradition? Second, why should you understand constitutionalism to be entwined with the Common Law tradition?

Regarding the first question, it might be enough to remind you of the peripheral exposure to the Common Law tradition you received in my presentation of the Civil Law tradition in Chapter 2. Remember that many comparative law scholars regard the Civil Law and Common Law traditions as antipodes. That's why Grosswald Curran, in an excerpt I presented in Chapter 2, argued that the Civil Law tradition expresses Enlightenment values while the Common Law tradition expresses the values of Romanticism. Glenn marvelously insisted that there can be no single Common law tradition. But he understood that, for most scholars of comparative law, the Common Law tradition is "often defined as case law, with its attendant notions of precedent, *stare decisis*, and *ratio decidendi*, and is often contrasted with the written or codified law found in many jurisdictions described as civilian in character."[6] So, for our purposes, the Common Law tradition entrusts the development of the law to judges and not the codifying legislator (which, as we have learned, is aided by the "scientific" gloss of scholars). Judge-made law in the Common Law tradition involves an inductive process, in which the court derives a generally applicable rule from the specific facts of the case, usually by closely following previous court rulings (when bound by precedent to do so), by analogizing to judgments in similar cases (when no controlling precedent applies), or by resolving the matter according to equity, logic, or the pursuit of a particular policy outcome. In this way, the law is dynamic and flexible, but also not at all systematic and sometimes not even very rational. The Common Law tradition is not the legal science of the Civil Law tradition. As US Supreme Court Justice Oliver Wendell Holmes explained, the life of the Common Law tradition "has not been logic: it has been experience."[7] Rejecting most of the ambitions of the Civil Law tradition (including scientific coherence, objectivity, and insulation from politics or morality), Holmes counted temporal necessity, morality, prejudice, and public policy among the determinants of a prevailing rule in the Common Law tradition. The Common Law tradition embraces the understanding – contrary to the Civil Law tradition – that the law "cannot be dealt with as if it contained only the axioms and corollaries of a book of mathematics."[8]

That portrayal of the Common Law tradition already points to the answer to the second question. The Common Law tradition prioritizes judges in the development of the law. And constitutionalism calls for an expansive role for judges in the exercise of judicial review. That symmetry led Thomas Poole to conclude that constitutional law is "grounded in fundamental common law principles" and that it is "structured around the institution of the common law court."[9] Poole argued that the core features of constitutionalism (perhaps including Raz's list) "are most consistently recognized and protected by the common law, particularly in the context of judicial review."[10] In fact, many scholars simply refer to the "constitutional common law."[11]

Walter Murphy, one of the pioneers of the comparative study of constitutional law, made an even stronger claim. On the one hand, he argued that constitutionalism is an expression of the Common Law tradition. On the other hand, he argued that the Civil Law tradition raises barriers to constitutionalism. I summarized Murphy's views elsewhere:

> Murphy advances the fundamental argument that the character of the civil law is at odds with constitutionalism and that the character of the common law is aligned with constitutionalism. He contrasts "the civil law's tense commitment to order" with the common law's embrace of chaos. The civil law, Murphy concludes, "leaves judges no respectable room to maneuver," while the common law instructs judges "to walk around rather than try to fill in the abyss, to hunker down when the great wind blows rather than to attempt to contain it." The common law's inductive, case-by-case approach, Murphy concludes, involves a "supple pragmatism over tight logic" that is inherent in the "messiness of constitutional politics."[12]

I don't intend to go as far as Murphy and express skepticism about the compatibility of the Civil Law tradition with constitutionalism. Still, your familiarity with the Civil Law tradition (perhaps first acquired in this book) allows you to see how constitutionalism's embrace of enduring, hard-to-change, written charters calls for an elevated and empowered status for judges that is uncommon in the Civil Law tradition. This understanding is what encourages me to imagine Germany's now-thriving constitutionalism as the Common Law's beachhead in the German legal system.

Let me conclude this introduction with an appeal. Because most of us come from legal systems that have a constitution (by one count 193 of the world's 195 countries have such a charter), you unavoidably begin this encounter with all the familiarity, understanding, and assumptions about constitutionalism that you have assimilated in your primary or "national" legal system. But recall the last of Raz's fundamental features of constitutional law: A constitution shapes and expresses a polity's identity. A constitution is a particularly local and contextual legal framework, shaped by history, culture, religion, the economy, demographics, geography, and much else besides. As one scholar put it, "societies largely invent their constitutions [...]."[13] As you engage with German constitutional law in this chapter I hope you will remain aware of this fact and that you'll strive to understand the Basic Law in its distinct social and legal context. Do some of the "differencing" that Frankenberg prescribed in the excerpt of his article included in Chapter 1. Allow German constitutional law to speak for itself. After all, it has a remarkable story to tell.

8.1 Constitutional Supremacy: The German Basic Law

As you saw in the brief history of German constitutional law presented in Chapter 4, Germany has known many constitutions. Nationally, the

Paulskirchenverfassung (St. Paul's Church Constitution) of 1849 and the *Weimarer Reichsverfassung* (Weimar Imperial Constitution) of 1919 are the most prominent manifestations of the democratic constitutional impulse in Germany history. But before and alongside these earlier, ill-fated constitutional experiments, many of Germany's constituent principalities and free cities – and later the states out of which the Allies cobbled together the postwar Federal Republic – had their own local, liberal constitutions.[14] All of these other, older German constitutions (national and local) have echoes in the Basic Law that was drafted in the ruins of post-World War II West Germany.[15] Following the unification of East and West Germany in 1990, the Basic Law's preamble was amended to provide that the West German constitution would now "apply to the entire German people."[16]

Donald Kommers was the most prominent comparative law scholar of postwar German constitutionalism. In the following canonical article he described the Basic Law's structure, content, and values.

Donald P. Kommers
German Constitutionalism: A Prolegomenon
40 EMORY LAW JOURNAL 837, 837–839, 845–846, 855–860 (1991)[*]

Introduction

* * *

Germany's written constitution is known as the Basic Law (*Grundgesetz*), so labeled because it was conceived in 1949 as a transitional document pending national unification. The more dignified term "constitution" (*Verfassung*) would be reserved for a governing document applicable to the nation as a whole and designed to last in perpetuity. Yet, over the years, having survived the test of time, the Basic Law has taken on the character of a genuine constitution. In fact, following the bloodless coup of March 18, 1990 – the day on which East Germans voted to end Germany's division – a new and freely elected East German government chose to accede to the Federal Republic of Germany within the framework of the Basic Law. This decision and the Unification Treaty signed later by East and West Germany transposed the Basic Law from a temporary instrument of governance for one part of Germany into a document of force and permanence for the entire German nation.

[... The] Basic Law draws much of its inspiration from previous German constitutions in the democratic tradition. In its original form, the Basic Law consisted of eleven sections and 146 articles; numerous amendments over the years [...] produced a document of 171 articles, not to mention the five articles of the Weimar Constitution (Articles 136–139 and 141) on church-state relations absorbed into the Basic Law under the terms of Article 140. Seven of the Basic Law's fourteen sections, representing no fewer than sixty-five articles, spell out in detail the powers of federal and state governments and their duties to each other. [...]

[...] [The] focus here is on the "new constitutionalism" reflected in the Basic Law, that is, on those of its features that represent significant departures from Germany's past. [...]

---

[*] Excerpt reproduced with permission of the *Emory Law Journal*.

8.1 Constitutional Supremacy: The German Basic Law

* * *

The New Constitutionalism of the Basic Law
Supremacy of the Constitution

The Basic Law marks a radical break with Germany's past. Previous constitutions in the democratic tradition were easily amended and not regarded as binding in all respects. By contrast, the Basic Law is a binding document. As several of its provisions make clear, it controls the entire German legal order, in which respect Articles 1, 19, 20, and 79 are particularly relevant. Article 1, paragraph 3, declares that the fundamental rights listed in the Basic Law, including the inviolable principle of human dignity, "shall bind the legislature, the executive, and the judiciary as directly enforceable law." In reinforcing this provision, Article 20 subjects "legislation" to the "constitutional order" and *binds* "the executive and the judiciary to law and justice."

In binding executive and judicial authority to "law" (*Gesetz*) and "justice" (*Recht*), the Basic Law's founders were recreating the formal *Rechtsstaat* – a state based on the rule of positive law (i.e., *Gesetz* or *Rechtspositivismus*) – but now, unlike the situation under previous constitutions, positive law is subject to the supra-positive notion of justice or *Recht*, a notion that appears to include unwritten norms of governance. In one of its landmark decisions the Federal Constitutional Court declared that laws "must also conform to unwritten fundamental constitutional principles as well as to the fundamental decisions of the Basic Law, in particular the principles of the rule of law and the social welfare state." In short, the *Rechtsstaat*, far from being an end in itself, now serves the constitutional state (*Verfassungsstaat*).

Articles 19 and 79 carry the principle of the Basic Law's supremacy even further. Article 19, paragraph 2, bans any law or governmental action that invades "the essential content of [any] basic right." But this is not all. Article 79, paragraph 3 – the so-called "eternity clause" – bars any amendment to the Basic Law that would tamper with the principle of federalism or impinge upon "the basic principles laid down in Articles 1 and 20." Article 1, as already noted, sets forth the principle of human dignity and imposes upon the state an affirmative duty "to respect and protect it," whereas Article 20 proclaims the basic principles governing the polity as a whole – that is, federalism, democracy, republicanism, separation of powers, the rule of law, popular sovereignty, and the social welfare state. The Basic Law's framers believed, quite clearly, that the best way to realize human dignity, now and in the future, is to freeze certain principles of governance into the constitutional structure itself.

The Structure of Rights and Values
The Primacy of Rights

The [...] German Basic Law takes rights seriously. It leads off by proclaiming that "[t]he dignity of man is inviolable" and then, in the very next sentence, commands the state to respect and protect it (Article 1 [1]). All of the ensuing rights enumerated in the remaining eighteen articles of the Bill of Rights are designed to actualize this crowning principle of human dignity. Human dignity, as the Constitutional Court repeatedly emphasizes, is the highest value of the Basic Law, the ultimate basis of the constitutional order, and the foundation of guaranteed rights. All other rights proceed in logical succession, moving from the general to the particular. Article 2 secures to every person "the right to the free development of his [or her] personality" and the right to personal inviolability. Article 3 contains a general equality clause together with provisions forbidding discrimination based on gender, race, national origin, language, religion, and political affiliation. The remaining articles guarantee all the rights and liberties commonly associated with liberal constitutionalism.

These include the freedoms of religion, speech, assembly, association, and movement as well as the rights to property, privacy, and petition. Conscientious objection to military service and the right to choose a trade or occupation round out this list of fundamental rights.

The Bill of Rights, however, includes more than these personal liberties. It also protects communal interests such as marriage and the family and the right of parents to decide whether their children shall receive religious instruction in public schools. In sharp contrast to the United States Constitution, the German Bill of Rights speaks of duties and responsibilities as well as rights. Article 6, for example, tells parents that it is their "natural right" and "duty" to care for their children while simultaneously instructing the "national community" to "watch over their endeavors in this respect." Article 14 declares that the right to property "imposes duties" and should "serve the public weal." Under Article 12a, finally, all men eighteen years or older are subject to military service or, if a male citizen refuses induction because of conscience, he may be required to serve society in an alternative civilian capacity for a period equal to the time he would have spent in the military. While Article 20 is not part of the Bill of Rights it nevertheless incorporates the concept of the social welfare state in terms of which basic rights are often interpreted. German constitution-makers thus believed – and have always believed – that any realization of human dignity implies a fusion of individual rights and social responsibilities.

A close look at the Basic Law discloses an interesting hierarchy of rights. Some are cast in unqualified language, others in conditional language. In actuality, however, no right under the Constitution is absolute. A right framed in unconditional language may conflict with another express constitutional right in which case the task of the Court is to apply a balancing test [...]. The broad principle of human dignity, for example, which under the explicit terms of Article 1 (1) binds all state authority, may also serve to limit the exercise of a so-called unconditional right.

In addition, all rights, including those cast in more absolute terms, are limited by the architectonic political principle that informs the Basic Law as a whole, namely, the "free democratic basic order." [...] [T]his normative view of constitutionalism [...] implies a sturdy defense of certain principles of political obligation. [...]

All [...] rights [...] fall into three categories. First are those rights which can only be limited by the terms of the Basic Law itself. These rights, like those framed in unconditional terms, are the object of the Constitutional Court's special vigilance. The state has the burden of showing that any limitation upon such rights falls within the explicit exceptions mentioned in the Constitution, examples of which may be drawn from the rights of speech and personality. Article 5 (2) declares that speech rights "are limited ... by the ... provisions of law for the protection of youth and by the right to the inviolability of [one's] personal honor," just as Article 2 secures the general right to the development of one's personality so long as "he [or she] does not violate the rights of others or offend the constitutional order or the moral code." These reservation clauses also have the distinctive merit of providing the Federal Constitutional Court with interpretive guidelines.

The second category of conditional rights are those whose contours are to be defined by law. For example, the right to life and to the inviolability of one's person, under the terms of Article 2 (1), "may only be encroached upon pursuant to a law." Numerous other rights (e.g., the rights to privacy of posts and telecommunications, open-air assemblies, practice of a trade, conscientious objection to military service, inviolability of the home, and property) can only be limited by means of a special legislative enactment. Here too the Basic Law seeks to circumscribe legislative power, for under Article 19 (1), any basic right "restricted pursuant to a law [...] must apply generally [...] and name the basic right, indicating the Article concerned." Finally, certain rights may be restricted by the "general laws." The reference here is to the general provisions of the civil and criminal code. No specific legislation is required here to restrict the applicable right, but in the case of speech rights, for example, they "are limited by provisions of the general laws" (e.g., libel and slander), just as the right to association – to take another example – is limited by general criminal law.

An Objective Order of Values

[... The] Constitutional Court envisions the Basic Law as a unified structure of *substantive* values. The centerpiece of this interpretive strategy is the concept of an "objective order of values," a concept that derives from the gloss the Federal Constitutional Court has put on the text of the Basic Law. According to this concept, the Constitution incorporates the "basic value decisions" of the founding fathers [and mothers], the most basic of which is their choice of a free democratic basic order – that is, a liberal, representative, federal, parliamentary democracy – buttressed and reinforced by basic rights and liberties. These basic values are objective because they are said to have an independent reality under the Constitution, imposing upon all organs of government an affirmative duty to see that they are realized in practice.

The notion of an objective values order may be stated in another way. Every basic right in the Constitution – for example, freedom of speech, press, religion, association, and the right to property or the right to choose one's profession or occupation – has a corresponding value. A basic "right" is a negative right against the state, but this right also represents a "value," and as a value it imposes an obligation on the state to ensure that it becomes an integral part of the general legal order. One example may suffice: The *right* to freedom of the press protects a newspaper against any action of the state that would encroach upon its independence, but as an objective value applicable to society as a whole the state is duty-bound to create the conditions that make freedom of the press both possible and effective. In practice, this means that the state may have to regulate the press to promote the value of democracy; for example, by enacting legislation to prevent the press from becoming the captive of any dominant group or interest.

* * *

The Justices of the Federal Constitutional Court have not only postulated an objective order of values; they have also arranged these values in a hierarchical order crowned by the principle of human dignity. [...] That the Basic Law is a value-oriented – not a value-neutral – constitution is a familiar refrain in the Constitutional Court's case law. Early on in its jurisprudence the Court spoke of certain "unwritten" or "supra-positive" norms that presumably govern the entire constitutional order. Justices intellectually rooted in the Christian natural law tradition adhered to this view. Today the Court is more inclined to speak of the value system inherent in the Basic Law itself. The objective values of the Basic Law define a way of life to which the German people, as a nation, are committed. The task of the Court in adjudicating constitutional controversies is one of integrating these values into the common culture and common conscientiousness of the German people. The task is no less than creating and maintaining a nation of shared values.

* * *

Questions/Comments

- Which of the fundamental elements of constitutionalism identified by Raz does Kommers describe in respect to the German Basic Law?
- For Raz, the protection of individual or basic rights was not a necessary feature of constitutionalism. Still, many constitutions contain an enforceable

catalogue of rights. As Kommers highlights, perhaps no constitution does this with more rigor and with such emphasis as the German Basic Law. Even before enumerating and empowering the institutions and organs of the state, the Basic Law's first nineteen articles provide an impressive framework of rights protection, crowned by the declaration in Article 1(1) that "human dignity is inviolable."[17] As a contrast, the US Constitution of 1787 didn't contain a catalogue of rights. The protections provided by the Bill of Rights were added to the Constitution as amendments (albeit by the first Congress convened under the new constitution). Why did the founders of the Federal Republic "take rights so seriously"?[18]

- Why does human dignity hold such a prominent place in German constitutionalism?[19] What does human dignity encompass? What consequences does the prioritization of human dignity have for other rights, and for Germans' self-understanding? The Federal Constitutional Court has explained that the Basic Law's absolute protection of human dignity is to be understood as a direct response to the horrors of the Nazi regime.[20] It has resorted to several theories when giving force to that constitutional commitment.[21] Dignity is understood as an expression of human autonomy and rationality. Dignity also accounts for humans' efforts to fashion an identity and self-understanding – especially against the power of the state. Finally, dignity encompasses interactions among humans, as life in society is understood to be an essential part of the human condition. Kingreen and Poscher explain that the Constitutional Court's human dignity jurisprudence provides three core protections: human subjectivity, including spiritual and mental integrity; fundamental equality of all humans; and an assurance of the minimum resources needed for a meaningful human existence.[22] These values have led to an expanding range of concrete protections under Article 1 of the Basic Law, including prohibitions on torture, slavery, systematic discrimination, and intrusions on human intimacy. We will get a chance to consider some of the practical implications of this profound constitutional right in Chapter 10, which introduces German criminal law. But let me offer a final insight into this most important provision of the German constitution. In applying Article 1(1), the Federal Constitutional Court often makes use of the *Objektformel* (object formula). Informed by the teachings of the German philosopher Immanuel Kant, the *Objektformel* demands that no human be treated as a mere object or as a means to some end, but rather, that humans must be regarded as ends unto themselves. Can you think of examples of state action (or even private interactions) that might risk violating the *Objektformel*, that is, potentially reducing a person to a mere means to an end?

- What difference was Kommers stressing when he insisted, in another article, that "the Basic Law [is] a constitution of dignity and the American document [is] a constitution of liberty"?[23] Would you be helped in answering that question if you learned that many comparative law scholars portray the

Basic Law as a "substantive" constitutional order, while the American constitutional scheme is portrayed as a "procedural" constitutional regime?
- In what ways might the German constitutionalism described by Kommers be ill at ease in a system extensively influenced by the Civil Law tradition? What do you make of the systematic structure Kommers attributes to the Basic Law's protection of rights: first providing a grand statement of the constitution's values (Article 1 – "human dignity"), followed by slightly more concrete commitments derived from that value (Article 2 – "personal freedom"; Article 3 – "equality"), followed in turn by sixteen specific, more detailed protections (covering, *inter alia*, freedom of religion, freedom of speech, a right to property, freedom to choose a vocation)? In what other ways can the rights protected by the Basic Law be classified? The Basic Law's impressive catalogue of basic rights is represented in the icons in Figure 8.1.
- Kommers mentions Germany's military draft as an example of the way in which the Basic Law also imposes "duties and responsibilities" on Germans. But Article 12a only provides that eighteen-year-old men "may" be conscripted. In 2011, after fifty-five years of obligatory military service for men (and an impressive range of jurisprudence and policies seeking to accommodate the rights of conscientious objectors), Germany suspended the draft in an effort to trim defense spending and modernize its armed forces.
- Kommers noted that constitutionalism in Germany has been identified with "unwritten" or "supra-positive" norms, and that "the positive law is subject to the supra-positive notion of justice or *Recht*, a notion that appears to include unwritten norms of governance." Was this the understanding of the law advocated by Radbruch, whose work was presented in Chapter 3?
- It might seem odd that the Basic Law's supremacy is one of the key features of what Kommers celebrated as Germany's "new constitutionalism." Americans probably take the US Constitution's supremacy for granted. But it is important for Americans to recall that this was not a given at the founding of the United States. The text of the US Constitution makes federal law – the constitution, federal legislation and treaties – supreme over the law of the several states. But it does not textually establish the constitution's priority above rival forms of federal law. Chief Justice John Marshall secured the supremacy of the 1787 Constitution with his opinion in the seminal case *Marbury v. Madison* (1803):

> To what purpose are powers limited, and to what purpose is that limitation committed to writing [in a constitution]; if these limits may, at any time, be passed by those intended to be restrained? [...] The distinction between a government of limited and unlimited powers is abolished, if those limits do not confine the persons on whom they are imposed, and if acts prohibited and acts allowed are of equal obligation. [...] Between those two alternatives there is no middle ground. The constitution is either a superior, paramount law, unchangeable by ordinary means, or it is on level with ordinary legislative acts. [...] Certainly all those who have framed written constitutions contemplate

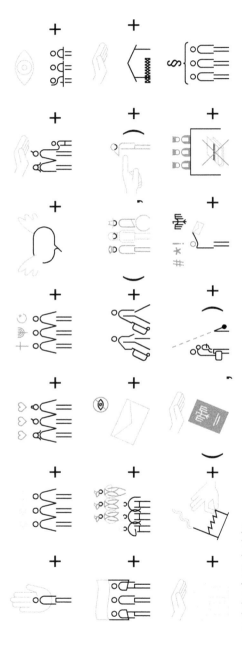

Depicting the Basic Rights

The Basic Law opens with an extensive catalogue of protected basic rights (Articles 1-19). Can you guess what those protections are from this graphic? You can study the online, English-language translation of the Basic Law to check your answers: www.gesetze-im-internet.de/englisch_gg/englisch_gg.html. Many of the basic rights contain limiting clauses that anticipate statutorily enacted restrictions on those rights. An example is Article 14(1), which provides: "(1) Property and the right of inheritance shall be guaranteed. *Their content and limits shall be defined by the laws*" (emphasis added).

Figure 8.1 The Basic Rights

Source: Illustration Grundrechte permission granted by Brandenburgische Landeszentrale für politische Bildung (Potsdam) and Großstadtzoo (Berlin)

them as forming the fundamental and paramount law of the nation [...]. [To reject the supremacy of the constitution] thus reduces to nothing what we have deemed the greatest improvement on political institutions – a written constitution [...].[24]

- The German Basic Law enjoys supremacy in its jurisdiction. Article 1(3) unequivocally declares: "The following basic rights shall bind the legislature, the executive and the judiciary as directly applicable law."[25] Article 20(3) further establishes that "[t]he legislature shall be bound by the constitutional order [...]."[26] As Kommers noted, a number of other Basic Law provisions work alongside Article 1(3) to secure the constitution's supremacy. Germany's muscular commitment to this fundamental element of constitutionalism is all the more meaningful when one reflects on the pernicious, cynical, and brutal disregard Hitler's National Socialists showed for the Weimar Constitution. The Basic Law, as one commentator explained, "was meant to be an answer to the destruction of the Weimar Constitution of 1919. To this end, the Basic Law was designed to block any possible relapse into a regime of terror similar to that of National Socialism or Stalinism."[27] At the individual level, the robust protection of basic rights makes a significant contribution to that aim. The Basic Law also pursues this agenda at the social, political, and institutional level. Finally, through a framework referred to as *wehrhafte Demokratie* (defensive democracy or militant democracy), the constitution seeks to control and oversee political movements, the popular will, and the government. To do this it provides illiberal and undemocratic tools for the protection of liberalism and democracy. For example, Article 21(3) of the Basic Law allows the state to ban political parties that pose a threat to the "free, democratic, basic order." Would you prefer to live in a constitutional system that conditions and controls outcomes in this way, in order to preserve a range of values thought to be existential, or in a constitutional system that enforces the democratic and procedural rules of the game without attempting to dictate a winner?
- Perhaps the strongest signal of constitutional superiority in the German scheme is provided by Article 79(3), which makes a handful of constitutional provisions unamendable and "eternal."[28] That is, some parts of the Basic Law can never be changed or abandoned, not by a super-majority of the Federal Parliament, not by unanimous demand of the federal states, and not by a popular uprising from the people. Which constitutional provisions and commitments do you think are given this "eternal" status? If some features of modern German constitutional law are unamendable, what recourse might nevertheless exist to change or abandon them?
- One of the provisions covered by the "eternity clause" of Article 79(3) is Article 20, which declares the essential character of the German state: "The Federal Republic of Germany is a democratic and social federal state."[29] But Kommers identifies another definitive characteristic of the system constituted by the Basic Law. Germany is a *Rechtsstaat*. It is a difficult term

(and concept) to translate. Literally, it means something like a "law state." It is often translated as the "rule of law," or clumsily as "a state governed by the rule of law." Kommers tells us that in German the concept has two dimensions: committing the state to governance by law (*Vorrang und Vorbehalt des Gesetzes*) as well as to justice (*Gerechtigkeit*). Curiously, the only references to the *Rechtsstaat* in the text of the Basic Law are linked to the conditions of government in other contexts: as a limit on the extradition of Germans to other countries; as a mandate for Germany's integration into the European Union system; and as a requirement for the governance exercised by the German federal states.[30] The Federal Constitutional Court derived the enforceable federal constitutional commitment to the *Rechtsstaatprinzip* (rule of law principle) from the values and terms of the Basic Law generally. It consists of a range of discrete assurances. For example, it requires that public power be exercised under the authority and within the scope of a statutory mandate. It also includes, among other commitments, the right to be heard by a court, the principle of the separation of powers, and the principle of proportionality. We'll learn more about the last of these expressions of the *Rechtsstaat* later in this chapter.

8.2 Judicial Review: The Federal Constitutional Court

A constitution's supremacy depends entirely on the presence of a legitimate and powerful entity of state authority charged with interpreting and enforcing the constitution. Under the US Constitution this responsibility might have fallen to the legislature or the executive. The 1787 Constitution is silent on the matter. But, in the facet of *Marbury v. Madison* for which the case is best known, Chief Justice Marshall claimed this role for the judiciary, especially the Supreme Court. He insisted that "it is emphatically the province and duty of the judicial department to say what the law is." Some accuse Chief Justice Marshall of political chicanery and institutional bias, but the result was that he conferred the authority to enforce the constitution's supremacy – as well as the power to definitively interpret the constitution – on the courts. Not unlike the "shot heard round the world" – the salvo between American revolutionaries and British soldiers that started the American Revolution in 1775 – Chief Justice Marshall's principle of judicial review has reverberated far beyond the US constitutional landscape.

The concept of judicial review, as a fundamental element of constitutionalism, has touched Germany in a most spectacular way. Uwe Wesel began his delightful book about German constitutional history with a chapter entitled "John Marshall and his Judgment in the Case *Marbury v. Madison*."[31] Tracing the direct influence of *Marbury v. Madison* on Germany's post-war constitutional order, Wesel explained that constitutional review was vested by the Basic Law in a special entity known as the Federal Constitutional Court. Article 92 of the Basic Law creates the Federal Constitutional Court. Article 93 of the

8.2 Judicial Review: The Federal Constitutional Court

Basic Law, through an astounding number of detailed jurisdictional competences, expressly makes the Constitutional Court the "guardian of the constitution ("*der Hüter der Verfassung*"). Many more details relating to the Federal Constitutional Court are resolved in the *Bundesverfassungsgerichtsgesetz* (BVerfGG or Federal Constitutional Court Act).

Donald P. Kommers & Russell A. Miller
Das Bundesverfassungsgericht: Procedure, Practice and Policy of the German Federal Constitutional Court
3 JOURNAL OF COMPARATIVE LAW 194, 197–203, 207–208 (2008)[*]

* * *

The most important structural feature of the [Federal Constitutional] Court is its division into two senates with mutually exclusive jurisdiction and personnel. The Plenum – the two senates sitting together – meets periodically to resolve jurisdictional conflicts between the senates and to issue rules on judicial administration. Justices are elected to either the First Senate or the Second Senate, with the Court's President presiding over one senate and the Court's Vice President presiding over the other.

[…] The Second Senate was designed to function much like the *Staatsgerichtshof* of the Weimar-era. It would decide political disputes between branches and levels of government, settle contested elections, rule on the constitutionality of political parties, preside over impeachment proceedings, and decide abstract questions of constitutional law. The First Senate was vested with the authority to review the constitutionality of laws and to resolve constitutional doubts arising out of ordinary litigation. More concerned with the "nonpolitical" side of the Court's docket and the "objective" process of constitutional interpretation, the First Senate would hear the constitutional complaints of ordinary citizens as well as referrals from other courts.

This division of labor resulted initially in a significant imbalance between the workloads of the two senates. As a consequence, the *Bundestag* (Federal Parliament) amended the [Federal Constitutional Court Act – FCCA] in 1956 to distribute the caseload more evenly. Much of the First Senate's work was transferred to the Second Senate, thus eroding the original rationale of the two-senate system. The Second Senate, while retaining its "political" docket, would henceforth decide all constitutional complaints and concrete judicial review cases dealing with issues of civil and criminal procedure. The First Senate would continue to decide all such cases involving issues of substantive law.

The number of Justices serving on the two senates has also changed over the years. The FCCA originally provided for twelve members per senate. In 1956, the number was reduced to ten; in 1962, it was further reduced to eight, fixing the Court's total membership at sixteen. Considerations of efficiency, coupled with the politics of judicial recruitment, prompted these reductions.

* * *

Machinery for Judicial Selection

The Basic Law provides that half the Court's members be elected by the *Bundestag* and half by the *Bundesrat* (Federal Council of States). The participation of the *Bundestag* in the selection of the Court's justices underscores the significant role the Court plays in

---

[*] Excerpt reprinted with permission of the author.

reviewing the content and democratic quality of the decisions of the popularly elected federal parliament. It seems appropriate, then, that the *Bundestag* plays some role in staffing the Court. Similarly, the participation of the *Bundesrat* in the selection of the Court's justices was meant to ensure that the Court was, at least with respect to its staffing, steeped in Germany's federalism.

Under the FCCA the *Bundestag* elects its eight justices indirectly through a twelve-person Judicial Selection Committee (JSC) known as the *Wahlmännerausschuss*. Party representation on the JSC is proportional to each party's strength in the *Bundestag*; eight votes – a two-thirds super-majority – are required to elect. The *Bundesrat* votes as a whole for its eight justices, with a two-thirds vote also being required to elect. The two chambers alternate in selecting the Court's president and vice president.

The process of judicial selection is highly politicized. The JSC, which consists of senior party officials and the top legal experts of each parliamentary party, conducts its proceedings behind closed doors and after extensive consultation with the *Bundesrat*. The two-thirds majority required to elect a justice endows opposition parties in the JSC with considerable leverage over appointments to the Constitutional Court. Social and Christian Democrats are in a position to veto each other's judicial nominees, and the Free Democratic and Green parties, when in coalition with one of the larger parties, have won seats for their nominees through intra-coalition bargaining. Compromise is a practical necessity.

Compromise among contending interests and candidacies is equally necessary in the *Bundesrat*, where the interests of the various states, often independent of party affiliation, play a paramount role in the selection of the justices. An advisory commission consisting of the state justice ministers prepares a short list of potentially electable nominees. The justice ministers on the commission, like certain state governors (*Ministerpräsidenten*) and members of the *Bundestag's* JSC, are often themselves leading candidates for seats on the Constitutional Court. Informal agreements emerge from the commission's proceedings, specifying which states shall choose prospective justices and in what order. Throughout this process, the commission coordinates its work with that of the JSC. It is important to avoid duplicate judicial selections, and the two chambers need to agree on the particular senate seats each is going to fill and which of these seats are to be filled with justices recruited from the federal high courts.

For all its opacity, the German process, largely as a consequence of the super-majority required for election, has consistently produced a Court reflective of Germany's most prominent political parties, regional divisions, and confessions. In one respect, however, the Court has been less than representative of German society. The recently concluded Constitutional Court Presidency of Jutta Limbach, the first woman to hold the position, draws attention to the fact that the Court continues to be dominated by men. In 1951 the remarkable Erna Scheffler, who participated in the Parliamentary Council, was elected as one of the Court's first Justices. In the subsequent half-century, only ten other women have found their way onto the Court.

Jurisdiction

The Basic Law enumerates the totality of the Court's jurisdiction, with elaboration where necessary in the FCCA. The most important of these competencies are described briefly here.

Prohibiting Political Parties

The Court's function as guardian of the constitutional order finds its most vivid expression in Article 21(2) of the Basic Law. Under this provision, political parties seeking "to impair or abolish the free democratic basic order or to endanger the existence of the Federal Republic of Germany shall be unconstitutional." The article goes on to declare that only the Federal Constitutional Court may declare parties unconstitutional. The Court has received only eight party-ban petitions from the other federal organs and it has decided just five of those cases. In only two, concluded early on, did the Court sustain the petitions: in 1952 when it banned the neo-Nazi Socialist Reich party, and in 1956 when it ruled the Communist party unconstitutional.

Disputes between High Federal Organs

Conflicts known as *Organstreit* proceedings involve constitutional disputes between the highest "organs," or branches, of the German Federal Republic. The Court's function here is to supervise the operation and internal procedures of these executive and legislative organs and to maintain the proper institutional balance between them. The governmental organs qualified to bring cases under this jurisdiction are the *Bundespräsident* (Federal President), *Bundestag* (Federal Parliament), *Bundesrat* (Federal Council of States), *Bundesregierung* (Federal Government), and units of these organs vested with independent rights by their rules of procedure or the Basic Law. Included among these units are individual members of the *Bundestag*, any one of whom may initiate an *Organstreit* proceeding to vindicate his or her status as a parliamentary representative. These units also include the parliamentary political parties. An *Organstreit* proceeding is not available, however, to administrative agencies, governmental corporations, churches, or other corporate bodies with quasi-public status.

Federal-State Conflicts

Constitutional disputes between a *Land* (state) and the *Bund* (federation) ordinarily arise out of conflicts involving a state's administration of federal law or the federal government's supervision of state administration. Proceedings may be brought only by a state government or by the federal government.

Concrete Judicial Review

Concrete, or collateral, judicial review arises from an ordinary lawsuit. If an ordinary German court is convinced that a relevant federal or state law under which a case has arisen violates the Basic Law, it must refer the constitutional question to the Federal Constitutional Court before proceeding to a resolution of the case. Judicial referrals do not depend on the issue of constitutionality having been raised by one of the parties. An ordinary court is obliged to make such a referral when it is convinced that a law under which a case has arisen is in conflict with the Constitution.

Abstract Judicial Review

The Court may decide differences of opinion or doubts about the compatibility of a federal or state law with the Basic Law on the mere request of the federal or a state government or of one-third of the members of the *Bundestag*. Oral argument before the Court, a rarity in most cases, is always permitted in abstract review proceedings. The question of the law's validity is squarely before the Court in these proceedings, and a decision against validity renders the law null and void.

Constitutional Complaints

A constitutional complaint may be brought by individuals and entities vested with particular rights under the Constitution. After exhausting all other available means to find relief in the ordinary courts, any person who claims that the state has violated one or more of his or her rights under the Basic Law may file a constitutional complaint in the Federal Constitutional Court. Constitutional complaints must be lodged within a certain time, identify the offending action or omission and the agency responsible, and specify the constitutional right that has been violated. The FCCA requires the Court to accept for decision any complaint if it is constitutionally significant or if the failure to accept it would work a grave hardship on the complainant. "Any person" within the meaning of this provision includes natural persons with the legal capacity to sue as well as corporate bodies and other "legal persons" possessing rights under the Basic Law.

The procedure for filing complaints is relatively easy and inexpensive. No filing fees or formal papers are required. Most complaints are prepared without the aid of a lawyer (attorneys prepare about a third). No legal assistance is required at any stage of the complaint proceeding. As a consequence of these rather permissive standing rules, the Court has been flooded with complaints, which have swelled in number from well under 1,000 per year in the 1950s, to around 3,500 per year in the mid-1980s, and rising from around 5,000 per year in the 1990s to nearly 6,000 in 2006. The Court grants full review to barely more than 1 percent of all constitutional complaints, but such complaints result in some of its most significant decisions and make up more than 50 percent of its published opinions.

* * *

The Federal Constitutional Court and the Polity
Practice of Judicial Review

[…] [T]he Court has accumulated a considerable store of moral authority and public approval. A series of public opinion polls taken in recent years shows that the Court enjoys substantially more public trust than any other major political or social institution, including parliament, the military establishment, the regular judiciary, the television industry, and even churches and universities. It relies on this goodwill when, as it often does, it wades into Germany's most contentious issues.

Among the many reasons for the widespread acceptance the Court enjoys are its passive posture in the scheme of separation of powers and the restraint is has typically shown when it does act.

With respect to its passive posture, it is often noted that, although the Court enjoys equal standing alongside the other "high" federal organs that have principle responsibility for governing Germany (*Bundestag, Bundesrat, Bundesregierung* and *Bundespräsident*), it is unique in that it cannot call itself to action. It is bound, instead, to dispose of the cases and controversies that find their way to its door.

Even when summoned to service, in numerous ways the Court shows considerable restraint. First, the Court traditionally has refrained from anticipating a question of constitutional law in advance of the necessity for deciding it. While every case properly before the Court involves a constitutional question, the Court usually refrains from deciding ancillary constitutional issues not yet ripe for decision. Second, the approach the Court takes towards statutory interpretation exemplifies its reserve. A leading principle of judicial review in Germany obliges the Court to interpret statutes, when possible, in conformity with the Basic Law (*Pflicht zur verfassungskonformen Auslegung*). Additionally, the Court frequently has stated that it will not substitute its judgment of sound or wise public policy for that of the legislature. The Court also will not overturn statutes simply because the legislature may have inaccurately predicted the consequences of social or economic policy. Third, the Court abides by several rules that limit the number of concrete judicial review referrals from ordinary courts. Fourth, while the Court does not enjoy discretion akin to the *certiorari* power of the United States Supreme Court, it does have limited control over its docket through the three-justice Chambers. This admissibility review can, to no small degree, be instrumentalized to serve the Court's interests, including its interest in preserving its moral authority.

The Court's Impact

The Court's record, in spite of the modesty just described, reveals a self-confident tribunal deeply engaged in Germans' lives and politics. By January 1 2007, the Court had invalidated 596 laws and administrative regulations (or particular provisions thereof) under the Basic Law. The large majority of these rulings admittedly involved minor legal provisions, but a fair number featured important public policies. The number and range of cases in which the Federal Constitutional Court has acted to dramatically impact German politics are too great to systematically or comprehensively recount in this brief introduction. As already noted, the Court has banned political parties as unconstitutional, policed federal-state relations, monitored the democratic process, overseen the dissolution of parliament, supervised the unification of West and East Germany, shaped education policy, delineated Germany's social market economy and cradle-to-grave welfare regime, and defined and enforced a regime of basic liberties.

* * *

Questions/Comments

- The judiciary benefits from the supremacy of the Basic Law because the justices of the Federal Constitutional Court are charged (by the Basic Law itself) with interpreting, defining, and effectuating the constitution. The Court's interpretations of the Basic Law must be followed by others – in the judicial, executive, and legislative branches – as directly enforceable constitutional law. Kommers' conclusion that much of the Basic Law's regime derives from "the gloss the Federal Constitutional Court has put on the text of the Basic Law" describes a role for the judiciary that is far removed from the formalistic – almost mechanistic – judicial function typical in systems influenced by the Civil Law tradition. Instead, as I suggested earlier in this chapter, the kind of judging the Constitutional Court is empowered to do seems to be more closely aligned with the role the Common Law tradition assigns to the judiciary.
- Kommers credited the justices of the Federal Constitutional Court with having "created and maintained a nation of shared values." From this perspective the Constitutional Court, not political institutions or private actors, has been the defining force in modern Germany. One prominent commentator even wondered if it might be better to refer to the Federal Republic as the "Karlsruhe Republic," as a nod to the quaint, southwestern German city where the Court is based.[32] It is common in German politics to hear the phrase "*wir sehen uns in Karlsruhe!*" ("I'll see you in Karlsruhe!"). This expresses the idea that political debates aren't finally settled until the Constitutional Court has ruled on the matter. And the Constitutional Court is consistently called on to decide

The Federal Constitutional Court

The Federal Constitutional Court resides at Schlossbezirk 3 in Karlsruhe, Germany. The Court's location, far from the seat of the federal government and federal parliament (in Bonn as the capital of West Germany, and in Berlin after reunification), establishes distance and independence (literal and symbolic) between the justices and the country's politics. Paul Baumgarten's Bauhaus design featured wood (suggesting the living and flexible character of the law), luminous glass (signaling the openness and transparency of justice), and concrete (exuding the Court's strength and stability). The effect is a modern home for Germany's post-war constitutional tradition.

Figure 8.2 Federal Constitutional Court: Guardian of the Constitution
Source: Shutterstock

the fate of prominent or divisive policy. The Court's concrete, steel, glass, and wood-trimmed building can be seen in the photo in Figure 8.2. The design and materials are highly symbolic – signaling modernity, transparency, solidity and stability, suffused with a measure of dynamism and flexibility.

- Judicial review and a powerful court may be an essential feature of constitutionalism. The Constitutional Court has not shied away from this prominent, political role. It is only symbolic of that power, but, as depicted in Figure 8.3 later in this chapter, the Constitutional Court justices appear at their rare oral hearings wearing dramatic, scarlet red robes. There is nothing modest about that solemn, almost ecclesiastical style. But, could constitutionalism's empowerment of the judiciary be taken too far? Is it a good thing, as Kommers and Miller reported, that the Constitutional Court is held in higher regard in Germany than "any other major political or social institution, including Parliament"?
- The Federal Constitutional Court enjoys sweeping and wide-ranging jurisdiction, which is outlined in detail in the Basic Law and the Federal

Constitutional Court Act. The full range of these paths to the Court's jurisdiction is presented in Table 8.1. Which of these jurisdictional provisions most dramatically insert the Court into policymaking? Does the Federal Constitutional Court enjoy forms of jurisdiction that the apex court in your primary or "national" legal system does not?

- In recent years, concern about the extreme politicization of the US Supreme Court prompted serious consideration of reforms. At the same time, many observers pointed to the German Federal Constitutional Court as a model for judiciousness and judicial integrity. Two factors contribute to the Court's seeming political balance and acceptance. First, the appointment process described by Kommers and Miller is less crudely partisan. The key element of that process is the requirement of a two-thirds super-majority (in the *Bundestag* or *Bundesrat*) for the empanelment of a justice at the Court. A second factor limiting partisanship at the Constitutional Court is the statutory limit on justices' tenure. Justices may serve only a single twelve-year term (or fewer years if affected by mandatory retirement at age sixty-eight). The frequent, predictable, and orderly rotation of the justices seems to have lowered the political heat around the process. Despite the hopes heaped on the Constitutional Court's appointment process by American reformers, the pathway to the Constitutional Court remains troublingly opaque. The order in which the parties take their turn appointing justices, not to mention the parties' commitment to approving any specific appointee, is settled by veteran politicians in smoke-filled cloakrooms at the *Bundestag* and *Bundesrat*.
- The *Bundestag* vets its share of the appointments to the Constitutional Court in a parliamentary committee once known as the *Wahlmännerausschuss* (committee of electors). In recognition of the masculine gender assigned to the German word for "elector," since 1994 the committee has had the more gender-neutral title *Wahlausschuss* (electing committee). That cosmetic change has been accompanied by a remarkable demographic development at the Court: By 2022 more than half the Constitutional Court's justices were women. Still, other barriers must fall. No German who identifies with, or who has a background in, one of Germany's vibrant and well-integrated migrant communities has yet been appointed to the Court.
- The German Constitutional Court receives about the same number of newly docketed cases each year (from a country of 80 million people) as the US Supreme Court receives (from a country of 320 million people). Kommers and Miller explain that the Constitutional Court must rule on nearly all of the 5,000 constitutional complaints it receives annually. At the same time, the US Supreme Court decides roughly seventy cases each year. What explains this large discrepancy between the two courts' output?
- The Constitutional Court's interpretation of the Basic Law is central to the meaning and implementation of the constitution. But the Court's interpretive practice does not attract the same attention and theoretical scrutiny

Table 8.1 Procedures before the Federal Constitutional Court

Forfeiture of Basic Rights	Art. 18 Basic Law; Section 13(1) BVerfGG	By application of the Federal Parliament, the Federal Government, or a state government, anyone who has abused select basic rights in order to undermine the "free democratic basic order" may have his or her rights revoked by the Constitutional Court.
Unconstitutionality of Political Parties	Article 21(2) Basic Law; Section 13(2) BVerfGG	By application of the Federal Parliament, the Federal Council of States, or the Federal Government, a political party that seeks to undermine or abolish the "free democratic basic order" may be banned.
Exclusion of Political Parties from Public Funding	Article 21(3) Basic Law; Section 13(2a) BVerfGG	By application of the Federal Parliament, the Federal Council of States, or the Federal Government, a political party that seeks to undermine or abolish the "free democratic basic order" may be excluded from the system of state support for political parties.
Election Review	Article 41(2) Basic Law; Section 13(3) BVerfGG	The Federal Parliament resolves election disputes. But its decisions are reviewable by the Federal Constitutional Court.
Political Party Status	Article 93(1)[4c] Basic Law; Section 13(3a) BVerfGG	The Federal Parliament, through the Federal Election Committee, certifies which civil society organizations may campaign for Bundestag election as "political parties." The Committee's decision to refuse to certify an organization may be challenged before the Federal Constitutional Court. Prior to the 2021 federal elections the Committee did not certify 44 organizations.
Proceedings for the Impeachment of the Federal President	Article 61 Basic Law; Section 13(4) BVerfGG	On an application of at least one-quarter of the Federal Parliament or the Federal Council of State the Federal Constitutional Court will decide whether to impeach the Federal President for a "willful violation" of the Basic Law or another federal law.

Table 8.1 (cont.)

Disputes Concerning the Rights and Duties of High Federal Organs	Article 93(1)[1] Basic Law; Section 13(5) BVerfGG	The Federal Constitutional Court supervises and the operation of the High Federal Organs (Federal Parliament or party fractions within the parliament, Federal Council of States, Federal Government, Federal President) to ensure that their activities conform to the Basic Law. There have been 353 of these applications before the Federal Constitutional Court.
Abstract Judicial Review	Article 93(1)[2] Basic Law; Section 13(6) BVerfGG	On an application of the Federal Government, the government of a state, or at least one-quarter of the members of the Federal Parliament, the Federal Constitutional Court may resolve doubts or disagreements about the constitutionality of newly enacted federal or state law.
Federalism Disputes	Articles 93(1)[2a], 126; Sections 13(6a) and (6b) BVerfGG, 13(14)	Article 72(2) of the Basic Law grants the Federation legislative priority over the states with respect to a limited range of concurrent competences, so long as federal action is necessary for the "establishment of equivalent living conditions throughout the federal territory or the maintenance of legal or economic unity." The Federal Council of States, a state government, or a state parliament can challenge the necessity for federal action (or assert the expiration of a previously existing necessity for federal action) before the Federal Constitutional Court. In the wake of major federalism reform in 2006, the Federal Constitutional Court has the authority to determine whether federal legislative competences exercised before the reform have been superseded and now involve competences over which the states have priority.

Table 8.1 (cont.)

Federal-State Disputes	Articles 93(1)[3], 93(1)[4], 84(4)[2]; Sections 13(7), 13(8) BVerfGG	The Federal Constitutional Court adjudicates public law disputes between the federation and the states, between the states, and within a state. These proceedings particularly concern the implementation of federal law by the states.
Constitutional Complaints	Article 93(1)[4a] and [4b] Basic Law, Section 13(8a) BVerfGG	The Basic Law grants every person a right to complain to the Federal Constitutional Court about an infringement on his or her basic rights by public authority. In a similar manner, municipalities may complain to the Federal Constitutional Court about infringements on their right to self-government. This is the largest and most demanding part of the Court's docket, with around 5,000 individual constitutional complaints filed each year.
Judicial Impeachment Proceedings	Article 98(2) and (5) Basic Law; Section 13(9) BVerfGG	On an application from the Federal Parliament or state authorities, the Federal Constitutional Court may rule on the impeachment of a federal or state judge for an infringement on "the principles of this Basic Law or the constitutional order of a state."
Referral of a Constitutional Dispute from a State	Article 99 Basic Law; Section 13(10) BVerfGG	A state law may assign the adjudication of internal constitutional disputes to the Federal Constitutional Court.
Concrete Judicial Review: Constitutional Law	Article 100(1) Basic Law; Section 13(11) BVerfGG	If an ordinary court concludes that a law that will be determinative in a case is unconstitutional, then the proceedings must be stayed and a final decision on constitutionality must be obtained from the Federal Constitutional Court. This is the primary mechanism for classical judicial review in the German constitutional system. It underscores, however, the Federal Constitutional Court's exclusive (specialized) jurisdiction over the interpretation of the Basic Law. This is the second most frequent proceeding before the Court. There have been more than 4,000 concrete judicial review cases.

Table 8.1 (cont.)

Committee of Inquiry Cases	Section 36(2) Committees of Inquiry Act	The Federal Constitutional Court may determine whether the Federal Parliament's decision to establish a committee of inquiry is compatible with the Basic Law.
Concrete Judicial Review: International Law	Articles 100(2) and 25 Basic Law; Section 13(12) BVerfGG	If a court has doubts about the direct, domestic applicability of a provision of public international law, including whether the international norm establishes individual rights or duties, then the proceedings must be stayed and a final decision must be obtained from the Federal Constitutional Court.
Concrete Judicial Review: State Constitutional Law	Article 100(3); Section 13(13) BVerfGG	If a state constitutional court proposes to deviate from a holding of the Federal Constitutional Court, then the proceedings must be stayed and a final decision must be obtained from the Federal Constitutional Court.
Preliminary Injunctions	Section 32 BVerfGG	In a dispute before the Federal Constitutional Court, the Court may provisionally decide a matter by way of a preliminary injunction if this is urgently required. The preliminary injunction may be issued without an oral hearing. A preliminary injunction is not a formal resolution of the underlying issues. Still, granting an injunction tips the Court's hand regarding the merits of the case. There have been more than 4,000 preliminary injunction proceedings.

given to the US Supreme Court's approach to constitutional interpretation. In the US system this is partly due to the very broad nature of the text of the 1787 Constitution. That leaves, as they say, a lot to interpretation. One prominent American constitutional law scholar even suggested that the method of interpretation – more than the text itself – *is* the constitution.[33] There is plenty of broadly framed and open-textured language in the Basic Law, too. For example, earlier we considered how to make sense of the Basic Law's demand that "human dignity" be shown absolute respect. But it is also true that the Basic Law is a long, and in some places exceedingly detailed, constitution. In those provisions the Basic Law seems a lot like a carefully constructed statute, or even a code. The presence of that kind of coverage might explain why, in the German constitutional practice, the accepted modalities of interpretation are uncontroversial and more-or-less systematically applied. As discussed in Chapter 6, they include: textual or grammatical interpretation (deriving meaning from the words and the impact of the related grammar); systemic interpretation (deriving meaning from a term's usage or location in the broader constitutional text); historical interpretation (deriving meaning from the considerations and debates that informed the enactment of the provision); and teleological interpretation (deriving meaning from the norm's object and purpose).

One interpretive tool used by the Constitutional Court merits special attention, not the least because it is thought to have been adopted by nearly all rights-protecting legal regimes in the world (both domestic constitutional law and international human rights law). When deciding whether a basic right has been violated the Constitutional Court invariably employs a formalized and systematic proportionality analysis. This is the analytical expression of the proportionality principle, which, as I noted earlier, is a component of the constitutionally mandated *Rechtsstaatprinzip*. That is a convoluted way of saying that the proportionality analysis itself has acquired constitutional significance, even as its function is to give meaning and force to substantive constitutional rights. The proportionality analysis embraces a distinct understanding of basic rights. The American constitutional tradition treats basic rights as absolutes and (at least in principle) the Supreme Court enforces them as all-or-nothing commands. Informed by an underlying suspicion towards the state, it is thought that this approach is the only way to be sure that the powerful state cannot disturb individual liberty. A right, Ronald Dworkin insisted, should be a categorical and absolute "trump."[34] The German tradition, however, is less skeptical of the state. There is a deep history of paternalism in relations between public power and the German people, perhaps dating back to the "fatherly" role played by clan or tribal chiefs, but certainly present in the nature of the feudal society that dominated most of Europe in the Medieval age. Today, acceptance of the state is conditioned by the understanding that public authority is democratically legitimated and constitutionally constrained. It seems unfortunate that every degree of the benefit intended by a public policy must be lost in order to realize any degree of constitutional rights protection. Faced with that troubling calculus, and recognizing that many of the Basic Law's rights contain explicit limitations clauses, Robert Alexy urged that basic rights be regarded as "principles" that can be satisfied in varying degrees in order to "optimize" both public policy and basic rights.[35] In this approach, an intrusion upon a basic right can be tolerated so long as it is "proportional."

I referred to the proportionality analysis when discussing legal method in Chapter 6. It merits a second look here because it plays such a significant role in the work of the Federal Constitutional Court and the life of the Basic Law.

The proportionality analysis makes a modulated rights jurisprudence possible. In the German practice, four concerns are addressed: (1) whether the intrusion on a right is justified by a *legitimer Zweck* (legitimate policy aim); (2) whether the means chosen are *geeignet* (suitable for achieving the aim); (3) whether the means chosen are *erforderlich* (necessary, or are the least intrusive possibility for achieving the aim); and (4) whether the benefits of the policy are *angemessen* (proportional to the burden that results from the intrusion on a basic right). If the answer to these questions is "yes," then the policy producing the infringement on a basic right is not regarded as constitutionally problematic. It is a "proportional" intrusion on the constitutional right. Especially in the fourth step of this analysis, building from an unstated assumption that the policy (enacted or mandated by the democratically legitimated legislature) should survive constitutional review, it is possible for the court to conceive of modest adaptations, corrections, or limitations that retain many of the policy's benefits while also minimizing the constitutional harm done. This step is often called *Verhältnismäßigkeit im engeren Sinne* (proportionality in the narrower sense), and it involves a straightforward balancing assessment: do the scales tip too heavily towards the intrusive policy or too heavily towards the basic right?

The balancing that takes place in the fourth step of the proportionality analysis produces what some refer to as the "yes ... but" jurisprudence of the Constitutional Court: *Yes*, an intrusive policy may be constitutionally acceptable; *But* only if the legislature revisits its terms to refine and limit the degree to which the policy intrudes upon a basic right. One example (of many) of this "yes ... but" praxis comes from the Court's review of challenges to new and extensive security and surveillance measures granted to the German Federal Criminal Police Office.[36] The Court found that the new measures were acceptable. But the extent of the intrusion on Germans' household and telecommunications privacy (protected by Articles 3 and 10 of the Basic Law) had to be further limited by a newly enacted version of the legislation that included the new, refined rights protections the Court had outlined in detail in its eighty-page judgment. Those statutory assurances included, *inter alia*: provisions strictly precluding the deployment of the new investigative powers in the home or in the context of highly protected relationships; provisions establishing a heightened standard for and judicial approval of the use of the new surveillance powers; and provisions requiring that notice of the measures be given to the surveillance subjects, that the data obtained be stored and registered in a protocol, that the data obtained be used only for the original purpose for which it was gathered, and that the data be deleted after a set period of time.[37] The parliament promptly made the changes and the law entered into force, now proportionately advancing the policy concerns around security while preserving a slightly greater degree of personal privacy.

The proportionality analysis places the Court in a policymaking posture that is sometimes hyper-legislative. The Court has not hesitated to extensively "rewrite" the challenged legislation (as in the example of the *BKA Act Case*), dictating to the parliament the exact amendments needed in order for the law to achieve the required balance. As a constitutionally mandated standard for the exercise of state authority, the proportionality principle and its accompanying proportionality analysis play a central role in the judicial oversight of the administrative state. This dynamic will be considered in more detail in Chapter 9, which presents German administrative law.

The proportionality approach to the judicial review and enforcement of basic rights – conceptualized and perfected by the German Federal Constitutional Court – has proven so appealing that many scholars regard the "proportionality paradigm" as the definitive method for adjudicating rights guarantees all around the world.[38] In any case, the proportionality analysis is now so thoroughly ingrained in the German jurisprudence and practice of constitutional rights that you are likely to get a more lively debate about the subtleties of its implementation than you are about the substantive meaning or scope of a basic right. Still, there are a very limited number of basic rights contexts to which the Constitutional Court does not apply the proportionality analysis. These contexts involve the Basic Law's rare absolutist protection of a right, most prominently the inviolable protection of human dignity pursuant to Article 1(1).

The materials I've presented so far have underscored the importance of two fundamental elements of constitutionalism in the German legal system: constitutional supremacy and judicial review by a powerful court. In a commemoration written on the 200th anniversary of *Marbury v. Madison*, former Federal Constitutional Court Justice Wolfgang Hoffmann-Riem recognized those features of modern German constitutionalism. Hoffmann-Riem attributes their emergence in the United States to "historical conditions" at the time the US Supreme Court decided *Marbury* that "enabled a change in paradigm; a new design of legislative reality [...]."[39] The paradigm shift, he argued, required the acceptance of higher-ranking constitutional law and the judiciary's right of constitutional review.[40] With the supremacy of the post-war Basic Law, as interpreted and enforced by the Federal Constitutional Court, Hoffmann-Riem concluded that this paradigm shift finally and decisively has overtaken Germany.

Wolfgang Hoffmann-Riem
Two Hundred Years of Marbury v. Madison: *The Struggle for Judicial Review of Constitutional Questions in the United States and Europe*
5 GERMAN LAW JOURNAL 685, 697–698 (2004)[*]

* * *

[...] German history has been marked by unsuccessful or even failing attempts to establish the rule of law, which reached a low point in the totalitarian dictatorship of the Nazi era. In 1949, there was a totalitarian regime in East Germany, and West Germany was

---

[*] Excerpt reprinted with permission of the author.

under military rule. It seemed appropriate to ratify the long overdue change of political paradigm with a new constitution.

[…] Articles 1(3) and 20(3) of West Germany's Basic Law established the supremacy of the constitution over other laws. […] All courts could review laws for constitutionality. However, only the Federal Constitutional Court had jurisdiction to reject laws as unconstitutional (Art. 100 of the Basic Law). This Court is a special authority entrusted with ensuring that sovereign power was exercised in accordance with the constitution (Art. 93 et seq. of the Basic Law). […]

Apparently in response to previous failed attempts to establish the rule of law, the jurisdiction of this court is particularly wide-ranging. Not only is there a separate constitutional court, but it was given an abundance of responsibilities not possessed by any other constitutional court of the time. For one thing, it has considerably greater review jurisdiction than the U.S. Supreme Court. This includes the legal power to review of laws (in the absence of a specific controversy) and to institute a constitutional complaint, even against laws (arg. Art. 93(3) of the Federal Constitutional Court Act, BVerfGG). Finally, unconstitutional laws are void, and not, as in the United States, only no longer applicable.

Supported by this institutional framework, impelled by its experience with totalitarian injustice, and spurred on by the public's growing recognition of its role, the Federal Constitutional Court has been proactive in realizing the idea of the constitutional state and the inalienability of fundamental rights. It did not bend when it came under sharp criticism in the 1990s and was confronted with proposals for institutional change – in the spirit of President Roosevelt's court-packing plan – which were never carried out.

Moreover, the Federal Constitutional Court has continually expanded its identity as the protector of the constitution and has enforced constitutional rights more vigorously than other courts, including the higher federal courts. It has overturned many of their decisions as unconstitutional. The constitutional court has always been subject to criticism. This includes the thesis, formulated by Carl Schmitt, that the power to review laws for constitutionality juridifies politics and politicizes the judiciary, resulting in a situation where neither win and both lose. Setting aside Schmitt's conclusion, it can, nevertheless, not be denied that a constitutional court with such strong jurisdiction is a political factor to be reckoned with. The Federal Constitutional Court has never denied this. The judicial right to review laws has been a political issue since its inception in 1803. The refusal to reject an unconstitutional law can also be a political issue. If the constitutional legal system leaves leeway for application of the law, which is indisputably the case, this becomes a political issue. The legal power to make the final binding decision is coupled with the highest responsibility.

A look at the history of jurisdiction over constitutional issues in the Federal Republic of Germany shows that the political culture in Germany was initially not strong enough to assure that the legal system would conform to the constitution without a special institution for that purpose. With this oversight, however, a high standard of constitutional review and of constitutional law has been developed.

* * *

Hoffmann-Riem, a former Federal Constitutional Court Justice, confirmed the enhanced role of the Federal Constitutional Court when he concluded that "the jurisdiction of this court is particularly wide-ranging" and considerably greater than the review jurisdiction of the US Supreme Court. The Federal Constitutional Court, Hoffmann-Riem said, "has been proactive" and has "continually expanded its identity." This has placed it, unbending, in conflict with what Hoffmann-Riem called the higher federal courts. Referring to Figure 5.4 – the chart of the German court system in Chapter 5 – these are the federal courts that sit atop Germany's various subject-matter jurisdictions. They are the courts of last instance charged with definitively interpreting and applying statutory law and the respective codes. These courts are bastions of an approach to law that remains heavily influenced by the Civil Law tradition. This is especially true of the *Bundesgerichtshof* (BGH or Federal Court of Justice), which is responsible for "ordinary" legal disputes arising from the civil and criminal codes. Basil Markesinis and Hannes Unberath described the judgments of the Federal Court of Justice as formulaic, abstract, "highly conceptual, even metaphysical," and containing "detailed consideration of the views of contemporary (and past) academic writers."[41] That sounds a lot like the Civil Law tradition. It also sounds like a jurisprudence that was bound to clash with Germany's new common law constitutionalism.

8.3 Horizontal Effect (*Drittwirkung*): The Encounter between Common Law and Civil Law

Now you understand that an encounter between the Federal Constitutional Court (interpreting and enforcing the Basic Law) and the Federal Court of Justice (interpreting and enforcing the Civil Code) would also be an example of the broader encounter taking place between the Common Law tradition and the Civil Law tradition in the German legal system. The odd-sounding doctrine known as *Drittwirkung* has sought to chaperone – to manage or negotiate – the rendezvous between those regimes and traditions. *Drittwirkung* refers to the indirect application of the constitution's basic rights protections (and, by implication, the Common Law frame of mind) in German private law, including with respect to the Civil Code (which is so thoroughly influenced by the Civil Law tradition). This is a dramatic suggestion. Traditionally, it was understood that a constitution does not apply to "horizontal" relationships between private parties. Instead, constitutions were chiefly meant to protect individuals in their "vertical" relationship with a potentially overbearing state, especially where it risked intruding on individual liberty. The doctrine of indirect horizontal effect was a response to a number of jurisprudential forces indigenous to the German legal system, not the least being the reverence shown to the German Civil Code, which is thought to comprehensively regulate private relations.

Knut Wolfgang Nörr
From Codification to Constitution: On the Changes of Paradigm in German Legal History of the Twentieth Century
60 TIJDSCHRIFT VOOR RECHTSGESCHIEDNEIS 145, 147–148, 152–154 (1992)[*]

* * *

---

[*] Excerpt reproduced with permission of Martinus Nijhoff/Brill.

8.3 Horizontal Effect (*Drittwirkung*)

[...] When we overlook the development of the German legal system in the periods formed by the *rule of law*, following the great lines from the last third of the nineteenth century to the present, we may notice a significant difference in the fundamental orientation of [German] law, a crucial change of *Leitbild* or paradigm. This change may be summarized in the formula of the change from Codification to Constitution.

* * *

[...] Only later an identity comparable with the other great legal systems [including English Common law and Napoleon's Code Civil of 1804] moulded slowly and step by step, in the form of the Codification drawn up in the last third of the nineteenth century.
[...] [A] great corpus of law had been created [...].
For the civil code was the code regarded as the core, the centrepiece of Codification. What was the reason for this estimation? [...] [W]e have to remember that in Germany [scholarly commentary] was still considered the decisive factor in shaping the law. Now, [scholars] saw Roman law, the way it presented itself in the Digest, as the ideal model for a rational unfolding of law, as the emanation of the reason of law itself. The Digest, however, contained almost exclusively civil law, *bürgerliches Recht*. The second [...] factor was the [French] Code Civil of 1804 whose high reputation impressed and encouraged the German [scholars] as well; it consisted also of civil law.

* * *

[It could not be assumed that the announcement of the Basic Law in 1949 meant a completely new beginning. Codification might have hoped to survive as the *Leitbild* of German law. After all, the Civil Code had survived the Nazi regime, as Nörr says, "at least in its outward shape."]
[...] Thus, with the formation of [West Germany] the question could have emerged again where the legal system of the Federal Republic would find its identity, whether it would go back to the Codification or turn to the Basic Law. This has not remained an open question for long. Within a few years the Basic Law became the point of reference for the [West German] legal system and in this function superseded the Codification: for good, it seems.
This process can be gathered from several phenomena [...].

* * *

The third symptom showing us the orientation of the legal system towards the Constitution leads us into substantive law. We mentioned the general clauses of the Codification above, that is the [principles of public policy and good faith]. We commented on their function as correctives of norms. Now we are dealing with another function. The general clauses have also been a pivotal instrument for the development of law. Whenever new facts emerged, the general clauses which by their very nature represent blank forms could be filled with new contents; hence, new norms could be developed. Of course, the question came up from which source the new norms should be taken. One usually turned to the values of the Codification, of the codes themselves to extract from them the standards for the development of law. In this respect a crucial change occurred [after the promulgation of the Basic Law]. Certain constitutional jurists founded the doctrine of the general clauses being the link between the Codification and the Basic Rights of the Constitution [so-called *"Drittwirkung der Grundrechte"*]. The doctrine maintains that also the relationship between individuals ought to be measured to a certain extent by the standards of the Basic Rights. Whereas according to the traditional view the Basic Rights serve to protect the citizen against the power of the state, now they shall protect one citizen against the other. The Constitutional Court in 1958 has adopted this theory [in the *Lüth Case*, BVerfGE 7, 198]. In this way, the Constitution – through the general clauses of the Codification – found its way into the Codification itself, and right into its zones of growth.

In connection with this the so-called objective order of values of the Basic Rights was developed as a conception that should extend over the whole legal system. This re-definition went hand in hand with a monopolization; for all the standards were now taken from the Basic Law; the fact, however, that the Codification also contained decisions for certain values or elementary notions of order was hardly noticed any more. Thus, the way was blocked for a theory which would have linked the fundamental principles of [the German] legal system not only to the Basic Rights but also to the leading ideas of the Codification.

As a result we have to record that the change of orientation from Codification to Constitution seems to have taken place definitively and irreversibly. The Basic Law has secured its position, the era of the Codification as *Leitbild* of the legal system seems to be over. [...]

* * *

Questions/Comments

- Nörr says that the paradigm shift from codification (the Civil Law tradition) to constitution (the Common Law tradition) was achieved through the Federal Constitutional Court's invention of the doctrine of indirect horizontal effect in the *Lüth Case*.[42] That's the case I presented in Chapter 3 as an example of the episodic – but recurring – resistance in Germany to the Civil Law tradition's predominance. Just how significant a disruption the case represented should now be coming into focus. In Chapter 3 I noted that *Lüth* achieved the ascendance of Basic Law's "objective order of values" in the German legal system. Nörr refers to a major consequence of that achievement in *Lüth*: The notion that the "objective order of values" has indirect horizontal – or radiating – effect in private law relations. Those two major doctrinal developments confirm why the *Lüth Case* is widely viewed as the most iconic of the Federal Constitutional Court's decisions.[43] Jacco Bomhoff explained that:

  > [t]he judgment [...] stands at the origin of the phenomenal spread in the acceptance of doctrines on the "horizontal effect" of constitutional norms. With its principled and affirmative answer to "the fundamental question of whether Constitutional norms affect private law," the [Federal Constitutional Court] set in motion an expansion of the sphere of influence of rights that has rippled through countries as diverse as South Africa and Canada, and that has arguably culminated in last year's decision of the Court of Justice of the European Communities on the "horizontal effect" of Community rules on freedom of movement.[44]

- *Lüth* is remarkable for several other reasons that distinctly characterize German constitutionalism. First, *Lüth* is one of several (still frequent) examples of the Federal Constitutional Court's explicit use of Germany's Nazi past as a foil for the new rights-respecting order ushered in by the Basic

8.3 Horizontal Effect (*Drittwirkung*)

Law. Although a number of new constitutional democracies rely on their undemocratic pasts as a buttress for a more democratic future, few rival the infamy of the Third Reich and the constructive use to which the Basic Law and the Federal Constitutional Court have put Germany's historic national disgrace.[45] As my presentation of the case in Chapter 3 establishes, that history played a central role in *Lüth*.

- *Lüth* is also an early and dramatic example of the Federal Constitutional Court's use of the proportionality analysis when interpreting and applying basic rights. In that approach, especially in the fourth step of the analysis, the Constitutional Court's justices weigh competing values in a particular case. That is a fact-specific undertaking that looks more like Common Law judging, which Holmes said is driven by the moral and policy implications of a case. But such a significant and policy-oriented role for judges, although typical of the Common Law tradition, raises concerns about the democratic legitimacy of the development of the law. Judges, after all, usually don't enjoy a directly elected, republican mandate. At least in democratic-parliamentary systems, such as Germany's, the Civil Law tradition's emphasis on enacted statutes and codes provides a reassurance of the democratic legitimacy of the law. Concerns about "judicial activism" are amplified by the seemingly unguided balancing that takes place in the proportionality analysis.[46] This led one commentator to conclude that a balancing analysis "is no more protective [of constitutional rights] than the judges who administer it."[47] The Federal Constitutional Court's fondness for balancing has stirred a lot of criticism. "Numerous authors," Alexy explained, "have raised the objection that balancing is both irrational and subjective."[48] One of the most critical observers of the Federal Constitutional Court's booming balancing business has been the constitutional law scholar Bernhard Schlink. Responding directly to Alexy, Schlink complained that rights susceptible to balancing are not absolute protections at all:

> as rules of optimization, fundamental rights [...] guarantee the citizen entitlements only in accordance with what is legally and actually possible. In this view, because conflicts are unavoidable among fundamental rights, as well as between fundamental rights and state interests, the entitlement to a fundamental right does not go beyond its enforcement in the conflict. The degree of enforcement will be more in one conflict, less in another; it is as much as possible and, to the extent possible, the optimum.[49]

To bring the discussion full circle, Schlink noted that the trajectory in German constitutional law towards balancing – including the concomitant enhancement of the Federal Constitutional Court's "activist" authority to "affect and legitimize change in the legal system or social order" – has its roots in "a spectacular case in the 1950s concerning a call for a boycott [...]."[50] That was the *Lüth Case*. Considering the new dimensions of the case mentioned here, it would pay to revisit the excerpt of that case presented in Chapter 3. After all, some regard it as the most important case in the history of the German Federal Constitutional Court.

The Federal Constitutional Court relied on the theory of indirect horizontal effect when it affirmed Lüth's complaint. Recall that Lüth had argued that the filmmaker Veit Harlan and his film distribution company – as private parties – infringed his free speech rights when they obtained an injunction under the Civil Code against Lüth's call for a boycott of Harlan's new film. The Constitutional Court held that the basic rights articulate an "objective order of values." Now you understand that the Constitutional Court also insisted, through the doctrine of *Drittwirkung*, that this objective order of values informs all law, including private law. "Every provision of private law," the Court said, "must be compatible with this system of values, and every such provision must be interpreted in its spirit." While private relations and transactions on the horizontal plane between individuals continue to be governed exclusively by private law norms such as the Civil Code, the Court demanded that the interpretation and application of those norms by the ordinary courts take the constitution's objective order of values into consideration. This is especially true, the Court explained, of the Civil Code's general clauses, which, as discussed in Chapter 7, permit consideration of broader social and ethical interests in the application of the detailed and systematic Civil Code. The general clauses, the Court said, are the "points where constitutional rights enter the domain of private law." The Constitutional Court charged the ordinary civil courts with the responsibility of ensuring that their interpretation and application of the private law takes account of the Basic Law's value decisions. And the Court threatened to review and reverse the private law decisions of those courts when they fail to adequately carry forward the Basic Law's values.

Pursuant to the doctrine of indirect horizontal effect announced in *Lüth*, the Basic Law's constitutional rights apply to all private law and have indirect effect on private actors whose legal relationships are regulated by that law.[51] Nörr remarks that the horizontal effect doctrine constituted a shift in Germany's legal paradigm because it made the Civil Code a subject of the Basic Law's new constitutional order. This was no small feat. Stephen Gardbaum noted that "the German Civil Code of [1900] had been viewed since its inception as the crowning glory of the legal system, a definitive and authoritative written document with a cultural status and prestige not dissimilar to that of the Constitution of the United States."[52]

8.4 Application of *Drittwirkung* by the Constitutional Court: The *Suretyship Case*

Drittwirkung has proven a practical as well as symbolic force, exposing every aspect of the law to potential constitutional review, even the private law regime established by the sacred Civil Code. As the following excerpt from the *Suretyship*

8.4 Application of *Drittwirkung*: The *Suretyship Case*

Case demonstrates, the suretyship contracts we examined in Chapter 7 are no exception to this development. In fact, they have often come in for constitutional scrutiny under the *Drittwirkung* doctrine.

A flurry of claims raised in the ordinary civil courts in the 1980s and 1990s challenged the binding force of suretyships obtained by banks from the primary creditors' relatives or partners. In many of these cases young, inexperienced sureties signed suretyship declarations for credit sums worth vastly more than their actual, and arguably their potential, net worth. In these cases, § 138 and § 242 – the general clauses representing "drops of social oil" in the Civil Code – served as the window through which the Basic Law's objective order of values radiated into the field of private law. The sureties invoked these provisions in their attempts to have the contracts declared void as "contrary to public policy" or to have their enforcement adjusted to reflect the banks' "duty to perform according to the requirements of good faith." The Federal Court of Justice (the last instance court for civil and criminal law) persisted in interpreting the relevant Civil Code provisions narrowly and formalistically. The sureties' claims for relief were rejected. Following the Federal Court's lead, that was the position the Hamburg Regional Court adopted in the suretyship case we considered in Chapter 7. In these cases, the Federal Court of Justice reasoned that it was enforcing the important notion of *Privatautonomie* that animates the prominent and proud Civil Code regime. In their constitutional complaints, however, the sureties argued that the formalistic interpretation the Federal Court of Justice was giving to § 138 and § 242 – even if consistent with the liberal, individualistic spirit of the Civil Code and with the nature of judging in the Civil Law tradition – failed to adequately account for the Basic Law's objective order of values. They insisted that problematic suretyship agreements might constitute a violation of human dignity, as that inviolable right is expressed in the general right to personal freedom secured by Article 2(1) of the Basic Law. The Federal Court of Justice, the sureties argued, should have interpreted and applied § 138 and § 242 with an awareness of those constitutional commitments. In the *Suretyship Case* the Federal Constitutional Court agreed with those views.

Federal Constitutional Court
Suretyship Case
BVerfGE 89, 214 (1993)[*]

[Translation by Russell A. Miller]

Facts

The constitutional complaint requires us to determine the degree to which the constitution obliges the civil courts to subject suretyship contracts with banks to substantive review when relatives with no income or assets undertake high liability risks as sureties on behalf of the debtors.

---

[*] Permission granted by the Federal Constitutional Court.

Bank contract law is not regulated by special statutes. It is governed by the contract law of the BGB [...].

In granting credit, banks use contractual forms that are largely uniform. [...] In the security practice of credit institutions, especially in the case of consumer credit and business credit involving medium-sized undertakings, banks typically conclude suretyship contracts with family members. The income and assets of these sureties are frequently not investigated. The purpose of such contracts is not exclusively to increase the assets available as a guarantee for the credit. It also addresses asset transfer issues and makes recipients of credit exercise greater care in their business dealings by bringing their relatives into the matter.

For the last ten years the civil courts have been increasingly concerned with cases in which young adults have become hopelessly overburdened with debt because they provided guarantees for high bank loans to their partners or parents, even though they only had small incomes.

The courts of first instance subjected the contracts concluded according to this practice to extensive substantive review. [...]

This jurisprudence was largely rejected on appeal by the ninth civil senate of the *Bundesgerichtshof* [Federal Court of Justice]. The third civil senate has confirmed the ninth senate's approach. The Federal Court of Justice has concluded that suretyship contracts should not be found to have violated "public policy" just because they are likely to overwhelm a surety with debt. The Federal Court of Justice explained that the freedom to formulate contracts includes, for everyone of full legal capacity, the legal power to take on high-risk obligations that can be satisfied only under especially favorable conditions. According to the Federal Court of Justice, the business inexperience of a surety is no ground for imposing duties of explanation and advice on credit institutions. A person is assumed to know, even without special instructions, that giving a guarantee declaration represents a risky transaction. The Federal Court of Justice has held that a bank can assume that a person who offers a surety knows the significance of this action and has independently assessed the risk. Different considerations would apply, the Federal Court of Justice explained, if the bank's actions caused the surety to make a mistake by which the risk of liability was increased. This would be the case at least with regard to actions that the bank could recognize as having this effect.

These cases from the Federal Court of Justice have found reserved approval in the academic literature. But they have predominantly been rejected by scholars. Even some first instance courts have failed to follow this jurisprudence. The criticism argues that the Federal Court of Justice has interpreted the rule requiring the courts' review of the content of suretyship contracts in a too-inflexible and too-indiscriminate manner. By doing so, the critics argue that the Federal Constitutional Court has failed to fulfill a basic decision taken by the Constitution. [...]

* * *

The complainant's father operated as a real estate broker; he erected and sold flats for owner occupation. In 1982 he asked the City Savings Bank C. for a doubling of his credit limit from DM 50,000 to DM 100,000. When the bank demanded a guarantee the complainant, who at that time was 21 years old, signed a pre-printed suretyship document on 29 November 1982 guaranteeing a maximum sum of DM 100,000 plus additional obligations [...].

* * *

The increase in credit was granted. The complainant received a right of signature for her father's credit account but had no assets herself. She had no vocational training, was

8.4 Application of *Drittwirkung*: The *Suretyship Case*

mainly unemployed, and at the time she signed the guarantee declaration earned DM 1,150 net per month in a fish factory.

In October, 1984, the complainant's father gave up his real property business and operated as a shipowner. The bank financed the purchase of a ship with DM 1.3 million. In December 1986 the bank terminated the outstanding credit (about DM 2.4 million) and informed the complainant that a claim would be made against her under the suretyship declaration.

The complainant at first claimed that her surety was invalid. The bank then raised a counterclaim for payment of DM 100,000 with interest. The *Landgericht* [Regional Court] granted the bank's counterclaim.

On the complainant's appeal the *Oberlansdesgericht* [Higher Regional Court] revised the Regional Court's decision and rejected the counterclaim. Citing flaws in the contractual negotiations the Higher Regional Court ruled that the bank was obliged to release the complainant from the surety. In particular, the Higher Regional Court found that the bank had violated its duty to provide information during the contractual negotiations. The Higher Regional Court recognized that in general creditors do not have to explain risks to sureties. But an exception from this principle, the Higher Regional Court explained, was required when the creditor's conduct recognizably caused the surety to make a mistake. This, in essence, is what a credit institution does when it influences an inexperienced surety's decision by trivializing the type and scope of liability assumed under a suretyship contract. The Higher Regional Court found that this happened in the present case. The evidence established that the representative of the bank essentially said to the complainant: "Here, please, just sign this. It doesn't mean you're entering into any big obligation. I just need it for my records." On these facts the Higher Regional Court found that the bank's representative had substantially "glossed over" and trivialized the complainant's actual risk. The bank could not have assumed, on any realistic assessment, that the complainant was prepared to take on the surety.

In the judgment that is now being challenged the Federal Court of Justice quashed the decision of the Higher Regional Court and rejected the complainant's appeal against the judgment of the Regional Court. The Federal Court of Justice held that suretyship contracts are legal transactions creating one-sided obligations for which the creditor as a rule has neither a duty of explanation nor a duty to obtain information about the state of the surety's knowledge. A person who is over 18 years old and therefore of the age of majority according to statute law, is assumed to know that a surety declaration gives rise to liability risks. The Federal Court of Justice found that special experience in business matters is not necessary for this general knowledge. The Federal Court of Justice concluded that a surety cannot make his or her expectation that no claim would be raised on the basis of the guarantee the basis of a rational business transaction. The representative of the bank, the Federal Court of Justice explained, had done nothing that would have influenced the surety's assessment of her risks. At the time the guarantee declaration was signed, the Federal Court of Justice explained, the principal debtor's credit was good and the information given by the bank employee suggesting that the guarantee was likely not to be consequential was, in fact, correct. Finally, the Federal Court of Justice reasoned that the complainant, as surety, should have kept an eye on the further development of her father's business affairs and the risk of any future liability. To this end, express reference had been made in the suretyship contract to the possibility of giving notice of termination of the surety.

In her constitutional complaint the complainant alleges violations of her basic rights under Article 1(1) and Article 2(1) of the Basic Law, in combination with the principle of the social state. [...].

* * *

[...] At the time she entered into the guarantee contract the complainant's available (*pfändbar*) income consisted of DM 413.70. Since October 1991 the complainant had been the single mother of a son. She lived on social assistance and public child-support benefits (*Erziehungsgeld*). As of January, 1992, a debit balance calculated at DM 160,000 had accumulated. The complainant argues that in these circumstances there can be no expectation that she could ever satisfy her obligation. [...]

* * *

Reasoning

In so far as the complainant's constitutional complaint is admissible, it is also successful.

The constitutional complaint is directed against a civil court judgment for the payment of money. The normative foundations that support the judgment are not challenged. No objection is raised against the determinative provisions of the BGB. The complainant's objections are concerned instead with the interpretation and application of the general clauses, which require the civil courts to undertake review of the substance of contracts, primarily §§ 138 and 242 BGB. In concretizing these clauses the basic right guarantee of private autonomy and the general right of personality should have been considered and the civil courts failed to recognize this in the initial proceedings.

The Basic Law contains in its basic rights section fundamental decisions in constitutional law that apply to all areas of the law. These fundamental decisions develop through and are realized in the medium of ordinary legal provisions that directly control the area of law in question. Above all, this is true with respect to the interpretation of the General Clauses in civil law (*see Lüth*, BVerfGE 7, 198 [1958]; [...]). When § 138 and § 242 BGB refer quite generally to "public policy", "custom" (*Verkehrsitte*) and "good faith," they declare standards and principles that require concretization by the courts in accordance with the value concepts that are primarily determined by the constitution. Therefore, the civil courts are constitutionally obliged to consider the basic rights as "guidelines" in the interpretation and application of the General Clauses. If they fail to fulfill this obligation and therefore make a decision that disadvantages a party to the proceedings, then the civil courts violate that party's basic rights (*see Lüth*, BVerfGE 7, 198 (206 *et seq*.)).

Yet the Federal Constitutional Court does not examine the interpretation and application of ordinary law. It is merely obliged to ensure that the ordinary courts observe the norms and standards of the basic rights. The Federal Constitutional Court cannot object to a legally effective civil court decision just because it would have put the emphasis elsewhere in the assessment of conflicting basic rights positions and would have reached a different result. The threshold at which a violation of the constitution takes place, necessitating correction by the Federal Constitutional Court, is only reached when the challenged decision reveals mistakes in interpretation that are based on the ordinary court's incorrect conclusion about the significance of a basic right (in particular the scope of a basic right's protective area). These mistakes also must be of some material significance for the case at hand. Measured by this standard, the judgment of the Federal Court of Justice in the present case cannot survive the complainant's challenge. [...]

The suretyship contract that the Federal Court of Justice had to assess differed significantly from everyday credit assurances. The complainant undertook an extraordinarily high risk without having an economic interest of her own in the credit secured. The contract renounced almost all the protective provisions of the BGB that can be removed by agreement and she therefore gave an unconditionally enforceable surety of her father's entrepreneurial risk to an extent that went far beyond her economic circumstances. It was foreseeable from the start, and easy for the credit institution to establish, that if liability arose the complainant would probably not be in a position at any point in her life to free herself from the burden of indebtedness which she had undertaken. In such a situation the civil courts should have examined the prerequisites as well as the reasons for concluding the contract. This is especially true because the party's submissions to the courts concentrated on these concerns. The complainant claimed in the trial courts that the bank had violated pre-contractual duties of showing due respect and had pursued its own interests in exploiting her lack of business experience. The Higher Regional Court accepted this view in reaching its judgment in the case. The Federal Court of Justice, however, saw no cause to review the content of the suretyship contract. It did not ask whether and to what degree the contracting partners could freely decide about the conclusion and content of the contract. This constituted a misunderstanding of private autonomy as guaranteed by the basic rights.

According to the consistent case law of the Federal Constitutional Court, formulation of legal relationships by the individual in accordance with his or her intentions is a part of the general freedom of action. Article 2(1) of the Basic Law guarantees private autonomy, defined as "self determination by the individual in the legal world."

Private autonomy, however, must be positively articulated by the law. Private law consists of a calibrated system of coordinated rules and methods for the articulation of private autonomy, which must, in turn, fit into the constitutional order. But this does not mean that private autonomy can be dealt with by the legislature as it pleases, and certainly not in a manner that leads to the evisceration of the content of this basic right. In the necessary articulation of rules providing for private autonomy the legislature must be guided by the objective values of the basic rights. The legislature must open up an appropriate area of activity in the legal world for the individual's self-determination. Private autonomy must be secured by the state. Its guarantee is realized juristically. The legislature is bound to make available methods for concluding transactions that must be treated as legally binding and, in the case of a dispute, form the basis of enforceable legal positions.

The duty to shape the private law system gives the legislature a problem of practical concordance. Equally ranking holders of basic rights take part in civil law transactions and they pursue differing interests and (frequently) opposing goals. All participants in civil law transactions enjoy the protection of Article 2(1) of the Basic Law and can appeal to the basic right guarantee of their private autonomy to the same extent. For this reason, civil law cannot simply be governed as the right of the stronger party. The conflicting basic right positions should be seen in their reciprocal effect on each other and should be limited in such a way that they are effective for all participants as extensively as possible. In procedural law the proper reconciliation of interests derives from the coinciding intentions of the contracting partners. They bind themselves and, therefore, together make use of their individual freedom of action. However, if one of the contracting parties is in such a disproportionate position of strength that he or she can, in fact, unilaterally determine the contractual content, then this results in the stronger party dominating and directing the will of the weaker party. In this circumstance, and contrary to the basic right guarantee, the weaker party is not self-determining but is being determined *by another*. Admittedly the legal system cannot provide for all situations in which equilibrium in negotiations is more or less impaired. Out of respect for legal certainty a contract should not subsequently be put into doubt or corrected every time inequality in negotiations might have existed. But if it is a question of a categorizable case that reveals a structural inferiority of one of the contracting parties, and if the consequences of the contract are unusually burdensome for the inferior contracting party, then the civil law system must provide a way to correct this situation. This follows from the basic right guarantee of private autonomy (Article 2(1) of the Basic Law). […]

* * *

Current contract law satisfies these requirements. The authors of the BGB proceeded on the basis of a model of formally equal participants in private law transactions, even while they created various norms for the protection of a weaker party in legal transactions. But even the *Reichsgericht* [Court of the German Empire] abandoned this strictly liberal approach and instead adopted "a material ethic of social responsibility." Today there is extensive agreement that contractual freedom only works in the case of an approximately balanced relationship in the strength of the parties. This ensures an appropriate reconciliation of interests. Thus, one of the chief tasks of current civil law is the resolution of a lack of contractual parity. Large parts of the BGB can be viewed as serving this objective. In this connection the General Clauses of the BGB have central significance. The wording of § 138(2) BGB expresses this particularly clearly. It describes the typical circumstances that automatically lead to the inferiority of one contracting party in negotiations, including a lack of experience. If a stronger party exploits this weakness in order to promote his or her interests unilaterally in a conspicuous manner, then the contract can be invalidated. Section 138(1) links invalidity quite generally to a violation of "public policy." However, more nuanced legal consequences are provided by § 242 BGB. Civil law jurisprudence on the matter takes the view that the principle of "good faith" describes an inherent boundary to the contractual power of formulation, and forms the basis of the authority for judicial review and revision of the contract's substance.

There is disagreement in the academic literature about the prerequisites for and the intensity of this substantive review. However, for the assessment in constitutional law it is sufficient to establish that existing law has instruments available that make it possible to react appropriately to structural problems with contractual parity. For the civil courts a duty follows from the existence of these civil law provisions to ensure, in the interpretation and application of the general clauses, that contracts do not become a means for determining the will of another. If the contracting partners have agreed to a regime that, in itself is permissible, then a more extensive control of content will normally be unnecessary. But, if the content of the contract is unusually burdensome for one party, and obviously inappropriate as a reconciliation of interests, then the courts should not content themselves with saying: "a contract is contract." Instead, they must determine whether the regime is a consequence of structurally unequal negotiating strength and, if necessary, intervene to correct it within the framework of the general clauses of the civil law. How they must proceed here and what conclusion they should reach is primarily a question of ordinary law for which the constitution recognizes a wide margin of discretion. But it is necessary for the Constitutional Court to consider whether there is a violation of the basic right guarantee of private autonomy if the civil courts have not seen the problem of a lack contractual parity or if its resolution is sought by unsuitable methods.

The disputed decision of the Federal Court of Justice is marked by such a violation. The suretyship declaration signed by the complainant was assessed by the Federal Court of Justice as if a normal contract with corresponding interests and comprehensible risks had been made. All the arguments by which the [...] complainant tried to prove her weakness in negotiations were rejected by reference to the fact that she was of the age of majority and should have ascertained the risks.

That is not sufficient. The risk of liability that the [...] complainant undertook by the suretyship contract, without having any economic interest of her own, was unusually high. Besides this the contract was extraordinarily hard to evaluate. The guaranteed sum only described a maximum for the primary debt; the considerable costs and interest on the credit were to be added to this without the basis of their calculation being shown in the suretyship contract. Above all, however, there was no limitation on the business obligations secured. In addition, the contract's waiver of the statutory protections provided for suretyship contracts makes clear that the complainant was to be liable, for all practical purposes, as her father's partner. Even people experienced in business could scarcely have evaluated the meaning and the extent of this risk. For the 21 year-old [...] complainant, who had no skilled vocational training, the meaning and extent must have been incomprehensible.

In a case in which one of the contracting parties is so profoundly inferior, the decisive issue is the way in which the contract came into existence and in particular how the superior contracting partner has behaved. Yet, the Federal Court of Justice found that the bank had no duty to explain the contract or provide the complainant guidance in understanding its terms. The Federal Court of Justice even regarded as insignificant the pressure exerted by the bank employee's statement "You're not entering into any big obligation." The Federal Court of Justice merely sees in this – contrary to the findings of the Higher Regional Court – provisional information about the complainant's father's creditworthiness that could have no influence on the negotiating position of the complainant. That does not do justice to the problematic nature of this case and it fails to meet the basic right guarantee of private autonomy so fundamentally that the decision [of the Federal Court of Justice] cannot stand.

* * *

Questions/Comments

- In the *Suretyship Case* the Constitutional Court found that the Federal Court of Justice's ruling on the scope of the Civil Code's general clauses had not adequately accounted for the constitutional protection of "personal freedom" secured by Article 2(1) of the Basic Law. Article 2(1) states: "Every person shall have the right to the free development of his or her personality insofar as he or she does not violate the rights of others or offend against the constitutional order or the moral law." This broadly framed right has been interpreted to encompass two interests: a right to freedom of action and a right to freely develop one's personality.[53] The latter interest is understood to be a clarification and concretization of the broader, inviolable commitment the Basic Law makes to human dignity in Article 1(1). For this reason, when complainants invoke their Article 2(1) rights they often do so by formally claiming a violation of "Article 2(1) in connection with Article 1(1)." As I described earlier in this chapter, human dignity is concerned with human self-realization and self-determination. The right to "freely develop one's personality" as part of the personal freedom guaranteed by Article 2(1) clearly serves that end. Can you identify the "dignitarian" reasoning in the Court's *Suretyship Case*? Even if only implicit and imprecise, do you see an engagement with the *Objektformel* in the Court's critique of the judgment from the Federal Court of Justice?
- Alexy called *Lüth* "the big bang" in an explosion of constitutional law in Germany.[54] Does the *Suretyship Case* support that claim? That is, are you surprised to see the Federal Constitutional Court involved in the dispute implicated by that case? Think of all the many private law relations in which

Federal Constitutional Court

The justices of the Federal Constitutional Court appear in their rare oral proceedings wearing resplendent red robes. A massive, wood-carved Federal Eagle (*Bundesadler*) presides over the Court's light-filled hearing chamber (partly visible in this photo's upper-left corner). The Eagle's wings are folded in a protective posture, indicating the Court's role in securing Germans' basic rights.

Figure 8.3 Decisions of the Federal Constitutional Court
Source: Getty Images

you are involved: intimate-partnership status, such as marriage; rental agreements; the terms-and-conditions agreements you conclude with IT firms and web-based services. Would you have imagined that any (not to mention all) of those relations and interactions potentially involve constitutional law concerns?
- Is the indirect horizontal effect announced in *Lüth* and applied in the *Suretyship Case* really all that exceptional? Does it differ conceptually or in degree from the "state action doctrine" in American constitutional law? According to that doctrine, US constitutional law only applies as a limit on policy or conduct of public authorities.[55] The US Supreme Court has strictly enforced this doctrine and narrowly construed the few potential exceptions to the rule. Despite the dramatic role he attributed to the doctrine of *Drittwirkung* in the encounter between constitutionalism and the Civil Law tradition in Germany, Gardbaum thinks that the German doctrine of indirect horizontal effect represents just one response from among a spectrum of responses, to a phenomenon that is present in all constitutional systems, namely: "the scope of application of individual rights provisions, in

8.4 Application of *Drittwirkung*: The *Suretyship Case*

particular, their reach into the private sphere."[56] How is that issue addressed in the constitutional regime of your primary or "national" legal system?

- If one had to pick just one article from the Basic Law for discussion (in exactly the way that writing a textbook survey requires!), then a strong case can be made for Article 1. It contains the substantive protection of "human dignity," which the Federal Constitutional Court has placed atop Germany's normative hierarchy. This human rights protection is the driving force behind the judge-empowering, amorphous "objective order of values" declared by the Federal Constitutional Court in *Lüth*. At the same time, the third paragraph of Article 1 provides the textual basis for the doctrine of the constitution's indirect horizontal effect. In that way, Article 1(3) is the textual source for the increasing priority enjoyed by constitutional law in Germany. It provides: "The following basic rights shall bind the legislature, the executive and the judiciary as directly applicable law." Yet, Article 1(3) of the Basic Law unmistakably speaks only to state power. For this reason, in formal terms, *Lüth* does not make the constitution's basic rights *directly* applicable in the horizontal relations among individuals. Neither Veit Harlan and the film distributor in *Lüth*, nor the bank in the *Suretyship Case*, was found to have violated the constitution. Instead, pursuant to Article 1(3), "an indirect application of constitutional rights to private actors takes place through the state's interpretation of private law, performed by the individual civil judge. If the judge does not act accordingly, in his role as a public official [covered by Article 1(3) of the Basic Law], he deprives the citizen of his constitutional rights and contravenes the Basic Law."[57] Finally, the importance of Article 1 is established in another way. Along with Article 20, it is the other provision granted "eternal" and unamendable status by Article 79(3).

- Peer Zumbansen identified a constitutional dilemma in the *Suretyship Case* that goes beyond the question of the Basic Law's colonization of the private law.[58] He noted that freedom of contract is a principle that is not only secured by the Civil Code, it is also a constitutional guarantee that is derived from the personal freedom secured by Article 2(1) of the Basic Law. Thus, the *Suretyship Case* actually represented the Federal Constitutional Court's resolution of the tension between two potentially conflicting *constitutional* values: personality rights (to freely form contracts – the Civil Code's *Privatautonomie*) and self-determination (to freely develop one's personality – the Basic Law's rights to personality and dignity). In the balancing mode typical of the proportionality analysis, the Federal Constitutional Court gave preference to the latter interest. Why do you think the Court made that choice between the conflicting constitutional values? How expansive is the constitutional intrusion into the private law? What evidence is there that the Constitutional Court intends the doctrine of *Drittwirkung* to be a limited jurisprudence? What standard does the Constitutional Court articulate and apply in the case? Is it the same as the standard the Court applied forty years earlier in the *Lüth Case*?

8.5 Conclusion

What a terrible assignment – to try to summarize and survey a complex and historic constitutional regime in a mere handful of pages. The same might be said of any of the fields of law covered by this book. They also receive just one short chapter. But a constitution is different. It looks back at a society's past and it looks forward to the future.[59] A constitution tells the story of a distinct polity – its distinct hopes, conditioned as they are by a distinct past. A constitution expresses a people's identity even while it strives to reshape that identity for a better future. The opening lines of the Basic Law's preamble point towards the past and the future: "Conscious of their responsibility before God and man, [and] inspired by the determination to promote world peace as an equal partner in a united Europe, the German people, in the exercise of their constituent power, have adopted this Basic Law."

The "responsibility" to which the preamble refers must be clear to everyone. Auschwitz casts a long and dark shadow across modern Germany. The Basic Law does not shy away from that burden. Instead, it makes the bitter and brutal lessons of the Holocaust the spirit of Germany's constitutional future as a peaceful, cooperative, and dignity-respecting participant in a "united Europe." There are many ways in which the Basic Law codifies and instrumentalizes German responsibility in pursuit of that better future. I could touch on only a few of them here: the crowning commitment to human dignity; the demand for a government adhering to the *Rechtsstaatsprinzip*, including the requirement that state action be proportional; the militant resolve to protect and reinforce democratic institutions and processes; the "eternal" security of the regime's core values and features; and the insistence that those values shape all of life and law in Germany.

Rounding out this picture, recall that in Chapter 5 you were given a glimpse of the democratic institutional framework established by the Basic Law. And, in Chapter 12, we will consider the Basic Law's profound mandate for Germany's integration into the European Union.

The constitution is doing all of that and much more. But the Basic Law's longevity and success are triumphs in their own right. Now, after seventy-five years, it is safe to say that the *Grundgesetz* has broken the curse that plagued German constitutionalism across the centuries. It has managed to entrench constitutionalism in Germany – especially constitutional superiority and judicial review. I have argued that, by doing this, Germany's post-war constitutional regime also has added new threads, new colors, to the tapestry of German legal culture. Even if the Civil Law tradition remains the dominant frame, the Basic Law clearly gives scope and meaning to the Common Law tradition in Germany.

Jürgen Habermas, the great German philosopher of the post-war era, envisioned a new kind of unifying force for society, one that is not dependent on the contingencies of historical or national continuities. Instead, Habermas called for "constitutional patriotism," which would stitch together a new

8.5 Conclusion

identity based on pride in constitutional rights secured, confidence about vital democratic procedures, and the personal security created by a functioning *Rechtsstaat*.[60] Those don't have to be uniquely German achievements. And Habermas meant his theory of constitutional patriotism to be a universal summons. But there can be no doubt that he found inspiration in the *Wunder* that is the 1949 German *Grundgesetz*.[61]

Further Reading

- *Dieter Grimm – Advocate of the Constitution* (Oliver Lepsius *et al.* eds.) (Justin Collings trans.) (Oxford University Press) (2020)
- *The German Federal Constitutional Court: The Court without Limits* (Matthias Jestaedt *et al.* eds.) (Jeff Seitzer trans.) (Oxford University Press) (2020)
- Christian Bumke & Andreas Vosskuhle, *German Constitutional Law: Introduction, Cases, and Principles* (Oxford University Press) (2019)
- *Habermas and Law* (Hugh Baxter ed.) (Routledge) (2017)
- Gerhard Robbers, *Constitutional Law in Germany* (Wolters Kluwer) (2017)
- Dieter Grimm, *Constitutionalism: Past, Present, and Future* (Oxford University Press) (2016)
- Justin Collings, *Democracy's Guardians – A History of the German Federal Constitutional Court, 1951–2001* (Oxford University Press) (2015)
- Michaela Hailbronner, *Traditions and Transformations: The Rise of German Constitutionalism* (Oxford University Press) (2015)
- Jo Eric Khushal Murkens, *From Empire to Union: Conceptions of German Constitutional Law since 1871* (Oxford University Press) (2013)
- Aharon Barak, *Proportionality – Constitutional Rights and Their Limitations* (Cambridge University Press) (2012)
- Donald P. Kommers & Russell A. Miller, *The Constitutional Jurisprudence of the Federal Republic of Germany* (Duke University Press) (3rd ed. 2012)
- Werner Heun, *The Constitution of Germany – A Contextual Analysis* (Hart Publishing) (2010)
- Jan-Werner Müller, Constitutional Patriotism (Princeton University Press) (2009)
- Georg Vanberg, *The Politics of Constitutional Review in Germany* (Cambridge University Press) (2004)
- David P. Currie, *The Constitution of the Federal Republic of Germany* (University of Chicago Press) (1994)

Notes

1 Miguel Schor, *Judicial Review and American Constitutional Exceptionalism*, 46 OSGOODE HALL L. J. 535 (2008).
2 H. PATRICK GLENN, LEGAL TRADITIONS OF THE WORLD 260 (5th ed. 2014).

3. H. Patrick Glenn, *Comparative Legal Families and Comparative Legal Traditions*, in THE OXFORD HANDBOOK OF COMPARATIVE LAW 421, 435 (Mathias Reimann & Reinhard Zimmermann eds., 2nd ed. 2019).
4. JOSEPH RAZ, BETWEEN AUTHORITY AND INTERPRETATION 324–25 (2009).
5. *Id.*
6. H. Patrick Glenn, *Common Law*, 66 MCGILL L. J. 19 (2020–2021).
7. OLIVER WENDELL HOLMES, THE COMMON LAW 1 (1881).
8. *Id.*
9. Thomas Poole, *Questioning Common Law Constitutionalism*, 25 LEGAL STUD. 142, 142 (2005).
10. *Id.*
11. *See* Henry P. Monaghan, *The Supreme Court Term 1974 – Foreword: Constitutional Common Law*, 89 HARV. L. REV. 1, 3–4 (1975); Abigail R. Moncrieff, *Validity of the Individual Mandate*, 92 B.U. L. REV. 1245, 1248 (2012); Adrian Vermeule, *Common Law Constitutionalism and the Limits of Reason*, 107 COLUM. L. REV. 1482, 1482 (2007).
12. Russell A. Miller, *Germany's German Constitution*, 57 VA. J. INT'L L. 95, 110 (2017) (quoting Walter F. Murphy, *Civil Law, Common Law, and Constitutional Democracy*, 52 LA. L. REV. 91, 96 (1991)).
13. S. F. C. MILSOM, HISTORICAL FOUNDATIONS OF THE COMMON LAW ix (1969).
14. DONALD P. KOMMERS & RUSSELL A. MILLER, THE CONSTITUTIONAL JURISPRUDENCE OF THE FEDERAL REPUBLIC OF GERMANY 4–10 (3rd ed. 2012); DAVID P. CURRIE, THE CONSTITUTION OF THE FEDERAL REPUBLIC OF GERMANY 1–8 (1994); MACK WALKER, GERMAN HOME TOWNS: COMMUNITY, STATE, AND GENERAL ESTATE 1648–1871 18–26 (2014).
15. Kommers & Miller, *supra* note 14, at 44.
16. GRUNDGESETZ FÜR DIE BUNDESREPUBLIK DEUTSCHLAND [GG] [BASIC LAW], pmbl.
17. GRUNDGESETZ FÜR DIE BUNDESREPUBLIK DEUTSCHLAND [GG] [BASIC LAW], art. 1(1).
18. *See, e.g.,* RONALD DWORKIN, TAKING RIGHTS SERIOUSLY (1977).
19. *See, e.g.,* Ernst Benda, *The Protection of Human Dignity (Article 1 of the Basic Law)*, 53 SMU L. REV. 443 (2000).
20. *Id.* at 445.
21. *See* THORSTEN KINGREEN & RALF POSCHER, GRUNDRECHTE STAATSRECHT II 132–133 (37th ed. 2021).
22. *Id.*
23. *See* Donald P. Kommers, *Can German Constitutionalism Serve as a Model for the United States?*, 58 ZEITSCHRIFT FÜR AUSLÄNDISCHES ÖFFENTLICHES RECHT UND VÖLKERRECHT 787 (1998).
24. Marbury v. Madison, 5 U.S. (Cranch) 137 (1803).
25. GRUNDGESETZ FÜR DIE BUNDESREPUBLIK DEUTSCHLAND [GG] [BASIC LAW], art. 1(3).
26. GRUNDGESETZ FÜR DIE BUNDESREPUBLIK DEUTSCHLAND [GG] [BASIC LAW], art. 20(3).

27 GÜNTER FRANKENBERG, GRUNDGESETZ 5 (2004) (Russell A. Miller trans.).
28 "Amendments to this Basic Law affecting the division of the Federation into Länder, their participation on principle in the legislative process, or the principles laid down in Articles 1 and 20 shall be inadmissible." GRUNDGESETZ [GG] [Basic Law or Constitution] art. 79(3).
29 GRUNDGESETZ FÜR DIE BUNDESREPUBLIK DEUTSCHLAND [GG] [BASIC LAW], art. 20(1).
30 GRUNDGESETZ FÜR DIE BUNDESREPUBLIK DEUTSCHLAND [GG] [BASIC LAW], arts. 16(2), 23(1), 28(1).
31 UWE WESEL, DER GANG NACH KARLSRUHE 19 (2004) (Russell A. Miller trans.).
32 Gerhard Casper, *The "Karlsruhe Republic – Keynote Address at the State Ceremony Celebrating the 50th Anniversary of the Federal Constitutional Court*, 2 GER. L. J. (2001), www.germanlawjournal.com/index.php?pageID=11&artID=111.
33 PHILLIP BOBBITT, CONSTITUTIONAL FATE (1982).
34 *See* DWORKIN, *supra* note 18.
35 ROBERT ALEXY, THE THEORY OF CONSTITUTIONAL RIGHTS (Julian Rivers trans., Oxford University Press, 2010).
36 BKA Act Case, BVerfGE 141, 220 (2016).
37 *See* Russell A. Miller, *A Pantomime of Privacy: Terrorism and Investigative Powers in German Constitutional Law*, 58 B.C. L. REV. 1545 (2017).
38 *See, e.g.,* AHARON BARAK, PROPORTIONALITY. CONSTITUTIONAL RIGHTS AND THEIR LIMITATIONS (2012); DAVID M. BEATTY, THE ULTIMATE RULE OF LAW (2004).
39 Wolfgang Hoffmann-Riem, *Two Hundred Years of Marbury v. Madison: The Struggle for Judicial Review of Constitutional Questions in the United States and Europe*, 5 GER. L. J. 685, 689 (2004).
40 *Id.* at 689–692.
41 BASIL S. MARKESINIS & HANNES UNBERATH, THE GERMAN LAW OF TORTS – A COMPARATIVE TREATISE 8-14 (4th ed. 2002).
42 Lüth Case, BVerfGE 7, 198 (1958).
43 *See* Hannes Rössler, *Harmonizing the German Civil Code of the Nineteenth Century with a Modern Constitution – The Lüth Revolution 50 Years Ago in Comparative Perspective*, 23 TULANE EUR. & CIV. L. FORUM 1 (2008).
44 Jacco Bomhoff, *Lüth's 50th Anniversary: Some Comparative Observations on the German Foundations of Judicial Balancing*, 9 GER. L. J. 121 (2008).
45 Rössler, *supra* note 43, at 4–5, 11–12.
46 *See* ALEXANDER BICKELL, THE LEAST DANGEROUS BRANCH (1962).
47 DAVID P. CURRIE, THE CONSTITUTION OF THE FEDERAL REPUBLIC OF GERMANY 181 (1994).
48 Robert Alexy, *Balancing, Constitutional Review, and Representation*, 3 INT'L J. CONST. L. 572 (2005).
49 Bernahd Schlink, *German Constitutional Culture in Transition*, 14 CARDOZO L. REV. 711, 714–15 (1993).
50 *Id.* at 718.
51 Stephen Gardbaum, *The "Horizontal Effect" of Constitutional Rights*, 102 MICH. L. REV. 387, 403 (2003–2004).

52 *Id.*
53 *See* KINGREEN & POSCHER, *supra* note 21, at 139–145.
54 Robert Alexy, *Verfassungsrecht und einfaches Recht – Verfassungsgerichtsbarkeit und Fachgerichtsbarkeit*, 61 VERÖFFENTLICHUNGEN DER VEREINIGUNG DER DEUTSCHEN STAATSRECHTSLEHRER 7, 9 (2002).
55 *See* Civil Rights Cases, 109 U.S. 3 (1883).
56 *See* Gardbaum, *supra* note 51, at 388.
57 Rössler, *supra* note 43, at 24.
58 Peer Zumbansen, *The Law of Contracts*, in INTRODUCTION TO GERMAN LAW 179 (Mathias Reimann & Joachim Zekoll eds., 2005).
59 Jan-Werner Müller & Kim Lane Scheppele, *Constitutional Patriotism: An Introduction*, 6 INT'L J. CONST. L. 67 (2008).
60 Jürgen Habermas, *Können komplexe Gesellschaften eine vernünftige Identität ausbilden?*, in ZUR REKONSTRUKTION DES HISTORISCHEN MATERIALISMUS 92 (1976); JÜRGEN HABERMAS, THE NEW CONSERVATISM: CULTURAL CRITICISM AND THE HISTORIANS' DEBATE (S. W. Nicholsen ed. and trans., 1991); JÜRGEN HABERMAS, DIE NACHHOLENDE REVOLUTION (1990).
61 *See* Jan-Werner Müller, *On the Origins of Constitutional Patriotism*, 5 CONTEMP. POL. THEORY 278 (2006); Müller & Scheppele, *supra* note 59, at 67.

9

German Public Law

Administrative Law

Key Concepts

- *Verwaltungsverfahrensgesetz*: The Federal Administrative Procedure Act establishes the general principles of German administrative law. The federal states, which have a significant administrative role in the German system, have independent administrative law regimes. But the Federal Act has helped impose unity and coherence across this system.
- *Verwaltungsakt*: The fundamental subject of administrative law is an "administrative act," involving the binding exercise of sovereign public authority in a concrete case.
- *Rechtsstaatsprinzip*: The Basic Law's commitment to the *Rechtsstaat* (rule of law) is enforced as a guarantee that the state acts pursuant to law and justice. Above all, the *Rechtsstaatsprinzip* ensures that the state does not act arbitrarily. The *Rechtsstaatsprinzip* is realized through a number of doctrines, including the principle of the separation of powers, the proportionality principle, the principle of equality, and the principle of legality.
- *Verhältnismäßigkeitsprinzip*: The proportionality principle is regarded as a fundamental component of the *Rechtsstaatsprinzip*. For this reason, it is an unamendable constitutional guarantee in the German system. The proportionality principle demands that state actions constituting a permissible infringement on an individual's basic rights nevertheless remain proportionate, exhibiting a balance between the state's policy interests, on the one hand, and the rights interests of the individual, on the other hand. The proportionality principle is largely realized through the judicial application of the proportionality analysis.
- *Legalitätsprinzip*: The principle of legality ensures that the government acts according to law and fulfills a core promise of the *Rechtsstaatsprinzip*. For example, the principle of legality requires that state action be carried out with a statutory mandate (*Vorbehalt des Gesetzes*) and in conformity with that mandate (*Vorrang des Gesetzes*).
- **Administrative Federalism**: As part of Germany's scheme of cooperative federalism, the competences to enact law (legislative power) and enforce law (executive power) are shared between the federation and the states. The

federation is largely responsible for legislation. The state administrations are responsible for implementing those federal policies. This protects against tyranny, as no sovereign can act alone in the exercise of its power. It also lends legitimacy to and promotes the effectiveness of the administration, which can be more responsive to local conditions.
- **Islamic Law**: *Sharia* (or *sharī'ah*) involves the divine norms and doctrine of the Muslim faith as articulated in primary sources (the Koran as the word of God revealed to the Prophet, and the Sunnah encompassing the tradition laid down by the Prophet) and secondary sources (respected scholarly opinion and interpretive gloss). *Sharia* includes dogmatic theology (with spiritual significance) and rules for the conduct of believers (with civic significance). "It specifies how the Muslim should conduct himself in accordance with his religion, without making any distinction in principle between duties towards others [...] and those towards God."[1] Among other distinctions, Islamic Law is different to other legal traditions due to its claimed divinity and the way in which morality is inherent to the norms it prescribes.
- **Halal**: An Arabic term for "permissible," halal has become synonymous with dietary rules in Islamic Law. In principle, all food is permitted except: pork, a few other carnivorous animals and birds, and any meat not slaughtered according to specific rules. For example, according to the Islamic Law rules an animal may not already be dead when the process of slaughtering begins and may not be slaughtered in the name of any other entity but Allah.

Study Tips

A translation of the *Verwaltungsverfahrensgesetz* (VwVfG or Administrative Procedure Act) is available from the German Ministry of the Interior and Community (www.bmi.bund.de/SharedDocs/downloads/EN/gesetztestexte/VwVfg_en.pdf?__blob=publicationFile&v=2).

The *Bundesverwalltungsgericht* (BVerfWG or Federal Administrative Court) has a searchable database of a collection of recent judgements translated into English (www.bverwg.de/en/suche?lim=10&start=1&db=e&q=*).

Professor Susan Rose-Ackerman's "Comparative Administrative Law Initiative" at Yale Law School provides resources and insights (https://law.yale.edu/study-law-yale/areas-study/comparative-administrative-law-initiative/about-comparative).

For a number of reasons, it makes good sense that this survey should now tun to German administrative law.

First and foremost, this may be Germany's most enduring and characteristic contribution in the law. It has been remarked that, while the French were storming the Bastille, the Germans were busy formalizing their administrative law.[2] And surely the persistent stereotype of a professional – and pervasive – German bureaucracy is rooted in the long and mostly commendable history of Germany's civil service.[3] Ensuring the effectiveness and accountability of that bureaucracy has been the mandate of administrative law since before the enactment of the German Civil Code. German administrative law long predates the modern constitutional regime established by the Basic Law.[4] Perhaps the pedigree of German administrative law is best captured by Otto Mayer's oft-referenced reflection: "*Verfassungsrecht vergeht, Verwaltungsrecht besteht*" ("constitutional law comes and goes, administrative law remains").[5] In any case, with the ascendance of the modern welfare state (especially in its extensive form in Germany), the administration has become indispensable. Revolutionaries and the discontented might still dream of overthrowing their governments.[6] But it no longer would be practicable for them to dispose of the administration and the legal framework supporting it.[7] That's especially true for Germany!

A second reason for engaging with German administrative law at this time is that it makes for a fitting progression from the preceding chapters in which we examined the Civil Code (embodying the Civil Law tradition) and constitutionalism (embodying the Common Law tradition). In German administrative law we find a confluence of those traditions – the "Civilian" confidence in statutes and the Common Law's confidence in judges. That makes Germany's administrative law its own distinct, intertwined thread in the tapestry of German legal culture. Armed with that insight, I consider a distinguishing hallmark of German administrative law. Different to the approach taken in the American administrative law framework, German administrative law extends public authorities considerable *ex ante* discretion to develop and enforce policy. But, as you will see, that relative autonomy comes with a price. While American administrative law seeks to limit the authority of courts to review administrative actions,[8] the German regime empowers the judiciary to conduct thoroughgoing, substantive *ex post* review of state conduct. We will consider whether that is an effective way to foster productive policy and to constrain the power of the state. However you answer that question, you should see that the system avails itself of Civil Law and Common Law impulses. On the one hand, it relies on statutory positivism in order to justify the *ex ante* discretion afforded the administration. On the other hand, it relies on extensive *ex post* judicial review to constrain the administration, especially out of respect for basic rights.

I conclude the chapter with a presentation of the divisive and notorious *Ritual Slaughter Cases*. That case study involves the discrete subfield of administrative law concerned with *Tierschutz* (animal protection). German administrative agencies refused to grant Muslim butchers the right to ritually slaughter animals in conformity with *halal* dietary obligations. Those are the Muslim norms governing the preparation and consumption of food. Besides serving as a useful glimpse of German administrative law in practice, the *Ritual Slaughter Cases* allow us to consider whether Islamic Law – as yet another legal tradition – is being plaited into the rich and colorful fabric of German law.

9.1 The Common Law and Civil Law Qualities of German Administrative Law

The constitutional (and Common Law) character of German administrative law is pronounced. Constitutional law and administrative law, taken together, are considered to be *Öffentliches Recht* (public law) in the sharp divide between public law and private law maintained by the German legal system. Administrative law, which regulates the exercise of state power by public authorities, is a jurisdictionally specialized extension of constitutional law. At one level, constitutional law establishes public authority, erects or recognizes administrative institutions, and provides the broad values and principles for the state's operation. At another level, administrative law serves as the detailed rulebook for ensuring that public authorities' conduct – especially when it affects citizens – is "legal." That is, administrative law demands that executive action is legally mandated, that it remains within its legally mandated scope, and that it be carried out proportionally. It is administrative law that matters in all the constant and myriad ways in which Germans interact with the state. Administrative law is the day-to-day, ordinary expression of constitutional law. It is constitutional law for the streets!

At the most abstract level, pursuant to the doctrine of the separation of powers, the Basic Law divides the state's power into legislative, judicial, and administrative (or executive) competences.[9] That is a foundational source of administrative law, not the least because it marks the executive branch as distinct and therefore meriting distinct legal concern. More specifically, the historical prominence of the civil service in the German polity meant that the administration was explicitly recognized in the Basic Law.[10] Article 33(4) declares: "The exercise of sovereign authority on a regular basis shall, as a rule, be entrusted to members of the public service who stand in a relationship of service and loyalty defined by public law." Ultimately, the more meaningful connection between constitutional law and administrative law comes from the negative limits and positive obligations the Basic Law imposes on the exercise of public authority. Those limits and duties are partly a consequence of the role the administration played in the Nazi regime.[11] Article 20(3) of the Basic Law, for example, requires the administration to act in compliance with "law and justice." And, pursuant to Article 1(3) of the Basic Law, every administrative action must conform to the constitution's basic rights. Article 19 reinforces these protections against state power in two ways. It insists that no state action (however well-justified) may infringe on the core of a basic right (Article 19(2)). And it ensures that, "should any person's rights be violated by public authority [he or she] must have recourse to the courts" (Article 19(4)). Finally, drawing on these and other provisions, the Constitutional Court has concluded that the Basic Law makes the *Rechtsstaatsprinzip* an essential feature of German constitutionalism. As discussed in Chapter 8, the Federal Constitutional Court has found that the *Rechtsstaatsprinzip* imposes strict standards for the exercise of public authority, especially including the executive branch. Those standards include the principles of legality (including *Vorbehalt des Gesetzes* and *Vorrang des Gesetzes*) and proportionality (*Verhältnismäßigkeitsprinzip*).

As is the case with constitutionalism generally, the constitutional elements of German administrative law give judges and judicial review a significant role. An examination of just how extensive that role is will be a key part of this chapter's coverage. In any case, it seems that administrative law is the first and most affected heir to the Common Law influence ushered into the German legal culture by the success of Germany's post-war constitutionalism.

Yet, some features of German administrative law show the lingering influence of the Civil Law tradition. In two ways, the regime expresses deep confidence in statutory law.

First, the field is framed by statutory law to such a degree that it can be portrayed as a kind of "patch-work codification."

The general principles of administrative law are framed in the *Verwaltungsverfahrensgesetz* (Administrative Procedure Act). Edward Eberle explained that the German Administrative Procedure Act "regulates the legal relationship between administrative agencies and citizens, further guarantees citizens access to the administrative decision-making process, and lends a necessary degree of clarity and unity to a complex procedural area."[12] The Administrative Procedure Act promotes the efficacy of German policymaking and implementation, ensures popular access to and political oversight of policymaking processes, and reinforces the protection of basic rights. It requires public authorities to "evaluate all pertinent facts, provide affected persons with an opportunity to be heard, and coordinate their activities with those of other administrative departments and bodies."[13]

In ways that are reminiscent of the general coverage of the Civil Code's First Book, the Administrative Procedure Act resolves general and fundamental issues. In doing so, it integrates and harmonizes the practice of the federal and state administrations. As you learn about Germany's so-called "administrative federalism" later in this chapter, it will become clear just how challenging and important that role is for the Administrative Procedure Act. But here, let me offer just one example of the way the Administrative Procedure Act frames the field's general elements. Every discussion of German administrative law begins with a discussion of the relevant subject of administrative law, which is identified in Section 35 of the Administrative Procedure Act as the *Verwaltungsakt*: "Any order, decision or other sovereign measure taken by an authority to regulate an individual case in the sphere of public law and intended to have a direct, external legal effect on the enforceable exercise of public authority."[14] Once again, the similarity to the Civil Code is evident. Recall from Chapter 7 that the Civil Code is chiefly concerned with the fundamental concept of a *Rechtsgeschäft*.[15] The scholarly energy devoted to commenting on the *Verwaltungsakt* as a threshold concept, and the legal consequences of those doctrinal efforts, also echo the Civil Law tradition's *Begriffsjurisprudenz* (conceptual jurisprudence).

The field is not subject to a comprehensive, contained, and coordinated statutory framework in the way that the Civil Code occupies the field of private law. Still, the Administrative Procedure Act operates something like administrative law's "*allgemeiner Teil*" (general part or Book One) of the Civil Code. And, a large number of subsidiary statutes provide the substantive rules for various administrative law subfields in much the same way that the "*besondere Teile*" (special parts) of the Civil Code address several discrete subfields of private law. Table 9.1 depicts the statutory framework for administrative law as if it were a "codification."

Below this statutory framework, public authorities themselves can promulgate legally binding *Rechtsverordnungen* (statutory instruments) and *allgemeine Verwaltungsvorschriften* (administrative regulations). *Rechtsverordnungen* involve a delegation of the lawmaking competence to the administration. These generally applicable norms – binding citizens, the executive branch, and the judiciary – are anticipated, and strictly conditioned, by Article 80(1) of the Basic Law:

> The Federal Government, a Federal Minister, or the state governments may be authorized by a law to issue statutory instruments. The content, purpose and scope of the authority conferred shall be specified in the law. Each statutory instrument shall contain a statement of its legal basis. If the law provides that such authority may be further delegated, such sub-delegation shall be accomplished by statutory instrument.

Verwaltungsvorschriften involve internal regulations that govern the organization and functioning of the administration itself.[16] But, as the administration is in regular (or nearly constant) contact with individuals, its internal operations have indirect significance for citizens as well.

The second way in which German administrative law expresses a Civil Law confidence in statutes is that the field places great faith in the capacity of statutes to condition and constrain the power wielded by public authorities. This is clearly expressed, for example, by Article 80(1) of the Basic Law. The constitution permits the delegation of lawmaking authority to the administration, but envelops that power in statutory reassurances. It requires: statutory authorization; statutory framing of the administrative act's content, purpose, and scope; and a formalistic reference to the underlying enabling statute. This faith is clearly informed by the Civil Law appreciation for statutory positivism and formalism. That is the jurisprudential posture that informed Kantorowicz's "ideal image" of the German jurist as a machine operator (see the Kantorowicz excerpt in Chapter 3). Kantorowicz was describing the German jurist, but administrative law's confidence in the force of statutes to limit state power overlays that image on public authorities. They can be given discretion when making and implementing policy because, due to the principle of legality and the Civil Law ethos, they can be expected to act – only and strictly – under the authority, and within the scope, of a statutory mandate (*Vorrang des Gesetzes* and *Vorbehalt des Gesetzes*). And, paraphrasing Kantorowicz, the civil servant is able to "deduce his or her conduct from the legal code predetermined by the legislature." In the excerpt provided later, Nolte emphasizes that statutes and statutory positivism once dominated German administrative law in the same way that those features (as an expression of the Civil Law tradition) still dominate German private law.

These influences – confidence in statutes *and* extensive judicial review – make German administrative law a unique mixture of the Civil Law tradition and the Common Law tradition.

Table 9.1 The German Administrative Law "Code"

Grundgesetz (Basic Law)	The constitution establishes and empowers German executive authority at the federal and state levels. It also recognizes and secures the status of the traditional German civil service. Other constitutional commitments have significance for administrative law, such as the principle of the separation of powers, the *Rechtsstaatsprinzip*, and the proportionality principle. Finally, the basic rights protect individuals against harmful intrusions resulting from the conduct of pubic authorities. Often that involves the state's administrative functions.	General Parts
Verwaltungsverfahrensgesetz (Administrative Procedure Act)	Federal law establishing the general principles of administrative law and procedure.	
Polizeirecht (Police Law)	Governed by individual states, each with its own statutory framework.	
Kommunalrecht (County and Municipal Law)	Constitutional guarantee of municipal self-administration under the authority of the states (Art. 28 Basic Law), so long as the framework established respects the principles of republicanism, democracy, the *Sozialstaat*, and basic rights protection. Expressed in state constitutions and a wide range of state statutes.	Special Parts
Baurecht (Building and Zoning Law)	The strict regime limiting where and how construction can proceed in Germany is regulated by state law.	

Table 9.1 (cont.)

Ausländerrecht (Foreigners Law)	Governed by the federal *Aufenthaltsgesetz* (Foreigners' Residency Act).
Melde- und Passerecht (Registration and Passport Law)	Everyone with a residence in Germany must register with public authorities pursuant to the *Bundesmeldegesetz* (Federal Registration Act).
Datenschutzrecht (Data-Protection Law)	The *Bundesdatenschutzgesetz* (Federal Data Protection Act) secures constitutional privacy protections (Arts. 2(1) and 1(1) Basic Law) and data-protection mandates from the European Union.
Recht des öffentlichen Dienstes (Law Concerning Public Service)	The German civil service, which enjoys high status and secure tenure, is recognized and protected by the constitution (Art. 33 Basic Law). The details of civil service are regulated by federal and state law, including the *Beamtenstatusgesetz* (Civil Servant Act).
Kulturverwaltungsrecht (Law Concerning the Administration of Culture)	Involving the state law governing the administration of schools and universities, as well as the extensive, state-subsidized cultural offerings Germans enjoy.
Medienrecht (Media Law)	The constitution guarantees freedom of the press (Art. 5 Basic Law). The states thoroughly regulate broadcast and communications/IT matters, including Germany's well-known rules providing public funding and public oversight of broadcasting. The states coordinate governance in these matters with interstate agreements.
Straßenverkehrsrecht (Traffic Law)	Extensively regulated by a number of federal statutes, including *Straßenverkehrsgesetz* (Road Traffic Act) and the *Straßenverkehrsordnung* (Road Traffic Regulation).

Table 9.1 (cont.)

Sozialrecht (Law Concerning Social Welfare and Entitlements)	Germany's wide-ranging and generous social welfare regime is mandated by the constitution's *Sozialstaat* principle (Art. 20 Basic Law). The extensive details, covering substance and process, are provided in the thirteen sections of the federal *Sozialgesetzbuch* (Social Code).
Wirtschaftsverwaltungsrecht (Law Concerning Economic Regulation)	Freedom of economic activity is ensured by the constitution (contracting – Art. 2 Basic Law; occupational freedom – Art. 12 Basic Law; property – Art. 14 Basic Law). But these rights are limitable or are accompanied by constitutionally imposed responsibilities. The federal *Gewerbeordnung* (Trade Regulation) is an example of the extensive regulation of economic activity in Germany.
Umweltrecht (Environmental Law)	The constitution contains a mandate for environmental and animal protection (Art. 20a Basic Law). The realization of that mandate encompasses a large number of federal statutes, concerned with, *inter alia*: emissions, clear air, clean water, the protection of nature, the protection of animals, and industrial practices (in the energy and chemical sectors).
Steuerrecht (Tax Law)	There are many different forms of tax regulated by scores of federal statutes.

9.2 German Administrative Law: Substance Not Process

Globalization – and the attending global wave of governmental privatization of the last quarter-century – may have shaken or altered the modern administrative state. But it has not displaced it as the predominant social and political institution.[17] Rather, the regulations it promulgates, the vast range of services it provides, and the extensive demands it makes, have led some theorists to worry about the state's colonization of the individual's "life-world."[18] It might be less worrisome if the state's deep involvement in our lives was carried out by our most directly accountable institutions. Instead, it is the confounding reality that the nuance and complexity of the responsibilities the modern administrative state has assumed requires expertise, flexibility, and efficiency. But those are qualities not well matched with elected, democratically accountable parliamentary representation. Everywhere states have responded by ceding the power to set and implement complex public policy to administrative authorities. Some now refer to these agencies as the "fourth branch."

Susan Rose-Ackerman concluded that the fundamental tension at the core of administrative law is the struggle to "strike a balance between popular control and expertise."[19]

What makes the field interesting as an object of comparison, then, is not so much *where* different societies draw the line between popular control and expertise (which might be little more than a question of degree) but *how* that line is enforced. Georg Nolte (who now serves as the German judge at the International Court of Justice) explains in the following excerpt that the German approach, characterized by *ex post* judicial review of the substance of administrative policymaking and the actions of public authorities, is evidence of Germany's post-war commitment to the *Rechtsstaatsprinzip*. As the highest order of law in Germany, it should not be surprising that the constitution – specifically its catalogue of basic rights – frequently emerges as the "rule" to which the administrative state is made to submit. This means that, in a function more closely aligned with the Common Law tradition, judges review administrative action for its conformity with the Basic Law.

Georg Nolte
General Principles of German and European Administrative Law – A Comparison in Historical Perspective
57 MODERN LAW REVIEW 191, 198–205 (1994)[*]

* * *

Historical Sources of German Administrative Law

[...] The truth is that German administrative law [...] is largely a product of recent impulses coming from constitutional law, and in particular from decisions of the Bundesverfassungsgericht [German Federal Constitutional Court]. It is therefore a rather

---

[*] Excerpt reproduced with permission of *The Modern Law Review* Limited, John Wiley & Sons, and the author.

young and somewhat political law and not, like English administrative law, the product of a more evolutionary legal tradition.

The Establishment of Judicial Review

Under their political slogan "Rechtsstaat" the German liberals (Bürgertum) strove during most of the nineteenth century to establish legal structures which would limit the unfettered exercise of state power by the monarchs of the various German states. Their first success was the establishment, by some monarchs, of more or less representative assemblies whose consent was necessary for the levying of taxes and for all state action which infringed on the "liberty and property" of citizens. Although this system of "constitutionalism" (Konstitutionalismus) provided for a fair degree of cooperative decision making and legal security, it for the most part did not yet entail any independent, let alone judicial control over the exercise of administrative power. When, some years after the failed Paulskirche revolution of 1848, the political conditions were ripe to seriously address the question, a famous debate took place between Otto Bähr and Rudolf von Gneist on how to achieve this goal. This debate is of some relevance here since it marks the point of departure for a self-conscious science and practice of German administrative law.

Bähr proposed to entrust the ordinary courts with the responsibility of reviewing the exercise of administrative power. He thereby articulated the more liberal position which distrusted any form of self-control of the (monarchical) administration. Gneist, on the other hand, suggested a compromise solution which ultimately prevailed in most states, Prussia in particular. Without denying the need for judicial review, Gneist maintained that the most important problem of administrative law, the possible abuse of discretion, could not satisfactorily be dealt with by giving courts the power of judicial review. According to Gneist, courts could only determine whether acts of the administration were *ultra vires* and not whether they were taken in a spirit which was true to the law's intentions. He therefore advocated following what he perceived to be the English example and to provide, in certain important areas, for less hierarchical, more collegiate decision-making organs which would be staffed partly by professional administrators and partly by respected citizens. Gneist thought that if such a structure existed at the first two levels of the administration this would ensure, better than any courts, that the law was applied independently from the political bias which he expected to come from the higher governmental organs. Only the third and last levels of control should rely on an institution which would be staffed by independent lawyers and act in a purely judicial fashion, however separate from the ordinary courts. Gneist's ideas were ultimately implemented in Prussia in 1872–86 with the "Preussisches Oberverwaltungsgericht" (Prussian Supreme Administrative Court) being established as the judicial head of a three-tier Prussian administrative organisation.

The "Formal Rechtsstaat"

The history of the establishment of judicial review in Prussia and in most other German states of the Bismarck-Reich shows that, initially, a very strong scepticism prevailed with regard to the efficacy of judicial review of the discretionary powers of the executive. And, during the almost sixty years of its existence, the Preussisches Oberverwaltungsgericht hardly began to develop those principles which became so well known after the Second World War as characteristic of German administrative law. The lack of development of more substantive principles of administrative law can be explained by the general legal theory and the understanding of "Rechtsstaat" which prevailed unchallenged until almost the end of the Weimar Republic. As in other western countries at that time, the dominant legal theory was that of positivism, and the term "Rechtsstaat" had therefore acquired a rather restricted meaning. While Kant and the early liberals of the first half of the nineteenth century had still associated some notions of substantive justice with the principle of "Rechtsstaat," after the failed Paulskirche revolution of 1848 a different concept of "Rechtsstaat" emerged which was limited to the requirements that the state must act within the framework of the law and that the law must be precise, calculable and enforceable. This concept of "Rechtsstaat" was later called "formal Rechtsstaat" since it did not entail any "higher" or "inalienable" values such as fundamental rights or basic principles of justice. This "value-free" concept also reflected the situation of political compromise which was characteristic of the "constitutionalist" system which existed in Germany until the First World War. Any value-inspired jurisprudence by the courts might have endangered the delicate balance between the liberal and the conservative-monarchist forces.

"Substantive Rechtsstaat"

The formal understanding of "Rechtsstaat" prevailed until the Nazi regime. It had, however, already started to fall into disrepute during the Weimar Republic. Although the fundamental rights proclaimed in the Weimar constitution were subjected to potentially unlimited legislative restrictions, some academics began to assert that substantive limits on legislative power did in fact exist. In 1925, the Reichsgericht (Federal Supreme Court) asserted the power of judicial review over acts of legislation, but never actually declared an Act of Parliament to be void. These first signs of reorientation, however, were overtaken in 1933 with the coming to power of the Nazis. The new regime could draw on perverted positivistic attitudes in the population that "law is law" and that it had to be respected no matter what its content. Then, as a reaction to the abuses of the legal system under the Nazis, a resurgence of "substantive" or natural law thinking took place among German lawyers after 1945. This "turn" is often said to be personified by Gustav Radbruch who had been a leading positivist legal philosopher, as well as a minister of justice during the Weimar period. In an article which was to influence not only many lawyers but also the highest German courts, Radbruch argued in 1946 that those laws and acts of the Nazi regime which manifestly contradicted the idea of "justice" (Gerechtigkeit) could not be recognised as valid in law.

This resurgence of value-oriented legal thinking, or natural law, also had a strong impact on the concept of "Rechtsstaat." Now it was held that the term also contained a minimum degree of "justice." This development was not necessarily to be expected since the Basic Law (Grundgesetz) is actually quite traditional. It contains neither an explicit reference to the principle of proportionality nor to the principle of legitimate expectations ("Vertrauensschutz"). Its equal protection clause has the same wording as the parallel guarantee in the Weimar constitution. But there were some innovations: a somewhat hidden reference to the principle of "Rechtsstaat" (Article 28(1)), an introductory clause concerning the protection of human dignity (Article 1(1)), the principle that the legislature is bound by the fundamental rights (Article 1(3)) and the guarantee that the "essence" of fundamental rights may never be infringed upon by law (Article 19(2)). What happened was that the Bundesverfassungsgericht took these provisions together with some more classical principles and held that they expressed a wider and more substantive concept of "Rechtsstaat." Ultimately, this, together with other decisions, led to profound changes in German administrative law. In 1959, the President of the Federal Administrative Court, part in observation, part in prophecy, remarked that administrative law was in fact "konkretisiertes Verfassungsrecht" (concretised constitutional law).

Constitutional Law Influences upon Administrative Law

In this context, the point to stress is that constitutional law has helped shape [...] principles of German administrative law [...].

The Principle of Proportionality

Before the Nazi regime came to power, the principle of proportionality only served to limit certain excesses in the exercise of police powers. It was not considered to be a general principle of administrative, let alone of constitutional law. Although it is often claimed that the Preussisches Oberverwaltungsgericht had already recognised the principle of proportionality, this is only true in a terminological sense. A thorough analysis of its case law leads to the conclusion that the court understood and applied the requirement of Verhältnismäßigkeit (proportionality) very differently from contemporary German practice. Essentially, there were only two situations in which a measure would be deemed disproportionate: if the measure could not contribute to achieving its aim; or if a less restrictive measure would clearly have been available. In actual practice the most important instance of the latter was when the person at whom the measure was addressed offered to provide an alternative means which would be as effective in achieving the aim. Thus, what is considered today to be the characteristic feature of the principle of proportionality – that the court determines freely whether a less restrictive means exists or whether the chosen means is unduly burdensome – was, at best, recognised only in embryo. This changed under the Basic Law (Grundgesetz). Beginning in 1958, the Bundesverfassungsgericht declared the principle of proportionality to be of central and general importance. The relevant case concerned a law which limited the number of pharmacies within a district in order to avoid the "harmful" effects of competition. The Bundesverfassungsgericht held that such a measure constituted a disproportionate restriction on the freedom to choose one's profession (Article 12, Grundgesetz). Today the principle of proportionality is always applied as the last and decisive test of the validity of any restriction on the general principle of freedom of action (Article 2(1), Grundgesetz). This, in turn, has led to its overextension. The Federal Administrative Court, for example, has dealt repeatedly with the question of under what circumstances the police have the power to remove cars parked in violation of traffic regulations. In one case the court held that it could be disproportionate to remove a car if it was parked only for a short time or if it was standing at a place where it did not disturb the flow of traffic, provided that there was no danger that other drivers would feel tempted to follow the bad example. Since the principle of proportionality is a rule of constitutional law, it is possible that a car owner could successfully challenge a removal order before the Bundesverfassungsgericht.

The Principle of Equality

Writing in 1931, the author of the leading treatise on German administrative law, Walter Jellinek, observed that the constitutional principle of equality (Article 109 of the Weimar Constitution) was referred to only very rarely in judgments dealing with abuse of discretion by the administration. Jellinek's observation is characteristic of the entrenched division between constitutional and administrative law at the time. As a principle of constitutional law the principle of equality traditionally meant no more than the requirement of the equal application of the laws. But in the sphere of administrative law, it was generally recognised that the principle of equality was nothing other than the prohibition of arbitrary action – a rule which, it is suggested, was comparable to the English test of unreasonableness. One of the early implications of the administrative principle of equality was that the administration could not in certain cases deviate without good reason from an established pattern of behaviour even if, in principle, it had the power to do so. After the Second World War, however, the constitutional principle of equality before the law (Article 3(1), Grundgesetz) served as a justification, in practical as well as in theoretical terms, for a vast extension of this rule concerning the "self-binding" of the administration. Now the courts held that the administration had already violated the principle of equality when it did not act in conformity with those circulars or administrative rules which, without having the force of legally binding rules, served as guidelines for the exercise of its discretion. This development is explained on the basis that every deviation from the pattern established by these rules violates the principle of equality.

* * *

Administrative Discretion

Most importantly, until the second half of this century, there was no dogma about the one and only correct solution concerning the interpretation of "indeterminate legal concepts." Indeed, during the Weimar Republic it was still recognised that the administration possessed discretion not only where this was expressly provided for but also if this was to be reasonably expected under the circumstances. Since the unique duty of the German administrative courts to gather evidence *de novo* existed prior to the Second World War, the origin of the dogma must lie elsewhere. The most obvious explanation is, once again, the post-war "substantive" understanding of Rechtsstaat. As late as 1956 the Federal Administrative Court refused to impose limits upon administrative discretion when asked to determine whether the licensing of a private bus line would "adversely affect the interests of public transportation." However, subsequently the court adopted the approach that discretion would only exist where it was expressly provided for, except in certain exceptional cases. The Bundesverfassungsgericht has repeatedly confirmed that the right to effective judicial review (Article 19(4), Grundgesetz) mandates this rule. It should be noted that its constitutional underpinning makes the dogma highly resistant to change.

Procedural Rights

Procedural rights have traditionally played a less important role in German administrative law than in the United Kingdom. This explains why the "constitutionalisation" of the law of administrative procedure occurred later than the other developments which have been referred to. Only in the last twenty years has the Bundesverfassungsgericht begun to insist that certain substantive fundamental rights also have an impact in the field of administrative procedure. It is sufficient to mention only the two most important decisions. First, in 1979, the Court held that the obligation of the state to protect the health of its citizens required that the licensing procedures for nuclear power plants permit private individuals to challenge any non-compliance with technical safety rules. Since judicial review of administrative action in Germany is, in principle, limited to the protection of the rights or legally protected interests of the directly affected individual, this development was a remarkable one. Second, in 1983, the Court held that the threat which modern data processing poses to the legitimate privacy interests of the individual required the enactment of rules of administrative procedure which ensure the proper use of collected data. Both decisions show that there is a growing awareness of the importance of procedural rules for the effective protection of rights. So far, however, procedural rules have not acquired a practical importance comparable to the substantive limits on administrative action.

The German Principles in Perspective

[These] German principles [of administrative law] [...] are part of a strong general tendency which began after the Second World War. This tendency is characterised by an intensification of substantive judicial review; an intensification which has its source not within a quasi-autonomous sphere of administrative law, but within constitutional law. "Correcting" the perceived failures of the legal system which, as it was held, had contributed to the rise to power of the Nazi regime, and, of course, the abuses of that regime, this new constitutional thinking is characterised by its orientation towards substantive justice. Deciding in a similar spirit, both the Bundesverfassungsgericht and the Federal Administrative Court, through their reinterpretation of the classical principle of "Rechtsstaat" which included taking fundamental rights seriously, have developed the tools which now enable the courts to scrutinise closely the actual results of administrative decisions. This has contributed to the paradoxical result that the traditional continental distinction between administrative courts and ordinary courts, a distinction which originally symbolised that administrative action was only subject to a lesser form of judicial review, in Germany now has the opposite effect of encouraging specialised judges to conduct a very searching form of review. It is true that in the last few decades English administrative law has also witnessed a certain tendency to increase judicial review of administrative action, especially with respect to the control of administrative discretion. This tendency, however, appears to be not nearly as revolutionary as its German counterpart.

* * *

Questions/Comments

- What does Nolte mean when he claims that German administrative law has features of the "formal *Rechtsstaat*" and, since the post-war period, an "intensification" of the "substantive *Rechtsstaat*"? Nolte refers to Gustav Radbruch, one of the scholars we discussed in Chapter 3. Does Nolte believe that Radbruch is aligned with the formal or the substantive *Rechtsstaat* – or maybe both?
- Based on the excerpt from Nolte, how would you describe the German solution to administrative law's "'central tension' [...] between technical competence and democratic legitimacy"?[20] Rose-Ackerman argued that Germany and the United States diverge sharply: "The German public law system focuses mainly on the protection of individual rights against the state, rather than [as in the United States] on the oversight of executive process."[21] German administrative law extends considerable *ex ante* freedom to the administration in making and implementing policy. This must be, at least in part, a consequence of Germans' historical confidence in the state bureaucracy.[22] As I suggested earlier, it also seems to reflect the influence of the Civil Law tradition, which is characterized by a profound confidence in legislative control through statutes. The foundational tenets of German administrative law similarly focus on the "legality of administration" – the notion that the administration is (adequately) bound by the popularly elected

parliament through the enactment of detailed statutes. This understanding finds its expression in the constitutionally rooted *Legalitätsprinzip* (principle of legality). The principle of legality is one of German administrative law's most important commitments. It means that the state can act only pursuant to and within the scope of a statute. "Legality" consists of two elements: "subjection to the law (*Vorbehalt des Gesetzes*), [which] obliges the administration to act upon statutory authorization only," and "the precedence of law (*Vorrang des Gesetzes*), [which requires that] all administrative actions [...] comply with the law and therefore must not violate superior rules."[23]

- The principle of legality is a component of the constitutional value known as the *Rechtsstaatsprinzip*. Nolte highlights the *Rechtsstaatsprinzip* as a major element of German administrative law. Can you list the other major elements of the *Rechtsstaatsprinzip*? Is the American notion of "due process" a parallel to the *Rechtssaatsprinzip*? How do these distinct concepts – *Rechtssaat* in Germany and due process in the United States – embody the different approaches to administrative law that Rose-Ackerman identified? Finally, I must point out that the *Legalitätsprinzip* has a meaning and role in administrative law that is different to the *Legalitätsprinzip* that is central to German criminal procedure. That version of the concept will be discussed in Chapter 11.

- Having left the administration to its work relatively undisturbed within its statutory mandate, German administrative law nonetheless makes the substance of those actions fully reviewable by the courts after the fact. The courts are not burdened with a doctrine requiring deference to the administration. US administrative law is preoccupied with controlling the processes of administrative decision-making.[24] That emphasis on *ex ante* process justifies showing deference to public authority and limiting American courts' review of administrative actions. Thus, American administrative law extends less freedom to the public administration to formulate policy. But, in light of the strictly enforced procedures the administration must follow, American administrative law demands greater deference from the courts in their review of public authorities' policymaking. The opposite is true for German administrative law, which extends considerable freedom to the administration to formulate policy, but extends little deference from the courts in their review of state action. What historical or social factors might account for the different approaches taken by the United States and Germany? Does the difference reveal something about how the two societies view public authority and the judiciary? Is the difference rooted in the two systems' orientation towards the Civil Law tradition or the Common Law tradition?

- When I say that the German judiciary has a prominent role in reviewing administrative action, I mean that the courts test the substance of policy and its implementation against the underlying subsidiary legislation, the general principles of administrative law framed by the Administrative Procedure Act, and the basic rights secured by the Basic Law. Especially when assessing whether state action has infringed on a basic right secured by the Basic Law, the courts' review involves an application of the proportionality analysis described in Chapter 8. Proportionality is another component of the *Rechtsstaatsprinzip*. Nolte explains that, in implementing the proportionality analysis, "the court determines freely whether a less restrictive means exists or whether the chosen means is unduly burdensome." Why is Nolte concerned about the "overextension" of the proportionality analysis in German administrative law? What alternatives exist to the courts' proportionality review of administrative action?

- To this point I have recklessly blurred the distinct history and sociology of administrative law in the many German principalities that eventually came to form the modern, united German state. In doing so I have equated Prussia – and the Prussian administrative tradition – with an all-German administrative tradition. But, as any Bavarian will quickly and vigorously point out, Germany is *not* Prussia. Nonetheless, modern Germany's administration and civil service owe a great debt to Prussia, a fact that led a pair of prominent commentators to refer to the field as "*Dieses (preußisch) deutsch Verständnis von Verwaltung*" ("this (Prussian) German understanding of administration").[25] Mahendra Singh's survey of the history of German administrative law also emphasized Prussian developments.[26] And, as Nolte made clear, the foundational jurisprudential debate that led to the emergence of modern German administrative law was carried out between Otto Bähr and Rudolph von Gneist. Naturally, they were both Prussians.

Most of Germany's administration is based in the *Bundesländer* (federal states), which are charged by the Basic Law with implementing federal law as well their own laws.[27] This peculiarity – known as "administrative federalism" – will be examined as part of the next excerpt from Peter Lindseth. For present purposes it is sufficient to note that the German states typically operate at least three levels of bureaucracy for making and implementing policy: *Landesbehörden* (state-wide authorities, such as the state government, the state premier minister (governor), and the state ministries headed by a cabinet minister); *Landesmittelbehörden* (local authorities, such as county governments or the city mayor); and *untere Landesbehörden* (lower-level local authorities, such as the local police department or the local school superintendent).

As is apparent from Figure 5.4 in Chapter 5, which charts the German judicial system, judicial review of administrative matters takes place across three levels of the specialized administrative courts. The first-instance courts are simply called *Verwaltungsgerichte* (administrative courts). The intermediate appellate level consists of fifteen *Oberverwaltungsgerichte* or *Verwaltungsgerichtshöfe* (Higher Regional Administrative Courts). There are only fifteen of these courts, despite the fact that there are sixteen federal states, because Berlin and Brandenburg have a shared *Oberverwaltungsgericht*. The last-instance appeals

Federal Administrative Court in Leipzig
Renaissance style architecture imbues the Federal Administrative Court—and the field of administrative law—with a sense of enduring tradition. Especially when this court is compared to the Federal Constitutional Court's modern, post-war home in Karlsruhe, it's easy to see why Germans sometimes say: "constitutional law comes and goes, administrative law remains."
Figure 9.1 Federal Administrative Court

court is the *Bundesverwaltungsgericht* (BVerwG or Federal Administrative Court). The Federal Administrative Court has its seat in the building in Leipzig that, from 1879 to 1945, housed the *Reichsgericht* (Imperial Court). As you can see in the photo in Figure 9.1, the building is a grand example of the monumental Wilhelmine style, featuring neo-baroque and neo-renaissance flourishes. The *Reichsgericht* was the Empire's court of last instance in private law and criminal law matters. That is, for more than sixty years it was the highest court in the fields covered by Germany's two great codifications: the Civil Code and the Criminal Code. Maybe that's another source of the Civil Law influence in German administrative law. The "Civilian" ethos echoes from the walls and rafters of the Federal Administrative Court's home.

It was in the Leipzig *Reichsgericht* that the Nazis conducted the cynical show-trial of the communist sympathizers who were accused of setting fire to the *Reichstag* (Federal Parliament) building in 1933. Hitler used the *Reichstag* fire to justify the implementation of emergency laws that suspended many constitutional limits on his power as the chancellor. That history makes it all the more meaningful that the Leipzig courthouse now hosts the highest court of the respected and effective legal regime that controls and constrains German state power.

Alongside the Federal Administrative Court, the Federal Constitutional Court (described in Chapter 8) may be called upon to review administrative law matters when decisions of the administrative courts are alleged to have violated the Basic Law.

Rose-Ackerman argued that German administrative law dangerously favors expertise at the expense of democratic legitimacy and effective governance. The principle of legality, she explained, does not adequately limit administrative discretion because "German statutes are not precise statements of policy, but are full of vague and undefined terms that require further interpretation before the acts can be implemented."[28] Against that backdrop Rose-Ackerman saw only a range of easily disregarded informal safeguards that are meant to check the administration in Germany. Finally, Rose-Ackerman argued that Germany's preference for *ex post* substantive judicial review does not resolve the risks created by the administration's *ex ante* autonomy. "The judiciary's task," she said, "is [...] to prevent the state from riding roughshod over individuals as the state pursues broad public goals. The German administrative courts devote most of their time to protecting individual rights, rather than to monitoring political and policymaking activities of government."[29] But this admirable protection of individuals does not address more pragmatic questions like the efficacy of broad, underlying administrative policies. "Individuals," Rose-Ackerman explained, "can defend only their own particular interests, not public interests."[30]

Peter Lindseth, one of the most accomplished scholars of comparative administrative law, disagreed with Rose-Ackerman. He said that she ignored German administrative law's cultural embeddedness and that she neither fully nor fairly surveys the field. In particular, Lindseth says that Rose-Ackerman neglected a number of additional checks on executive authority, most significantly, Germany's federalism.

Peter L. Lindseth
Review Essay – Comparing Administrative States: Susan Rose-Ackerman and the Limits of Public Law in Germany and the United States
2 COLUMBIA JOURNAL OF EUROPEAN LAW 589, 601, 603 (1995–1996)[*]

* * *

Prof. Rose-Ackerman's treatment of German federalism, a principle deeply embedded in German constitutional law, history, and culture, illustrates the limitations of her approach. From her analytical standpoint, the "German constitution's assignment of environmental tasks does not make policy sense." The problem she sees is that the German *Grundgesetz* (GG) fails to apportion responsibilities according to the nature of substantive environmental problems, in which truly "local" problems (those with costs and benefits concentrated in one jurisdiction) could be rationally regulated in that jurisdiction alone, and "regional" or "global" issues (those with costs and benefits that cross

---

[*] Excerpt reproduced with permission of the *Columbia Journal of European Law* and the author.

Länder or national borders) would require federal, European or international regulation. The *Grundgesetz* makes, from a cost-benefit perspective, an arbitrary distinction between those issues for which concurrent federal-Länder authority exists, and those which permit only federal framework laws that leave the Länder free to fill in the legislative details with their own statutes. The net effect of these constitutional provisions is to make the *Länder* primarily responsible for the day-to-day implementation of many of the most important federal regulatory statutes.

* * *

Leaving aside the question of consultation, there are several structural and functional checks in the German system that could lead a reasonable observer to precisely the sort of "superficial" view [Rose-Ackerman] criticizes. German federalism, for example, imposes significant checks on the exercise of delegated legislative power at the federal level. Indeed, federal regulatory power is purely normative, lacking any direct enforcement authority, which is the responsibility of the Länder. The federal government cannot threaten takeover of regulatory enforcement at the state level (in fact, it does not have any regional offices). Even the normative power of the federal government is significantly constrained: federal laws, regulations and administrative guidelines that are to be implemented by the Länder (i.e., the major ones) must receive the consent of the Bundesrat. Depending on the composition of Länder governments, the Bundesrat may be controlled by opposition parties. Moreover, many of the major environmental statutes also provide for a veto by the Bundestag over major regulations. The effect is to involve members of the Bundestag and state government ministers in the drafting of important regulations. Although Prof. Rose-Ackerman acknowledges how these checks might limit the federal bureaucracy's operation, she argues that they "are not necessarily conducive to good policy-making," potentially leading to an overemphasis on administrative convenience and interstate uniformity "where neither will produce sensible policy."

* * *

Lindseth's reaction to Rose-Ackerman requires us to pause, briefly, to highlight Germany's "administrative federalism." David Currie concluded that it is "one of the most startling aspects of the German Basic Law [that] most federal laws are carried out by the states." As you consider this unique feature of German constitutional and administrative law you should ask yourself if you find it – when working in conjunction with Germany's extensive *ex post* judicial review – to be an adequate limitation on the state's implementation of its policy. Recall that Rose-Ackerman worried that "German law places few limitations on governmental rulemaking procedures"[31] and that, ultimately, the judicial review applied to executive-branch policymaking has an "anemic quality."[32] She also easily dismissed the control potential of administrative federalism, remarking that

> [b]ecause Germany' federal system delegates most implementation to the states, the *Bundesrat* enjoys veto power over a wide range of executive branch activity, including all major environmental initiatives. As state government officials, *Bundesrat* members are, however, generally more concerned with the ease of implementation than with the merit of the substantive policies.[33]

The following excerpt explains Germany's "administrative federalism."

9.2 German Administrative Law: Substance Not Process

David P. Currie
THE CONSTITUTION OF THE FEDERAL REPUBLIC OF GERMANY 61–69 (1994)*

* * *

[...] [T]he list of federal lawmaking powers is impressively long; despite faithful judicial enforcement of many of the limits on federal authority, most significant legislation in Germany is federal. Yet it would be wrong to conclude that the Länder play a minor role in this field. Even though the Länder enact few important statutes of their own, they take a substantial part in the enactment of federal legislation. For while the members of the federal Parliament ("Bundestag") are directly elected by the people, no federal law can be enacted without being submitted to a separate body called the Bundesrat (Council of State Governments), which represents the states themselves. It is not merely that, as was originally the case of the U.S. Senate, members are chosen by some branch of state government. The members of the Bundesrat are *members* of state governments, appointed and subject to recall by the states; they are there as representatives of the Länder.

The details have varied over time, but every German constitution since 1849 has provided for a similar body through which the states play a role within the central government. Under the Basic Law a variety of federal executive actions affecting the Länder require Bundesrat approval, and the Bundesrat selects half the members of the Federal Constitutional Court. The most important powers of the Bundesrat, however, are those respecting federal legislation.

The basic provision is Article 77, which gives the *Bundesrat* a suspensive veto over federal legislation generally. Normally the *Bundestag* may override this veto by a majority vote; but if the veto is passed by a two-thirds majority [in the *Bundesrat*], [then] a two-thirds vote is required [in the Bundestag to override the veto]. In a number of instances, however, the Bundesrat has an absolute veto; no federal statute may become law without Bundesrat approval. Provisions to this effect are inconveniently scattered throughout the Basic Law. Predictably, they tend to involve matters of particular concern to the Länder: [...] [including] state administrative agencies [...].

Originally it was expected that the requirement of Bundesrat consent would be the exception, not the rule. According to recent estimates, however, somewhere between fifty-five and sixty percent of all federal statutes now require such consent. In part this high percentage is attributable to the fact that constitutional amendments giving the Federation additional powers commonly mitigate the incursion on state authority by giving the Bundesrat an absolute veto. The most fertile source of laws requiring Bundesrat approval, however, is Article 84(1), whose interesting development merits closer examination.

[...] [M]ost federal laws in Germany are carried out by the Länder. Because the Federation has an obvious interest in the execution of its laws, Article 84(1) permits it to regulate the organization and procedure of state agencies administering federal law. Because such regulations plainly impinge on the interests of the Länder, they may be enacted only with Bundesrat consent.

Many federal statutes contain provisions regulating state administrative organization and procedure. Moreover, the Constitutional Court very early concluded that a statute was to be treated as a unit for this purpose: If any provision of the statute regulated state administration, the entire statute required Bundesrat approval. Thus the Bundesrat may base its rejection of a law regulating state procedure on objections to substantive provisions of the same statute; and thus the Bundesrat has veto power over many substantive provisions not independently requiring its approval.

---

* Used with permission of University of Chicago Press – Books, through Copyright Clearance Center, Inc.

* * *

Thus, the interpretation of the various provisions respecting *Bundesrat* approval of federal legislation has presented a continuing challenge, and the requirement of state participation in the enactment of federal laws remains an important safeguard for the interests of the Länder. Because it is the *executive* branch of state government that is represented in the Bundesrat, moreover, this requirement also assures that practical questions of administration receive adequate consideration in the legislative process. Finally, because Bundestag and Bundesrat have often been controlled by different parties, the participation of the latter has sometimes provided a political check as well. [...]

To an observer from the United States, one of the most startling aspects of the German Basic Law is [the aforementioned principle that] most federal laws are carried out by the states. Article 83 declares the basic principle: "The *Länder* shall execute federal laws as matters of their own concern insofar as this Basic Law does not otherwise provide or permit." Article 83 [...] is riddled with exceptions [...] [but] [m]ost legislative power in Germany is federal; most executive power is not.

It is hard to imagine that Congress would ever trust the states to enforce federal law to the same extent in the United States. The usual reason federal laws are enacted is that the states have proved unwilling to tackle the problem; the same political pressures that produced legislative reluctance seem likely to produce executive footdragging as well. In order to reduce federal bureaucracy and permit diversity, some federal statutes in [the United States] do provide for state participation in their enforcement; but they generally provide for federal intervention in case the states do not do the job.

* * *

State administration of federal law in Germany is motivated in part by the same considerations that underlie [America's] separation of legislative and executive powers. The dangers of an all-powerful federal executive were all too vividly illustrated during the Nazi period; the risk of inadequate enforcement is the price of protection against prosecutorial abuse. The Basic Law goes beyond our Constitution by taking enforcement not only out of legislative hands but largely out of federal hands as well; in a parliamentary system this may be necessary to assure effective freedom from legislative control.

State enforcement of federal law had been the norm under earlier constitutions; the willingness of the framers of the Basic Law to reinstitute and even to strengthen it suggests that it had worked reasonably well. Apparently it has also worked well enough since; although one hears periodic complaints about an enforcement deficit ("*Vollzugsdefizit*"), virtually no one seems to attribute it to the allocation of enforcement authority to the *Länder*. The fact that so many federal laws can be enacted only with the consent of the *Länder* (though not necessarily of all of them) may help to reduce the danger of inadequate enforcement, as may the possibilities of federal intervention already described. Another possible inference is that most *Länder* officials (presumably like most state officials in this country) take their constitutional obligations seriously.

* * *

Questions/Comments

- Does administrative federalism tilt Germany's administrative law in the direction of judge-empowering judicial review (of the kind Nolte described) and the Common Law tradition? Or is it a manifestation of the Civil Law tradition's influence on German administrative law? Maybe it is not related to either of these traditions?

- One unexpected development in Germany's post-war constitutional politics was the increasingly recurrent phenomenon that one major party held a large share of the seats in the parliament and, thus, controlled the federal government, while the major opposition party led a number of state governments and therefore occupied a large share of the seats in the *Bundesrat*. In these circumstances, wielding the veto authority described by Currie, the *Bundesrat* emerged as a major check on federal policymaking. Again, the main vehicle for the *Bundesrat's* interest in federal legislation was the fact that the states, pursuant to administrative federalism, bore the bureaucratic burden of implementing newly enacted federal policy. The *Bundesrat's* obstructionism, at least partially motivated by partisanship, became so problematic that it was blamed for blocking much-needed reform being pursued by the Federal Government and its majority in the *Bundestag*. In 2006 a "grand coalition" of the two major parties in the *Bundestag* overhauled the Basic Law's federalism scheme in what was called the "mother of all reforms." It was hoped that the reform would significantly reduce the *Bundesrat's* ability to thwart the parliamentary majority's will. It seems that the federalism overhaul did less to streamline federal policymaking than was desired.[34] Does administrative federalism represent an important limit in Germany's administration, as Lindseth insists? Doesn't that question require you to reflect on who – or what institution – might be harmed by unchecked policymaking and the unconstrained implementation of policy?

Germany's administrative federalism made a cameo appearance in US constitutional law, if only to play the part of a counterfactual to the American system. The American constitution provides for dual federal and state administration of separate federal and state laws. In *Printz v. United States* the US Supreme Court ruled that a federal law that required state and local law enforcement officers to implement parts of a new federal handgun registration policy was unconstitutional.[35] The majority of the Court was concerned that, by "commandeering" the state governments' administrative officers for the implementation of a federal policy, the law dangerously eroded the constitution's principle of dual federalism. Justice Breyer, in a dissenting opinion, argued that Swiss, German, and European Union administrative federalism proved the majority's concern to be exaggerated.[36]

Critics strenuously objected to the relevance of the comparison. Daniel Halberstam regretted that Justice Breyer failed to adequately develop "the comparison between the U.S. and European systems […] [ignoring] countervailing institutional dynamics that complicate any reliance on the European example."[37] Specifically, Halberstam criticized Justice Breyer for not fully accounting for the extensive role played by Germany's state governments, via their representatives in the *Bundesrat*, in forming federal policy that ultimately will be implemented by state-level bureaucracies. By pressing this criticism, Halberstam seemed to be supporting Lindseth's view that there is more bite to Germany's administrative federalism than Rose-Ackerman recognized. In a blog essay, Rick Hills asked whether "Breyer's pro-commandeering argument in *Printz* [is] the worst comparative constitutional law ever?"[38] As one might expect, Hills' answer to that blustery question was a resounding "yes." Even if he used more collegial rhetoric and couched his commentary in informed, scholarly terms, Halberstam's criticism expressed similar disappointment in Justice Breyer's use of comparative constitutional law.

Halberstam's critique provides valuable insight into the true force and effect of Germany's administrative federalism as a central component of German administrative law. In light of that insight, are you able to say who or what is policing the very extensive deployment of executive power in the German system? At the same time, Halberstam's disagreement with Justice Breyer's approach is a useful reminder – deep into our comparative law journey into the German legal culture – of the challenges and sensitivities involved in thoughtful comparative legal studies. Justice Breyer, had he reflected on the issues we considered in Chapter 1, might have avoided these stinging reactions.

9.3 Administering Islamic Law in Germany

The foregoing materials highlight three distinct ways in which German administrative law imposes checks on the exercise of state authority: the principle of legality (with its Civil Law confidence in statutes); the extensive *ex post* substantive review exercised by administrative courts (reflecting constitutionalism and the Common Law tradition); and the principle of administrative federalism. There are other *ex ante* limits that apparently failed to reassure Rose-Ackerman, including limitations arising from the statutory assignment of administrative competences, and the requirement that administrative authorities act only pursuant to one of an established set of administrative mechanisms (*Verwaltungsakte* such as statutory instruments or administrative regulations). The impetus for consensus in German policymaking is another *ex ante* check on the German administration, especially as it provides more-or-less formal roles in administrative undertakings for "private norm-setting organizations" and stakeholder "advisory committees."[39]

For all their disagreement, Nolte nevertheless seemed to confirm Rose-Ackerman's thesis that the most important limit on the German bureaucracy is the extensive *ex post* substantive review German administrative courts undertake to enforce a range of constitutional law and administrative law principles. Curiously, even as it represents the kind of judicial empowerment characteristic of the Common Law tradition, there is no equivalent to this broad scope of substantive review of administrative actions in the administrative jurisprudence of legal systems that are predominantly influenced by the Common Law tradition.[40] Its extent, as Singh explained, is sweeping.

[The German administrative courts may] invalidate an administrative action if it is in excess of [an assigned competence, or] they may also check illegalities committed within the [assigned competence] and [they] may also modify or change the administrative determination to bring it in conformity with the law. Their jurisdiction is not confined to jurisdictional questions. They can go into all questions of legality whether apparent on the face of the record or hidden in or behind it and [they] may also replace the administrative determination by their own in appropriate cases.[41]

As part of the *Rechtsstaatsprinzip*, the comprehensive judicial review of administrative actions in Germany is mandated by the constitution.[42] The Federal Constitutional Court and the Federal Administrative Court have concluded that "the administrative courts generally have the power and obligation to completely review administrative decisions. Otherwise the procedural guarantee of [Article 19(4) of the Basic Law] and an effective protection of basic rights would be endangered."[43] Nolte identifies the central constitutional principles against which the courts will test administrative actions, including proportionality, equality, and the abuse of discretion. But, as will be seen in the following case study, the administrative courts also review administrative policymaking and actions for unconstitutional infringements on basic rights, such as the guarantee of personal freedom enshrined in Article 2 of the Basic Law. The administrative courts also review administrative policymaking and actions for their compliance with principles of administrative law, including conformity with procedural requirements, the competence to act, exceeding assigned competences, or substantive defects.

The last point in that list is remarkable enough to merit emphasis. It proposes that the courts should assess the integrity of the substantive policy conclusions reached by administrative authorities. That's remarkable because states turn to the administration precisely because other branches of government lack the expertise, efficiency, and flexibility to resolve complex regulatory matters. The *Ritual Slaughter Cases* show how far-reaching – but also how variable – courts' substantive review of policy can be in German administrative law.

In the following case study the courts were asked to determine whether the administrative authorities committed a substantive – *factual* – error in concluding that the circumstances did not justify the application of a statutorily created exception to the relevant rule. The case study confirms Singh's conclusion that "[t]he German administrative courts have unlimited jurisdiction to look into the factual basis of an administrative action. They can assess themselves [...] to find out whether the facts justify an action. If they find such justification missing they will invalidate the action."[44]

This case study does not involve a run-of-the-mill administrative law dispute. Even so, the basic components of the judicial review of administrative action just discussed – a purported constitutional violation and a purported substantive error in the administrative agency's decision – are central to its outcome. The cases are exceptional because they implicate the thorny intersection of Germany's Christian (although now largely secular) cultural and legal tradition and the country's growing Muslim population, which includes many Muslims who seek to reconcile respect for the tenets of Islamic Law (*Sharia*) with their legal rights and duties under German law.

Described in the reactionary press and by some scholars as a "clash of civilizations," the cultural negotiation between Western and non-Western law and values is not unique to Germany or even Europe.[45] Still, the issue seems to have particular resonance in Europe where "Muslims constitute the majority of immigrants [...], including [in] Belgium, France, Germany, and the Netherlands, and the largest single component of the immigrant population in the United Kingdom [...]."[46] Overall, the number of Muslims in Europe remains small, even after the arrival of millions of Muslim asylum seekers in Europe between 2015 and 2017. The Pew Research Center found that Muslims constitute just 5 percent of Europe's population, but noted that "in some countries [...] the Muslim share of the population is higher. And, in the coming decades, the Muslim share of the continent's population is expected to grow – and could more than double."[47] The Pew study from 2016 found that Germany's 5 million Muslims accounted for just 6 percent of the country's population.[48] By 2021 these numbers had risen to 5.5 million and nearly 7 percent of Germany's population.[49]

A number of headline-grabbing developments demonstrate the complexity and intensity of the social and legal issues resulting from the growth of Europe's Muslim population. France has banned "conspicuous" religious symbols in a move that seemed aimed at Muslim women wearing the traditional headscarf. If there was any doubt about the law's aim, it was answered when, in 2011, France formally outlawed face-coverings in public.[50] In the last decades, legal systems across Europe have had to come to grips with an increasing number of so-called "honor-killings," murders often attributed to fundamentalist Muslims who kill women relatives for perceived Western slights of traditional values.[51] In 2008 the Archbishop of the Church of England was embroiled in controversy after suggesting that Muslims in Britain should be able to have *Sharia* norms applied to a discrete number of private concerns by independent Islamic courts.[52] In a national referendum, Switzerland voted to ban the construction of minarets.[53] Other European countries have added to the strained dynamic with bans on engaging in Muslim worship in public, and with the criminalization of circumcision.[54]

Germany's Federal President Christian Wulff sparked widespread debate around the issues of demographic change, integration, and religious tolerance when, at the ceremony marking the twentieth anniversary of Germany's reunification in 2010, he declared: "The future belongs to nations that are open to cultural diversity, for new ideas and coming to terms with strangers. [...] Christianity doubtless belongs in Germany. Judaism doubtless belongs in Germany. That is our Judeo-Christian history. But now, Islam also belongs in Germany."[55] Those sentiments were countered by unashamed xenophobic antagonism from some quarters.[56] There is a troublingly high number of hostile incidents directed towards Muslims in Germany each year,[57] including acts of violence and murder.[58] Even amongst mainstream public figures and politicians, President Wulff's comments were met with restraint and qualification. In response to President Wulff, Chancellor Angela Merkel insisted that "Muslims living in Germany [must] conform to 'fundamental German values.'"[59]

The following administrative law cases represented a test of all these social forces and beliefs. They arose out of German administrative agencies' refusal to grant Muslim butchers the right to slaughter animals in conformity with their views of Muslim *halal* dietary restrictions.

One of the provisions of Germany's *Tierschutzgesetz* (TSchG or Animal Protection Act) of 1986 requires that warm-blooded animals be stunned or anesthetized before they are slaughtered – §§ 1 and 4a(1).[60] But the law provides an exemption to this general prohibition, to the extent *necessary* to meet the needs of religious groups whose dietary laws *mandate* the consumption of the meat of animals that are ritually slaughtered, that is, animals that are not stunned or anesthetized prior to being slaughtered – § 4a(2)[2] (emphasis added).

Animal Protection Act[*]

Section 1

The aim of this Act is to protect the lives and well-being of animals, based on the responsibility of human beings for their fellow creatures. No one may cause an animal pain, suffering or harm without good reason.

Animal Protection Act[*]

Section 4a

(1) Warm-blooded animals may be slaughtered only if stunned before exsanguination.
(2) By way of derogation from paragraph (1), no stunning shall be required if:
   1. it is impossible under the circumstances in the case of an emergency slaughter;
   2. the competent authority has granted an exemption for slaughter without stunning (ritual slaughter); this exemption may be granted only where necessary to meet the requirements of members of religious communities in the territory covered by this Act whose mandatory rules require ritual slaughter and prohibit consumption of meat of animals not slaughtered in this way;
   3. this is meant as an exemption by ordinance under Article 4b (3).

---

[*] Translation reprinted with permission of Michigan State University College of Law.
[*] Translation reprinted with permission of Michigan State University College of Law.

The first of the two *Ritual Slaughter Cases* presented here is a decision of the Federal Administrative Court. The Court rejected the last-instance appeal of a butcher who was denied an exemption from the Animal Protection Act's requirement that animals be stunned or anesthetized before being slaughtered. The administrative agency that denied the requested exemption, and the lower administrative courts that upheld that decision, concluded that the applicant's case did not fulfill the terms of § 4a(2)[2] because, based on the learning of established experts in Islamic Law, Islam does not *mandate* a form of ritual slaughter that is incompatible with, for example, stunning animals electronically before they are slaughtered.

As you read the following decision try to identify the kinds of review undertaken by the court. That will help you see the ways in which the general principles of administrative law operate in practice to direct and constrain public authority in Germany.

Federal Administrative Court
Ritual Slaughter Case

[Translation by Russell A. Miller]

BVerwGE 99, 1 (1995)

* * *

The appeal is not justified. [The Higher Regional Administrative Court's decision, which found that the complainant is not entitled to a special permit to slaughter warm-blooded animals without stunning them as provided by § 4a(2)[2] of the Animal Protection Act, does not violate federal law.]

Section 4a(2)[2] of the Animal Protection Act permits exemptions to the general requirement of § 4a(1) that warm-blooded animals be stunned before they are slaughtered "only where necessary to meet the requirements of members of religious communities in the territory covered by this Act whose mandatory rules require ritual slaughter and prohibit consumption of meat of animals not slaughtered in this way; [...]." The purpose of the initial legal challenge to the administrative agency's refusal to grant such an exemption in this case was the complainant's desire to supply customers with meat that comes from animals that were not stunned before they were slaughtered. The complainant views ritual slaughter as a binding and effective tenet of Islam. At issue in this case are the needs of people, like the complainant's customers, who believe themselves to be prohibited from eating the meat of animals that were not stunned before they were slaughtered [...].

* * *

The conditions for granting an exemption under § 4a(2)[2] of the Animal Protection Act are not fulfilled. The legal norm only allows for an exemption if binding rules of a religious community prohibit its members from consuming the meat of animals that were not stunned before they were slaughtered. This does not apply to the complainant's customers, in whose interest the complainant asserts and justifies the request for the exemption.

The complainant's customers do not belong to a religious community that prohibits, by means of binding rules, its members from consuming the meat of animals that are not stunned before they were slaughtered.

[Definition of the Term "Religious Community"]

A religious community is understood in Church Law [*Staatskirchenrecht*] as a collective that unifies members of the same creed – or several related creeds – to the fulfilment of certain actions. This definition's validity as regards § 4a(2) of the Animal Protection Act need not be debated. The term "religious community" is, in any event, submitted by the legislature to the judgement of the relevant administrative authority, which is charged with evaluating a "religious community" on the basis of its current realization in daily life, its cultural tradition, and common as well as theological understanding of its tenets. This assessment eventually becomes a matter for the courts, which must interpret § 4a(2) of the Animal Protection Act in order to determine whether the respective religious community must clearly distinguish from non-members so that it is in a position to impose binding rules on its members.

As the predicate religious community, the complainant offers the Sunni branch of Islam. The complainant does not refer to any other religious community to which these customers might belong. And no other religious community is plausible in this case. In particular, as the complainant confirmed during the oral hearing in this case, these customers do not constitute a separate religious community apart from Sunnite Islam. For this reason, they represent neither a more distinct and clear separation from the outside world, nor do they possess the necessary internal coherence.

Section 4a(2)[2] of the Animal Protection Act requires the objective conclusion that there are binding rules of a religious community regarding the prohibition on slaughtering stunned animals. The concerned religious community must have clear rules that, in the administration's and courts' assessment, are regarded as binding in the self-conception of the community [...].

* * *

[Teleological Interpretation]

An individual point of view that relies solely on the subjective – albeit not seen as binding – religious belief of the members of a religious community is incompatible with the intention and purpose of the act as expressly stated in § 1 of the Animal Protection Act. According to this paragraph the act intends to make the life and wellbeing of animals part of humanity's responsibility and to prohibit that any animal be harmed or suffer pain, affliction or damage without good cause [...]. The legislature's intention to protect animals – and to prohibit slaughtering animals without first stunning them as part of this intention – would be undermined to a large degree if its observance were left to be decided upon by individuals as a result of a less-strict interpretation of § 4a(2)[2] of the Animal Protection Act.

[Historical Interpretation]

This interpretation of the norm is confirmed by the history of its promulgation. The norm was added to the Animal Protection Act of 1972 by an amending law enacted on 12 August 1986. During the debates on this amending law the Legal Committee of the *Bundestag* insisted that an exemption to the prohibition on butchering without stunning animals should be granted only if ritual slaughter was binding for members of a religious community. The Committee for Nutrition, Agriculture and Forestry rejected this position in its report on the law. The Committee for Nutrition, Agriculture and Forestry argued that the ambiguity of the word "binding" would require administrative agencies to interpret and assess the rules of religious communities. The Committee for Nutrition, Agriculture and Forestry concluded that this would not be acceptable in a religiously neutral *Rechtsstaat*. Against this decision the *Bundesrat* called upon the Mediation Committee [which negotiates disputes between the *Bundestag* and the *Bundesrat*] with the intention of clarifying in the law that the exemption from the general prohibition would be permitted only for "slaughtering techniques that are binding for members of certain religious communities." The *Bundesrat* also hoped to clarify in the law that ritual slaughter should only be permitted if required in cases accounted for by Article 4 of the Basic Law [which provides that "freedom of faith and of conscience, and freedom to profess a religious or philosophical creed, shall be inviolable" and that the "undisturbed practice of religion shall be guaranteed."]. In this respect, the *Bundesrat* underscored the fact that in some countries ritual slaughter would be the general slaughtering technique and that ritual slaughter would be an independent component of religious belief [and thus protected by Article 4 of the Basic Law] only in discrete cases.

The *Bundesrat* could not see the full extent of its proposals implemented [...]. The requirement that "binding rules of a religious community" serve as a predicate for the exemption was included in the amending law. [...]

This facet of the rule does not violate the constitution. In particular, it does not violate the basic rights of religious freedom laid down in Article 4(1) and (2) of the Basic Law.

This constitutional freedom certainly includes the (inner) freedom to believe or to not believe and it also includes the exterior freedom to manifest one's religious beliefs, to confess and to spread them [...]. This right, however, is not infringed by the denial of an exemption from the prohibition of ritual slaughter if the beliefs of those affected only prohibit them from the consumption of such meat [...].

The prohibition [...] does not infringe upon the possibility of an active realization of a religious commandment.

If the religion only prohibits the consumption of the meat of animals not ritually slaughtered, then the members of this religious community are not prevented from leading a certain way of life. They are neither factually nor legally bound to consume such meat contrary to their religious beliefs. With the prohibition, the consumption of *halal* meat is not prohibited. They may either resort to food of vegetable origin or rely upon meat imports from countries without such a prohibition. Certainly, meat may represent a common dish in our present-day society. Nevertheless, the abandonment of this type of food is not an unreasonable limitation of personal possibilities of development. The resulting difficulty in arranging a diet is reasonable if weighed against Article 2(1) of the Basic Law [Personal Freedom, general liberty clause] [...].

* * *

Questions/Comments

- Can you summarize the court's reasoning in the case? Why does the complainant lose his appeal?
- Does the Federal Administrative Court's decision, in style and approach, seem to be influenced by the Civil Law tradition or the Common Law tradition? Can you see evidence of both traditions in the judgment?
- The court concludes that enforcement of the prohibition on ritual slaughter was "reasonable" when "weighed against" the complainant's constitutional

9.3 Administering Islamic Law in Germany

right to personal freedom (Article 2(1) of the Basic Law). This is an example of the assessment of "proportionality in the narrower sense," which is the fourth and final step in the formalistic proportionality analysis described in Chapter 8.

- The Federal Administrative Court continued, in a portion of the decision not included here, by examining Article 3 of the Basic Law and concluded that, for two reasons, no unconstitutional inequality resulted from the enforcement of the Animal Protection Act's prohibition of ritual slaughter in this case. First, the underlying rule does not rely on the distinct content of a particular religious belief. Second, the criteria of an objectively identifiable, binding theological obligation is necessary to achieve the differentiation that satisfies the purpose of the animal protection rule. The court's consideration of the constitution's equality provisions represents yet another dimension of the *Rechtsstaatsprinzip*.

Consistent with the Federal Administrative Court's ruling, administrative authorities throughout Germany continued to reject applications for an exemption to the ban on ritual slaughter based on Muslims' understanding of the precepts of *Sharia*. At the same time, these authorities regularly granted the exemption to butchers who invoked Judaism's *kosher* dietary obligations. The different treatment given to Muslims and Jews, as becomes clear in the following case excerpt, is at least partially a result of the fact that Germany's small but growing Jewish community is rather denominationally cohesive and effectively represented in German society by a single organization, the Central Council of Jews in Germany (*Zentralrat der Juden in Deutschland*).[61] This means that experts summoned by administrative authorities or courts seeking to clarify the mandatory nature of *kosher* doctrine in Judaism in support of applications for exemptions under § 4a(2)[2] of the Animal Protection Act were less likely to give diverse or conflicting opinions.

Germany's Muslims, by contrast, are much greater in number and are a varied and denominationally diverse population. In that sense they are like Muslims everywhere. Perhaps the most significant of these divisions is the difference between Sunni Islam and Shia Islam. Although there are sects with varying degrees of orthodoxy in both of these denominations, one might generally expect a Sunni Muslim to more rigidly adhere to rules of Islamic Law such as the *halal* dietary restrictions. In any case, the broad interpretive range that exists in Islam generally, and within the denominations specifically, frequently leads to conflicting opinions regarding the mandatory nature of *halal*. German administrative authorities, impressed by these objective discrepancies, concluded that applications for exemptions to the ban on ritual slaughter need not be granted to Muslims, regardless of how strong the applicants' subjective religious conviction was regarding the *halal* dietary restrictions.

This is precisely what happened when administrative authorities in Hesse rejected Rüstem Altinküpe's application for an exemption from the Animal Protection Act's ban on ritual slaughter. A pious Sunni Muslim and butcher,

Altinküpe was a non-German who had operated a butcher shop in Germany for twenty years. The administration's denial was based on the conclusion that ritual slaughter was not "mandatorily required by the highest representatives of Sunni Islam," although Altinküpe and his customers believed themselves to be religiously bound to consume only the flesh of ritually slaughtered animals. Altinküpe ultimately filed a constitutional complaint with the Federal Constitutional Court against the administrative agency's denial of the exemption. The denial of an exemption had been confirmed by the lower administrative courts, and again in a final decision of the Federal Administrative Court. Altinküpe pointed out in his complaint to the Federal Constitutional Court that Jewish butchers had routinely been granted the exemption and he argued that he and his customers were entitled to the same treatment. Altinküpe challenged the rulings against him on the basis of: personal freedom (Article 2(1) of the Basic Law); equality (Article 3(1) and (2) of the Basic Law); religious liberty (Article 4(1) and (2) of the Basic Law); and occupational freedom (Article 12(1) of the Basic Law).

The case is a clear example of the significant role constitutional law and the Federal Constitutional Court play in German administrative law. How does the Federal Constitutional Court's *ex post* review of this administrative matter differ from the reasoning and standards used by the Federal Administrative Court in the preceding *Ritual Slaughter Case*?

Federal Constitutional Court
Ritual Slaughter Case
BVerfGE 104, 337 (2002)[*]

* * *

Judgment of the First Senate. [...]

* * *

The constitutional complaint is well-founded. The applicable provisions of the Animal Protection Act are compatible with the Basic Law. In this case, however, the challenged decisions do not stand up to review by the Federal Constitutional Court.

The Federal Constitutional Court's basis for review is, first and foremost, Article 2(1) of the Basic Law. In the original proceedings the complainant, a pious Sunni Muslim, sought and was denied an exemption from § 4a(1) of the Animal Protection Act. That provision prohibits the slaughter of animals that have not been stunned or anesthetized. The complainant sought the exemption in order to ensure that, in the practice of his occupation (butcher), his customers would be able to purchase and consume the meat of ritually slaughtered animals, that is, animals that had not been stunned or anesthetized before they were slaughtered. [...]

Because the complainant is not a German, but a Turkish, citizen, this activity is not protected by Article 12(1) of the Basic Law [providing that "all *Germans* shall have the

---

[*] Translated and permission granted by the Federal Constitutional Court.

right freely to choose their occupation or profession."]. The relevant provision in this context, then, is Article 2(1) of the Basic Law, particularly the protection that results from the special nexus between Article 12 of the Basic Law, which only applies to Germans, and Article 2(1), which applies to non-citizens. For the complainant, however, ritually slaughtering animals is not only a means for obtaining and preparing meat for his Muslim customers and himself. According to his statements it is also an expression of a basic religious attitude, which, for the complainant as a pious Sunni Muslim, includes the duty to slaughter animals in accordance with the rules of his religion. He regards these rules as binding. The complainant's statements to this effect were not cast into doubt in the challenged decisions. Even if ritually slaughtering animals is not seen as a religious act or practice in objective terms, the complainant's subjective view that it constitutes a religious practice must nonetheless be given consideration as part of and enhancing the protection of his occupational freedom under Article 2(1). His view of ritual slaughter as a religious practice enhances his occupational freedom because it constitutes a special liberty right (*Freiheitsgehalt*) of the kind that are protected as fundamental rights under the freedom of religion guaranteed by Article 4(1) and (2).

The general prohibition on ritually slaughtering animals encroaches upon the fundamental right under Article 2(1) [occupational freedom for non-citizens] in conjunction with Articles 4(1) and (2) [religious freedom] because it permits a Muslim butcher like the complainant to ritually slaughter animals only as an exception from the general requirement that slaughtered animals be stunned or anesthetized and only when the restrictive conditions established by § 4a(2) [2] of the Animal Protection Act have been found to exist. This encroachment, on its own, is not constitutionally objectionable because it can be adequately justified.

* * *

Recognizing humankind's responsibility for animals as our fellow creatures, the Animal Protection Act's purpose is to protect the life and well-being of animals. To that end, no one may inflict pain, suffering or damage upon an animal (§ 1 of the Animal Protection Act) without reasonable cause. The protection of animals secured by the Animal Protection Act is based on ethical principles, which are served by the general prohibition on ritual slaughter found in § 4a(1) in conjunction with the exemption to that general prohibition carved out by § 4a(2)[2]{2}. […] This is a legitimate aim for regulation of this sort, which takes the feelings of broad sections of the population into consideration, especially with a view to the ritual slaughter of animals.

* * *

The regulation is suitable and necessary for achieving the purpose of the regulation, that is, for extending the desired, ethical protection of animals to warm-blooded animals facing slaughter.

> [In this section of the opinion, the Court examined the Animal Protection Act and its supporting legislative justification. The Court held that the Act satisfied all the standards of constitutionality, including the principle of proportionality. The act was seen as a legitimate effort to minimize animal cruelty and suffering, while simultaneously carving out an appropriate exemption for religious persons who otherwise would be "unreasonably restricted" in the exercise of their fundamental rights by a general prohibition of ritual slaughter. As for the exemption, the Court concluded that it validly "requires exceptional permission because the parliament wanted to submit ritual slaughter to increased supervision by the state."]

* * *

[...] The parliament intended to ensure, through the collateral clauses to the exemption, that animals bound for slaughter are spared avoidable pain and suffering during their transport, immobilization, and the act of ritual slaughter itself. These safeguards are separate and apart from other regulations concerned with a butcher's expertise and personal aptitude. Over all, the parliament sought to achieve its aims by setting rules for the suitable premises, equipment, and other devices used when ritually slaughtering animals. Thus, the regulation intends to prevent, wherever possible, the domestic or other private performance of ritual slaughter. These settings, the parliament concluded, often do not ensure an effective and proper ritual slaughter. These settings can result in particularly acute suffering on the part of the animals involved. Instead, the parliament intended to promote slaughtering in approved slaughterhouses [...].

Apart from this, the prerequisite for the grant of an exemption is that, in the specific case, the needs of adherents of a religious group are to be met. It is the parliament's intent that these needs arise only out of mandatory provisions of a group's religion, that is, that the group's religion prohibits its adherents from consuming the meat of animals that are not ritually slaughtered. The fact that the law grants an exemption to its general prohibition on ritual slaughter only if this prerequisite is fulfilled inevitably means that some desired exemptions will not be granted. In the case of Islam, it must be acknowledged that the religion requires that animals be killed as gently as possible. This tenet was outlined in the expert opinion presented to the Court by the Muslims' Central Council in Germany. Thus, according to the rules of Islam, animals must be slaughtered in such a way that the death of the animal is accomplished as speedily as possible and that the animal's suffering is restricted to a minimum, with any kind of cruelty to the animal being avoided. [...]

* * *

The encroachment upon Muslim butchers' fundamental right to occupational freedom, however, is grave. Without the exemption provided by the Act it would not be possible for pious Muslims, like the complainant, to practice their occupation in the Federal Republic of Germany. Without an exemption they would have to restrict themselves to selling imported meat from ritually slaughtered animals, to choose to sell meat of animals that were not ritually slaughtered, or consider finding an altogether new occupation. These options, however, would lead to far-reaching consequences for the exercise of a butcher's freely chosen occupation. The decision to only market the imported meat of ritually slaughtered animals as a sales outlet would mean foregoing the craft of slaughtering animals but might also create uncertainty over whether the meat offered for sale really comes from ritually slaughtered animals and is, thus, suitable for consumption in accordance with the rules of the butcher's faith and that of his [or her] customers. The alternative possibility, namely to convert the butcher's business into a sales outlet for the meat of animals that were not ritually slaughtered, is even more intrusive. It would require the former butcher to win new customers. Finally, a complete occupational reorientation, provided that it is still possible in the specific situation of the individual concerned, would mean asking the former butcher to make a completely new start with his occupation and career.

The ban impacts the Muslim butcher and his customers. When they demand meat of animals that were ritually slaughtered, this is obviously based on the fact that they are convinced that their faith prohibits them, in a binding manner, from eating other meat. If they were required to forgo the consumption of meat as a result of the lack of available meat from ritually slaughtered animals, then the eating habits and preferences of the residents of the Federal Republic of Germany would not be properly accounted for. In Germany meat is a common food and it can hardly be regarded as reasonable that discrete populations might be required to involuntarily renounce its consumption. It is true that the consumption of imported meat makes such total renunciation unnecessary. But importing the meat of ritually slaughtered animals cannot replace the confidence customers have that religious rules have been satisfied that results from personal contact to the butcher. The consumption of imported meat must be plagued by doubts that the meat complies with the commandments of Islam.

These consequences for pious Muslim butchers and their pious customers must be weighed against the fact that Germans regard the protection of animals as a public interest of great importance. The Parliament has taken this into consideration by not regarding animals as objects but as fellow creatures, which also feel pain, and by protecting them with special laws [...]. Such protection is, above all, enshrined in the Animal Protection Act. [...]

* * *

Yet, an exemption from the requirement that warm-blooded animals be stunned or anesthetized before their blood is drained cannot be precluded if the intention connected with this exemption is to facilitate, on the one hand, the practice of a profession with a religious character, which is protected by fundamental rights, and, on the other hand, the observation of religious dietary laws by the customers of the person who practices the occupation in question. Without such exemptions the fundamental rights of those who want to slaughter animals without stunning them as a matter of their occupation would be unreasonably restricted, and the interest in protecting animals would, without a sufficient constitutional justification, be given priority in a one-sided manner. What is necessary, instead, is a regulation that, in a balanced manner, takes into consideration: (1) the fundamental rights that are affected; and (2) the aims that justify the ethical protection of animals.

* * *

[...] The Federal Administrative Court held that, in the case at hand, the prerequisites established by the Animal Protection Act for granting an exemption had not been satisfied because Sunni Islam, of which the complainant is an adherent, like Islam in general, does not mandate that Muslims consume only the meat of animals that were ritually slaughtered.

* * *

This interpretation does not live up to the meaning and the scope of the fundamental right secured by Article 2(1) in conjunction with Article 4(1) and (2) of the Basic Law. The result of this interpretation is that § 4a(2)[2]{2} of the Animal Protection Act is rendered ineffective for Muslims irrespective of their subjective religious convictions. This interpretation prevents butchers who intend to ritually slaughter animals from exercising their occupation [...] because these butchers, with a view to the faith to which they and their customers adhere, want to ensure the supply of meat from ritually slaughtered animals. This is an unreasonable burden for the persons concerned, which, in a one-sided manner, only considers the interests of the protection of animals. If it were interpreted in this manner, § 4a(2)[2]{2} of the Animal Protection Act would be unconstitutional on its face.

This result, however, can be avoided by interpreting the legal elements "religious group" and "mandatory provisions" in a manner that takes into account the fundamental right under Article 2(1) in conjunction with Articles 4(1) and (2). [...]

* * *

[...] In the case of a religion that, as Islam does, takes different views regarding whether ritual slaughter is mandatory, the point of reference of an assessment under the terms of the exemption is not necessarily Islam as a whole, or the Sunni or Shia denominations of this religion. The question whether tenets are to be regarded as mandatory must be answered with a view to the specific religious group in question, which may also exist as a subset of a particular denomination.

* * *

The challenged decisions issued by the administrative authorities and courts violate the complainant's fundamental right under Article 2(1) in conjunction with Article 4(1) and (2) of the Basic Law. The administrative authorities and courts misjudged the necessity and the possibility of a constitutional interpretation of § 4a(2)[2]{2} of the Animal Protection Act. In doing so they restricted the above-mentioned fundamental right in a disproportionate manner with their strict application of the Act's exemption to the ban on ritually slaughtering animals. The administrative authority's denial of the complainant's application for an exemption, and the administrative courts' endorsement of that denial were a result of this disproportionate restriction of the complainant's constitutional right. It cannot be ruled out that the complainant's customers, like the complainant himself, are members of a religious group that mandates that meat come from animals that were ritually slaughtered, and that, if the decision had been based on this fact, the complainant would have been granted the exemption in order to facilitate the consumption of the meat of ritually slaughtered animals by him and his customers.

As regards the challenged decisions, they are overturned pursuant to § 95 (2) of the *Bundesverfassungsgerichtsgesetz* [BVerfGG – Federal Constitutional Court Act]. The matter is referred back to the Federal Administrative Court because it can be expected that the dispute on a point of administrative law will be terminated there on the basis of the present judgment. [...]

* * *

Questions/Comments

- Proportionality is among the bases of constitutional review of administrative actions identified by Nolte, who described the Constitutional Court's proportionality analysis as "the last and decisive test of the validity of any restriction on the general principle of freedom of action (Article 2 (1), Grundgesetz)." In this chapter and in Chapter 8, I have pointed out that the proportionality analysis, as part of the broader proportionality principle, is one dimension of the Basic Law's fundamental commitment to the *Rechtsstaatsprinzip*. How does the Court use the proportionality analysis in the *Ritual Slaughter Case*?
- In 2002 an animal protection clause was added to the German Basic Law. Article 20a reads: "Mindful also of its responsibility toward future generations, the state shall protect the natural foundations of life and animals by legislation and, in accordance with law and justice, by executive and judicial action, all within the framework of the constitutional order." How would the elevation of animal protection from a mere statutory mandate to a constitutional value alter the Federal Constitutional Court's proportionality analysis in the *Ritual Slaughter Case*? Revisit Nolte's description of the exaggerated role the proportionality analysis has assumed in constitutional

9.3 Administering Islamic Law in Germany

and administrative law. Does such an ambiguous standard give the courts too much authority in German administrative law? Does the judiciary's role undermine both poles in Rose-Ackerman's dichotomy "between popular control and expertise"?

- Although the "undisturbed practice of religion" was a critical element in the case, the Federal Constitutional Court's decision rested mainly on the right to personal freedom under Article 2(1). The religious issue largely turned on whether the "objective" position of the Sunni denomination of the Islamic faith should trump the "subjective" theological views of the butcher and his customers. Why do you think the Court emphasized occupational freedom (Article 12 of the Basic Law) and personal freedom (Article 2 of the Basic Law) rather than engaging more extensively with the right to freedom of religion (Article 4 of the Basic Law)?

- Perhaps the following update on the case sheds additional light on the preceding question. Seven years after the Constitutional Court ruled in his favor, Altinküpe was still having difficulty obtaining an exemption to the Animal Protection Act's prohibition on ritual slaughter. One press report described the situation as a "regime of harassment" with local administrative authorities and courts competing with each other to create new barriers to the butcher's *de facto* enjoyment of the rights identified and reinforced in the Constitutional Court's 2002 decision.[62] A repeated tactic of the administrative authorities and lower administrative courts had been to delay deciding Altinküpe's application for an exemption and his appeal of the extraordinary requirements often imposed as part of a granted exemption. In one case, for example, he was ordered to have a veterinarian in attendance when performing the ritual slaughter. As the exemption is issued for only one year at a time, even the shortest delay in deciding the case rendered the matter moot when the year for which the exemption had been requested lapsed. In 2009, a three-justice chamber of the Federal Constitutional Court ruled that the difficulty and delay with which Altinküpe was confronted amounted to a violation of his right to an effective legal remedy guaranteed by Article 19(4) of the Basic Law.[63] It is precisely this constitutional provision that facilitates the extensive *ex post*, substantive judicial review that is characteristic of the Common Law nature of German administrative law.

- In reference to other issues arising from the nexus of the Basic Law and religion, Christoph Möllers remarked that "religious communities with a stable and defined organization are best situated to participate in a structured relationship with the state – in practice this means the Christian Churches. And it is not always easy to distinguish between factual disadvantages and conscious discrimination."[64]

- It must be said that Altinküpe, pictured in Figure 9.2 during the hearing of his case before the Federal Constitutional Court, seems to have been a victim of anti-Muslim sentiment, especially when one considers the fact that Jewish butchers faced considerably less bureaucratic difficulty when applying for the exemption to the ban on ritually slaughtering animals.

Rüstem Altinküpe, the German-Turkish butcher at the Federal Constitutional Court

Rüstem Altinküpe's attempts to obtain a *halal* exemption to the Animal Protection Act highlighted the challenges of accommodating the Islamic Legal tradition in the German legal culture. In addition to the long legal action Altinküpe pursued against obstructionist administrative authorities, his butcher shop was damaged by an arson attack in 2004.

Figure 9.2 Ritual Slaughter: The Intersection of German Administrative Law and Islamic Law
Source: Getty Images

Yet, even as the *Ritual Slaughter Cases* suggest that there is persistent and institutionalized suspicion towards Muslims in Germany, the cases also serve as evidence that the mere presence of a vibrant Muslim community (animated by the admirable persistence of advocates for religious freedom and equality such as Rüstem Altinküpe) is nudging Germany toward pluralism and integration. One aspect of this halting, progressive process is that it calls upon Germany's state-based, secular legal culture to engage with the tradition of Islamic Law. For many of Germany's Muslims, the dictates of Islamic Law have a normative force – creating rights and obligations – that are every bit as binding as the rules contained in the Civil Code or all the rest of Germany's state-based, secular law. This raises the prospect that, alongside the Civil Law tradition, the Common Law tradition, and the echoes of the Socialist Law tradition, the tradition of Islamic Law is yet another thread being woven into the tapestry of German legal culture.

The Islamic Law tradition is different to the predominant Civil Law tradition in ways that are more fundamental than the differences presented by the Common Law tradition. A starting point for any summary of the Islamic Law tradition must underscore that it is not a single, coherent social and normative system. Just as I insisted in Chapter 2 that the Civil Law tradition takes different forms, in different times and contexts, we also have to speak of traditions of Islamic Law. Diversity springs from the different interpretations generally applied by the religion's two grand denominations, Shia and Sunni Islam.[65] And it is the product of the prominent theological schools engaging with Islam's religious doctrine and law.[66] Diversity in Islamic Law also results

9.3 Administering Islamic Law in Germany

from the joints in the theology where religious doctrine and the law might be interpreted to respond to discrete or case-specific concerns. Finally, Islamic Law today shows the diversity that has resulted from its varied encounters with the state. In some Muslim-majority states that has involved Islamic Law as a consecrator of, or cohabitating with, state-based law.[67]

Still, it is possible to identify a number of features that distinguish Islamic Law as a distinct tradition. I will mention two of them here.

One distinct characteristic is that the sources of Islamic Law are regarded as divine, originating outside or beyond the state.[68] One consequence of *Sharia's* divinity is that it is final and definitive, at least with respect to its primary sources (the Koran and the Prophet's edicts known as the *Sunnah*). Even if they are nearly unchangeable in practice, codes and constitutions (as expressions of the Civil Law tradition and the Common Law tradition) are nevertheless quite dynamic. They can be changed by humans and human institutions through amendments, new statutory processes, and judicial interpretation. But the words of the Prophet are final and immutable.

Another difference is that Islamic Law blends law and morality in a way that is unknown to the political and positivist Western expression of law in the Civil Law tradition and the Common Law tradition. Recall, for example, that Kelsen's separation thesis (presented as archetypical of the Civil Law tradition in Chapter 3) demanded the strict separation of morality and law so that the task of the "pure law" jurist is to simply identify the properly postulated rule without regard for its justness. You'll recall (also from the discussion in Chapter 3) that Radbruch agonized over the moral bankruptcy of the positivists' insistence during the Nazi era that "the law is the law." Moral indifference of this kind is impossible in Islamic Law. As religious law, it addresses theology and ethics. But those facets are fully a part of *Sharia's* parallel legal function. Kamali explained that Islamic Law consists of "the totality of guidance that God has revealed to the Prophet Muhammad pertaining to the dogma of Islam, its moral values, and its practical legal rules."[69] This lends *Sharia* a logic and legitimacy that is different to other legal traditions, which must depend for their legitimacy on their democratic provenance, their alignment with social facts, their inherent logic, or their practical efficacy. Islamic Law is a regime of duties, in contrast to the rights created by statutes and contracts in secular legal traditions. And those duties have spiritual as well as legal consequences. In the former case, *Sharia* refers to conduct that is "recommended," "reprehensible," or "permissible."[70] In the latter case, *Sharia* speaks of "obligations," or "prohibitions." It is one system, but it accounts for both piety and legality.

Is there an irreconcilable conflict between the character of and values implicated by *Sharia*, on the one hand, and those inherent in Western legal traditions, on the other hand? The *Spiegel Online* article that follows suggests that there is. It reports on a case in Germany in which a judge denied an expedited divorce to a Muslim woman who had been physically abused by her Muslim husband. The judge in the case cited provisions of the Koran that can be interpreted as permitting husbands to physically abuse their wives in reaching the conclusion that the woman should have expected to live with violence in her marriage. The decision, much like the *Ritual Slaughter Cases*, set loose a storm of reactions and underscored the dilemma Germany faces in reconciling its traditional values (and the legal culture that help give them force) with those of its growing Muslim population. The article concludes that a "disturbing number of rulings are helping to create a parallel Muslim world in Germany that is welcoming to Islamic fundamentalists."

Does the following excerpt provide additional insight into the possibility that Altinküpe had been treated unfairly by the administrative authorities and courts?

Matthias Bartsch *et al.*
German Justice Failures: Paving the Way for a Muslim Parallel Society

[Translation by Christopher Sultan]

SPIEGEL ONLINE*

* * *

[…] Germany's only minister of integration at the state level, Armin Laschet, a member of the conservative Christian Democratic Union (CDU) from the state of North Rhine Westphalia, sees the [divorce court] ruling as the "last link, for the time being, in a chain of horrific rulings handed down by German courts" – rulings in which, for example, so-called honor killings have been treated as manslaughter and not murder.

This, says Berlin family attorney and prominent women's rights activist Seyran Ates, is part of the reason one should "be almost thankful that [the divorce court judge] made such a clear reference to the Koran. All she did was bring to the surface an undercurrent that already exists in our courts." Out of a sense of misguided tolerance, says Ates, judges treat the values of Muslim subcultures as a mitigating circumstance and, in doing so, are helping pave the way for a gradual encroachment of fundamentalist Islam in Germany's parallel Muslim world. It's an issue Ates often runs up against in her cases. [In the divorce case], she says, "someone expressed openly for the first time what many are already thinking."

Does Germany Already Have Sharia Law?

Ursula Spuler-Stegemann, an Islam expert from the central German university town of Marburg, has a similar take on the matter. "Do we already have *Sharia* here?" she asks, adding that the [divorce] case shows that "things are getting out of hand here."

Does the unspeakable decision by a single [divorce] court judge truly mark a new stage in the German judiciary's unspoken policy of appeasement toward aggressive Muslims? Or is the collective outcry so loud and nonpartisan this time because the case is so clear? Is it because everyone believed that the debate, raging for years and still unresolved, over the issue of how much immigration the Germans should tolerate and how much assimilation they can expect was finally coming to an end? And because this particular case was

---

* www.spiegel.de/international/germany/german-justice-failures-paving-the-way-for-a-muslim-parallel-society-a-474629.html. Excerpt reproduced with permission of *Der Spiegel*.

about violence, the lowest common denominator on which everyone from left-leaning feminists to neoconservatives could agree?

And now that the danger has been recognized, is it being addressed quickly? Not exactly.

* * *

Violating the Principles of Equal Treatment

For far too long, Germany's Muslim immigrants were not asked to put much effort into integrating. For decades, German judges essentially paved the way for Islamic fundamentalists to form a parallel society. They raised little opposition to the strategy employed by Islamic groups to demand their supposed religious freedom in court until they got it. But the judges must have known, argues Johannes Kandel, that "giving preferential treatment to groups violates the principle of equal treatment in a secular legal system." Kandel heads the intercultural dialogue group at the political academy of the Friedrich Ebert Foundation, which is closely aligned with the center-left Social Democrats.

Citing the freedom of religious expression guaranteed under the German constitution, judges in Germany permitted Muslims to withdraw their children from swimming lessons or to forbid them from taking part in school celebrations or school trips. This allowed outdated concepts of chastity from places like Turkey's highly traditional eastern Anatolia region to survive in an otherwise enlightened Europe. But religious freedom, says Udo Di Fabio, a judge on Germany's Federal Constitutional Court, the country's highest judicial institution, is no "basic right deluxe," but rather one of many constitutional rights – and one that constantly has to be weighed against other rights.

"We were far too negligent for much too long," says Andreas Jacobs, the coordinator for Middle East policy and Islamic countries at the Konrad Adenauer Foundation, which is aligned with the conservative Christian Democrats. Wolfgang Bosbach, the deputy chairman of the CDU's parliamentary group says he sees the [divorce] ruling as an indication "that we are gradually putting our own concepts of the law and values up for grabs." But Jacobs believes it is instead a kind of aftershock of the naïve multicultural illusions of recent decades.

A Much-Delayed Wake-Up Call

* * *

The clash of cultures [has drawn] Germany's attention to conditions that many had preferred to play down as "cultural diversity." Suddenly Germans were waking up to the creeping Islamicization on the fringes of their society, and to the existence of parallel worlds in German cities. Ironically, until only a few years ago all of this was happening with the enthusiastic support of the constitutional state and its servants.

German judges were accommodating Muslims in many minor rulings, and often with good reason. In 2002, the state labor court in the northern city of Hamm ruled that prayer breaks are permissible during working hours, but must be coordinated with the employer. The case had come to the fore after a company reprimanded a Muslim worker who wanted to pray several times a day. The worker demanded his rights, citing religious freedom.

In a number of cases dealing with halal butchering, German courts were forced to grant exceptions to Muslim butchers similar to those applied to butchers who adhere to Jewish kosher butchering rituals. In 2002, the Federal Constitutional Court issued a landmark decision allowing butchering according to Muslim ritual, after Rüstem Altinküpe, a butcher [...] filed a lawsuit.

* * *

Europe at a Crossroads

Berlin attorney Seyran Ates says: "We are at a crossroads, everywhere in Europe. Do we allow structures that lead straight into a parallel society, or do we demand assimilation into the democratic constitutional state?"

The answer is clear, at least if one studies the literature of conservative Muslims. For example, in his book "Women in Islam," Imam Mohammed Kamal Mustafa of Spain recommends how women should be beaten. If you beat their hands and feet with "whips that are too thick," he warns, you risk leaving scars. Abdelkader Bouziane, an Algerian imam who calls two women his own, recommends handing out beatings in such a way that the consequences are not apparent to infidels.

Although Islamic groups do their best to condemn marital violence, there are clear indications of how ubiquitous beatings are in many Muslim marriages. Experts say that a disproportionately high percentage of women who flee to women's shelters are Muslim. This sort of domestic violence in the family has even ended in death for more than 45 people in Germany in the last decade. According to an analysis by the Federal Office of Criminal Investigation on the "phenomenon of honor killings" in Germany, woman are often slaughtered in the most gruesome of ways for violating archaic concepts of morality. In many cases an entire family council has ruled on the execution of a rebellious female family member.

In 2005, Hatun Sürücü, a young Berlin woman, was killed because she was "living like a German." In her family's opinion, this was a crime only her death could expiate. Her youngest brother executed her by shooting her several times, point blank, at a Berlin bus stop. But because prosecutors were unable to prove that the family council had planned the act, only the killer himself could be tried for murder and, because he was underage, he was given a reduced sentence. The rest of the family left the courtroom in high spirits, and the father rewarded the convicted boy with a watch.

It is by no means unusual for people put on trial for honor killings in Germany to be convicted on the lesser charge of manslaughter in the end. In 2003 the Frankfurt District Court handed down a mild sentence against a Turkish-born man who had stabbed his German-born wife to death. She had disobeyed him and was even insolent enough to demand a divorce.

Muslim Moral Precepts as Mitigating Factors

The court argued that one could not automatically assume that the man's motives were contemptible. He had, after all, acted "out of an excessive rage and sense of outrage against his wife" – who he had regularly beaten in the past – "based on his foreign socio-cultural moral concepts." According to the court's decision, the divorce would have violated "his family and male honor derived from his Anatolian moral concepts." The Federal Constitutional Court reversed the decision in 2004.

Even though higher courts usually reverse these sorts of rulings, judges are still handing down sentences based on the same logic. For example, the municipal court in the western city of Leverkusen sentenced a Lebanese man to probation in 2005 after he had severely beaten his daughter several times for resisting his efforts to force her into an arranged marriage. He hit her on the head with a stick. When it broke he choked her and threatened to stab her to death. The court argued that the fact that his actions were based on his Muslim moral concepts served as a mitigating factor.

The district court in Essen was equally lenient when, in 2002, it sentenced a Lebanese man who had applied for asylum – and who routinely beat his children and wife with a belt and also raped his spouse – to nothing more than probation. The judge cited the man's cultural background as a mitigating circumstance. In commenting on his crimes, the man said: "I am a Muslim, a normal person. I pray, fast and fulfill my duties."

* * *

Questions/Comments

- The article mentions in passing the administrative law cases involving ritual slaughter. The other cases featured are drawn from private law, labor law, and criminal law. This suggests the breadth of the phenomenon. The German legal system is encountering Islamic Law in every jurisdiction and field of law where devout Muslims are living and working in German society. I will seize upon the article's references to criminal law to note that we will consider that field in Chapter 10. But the article's central case study – the abused wife who was denied an expedited divorce – involved family law. That is a part of the private law covered by the Civil Code. Would it be more acceptable to accommodate *Sharia* in private law than it would be in public law (such as administrative law)? Would your answer to that question change if you knew that many scholars believe that *Sharia* has a more developed tradition of private law than public law?[71]
- The story of the *Ritual Slaughter Cases* and the conditions portrayed by the *Der Speigel* article seem to contradict one another. On the one hand, the *Ritual Slaughter Cases* seem to expose deep and perhaps even conscious bias towards Muslims in Germany. On the other hand, the article claims that German society and institutions have been overly tolerant towards Muslims. The article suggests that tolerance towards Islam (and the dictates of the tradition of Islamic Law) is acceptable in the context of *halal* dietary rules and the right to pray at work. But an essential common denominator, the article says, must be the rejection of violence. Reflecting on the coverage of German constitutional law in Chapter 8, can you frame that argument in constitutional terms? Does that distinction justify the anxious tone of the article, or does the article expose the existence of a broader form of intolerance? Societies everywhere are becoming more diverse. There is also a profound new awareness of social injustice and discrimination that has given rise to new political movements. Is that true in your primary or "national" legal system? How is your primary or "national" legal system accommodating difference, correcting past and entrenched discrimination, and integrating new understandings of and approaches to law? Is the state involved in those efforts – perhaps through the authority exercised by the administration? If so, then administrative law is likely playing a key role in that encounter.

- Observant Muslims in these cases argue that German law must adapt to and accommodate the dictates of *Sharia* that guide their lives (as theology, morality, and law). The legal instrument for making that demand is the Basic Law's protection of religious freedom (Article 4). The article quotes former Constitutional Court Justice Udo Di Fabio as saying that religious freedom is not a preferred or prioritized right. Instead, he notes that rights must be weighed and balanced against one another. You now know that he is referring to the proportionality analysis, which, in the fourth step, calls for a weighing of the interests in a case (proportionality in the narrow sense). If German administrative law is influenced by and part of German constitutional law, then the extensive *ex post* judicial review that characterizes German administrative law will very often involve the courts' application of the proportionality analysis to competing rights. In fact, Nolte suggested that proportionality is the essence of German administrative law.

9.4 Conclusion

German administrative law, with its mix of statutory positivism and extensive substantive judicial review, seems to be a compelling example of the thesis that legal systems are the site of encounters between different legal traditions. From some vantage points the Civil Law tradition might seem more prominent in German administrative law. From other angles German administrative law's extensive reliance on *ex post* (and often constitutional) judicial review gives the jurisprudence a decidedly Common Law feel. German administrative law has served as a medium for the reconciliation (even hybridization) of those distinct legal traditions. At the same time, administrative law (and many other fields of law) seems to be struggling with the claim, raised by some German residents and citizens, that the state should respect and accommodate their desire that Islamic Law also play a role in organizing their lives. That negotiation may determine the future of German society. It certainly ensures the dynamism and diversity of German legal culture.

Further Reading

- Mashood A. Baderin, *Islamic Law: A Very Short Introduction* (Oxford University Press) (2021)
- *Oxford Handbook of Comparative Administrative Law* (Peter Crane & Peter L. Lindseth eds.) (Oxford University Press) (2021)
- *Comparative Administrative Law* (Susan Rose-Ackerman, Peter L. Lindseth & Blake Emerson eds.) (Edward Elgar) (2nd ed. 2017)
- Andrea Büchler, *Islamic Law in Europe? Legal Pluralism and Its Limits in European Family Laws* (Routledge) (2016)

- *The Judge and the Proportionate Use of Discretion: A Comparative Administrative Law Study* (Boudewijn de Waard & Sofia Ranchordás eds.) (Routledge) (2015)
- *Debates in German Public Law* (Christian Waldhoff & Hermann Pünder eds.) (Hart Publishing) (2014)
- Benedikt Pirker, *Proportionality Analysis and Models of Judicial Review: A Theoretical and Comparative Study* (Europa Law Publishing) (2013)
- Mohammed Hasim Kamali, *Shariʿah Law: An Introduction* (Oneworld Publications) (2010)
- *Islam and Muslims in Germany* (Ala Al-Hamarneh & Jörn Thielmann eds.) (2008)
- Martina Künnecke, *Tradition and Change in Administrative Law: An Anglo-German Comparison* (Springer) (2007)
- Mahendra P. Singh, *German Administrative Law in Common Law Perspective* (Springer) (2001)

NOTES

1 RENÉ DAVID & JOHN C. BRIERLEY, MAJOR LEGAL SYSTEMS IN THE WORLD TODAY 455 (3rd ed. 1985).
2 The dates do not match perfectly but Mahendra P. Singh confirmed that "[i]n 1808 Prussia transferred competence to adjudicate [some administrative disputes] to the ordinary civil courts leading to a separation between adjudication and the administration." MAHENDRA P. SINGH, GERMAN ADMINISTRATIVE LAW IN COMMON LAW PERSPECTIVE 22 (2001). This less-than-revolutionary engagement with the liberal spirit coursing through Europe and America at the end of the eighteenth century was a result of the Germans' "more positive relationship between the individual and the state, [the rejection of] political violence on the French scale and [a more ready deference] to king and country ... Germany's educated elite both challenged and defended established society. Therein lay a predilection for carefully controlled change, progress with good order – a society that could be both liberal and conservative at once." STEVE OZMENT, A MIGHTY FORTRESS 152, 161 (2004).
3 "[T]he civil service [...] has stood out for generations as one of the most influential forces in German life [...] looked upon by foreign observers as Germany's greatest contribution in the field of political organization and as an encouraging example for the whole world. It was indeed the German civil service which, long before Germany entered the era of industrialization with all its new governmental responsibilities, had already 'vitalized the state on its constructive side and its active rather than its passive aspects.'" Fritz Morstein Marx, *German Bureaucracy in Transition*, 28 AM. POL. SCI. REV. 467–468 (1934).
4 In 1872 the Prussian Supreme Administrative Court began its service, twenty-eight years before the German Civil Code entered into force.
5 OTTO MAYER, 1 DEUTSCHES VERWALTUNGSRECHT (3rd ed. 1924) (cited and translated in Georg Nolte, *General Principles of German and European*

Administrative Law – A Comparison in Historical Perspective, 57 MOD. L. REV. 191, 198 (1994)).

6 *See, e.g.,* GRUNDGESETZ FÜR DIE BUNDESREPUBLIK DEUTSCHLAND [GG] [BASIC LAW], art. 20(4) ("All Germans shall have the right to resist any person seeking to abolish this constitutional order if no other remedy is available.").

7 Marx, *supra* note 3, at 468–469. *See, e.g., "I'm from the Taliban and I'm Here to Help,"* THE ECONOMIST (July 7, 2022), www.economist.com/asia/2022/07/07/im-from-the-taliban-and-im-here-to-help.

8 That is a contested and fast-changing tradition in American administrative law. *See, e.g., Administrative Law Reform Legislation in the 116th Congress*, CONG. RSCH. SERV. (July 23, 2020), https://crsreports.congress.gov/product/pdf/LSB/LSB10523.

9 *See* GRUNDGESETZ FÜR DIE BUNDESREPUBLIK DEUTSCHLAND [GG] [BASIC LAW], arts. 1 (3) and 20 (3).

10 *See, e.g.,* Walter L. Dorn, *The Prussian Bureaucracy in the Eighteenth Century*, 46 POL. SCI. Q. 403, 404 (1931) ("[N]o one conversant with the evolution of modern Prussia can fail to see that the Prussian bureaucracy was for many decades the most creative force in Prussian history ... this bureaucracy not merely reformed itself but adapted the Prussian state to the conditions of modern life [...]."); GREG NEES, GERMANY: UNRAVELING AN ENIGMA 38–40 (2000).

11 *See, e.g.,* Dan P. Silverman, *Nazification of the German Bureaucracy Reconsidered: A Case Study*, 60 J. MOD. HIST. 496 (1988).

12 Edward J. Eberle, *The West German Administrative Procedure Act: A Study in Administrative Decision Making*, 3 DICK. J. INT'L L. 67 (1984).

13 *Id.*

14 *See* Verwaltungsverfahrensgesetz [VwVfG] [Administrative Procedure Act] May 25, 1976, revised Jan. 23, 2003, BGBl I at 2154, last amended by Act, May 5, 2004, BGBl. I at 718, art. 4.

15 The fundamental basis for the Civil Code's normative regime, a *Rechtsgeschäft* (an act with legal significance or a legal transaction) involves one or more person's declared intention that a legal obligation should be formed.

16 *See* Michael Ronellenfitsch, *Öffentliches Recht*, in EINFÜHRUNG IN DIE RECHTSWISSENSCHAFT 249, 355 (Kristian Kühl *et al.* eds., 3rd ed. 2019).

17 *See* Florian Hoffmann, *In Quite a State: The Trials and Tribulations of an Old Concept in New Times*, in PROGRESS IN INTERNATIONAL LAW 263 (Russell Miller and Rebecca Bratspies eds., 2008).

18 JÜRGEN HABERMAS, II THEORY OF COMMUNICATIVE ACTION (Thomas McCarth trans., 1981).

19 Susan Rose-Ackerman, *American Administrative Law under Siege: Is Germany a Model?*, 107 HARV. L. REV. 1279 (1993–1994).

20 Peter L. Lindseth, *Review Essay – Comparing Administrative States: Susan Rose-Ackerman and the Limits of Public Law in Germany and the United States*, 2 COLUM. J. EUROPEAN L. 589, 590 (1995–1996).

21 Rose-Ackerman, *supra* note 19, at 1281.

22 *See, e.g.,* HANS-ULRICH WEHLER, GERMAN EMPIRE 1871–1918 65–71 (Trans., 1985); Hans-Ulrich Derlien, *Public Administration in Germany:*

Political and Societal Relations, in BUREAUCRACY IN THE MODERN STATE: AN INTRODUCTION TO COMPARATIVE PUBLIC ADMINISTRATION 64, 89 (1995) ("Contrary to the Anglo-Saxon world, in Germany bureaucracy preceded democracy. This has had a lasting impact on the importance attributed to expertise ...").

23 Michael Nierhaus, *Administrative Law*, in INTRODUCTION TO GERMAN LAW 87, 88 (Mathias Reimann and Joachim Zekoll eds., 2005).
24 Chevron U.S.A., Inc. v. Natural Resources Defense Council, Inc., 467 U.S. 837 (1984).
25 Armin von Bogdandy & Peter M. Huber, *Staat, Verwaltung and Verwaltungsrecht in Deutschland*, in III IUS PUBLICUM EUROPAEUM: VERWALTUNGSRECHT IN EUROPA – GRUNDLAGEN UND WISSENSCHAFT (Armin von Bogdandy *et al.* eds., 2010).
26 SINGH, *supra* note 2, at 20–26.
27 *See* GRUNDGESETZ FÜR DIE BUNDESREPUBLIK DEUTSCHLAND [GG] [BASIC LAW], art. 83 ("The Länder shall execute federal laws in their own right insofar as this Basic Law does not otherwise provide or permit.").
28 Rose-Ackerman, *supra* note 19, at 1288.
29 *Id.* at 1297.
30 *Id.* at 1299.
31 *Id.* at 1289.
32 *Id.* at 1300.
33 *Id.* at 1289.
34 CHRISTOPH MÖLLERS, DAS GRUNDGESETZ 86 (2009).
35 Printz v. United States, 521 U.S. 898 (1997).
36 *Id.* at 976–978 (Breyer, J., dissenting).
37 Daniel Halberstam, *Comparative Federalism and the Issue of Commandeering*, in THE FEDERAL VISION 213, 216–217 (Kalypso Nicolaidis and Robert Howse eds., 2001).
38 Rick Hills, *Is Breyer's Pro-commandeering Argument in Printz the Worst Comparative Constitutional Law Ever?*, PRAWFSBLAWG, Sept. 9, 2008, http://prawfsblawg.blogs.com/prawfsblawg/2008/09/is-breyers-pro.html.
39 Rose-Ackerman, *supra* note 19, at 1290–1294.
40 SINGH, *supra* note 2, at 181 ("The wider judicial review of the indefinite legal concepts by the German courts is commensurate with their overall jurisdiction to review administrative decisions which is certainly wider than the judicial review jurisdictions of the courts in the common law countries.").
41 SINGH, *supra* note 2, at 121.
42 GRUNDGESETZ FÜR DIE BUNDESREPUBLIK DEUTSCHLAND [GG] [BASIC LAW], art. 19(4); *see* SINGH, *supra* note 2, at 123 ("In the German law the judicial review of administrative action stands on a much more clear and solid basis. Not only the Basic Law guranatees certain judicially enforceable basic rights but among such rights is also include the right to approach the courts in case any right of a person, including the rights other than the basic rights, is violated by public authority.").
43 NIGEL G. FOSTER & SATISH SULE, GERMAN LEGAL SYSTEM & LAWS 257 (4th ed., 2010).

44 *Id.* at 145.
45 James C. McKinley, Jr., *Oklahoma Surprise: Islam as an Election Issue*, N.Y. Times (Nov. 14, 2010), www.nytimes.com/2010/11/15/us/15oklahoma.html?ref=shariaislamiclaw.
46 Robert S. Leiken, *Europe's Angry Muslims*, 84 Foreign Aff. 120, 122 (2005).
47 Conrad Hackett, *5 Facts about the Muslim Population in Europe*, Pew Research Center (Nov. 28, 2017), www.pewresearch.org/fact-tank/2017/11/29/5-facts-about-the-muslim-population-in-europe/; *see also* Houssain Kettani, *Muslim Population in Europe: 1950–2020*, Int'l J. Env't Sci. & Dev. (Jan. 2010), www.researchgate.net/publication/241278288_Muslim_Population_in_Europe_1950_-_2020.
48 Hackett, *supra* note 47.
49 *Muslim life in Germany is diverse*, Federal Office for Migration and Refugees (Oct. 28, 2021), www.bamf.de/SharedDocs/Meldungen/EN/2021/211028-am-mld2020.html?nn=285460.
50 *Parliament Approves Ban on Full Veil in Public*, France 24 (Sept. 14, 2011), www.france24.com/en/20100914-french-parliament-approves-ban-full-veil-public-senate-law-fine-sarkozy-islam; Steven Erlanger, *France Enforces Ban on Full-Face Veils in Public,* N.Y. Times (Apr. 11, 2011), www.nytimes.com/2011/04/12/world/europe/12france.html.
51 *Europe Grapples with "Honor Killings,"* DW (June 24, 2004), www.dw.com/en/europe-grapples-with-honor-killings/a-1244406.
52 Paul Majendie, *Sharia Law in Britain Unavoidable: Archbishop*, Reuters (Feb. 9, 2008, 6:47 AM), www.reuters.com/article/us-religion-sharia/sharia-law-in-britain-unavoidable-archbishop-idUSL0790681320080209; *Archbishop's Lecture – Civil and Religious Law in England: A Religious Perspective,* Dr. Rowan Williams 104th Archbishop of Canterbury (Feb. 7, 2008), http://rowanwilliams.archbishopofcanterbury.org/articles.php/1137/archbishops-lecture-civil-and-religious-law-in-england-a-religious-perspective.html.
53 Nick Cumming-Bruce & Steven Erlanger, *Swiss Ban Building of Minarets on Mosques,* N.Y. Times (Nov. 29, 2009), www.nytimes.com/2009/11/30/world/europe/30swiss.html.
54 Jeff Diamant, *Europe Experienced a Surge in Government Restrictions on Religious Activity over the Last Decade*, Pew Research Center (July 29, 2019), www.pewresearch.org/fact-tank/2019/07/29/europe-experienced-a-surge-in-government-restrictions-on-religious-activity-over-the-last-decade/.
55 *German President's Call for Religious Tolerance Meets with Praise and Criticism,* DW (Apr. 10, 2010), www.dw.com/en/german-presidents-call-for-religious-tolerance-meets-with-praise-and-criticism/a-6070436.
56 *"Germany Does Away with Itself" – Thilo Sarrazin's Inflammatory Book*, DW, www.dw.com/en/germany-does-away-with-itself-thilo-sarrazins-inflammatory-book-03092010-people-and-politics/av-5970520.
57 *Germany Sees Almost 1,000 Anti-Muslim Crimes in 2017*, DW (Mar. 3, 2018), www.dw.com/en/germany-sees-almost-1000-anti-muslim-crimes-in-2017/a-42810445; *Attacks on German Muslims "Becoming More Violent,"* DW (Aug. 18, 2017), www.dw.com/en/attacks-on-german-muslims-becoming-more-violent/

a-40152226; *Muslims Face Increase in Online Attacks in Europe*, DW, www.dw.com/en/muslims-face-increase-in-online-attacks-in-europe/a-58201471.

58 *After Hanau Attack, Germany Steps up Protection of Muslims*, DW (Feb. 21, 2020), www.dw.com/en/after-hanau-attack-germany-steps-up-protection-of-muslims/a-52470189.

59 *German President's Call for Religious Tolerance Meets with Praise and Criticism*, *supra* note 55.

60 Tierschutzgesetz [TierSchG] [Animal Protection Act], May 18, 2006, BGBl. I at 1206, 1313, last amended by Act, Dec. 9, 2010, BGBl. I at 1934. These excerpts come from an excellent English-language translation of the Act. *See* www.animallaw.info/nonus/statutes/stdeawa1998.htm.

61 *See Central Council of Jews in Germany*, www.zentralratdjuden.de/en/topic/2.html.

62 Patrick Bahners, *Regime der Schikanen*, FRANKFURTER ALLGEMEINE ZEITUNG 31 (Oct. 8, 2009).

63 Bundesverfassungsgericht, 1BvR, Sept. 28, 2009, www.bundesverfassungsgericht.de/entscheidungen/rk20090928_1bvr170209.html.

64 MÖLLERS, *supra* note 34, at 105 (authors' trans.).

65 *See* MOHAMMAD HASHIM KAMALI, SHARI'AH LAW: AN INTRODUCTION 159 (2008)

66 *Id.* at 159.

67 *See* MASHOOD A. BADERIN, ISLAMIC LAW: A VERY SHORT INTRODUCTION 19 (2021).

68 *Id.*; Kamali, *supra* note 65, at 45.

69 Kamali, *supra* note 65, at 99.

70 *Id.* at 113.

71 Kali Robinson, *Understanding Sharia: The Intersection of Islam and the Law*, COUNCIL ON FOREIGN RELATIONS (last updated Dec. 17, 2021, 2:00 PM), www.cfr.org/backgrounder/understanding-sharia-intersection-islam-and-law.

10

German Criminal Law

Key Concepts

- ***Strafgesetzbuch***: The German Criminal Code enacted in 1871, shortly after Prussia unified Germany. The Criminal Code is still in force and largely unchanged. It consists of two parts. A general part (*Allgemeiner Teil*) addresses broad principles or issues potentially applicable to any crime. A special part (*Besonderer Teil*) identifies specific crimes (including their elements and the prescribed punishments) arranged in categories, such as "crimes against the democratic rule of law," "crimes against the person of a sexual nature," or "crimes against another person's property."
- ***Straftatsystem***: Three-step framework for determining whether a suspect acted criminally and must suffer a criminal sanction. The steps of the analysis include: (1) *Tatbestand* – whether the facts align with the statutory elements of a crime (*actus reus* and *mens rea*); (2) *Rechtswidrigkeit* – whether fulfillment of the elements of a crime also were unlawful because no objective justification for the conduct exists (such as self-defense); and (3) *Schuld* – whether the suspect is blameworthy because no subjective excuse exists.
- ***Schuld***: Blameworthiness is a central concept in German criminal law. It is the third of three elements of a crime in the German *Straftatsystem*. Out of respect for a suspect's humanity, a court will not find that a suspect acted criminally if a subjective excuse diminishes his or her blameworthiness. Statutorily established excuses include necessity (as a defense), a lack of responsibility due to mental illness, or a mistake of law.

Study Tips

The Ministry of Justice and Federal Office of Justice provide English-language translations of a number of important German codes and statutes at the website "Gesetze im Internet" (www.gesetze-im-internet.de/). This includes the *Strafgesetzbuch* (StGB or German Criminal Code).

German law has served as an export to, or model for, other legal systems around the world. The German Civil Code has a wide sphere of influence. And many of the world's high courts are modeled on Germany's Federal Constitutional Court.

But some suspect that all of that interest in German law is rather modest when compared to the immense global impact of German criminal law. One prominent scholar of comparative criminal law pointed out that "German criminal law theory has been particularly influential in Spain, Latin America, Japan, South Korea, and Taiwan, as well as in several Eastern and Southern European countries." This led him to conclude that "the sun never sets on German criminal law theory."[1] The influence of German criminal law now also extends to a "decisive" impact on international criminal law.[2]

These claims for the global prominence of German criminal law already point to some of its key features. For example, in the quote above it is referred to as "German criminal law theory," and not merely as "German criminal law." That suggests the richly (perhaps excessively) theoretical and abstract nature of German criminal law. Those "scientific" qualities are confirmed by the ease with which German criminal law – functioning something like a neutral operating system – could be taken up in so many other jurisdictions.

The system is primarily expressed through the *Strafgesetzbuch* (StGB or German Criminal Code), which has been in operation in more or less the same form since 1871. That makes it three decades older than the revered German Civil Code. The German Criminal Code consists of two highly systematized books. The first is the *Allgemeine Teil* (general part), which addresses issues relevant to all crimes, such as the problem of "attempt," the framing of defenses and justifications to criminal conduct, statutes of limitations on prosecution, and the framework of criminal punishments. The second book, known as the *Besonderer Teil* (special part), provides concrete elements for scores of discrete crimes that are arranged in more than thirty categories. These are as typical as "offenses against life" and "forgery of documents." And they are as distinctly German as "offenses against the environment" and "insult." Somewhat counterintuitively, German criminal law practice often starts with an application of the facts of a case to the elements of a discrete crime outlined in a paragraph of the special part (second book) before moving on to resolve the more abstract issues covered by the general part (first book).

Like so much else in German law, the analysis and application of criminal law under the Criminal Code is formalistic, even formulaic. That quality aims at eliminating (or at least reducing) politics, power, prejudice, arbitrariness, emotion, and irrationality from the criminal justice enterprise. This ambition is an echo of two factors. First, it is the Enlightenment's correction on the unlimited power of the king. Second, in the post-war era, it is positive law's correction on the unlimited power wielded by the Nazis. The answer to both of these troubling expressions of arbitrary power in criminal law has been the hope that, if constructed carefully enough, the German Criminal Code could channel and constrain the ominous power the state wields when enforcing order. In that sense, it is related to the statutory positivism that characterizes one part of German administrative law (as discussed in Chapter 9). The Criminal Code's "rational principles [should serve as] the guarantors of civil liberties" and fulfill a uniquely German yearning for legal certainty.[3] In this sense, Germans believe that the Criminal Code makes it possible to arrive at a "correct solution" to a criminal case similar to the way that math problems have a correct answer.

The Enlightenment fostered the enduring aspiration for rationality in German criminal law. It also elevated the autonomous individual as the key subject of the criminal law regime.[4] Once again, the opposite side of that coin is the diminishment of the state's prerogative over criminal law. This is what Vormbaum and Bohlander referred to as the "humanization" of German criminal law. It called for greater respect – even sympathy – for the accused.[5] That priority in German criminal law was strengthened after World War II. Germany's commitment to a "humanized" criminal law takes many forms. Perhaps most conspicuous for an American encountering the system are the comparatively mild punishments German criminal law imposes.[6] The aim of German criminal punishment is "positive general prevention" oriented to the entire community, and not retribution or incapacitation focused only on the criminal. But more profoundly, as you'll see in this chapter, the centrality of the autonomous individual in German criminal law is especially realized through the *Schuldprinzip* (principle of blameworthiness), which requires the criminal court to assess the extent of the defendant's "blameworthiness" as a distinct component of the crime, as well as a factor in determining a punishment.

Even if the German Criminal Code is old and entrenched, it is better to understand German criminal law as a history of continual reform. These efforts, involving scholars as much as parliamentarians, often take decades. That means the reforms sometimes arrive already having missed the moment in history and jurisprudence to which they were meant to respond. So, the process of reform starts over – most recently in the wake of reunification with a major reform enacted in 1998.

All of this suggests that German criminal law is *scientific*, *systematic*, and *sympathetic*. That contrasts sharply with American criminal law, which could be characterized as *parochial*, *political*, and *punitive*. Yet, in keeping with this book's vision, I will urge you to consider whether there are currents of contingency in Germany's criminal law regime. The rational, scientific, and objective edifice has cracks that sometimes permit a more politicized, emotional, and unpredictable approach to criminal law. That would allow me to argue that this is another unexpected, unorthodox thread woven into the tapestry of German law. Ironically, as this chapter's presentation of the infamous *Frankfurt Police Torture Case* reveals, that development has in part been facilitated by the *Schuldprinzip*, which is the most German of all theoretical criminal law concepts.

10.1 The Theory and Logic of German Criminal Law

German criminal law has a long history marked by theoretical and scholarly innovation, codification, and periodic reform. Like all other parts of German legal culture, German criminal law also was marked by the perversions of the National Socialist dictatorship and the post-war division of the country. But the values and logic established by the 1871 *Strafgesetzbuch für das Deutsche Reich* (Criminal Code for the German Empire) have persisted – now as the *Strafgesetzbuch* – even while they have been subject to refinement.[7]

The Prussian Criminal Code from 1851 served as a functional framework for the criminal law regime implemented in the German Reich after 1871. Building from that Prussian model, the new all-German Criminal Code was drafted and debated in just three years – a relative sprint when compared to the three decades it took to finalize the German Civil Code. In terms that echo the admiration lavished on the German Civil Code, Vormbaum and Bohlander characterize the Criminal Code as "one of the last great works" of the "liberal age of criminal law."[8] It seems that Germans are quite proud of their law codes!

One of the new Criminal Code's achievements was to give the accused's culpability a more complex theoretical framing. This extends to the differentiation between intent and negligence in various ways with respect to various crimes. Vormbaum and Bohlander explain that it also involves the theoretically subtle principle of *Schuld* (blameworthiness), which came into focus in German criminal law in the second half of the twentieth century.

> In the tradition of Kantian philosophy, it was assumed that the offender was autonomous, and thus the psychological concept of [*Schuld*] blameworthiness forms the basis of the Code [...]. An offender who could not be held responsible was thus to be acquitted and was thus no longer the responsibility of criminal justice [...].[9]

Markus Dirk Dubber, a renowned comparative criminal law scholar, provided an excellent introduction to the *Schuldprinzip* and other key features of German criminal law.

Markus Dirk Dubber
The Promise of German Criminal Law: A Science of Crime and Punishment
6 GERMAN LAW JOURNAL 1049, 1049–1057, 1060, 1066–1069 (2005)[*]

Introduction

* * *

[...] [S]ome features of German criminal law theory have attracted considerable attention among Anglo-American criminal law scholars, most notably the German system for the analysis of criminal liability, or "criminal offense system" (Straftatsystem). [The

---

[*] Excerpt reprinted with permission of the author.

tripartite (or "structured") system of analysis appears in American casebooks, textbooks, and court opinions, though its German origins are not always acknowledged. Developed in the early twentieth century,] [t]he *Straftatsystem* distinguishes between three levels of inquiry: satisfaction of all offense elements as defined in the statute (*Tatbestandsmäßigkeit*), wrongfulness (*Rechtswidrigkeit*), and culpability (*Schuld*). This general analytic system applies to all questions of criminal liability, no matter what the offense. Underlying it is the notion that there is such a thing as a general part of criminal law – and of a criminal *code* – that contains the general principles of criminal liability governing all offenses defined in the criminal law's – and the criminal code's – special part.

The common law of crimes, by contrast, concerned itself with crimes, as its name suggests. Such "general part" matters as self-defense, public duty, law enforcement, and crime prevention were instead thought of as questions of the law of particular offenses, most importantly homicide.

Under the German tripartite system, the inquiry into criminal liability begins with the special part. Once a potentially applicable offense definition [*Tatbestand*] has been found there – say, because someone has intentionally caused the death of another human being, thus satisfying the definition of murder, at least on its face – the inquiry proceeds to the second level, wrongfulness [*Rechtswidrigkeit*]. Here the question is whether the conduct in question was not only facially criminal, but unlawful (or wrong, in a legal sense – *rechtswidrig*, contrary to law) as well. In terms of Anglo-American criminal law, the question is whether the conduct is justifiable. (So, to stick with our example, the question might be whether the accused killed in self-defense, i.e., in order to prevent a deadly unlawful attack against him.)

Eventually, assuming the conduct matches the definition of some offense and is unlawful, the inquiry turns to the third, and final, step, which homes in on the actor's responsibility [*Schuld*] for her concededly criminal and unlawful conduct. Here Anglo-American criminal law, with its traditional procedural approach, considers whether the defendant can raise an excuse "defense." (For instance, instead of claiming self-defense as justification, the accused might be entitled to the insanity defense on the ground that he cannot be held responsible for his criminal and unlawful conduct because he lacked some minimum capacity to appreciate the wrongfulness of his conduct or to exercise sufficient self-control.)

* * *

The Idea of Criminal Law as Science

An eminent Spanish criminal law scholar recently praised the German system of criminal law as "an imposing construct that must be considered one of the great achievements of the human sciences." The results of two centuries of German criminal law theorizing, and of well over a century of concerted doctrinal systematizing (beginning in earnest with the creation of the German Empire and its German Criminal Code in 1871), are indeed impressive. Assembled by generations of scholars and their stables of assistants, who themselves join the professoriate after producing – as is the German custom – two book-length monographs on a criminal law subject, the German system of criminal law is unparalleled in comprehensiveness and complexity.

The serious and sustained attention criminal law theory has received in Germany frequently has been contrasted with the comparative neglect of this subject in Anglo-American jurisprudence, which traditionally has taken a greater interest in matters of private law and, at least in the United States, of constitutional law.

10.1 The Theory and Logic of German Criminal Law

It's not uncommon, in fact, to find German criminal law defining itself, and occasionally its scientific achievements, in explicit contrast to Anglo-American criminal law. This contrast has not gone unnoticed in the German literature. A popular treatise, for example, justifies the very project of German criminal law theory by citing the famous nineteenth-century English case of *Regina v. Dudley & Stephens*, about murder and cannibalism after a shipwreck on the high seas. We need a theory of crime that attempts to "theoretically capture punishable conduct in its entirety through the enumeration of general characteristics," the authors explain, precisely because without it the "solution of this case remains uncertain and dependent upon emotional considerations." The English judges would have been better off, so the argument goes, had they enjoyed the benefit of the tripartite analysis of criminal law developed by German criminal law theory (decades after the decision in *Dudley & Stephens*), with its "differentiation of the concept of crime into offense definition, illegality, and guilt and the further distinctions connected to it, such as that between necessity as a justification and as an excuse." Had they not proceeded upon the – it turns out, incorrect – assumption that necessity could only justify, but not excuse, the authors suggest, the English judges would have solved the case correctly, namely by acquittal on the ground of necessity as an excuse, rather than sentencing the defendants to death for murder, only to see the sentence reduced to six months by way of royal pardon later on.

Now the notion that there could be such a thing as a *solution* to a case, which might be correct or not, is quite foreign to Anglo-American law, which instead emphasizes that there are always different ways of analyzing a case, and different ways of resolving it, depending not only on the formulation of the relevant legal norms but also, equally important, on the statement of the facts of the case. Similarly unfamiliar is the idea that a system of criminal law would qualify as a *scientific* achievement (never mind one that would rank among "the great achievements of the human sciences"). These two features of German criminal law are related: there is a solution to every case because law is a science. [It is the job of a system of criminal law, as a body of scientific knowledge, to solve cases.]

* * *

The Role of the Professoriate

* * *

The German Criminal Code [...] is remarkably short. It's noteworthy not so much for what it contains, but for what it leaves out. One example is the definition of the various types of *mens rea* – intention (*Vorsatz*) and negligence (*Fahrlässigkeit*). The American Model Penal Code devotes great effort to this task. It would be no exaggeration to say, in fact, that the section defining the four mental states (purpose, knowledge, recklessness, and negligence) is the core of the entire Model Code, and its most important contribution to law reform. The German criminal code, by contrast, does not define the mental element of crime. Definitions were proposed on the occasion of the basic reform of the general part of the German code in the 1970s. They were removed, however, for the explicit purpose of leaving their continued refinement to the development of legal science.

Although the influence of the professoriate waned in the late twentieth century, it remains considerable to this day. German law students are required to take three semesters of substantive criminal law, and at least one semester of criminal procedure. These comprehensive courses traditionally have followed a strict lecture format, with the professor often sticking so closely to a prepared script that students' lecture notes are bound and sold to incoming students. The primary teaching tools are not collections of court opinions, but textbooks written by professors and, for more ambitious students, treatises.

***

The professoriate's influence on the doctrine of criminal law, however, goes beyond the training, and official examination, of its practitioners. Traditionally, criminal law professors have played an important role in criminal code drafting and reform. The Bavarian Penal Code of 1813, hailed as the first modern German criminal code, was drafted by a professor, Paul Johann Anselm Feuerbach, who is considered the founder of modern German criminal law. Feuerbach's draft in turn resulted from his criticism of a draft submitted by another professor (by the curious name of Gallus Aloys Kleinschrod). Professors took part in the fundamental reform of the German criminal code in the 1970s not only directly, through participation in the official parliamentary drafting commission, but also indirectly, through the development and publication of a comprehensive, and influential, "Alternative Draft." Unlike the American Model Penal Code, which was drafted by the American Law Institute from 1952 to 1962 under the direction of Professor Herbert Wechsler of Columbia Law School with the significant contribution of leading judges like Learned Hand, the authors of the Alternative Draft had no institutional affiliation, or backing, beyond their status as criminal legal scientists.

To their great chagrin, the German professoriate had little influence on the recent revision of the code's special part, raising the specter of "Legislation Without Criminal Legal Science." Legislatures' failure to pay sufficient heed to advancements in German criminal legal science has become a common complaint among German criminal law professors [...].

***

The professoriate's greatest influence on German criminal law, however, has come not through teaching, state examinations, legislation, or adjudication, but through the publication of treatises, textbooks, and code commentaries. The doctrinal literature on German criminal law, which has been accumulating since the early nineteenth century, is vast in every respect. Not only does it reach every nook and cranny of doctrine; it creates, or rather discovers, the nooks and crannies in the first place. The comprehensive and complex artifice that is German criminal law is almost entirely a creation of the German professoriate. Even though the influence of the judiciary has increased over the past century, it still cannot match the scope and depth of the professoriate's continuing scientific output.

In the traditional German model of criminal law as science, to the extent that the judiciary participates in the construction of criminal law doctrine, it does so mostly by adopting a particular solution, or approach, favored by a particular scientific school. In fact, German judicial opinions in criminal law, of which there are many because every decision in every case must be supported by reasons in writing, read more like expert reports than like opinions of common law courts. They closely follow the tripartite analytic structure of criminal law science, which has remained more or less unchanged since it was developed by professors – not the judiciary or the legislature – in the early twentieth century. Generally short on facts, and long on legal rules, these opinions reflect the abstract style traditionally favored by German criminal law science.

[The following text was included in an original draft of the article at footnote number 34: Judges, it should be noted, are appointed immediately upon graduation from university primarily on the basis of their performance on the state exams. They have no practical legal experience apart from the two-year apprenticeship sandwiched between the first and second set of state exams. Upon appointment, judges are promoted through the ranks from trial to appellate courts based on their performance, as evaluated by their superiors in the judicial hierarchy.]

It has been said that civil-law court opinions are addressed not so much to the public but to fellow judges. Although an obvious oversimplification, there is some truth in this observation, except that in the case of German criminal law, the audience includes not only one's judicial superiors, but the professoriate as well.

Substance and Procedure

* * *

[…] The heart of substantive German criminal law, by contrast, is its "general theory of crime" which lays out the "general legal prerequisites of punishability."

In German criminal law, substance takes priority over procedure. Substantive criminal law concerns itself with the legal principles that are then, subsequently, applied in the criminal process. How these principles are applied, or by whom, is irrelevant for purposes of determining what they are, or should be. Considerations of evidentiary convenience, for instance, are therefore *by definition* out of place in discussions of substantive criminal law.

* * *

Criminal Law as Taxonomy

* * *

[The] classificatory approach to criminal law science has three main effects […].

* * *

[Most significantly], the taxonomical mode of German criminal law lends itself to a certain formalism. Arguments are not infrequently resolved by definition, or rather by classification. Once an issue has been properly classified, it has been properly resolved. Given the care with which it has been assembled, and continues to be maintained, it is perhaps not surprising that the classificatory system of German criminal law is asked to do considerable rhetorical work. If the categories are correct, and an issue has been correctly categorized, then the issue has been correctly resolved, or so the syllogism goes. In other words, the time that common criminal lawyers spend on fretting over the proper resolution of a particular case, German criminal lawyers instead dedicate to the correct construction of a system for the resolution of all cases. The more effort goes into the building and quality control of the juridical apparatus, the less effort need go into output control. And so indefinite preventive detention, for instance, is legitimate *because* it is classified not as a "punishment," but as a "measure," and large fines against corporations are legitimate *because* they are classified as "monetary fines" (or, once again, as a "measure") for "order violations" rather than as "punishments" for "crimes," and so on.

* * *

The danger of this taxonomical formalism is, of course, that it may deflect attention from the search for justification, and ultimately legitimation. If the task of the criminal law scientist consists exclusively of identifying – and then filling – gaps within the entirely autonomous system of criminal law, the scientific achievements of German criminal law will be appreciated only by fellow practitioners. Outside observers – including legislators, the public, and even Anglo-American criminal law scholars – may find themselves mystified and, ultimately, unconvinced.

* * *

Questions/Comments

- At the end of this excerpt Dubber wonders if German criminal law's self-referential practice, which contributes to its impressive complexity and theoretical sophistication, makes it less appealing to "outside observers." But Dubber and many others have noted the roaring export success of German criminal law, which has influenced legal systems all over the world. How would you reconcile these seemingly contradictory claims?
- As you've seen with other areas of the law, German criminal law is thought to be "scientific." What does Dubber point to as evidence of this? Is the idea that there is a "correct solution" to a criminal case familiar to you? Is it realistic? Why would it be particularly desirable to think about criminal law (as opposed to private law or public law) in that way? At the same time, Dubber claims that German criminal law's scientific character can be contrasted with the general lack of theoretical (scientific) grounding for Anglo-American criminal law. If that portrayal is justified, then what force or logic might animate the foundation and development of Anglo-American criminal law? Dubber says some German critics of Anglo-American criminal law worry about the "uncertain" outcomes that tradition produces as a result of the weight given to "emotional considerations." Are flexibility and the accommodation of emotion negative attributes in a criminal law regime?
- How do legal scholars influence and impact German criminal law? Dubber gives Germany's criminal law scholars pride of place with respect to the field's development and reform. Another celebrated comparative criminal law scholar paints a more complex picture. George Fletcher noted that reform of German criminal law is not achieved through abruptly enacted changes to the Code, as might be the case in the more politicized American context. Instead, Fletcher explained:

> It is important to understand that this is not the current Continental mode, particularly not the German mode, of legal development. The function of legislation is not to slash through Gordian knots. These knots must come unraveled slowly, with painstaking care, first in the theoretical literature and then in the courts. The final stage of development is recordation of the prevailing view in a new statute. [Reform results from] a consensus reached after intensive theoretical debate, adjudication and finally the emergence of what the Germans call a "prevailing theory" (*herrschende Lehre*).[10]

Fletcher describes a process in which interpretation and innovation by the courts play a fundamental role in the evolution and refinement of the criminal law. In fact, Dubber seems to concede as much when he acknowledges that scholars face a diminishing role in the German criminal law enterprise. Does an increased role for judges in law's development fit with your understanding of a legal system predominantly influenced by the Civil Law tradition? The main judicial protagonist in German criminal law is the *Bundesgerichtshof* (BGH or Federal Court of Justice). The Federal Court of

10.1 The Theory and Logic of German Criminal Law

Justice, discussed more fully in an excerpt in Chapter 5, is the last-instance court in criminal matters and it is the definitive interpreter of the Criminal Code. Four of its senates are based at the Court's main home in Karlsruhe. But, since reunification, a fifth senate has also been based in Leipzig.

- Dubber explains that in German criminal law, substance takes priority over procedure. He calls this the "substantiveness of German criminal law." How would the alternative – procedural criminal law – function? How do the two approaches protect the rights and interests of the accused? A key factor in the reduced importance of procedure in German criminal justice, Dubber explains, is the absence of a lay jury. Many German criminal proceedings are administered by professional judges who are accompanied by *Schöffen* (lay judges). The lay judges develop extensive experience and familiarity with the law through long terms of service at the court. Still, there is a tendency for the lay judges to defer to their professional colleagues on the bench. This makes procedural and evidentiary issues less important because, "without a group of impressionable and confusable lay people [...] there is less of a need to carefully limit what evidence is introduced and, once introduced, how it is to be presented, and weighed." Dubber goes on to conclude: "Not only the jury is missing [...] so is the adversarial process." The meaning of this point – and the distinction it implies between "adversarial process" (typical in countries influenced by the Common Law tradition) and "inquisitorial process" (typical in countries influenced by the Civil Law tradition) – will be considered in Chapter 11.

- The German Criminal Code entered into force in 1871. What would have prompted the promulgation of a new criminal code in that era? The answer to that question underscores the important social and political function criminal law plays in shaping a national culture and reinforcing a state's authority. This was confirmed in 2009 when, in a major decision establishing limits on Germany's integration into the European Union, the German Federal Constitutional Court ruled that criminal law must remain a *national* German legislative competence and may not become a competence of the *supranational* European Union. The Court reasoned: "Particularly sensitive for the ability of a constitutional state to democratically shape itself are decisions on substantive and formal criminal law [...]. [The] administration of criminal law depends on cultural processes of previous understanding that are historically grown and also determined by language, and on the alternatives that emerge in the process of deliberation which moves the respective public opinion."[11] Doesn't this view conflict with German criminal law's scientific (objective and universal) aspirations? How is the criminal law in your primary or "national" legal system representative of that jurisdiction's "historically grown" culture?

- Dubber suggests that the priority on classification and conceptualization in German criminal law give the system a formalistic character. The cost of this, he notes, might be the field's reduced legitimacy. Why might German

criminal law's yearning for scientific objectivity and systematic predictability fail to inspire Germans' confidence, not to mention their allegiance?
- Based on the excerpt from Dubber, what would you say the fundamental characteristics of German criminal law are?

Dubber praises the theoretical integrity of the German Criminal Code, which he calls "comprehensive and complex." The finely tuned system advances its vision of objectivity and restraint wherever the state seeks to exercise its monopoly on violence through the medium of criminal sanctions. But it has not always been possible to hold a more politicized and contingent approach to criminal law at bay. Vormbaum and Bohlander note that supplementary criminal law provisions have often been enacted alongside the Criminal Code. In the middle of the twentieth century, for example, the Nazis enacted *Strafrechtliche Nebengesetze* (supplementary criminal laws) to help them seize control of the economy and to advance their racist agenda.[12] At the turn of this century new offenses concerned with intellectual property, economic matters, immigration, the social welfare regime, and the shipping and transport sectors were added.[13] Vormbaum and Bohlander report that this alternative universe of more politically responsive criminal law has taken the form of a large number of *Bekämpfung* acts aimed at "combatting" the social problems of the moment, often in response to popular alarm stoked by the tabloid press, including: drug crimes, the protection of children, crimes related to the accessibility of East German *Stasi* files, anti-terrorism measures, and Germany's domestic implementation of an International Criminal Code in support of the Rome Statute and the newly established International Criminal Court.[14] This tradition of popular and political uses of the criminal law, although measured when compared with American criminal law's practice of enacting harsh, reactive criminal legislation, points to gaps and outgrowths in the regime established by the Criminal Code. This might suggest the erosion of the system's pursuit of scientific objectivity and certainty.

Nevertheless, the Criminal Code dominates the field of criminal law. Much like its venerated younger sibling (the Civil Code), the Criminal Code remains in force today in more or less the same form as when it was enacted in the late nineteenth century. But the Code has undergone periodic reform and revision, with at least six omnibus reforms enacted since the founding of the postwar Federal Republic. Some of this reform was aimed at removing the changes imposed on the Criminal Code by the National Socialists. Those were sinister, but piecemeal, intrusions on the old Code that often sought to entrench the Nazis' "race theory and ideas of social hygiene."[15] As noted, many of the Nazi regime's most infamous and grotesque criminal provisions were enacted outside the Criminal Code's framework as supplementary provisions, including the notorious Law for the Protection of German Blood and German Honor.[16] As a general matter, however, the National Socialists sought to free German criminal court judges from the constraints of the positive law, which didn't adequately encompass and embrace Nazi ideology. They were encouraged to punish all "criminal" conduct, even if a statutory basis was lacking. This required the exercise of analogical reasoning, an approach to interpreting and applying the law that would be familiar to jurists in the Common Law tradition. In the Nazis' hands it meant that defendants should be convicted and punished if their actions could be analogized to a codified crime.[17] The Nazis' ambitions for a comprehensive overhaul of the Criminal Code foundered due to the demands and distractions of the war Germany had unleashed on the world.

One of the proudest and most prominent products of the centuries of intense "scientific" refinement of German criminal law is the system's renowned tripartite analysis. Dubber described this by referring to the three steps of an inquiry in a criminal law case:

- Step 1 – *Tatbestandsmäßigkeit* (consideration of the facts of a case to determine whether the formal elements of a crime as outlined in the Criminal Code's Special Part have been met)
- Step 2 – *Rechtswidrigkeit* (consideration of the wrongfulness of the defendant's actions, or whether the actions might have been objectively justifiable)
- Step 3 – *Schuld* (consideration of the defendant's blameworthiness, or whether the defendant might have a subjective excuse for his or her actions)

This distinct analytical framework merits closer attention. Appreciating the tripartite system is essential to understanding a German criminal law judgment. Its formal and systematic application – almost regardless of the facts involved in a case – also confirms German criminal law's scientific ambitions. Albin Eser's explanation should help you to better understand this system of criminal law analysis.

Albin Eser
Justification and Excuse
24 AMERICAN JOURNAL OF COMPARATIVE LAW 621, 622–631, 634–637 (1976)[*]

* * *

[...] According to the new general part of the German Penal Code [*Strafgesetzbuch*], the distinction between (objective) justification of the act and mere (subjective, individual) excuse of the actor is now expressly recognized as a matter of principle, even though some minor problems persist – in particular, the unavoidable question where to draw the line. The most obvious example is the distinction between "justifying necessity" (§ 34) [*Rechtswidrigkeit*] and "excusing necessity" (§ 35) [*Schuld*]. In § 34 the law calls the act *nicht rechtswidrig* (not unlawful) if it is committed for the purpose of saving a prevailing legal interest from imminent danger. On the other hand, § 35 deals with the situation in which the act remains unlawful since the interest violated may objectively prevail, but the actor may be held to act *ohne Schuld* (without guilt, in the sense of personal blameworthiness) if he intended to save his or his relative's life, limb, or liberty. Similarly, an act committed in self-defense is considered "not unlawful" (§ 32), provided the actor has not exceeded the bounds of necessary defense; but even if he has done so (e.g., by killing

---

[*] Excerpt reproduced with permission of the American Journal of Comparative Law.

instead of only wounding the aggressor) and therefore his act was unlawful, he might "not be punishable" (i.e., he would be *excused*) if he exceeded the bounds of the defense by reason of emotion, fear or fright (§ 33).

* * *

The Triple Elements in the German Concept of Crime

Justification and excuse can hardly be explained without regard to the distinction between unlawfulness (of the act) [*Rechtswidrigkeit*] and blameworthiness (of the perpetrator) [*Schuld*]. [...]

A fundamental prerequisite for distinguishing justifying defenses from exculpating defenses was the rise of *Rechtswidrigkeit* (unlawfulness of the act) and *Schuld* (guilt in the sense of subjective individual blameworthiness, not in the procedural sense of guilty plea) as systematic and distinct elements in the concept of crime. [...]

* * *

Although the development considered so far was primarily directed at separating wrongfulness from guilt, Beling's attention turned to wrongfulness as distinct from the fulfillment of penal law provisions. In his famous *Lehre vom Verbrechen* (1906), Beling developed the so-called *Tatbestand* as a comprehensive set of the statutory elements which constitute the various types of crimes. As such, *Tatbestandsmässigkeit* (in the sense of the act's statutory type) is an independent notional element of crime. And since *Tatbestandsmässigkeit* was thought of as indicating only the type of an act, without implying any final normative judgment as to its wrongfulness, the tripartite system of the German crime concept emerged: *Tatbestandsmässigkeit* (as the fulfillment of the statutory elements of a provision of penal law), *Rechtswidrigkeit* (as the objective conclusion that the act is unlawful) and *Schuld* (as subjective imputability of the act to the perpetrator).

Based on this tri-partition, F. von Liszt, in his own and still more refined system defined crime as an act (*Handlung*, in the sense of a willful physical motion) which is typified by a penal provision (*Tatbestandsmässigkeit*), unlawful (*Rechtswidrigkeit*), and guilty (*schuldhaft*, in the subjective sense). Thereby unlawfulness was related to the *objective* elements of the act, whereas "guilt" [*Schuld* or blameworthiness] was understood as the *subjective* prerequisite for a criminal sanction. In later writings, v. Liszt clarified guilt in a more psychological sense: guilt [*Schuld* or blameworthiness] as the subjective relation of the perpetrator to the proscribed harm. Thus by dividing the objective from the subjective elements of the crime, a system characterized by a hitherto-unknown clarity was established. It was acknowledged as a great doctrinal development compared with the criminal theories of the nineteenth century.

* * *

The Final Step

Yet the distinction between guilt and unlawfulness did not lead *eo ipso* to an adequate separation and clarification of grounds for justification and excuse [...].

[...] Just as the unlawfulness of the violation of a legal norm can be waived by reason of justification, the violation of a norm of responsibility may be held not blameworthy if the perpetrator can invoke a ground of exculpation through which his personal responsibility is excluded [...].

* * *

Rationale and Grounds of Justification

The new Code leaves no doubt that an act, although fulfilling the statutory elements of a penal provision, is held "not unlawful" (*nicht rechtswidrig*) if supported by a rule of justification. In short, a justified act is deemed legal.

* * *

To get an idea of its broad range, we should point out some of the more important grounds of justification recognized by German law. Keep in mind that the permissive rules by which a criminal act may be justified are not only found in criminal law. According to the principle of "unity of the legal system," any permitting norms regardless of where they may be found – in criminal, administrative, or even private law – have to be taken into consideration. If we classify the grounds of justification with respect to their source or purpose, we can distinguish four main groups:

1) *Consent* (express or implied) of the injured person as proof that he waives protection of his interest. The result is an "absent interest."
2) Rights of defense against some invasion: particularly self-defense (§ 32 StGB or § 227 BGB).
3) Acting in a state of necessity or conflict of interests: in addition to "justifying necessity" (§ 34 StGB) or collision of duties (*Pflichtenkollision*, not yet regulated by law), we should also mention "aggressive necessity" (§ 904 BGB) by which destruction or other damage to another's property is justified if necessary for preventing other, disproportionate damage.
4) Lastly we can group together those grounds of justification in which the actor violates a penal norm by exercising a certain right (such as freedom of opinion (§ 193 StGB) offending another's social reputation) or by fulfilling a legal duty (e.g., acting *pro magistratu* or similar cases of public or domestic authority).

* * *

Necessity

Although the wording of the self-defense provision (§ 32) does not explicitly require a balancing of interests, but does so by interpretation, justifying necessity (§ 34) provides a clear case of justification by reason of superior interest. […] [T]hese legal provisions were sufficient grounds for the general principle, already developed by the courts, that the actor may be justified if, balancing the interests at stake, he was furthering the greater value. Once recognized by the *Reichsgericht* in such a general way, this *übergesetzliche Notstand* (extra-statutory necessity) came to be invoked in a long line of cases.

Thus the new § 34 is actually nothing more than a formal codification of a very well established ground of justification by balancing conflicting interests. […]

Regardless of which interpretation of the adequacy clause is correct, the wording of § 34 leaves no doubt that justification requires more than simply a balancing of conflicting legal interests, such as where a comparison is made between the life of the fetus and the life or limb of the mother (mere *Güterabwägung*). What is called for is a comprehensive evaluation of all significant interests, such as the degree of risk or damage, the cause of danger, the legal duty to accept a risk, etc. (*Gesamtinteressenabwägung*). If after a comprehensive balancing of all values involved the act can be deemed to have served the clearly superior interest, the act can be treated as justified, with the consequence of legalizing behavior otherwise falling into the criminal category.

Rationale and Grounds of Excuse

Unlike justification, excuse does not affect the unlawfulness of the act; it merely removes the personal blameworthiness of the actor: he is (only) excused. Excuse is granted only to those participants who are acting under excusing conditions; all other participants remain punishable for the illegal act. Contrary to the common law tradition, which seems to limit excuse to insanity, duress and to some extent mistake of law, German law has recognized for quite some time that excessive self-defense by reason of distress, fear or fright (§ 33), necessity (§ 35), and conflict of duties are also grounds of excuse. German criminal theory [...] [refers to] *Entschuldigungsgründe* which excuse an act that is unlawful and "guilty" since committed with *mens rea*. Only in this [...] group (duress, necessity, conflict of duties or excessive self-defense by reason of fear) can we speak of an excuse for an otherwise "culpable" act. And only these grounds of "excuse" are of major concern in our present context.

Although the grounds for exclusion of guilt (*Schuldausschliessungsgründe*) are characterized by a lack of cognitive (mistake of law) and/or willed (insanity) elements of guilt, grounds of excuse (*Entschuldigungsgründe*) are rooted in extraordinary psychological pressure on the perpetrator. [...]

In order to consider at least one ground of excuse in some detail, we should perhaps choose "excusing necessity" (§ 35) as distinct from "justifying necessity" (§ 34), which we earlier discussed as a ground for justification. In contrast to justifying necessity, which permits an act in promotion of *any* legal interest, excusing necessity is restricted to the saving of life, limb or liberty. This restriction might at first appear paradoxical unless we keep in mind that justifying necessity requires protection of a superior interest, whereas § 35 does not require a predominance of the protected over the damaged value. Therefore excusing necessity may even be granted in cases where life stands against life. However this gap in the objective balance of interests has to be supplemented – and this is the essential feature of excuse – by the presence of personal danger: the actor is required to have acted for the sake of his own or a relative's life, limb or liberty. This requirement of extraordinary personal danger is expressly stressed by § 35(2) which states that excuse may not be granted if, under given conditions, the actor must be expected to cope with the danger (*zumutbar*). That is to say, exculpation is primarily based on considerations personal to the perpetrator. [...]

* * *

In sum, by granting justification the law permits the furtherance of the objectively greater value, while by granting excuse it recognizes a subjectively overwhelming motivation. But as with all exemptions, these are tolerable only so long as they do not become the rule.

* * *

Questions/Comments

- German criminal law's distinction between justification and excuse, between *Rechtswidrigkeit* and *Schuld*, is technically and theoretically complex. Complicating the matter is the fact that, while some elements of both are explicitly outlined in the Criminal Code, other elements have emerged

10.1 The Theory and Logic of German Criminal Law

from scholarly commentary, judicial interpretation, and longstanding practice. Clouding things further, the concept of "necessity" can serve as the basis for justification (*Rechtswidrigkeit*) as well as for excuse (*Schuld*). Eser helpfully focuses on the different forms of necessity in his effort to explain and illustrate the system. He notes that "justifying necessity" is codified in § 34 of the Criminal Code[18] while "excusing necessity" is codified in § 35 of the Criminal Code.[19] Eser explains that a "justifying necessity" strips otherwise criminal conduct of its illegality (*Rechtswidrigkeit*) if the conduct was undertaken to promote an objectively greater legal interest (such as the life, limb, or liberty of another person). This balancing exercise, Eser explains, involves a consideration of the totality of the circumstances. "Excusing necessity" is different. It precludes punishment for illegal conduct when the offender cannot be subjectively blamed (*Schuld*) for his or her actions. That also involves a form of balancing. The former (justifying necessity) is concerned with an objectively superior interest justifying criminal conduct. The latter (excusing necessity) accounts for extraordinary subjective circumstances that excuse the offender for failing to conform his or her conduct to the criminal law.

- The balancing analysis called for by the *Schuldprinzip* allows for flexibility and variation in the application of the formal, positive law. That might open the criminal law up for unpredictability, perhaps even based on emotional or political considerations. The *Schuldprinzip* promotes the human autonomy of the defendant. But it might frustrate German criminal law's ambitions for scientific objectivity and certainty. Can law be reduced to an objective system as long as it must engage with humankind's varied conditions and experiences?

- Germany's tripartite criminal law analysis is sketched in Figure 10.1. In telling the story of the emergence of that framework, Eser wondered why the systematic and conceptual distinction between act, justification, and guilt "has not been accepted in one legal system while it developed in another?" Are you willing to offer Eser an answer to that question? What does German criminal law gain by adding the third step – the *Schuldprinzip* – to its criminal law practice? What values inform the insistence on addressing "blameworthiness" in such a formal and fundamental way? It is widely understood that the Anglo-American legal systems have not adopted a tripartite framework for criminal law. Instead, they rely on a bipartite analysis: first, have the elements of a crime been met; and second, is there a defense for that conduct. But Dubber and Fletcher insist that there is evidence of the *Schuldprinzip* (the third element in the Germany trinity) in American criminal law. What does Dubber say counts as the consideration of *Schuld* (blameworthiness) in the American criminal law practice?

German Criminal Law

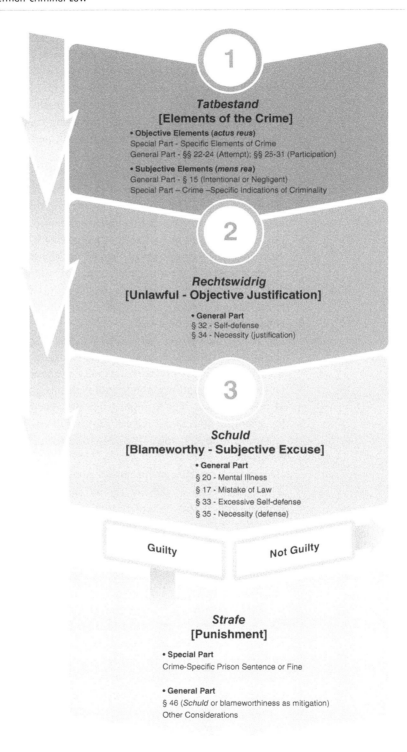

Figure 10.1 German Criminal Code: The *Straftatsystem*

10.1 The Theory and Logic of German Criminal Law

It is one thing to understand what the latter two elements in German criminal law are (illegality/justification and blameworthiness/excuse). The following excerpt seeks to explain why German criminal law constructed them.

Tatjana Hörnle
Guilt and Choice in Criminal Law Theory – A Critical Assessment
4 BERGEN JOURNAL OF CRIMINAL LAW & CRIMINAL JUSTICE 1, 1–3 (2016)[*]

* * *

In Germany and other European countries, courts and legal scholars assume that the Principle of Guilt (*Schuldprinzip*) is of central importance for the legitimisation of criminal punishment. The German Federal Constitutional Court (*Bundesverfassungsgericht*) assigns the Principle of Guilt constitutional status. Although it is not mentioned in the German Constitution (the *Grundgesetz* from 1949), the Federal Constitutional Court refers to it in several judgments such as the following (the Lissabon-decision) from 2009:

> Criminal law is based on the principle of guilt. This principle presupposes a human being's own responsibility, it presupposes human beings who themselves determine their actions and can decide in favour of right or wrong by virtue of their freedom of will. The protection of human dignity is based on the idea of Man as a spiritual and moral being which has the capabilities of defining himself, and of developing, in freedom. [...] In the area of the administration of criminal law, Article 1.1 of the Basic Law determines the idea of the nature of punishment and the relationship between guilt and atonement [...]. The principle that any sanction presupposes guilt thus has its foundation in the guarantee of human dignity under Article 1.1 of the Basic Law [...].

The Constitutional Court did not invent the Guilt Principle – it traces back to older developments in post-war criminal law doctrine. In a ruling from 1952, the German Federal Court of Justice (*Bundesgerichtshof*, the highest appellate Court for criminal and civil cases) emphasised the importance of the Guilt Principle (in a rather brief way, obviously meaning to express a self-evident truth):

> Judgments about guilt blame the offender for not having behaved in the legally required way, for having decided in favour of wrongdoing, although he could have acted in a legally required way and could have decided in favour of the law.

Criminal law theorists have pointed to the historical background of this 1952-decision, arguing that its underlying "pathos of freedom" has to be read as a rejection of, and statement against, the [Nazi] regime. References to the historical context can, however, not, or at least not fully, explain the central role of guilt within German criminal law doctrine. Underlying assumptions about personal responsibility and the legitimacy of blame are neither based on a particular German tradition, nor are they to be found uniquely in the area of the criminal law. Rather, it is a widespread notion in modern (broadly speaking) 'Western societies' that moral and legal blame for human conduct is only legitimate if the person blamed could have acted otherwise.

This notion has been spelled out as the Principle of Alternate Possibilities (PAP) in the philosophical literature. Harry Frankfurt used this expression in his seminal article "Alternate Possibilities and Moral Responsibility," describing its content with the sentence: "*An agent is morally responsible for an action only if that person could have done otherwise.*" The point of Frankfurt's article is to shed doubt on the thesis that "*could have done otherwise*" is a necessary requirement for moral blame. However, Frankfurt

---

[*] Excerpt reprinted with permission of the author.

acknowledges that the Principle of Alternate Possibilities is firmly rooted in everyday moral attitudes, and the intensity of reactions to Frankfurt's attempt to debunk the Principle of Alternate Possibilities underscores this point.

The German courts (in the decisions cited above) use a somewhat narrower concept of alternate possibilities than Frankfurt. While his focus is on alternate actions ("*could have done otherwise*"), the crucial point is the possibility of alternate decisions ("*could have decided otherwise*"). To distinguish between a broader Principle of Alternate Possibilities and a somewhat narrower Principle of Alternate Decisions is helpful for an analytical purpose. It allows separating internal freedom from external freedom – that is freedom from coercion, by persons or other sources of imminent danger.

For those who are familiar with the English literature on the subject of criminal responsibility, the general reasoning behind the German insistence on a Principle of Alternate Decisions [in the form of the Guilt Principle] must appear familiar, too. It is a common assumption in contemporary legal theory that the foundation for criminal responsibility is *choice*. Modern conceptions of individual fault are deeply rooted in subjectivism and the notion of having made the wrong choice.

* * *

Questions/Comments

- The desire to recognize and realize human autonomy and agency – we might refer to it as "free will" – helps to justify the *Schuldprinzip* in German criminal law.[20] Hörnle links this element of German criminal law theory to the post-war emphasis on human dignity in German law. We've seen this commitment throughout this survey of German law and legal culture, especially the discussion of Article 1 of the Basic Law in Chapter 8. It is justified, in part, as a categorical rejection – also in criminal law – of the Nazis' arbitrary and inhumane world view, governance, and jurisprudence.
- The "excuse" element captured by the *Schuldprinzip* ensures that "the suspect, in light of his abilities and opportunities, was in a position to conform his behavior to the law."[21] For example, children or those suffering from a mental disability might lack "blameworthiness" in this sense. The same might be true for someone confronted with exceptionally frightful circumstances or facing extraordinary personal danger. Does the criminal law in your primary or "national" legal system account for free will, with or without a settled role for an analytical element such as the *Schuldprinzip*? If not, then would you say that individual autonomy and free will are not a centerpiece of your system's criminal law? It is uncontroversial amongst philosophers to debate the merits of the notion of free will, which, as Hörnle notes, is a traditional explanation for recognizing merit (for good choices leading to positive outcomes) or culpability (for bad choices leading to negative outcomes). Determinists dispute the possibility of free will, arguing instead that material factors (whether biological or social) decisively condition (determine) our behavior. Most philosophers have settled on a compromise, "compatibilist" position that holds that we exercise free will within determinate conditions. In which of these directions does Germany's criminal law system point?

- The concern for human autonomy advanced by the *Schuldprinzip* is enhanced by the fact that the legal-political principle of blameworthiness has a multifaceted function in German criminal law. It has the role described above as the third part of the tripartite analysis used to confirm a criminal conviction. But it also plays a role at sentencing as a factor in determining what the criminal punishment for a conviction should be. That is, the defendant's "blameworthiness" is assessed when assigning guilt and again when the court sets the punishment. In the latter context the question is not whether the defendant had the subjective capacity to be blameworthy. The question is: to what extent did the defendant's acts disturb the legal order?

10.2 An Example of German Criminal Law: The *Frankfurt Police Torture Case*

Both of the facets of the *Schuldprinzip* (guilt and sentencing) played a prominent role in the infamous *Frankfurt Police Torture Case*. The case is also referred to as the *Gäfgen Case* – for the name of one of the defendants involved in what is a complex and distressing story. The facts of the case were usefully summarized by the European Court of Human Rights, which eventually became involved in the matter.

European Court of Human Rights
Case of Gäfgen v. Germany
Application no. 22978/05 (2010)

* * *

J. was the youngest son of a banking family in Frankfurt am Main. He got to know the applicant [Gäfgen], a law student, as an acquaintance of his sister. On 27 September 2002 [Gäfgen] lured J., aged 11, into his flat in Frankfurt am Main by pretending that the child's sister had left a jacket there. He then killed the boy by suffocating him.

Subsequently, [Gäfgen] deposited a ransom note at J.'s parents' place of residence stating that J. had been kidnapped and demanding one million euros. The note further stated that if the kidnappers received the ransom and managed to leave the country, then the child's parents would see their son again. [Gäfgen] then drove to a pond located on a private property near Birstein, approximately one hour's drive from Frankfurt, and hid J.'s corpse under a jetty.

On 30 September 2002 at around 1 a.m. [Gäfgen] picked up the ransom at a tram station. From then-on he was under police surveillance. He paid part of the ransom money into his bank accounts and hid the remainder of the money in his flat. That afternoon, he was arrested at Frankfurt am Main airport with the police pinning him face down on the ground.

After having been examined by a doctor at the airport's hospital on account of shock and skin lesions, [Gäfgen] was taken to the Frankfurt am Main police headquarters. He was informed by detective officer M. that he was suspected of having kidnapped J. and was instructed about his rights as a defendant, notably the right to remain silent and to consult a lawyer. He was then questioned by M. with a view to finding J. Meanwhile, the police, having searched [Gäfgen's] flat, found half of the ransom money and a note concerning the planning of the crime. [Gäfgen] intimated that the child was being held by another kidnapper. At 11.30 p.m. he was allowed to consult a lawyer, Z., for thirty minutes at his request. He subsequently indicated that F.R. and M.R. had kidnapped the boy and had hidden him in a hut by a lake.

Early in the morning of 1 October 2002, before M. came to work, D., Deputy Chief of the Frankfurt Police, ordered another officer, E., to threaten [Gäfgen] with considerable physical pain, and, if necessary, to subject him to such pain in order to make him reveal the boy's whereabouts. D.'s subordinate heads of department had previously and repeatedly opposed such a measure [...]. Detective Officer E. thereupon threatened [Gäfgen] with subjection to considerable pain at the hands of a person specially trained for such purposes if he did not disclose the child's whereabouts. According to [Gäfgen], E. further threatened to lock him in a cell with two huge black men who would sexually abuse him. The officer also hit him several times on the chest with his hand and shook him so that, on one occasion, his head hit the wall. The Government disputed that [Gäfgen] had been threatened with sexual abuse or had been physically assaulted during the questioning.

For fear of being exposed to the measures with which he was threatened, [Gäfgen] disclosed the whereabouts of J.'s body after approximately ten minutes.

[Gäfgen] was then driven with M. and numerous other police officers to Birstein. He had refused to go with E. The police waited for a video camera to be brought to the scene. Then, [Gäfgen], on the communicated order of the police officer in command and while being filmed, pointed out the precise location of the body. The police found J.'s corpse under the jetty at the pond near Birstein as indicated by [Gäfgen]. [Gäfgen] claimed that he had been obliged to walk without shoes through woods to where he had left the corpse and, on the orders of the police, he had had to point out its precise location. The Government disputed that [Gäfgen] had had to walk without shoes.

Upon forensic examination of the scene, the police discovered tyre tracks left by [Gäfgen's] car near the pond near Birstein. Under questioning by detective officer M. on the return journey from Birstein [Gäfgen] confessed to having kidnapped and killed J. He was then taken by the police to various other locations indicated by him where they secured J.'s school exercise books, a backpack, J.'s clothes and a typewriter used for the blackmail letter in containers. An autopsy carried out on J.'s corpse on 2 October 2002 confirmed that J. had died of suffocation.

Having returned to the police station, [Gäfgen] was then permitted to consult his lawyer, who had been instructed to act on his behalf by his mother and who had tried, in vain, to contact and advise [Gäfgen] earlier that morning.

In a note for the police file dated 1 October 2002, Deputy Chief D. stated that he believed that that morning J.'s life had been in great danger, if he was still alive at all, given his lack of food and the temperature outside. In order to save the child's life, D. had therefore ordered [Gäfgen] to be threatened by Detective Officer E. with considerable pain, which would not leave any trace of injury. D. confirmed that the treatment itself was to be carried out under medical supervision. Daschner further admitted that he had ordered another police officer to obtain a "truth serum" to be administered to [Gäfgen]. According to the note placed in the file, the threat to [Gäfgen] was exclusively aimed at saving the child's life rather than furthering the criminal proceedings concerning the kidnapping. As [Gäfgen] had disclosed the whereabouts of J.'s body, having been threatened with pain, no measures had in fact been carried out.

* * *

In January 2003 the Frankfurt am Main public prosecutor's office opened criminal investigation proceedings against Deputy Chief D. and Detective Officer E. on the basis of [Gäfgen's] allegations that he had been threatened on 1 October 2002.

* * *

10.2 The *Frankfurt Police Torture Case*

Frankfurt Police Torture Case

A German television film from 2012 dramatized the Frankfurt Police Torture Case, confronting audiences with a real-life example of the *Schuldprinzip*. Had Deputy Chief Daschner committed a crime? The facts clearly matched the statutory elements (*Tatbestandsmässigkeit*). He lacked a justification and, therefore, acted wrongfully (*Rechtswidrigkeit*). But did the pressure to find the victim mean that Officer Daschner was not blameworthy (*Schuldhaftigkeit*)?

Figure 10.2 *Frankfurt Police Torture Case*
Source: Image from the TV film production *Der Fall Jakob von Metzler*, reprinted with permission of ZDF and Hans-Joachim Pfeiffer

The criminal judgment presented below *does not* address the kidnapping and murder of the boy. That case resulted in Gäfgen's conviction on several counts, including murder (§ 211 Criminal Code) in connection with kidnapping (§ 234 Criminal Code), and casting false suspicion (§ 164 Criminal Code) in connection with unlawful imprisonment (§ 239 Criminal Code). The trial court found Gäfgen to be especially *schuldig* (blameworthy) (§ 57a(1)[2] Criminal Code) and departed from the statutorily prescribed fifteen-year penalty, instead imposing a lifelong prison sentence.

The following excerpt concerns the criminal charges brought against the two Frankfurt police officers who threatened Gäfgen with torture during his interrogation. News of their conduct and their eventual trial stirred a wide-ranging, passionate debate about the possible permissibility of torture in a ticking-timebomb scenario such as the one Deputy Chief Daschner believed he faced during the questioning of Gäfgen.[22] The case even inspired a TV film entitled *Der Fall Jakob von Metzler* (*The Case of Jakob von Metzler*), which was promoted with the poster presented in Figure 10.2. One headline from that time period summed up the moral and legal dilemma raised by Daschner's conduct: "Hero or Torturer?"[23] Another headline assumed a less neutral posture, criticizing Daschner as "The Man without Regret."[24]

The officers were charged with coercion (§ 240 Criminal Code), and Daschner was separately charged with inciting a subordinate to commit an offense (§ 357 Criminal Code).

Criminal Code

Section 240
Coercion (*Nötigung*)

(1) Whoever unlawfully, by force or threat of serious harm, compels a person to do, acquiesce to or refrain from an act incurs a penalty of imprisonment for a term not exceeding three years or a fine.

Criminal Code

Section 357
Incitement of subordinate to commit offence

(1) Superiors who incite or undertake to incite a subordinate to commit an unlawful act in public office or allow such an unlawful act to be committed by their subordinate incur the penalty provided for this unlawful act.

Criminal Code

Section 59
Conditions for warning with sentence reserved

(1) If a person has incurred a fine not exceeding 180 daily rates, the court may issue a warning at the time of conviction, may indicate the sentence and reserve imposition of the penalty if it is to be expected that the offender will commit no further criminal offences even without the immediate imposition of the sentence, following an overall evaluation of the offence and the offender's character, special circumstances are deemed to exist that render the imposition of a sentence unnecessary and the defence of the legal order does not demand the imposition of a penalty.

10.2 The *Frankfurt Police Torture Case*

The following is an excerpt from the Frankfurt Regional Court's judgment in the case against Deputy Chief Daschner and Officer Ennigkeit. Notes highlighting the steps in the tripartite analysis have been added so you can see how the court closely follows that scheme.

Regional Court Frankfurt (27th Criminal Chamber)
File No.: 5/27 KLs 7570 Js 203814/03 (4/04), 5–27 KLs 7570 Js 203814/03 (4/04)
20 December 2004

[Translation by Russell A. Miller]

* * *

[*Tatbestand*]

The defendant committed the crime of "coercion," as defined by § 240(1) of the Criminal Code. On the morning of 1 October 2002 he threatened to inflict serious pain on [Gäfgen], albeit under medical supervision and without causing injury, in order to force [Gäfgen] to disclose the location of the abducted boy. While doing this the defendant made it clear that he would not be the one carrying out the threatened harm. But, because he was speaking on behalf of the Department's leadership, the defendant clearly had the authority to order that the threats be realized.

The defendant committed the crime of "inciting a subordinate to commit an offence," within the meaning of § 357(1) – read in conjunction with § 240(1) – of the Criminal Code. As Deputy Chief of Police, the defendant was [Officer Ennigkeit's] superior and he instructed [Officer Ennigkeit] to commit the act. [Officer Ennigkeit] complied with the defendant's directions.

* * *

[*Rechtswidrigkeit*]

The police law provisions of the Hessian Law on Security and Order do not provide a legal basis for coercing someone to give a statement. Instead, those provisions of the law prohibit it. The state and its institutions, such as the police, have a general duty to protect. But that duty does not constitute a legal basis for coerced statements. The state's duty to save human lives only operates within the boundaries set for the state's functions. Because of Article 20(1)[2] of the Basic Law, the Executive Branch's failure to comply with the law is not only a breach of ordinary law, it is also an unconstitutional act.

* * *

Even if one applies to these exercises of state authority the legal justifications applicable to individuals, the actions of [the defendants] cannot be justified as a "defense of a third party" (§ 32) or as "necessity" (§ 34).

"Defense" within the meaning of § 32 of the Criminal Code requires a situation of defense at the time when the justified action takes place. Both defendants believed that the child could still be saved. But the conditions for the "defense of a third party" did not exist because the child was already dead. The defendants also cannot claim to have been mistaken about the actual requirements for asserting "defense" as a justification. Within the meaning of § 32 of the Criminal Code a defensive action is necessary if, on the one hand, it is suitable for defense and, on the other hand, it is the mildest possible measure.

The threat of inflicting pain on [Gäfgen] was not the mildest possible measure. Pursuant to the "step concept" other, milder, measures were conceivable.

Section 34 of the Criminal Code ["necessity"] would have provided a justification for criminal conduct if the threat to the child's life cannot otherwise be averted and if the defensive action taken constitutes an appropriate measure. Neither of these elements were fulfilled in this case. As noted, there were other, milder defensive means available. For example, [Gäfgen] could have been confronted with the victim's siblings. That strategy had not been carried out before the defendants resorted to their actions.

Additionally, the threatened harm was neither required, within the meaning of § 32 of the Criminal Code, nor appropriate, within the meaning of § 34 of the Criminal Code. That's the case because the threats constituted a violation of Article 1(1)[1] of the Basic Law.

This fundamental commitment of the Constitution is also reflected in Article 104(1)[2] of the Basic Law, which provides that detained persons may not be mentally or physically mistreated. According to Article 1(1)[1] of the Basic Law, human dignity is inviolable. The state may not treat a person as a mere object.

This legal concept has also found expression in international treaties and conventions, such as Article 3 of the European Convention on Human Rights, which is in force in Germany.

Respect for human dignity is a foundation of the *Rechtsstaat* [state governed by the rule of law]. The founders deliberately placed this value at the beginning of the constitution. The right to life and physical integrity has secondary status. It is enshrined in Article 2(2) of the Basic Law. The reason for the distinction between these commitments is the history of this State. Documents from the time of the founding of the Federal Republic of Germany make it abundantly clear that the atrocities committed by the National Socialists were still very much in the minds of the participants at the Parliamentary Council [Constitutional Convention]. Its fundamental concern was to prevent something like [the Nazi terror] from ever happening again and to categorically stamp out any temptation to return to those atrocities. Thus, human beings cannot again be treated as the mere carriers of knowledge to be extracted by the state, not even in the name of justice. This explains why Article 1(1)[1] of the Basic Law is unalterable. The founders expressed the idea of "*Wehret den Anfängen*" [nip it in the bud] in Article 79(3) of the Basic Law, which is also referred to as the "eternity clause." The strict prohibition of even a threat to inflict pain on a suspect results from the founders' consideration of all the relevant interests when they drafted the Basic Law. Respect for and the functionality of the criminal justice administration also are a key issue in this regard.

* * *

A departure from the clear legal situation would involve a breach of the absolute constitutional protection of human dignity and it would suggest that that constitutional value is open to a balancing of interests. But that would be like breaking a taboo.

Still, such exceptions have been considered in the context of circumstances involving terrorist attacks. Borderline cases have been described in which the protection of the perpetrator's human dignity has been weighed against the deaths, and thus the constitutionally protected lives, of thousands of people (ticking-timebomb cases). Among other claims, it has been argued that, in such a case, the human dignity of the victims requires the state to take every possible action to protect them, including the use of mental of physical pressure on the perpetrator. The argument is that, when weighing the interests involved, the human dignity of the perpetrator has lower priority.

* * *

[The court surveyed and summarized a wide range of scholarship on these questions, concluding that …]

In summary it can be said that even the advocates for relativizing human dignity are very cautious and restrictive in formulating the requirements for the extreme situations in which coercive pressure might be possible. Fundamental concerns remain. Even the abstract cases only allow coercion as *ultima ratio* if it would be very promising and only if the person subjected to the pressure is very likely the perpetrator.

* * *

[*Schuldprinzip* – **Conviction**]

There are no reasons to discount the defendant's *Schuld* (blameworthiness).

[The court dismissed several potential bases for discounting the defendants' blameworthiness, including "mistake of law" (§ 17 Criminal Code). The court noted that the defendants assumed that their actions were illegal and weighed the risk of facing a criminal process as a result. The court also noted that the defendants were confronted with objections to their conduct from their colleagues. Finally, the court concluded that the speed with which Gäfgen confessed after the defendants posed these threats points to their blameworthiness. It suggests, the court reasoned, that even Gäfgen knew the defendants' conduct was illegal and that he believed their conduct would shield him from criminal sanction in the kidnapping and murder case. The court emphasized the fact that the defendants were very experienced and high-ranking officers. On the basis of this analysis the court concluded that the defendants "knew that threats constituted an impermissible interrogation method." The court then continued its assessment of the defendants' blameworthiness.]

The ground for discounting blameworthiness provided by § 35 of the Criminal Code also is not applicable in this case. The defendants' responsibility for the abducted child resulted from the obligation the police have to avert danger. But this is not the "special legal relationship" required by § 35 of the Criminal Code. According to this provision, only relatives and persons in a close relationship with the victim can be excused for criminal conduct due to the personal relation and a situation of conflict situation. The defendants, as police officers, did not fit this status.

An emergency that might serve as a supra-statutory ground for discounting the defendants' blameworthiness did not exist. There was no irresolvable conflict of duties. As already discussed, the defendants' conduct was not the only means of action available to them.

* * *

In any case, courts should cautiously rely on an emergency as a supra-statutory ground for discounting blameworthiness. Invoking this concept to justify the action of state authorities could lead to a significant departure from the applicable law organizing public entities and granting them their competences. It poses the danger that, if an emergency can serve as a supra-statutory ground for discounting blameworthiness, then an emergency might come to serve as a "supra-constitutional ground for excuse and a general legal basis to cope with states of emergency." Every constitutional or statutory limitation on state power would then only be provisional.

Other grounds for discounting the defendants' blameworthiness are not relevant to the case. Criminal liability pursuant to § 240(1) of the Criminal Code has been established.

* * *

[*Schuldprinzip* – **Sentencing**]

Despite the existence of aggravating factors in the case, they are off-set by significant mitigating factors. These mitigating factors establish that it would be disproportionate to apply the heightened penalty-range of six months up to five years of imprisonment.

This confirms once again that this is an extremely difficult case.

The fact that both defendants were exclusively and urgently concerned with saving the life of the child speaks for a considerably more lenient punishment.

Among the mitigating factors is the fact that [Deputy Chief Daschner] felt a special responsibility while acting as the substitute for the Chief of Police. He was unfamiliar with that role and particularly burdened with the responsibility the case imposed on him. He spent the night thinking about the situation and the appropriate course of action. He felt he was confronted with a conflict of a kind he had not experienced before in his 40 years of service. In addition, he was under great pressure from his superiors and the public to find the abducted child.

The defendant had in mind his own children, who in part were the same age as the abducted child. He suffered with the thoughts that the abducted child might perish in miserable conditions. All of this weighed on him as he bore the responsibility in the case as Deputy Chief of Police while the Chief of Police was away on vacation.

Another mitigating fact for both defendants was [Gäfgen's] provocative and ruthless conduct during interrogation, conduct that severely strained the nerves of the investigators. Being trained in the law, [Gäfgen] knew how to formulate and present his false statements in such a way that they would constantly create uncertainty, hope, disappointment, and sow uncertainty. He gave the impression that he was deliberately playing with the child's life and steering the police, as they sought to act to rescue the abducted child, into the wrong direction. This created the impression that [Gäfgen] might be trying to stall as a way of causing the abducted child's death.

Additionally, the investigation was extraordinarily hectic and stressful. The police officers worked overtime; they were exhausted and tired. [Officer Ennigkeit] had worked through the night and [Deputy Chief Daschner] had only slept a couple of hours.

This tenseness reduces considerably the defendants' blameworthiness because it lowered the defendants' inhibition, thereby lowering the threshold to commit the act. Both defendants were at their limits. Additionally, both have impeccable records.

* * *

[The court documented a number of factors justifying a reduced penalty in the case. Officer Daschner, for example, documented the facts of the case and accepted responsibility for his decisions. The court also noted that the defendants were exposed to immense negative scrutiny in the public and in the media, to a degree approaching pillory. The criminal process to which the defendants were exposed also justified a lighter punishment. It was extremely long. And, in a humiliating turn of events, it involved the defendants being accused and confronted in court by Gäfgen, who by this time was a convicted murderer. The court was bothered that all of this pushed the memory of the true victim in the case – the abducted and murdered child – into the background. Finally, the court noted that the defendants already had suffered professional consequences for the episode as both were removed from front-line policing duties.]

For those reasons the range of punishment provided in § 240(1) of the Criminal Code [as opposed to the one of § 240(4)] is applicable. This provision allows for a penalty of imprisonment for a term not exceeding three years or a fine.

* * *

Considering all aggravating and mitigating factors, [Deputy Chief Daschner] is levied a fine of €120 per diem for 90 days and [Officer Ennigkeit] a fine of €60 per diem for 60 days.

Considering the aforementioned circumstances, the defendants will not be formally sentenced to imprisonment. Instead, making use of § 59 of the Criminal Code, a prison

10.2 The *Frankfurt Police Torture Case*

sentence will be indicated but its imposition will be suspended. The strict requirements of this provision are met. There are no doubts about a favorable social prognosis for both defendants. The overall assessment of the offense and the personality of both defendants result in special circumstances that allow for the suspension of a sentence. The act did not arise out of an unavoidable conflict because alternative measures were still available. But both defendants subjectively believed there was a situation at hand that was analogous to the circumstances that would give rise to justification and excuse [...].

Additionally, under § 59 of the Criminal Code, the enforcement of the legal order does not require the imposition of a prison sentence in this case. A serious impairment of the population's sense of justice will not result from suspending the sentence. Respect for the legal order called for a conviction. But it does not call for the imposition of a prison sentence. It must be clear that public authorities are obliged to respect and abide by existing laws and the constitutional principles embodied in them, even in situations in which it might seem very difficult to act in accordance with them. It is true that the defendant's conduct has complicated the criminal proceedings against [Gäfgen] immensely and thus affected the legal system. But similar to a Greek tragedy, the defendants' trial had a cathartic, that is, cleansing, effect. It sparked extensive public discussion. It helped to categorically establish that in such an unclear situation, where no facts have been fully established and promising measures were still to be taken, there is no room for ordering coercive measures to obtain information.

* * *

Questions/Comments

- You can see from this excerpt that the trial court assessed each of the steps in the tripartite analysis of a German criminal case. Is it surprising that the court devoted so little attention to *Tatbestandsmäßigkeit* (elements of the crime)? It often seems that a criminal case is dominated by the facts and a search for the truth in the matter. But that wasn't the case here. Is that because the defendants conceded most of the facts of the case (they only disputed Gäfgen's accusations of actual physical abuse and threatened sexual abuse)? Or, was the court's treatment of the facts and the concrete elements of the charges less central to the case because that part of a criminal law analysis in Germany is generally more straightforward and less theoretically challenging? Another explanation might be Germany's "inquisitorial process" for developing the facts of a case. That will be discussed in Chapter 11. But maybe the other parts of the tripartite analysis (*Rechtswidrigkeit* and *Schuld*) attract more of the court's attention because they raise more abstract and theoretical legal issues that are the natural domain of trained, professional jurists.
- One way to explore the application of the various parts of a criminal case analysis in Germany would be to consider the following questions. Are you able to identify the discrete elements (*Tatbestandsmerkmale*) of the crime of coercion under § 240(1) of the Criminal Code? At the same time, are you able describe the elements to be considered when assessing illegality (*Rechtswidrigkeit*) and blameworthiness (*Schuld*)? Could you reach

a conclusion about whether criminal conduct is *rechtswidrig* (there is no objective justification) and whether there is adequate *Schuld* (blameworthiness due to the absence of a subjective excuse) in order to convict? Would you get your answer to these questions from the Criminal Code or from some other source, such as court judgments from analogous cases, scholars' commentary, or perhaps your intuition, instincts, and values? German criminal law aims to eliminate uncertainty and arbitrariness (recall that Dubber worried about "emotion" in criminal proceedings). Do you think the second and third elements of the analysis – at least as implemented in this case – are formalistic and categorical enough to eliminate (or at least significantly reduce) political or emotional considerations in the implementation of criminal law? Is the aim of affirming the defendant's autonomy compatible with the aim of reducing criminal law to something like a math problem with a set, correct solution?

At least one institution was unimpressed with the Frankfurt Regional Court's compromise in the case. Gäfgen challenged his conviction as constitutionally flawed due to the officers' threatened torture. When the German Federal Constitutional Court rejected Gäfgen's complaints, he filed an application with the European Court of Human Rights in which he argued that his criminal process involved, among other concerns, a violation of Article 3 of the European Convention on Human Rights. Article 3 provides: "No one shall be subjected to torture or to inhuman or degrading treatment or punishment." The Convention is a regional international law treaty (not linked with the European Union) that obliges the signatory states (including Germany and more than forty other European countries) to protect human rights and to accept the jurisdiction of the European Court of Human Rights for the resolution of claims of rights violations brought by individuals. Treaties such as the Human Rights Convention can have force in German law because their ratification by the *Bundestag* (Federal Parliament) involves their domestication as national law. All of this is part of the "open" character of German constitutional law, which permits supranational and international law to play a role in the German legal order. This "open" system, and especially the relationship it has created between German law and European Union law, is the subject of Chapter 12 of this book. But for our purposes here, it explains why the Frankfurt Regional Court considered Article 3 of the Convention when analyzing the criminal case against the police officers. And it explains why the *Frankfurt Police Torture Case* eventually ended up before the Court of Human Rights.

A Chamber of the Court of Human Rights (sitting with seven judges) ruled that Gäfgen could not claim a violation of Article 3 because, with the criminal conviction of Daschner and Ennigkeit, the German state had fulfilled its obligation under the Convention, namely, the enactment of rules and procedures aimed at preventing the use of torture by German public officials.[25] In essence, the Chamber concluded that Gäfgen was no longer a victim of a violation of

Article 3 and that his claim was moot. Gäfgen appealed the Chamber ruling to the Grand Chamber of the Court of Human Rights (sitting with seventeen judges). The Grand Chamber ruled that, with the token and trivial sentences imposed on Daschner and Ennigkeit, Germany had failed to meet its obligations under the Convention to act robustly to preclude and prevent the use of torture. The Grand Chamber ordered Germany to pay a portion of Gäfgen's legal costs.[26]

The Grand Chamber conceded that it is not the European Court's task to determine the degree of the offender's guilt and its consequences for the punishment imposed. These issues, the Court explained, are the "exclusive concern of the national courts." But the Grand Chamber nevertheless found that the German court's assessment of guilt and the punishment in the case constituted a "manifest disproportion between the gravity of the guilt and the punishment imposed." The Court of Human Rights was more concerned with the relative weakness of the punishments imposed than it was with the officers' relative lack of blameworthiness (*Schuld*). In its reasoning, the Grand Chamber made only a passing reference to "a number of mitigating circumstances" in the case. By deemphasizing these concerns, the Court of Human Rights was narrowing the scope for a contingent outcome in the case. The German court seized upon the *Schuldprinzip* to realize German criminal law's concern for the defendants' (the police officers) individual autonomy. The European Court of Human Rights, for its part, worried that by doing so the German court had strayed too far from the rigorous certainty provided by the positive law, a move that imperiled Gäfgen's autonomy by failing to vigorously condemn torture.

Whether you agree with the approach taken by the Frankfurt Regional Court or are convinced by the judgment of the European Court of Human Rights, the case exposes the challenge German criminal law has in reconciling two of its key values: promoting scientific objectivity and certainty, on the one hand, and taking account of the humanity and individual autonomy of the defendant, on the other hand.

10.3 Criminal Law in German Popular Culture: *Terror*

Many commentators praised the Frankfurt Regional Court's Solomonic decision. German law's absolute protection of human dignity was reinforced with a clear criminal sanction for the defendants' threatened use of torture. But the heartrending facts of the case counseled against imposition of a severe punishment. Florian Jessberger summed up the court's maneuver in this way:

> Torture is a crime under domestic law (in our case, German law) and, if committed in the context of an armed conflict or as part of a widespread or systematic attack against a civilian population, under international law, even if it is resorted to in order to coerce a person to provide information required or expected to save innocent life [...] However, the specific and altruistic motivation of the perpetrator may only be taken into consideration in the determination of the

sentence. Here, the "guilty, but not to be punished" verdict of the *Daschner* Case provides an example of how to strike a balance between conflicting interests.[27]

Winfried Brugger, who was one of the most astute comparative scholars of German and American constitutional law, took a more daring step when he argued that the absolute prohibition on torture in German law should be reconsidered in order to permit exceptions in some extremely rare cases. This radical departure, Brugger explained, could be justified if three elements existed. First, the law must show a *Wertungslücke*, that is, a legal valuation that is in conflict with other values expressed in the law. Second, the availability of torture would be limited to a very narrow set of factual circumstances involving a clear, imminent, and severe danger. There also must be a strong factual likelihood that torture is necessary for obtaining the information needed to diffuse that danger. Third, this exceedingly rare exception must itself be codified in positive law to avoid its arbitrary use. Brugger argued that German constitutional law's absolute commitment to human dignity does not preclude the exception he proposed. Article 1 of the Basic Law provides a subjective, negative protection of an individual's dignity (e.g., the criminal suspect's dignity during interrogation) by prohibiting torture. But, Brugger noted, Article 1 also imposes an objective, positive duty on the state to support and strengthen the enjoyment of everyone's dignity, including those who would be harmed – or killed – by criminal conduct. Brugger noted that, because of the "long menacing shadow of the Third Reich," no post-war German law professor had ever dared raise these arguments. Still, he concluded, to his own surprise, that "German constitutional law would allow torture in exceptional cases."[28] Brugger could have been speaking directly to the trial court in the *Frankfurt Police Torture Case*, which pointed to the Nazi legacy when highlighting Article 1 and the protection of human dignity as the basis for insisting on convicting the two Frankfurt police officers.

How much leeway did the Frankfurt Regional Court have when considering the possible outcomes in the case? Which path would you choose as a judge in the case? Would you pursue a formalistic application of the criminal law, but perhaps issue a mitigated sentence? Or, would you adopt a novel exception to the controlling constitutional and statutory law to avoid a conviction in the case and, thereby, vindicate the justice that was achieved by the police officers' (formally criminal) decisions? Which of these two paths is closest to the spirit of German criminal law?

These challenging themes are at the heart of a popular play and film that were produced in Germany after the *Frankfurt Police Torture Case* stirred widespread debate. The play, simply entitled *Terror*, was written by the German criminal law attorney and author Ferdinand von Schirach. The play presents a hypothetical case in which a German Air Force pilot shoots down an airliner that has been hijacked by terrorists who intend to crash the commandeered aircraft into a sold-out soccer stadium. All 164 passengers and personnel on the plane are killed by the Air Force pilot's preventive intervention. The audience

10.3 Criminal Law in German Popular Culture: *Terror*

is presented with these facts and the legal arguments of the prosecutor and the Air Force pilot's defense counsel. Then the audience is asked to cast their vote: convict or acquit the pilot.

Ferdinand von Schirach
Terror 6, 8–9, 11, 32, 43–48, 51–52 (2017)[*]

[Translation by David Tuschingham]

Characters

- *Presiding Judge*
- *Lars Koch (Defendant)*
- *Biegler (Defence Counsel, male)*
- *Nelson (State Prosecutor, female)*
- *Christian Lauterbach*
- *Franziska Meiser*
- *Stenographer (female)*
- *Guard (male)*

Prologue

The Presiding Judge enters. The curtain remains closed behind him. He is wearing a dark suit, a white shirt and a white tie. He is carrying his gown over one arm. He speaks directly to the audience.

Presiding Judge: Good morning, ladies and gentlemen. I'm glad to see you all here on time. It's not easy parking round here and this building is a bit of a rabbit warren … Anyway, it's good that you've all managed to get here. Before we begin, I must ask you to forget everything that you have read or heard about this case. Yes, everything. It is you alone who have been called upon to judge this matter, you are the lay judges, the members of the public who today will sit in judgement on the defendant Lars Koch. The law grants you the power to determine the fate of a human being. Please take this responsibility seriously. You will judge solely what you hear in this courtroom. We lawyers describe this as "evidence gained from with the hearing itself." That means: only what is said by the defendant, the witnesses, the joint plaintiffs and legal experts in this courtroom, only the evidence which we gather here may provide the basis for your verdict. At the end of the trial you will be obliged to vote, and I shall announce the verdict that you have reached.

* * *

So make your judgement calmly and in your own time. And above all: remember that before you there is a human being, someone who has the same dreams as you, the same needs. He too, just like you, is trying to find happiness. And that's why in your judgement you should retain your own humanity.

Now, I'd like to begin, but we're still waiting for the Counsel for the Defence – he's late.

The Guard approaches the Presiding Judge from the rear, says something to him quietly. The Presiding Judge nods. The Guard exits once again.

I've just been told he's finally arrived. So, let us begin.

---

[*] Excerpt reprinted with permission of Faber Ltd.

The Presiding Judge exits, putting on his gown as he walks.

Act One

* * *

Presiding Judge: Then, if you please, State Prosecutor, the charge.

State Prosecutor: (*standing*) Lars Koch, whose personal details have just been specified, is charged under the German Criminal Code according to Section 154a, paragraph 1 of the Code of Criminal Procedure that on 26th May 2013 above the village of Oberappersdorf he did use deadly force to kill 164 people.

The charge states that on 26th May 2013 at 20:21 hours, using an air-to-air guided weapons system, he did shoot down a passenger aircraft type A320-100/200 manufactured by Airbus Industries belonging to Lufthansa German Airlines which was at that time flying from Berlin to Munich under flight code LH 2047, and did thereby kill the 164 persons on board. He is charged with the crime of murder according to Section 211, paragraph 2, group 2, variant 3.52, paragraph 1 of the German Criminal Code.

* * *

[The State Prosecutor and Counsel for the Defence offer their opening statements in the case. Evidence in the case begins with the testimony of German Air Force Lieutenant Colonel Christian Lauterbach. Lauterbach was the Duty Controller in charge of the NATO-monitored German airspace on the day of the hijacking. He testified to the events that took place and to the reactions of the civilian defense authorities, the military commanders, and the fighter-jet pilot Major Lars Koch who was dispatched to intercept the hijacked airliner. Lauterbach testified that he communicated to Major Koch the clear and unequivocal order that the airplane not be shot down. Lauterbach testified that this order was meant to comply with a recent judgment of the Federal Constitutional Court, which ruled that a new law permitting the Air Force to shoot down hijacked aircraft was unconstitutional. The Constitutional Court concluded that shooting down a hijacked aircraft and killing the innocent passengers aboard would violate the state's constitutional duty to protect and promote human dignity. During the defendant's testimony, the Prosecutor sought to question him about his familiarity with and view of that decision.]

State Prosecutor: Mr. Koch, I too have read your personal file. During your training you took a particular interest in matters of law. In light of this would you be prepared to give more reasons for your conclusion?

Defendant: I gave a lecture to young fighter pilots on the Federal Constitutional Court's ruling. I assume it's in the file.

State Prosecutor: Yes, that's right, there is a note of it. Then I ask you what was your understanding of this ruling. What legal conclusions did you …

Presiding Judge: Prosecutor, now I have to interrupt. You know that we do not debate matters of law with the defendant. We investigate the facts. And they are the basis on which we shall come to a ruling. That was also the reason why I did not ask Mr. Koch any further questions …

Defence Counsel: Excuse me please. Not only do I regard the State Prosecutor's question as admissible, I find it essential. If we are going to determine my client's guilt, then we need to understand his motivation. It is of relevance how Mr. Koch considered his own legal position. As we have heard, he took his decision anything but lightly.

10.3 Criminal Law in German Popular Culture: *Terror*

Presiding Judge: (*to the audience*) Ladies and gentlemen judges, the Defence Counsel points out that his client had considered his legal position and ought to be questioned about this. In this particular case his argument has some merit. We, like all modern states, have a law which is based on guilt. We punish a defendant according to his or her personal guilt. Earlier forms of law took the deed alone to be decisive. Anyone who killed a person would themselves be killed. Why the crime had been committed was irrelevant. Now, however, we want to understand this "why." We want to be able to comprehend what can have motivated someone to break the law. Did he kill to enrich himself? Out of jealousy? Out of pleasure in killing? Or did he have entirely different motives, possibly even ones with which we would agree? Our case today is such that the defendant's motives are evidently closely connected to his notion of the law. So we should hear his thoughts. [...]

* * *

Act Two

The entire court except the Presiding Judge is seated or standing in their places. The Guard walks to the front of the stage.

Guard: All those attending the trial please return to the courtroom, the proceedings are about to continue. All those attending the trial please return to the courtroom, the proceedings are about to continue.

The Presiding Judge enters the courtroom, everyone stands up.

Presiding Judge: Please be seated (*all sit*). Prosecutor, we will now hear your closing statement.

State Prosecutor: (*stands*) [...] This case does indeed revolve around one single question: are we allowed to kill innocent people? And is it a question of numbers? Can lives be weighed against each other at a point when, for the death of one person, four hundred others can be saved?

* * *

[...] What are the criteria by which we will decide whether the defendant was allowed to kill or not? We are actually deciding according to our consciences, according to our morals, according to our common sense. And there are other words to express this: the former Minister of Defence referred to an "extra-legal state of emergency." Some lawyers call it "natural law."

However, ladies and gentlemen, the terminology is irrelevant. The meaning is always the same: that we should decide on the basis of ideas which stand above the law, which are greater than the law, ideas, therefore, which replace the law. One has to ask: is this wise? I know each and every one of you believes that you can rely on your own morals and your own conscience. But that is not true.

* * *

We make mistakes, we make them over and over again. It is in our nature – we cannot help it. Morality, conscience, common sense, natural law, extra-legal state of emergency – each one of these terms is suspect, they shift, and it is in their nature that we cannot be certain what the correct course of action is today and whether we will draw exactly the same conclusions tomorrow.

So we need something more reliable than our spontaneous convictions. Something that we can use to judge by at any time and that we can hold on to. Something that provides us with clarity amid the chaos – a guideline which applies even in the most difficult situations. We need *principles*.

And, ladies and gentlemen judges, we have given ourselves these principles. They are our constitution. We have agreed to judge each individual case by it. Every case is to be measured by it and tested by it. By that constitution – not by our consciences, not by our morals, and certainly not by any other higher power. Law and morality must be kept strictly separate. […] Only what has become law may be binding for all. […] And moral views? Regardless of how correct they may appear to us – they bind no one. Only the law and nothing else can do that. And what is more: a "morally correct" view may never be placed above the constitution. At least not in a functioning democratic state based on justice.

* * *

Our constitution is a collection of principles which must always and unreservedly take precedence over morals, conscience, and any other notion. And the highest principle of the constitution is human dignity.

* * *

People are not objects. Life cannot be measured in numbers. It is not a market.

* * *

Lars Koch, ladies and gentlemen, is not a hero. He killed. He turned people into mere objects in his own hands. He denied them any opportunity to make a decision … he took away their human dignity.

* * *

I therefore move that the court find the defendant guilty of murder on 164 counts.

Presiding Judge: Thank you, Prosecutor. Counsel, do you need any more time to prepare?

Defence Counsel: No.

Presiding Judge: Good, then let's hear your closing statement.

Defence Counsel: (*stands up*) Ladies and gentlemen, did you hear the State Prosecutor? Did you understand what she was saying? She wants you to find Lars Koch guilty because of a *principle*. Really, that's exactly what she said – you should lock him up for the rest of his life because of a principle. Because of a principle 70,000 people should have died. I don't care what this principle is called – whether you call it "the constitution" or "human dignity" or anything else. All I can say is: thank God Lars Koch did not act on principle, instead he did what was right. I could actually finish my plea right now.

* * *

Ladies and gentlemen judges, I admit that this idea of choosing the lesser evil is more at home in other jurisdictions. However, and this is what really matters, it is reasonable.

* * *

Ladies and gentlemen judges, if you find Lars Koch guilty today, if you place a dubious constitutional principle above his individual case, by doing that you will be saying that we are not allowed to defend ourselves against terrorists. Perhaps the State Prosecutor is right, perhaps by doing that we are turning the passengers into objects and perhaps we are taking away their dignity. But we have to understand that we are at war. We did not choose it but we cannot change it. And, even if no one wants to hear this any more nowadays, there cannot be wars without victims.

For these reasons I move for a verdict of not guilty.

* * *

Presiding Judge: Ladies and gentlemen, you have now heard the evidence from the defendant, the witnesses and the closing statements from both the Prosecution and the Defence. You will also bear in mind the defendant's last words as you consider your decision. Now it is up to you alone to reach a just verdict. Do not let yourself be swayed by sympathy or antipathy towards the Defence Counsel of the State Prosecutor. Judge purely on the basis of what you consider to be right. You are now familiar with the arguments for both sides. I believe that the Prosecution and the Defence have each made their positions sufficiently clear. You must decide.

* * *

Legally, in making your decision you must know the following: there can be no doubt here that the defendant committed the act – even the Defence Counsel had not disputed this. Your deliberations should therefore focus on the question of whether the defendant was allowed to contravene the restrictions placed upon him by the Federal Constitutional Court and the constitution. That is the heart of the matter. It may be that some among you will be minded to convict the defendant though in light of the special circumstances of this case you don't wish him to have to serve a prison sentence. We judges have no possibility of first convicting the defendant because he has acted illegally and then subsequently pardoning him. That is the responsibility of other offices.

Once you have reached a verdict I shall announce it immediately. You alone will determine the outcome of this trial.

I know that this is a difficult decision but I am confident that you will succeed in judging the case of Lars Koch properly.

The Presiding Judge exits.

Questions/Comments

- How would you vote in the criminal case against Major Koch: guilty or not guilty? What values are implicated by your decision? Do the character and aims of German criminal law – scientific objectivity and certainty, on the one hand, and respect for the defendant's humanity and individual autonomy, on the other hand – clearly point to one outcome? Recall that German criminal law should provide a framework for reaching a "correct solution" in a case. What result would a case like this produce in your primary or "national" legal system? In 2016 a TV film production of the play entitled *Terror – Ihr Urteil* (*Terror – You Decide*) was viewed by nearly seven million Germans who could register their votes for the outcome in the case online or by telephone. More than 85 percent of those who cast a vote opted for Koch's acquittal.
- The play highlights the role of the *Schuldprinzip* in German criminal law. First, there is an insightful explanation of the principle offered by the Presiding Judge in Act One. Second, the closing arguments, and the charge

given to the judges by the Presiding Judge at the end of the trial, demonstrate that the conviction hinges on more than just a finding that the defendant's conduct meets the codified elements of the crime (*Tatbestandsmäßigkeit*) and that he lacked a statutory, objective justification (*Rechtswidrigkeit*) for his conduct. These points were not in dispute in the case. In order to convict in German criminal law, it is also necessary to find the defendant blameworthy (*schuldig*). As the Presiding Judge put it, the judges additionally must decide "whether the defendant was allowed to contravene the restrictions placed upon him" by the law. At this stage of the analysis, the Presiding Judge explained, the question of the defendant's *Schuld* is still a part of the determination of guilt, and not of the sentence the defendant should receive.

- Criminal law features prominently in German popular culture. Perhaps the best example is the long-running television series *Tatort* (*Crime Scene*). Now in its fiftieth year (with more than 1,200 episodes), *Tatort* tells the story of a criminal investigation, with each episode leading to the resolution of the investigation. The series features a rotating cast of detectives pursing their work in cities across Germany, Austria, and Switzerland. *Tatort* has been essential viewing on Sunday evenings for generations. As a "police procedural" *Tatort* focuses on the efforts of the police as they work to solve a crime. That is typical of German cultural engagement with criminal law, encompassing the beloved literary genre referred to as *der Krimi* (the crime novel), or more accurately, the subgenre known as *der Detektivroman* (the detective novel).[29] The investigator's search for the truth of the case seems to resonate with Germans' scientized world view. The German detective novel, one scholar explained, "is interested in the intellectual work of the detective."[30] German popular culture has been less preoccupied with criminal courtroom dramas. That makes *Terror* an exception, joined by the remarkable 2017 film *Aus dem Nichts* (*In the Fade*) from the celebrated German-Turkish filmmaker Fatih Akin. That film dealt with right-wing, racist terrorism in Germany and a major portion of the story unfolds during a criminal trial. Maybe detective dramas are favored over courtroom dramas in Germany because some have argued that the processes used in criminal, as well as civil, proceedings in Germany are "boring." Did you get a sense of that critique of German procedure in the excerpt from von Schirach's play? In any case, that's a theme we'll explore in the next chapter, which considers German procedural law.

10.4 Conclusion

German criminal law has a deep theoretical tradition that seems to be working towards two sometimes contradictory aims. On the one hand, criminal law should be scientifically objective and certain. This is achieved by the theoretical precision of the Criminal Code, which dominates the field and precludes arbitrary results. On the other hand, criminal law should actualize the humanity and individual autonomy of the defendant. This aim is advanced by the two uses of the *Schuldprinzip* (as an element of the conviction and as an element of sentencing). As the *Frankfurt Police Torture Case* demonstrates – with pointed correction from the European Court of Human Rights – concern for the defendant's individual autonomy can undermine the certainty that the formalistic positive law is meant to deliver. After all, no one would suggest that there was a single, mathematical "solution" to that case, or the fictional case of the hijacked airliner shot down by Major Koch. The Frankfurt Regional Court applied the famous (rather scientific) tripartite analysis while nevertheless grasping for a way to do justice in the case. This frustrating conflict of values – of legal traditions – in German criminal law promises this much: German criminal law scholars will continue to theorize about and tinker with the system so that it suitably restricts the possibilities for achieving justice while providing the flexibility that is sometimes needed to achieve that result.

Further Reading

- Kai Ambos, *National Socialist Criminal Law: Continuity and Radicalization* (Hart Publishing) (2019)
- Markus Dubber & Tatjana Hörnle, *Criminal Law: A Comparative Approach* (Oxford University Press) (2014)
- Richard F. Wetzell, *Crime and Criminal Justice in Modern Germany* (Berghahn Books) (2014)
- Thomas Vormbaum & Michael Bohlander, *A Modern History of German Criminal Law* (Margarte Hiley trans.) (Springer) (2013)
- Joy Wiltenburg, *Crime and Culture in Early Modern Germany* (University of Virginia Press) (2012)
- Michael Bohlander, *Principles of German Criminal Law* (Hart Publishing) (2008)
- George P. Fletcher, *The Grammar of Criminal Law: American, Comparative, and International – Volume One: Foundations* (Oxford University Press) (2007)

NOTES

1 Markus Dirk Dubber, *Comparative Criminal Law*, in THE OXFORD HANDBOOK OF COMPARATIVE LAW 1276, 1285 (Mathias Reimann & Reinhard Zimmermann eds., 2nd ed. 2019).
2 Claus Kress, *Germany and International Criminal Law: Continuity or Change?*, in THE NUREMBERG TRIALS: INTERNATIONAL CRIMINAL LAW SINCE 1945 235 (Herbert R. Reginbogin & Christoph Safferling eds., 2006); SALLA HUIKURI, THE INSTITUTIONALIZATION OF THE INTERNATIONAL CRIMINAL COURT 59 (2019).

3 Thomas Vormbaum & Michael Bohlander, A Modern History of German Criminal Law 25 (Margaret Hiley trans., 2014).
4 *Id.* at 19–32.
5 *Id.*
6 Article 102 of the German Constitution explicitly prohibits the death penalty. The most severe penalty provided by German Criminal Law is "life imprisonment." This applies, for example, to the crimes of high treason (§ 81 Criminal Code), engaging in relations which endanger peace (§ 100 Criminal Code), sexual abuse of children resulting in death (§ 176b Criminal Code), rape resulting in death (§ 178 Criminal Code), aggravated murder (§ 211 Criminal Code), or causing a nuclear explosion (§ 307 Criminal Code). Importantly, the German Federal Constitutional Court ruled that a lifetime prison sentence cannot preclude every possibility of parole. Even a life sentence must provide the opportunity, at least as a formality, for the inmate's rehabilitation, release, and reintegration into society. A fixed, invariable life prison sentence, the Court explained, constitutes a violation of the constitutional guarantee of human dignity. *See* Lifetime Prison Sentence Case, BVerfGE 45, 187 (1977). Otherwise, § 38 of the German Criminal Code provides that "(1) Imprisonment is for a fixed term, unless the law provides for imprisonment for life; and (2) The maximum term of a fixed-term period of imprisonment is 15 years, the minimum term one month."
7 Even if the German Criminal Code is old and entrenched, it is better to understand German Criminal Law as a history of continual reform. These efforts, involving scholars as much as parliamentarians, often take decades. That means they sometimes seem to arrive already having missed the moment in history and jurisprudence to which they were meant to respond. So the process of reform starts over, most recently in the wake of reunification with a major reform enacted in 1996.
8 Vormbuam & Bohlander, *supra* note 3, at 79.
9 *Id.* at 80.
10 George P. Fletcher, *Criminal Omissions: Some Perspectives*, 24 Am. J. Compar. L. 703, 710 (1976).
11 Lisbon Treaty Case, 123 BVerfGE 267, 359 (2009).
12 *Id.* at 185.
13 Vormbuam & Bohlander, *supra* note 3, at 134.
14 *Id.* at 252–253; *see* Cristinna Hoss & Russell Miller, *Domesticating International Criminal Law: The German High Courts and Bosnian War Crimes*, 44 Ger. Yearbook Int'l L. 576 (2002).
15 Vormbuam & Bohlander, *supra* note 3, at 173.
16 *Id.* at 185.
17 *Id.* at 176.
18 "Whoever, when faced with a present danger to life, limb, liberty, honour, property or another legal interest which cannot otherwise be averted, commits an act to avert the danger from themselves or another is not deemed to act unlawfully if, upon weighing the conflicting interests, in particular the affected legal interests and the degree of the danger facing them, the protected interest substantially outweighs the one interfered with. However, this only applies to the extent that the act committed is an adequate means to avert the danger."

10.4 Conclusion

19 "Whoever, when faced with a present danger to life, limb or liberty which cannot otherwise be averted, commits an unlawful act to avert the danger from themselves, a relative or close person acts without guilt. This does not apply to the extent that the offender could be expected, under the circumstances, to accept the danger, in particular because said offender caused the danger or because of the existence of a special legal relationship; the penalty may, however, be mitigated pursuant to section 49 (1), unless the offender was required to accept the danger on account of the existence of a special legal relationship."

20 GERHARD ROBBERS, EINFÜHRUNG IN DAS DEUTSCHE RECHT 119 (7th ed. 2019).

21 *Id.*

22 *See, e.g.,* Winfried Brugger, *May Government Ever Use Torture – Two Responses from German Law*, 48 AM. J. COMPAR. L. 661 (Fall 2000); Kai Ambos, *May a State Torture Suspects to Save the Life of Innocents?*, 6 J. INT'L CRIM. JUST. 261 (2008); Florian Jessberger, *Bad Torture – Good Torture: What International Criminal Lawyers May Learn from the Recent Trial of Police Officers in Germany*, 3 J. INT'L CRIM. JUST 1059 (2005).

23 Thomas Zorn, *Held oder Folterknecht*, FOCUS MAGAZIN (Nov. 15, 2004), www.focus.de/politik/deutschland/held-oder-folterknecht-prozess_id_1999532.html.

24 Steffi Dobmeier, *Der Mann ohne Reue*, TAZ (Aug. 4, 2011), https://taz.de/Frueherer-Polizei-Vize-Wolfgang-Daschner/!5114881/.

25 Case of Gäfgen v. Germany (Application no. 22978/05), Eur. Ct. H.R. (Chamber) (2008).

26 Case of Gäfgen v. Germany (Application no. 22978/05), Eur. Ct. H.R. (Grand Chamber) (2010).

27 Jessberger, *supra* note 22, at 1073.

28 Brugger, *supra* note 22, at 672.

29 Katharina Hall, *Crime Fiction in German: Concepts, Developments and Trends*, in CRIME FICTION IN GERMAN: DER KRIMI 1, 3 (Katharina Hall ed., 2016) (*quoting* Richard Alwyen, *Anatomie des Detektivromans*, in DER KRIMINALROMAN 52, 53 (Jochen Vogt ed., 1998)).

30 Hall, *supra* note 29 (*quoting* Heinrich Henel, *Der Indizienstil und die Haltung des Lesers*, in ANNETTE VON DROSTE-HÜLSHOFF, DIE JUDENBUCHE. MIT MATERIALIEN 82, 86 (Helmuth Widhammer ed., 1979)).

11

German Procedural Law

Key Concepts

- **Adversarial Procedure**: Often associated with legal systems influenced by the Common Law tradition, adversarial procedure emphasizes the role of the parties (and their lawyers) in the management of the legal process, including the development and presentation of evidence. Adversarial procedure fosters the creative and assertive pursuit of justice.
- **Inquisitorial Procedure**: Often associated with legal systems influenced by the Civil Law tradition, inquisitorial procedure emphasizes the role of the court in the management of the legal process, including the development and presentation of evidence. Inquisitorial procedure fosters the quick, predictable, and efficient pursuit of justice.
- **Zivilprozessordnung**: The Code of Civil Procedure (ZPO) entered into force in 1879. The Code governs all civil law proceedings.
- **Privatautonomie**: Private autonomy is the principle that individuals should be empowered to act upon their free will in their relationships with others and society. *Privatautonomie* is an expression of liberalism and the Enlightenment ideal of human rationality. This is a central value of the German Code of Civil Procedure, especially as the Code gives private law litigants considerable authority to direct and determine the invocation and prosecution of their rights. The Code's commitment to private autonomy is expressed by the *Dispositionsmaxime* (the parties are the masters of their claims and the process) and the *Verhandlungsmaxime* (the parties control the development and presentation of facts before the court).
- **Class Action**: An Anglo-American private law procedure that permits one or more plaintiffs to file and prosecute a lawsuit on behalf of a larger group, or "class." Put simply, the device allows courts to manage lawsuits that would otherwise be unmanageable if each class member was required to be joined in the lawsuit as a named plaintiff.[1] German civil procedure has only very limited possibilities for organizing a collective civil action. A reform in 2018, however, introduced the *Musterfeststellungsklage* (model declaratory proceedings) to expand the possibility for collective civil lawsuits in Germany.

The *Musterfeststellungsklage* sought to access the advantages of a class action without compromising on key features of the German civil procedure regime. For example, the case must be brought by a public interest organization and not by a law firm motivated by potential profit. The prized concept of private autonomy is preserved because the *Musterfeststellungsklage* only permits the establishment of a presumption of liability for the related claims. Individual litigants are left to pursue their own damages on the basis of that collective finding of liability.

- **Strafprozeßordnung**: The Code of Criminal Procedure (StPO) entered into force in 1879. The Code governs all criminal law proceedings.
- **Legalitätsprinzip**: The legality principle in German criminal procedure requires prosecutors to open an investigation (for the purpose of bringing charges) any time evidence suggests that a possible crime has been committed. By denying the prosecutor any discretion, this principle is evidence of the inquisitorial nature of German criminal procedure. This differs from the *Legalitätsprinzip* that operates in German administrative law.
- **Plea Bargain**: An Anglo-American criminal law procedure that allows defendants to bargain with the prosecution for a lighter punishment in exchange for an admission of guilt. Plea bargains are an efficient mechanism for managing courts' large criminal case dockets. The plea bargain device is criticized for several reasons. First, because it places a great deal of power in the hands of the prosecutor, who may over-charge a defendant in order to increase leverage in the bargaining process. Second, because it can motivate a defense attorney to focus exclusively on the opportunities and options associated with a potential plea agreement as opposed to the development of a rigorous defense case.

Study Tips

The Ministry of Justice and Federal Office of Justice provide English-language translations of a number of important German codes and statutes at the website "*Gesetze im Internet*" (www.gesetze-im-internet.de/). This includes the *Zivilprozessordnumg* (ZPO or Code of Civil Procedure) and the *Strafprozessordnung* (StPO or Code of Criminal Procedure).

A society's substantive norms say a lot about its history and values. For example, as you've learned in previous chapters, substantive German law places great weight on protecting human dignity. That substantive commitment is a direct consequence of the atrocities committed by Hitler's National Socialists and it has been stamped onto every field or framework of law in Germany. But there is another legal regime, other than substantive law, that helps us take the measure of a society. Procedural law doesn't declare that it is a crime to threaten to torture someone (as discussed in Chapter 10), or that a party cannot enforce a contract that is contrary to public policy (as discussed in Chapter 7). That's the work of substantive criminal law (§ 240 of the German Criminal Code, in the former case) and substantive private law (§ 138 of the German Civil Code, in the latter case). Instead, procedural law provides the rules that govern *how* a substantive legal right should be enforced or *how* it can be determined that a substantive legal duty has been violated. Procedural law is the "how" and not the "what" of a legal system. Among other things, procedural law encompasses the rules that establish the courts, determines when courts can do their work and for whom, sets the rules for conducting court proceedings, fixes the quality and quantity of evidence needed to confirm a fact, and provides the regime for enforcing courts' decisions.

Procedural law determines access to, and the functioning of, the justice system. When you think about it, that regime might have as much to do with the quality of justice in a society as the nature and character of the substantive rules themselves. After all, what good is a substantive right if the procedures in place make it difficult – or impossible – to reliably, efficiently, and fairly enforce it? With that in mind, some scholars even wonder if procedural law says more than substantive law about a society's values and its ambitions for justice. Medieval trial-by-combat looks strange and barbaric to us today. But it was shaped by and advanced the central elements of the prevailing world view.[2] Our courtroom processes and practices would be equally incomprehensible to our twelfth century ancestors. How strange, they would think, that the process for settling disputes is now oriented toward the rational search for truth through the examination of evidence with total disregard for the authority that should be given to the will and wisdom of the Almighty. The presentation of evidence, as opposed to the presentation of arms, speaks to the secular and rational values that shape most societies and their legal systems today.

So, there it is. Procedural law matters because it sets the rules for the pursuit of justice under law. And it matters because it is another basis for illuminating the social and historical character of a legal system. That, in turn, is another fruitful area of exploration for a comparative law undertaking like ours.

This encounter with German procedural law is meant to give you a glimpse into the way German lawyers assume the law ought to work. Not the "what" of German law, but the "how." As I have often done in this book, I'll use a comparative perspective to help bring the German approach into focus. For example, comparative law scholars widely accept the notion that German procedural law bears the traits of what is known as an "inquisitorial" model of legal process while the English and American systems are characteristic of an "adversarial" approach to legal process. To understand one (Germany's "inquisitorial" procedural law), it helps to consider it alongside the other (Anglo-American "adversarial" procedural law). After examining those two points of reference, I'll present some common threads and subtle distinctions that operate in German civil procedure and criminal procedure. In the field of procedural law, the German legal system will again look like it is the site of mingling traditions: quite a lot of inquisitorial justice, to be sure, but some elements of adversarial justice as well.

11.1 German Procedure: Inquisitorial or Adversarial Justice

Robert Kagan, the American political scientist, sociologist, and lawyer, wrote a marvelous book entitled *Adversarial Legalism: The American Way of Law* in which he tried to characterize "the distinctive qualities of governance and legal process in the United States."[3] He found that an illuminating way to do this was to compare American legal culture to the legal systems in "other economically advanced democracies, particularly in Western Europe."[4] His study confirmed an old understanding about the differences in procedural law between the US (and, to some extent, other legal systems heavily influenced by the Common Law tradition) and legal systems significantly shaped by the continental Civil Law tradition. The practice in comparative law has been to classify legal process in Anglo-American Common Law systems as "adversarial" and to classify legal process in the continental Civil Law systems, including Germany, as "inquisitorial." Maximo Langer thinks this habit is so entrenched that it has actually come to define and frame the field of comparative procedural law. "The influence and centrality of these categories," Langer argued, "shape comparative [procedural law] by reflecting and restricting the main theoretical trends and the main thematic interests of this field."[5] True to that tradition, Kagan found that these classifications still help portray and explain procedural law around the world, including Germany's procedural law.

Robert A. Kagan
ADVERSARIAL LEGALISM: THE AMERICAN WAY OF LAW 3, 11–12 (2nd ed., 2019)[*]

* * *

[Inquisitorial Legalism involves a] policy-implementing or decision-making process characterized by a high degree of hierarchical authority and legal formality [...] [and it] resembles the ideal-typical bureaucratic process as analyzed by Max Weber. Governance by means of bureaucratic legalism emphasizes uniform implementation of centrally devised rules, vertical accountability, and official responsibility for fact-finding. The more hierarchical the system, the more restricted the role for legal representation and influence by affected citizens or contending interests. In contemporary democracies the pure case of [...] [inquisitorial legalism] usually is softened in some respects, but it is an ideal systematically pursued [...]. Also tending toward this ideal are German and French courts, where judges are bureaucratically recruited and supervised – as contrasted with America's emphasis on election or political appointment. In court, these bureaucratically recruited and embedded judges – not the parties' lawyers and not lay juries – dominate both the evidence-gathering and

---

[*] © 2001 by the President and Fellows of Harvard College. Used by permission. All rights reserved.

the decision-making processes. Another illustration: in contrast to American criminal prosecutors' offices, in which individual assistant district attorneys usually make their own judgments about which charges to make and bargain with defense counsel about how much to reduce them in return for guilty pleas, prosecutors in [...] [systems characterized by inquisitorial legalism] are subject to detailed rules and close hierarchical supervision concerning the investigation of facts, determination of the proper charge, and the recommendation of penalties.

* * *

[Adversarial Legalism involves] policy-implementing and decision processes that are procedurally formalistic but in which hierarchy is relatively weak and party influence on the process is strong. Regulatory and antidiscrimination laws in the United States, for example, frequently are implemented and enforced not merely by government bureaucracies but also, and sometimes primarily, by means of lawsuits that are initiated by a decentralized array of private individuals, entrepreneurial lawyers, and advocacy organizations. American methods for compensating victims of highway and medical accidents prominently include a decentralized and adversarial tort law system driven by claimants and their lawyers, as contrasted with Western European compensation systems, which operate primarily through social insurance or benefit-payment bureaucracies. In American civil and criminal adjudication, the introduction of evidence and invocation of legal rules are dominated not by the judge (as in continental Europe) but by contending parties' lawyers. Even in comparison with the British adversarial system, hierarchical, authoritative imposition of legal rules is relatively weak in the United States. Trial court judges share decision-making power with lay jurors, whose decisions are not explained and largely shielded from hierarchical review, which reduces legal certainty and magnifies the influence of skillful legal advocacy. Hierarchical control of judges in the United States also is weakened by jurisdictional fragmentation between the federal and the fifty separate state judiciaries. Due to the large role of political parties and interest groups in the selection of judges, American judges, compared to more professionally selected and supervised judiciaries, more often are influenced by their political commitments, so that decisions are more often influenced by which judges decide the case or by which city or county court deals with the case.

* * *

Questions/Comments

- Amalia Kessler provided another, succinct way of framing the different approaches to procedural law: "The adversarial and inquisitorial models are distinguished primarily by whether the parties or the court control three key aspects of the litigation: initiating the action, gathering the evidence, and determining the sequence and nature of the proceedings."[6] Who do you think controls these elements of a legal process in an "adversarial" legal system? By contrast, who has control over these elements of a legal process in an "inquisitorial" legal system? Would you say that your primary or "national" legal system is inquisitorial or adversarial?
- Kessler explained that the inquisitorial approach to legal process is rooted in the "dark inquisitorial world of continental Europe" and that

11.1 German Procedure: Inquisitorial or Adversarial Justice

it is derived from the Roman-Canon tradition.[7] How have Europe's history, politics, and society informed its tilt towards inquisitorial justice? Can you imagine what the relationship is between the Civil Law tradition and an adjudicative process largely controlled by judges? Kagan aligns the adversarial approach to legal process with the Anglo-American Common Law tradition and approvingly quotes Seymour Lipset, who described American law and governance as singularly individualistic, anti-statist, legalistic, and rights-oriented.[8] How have America's history, politics, and society informed its tilt towards adversarial justice? Can you imagine what the relationship is between the Common Law tradition and an adjudicative process largely controlled by the parties?

You might have guessed that I am suspicious of the comparative law habit of classifying a legal system's procedural law as exclusively inquisitorial or adversarial. I share Kessler's view that the two approaches to procedural law are mere "models to which no actual legal system precisely corresponds, since all legal systems combine both adversarial and inquisitorial elements."[9] Kagan agrees with that insight, concluding that "no modern democratic legal system is characterized entirely" by these labels.[10] John Spencer has gone so far as to ask whether there is still a difference between inquisitorial and adversarial justice.[11] Despite those qualifications, it is true that German procedural law possesses many traits that would qualify it as an inquisitorial system. That will be evident in the following encounters with German civil procedure and criminal procedure. But these encounters will also reveal that the adversarial mode of adjudicating, typically linked to the Anglo-American systems influenced by the Common Law tradition, also is present in German law.

Whether, and to what degree, German procedural law fulfills the expectation that it is largely inquisitorial, depends on which legal process you're talking about. As you know, the German legal system is built on the foundation stones of several prominent codes and their accompanying distinct subject matter jurisdictions. Each of these enclosed fields of law have their own specialized courts (as discussed in Chapter 5 and depicted in Figure 5.4). Maybe it isn't surprising that, in this disaggregated legal framework, there are different procedural regimes that are meant to account for the distinct character of the relevant substantive law and the distinct interests of the courts adjudicating those regimes. That means that, when speaking of German procedural law, you should differentiate between the systems shown in Table 11.1.

The German Code of Civil Procedure draws on an old tradition, dating back to the Imperial Justice Acts of 1877. That pedigree and its association with the beloved Civil Code, have elevated civil procedure to prominence in German law. It is sometimes called the "mother of procedural law regimes."[12] Unless you specify, Germans are likely to assume that you mean civil procedure if you speak generally about "procedural law."

Table 11.1 German Procedural Law Framework

Substantive Law	Jurisdiction	Procedural Law
Constitutional Law (*Grundgesetz* – GG) (Basic Law)	Constitutional Court	*Grundgesetz* (GG) (Basic Law) and *Bundesverfassungsgerichtsgesetz* (BVerfGG) (Federal Constitutional Court Act)
Civil Law (*Bürgerliches Gesetzbuch*–BGB) (Civil Code)	Ordinary Courts	*Zivilprozessordnung* (ZPO) (Code of Civil Procedure)
Criminal Law (*Strafgesetzbuch* – StGB) (Criminal Code)		*Strafprozessordnung* (StPO) (Code of Criminal Procedure)
Administrative Law (Statutes and Regulations concerned with Farm Law, Municipal Law, Public Servants Law, Police Law, Environmental Law, and Law of the Economy)	Administrative Law Courts	*Verwaltungsgerichtsordnung* (VwGO) (Code of Administrative Court Procedure)
Fiscal Law (Statutes and Regulations concerned with the Administration Public Finances, including Tax Law)	Fiscal Courts	*Finanzgerichtsordnung* (FGO) (Code of Financial Court Procedure)
Social Law (*Sozialgesetzbuch* – SGB) (Social Code)	Social Law Courts	*Sozialgerichtsgesetz* (SGG) (Social Court Act)
Labor Law (Statutes and Regulations concerned with dependent employment)	Labor Courts	*Arbeitsgerichtsgesetz* (ArbGG) (Labor Court Act)

There is a lot of difference and variety across the distinct regimes of procedural law. But there are some overarching commonalities, too.

As I have already noted, in the assessment of most comparative law scholars, German procedural law is more inquisitorial than adversarial in character. Kagan would remind you that this means that German procedure "resembles the ideal-typical bureaucratic process [emphasizing] uniform implementation of centrally devised rules, vertical accountability, and official responsibility for fact-finding."[13]

The German constitution addresses a few general points of procedural law as well. As is the case in American law, the intersection between constitutional law and procedural law is thick and particularly meaningful in the context of criminal and administrative justice. But some Basic Law provisions are relevant to judicial processes in general, such as: Article 19(4) (providing a right to be heard by a court if public authority violates a basic right); Article 101 (banning extraordinary courts); and Article 103 (guaranteeing a right to raise a legal claim before a court).

As Table 11.1 confirms, German procedural law is statutory and codified law – exactly as you'd expect from a legal system so heavily influenced by the Civil Law tradition.

Cathrin Silberzahn identified a number of other elements that might form a "common regime of German procedural law," including the role procedure plays in enforcing individuals' rights, reinforcing the interests of the public, facilitating the development of the law, and securing legal order and legal certainty.[14] There is also a commitment across most German procedural law to elements such as oral hearings and public hearings.[15]

But there are limits to the cohesion of German procedural law, which is especially differentiated by the degree to which the rules empower the parties or the court to influence and steer the process. Criminal procedure and administrative procedure give greater power to the court while the parties are thought of as the "masters" of the proceedings under civil procedure. Already we are seeing that labeling German procedural law as "inquisitorial" may not be accurate, or at least not adequate. To get a general sense of German procedural law – including the different ways it inclines towards or away from inquisitorial justice – the rest of this chapter provides you with an introduction to civil procedure and criminal procedure. We'll be guided along the way by the renowned legal historian and comparative law scholar John Langbein, who had a special interest in and a unique perspective on German procedural law.

11.2 German Civil Procedure

In a provocative and influential article, John Langbein praised several features of German civil procedure, including judges' significant control over the case, and judges' control over the collection and evaluation of the evidence. That sounds rather inquisitorial. Langbein called the arrangement "a necessary and welcome" reduction in the role played by lawyers under American civil procedure. This, he concluded, constituted "the German advantage in civil procedure."

John H. Langbein
The German Advantage in Civil Procedure
52 UNIVERSITY OF CHICAGO LAW REVIEW 823, 826–830 (1985)[*]

* * *

There are two fundamental differences between German and Anglo-American civil procedure, and these differences lead in turn to many others. First, the court rather than the

---

[*] Excerpt reprinted with permission from the *University of Chicago Law Review* and the University of Chicago Law School.

parties' lawyers takes the main responsibility for gathering and sifting evidence, although the lawyers exercise a watchful eye over the court's work. Second, there is no distinction between pretrial and trial, between discovering evidence and presenting it. Trial is not a single continuous event. Rather, the court gathers and evaluates evidence over a series of hearings, as many as the circumstances require.

Initiation. The plaintiff's lawyer commences a lawsuit in Germany with a complaint. Like its American counterpart, the German complaint narrates the key facts, sets forth a legal theory, and asks for a remedy in damages or specific relief. Unlike an American complaint, however, the German document proposes means of proof for its main factual contentions. The major documents in the plaintiff's possession that support his claim are scheduled and often appended; other documents (e.g., hospital files or government records such as police accident reports or agency files) are indicated; witnesses who are thought to know something helpful to the plaintiff's position are identified. The defendant's answer follows the same pattern. It should be emphasized, however, that neither plaintiff's nor defendant's lawyer will have conducted any significant search for witnesses or for other evidence unknown to his client. Digging for facts is primarily the work of the judge.

Judicial preparation. The judge to whom the case is entrusted examines these pleadings and appended documents. He routinely sends for relevant public records. These materials form the beginnings of the official dossier, the court file. All subsequent submissions of counsel, and all subsequent evidence-gathering, will be entered in the dossier, which is open to counsel's inspection continuously.

When the judge develops a first sense of the dispute from these materials, he will schedule a hearing and notify the lawyers. He will often invite and sometimes summon the parties as well as their lawyers to this or subsequent hearings. If the pleadings have identified witnesses whose testimony seems central, the judge may summon them to the initial hearing as well.

Hearing. The circumstances of the case dictate the course of the hearing. Sometimes the court will be able to resolve the case by discussing it with the lawyers and parties and suggesting avenues of compromise. If the case remains contentious and witness testimony needs to be taken, the court will have learned enough about the case to determine a sequence for examining witnesses.

Examining and recording. The judge serves as the examiner-in-chief. At the conclusion of his interrogation of each witness, counsel for either party may pose additional questions, but counsel are not prominent as examiners. Witness testimony is seldom recorded verbatim; rather, the judge pauses from time to time to dictate a summary of the testimony into the dossier. The lawyers sometimes suggest improvements in the wording of these summaries, in order to preserve or to emphasize nuances important to one side or the other.

* * *

A related source of dispatch in German procedure is the virtual absence of any counterpart to the Anglo-American law of evidence. German law exhibits expansive notions of testimonial privilege, especially for potential witnesses drawn from the family. But German procedure functions without the main chapters of our law of evidence, those rules (such as hearsay) that exclude probative evidence for fear of the inability of the trier of fact to evaluate the evidence purposively. In civil litigation German judges sit without juries (a point to which this essay recurs); evidentiary shortcomings that would affect admissibility in our law affect weight or credit in German law.

Expertise. If an issue of technical difficulty arises on which the court or counsel wishes to obtain the views of an expert, the court – in consultation with counsel – will select the expert and define his role. [...]

Further contributions of counsel. After the court takes witness testimony or receives some other infusion of evidence, counsel have the opportunity to comment orally or in writing. Counsel use these submissions in order to suggest further proofs or to advance legal theories. Thus, non-adversarial proof-taking alternates with adversarial dialogue across as many hearings as are necessary. The process merges the investigatory function of [American] pretrial discovery and the evidence-presenting function of [an American] trial. Another manifestation of the comparative efficiency of German procedure is that a witness is ordinarily examined only once. Contrast the American practice of partisan interview and preparation, pretrial deposition, preparation for trial, and examination and cross-examination at trial. These many steps take their toll in expense and irritation.

Judgment. After developing the facts and hearing the adversaries' views, the court decides the case in a written judgment that must contain full findings of fact and make reasoned application of the law.

[…] [I]n German procedure the court ranges over the entire case, constantly looking for the jugular – for the issue of law or fact that might dispose of the case. Free of constraints that arise from party presentation of evidence, the court investigates the dispute in the fashion most likely to narrow the inquiry. A major job of counsel is to guide the search by directing the court's attention to particularly cogent lines of inquiry.

* * *

Questions/Comments

- This excerpt from Langbein's article obscures some of the most fundamental elements of German civil procedure. Ask any German lawyer about the central principles of civil procedure and he or she will mention the *Dispositionsmaxime* (the parties' authority over the process) and the *Verhandlungsmaxime* (the parties' responsibility for the facts of the case).[16] The *Dispositionsmaxime* provides that the decision whether to initiate a case, and the identification of the issues to be raised in the case, are matters exclusively for the parties. Private law is about private rights, the idea goes, so it is up to the individual holders of those rights to call on the court for help solving their legal disputes. This is an extension of the *Privatautonomie* (individual autonomy) that the Civil Code codifies, celebrates, and concretizes. The *Verhandlungsmaxime* builds on these notions by making it the parties' responsibility to identify and tender the relevant evidence needed to support their position in the case. One German textbook explains that "the court has no duty to establish the facts of the case."[17] Confusing, isn't it? The comparative law stereotype says that, as a system influenced by the inquisitorial tradition, the courts should dominate the process. And that's the understanding Langbein advances in his portrayal of German civil procedure. But that is not how many German lawyers see their civil process. Pointing to the revered *Dispositionsmaxime* and *Verhandlungsmaxime* they emphasize the parties' control over civil proceedings, a degree of control that looks to them a lot like adversarial justice.

- Two things might explain this seeming contradiction. First, both Langbein and the German lawyers in this scenario operate from positions that are colored by their embeddedness in their unique legal culture and training (recall our discussion of "distancing" and "differencing" in Chapter 1). For Langbein, the American trained "adversarialist," the significant role played by German courts in a civil process (even if moderated by the *Dispositionsmaxime* and the *Verhandlungsmaxime*) must look exaggerated. For German trained "inquisitorialists," however, the significant (but by no means exclusive) role the parties play in a civil process must look exaggerated. Second, this passage from Langbein's article is especially focused on the role of the judge in working with the evidence tendered to the court by the parties: reviewing and summarizing documents; examining and assessing witnesses; and ultimately drawing conclusions. Langbein is right that this effort is undertaken exclusively by the German judge in a manner that is remarkably hands-on by American adversarial standards. Langbein acknowledges, but nevertheless understates, the fact that the evidence with which a German judge is so intensively involved in a civil law dispute is almost exclusively limited to only that evidence which the parties identify and present to the court. That's the expression of the *Dispositionsmaxime* and *Verhandlungsmaxime* that impresses Germans so much.
- After reflecting on Langbein's conclusions about German Civil Procedure, and the debate his article stirred among comparative lawyers, an experienced German trial judge seemed to give the "advantage" to Langbein:

   German civil procedure shows a marked difference between theory and practice, even compared to the practice of maybe thirty years ago. In theory, the parties and their lawyers are supposed to adduce the facts of the case and the evidence and to do this as speedily as possible. In practice, the judge must urge them to comply with time limits and to disclose all the facts and evidence the court needs for its decision. The appellate courts over time have tightened their control over first instance courts considerably and now require [trial] judges to warn the parties of defects in the pleadings and state more or less explicitly how to mend them, regardless of whether they are represented by attorneys or appearing *pro se*. [...] The judge's role in pre-trial preparation and at the trial hearing is becoming more and more pro-active as a consequence of the abovementioned attitude of the appellate courts. Judges play a significant role in reaching settlements short of judgment by trying to mediate between the positions of the parties. The role of the lawyers is mostly reduced to a controlling function with regard to the court's actions. The modern civil trial in Germany could no longer be carried out on the lawyers' responsibility alone.[18]

- Langbein views the role of the lawyer in German private litigation as significantly limited when compared with the Anglo-American tradition. Nigel Foster and Satish Sule confirm this:

   The attorney's role [in German civil law proceedings] is mainly restricted to the preparation and the submission of written pleadings, more usual in civil

11.2 German Civil Procedure

law courts, plus some oral representation in the main court proceedings. [...] Litigation is thus often regarded as low-paid and dull work and is mainly left to the junior members and less experienced attorneys of a practice.[19]

- A telling indication of the more modest role of the lawyer in a German civil process might be the dearth of German literature, films, and television programs in which private lawyers star as the protagonist. No one like John Grisham has emerged to capture Germans' imagination with the tales of a civil litigator using private law to confront corporate power as a champion of the harmed, downtrodden, and dispossessed.[20] Aside from the fact that they do not contribute much to Germans' entertainment, Germany's "boring" lawyers might actually be part of the advantage Langbein attributes to German civil procedure. Kagan identifies other positive consequences of the German lawyer's low profile.

  > In terms of personal character, lawyers [working in an inquisitorial system] may be no less Machiavellian, on average, than are New York lawyers [presumably hardened by American law's brutal adversarialism]. But compared with the United States, professional codes of ethics in [legal systems influenced by the Civil Law tradition], more strongly enjoin lawyers to temper one-sided advocacy in the search for objective legal truth. Moreover, in the decentralized, adversarial American court system – with its long delays before adjudication, its weak hierarchical controls over lawyer-controlled pretrial discovery, its uncertainty, and its opportunities for forum shopping – lawyers have much stronger incentives to "see what they can get away with" than they do in [inquisitorial legal systems].
  >
  > [The American] civil justice system bloated by adversarial legalism thus is a twofold source of inequality: sophisticated litigants gain an advantage not only because they are better at withstanding the costs and uncertainties of adversarial litigation but also because they are better able to devise ways of circumventing it. More fundamentally, knowledge that the court system is too costly, complicated, slow, and uncertain to vindicate many legal rights and defenses must surely have a deeply corrosive effect on American citizens' faith in the justice system. The average citizen thinks it favors the rich.[21]

- Langbein might be excused for adopting the perspective he does. Many scholars and practitioners agree with him that the American tradition of "discovery" in civil proceedings – a process by which the parties painstakingly develop, share, and test the evidence relevant to a case before the trial begins and with only a minimal role for the court – is tedious, wasteful, time consuming, and expensive.[22] For example, one study concluded that, largely because of discovery, corporate litigation costs in the United States were between four and nine times higher than litigation costs outside the United States.[23] By involving the judge in the management of the collection and evaluation of the evidence, German civil procedure avoids those problems. That led Langbein to conclude that the Germans have the advantage when it comes to civil procedure. He credits the inquisitorial, judge-centered approach of German civil procedure as "a source of dispatch" and he praises "the comparative efficiency of German procedure." Yet, are speed and efficiency the only – or even the most – important measure of the quality of justice? What might the benefits of a more adversarial approach to procedural law be?

Whatever its advantages (or disadvantages), German civil procedure has struggled to respond to cases involving relatively modest harm suffered by a large number of possible claimants due to the conduct of a powerful defendant. In that kind of case, no single claimant may have the incentive to sue to enforce his or her individual rights, especially if doing so would mean squaring off against a big, wealthy opponent for a trivial potential recovery. These scenarios arise in the area of consumer protection, environmental harm, or securities regulation. They often involve large companies that are shielded from significant legal consequences because, out of respect for *Privatautonomie* and the parties' authority over proceedings, German civil procedure largely requires each claimant to bring a separate case. America's adversarial civil procedure has filled this gap in the framework of justice by allowing a handful of claimants – maybe just one – to file a suit on behalf of a large number of similarly situated individuals.[24] These "class action" lawsuits might even deny individual claimants the authority to determine their own legal fate. But they level the playing field in suits involving powerful defendants by combining the interests and harms of many potential plaintiffs into a single lawsuit.

According to Michael Halberstam the sprawling, costly, and time-consuming process of "discovering" evidence in American civil procedure is an essential part of class actions' success in advancing the cause of justice for the "little guy" in a world of corporate Goliaths.[25]

Michael Halberstam
The American Advantage in Civil Procedure: An Autopsy of the Deutsche Telekom Litigation
48 CONNECTICUT LAW REVIEW 817, 819–820, 823–824, 827–828, 830–831 (2016)[*]

* * *

Deutsche Telekom was accused in both the U.S. and German actions of misrepresenting the value of its real estate holdings in its financial disclosures and for failing to disclose negotiations for the acquisition of the U.S. company VoiceStream in its June 2000 global offering. [The company's] stock price declined substantially after news of the fifty billion Euro VoiceStream acquisition hit the markets, and again, in February of 2001, after the company took a two billion Euro write-down for a decline in its real estate assets. Shareholders in the United States and in Germany filed suit, claiming that the company had violated its securities disclosure obligations.

But the cases proceeded very differently and produced dramatically different outcomes. U.S. class action plaintiffs filed suit in the Southern District of New York in

---

[*] Excerpt reprinted with permission of the author.

December of 2000. After full discovery, plaintiffs negotiated a $120 million settlement with the Deutsche Telekom defendants. The settlement was approved by the court in June of 2005. Meanwhile, the parallel [individual] claims by German shareholders, the first of which were filed in 2001, were ultimately dismissed by the German courts in 2012, despite Germany's late-2004 adoption of a new and unprecedented aggregate litigation mechanism (dubbed "the Deutsche Telekom law") to afford thousands of complaining German shareholders a reasonable mechanism for pursuing a just and speedier resolution of their claims. The case was appealed to the Federal Supreme Court (*Bundesgerichtshof*), which published its decision on October 12, 2014, affirming the Higher Regional Court's judgment on the VoiceStream and real estate allegations, but finding fault with the by now fourteen-year-old lawsuit on grounds that the prospectus illegally classified certain transactions with a subsidiary involving Sprint shares as sales – an issue that was neither complained of nor litigated in New York. As of the publication date of this article, German shareholders have not received any monetary damages, due to further proceedings in the Frankfurt District Court.

* * *

According to Plaintiffs' attorneys, one major factor in the Deutsche Telekom case was the lack of discovery. In German civil actions, plaintiffs have a very hard time investigating company internal wrongdoing, because of fundamental principles of civil law adjudication that are deeply embedded in German civil procedure. Party-on-party discovery is prohibited. There are no interrogatories, no pretrial witness depositions, and no document discovery. For the most part, parties must obtain documentary evidence in support of their claims independently and extrajudicially. Defendants are not required, and cannot be forced, to produce relevant documents or electronic discovery to support a plaintiff's case. Based on these principles, as well as other principles of due process, the German court (and the U.S. court, acting on principles of comity upon receiving a letter from the German government) refused to allow German plaintiffs in the Deutsche Telekom litigation access to discovery materials that had already been produced in the U.S. litigation. German plaintiffs sought to obtain the documents and deposition transcripts pertinent to their case in U.S. proceedings under [rules of US civil procedure] and the German government went so far as to vehemently object to such disclosure.

* * *

Does the lack of adequate tools for fact investigation in private litigation in Europe (and other civil law jurisdictions) compromise the enforcement of shareholder rights – even in sophisticated jurisdictions like Germany, which Professor John Langbein famously advocated as a model of efficient fact-finding in his controversial article, "*The German Advantage in Civil Procedure*"?

* * *

Even as some European countries, like Germany, have passed legislation to do so, public enforcement remains the near exclusive venue for punishing and deterring issuer misconduct. In these debates, the costs of U.S.-style class actions, and in particular of litigation discovery, loom large.

The ability of U.S. plaintiffs to impose substantial discovery costs and burdens on corporate defendants is often viewed as a critical component of successfully prosecuting securities class actions. At the same time, the U.S. retreat from the "private attorney general" model in securities litigation is closely linked with the controversial theory that so-called "impositional discovery" enables plaintiff-side attorneys to pressure defendants to settle based on the threat of discovery rather than the merits of the case. Apart from encouraging meritless (and therefore unjust) strike suits, the critics of securities class actions maintain that the costs and burdens of discovery generate over-deterrence. Limiting plaintiffs' ability to obtain discovery has thus been the principal point of leverage for U.S. reforms.

Even as Europeans introduce aggregate litigation mechanisms into their domestic law, their reactions to litigation discovery in the U.S. class action setting are extreme. Discovery's purported excesses are viewed with nothing short of horror – the equivalent of "boiling the ocean to heat a tea kettle" in the words of one observer. Following Langbein, U.S. litigation discovery is considered to be an extremely inefficient way to acquire evidence for the resolution of civil disputes. The rise of electronic discovery has only heightened the sense that Americans are "nuts" when it comes to the scope and tools of litigation discovery, and the resources that are allocated to discovery.

The costs and burdens of litigation discovery are thus at the heart of the debate about how to find the right balance between public and private enforcement in the United States and in Europe. As already mentioned, this debate is longstanding.

In his 1983 article, Langbein championed the efficiency of German civil procedure. He argued that the German civil law process of evidence acquisition and fact-finding by a judge is far superior to the long and wasteful U.S. process of litigation discovery.

* * *

But in Europe, there is no litigation discovery. There is no specific phase of the litigation process dedicated to the exploration or collection of evidentiary materials in civil law systems. Nor is there a general right to obtain relevant information in connection with the proceedings. Party-on-party discovery is not permitted and any demand for information from a defendant must be approved and issued by a judge. The parties are thus expected to rely on their personal knowledge and any materials in their possession to make out their case. While there are some substantive and procedural rights to obtain information under certain circumstances – the main procedural tool is a shifting of the burden of proof – these are limited. A plaintiff must obtain evidence of corporate internal wrongdoing from other sources, like investigative journalism, government investigations, or whistleblowers. Plaintiff-side attorneys thus view companies as "black boxes" which they are able to penetrate only under special circumstances. German plaintiffs, like plaintiffs in other European countries, "practically have no access to ... [an issuer's] files" – "[o]nly prosecutors have the weapons to seize papers, question witnesses and find out what actually happened."

But Langbein's view of U.S. civil litigation, and especially discovery, appears still to be widely shared, especially in Europe. [...]

* * *

Questions/Comments

- In an essay published in 2021, two commentators noted that the German litigation in the Deutsche Telekom case was still grinding along: "To date, there are disputes before the Higher Regional Court of Frankfurt am Main and the BGH [Federal Court of Justice] as to whether the investors are actually entitled to compensation for damages [...]."[26]
- Europeans' suspicion about American-style civil litigation – and especially class action lawsuits – is partly stirred by the unseemly function played by

"entrepreneurial" plaintiffs' lawyers who, it is argued, are motivated to cobble together classes of claimants so that they can collect fees or a share of inflated punitive damages awards. This is the tawdry world of late-night, cable television advertisements pleading with viewers to call to register their grievances and injuries with a particular lawyer or law firm. Kagan acknowledges the "extortive potential" of "high-stakes lawsuits [such as those] in the realm of class actions by consumers, investors, and tort claimants."[27] He cites one critical study that concluded that "modern class action [...] has long been a context in which opportunistic behavior has been common and high agency costs have prevailed. Settlements have all too frequently advanced only the interests of plaintiffs' attorneys, not those of class members."[28] Most Americans, at some point in time, will receive an official-looking letter in the post advising them that they've been identified as a member of a "class" whose legal interests have been settled in a big class action case. The letter might inform them that they are entitled to claim their apportioned share of the damages: maybe just a few dollars. That is a result for which the class action lawyers may have been very handsomely compensated. The critique of all of this is that justice has been commodified and commandeered for the benefit of the lawyers with very little regard for the interests of the individual victims of misconduct. With this critique in mind it is necessary to concede that, in some important ways, American adversarial litigation would be a bad social fit for Germany. American plaintiffs' lawyers are given a slice of the big awards they win as a way of incentivizing them to bring these lawsuits. That's desirable because America's relatively unregulated market treats these lawyers (whether "self-interested" or acting as "social justice champions" depending on the case and your perspective) as *ex post* private regulators or "private attorneys general." There's considerably less need for that in Germany's more thoroughly regulated market, which seeks to constrain and conform conduct *ex ante*.

What happens in Germany when the strict respect shown for *Privatautonomie* by the civil procedure regime allows some harmful conduct to slip through the regulatory net? Nothing raised that concern more spectacularly than the so-called "Dieselgate" scandal that cast a thick smog of disrepute over the Volkswagen Auto Group in the 2010s, eventually spreading to most of the German auto industry. Based in Germany, VW is one of the world's biggest car companies. A major component of its success had been its development of remarkably fuel-efficient diesel engines that miraculously produced very little pollution. But, as is so often the case, if something seems too good to be true, then there is a good chance that it is a sham. VW's new diesel engines were just as dirty as older models. The company had merely coded the relevant software so that the pollution inhibiting technology (which significantly reduced fuel efficiency) was activated only when the cars' emissions systems were being tested as part of the periodic safety inspections required by most countries' transportation regulators. VW and other carmakers were simply cheating on the emissions tests and lying to consumers when they sold them "clean diesel" cars.[29] The scandal's harm went far beyond the marketing deceit, which allowed the manufacturers to sell the cars at a premium. The "poisonous" diesels posed a threat to public health, especially in their high concentration in European cities, because they far exceeded the legal limits for nitrogen oxide (NOx) emissions.

Under pressure from a massive, embarrassing, and costly class action lawsuit, VW quickly settled the case in a US federal court, agreeing to pay compensation to US consumers and to buy back the cars or to retrofit their emissions technology.[30] The legal remedies for Germans were much slower to materialize. None of the existing mechanisms for combining claims applied to the case or proved effective in forming a critical mass of claimants capable of confronting the country's industrial champion. One device permits the establishment of a *Musterklage* (model case) in the capital markets and securities sector. It was created in response to the Deutsche Telekom scandal referenced earlier in this chapter.[31] But that wasn't much help in the Dieselgate scandal, which involved a consumer protection problem. Other rules permit joinder of cases or the consolidation of parties. But all these elements of German civil procedure seek to maintain the tradition of *Privatautonomie*, on the one hand, and to prevent the emergence of dreaded, unsavory elements of adversarial American litigation (such as profiteering lawyers, a wasteful process for the development of evidence, and punitive damages), on the other hand.

The Dieselgate scandal nevertheless obliged the German parliament to act.

Katharina van Elten & Britta Rehder
How the Dieselgate Scandal Helped Bring American-Style Legal Conflict Resolution to Europe
BLOG – EUROPEAN POLITICS AND POLICY AT THE LONDON SCHOOL OF ECONOMICS (December 3, 2020)[*]

* * *

The Dieselgate emissions scandal is one of the largest and most far-reaching industrial scandals of the post-war period. It caused enormous financial damage and a considerable loss of reputation for the German car industry. However, it also had a substantial influence on consumer protection in Europe and Germany.

Consumers are now much more likely to assert their interests in court, since the scandal enhanced legal consciousness, opened the legal market to new players and led to the introduction of new collective redress rights in Germany and the EU. The events surrounding the scandal thereby contributed to the longstanding debate over whether European legal systems are becoming more American, specifically if the concept of "Adversarial Legalism" is transferring to Europe in a form of "Eurolegalism."

* * *

---

[*] https://blogs.lse.ac.uk/europpblog/2020/12/03/how-the-dieselgate-scandal-helped-bring-american-style-legal-conflict-resolution-to-europe/.

We argue that this process was fostered by Dieselgate for a variety of reasons. These include "backfiring corporatism," the marketisation of legal proceedings by new actors, and new opportunity structures and changing attitudes in the EU and the member states toward class action rules and collective redress rights.

Backfiring Corporatism

It has often been argued that corporatist networks prevent a turn to the legal system, and Germany is characterised by a pronounced and stable automotive corporatism. These networks were indeed very visible in the face of the scandal – partly to their disadvantage, though. The German government focused quite exclusively on damage limitation for the car industry. The blatant lobbying for the car companies (e.g., a further lowering of the emission limits at EU level) stood in stark contrast to the unwillingness to regulate the industry or show any political support for the affected customers. This led to a significant loss of legitimacy for automotive corporatism.

The Marketisation of Legal Proceedings

Since no support was to be expected at the political level, legal action offered an alternative to the pursuit of interests. This benefited a new alliance of actors. In Germany and Europe, so-called legal tech providers cooperated with consumer protection organisations, but most importantly with renowned American law firms and litigation financiers, in order to collect the claims of affected customers and negotiate them in a bundled manner.

Legal tech providers exploit the technical feasibilities of digitalisation to bring together plaintiffs from all over the European continent. They seek to build alliances with experienced (American) law firms and (international) financiers to handle mass compensation cases. This (to Europe) new business model is based on a legal grey area, in which the legal tech companies bear the cost risk and, if successful, retain up to 35% of the amount of damages claimed. In this respect, Dieselgate had a huge impact on the marketisation and juridification of conflicts.

New Opportunity Structures

Dieselgate created a window of opportunity for the (long demanded) introduction of collective rights of action in Germany and the EU. Long sceptical about collective redress rights, the German government felt compelled to introduce the so-called "Musterfeststellungsklage" (model declaratory proceedings), which allows public interest groups to bundle claims and take them to court.

At the EU level, litigation rights for consumers had been under discussion for some time, and the "New Deal for Consumers" created the first European collective redress mechanism. In both cases, efforts were made to prevent marketisation and a "litigation industry" by granting litigation rights exclusively to public interest groups and not to law firms.

The Lasting Effects of Dieselgate

These efforts were obviously aimed at preventing certain characteristics of the American system from spreading to Europe, specifically to contain the role of law firms and litigation financiers, but they will probably be unable to stop their growing influence. We argue that the dynamics triggered by the scandal will have a lasting effect.

The role of specialised law firms and the demand for collective litigation rights will probably expand for different reasons. The events around Dieselgate have increased legal consciousness enormously. Model declaratory proceedings have already been successfully applied by public interest organisations in Germany, not only against Volkswagen, but also in other cases, such as with respect to tenancy law. Legal tech providers have achieved a high level of awareness and are expanding their business in the legal market.

Many public interest groups have neither the resources nor the expertise to take on high profile cases and are dependent on law firms. Law firms can approach the organisations themselves and offer their services or look for first-mover-advantage. Furthermore, it has been shown that many affected persons try to achieve better results in court without participating in the collective legal action possibilities, further increasing the development of juridification of conflicts.

Recent developments show that the dynamics triggered have permanently changed the legal market and consumer protection, promoting Eurolegalism. This is underlined by the legal proceedings surrounding the latest scandals, bankruptcies and of course the Covid-19 pandemic: Legal tech companies, for example, were quick to try to take profits from the Thomas Cook bankruptcy and litigation financiers and the law firm Ernst & Young are already collecting claims for a class action suit in the Wirecard scandal.

* * *

In summary, we can say that the Dieselgate scandal has triggered processes that have encouraged the spread of Eurolegalism and increased the juridification of conflicts, especially in policy areas such as consumer protection. The increased legal consciousness, new actors and alliances in the legal market and the endowment of new collective rights of action mean that the mediation of interests in Europe will increasingly be carried out via legal strategies.

Questions/Comments

- Can you say why the class action process inherently points towards the adversarial procedural tradition? The authors of this report suggest that a key feature of class action proceedings is the prominent role played by profit-seeking plaintiff's lawyers. Why is the inquisitorial approach to procedure less likely to lead to the "marketization" of legal proceedings?
- It is worth emphasizing that the Dieselgate deception was discovered by graduate students in West Virginia in the United States.[32] There were millions more diesel cars on the road in Germany. And Germany is regarded by some as overregulated and bureaucratized. How is it possible that the German authorities didn't uncover the scandal? What do the authors of this report say the answer to this question is? Does adversarial or inquisitorial process make "corporatism" more or less likely?
- The report claims that the Dieselgate scandal prompted a new, more adversarial impulse in the German legal culture, albeit one adapted to its European context. It is labeled "Eurolegalism," in contrast to the "adversarial legalism" Kagan attributes to the United States. Based on this report, how does Eurolegalism incorporate elements of adversarial procedure? How does it try to retain some of the inquisitorial qualities expected from German procedural law?

- The report suggests that the movement towards adversarialism in German civil procedure has partly resulted from the influence of the growing number of American law firms operating in the German legal market. These firms may employ German-trained jurists. But the firms' practices and business models are influenced by the distinctly American practices and expectations of the home offices of the firms. One scholar, reflecting on Europe's tentative adoption of the American class action tradition, identified differences in lawyering culture "as one of the most important dissimilarities" that is likely to leave the German collective action process as a "peaceful creek" while American class actions have become a raging river. What is the fundamental difference in lawyering between the two systems? Csongor István Nagy explained:

  > The major difference between litigators on the two sides of the Atlantic is that "entrepreneurial lawyering" is virtually missing in Europe, where the lawyer is a counsel, normally paid on an hourly or a flat-rate basis, and contingency fee arrangements are rare, in some member states even prohibited or restricted. The lawyer usually does not take any risk in the action and law-suits are normally not financed (not even partially) by law firms. In contrast to this, US class actions are funded by lawyers and law firms, in exchange for a contingency fee. US litigators enter contingency fee arrangements and, hence, take enormous risks.[33]

  Reflecting on our discussion of German legal education and lawyering in Chapter 6, are you able to identify the features or impulses in German legal education that contribute to this difference? What about the predominant influence of the Civil Law tradition in the German legal system shapes the training and practice of lawyers in a way that discourages adversarial procedures like class actions?

- The *Musterfeststellungsklage* (model declaratory proceeding) rule enacted in reaction to the Dieselgate scandal extended Germany's modest collective action regime to consumer protection issues. It is lodged in §§ 606–614 of the Code of Civil Procedure. The process permits potential plaintiffs to "opt into" the class in the segment of the lawsuit concerned with establishing the defendant's liability. If the court issues a declaratory judgment establishing the existence of the preconditions of liability, then all members of the class can conclusively rely on that judgment in the separate and individual proceedings for determining their damages and any monetary award.[34]

We have seen that German civil procedure is a mix of inquisitorial and adversarial justice. The mix is dynamic and evolving, but maybe there is a trend towards Anglo-American style adversarial justice? That might erase Germany's "advantage" in civil matters. But German civil procedure always was ambiguously and ambivalently inquisitorial. Its *Dispositionsmaxime* and *Verhandlungsmaxime* give the parties a significant role in the proceedings. That shouldn't be the case for German criminal procedure, which is decisively inquisitorial in character. Or is it?

11.3 German Criminal Procedure

Thomas Weigend, the renowned scholar of comparative criminal law, spoke of "the German legal system's traditional reliance on the inquisitorial system."[35] In fact, the *Strafprozessordung* (StPO or Code of Criminal Procedure) makes the judge the master of criminal proceedings. Section 155(2), for example, provides that "the courts shall [...] act independently" and insists that the court "shall not be bound by the parties' applications when applying criminal law." Section 244(2) empowers the court to "*ex officio* extend the taking of evidence to all facts and means of proof which are relevant to the decision" in order to "establish the truth." One scholar concluded that the "German Code of Criminal Procedure is directly derived from the French Code of Criminal Examination,"[36] and there, too, "the French trial judge has an affirmative duty to make certain that all facts are revealed, developed and clarified, and for this purpose he is endowed with far greater authority than American law confers upon its judges."[37]

We can turn again to John Langbein for a sketch of Germany's inquisitorial criminal procedure.

John H. Langbein
Land without Plea Bargaining: How the Germans Do It
78 MICHIGAN LAW REVIEW 204, 206–212 (1979)[*]

* * *

The German Way of Trial

The Germans do without plea bargaining because they do not need it. German criminal procedure has resisted adversary domination and exclusionary rules of evidence. Trial procedure has been kept uncomplicated and rapid. Accordingly, all the reasons of principle that would (and in former times did) incline us to try our cases of serious crime can still be felt and obeyed in Germany.

* * *

Virtually all of the features of German court structure that strike an Anglo-American observer as distinctive have the effect of accelerating the conduct of trial by comparison with our own arrangements. Because it is so difficult to identify and to remedy error behind the one- or two-word verdict of an Anglo-American jury, we have concentrated over the last two centuries on devising prophylactic procedures to prevent error – for instance, the *voir dire* of prospective jurors, the vast exclusionary apparatus of the law of evidence, and the bewildering technique of multiple contingent judicial instructions to the jury ("If you find such-and-such, then …"). By contrast, the German system has no analogue to *voir dire* or to the law of jury control, despite having laymen sit on every trial for serious crime and despite extending the laymen's authority to matters of sentence as well as guilt determination. Professional judges speak to points of law only when legal issues become relevant in deliberations; important legal rulings show up in the written judgment and are available for scrutiny on appeal. The Germans also believe that the

---
[*] Excerpt reprinted with permission of the author.

presence of professionals in deliberations and the requirement of written findings of fact and law are sufficient safeguards against the misuse of potentially prejudicial varieties of evidence; accordingly, the general principle is that virtually all relevant evidence is admissible, and time is not spent arguing about exclusion and otherwise manipulating evidence in the familiar Anglo-American ways.

The non-adversarial character of the proof-taking further accelerates the oral public trial. To use our parlance, the presiding judge both "examines" and "cross-examines," after which he invites his fellow judges (professional and lay), the prosecutor, the defense counsel, and the accused to supplement his questioning. In examining, the presiding judge works from the official file of the case, the dossier, which contains the pretrial statements and public records gathered by police and prosecutors. These officials work under a statutory duty to investigate exculpatory as well as inculpatory evidence. This duty is reinforced in the pretrial phase by giving to the defense liberal rights to inspect the dossier, together with the right to motion the prosecution to investigate (at public expense) any defensive claims and evidence that might have been overlooked.

This thorough, open, and impartial pretrial preparation effectively eliminates surprise and forensic strategy from the trial. It also enables the presiding judge who determines the sequence of witnesses to control for relevance and to minimize needless duplication of trial testimony. Thus, the court that must decide the case conducts its own trial inquiry in a businesslike and undramatic fashion, overseen by prosecution and defense. Non-adversarial procedure recognizes no party burdens of proof. German law adheres to a standard of proof not materially different from our beyond-reasonable-doubt; but without the system of adversary presentation of evidence, there is no occasion to think of the "prosecution case" (or, indeed, of the defendant's burden of proving an "affirmative defense"). The only burden is the court's. In order to convict, the court must satisfy itself of the truth of the charges after taking the relevant evidence, including that requested by prosecution and defense.

A German trial begins with the examination of the accused. The presiding judge must instruct him about his right to remain silent, but for a variety of reasons the typical German accused feels little incentive to invoke his privilege against self-incrimination. In the Anglo-American system of adversary presentation of evidence and party burdens of poof, the accused is effectively silenced for the duration of the prosecution case. Our rule admitting past conviction evidence only if the accused speaks in his own defense further encourages him to rely wholly upon the intermediation of counsel. German procedure, being free of adversary domination of the proofs and of exclusionary rules of evidence, has a privilege against self-incrimination that is not overused. The German trial court thus typically hears from the accused, who is almost always the most efficient testimonial resource. This sequence is also an important time-saver: by speaking first with the accused, the court establishes at the outset of the trial precisely which (if any) matters charged by the prosecution are genuinely contested, thus limiting the range and depth of the subsequent proof-taking.

The accused frequently confesses some or all of the charges against him [...]. The important point for present purposes is that German procedure knows no guilty plea for cases of felony or grave misdemeanor. (For lesser offenses there is an analogue to our guilty plea, the penal order procedure discussed below.) By confessing to a major offense, an accused does not waive trial. Confession affects but does not abort the criminal trial. Confession shortens the trial by enriching the proofs but does not relieve the court of its duty of independent adjudication – its duty to satisfy itself of the accused's guilt beyond reasonable doubt.

* * *

The Rule of Compulsory Prosecution

Not only can the Germans do without plea bargaining, they want to do without it. That is the lesson of the German scheme for eliminating prosecutorial discretion in cases of serious crime.

Section 152(2) of the Code of Criminal Procedure prescribes the celebrated rule of compulsory prosecution (*Legalitätsprinzip*) that has been in force for a century. In the field of serious crime the German prosecutor must prosecute "all prosecutable offenses, to the extent that there is a sufficient factual basis." Paragraph 153(1) of the Code permits the counter-principle of discretionary non-prosecution (*Opportunitätsprinzip*) but only for misdemeanors (*Vergehen*) and then only if the culprit's guilt can "be regarded as minor" and "there is no public interest in prosecuting." Consequently, the German law requires that all felonies (*Verbrechen*) and all misdemeanors that cannot be excused under the two statutory criteria of pettiness must be prosecuted whenever the evidence permits.

The strongest incentives are created to enforce this rule of compulsory prosecution. If the prosecutor determines not to prosecute an offense that is subject to the rule – whether for want of sufficient factual basis or on grounds of legal insufficiency – the victim or kin may obtain departmental review of the determination; if the prosecutor's superiors uphold his decision, the citizen may appeal to the courts in a proceeding to compel prosecution. The prosecutorial corps is a career service with strictly meritocratic promotion standards. Prosecutors do not want their personnel records blotted with citizen complaints, especially successful complaints. Prudence counsels them to resolve doubts in favor of prosecution and trial.

A crucial corollary of this system is that the form of plea bargaining called charge or count bargaining in American practice can have no counterpart in German procedure. The prosecutor, who is duty-bound to prosecute in every case, lacks authority, for example, to offer to reduce the charge in return for a concession of guilt. The rule of compulsory prosecution requires him to take the case to trial in the strongest and most inclusive form that the evidence will support; if he does not, the court itself is empowered to correct his error. So strict is the rule that it prevents the Germans from employing that endemic device of Anglo-American prosecutorial practice, the grant of immunity for state's evidence.

Obviously, the German rule of compulsory prosecution of serious crime is no happenstance. The statutory standards, limitations, and remedies have been meticulously designed to fit the institutional structure and to serve the larger policies of the German criminal justice system. The rule is meant to achieve ends that are immensely important in the German tradition: treating like cases alike, obeying faithfully the legislative determination to characterize something as a serious crime, preventing political interference or other corruption from inhibiting prosecution, and more. The wisdom of these policies is not lost on Americans, but we lack the procedural institutions – above all a workable trial procedure – that would allow us to have a comparable rule of compulsory prosecution. As long as we depend upon plea bargaining to resolve our caseloads, we must give our prosecutors their bargaining chips.

* * *

German law forbids plea bargaining, and German legal professionals of all sorts – judges, prosecutors, academics, and (most importantly) defense counsel – consistently maintain that the law is obeyed. The disdain that American plea bargaining evokes in Germany is not confined to legal circles. Even in the ordinary press, American plea bargaining is regarded with astonishment bordering on incredulity.

* * *

11.3 German Criminal Procedure

Questions/Comments

- The Langbein excerpt touches on a number of fundamental elements of German criminal procedure. There are other elements that didn't make it into his survey. The accused enjoys a number of procedural protections, many of which are grounded in the constitution. These include the general procedural concerns mentioned earlier in this chapter.[38] But they also include the presumption of innocence, which is reinforced by the "beyond a reasonable doubt" standard of proof.[39] Langbein mentioned the right to remain silent and the accompanying privilege against self-incrimination. The accused enjoys a right to be assisted by counsel that he or she chooses.[40] In some serious cases, defense counsel must be appointed.[41] A person cannot be tried twice for the same crime (*ne bis in idem*).[42] These higher-level procedural protections are widely respected and enforced. That has not always been the case. The photographs in Figure 11.1 depict scenes from the intensely politicized criminal trials of left-wing domestic terrorists in Germany that were conducted in the late 1970s and early 1980s. Those criminal proceedings, carried out behind the walls of the prison in which the defendants were being held, involved problematic compromises of some fundamental procedural protections. Those and other rights of criminal procedure are not reinforced by a threatened exclusion of any illicit or illegally obtained evidence. Instead, as was the case in these exceptional terrorism trials, alleged violations of procedural rights (usually carried out on the basis of some statutory authority) can be litigated as constitutional violations before the powerful Federal Constitutional Court. This means that there's none of the party-driven evasion and strategy in gathering and presenting evidence that characterizes America's intensely adversarial, cat-and-mouse criminal process. Instead, Langbein describes a "thorough, open, and impartial" process for the development of the evidence. Most defendants choose to testify and many confess. There might be a tension here between Germany's inquisitorial criminal process and the protection of individual rights against intrusion and abuse by the state. Many Germans are sensitive to this perceived tension and defensively insist that their criminal process achieves an impressive mix of efficiency, the revelation of the truth, and the protection of the accused's constitutional and human rights. Do you think the German criminal process might prioritize one of those three interests? Can we regard a system as just if it features a confession from most defendants?
- Bohlander identified a number of "systematic principles" of criminal procedure, including the *Legalitätsprinzip* (legality principle), which Langbein defined in these terms: "The prosecutor, who is duty-bound to prosecute in every case, lacks authority [...] to offer to reduce the charge in return for a concession of guilt. The rule of compulsory prosecution requires him to take the case to trial in the strongest and most inclusive form that the evidence will support; if he does not, the court itself is empowered to correct

(a) RAF Terrorist Andreas Baader

Andreas Baader making his way to the courtroom at the Stuttgart-Stammheim prison. The courtroom at the prison was purpose-built for the sensational trials of the leaders of the Red Army Fraction (RAF) in the mid-1970s. The RAF was a domestic, urban-guerilla group that sought to provoke the West German state into crisis through terrorist violence that would force the government to betray its commitment to the rule of law. Baader, one of the group's founding leaders, was convicted of murder and terrorist activities and given a life-long prison sentence. He and several other RAF inmates were found dead in their prison cells in October 1977. The authorities labeled the deaths a group suicide but questions about the events have cast doubt on the official explanation.

(b) RAF Terrorism Trial

This courtroom sketch from the RAF trials, held at the Stuttgart-Stammheim prison complex, depicts the lawyers leading the state's case. The proceedings often neglected basic procedural rights, in part because of the antics of the accused and their lawyers. The defendants often had their microphones silenced during hearings. Their conversations with defense counsel were subject to surveillance.

Figure 11.1 Exceptional German Criminal Process – The Red Army Fraction (RAF) Trial
Source: Getty Images

his error." Markus Dubber argued that the legality principle's underlying ethos is a realization of the Enlightenment's recognition of individual autonomy, which, in turn, highlighted the "radical distinction between *Rechtsstaat* and *Polizeistaat*" [between a state governed by the rule of law and a police-state].[43] *Privatautonomie* features prominently in German civil procedure as the normative justification for empowering claimants to take a leading role in framing and raising their civil proceedings. How does German criminal procedure, which denies the accused the chance to bargain for a less severe charge or sentence, advance the principle of individual autonomy?

- You have learned that a *Rechtsstaat* is a state governed by law that is also committed to securing justice. Dubber suggests that German criminal procedure's insistence on the prosecution of all crimes promotes that ideal. There are no discretionary, arbitrary departures from the law. But doesn't that elevate the power of law enforcement? Every arrest and every charge will lead to a criminal process and, if the criminal conduct is confirmed, to the prescribed punishment. One check on that heavy hand is the quality and integrity of the underlying substantive criminal law. This is similar to the confidence German administrative law puts in statutes as the primary means for controlling the powerful state bureaucracy. In fact, a major subfield of administrative law in Germany is *Polizeirecht* (police law), which regulates the authority, activities, and relationships of law enforcement institutions. This suggests a dual statutory constraint on the power that the legality principle vests in the police. First, police law ensures that law enforcement does not abuse its power. Second, the legality principle only empowers the police to enforce codified substantive criminal law (discussed in Chapter 10). But what provides the assurance that the substantive German criminal law enforced by the police is fair and just, and deserving of invariable application? What other characteristics of German criminal justice does Langbein identify as helping to mitigate and moderate the effects of the duty to prosecute?

- The lack of discretion in Germany's criminal procedure regime might compel the blind application of the law without reflection on the justice (or political) implications of doing so in a particular case. That makes it sound like German criminal procedure operates according to the principle "the law is the law." I asked you to consider the complications and consequences of that approach to justice in Chapter 3. What was the context for that consideration of the issue? Which would you prefer: the expectation that the prosecutor has no choice but to dutifully apply the law in your case; or the opportunity to avail yourself of his or her discretion, perhaps to your benefit? Does your answer depend on whether you're guilty or innocent? Why has it been said: I would rather be guilty and tried in an American court and innocent and tried in a German court?

- Michael Bohlander defined the legality principle in this way:

    > The monopoly given to the prosecution to decide whom to prosecute requires a corrective mechanism to ensure that no arbitrary choices are being made. This is established in § 152(2), which requires the prosecution in principle to investigate, prosecute and indict any offence for which sufficient evidence exists. German doctrine therefore takes the opposite approach from that of England and Wales, famously expressed in 1951 by the former Attorney-General Sir Hartley Shawcross, who stated that "it has never been the rule in this country – I hope it never will be – that suspected criminal offences must automatically be the subject of prosecution." He added that a prosecution should occur "wherever it appears that the offence or the circumstances of its commission are of such a character that a prosecution in respect thereof is required in the public interest."[44]

- How are the legality principle in Germany, on the one hand, and the extensive use of plea bargaining in the United States, on the other hand, examples of the inquisitorial and adversarial distinctions in procedural law? To further consider the differences between the two approaches to criminal procedure, reflect on the images in Figure 11.2. How do they embody the

(a) Defense lawyer Atticus Finch in the film *To Kill a Mockingbird* (1962)
The image of the defense lawyer Atticus Finch is an archetype of an adversarial proceeding. The parties – and especially their lawyers – are at the center of the process.

(b) Medieval Inquisitor Konrad of Marburg
Inquisitorial procedure's roots in Europe's "dark past" can be seen in this depiction of Konrad of Marburg, "one of the middle age's first inquisitors." The judge–or inquisitor–is placed at the center of the proceeding in this tradition.

Figure 11.2 Mythological Depictions of Criminal Law Proceedings – Adversarial and Inquisitorial
Source: Getty Images

character and quality of the adversarial and inquisitorial traditions? How do they illuminate the strengths and weaknesses of the two traditions?

It was understood that the legality principle (and other commitments in constitutional law and criminal procedure) prohibited plea bargaining in Germany. But the German criminal justice system also suffers from large caseloads and limited resources. The pressure to fudge constitutional protections and streamline statutory procedures in order to promote efficiency is felt in the German criminal justice system, just as it is a strain in all legal systems. In fact, those pressures led to the gradual emergence of something like a plea bargain in German criminal procedure. Antonio Espisito and Christoph Safferling describe the practice, which came to be known as an *Absprache* (agreement):

> Plea-bargaining is a common phenomenon in German courtrooms or, rather, in the Judges' chambers. It is, however, not foreseen in the *Strafprozessordnung* (StPO – German Criminal Procedure Code), and is incompatible with the German procedural system. On the other hand, the bitter truth is that prosecutors and judges are, in practice, not capable of dealing properly with protracted and complicated proceedings in particular in the area of *Wirtschaftsstrafrecht* (economic criminal law). They are, thus, rather depending on an informal short-cut instead of implementing the formal procedure as foreseen in the procedural code in its pure form in order to come to terms with the masses of criminal prosecutions. Bargaining in the shadow of the StPO is more delicate and dangerous for the accused compared to the Anglo-American system because there is no guilty plea. Therefore, the bargain is about a full-scale confession on behalf of the defendant and not about a plea. Whereas the plea [in the Anglo-American approach] pertains to a certain charge, a confession

[obtained pursuant to the German approach] pertains to the facts and leaves the question of how to legally interpret the act up to the judge. The accused buys a pig in a poke. To reduce the risk, the judge usually offers some relatively precise insight into the possible sanction. Cases have been reported where the judge offered two-year imprisonment on probation in case of a confession [against the] predicted seven years imprisonment, should the accused decline cooperation. The threat, which is implied in this so called *Sanktionsschere*, leaves the accused in a case of Hobson's choice.[45]

The *Absprache* gambit differed from American plea bargains because it sought to streamline the criminal proceedings while respecting the legality principle and the Guilt Principle (which was discussed in Chapter 10). The accused's cooperation didn't lead to a change (or altogether abandonment) of the threatened charges and it left intact the court's duty to confirm the accused's (*Schuld*) blameworthiness. But it elevated the accused's confession to a decisive role in the court's assessment of the case, making it possible to speedily resolve the matter in exchange for expected leniency in sentencing. The practice of arriving at *Abspracheurteile* (agreed judgments) danced around the formal framework of German criminal procedure. Many commentators doubted that the practice of informal settlements was compatible with the inquisitorial nature of German criminal procedure. Espisito and Safferling explained that, over the years, the Federal Court of Justice sought to steer, manage, and constrain the practice:

> After several decisions, the BGH established [...] a number of basic provisions under which plea-bargaining can be realized. They are, e.g., that any participant of the trial must be involved in the bargain, the decision must be made public and written down on the record, and only the upper limit of the sentence may be promised by the court. In contrast, it is not allowed to deal with questions of guilt or the legal evaluation of the facts.[46]

As the Federal Court of Justice was forced again and again to tinker with this informal practice, which wasn't anticipated by and seemed clearly at odds with the Code of Criminal Procedure, a Grand Senate of the Court finally expressed its frustration, declaring in a seminal judgment that:

> the necessity of resolving all these questions – and those to which our answers will give rise – has proven especially difficult because the Code of Criminal Procedure does not anticipate a consensual process and therefore can serve neither as the basis for the establishment of such a process nor as the source for the relevant standards. Our efforts through caselaw to keep a plea-agreement process within the strict, formal boundaries required for criminal proceedings has brought us close to the outer-limit of the permissible judicial development of the law under constitutional separation of powers and the competences possessed by the legislative power and the judicial power.[47]

With the Federal Court of Justice's plea for legislative intervention ringing loud and clear, and a debate about "deals" raging, the parliament enacted legislation amending the Code of Criminal Procedure to formally permit plea bargains.

The following materials present the relevant provisions of the amended Code of Criminal Procedure (establishing the inquisitorial nature of German criminal proceedings [§ 244] and formally providing for a plea-agreement process as a carefully calibrated re-orientation of the system towards adversarialism [§ 257c]) and excerpts from the decision of the Federal Constitutional Court finding the new plea-agreement rule constitutionally sound.

Code of Criminal Procedure[*]

Section 244
Taking of evidence; inquisitorial system; rejection of applications to take evidence

(1) After examination of the defendant, evidence shall be taken.
(2) The court shall, in order to establish the truth, ex officio extend the taking of evidence to all facts and means of proof which are relevant to the decision.
(3) An application to take evidence shall be rejected if the taking of such evidence is inadmissible. In all other cases, an application to take evidence may be rejected only if the taking of such evidence is superfluous because the matter is common knowledge, if the fact to be proved is irrelevant to the decision or has already been proved, if the evidence is wholly inappropriate or unobtainable, the application is made to protract the proceedings or if an important allegation which is intended to offer proof in exoneration of the defendant may be treated as if the alleged fact were true.
(4) Except as otherwise provided, an application to take evidence by examining an expert may also be rejected if the court itself possesses the necessary specialist knowledge. The hearing of another expert may even be refused if the opposite of the alleged fact has already been proved by the first expert opinion; this rule shall not apply to cases where the professional competence of the first expert is in doubt, if his opinion is based on incorrect factual suppositions, if the opinion contains contradictions or if the new expert has means of research at his disposal which seem to be superior to the ones of an earlier expert.
(5) An application to take evidence by inspection may be rejected if the court, according to its duty-bound discretion, deems the inspection not to be necessary to establish the truth. Applications to take evidence by examining a witness may be rejected under the same condition if the witness has to be summoned from abroad. An application for the taking of evidence by reading out a source document may be rejected if, according to the court's duty-bound discretion, there is no reason to doubt that it corresponds in terms of content to the transmitted document.
(6) A court order shall be required if an application to take evidence is rejected. After concluding the ex officio taking of evidence, the presiding

---

[*] Translation reprinted with permission of the Federal Office of Justice.

judge may determine an appropriate period for the submission of applications to take evidence. A decision on applications to take evidence submitted after the end of the period determined may be given in the judgment; this shall not apply if it was not possible to submit an application to take evidence before the expiry of the period determined. If an application to take evidence is submitted after the end of the period determined, the facts which made it impossible to meet the deadline shall be substantiated in the application.

Code of Criminal Procedure*

Section 257c
Negotiated agreement

(1) In suitable cases, the court may reach an agreement with the parties on the further course and outcome of the proceedings in accordance with the following subsections. Section 244(2) shall remain unaffected.

(2) The subject matter of this agreement may only comprise the legal consequences which could be the content of the judgment and of the associated court orders, other procedural measures relating to the course of the underlying adjudication proceedings and the conduct of the parties during the proceedings. A confession shall be an integral part of any negotiated agreement. The verdict of guilty and measures of reform and prevention may not be the subject of a negotiated agreement.

(3) The court shall announce what the content of the negotiated agreement could be. It may, on free evaluation of all the circumstances of the case and general sentencing considerations, also indicate an upper and lower sentence limit. The parties shall be given the opportunity to make submissions. The negotiated agreement shall come into existence if the defendant and the public prosecution office agree to the court's proposal.

(4) The court shall cease to be bound by a negotiated agreement if legally or factually relevant circumstances have been overlooked or have arisen and the court is therefore then convinced that the prospective sentencing range is no longer appropriate to the severity of the offence or the degree of guilt. The same shall apply if the defendant's further conduct in the proceedings does not correspond to that upon which the court's prediction was based. The defendant's confession may not be used in such cases. The court shall give notification of any deviation without delay.

(5) The defendant shall be instructed as to the conditions for and consequences of the court deviating from the prospective outcome pursuant to subsection (4).

---

* Translation reprinted with permission of the Federal Office of Justice.

Federal Constitutional Court
Plea Bargains Case
BVerfGE 133, 168 (2013)[*]

* * *

The aim of criminal proceedings is to enforce the state's right to punish in the interest of protecting the legal interests of individuals and the general public by conducting judicial proceedings whilst guaranteeing effective protection of the accused's fundamental rights. [...] It is the central concern of criminal proceedings to establish the true facts of a case without which it is impossible to implement the substantive principle of individual guilt. It is necessary to prove in accordance with the rules of procedure the fact that the perpetrator committed the offence as well as the existence of guilt. An individual is presumed to be innocent until proven guilty.

* * *

Still, individuals charged with a criminal offence in the Basic Law's system governed by the rule of law may not be mere objects of criminal proceedings; instead they must be given the opportunity to influence the course and the result of the proceedings in order to protect their rights.

As an indispensable element of the conformity of criminal proceedings with the principles of the rule of law, the right to fair trial ensures that individuals charged with a criminal offence dispose of the necessary knowledge to make use of their procedural rights and opportunities to take appropriate steps in order to ward off infringements by government entities or other parties to proceedings. [...] It is primarily for the legislature to determine which specific procedural rights and assistance individuals charged with a criminal offence should be granted under the principle of fair trial and what form these rights should take. It is then up to the courts to make this determination in the individual cases, within the boundaries of the law, as part of their duty to interpret and apply the law. The right to fair trial is violated only if an overall assessment of the procedural law (including its interpretation and application by the courts) shows that conclusions that are compelling under the rule of law have not been drawn, or that rights that are indispensable under the rule of law have been waived. Such an overall assessment must also take into account the requirements of a functioning criminal justice system. Accordingly, procedural decisions that serve the interests of an effective criminal justice system do not automatically violate the constitutional right to fair criminal trial if the procedural position of the accused or the individual charged with a criminal offence is diminished in favour of a more effective criminal justice system.

* * *

On the basis of these standards, the Court currently cannot find that the Act on the Regulation of Plea Bargaining in Criminal Proceedings is unconstitutional. The legislature allowed plea bargaining in criminal trials merely within a limited framework and added specific safeguard mechanisms to its statutory framework, which, if interpreted and applied with the required specificity, may be expected to satisfy the constitutional requirements imposed on the design of criminal proceedings. [...]

The objective intent of the legislature, which is manifested in the wording and methodology of the Plea Bargaining Act, was not to introduce a new "consensual" class of proceedings. Instead, the Plea Bargaining Act integrates the forms of plea

---

[*] Reproduced with permission of the Federal Constitutional Court.

bargaining it allows into the existing system of criminal procedure with the aim of ensuring that criminal proceedings continue to be committed to ascertaining the substantive truth and to arriving at a just punishment that is commensurate with the crime. The legislature expressly stated that plea bargains as such may never constitute the sole basis of a judgment, but that instead the courts continue to be bound by their duty to investigate ex officio, which is laid down in § 244 sec. 2 StPO. Moreover, the legal evaluation of a case is not subject to a determination by the parties to a plea bargain. The Plea Bargaining Act comprehensively governs the permissibility of plea bargains in criminal proceedings; it thus prohibits what are euphemistically called "informal" approaches during plea bargaining. The legislature added specific safeguard mechanisms to its statutory framework, which guarantee that the steps leading to a plea bargain are completely transparent and that they are documented, thus enabling the exhaustive monitoring of the plea bargaining process by the public, the prosecution, and the appellate courts that was deemed necessary by the legislature. Finally, by imposing a limitation on the binding effect of plea bargains, the Act guarantees the court's neutrality. It also safeguards the interests of accused individuals by imposing a duty to instruct them that the plea bargain may have limited effect.

* * *

The clarification of § 257c sec. 1 sentence 2 StPO must be interpreted as a particular manifestation of the legislature's desire to integrate the possibility of plea bargaining into the existing system of criminal procedure while leaving "unaffected" the court's duty to investigate the facts *ex officio*, which is laid down in § 244 sec. 2 StPO. The wording of § 257c sec. 1 sentence 2 StPO is unambiguous; the provision prohibits any determination on the subject-matter and the scope of the court's *ex officio* duty to investigate the events on which the indictment is based. This stresses the fact that a plea bargain as such may never constitute the basis for a judgment, but that only the – adequately reasoned – conviction of the court concerning the facts it needs to establish remains decisive. The legislature was aware of the particularities of a confession that is based on a plea bargain, particularly of the increased likelihood of errors that is due to the incentives and temptations the accused individuals as well as their defence counsel face and, thus, of the risk of "false confessions. For this reason, the legislature made it explicitly clear that the court is bound by its *ex officio* duty to investigate, which is laid down in § 244 sec. 2 StPO. [...]

* * *

The provisions of the Plea Bargaining Act comprehensively govern the permissibility of plea bargains in criminal proceedings. Any "informal" agreements made outside the statutory framework are impermissible.

It already follows from the wording of § 257c sec. 1 sentence 1 StPO, which only permits plea bargaining "in accordance with the sections below", that every "informal" agreement, deal or "gentlemen's agreement" is prohibited. This prohibition achieves the statutory provision's objective, namely to provide clear framework conditions for plea bargaining in order to establish legal certainty and to guarantee the consistent application of the law through a "comprehensive and differentiated statutory framework."

* * *

By making plea bargains subject to the prosecution's consent, the legislature assigns the prosecution an active role in achieving the objective of guaranteeing effective monitoring of plea bargaining.

The prosecution is assigned the task of ensuring that proceedings are conducted in accordance with the principles of legality and that their results have a legal basis. Its duty of objectivity (§ 160 sec. 2 StPO) makes the prosecution a guarantor for conducting proceedings in conformity with the principles of the rule of law and the principles of legality; as the representative of the indictment it guarantees the effective functioning of the criminal justice system. [...]

In cases involving plea bargains, monitoring by the prosecution acquires particular importance because the accused and the court subject themselves to a commitment – albeit a limited commitment – as far as the possible results of the proceedings are concerned. The main purpose of including the prosecution in plea bargaining is to ensure that plea bargaining takes place in conformity with the principles of legality. The Plea Bargaining Act is based on the expectation that the prosecution will – in accordance with its role as "guardian of the law" – reject goings-on in connection with illegal plea bargains. The fact that the prosecuting system is hierarchically organised and includes reporting obligations, makes it possible to establish and enforce uniform standards for consenting to plea bargains and for exercising appellate rights. The prosecution is not only obliged to refuse its consent to illegal plea bargains, but is also obliged to appeal judgments that are based on such pleas (e.g., in cases in which it was initially unaware of the fact that the judgment was based on a plea bargain). [...]

* * *

The Plea Bargaining Act is compatible with the Basic Law. The Basic Law does not in principle preclude plea bargaining in criminal proceedings. The legislature took adequate precautions to guarantee that plea bargains meet the constitutional requirements on criminal proceedings.

* * *

Questions/Comments

- The complainants before the Constitutional Court argued that the process created by § 257c violated the "Principle of Guilt, and the mandate for equality and the Legality Principle that are derived from the constitutional commitment to the rule of law, all of which support the discovery of the true facts of the matter." But neither in the excerpts provided here, nor elsewhere in the long decision, does the Constitutional Court consider the risk the plea-bargain procedure poses to the legality principle. Why does Germany's plea agreement process seem to conform to the legality principle?
- In its *Plea Bargains Case*, the Constitutional Court explained that an unyielding application of the duty to prosecute risked making the accused a "mere object" of a criminal proceeding who is to be processed by the criminal justice apparatus without respect to his or her subjective interests or desires. This is one way of framing German constitutional law's absolute commitment to the protection of human dignity: the law must regard people as ends in themselves and not as the means to some end. The Constitutional Court underscored this concern in the *Life Imprisonment Case* (1977) in which it ruled that a lifelong prison sentence that allowed no possibility for parole or early release would violate human dignity:

In the area of criminal sanctions, which demands the highest degree of justice, Article 1(1) determines the nature of punishment and the relationship between guilt and atonement. [...] Every punishment must justly relate to the severity of the offence and the guilt of the offender. Respect for human dignity especially requires the prohibition of cruel, inhuman, and degrading punishments. The state cannot turn the offender into an object of crime prevention to the detriment of his or her constitutionally protected right to social worth and respect. [The state] must preserve the underlying assumptions governing the individual and the social existence of the human person.[48]

But there is a strong instrumental current running through the most prevalent justifications for criminal law: general deterrence (discouraging others from breaking the law) and specific deterrence (preventing the individual criminal from breaking the law again).[49] Doesn't all criminal law involve making the criminal a means to some end? The Constitutional Court, with its decisions in the *Life Imprisonment Case* and *Plea Bargains Case* suggests that the sting can be taken out of this fact by insisting that criminal procedure provide a fair process that actualizes the accused as a human. The Court explained: "Individuals charged with a criminal offense in the Basic Law's system governed by the rule of law may not be mere objects of criminal proceedings; instead they must be given the opportunity to influence the course and the result of the proceedings in order to protect their rights." In the context of plea agreements, the accused's engagement with the process might even include offering a confession that could animate some discretion on the part of the court regarding the punishment imposed.

- How does the Court justify its conclusion that the plea agreement process does not erode the inquisitorial nature of German criminal procedure? The Constitutional Court explained that nothing about the new plea bargain regime could strip the trial court of its exclusive responsibility to establish, *ex officio*, the facts upon which a conviction can be based. The parties' enhanced role in the proceedings does nothing to alter the trial court's status as "master of the case."
- In the *Plea Bargains Case* the Constitutional Court declared: "It is the central concern of criminal proceedings to establish the true facts." Which is better suited to achieving that aim – the inquisitorial approach to procedure or the adversarial approach to procedure? If one of these approaches is more oriented to discovering the "true facts," then what is the animating purpose of the other approach?
- In describing the parameters of a constitutionally adequate fair trial, the Constitutional Court identified these rights and protections: the *Schuldprinzip* (principle of individual guilt); the right to speedy trial; the right of individuals charged with a criminal offence to make statements or to remain silent and the prohibition on compelling an individual to incriminate him- or herself (*nemo tenetur se ipsum accusare*); the presumption of innocence; the right to be heard by an independent and impartial judge; the right of individuals charged with a criminal offence to be defended by an

attorney of their own choosing in whom they have confidence. Don't those protections point towards an adversarial dynamic in a criminal proceeding? How might German criminal proceedings maintain their inquisitorial character despite these protections?

11.4 Conclusion

Just as much as Germany's civil procedure shows some signs of intermingling inquisitorial and adversarial impulses, the country's inquisitorial criminal process also seems to be taking on some characteristics of the Anglo-American adversarial tradition. This may not surprise you at this stage of your work with this book. I have repeatedly sought to illuminate ways in which the German legal system is the site of intersections of various ways of thinking about and doing law. But especially when it comes to German procedural law – prized by Germans and foreign scholars for its efficiency, predictability, and accessibility – this dynamic dialogue of traditions and approaches might be lamented. After all, Professor Stephen Goldstein is reported to have remarked that the German "continental" approach to procedure consists of "a continuing process of exchange of written matter, punctuated when necessary by short proof-taking hearings, with no central, dramatic proof-taking event." This kind of process, he concluded, "would seem to need no explanation, for it represents the normal decision-making process." It is the adversarial Anglo-American trial, Goldstein urged, that is extraordinary, that needs explanation.[50]

Further Reading

- Michael Bohlander, *Principles of German Criminal Procedure* (Hart Publishing) (2nd ed. 2021)
- *Class Actions in Europe: Holy Grail or a Wrong Trail?* (Alan Uzelac & Stefaan Voet eds.) (Springer) (2021)
- Csongor István Nagy, *Collective Actions in Europe: A Comparative, Economic and Transsystemic Analysis* (Springer Open) (2019)
- Peter L. Murray & Rolf Stürner, *German Civil Justice* (Carolina Academic Press) (2015)
- Shawn Marie Boyne, *The German Prosecution Service: Guardians of the Law?* (Springer) (2014)
- *The Prosecutor in Transnational Perspective* (Erik Luna & Marianne Wade eds.) (Oxford University Press) (2012)
- *European Traditions in Civil Procedure* (C.H. van Rhee ed.) (Hart Publishing) 2005)
- John H. Langbein, *The Origins of Adversary Criminal Trial* (Oxford University Press) (2003)
- John H. Langbein, *Prosecuting Crime in the Renaissance: England, Germany, France* (Harvard University Press) (1974)

11.4 Conclusion

NOTES

1. *Class Action*, LEGAL INFORMATION INSTITUTE – CORNELL LAW SCHOOL, www.law.cornell.edu/wex/class_action#:~:text=A%20class%20action%20is%20a,group%2C%20or%20%22class%22.
2. "The word 'duel' suggests to modern audiences a conflict over honor, but although medieval trials by combat were likewise concerned with issues of reputation and shame, their purpose was judicial: a method of reaching a verdict when other methods could not. If evidence or testimony was not clear or was rejected by participants in a legal case, one could always turn to God." STEVEN MUHLBERGER & WILL MCLEAN, MURDER, RAPE, AND TREASON JUDICIAL COMBATS IN THE LATE MIDDLE AGES (2019).
3. ROBERT A. KAGAN, ADVERSARIAL LEGALISM: THE AMERICAN WAY OF LAW 3 (2nd ed. 2019).
4. *Id.* at 4.
5. *Id.* at 887–888.
6. Amalia D. Kessler, *Our Inquisitorial Tradition: Equity Procedure, Due Process, and the Search for an Alternative to the Adversarial*, 90 CORNELL L. REV. 1181, 1187 (2005).
7. *Id.* at 1183, 1185.
8. KAGAN, *supra* note 3, at 15 (quoting SEYMOUR MARTIN LIPSET, AMERICAN EXCEPTIONALISM: A DOUBLE-EDGED SWORD 21 (1996)).
9. Kessler, *supra* note 7, at 1187.
10. KAGAN, *supra* note 3, at 12.
11. John R. Spencer, *Adversarial vs. Inquisitorial Systems: Is There Still Such a Difference?*, 20 INT'L J. HUM. RTS. 601 (2016).
12. CATHRIN SILBERZHAN, DAS KONZEPT EINER ALLGEMEINEN PROZESSRECHTLEHRE IN GESETZGEBUNG UND RECHTSDOGMATIK 30 (2021).
13. KAGAN, *supra* note 3, at 12.
14. SILBERZHAN, *supra* note 13.
15. *Id.*
16. *See* GERHARD ROBBERS, EINFÜHRUNG IN DAS DEUTSCHE RECHTS 221–222 (7th ed. 2019).
17. *Id.*
18. Michael Bohlander, *The German Advantage Revisited: An Inside View of German Civil Procedure in the Nineties*, 13 TULANE EUR. & CIV. L. FORUM 25, 46 (1998).
19. NIGEL FOSTER & SATISH SULE, GERMAN LEGAL SYSTEM AND LAWS 98 (4th ed. 2010).
20. *But see*, JOHN GRISHMAN, THE RAINMAKER (1996); JOHN GRISHMAN, GRAY MOUNTAIN (2014).
21. KAGAN, *supra* note 3, at 118, 124.
22. *See* ALEXANDRA LAHAV, IN PRAISE OF LITIGATION 56 (2019).
23. *See Litigation Cost Survey of Major Companies*, www.uscourts.gov/sites/default/files/litigation_cost_survey_of_major_companies_0.pdf.
24. *See, e.g.,* Robert G. Bone, *The US Class Action form a Utilitarian Perspective: Balancing Social Benefits and Social Costs*, in THE CAMBRIDGE HANDBOOK

OF CLASS ACTIONS: AN INTERNATIONAL SURVEY 3 (Brian T. Fitzpatrick & Randall S. Thomas eds., 2021).

25 Michael Halberstam's article draws on an earlier article that makes the larger point systematically from a corporate law perspective. See Érica Gorga & Michael Halberstam, *Litigation Discovery and Corporate Governance: The Missing Story about the "Genius of America Corporate Law,"* 63 EMORY L. J. 1383 (2014).

26 Lars Röh & Tobias de Raet, *The Security Litigation Review: Germany*, THE LAW REVIEWS (June 7, 2021), https://thelawreviews.co.uk/title/the-securities-litigation-review/germany.

27 KAGAN, *supra* note 3, at 120.

28 *Id.* (quoting John C. Coffee, Jr., *Class Wars: The Dilemma of the Mass Tort Class Action*, 95 COLUM. L. REV. 1343, 1347–1348 (1995)).

29 *See* JACK EWING, FASTER, HIGHER, FARTHER: THE VOLKSWAGEN SCANDAL (2017).

30 *Id.*

31 *See* Kapitalanleger-Musterverfahrensgesetz [KapMuG] [Act on Model Case Proceedings in Disputes under Capital Markets Law], Oct. 19, 2012, BGBl. I at 2182, last amended by Act, June 23, 2017, BGBl. I at 1693, art. 24(1).

32 Philipp Oehmke, *The Three Students Who Uncovered "Dieselgate,"* SPIEGEL Internaitonal (Oct. 23, 2017), www.spiegel.de/international/business/the-three-students-who-discovered-dieselgate-a-1173686.html.

33 CSONGOR ISTVÁN NAGY, COLLECTIVE ACTIONS IN EUROPE 45–46 (2019).

34 *See* Zivilprozessordnung [ZPO] [Code of Civil Procedure], Dec. 5, 2005, BGBl. I at 3202, last amended by Act, Oct. 10, 2013, BGBl. I at 3786, art. 10; Nagy, *supra* note 33, at 80–81.

35 Thomas Weigend, *The Potential to Secure a Fair Trial through Evidence Exclusion: A German Perspective*, in DO EXCLUSIONARY RULES ENSURE A FAIR TRIAL? 61 (Sabine Gless & Thomas Richter eds., 2019).

36 A. ESMEIN, A HISTORY OF CONTINENTAL CRIMINAL PROCEDURE 580 (John Simpson trans., 1913).

37 Doris Jonas Freed, *Aspects of French Criminal Procedure*, 17 LOUISIANA L. REV. 730, 754 (1957).

38 *See* Grundgesetz [GG] [Basic Law], arts. 101 and 103, translation at www.gesetze-im-internet.de/englisch_gg/index.html.

39 GRUNDGESETZ FÜR DIE BUNDESREPUBLIK DEUTSCHLAND [GG] [BASIC LAW], art. 103(2); Para. 261 StPO; ROBBERS, *supra* note 17, at 138.

40 Strafprozessordnung [StPO] [Code of Criminal Procedure] paras. 137 and 138; ROBBERS, *supra* note 16, at 138.

41 Strafprozessordnung [StPO] [Code of Criminal Procedure] para 140; ROBBERS, *supra* note 17, at 138.

42 GRUNDGESETZ FÜR DIE BUNDESREPUBLIK DEUTSCHLAND [GG] [BASIC LAW], art. 103(3); ROBBERS, *supra* note 17, at 138.

43 Markus Dubber, *The Legality Principle in American and German Criminal Law: An Essay in Comparative Legal History*, in FROM THE JUDGE'S ARBITRIUM TO THE LEGALITY PRINCIPLE: LEGISLATION AS A SOURCE OF LAW IN CRIMINAL TRIALS 36 (Georges Martyn *et al.* eds, 2013).

44 MICHAEL BOHLANDER, PRINCIPLES OF GERMAN CRIMINAL PROCEDURE 25–26 (2nd ed. 2021).
45 Antonio K. Esposito & Christoph J. M. Safferling, *Report – Recent Case Law of the Bundesgerichtshof (Federal Court of Justice) in Strafsachen (Criminal Law)*, 9 GER. L. J. 683, 700–702 (2008)
46 *Id.* at 702.
47 50 BGHSt 40 (2005).
48 Life Imprisonment Case, 45 BVerfGE 187 (1977).
49 *See, e.g.,* Daniel S. Nagin, *Deterrence in the Twenty-First Century*, 42 CRIME & JUSTICE 199 (2013).
50 Jeremy Lever, *Why Procedure Is More Important than Substantive Law*, 48 INT'L & COMPAR. L. Q. 295 (*quoting* Stephen Goldstein, *The Anglo-American Jury System as Seen by an Outsider (Who Is a Former Insider)*, in 1 THE CLIFFORD CHANCE LECTURES: BRIDGING THE CHANNEL, 165, 170 (Basil S. Markesinis ed., 1996)).

12

The Europeanization of German Law

Key Concepts

- **Direct Effect**: European law principle established by the European Court of Justice. The principle of Direct Effect makes European primary law (the treaties) and some secondary law (Regulations) directly enforceable in the courts of the member states. The principle is based on the conclusion that the European project involves a *sui generis*, supranational legal system exercising the sovereign authority assigned to it by the member states.
- **Supremacy**: European law principle established by the European Court of Justice. According to the principle of Supremacy, European law supersedes and supplants the domestic law of the member states. The principle of Supremacy is informed by a teleological interpretation of the Treaties. Without the principle of Supremacy, the European Court of Justice concluded, the aims of the European project could be undermined and eroded by domestic law. The European Court of Justice cast the principle of Supremacy in absolute terms. Many of the member states, however, have accepted only a relative notion of the Supremacy of European law. The German Federal Constitutional Court, for example, has identified three bases upon which domestic law might prevail over European law: where the German constitution's protection of fundamental basic rights might be implicated; where the European Union (EU) might have expanded its range of competences on its own terms (*ultra vires* acts); and where EU policy intrudes upon the domestic "constitutional identity" of a member state.
- **Neoliberalism**: Neoliberalism is now generally thought to describe the philosophical view that a society's political and economic institutions should be robustly liberal and capitalist, but supplemented by a constitutionally limited democracy and a modest welfare state.[1]
- **Allgemeines Gleichbehandlungsgesetz**: AGG or General Act on Equal Treatment is a German law enacted in 2006 that established legally enforceable antidiscrimination policies. The Act prohibits discrimination in private economic matters on the basis of several characteristics, including: race or ethnic heritage, gender, religion or world view, disability, age, and sexual identity. The Act was part of a set of new laws that aimed to fulfill Germany's obligations under the EU's Anti-Discrimination Directive. There was significant resistance to the enactment of the AGG. Some argued that the Basic Law's equality provisions (Article 3) provided adequate protection against

discrimination, even if those provisions were largely applicable only to state action. Others argued that antidiscrimination law would undermine German private law's robust commitment to private autonomy.
- **Open Constitution** or **Open State**: The German Basic Law makes an essential commitment to the German polity's openness. This is expressed through *Völkerrechtsfreundlichkeit* (accommodation of international law) and *Europarechtsfreundlichkeit* (a mandate for participation in the process of European integration). The latter posture is required by Article 23 of the Basic Law.
- **Constitutional Identity**: As some of the core values of the member states started to become more recurrently affected by deepening European integration, national constitutional courts (primarily in Germany and Italy) emerged as defenders of these core (national constitutional) characteristics in their dialogue with the European Court of Justice.[2] Risk of infringements of Germany's constitutional identity now form the basis for review of EU action before the Federal Constitutional Court.

Study Tips

The Ministry of Justice and Federal Office of Justice provide English-language translations of a number of important German codes and statutes at the website "*Gesetze im Internet*" (www.gesetze-im-internet.de/). This includes the *Allgemeines Gleichbehandlungsgesetz* (AGG or General Act on Equal Treatment).

The European Court of Justice has produced a number of helpful introductory videos (www.youtube.com/c/CourtofJusticeoftheEuropeanUnion/featured).

In April 2008 the Berlin-based newspaper *Die Welt* (*The World*) published this short, tongue-in-cheek report:

New EU-Directive Regulates Lawnmowing

By Marc Lehmann
[Russell A. Miller translation]

Already in early April many garden enthusiasts are reaching peak form: with lawn mowers, lawn aerators, and chainsaws – the work begins and neighbors begin to get irritated. Thankfully the neighbors don't have to tolerate everything. European Union rules comprehensively regulate how much, where, and above all, when gardeners can make noise. German lawmakers have transposed an EU Directive dealing with the issue of noise into a German ordinance. The proper title of the ordinance is the *Geräte- und Maschinenlärmschutzverordnung* (Tool and Machine Noise Protection Ordinance). […] It regulates in detail when the 57 tools and machines it identifies can be used. Among the equipment covered are lawnmowers, hedge clippers, and drills. […]

The following rules regarding the times when these tools and machines can be used apply for residential areas, small housing developments, recreational areas, therapeutic areas, clinical areas, and areas used to accommodate tourists. Most

(a) Leipzig Physician Daniel Gottlob Moritz Schreber
Engraving of the Leipzig Physician and Professor, Daniel Gottlob Moritz Schreber. Schreber introduced and popularized the small "allotment" gardens used by German city-dwellers to grow produce and as a green-space escape from crowded urban living.

(b) German Garden Gnomes
Garden gnomes among the flowers at the Leipzig Schreber Gardens, the first "allotment gardens" in Germany. There is a three-year wait to claim one of these urban garden plots.

Figure 12.1 Germany's Schreber Gardens and the European Union
Source: Getty Images

of the 57 tools and machines identified may not be used at any time on Sundays and Holidays. They may not be used on weekdays between 8:00 pm and 7:00 am. For especially loud tools and machines there are additional restrictions. [...]

Those who prefer to mow the lawn by hand – that is, with their muscle-power – do not need to worry about these time restrictions. The EU Directive is concerned only with lawnmowers that rely on a combustion or electric motor to operate. [...]

Those using an old-fashioned push mower can cut loose at night, at least without worrying about running afoul of the *Geräte- und Maschinenlärmschutzverordnung.* [...][3]

No one who has traveled in Germany and encountered the small, colorful garden plots that create a green buffer around most of the country's densely populated cities will miss the article's irony – or its subtle-but-barbed political message. These immaculate *Schrebergärten* ("Schreber gardens"), credited to the nineteenth-century Leipzig medical researcher and wellness guru Daniel Gottlob Moritz Schreber (depicted in Figure 12.1), are compelling evidence of Germans' passion for gardening. They also seem to be the indigenous habitat of the mischievous German garden gnome (depicted in Figure 12.1). What an outrage, the article slyly suggests, that this deeply rooted German hobby – way of life – has fallen under the authority of the far-off, overly bureaucratic European Union.

This is a minor but representative matter. The point is that EU Law accounts for a significant part of the regulatory landscape in EU member states. It may have suited the editors of *Die Welt* to neglect the fact that domestic rules always imposed some noise limits in Germany. But, if it isn't lawnmowers, then there are plenty of other examples of EU Law's swelling role in the German legal system.[4]

There is no doubt that this "European Law" emanates from a mature, distinct legal system. It is only a small step farther to suggest that it also constitutes a distinct legal tradition in the sense that I have used that concept in this book. If that is the case, then it is worth examining European Law's increasing influence in the German legal system, in the same way that we have considered the Civil Law tradition, the Common Law tradition, Islamic Law, Socialist Law, and the traditions of inquisitorial and adversarial procedure. The process of "Europeanizing" the German legal culture has been profound and, at times, agonizing. The reality is that a large percentage of Germany's laws and regulations now originate with the EU. In fact, one of the EU's most remarkable achievements has been the gradual harmonization of some areas of law right across Europe. All of this makes European Law a new and prominent thread in the tapestry of German law.

This chapter examines the Europeanization of German law. First, it considers how EU Law, as it interacts with the law in the Union's member states, might be understood as a "legal tradition." Second, a specific example of an encounter between European Law and the German Civil Code is presented. Had space allowed it, similar scenes suggesting the Europeanization of other fields of law – both substantive and procedural – could have been presented.

These encounters have not always been smooth and uneventful. For example, with your newly won understanding of the preeminence of the Civil Code in Germany (and the Civil Law tradition it embodies), it will not surprise you to discover in the following materials that Europeanization has met with resistance where it has encountered German private law (but also criminal law, and anything implicating basic rights). Repeatedly, those sometimes rocky interactions between European Law and German law have come to a head in cases before the German Federal Constitutional Court, which has been asked if there is a constitutional limit to Germany's legal and political integration into the EU. That question has received varied answers over time, even if the consistent trend has been towards approving Germany's ever-deeper participation in the project of European integration. A survey of those Constitutional Court cases, presented at the end of this chapter, concludes that the Court's equivocal posture is the natural consequence of conflicting constitutional commands: securing Germany's "constitutional identity," on the one hand, and mandating Germany's participation in European integration, on the other hand.

There is one thing I cannot do in this brief chapter. I cannot provide a survey of the European project, including its fascinating history, its unique political institutions, and the complex legal regime that gives shape to and helps to realize the dream of an ever-closer European Union. That is a sweeping assignment meriting its own textbook. Fortunately, there are many excellent resources providing that background.[5] There is much more to my omission here. I will also not survey the regime that has built up around the European Convention on Human Rights and the European Court of Human Rights. I referred to a ruling of the European Court of Human Rights (ECtHR) in Chapter 10 (the ECtHR found a rights violation in the *Frankfurt Police Torture Case*). That system has also contributed to the Europeanization of German law. It is not part of the EU framework, but operates as part of the broader Council of Europe organization that is based in Strasbourg, France.[6] This chapter focuses only on the EU dimensions of the Europeanization process and for that discussion I have to assume that you have some familiarity with the EU and its legal regime.

Is it reasonable to treat the law of the EU as a "legal tradition"? I can resort to Glenn's deliberately ambiguous definition of the concept when suggesting that it is. At the very least, it is possible to think of European Law as "normative information."[7] It also might be susceptible to a more concrete understanding of what constitutes a legal tradition. Does European Law comprise, or consist of, "a set of deeply rooted, historically conditioned attitudes about the nature of law, about the role of law in the society and the polity, about the proper organization and operation of a legal system, and about the way law is or should be made, applied, studied, perfected, and taught"?[8] Two traits seem to distinguish EU Law as a distinct tradition: the supranational and supreme character of European Law; and persistent suspicions that the EU legal order is in the service of a neoliberal agenda that seeks to erode Europe's communitarian and social orientation.

Throughout the rest of this chapter you should consider whether these traits fairly represent EU Law and, if so, whether they meaningfully distinguish European Law from the other legal traditions we have considered in this book.

12.1 A European Legal Tradition: Supranational and Supreme

The principle of Direct Effect makes certain elements of European Law enforceable before the domestic courts of member states by both natural and legal persons. Direct Effect is not explicitly mentioned in the European treaties. Instead, the doctrine was established by the European Court of Justice in a 1963 decision known as *Van Gend en Loos*.

Van Gend en Loos (a postal and transportation company) imported a chemical from West Germany to the Netherlands. The Dutch customs authorities charged a tariff on the import. The company objected, arguing that the tariff was contrary to the European law applicable at the time. According to Article 12 of the Treaty of Rome (now Article 30 Treaty on the Functioning of the European Union (TFEU)), member states must refrain from introducing between themselves any new customs duties on imports and exports or any charges having equivalent effect, and from increasing those which they already apply in their trade with each other.

12.1 EU Law: Supranational and Supreme

The question before the European Court of Justice was whether Article 12 of the Treaty of Rome had direct application within the territory of a member state, in other words, whether individuals could lay claim, on the basis of a norm derived from an international regime, to individual rights that the domestic courts of the member states would be obliged to enforce.

Judgment of the Court of 5 February 1963
NV Algemene Transport- en Expeditie Onderneming van Gend & Loos v. *Netherlands Inland Revenue Administration*
Reference for a preliminary ruling: Tariefcommissie – Pays-Bas
Case 26–62

On the following questions:

1. Whether Article 12 of the EEC Treaty has direct application within the territory of a member state, in other words, whether nationals of such a State can, on the basis of the Article in question, lay claim to individual rights which the courts must protect;

THE COURT ... gives the following JUDGMENT ...

The first question

On the substance of the Case

The first question of the Tariefcommissie is whether Article 12 of the Treaty has direct application in national law in the sense that nationals of member states may on the basis of this Article lay claim to rights which the national court must protect.

To ascertain whether the provisions of an international Treaty extend so far in their effects it is necessary to consider the spirit, the general scheme and the wording of those provisions.

The objective of the EEC Treaty, which is to establish a common market, the functioning of which is of direct concern to interested parties in the Community, implies that this Treaty is more than an agreement which merely creates mutual obligations between the contracting states. This view is confirmed by the preamble to the Treaty which refers not only to governments but to peoples. It is also confirmed more specifically by the establishment of institutions endowed with sovereign rights, the exercise of which affects member states and also their citizens. Furthermore, it must be noted that the nationals of the States brought together in the Community are called upon to cooperate in the functioning of this Community through the intermediary of the European Parliament and the Economic and Social Committee. [...]

The conclusion to be drawn from this is that the Community constitutes a new legal order of international law for the benefit of which the states have limited their sovereign rights, albeit within limited fields, and the subjects of which comprise not only member states but also their nationals. Independently of the legislation of member states, Community law therefore not only imposes obligations on individuals but is also intended to confer upon them rights which become part of their legal heritage. These rights arise not only where they are expressly granted by the Treaty, but also by reason of obligations which the Treaty imposes in a clearly defined way upon individuals as well as upon the member states and upon the institutions of the Community. [...]

The wording of Article 12 contains a clear and unconditional prohibition which is not a positive but a negative obligation. This obligation, moreover, is not qualified by any reservation on the part of states which would make its implementation conditional upon a positive legislative measure enacted under national law. The very nature of this prohibition makes it ideally adapted to produce direct effects in the legal relationship between member states and their subjects.

The implementation of Article 12 does not require any legislative intervention on the part of the states. The fact that under this Article it is the member states who are made the subject of the negative obligation does not imply that their nationals cannot benefit from this obligation. [...]

It follows from the foregoing considerations that, according to the spirit, the general scheme and the wording of the Treaty, Article 12 must be interpreted as producing direct effects and creating individual rights which national courts must protect. [...]

* * *

Questions/Comments

- *Van Gend en Loos* raised questions about the direct domestic effect of European treaty law, which is referred to as the "primary" law of what is known today as the European Union. The European system also makes use of several "secondary" forms of law. The most prominent are Directives and Regulations. But there are also Recommendations and Decisions. A Directive is a legislative act of the European Union that requires member states to produce a particular result without dictating the means by which it might be achieved.[9] Directives, therefore, need to be enacted domestically ("transposed") as national law. For that reason, they are a more flexible instrument of European Law, policymaking, and integration. Does this indirect engagement by the European Union, which is "laundered" through the domestic legislation of the member states, mean that these European norms should not be counted as part of the process of Europeanizing German law and legal culture? Even if the impetus came from a European Directive, in the end, it was a *German* ordinance that sought to limit machine noise in the report at the start of this chapter. If Germany dithers (or even refuses outright) in fulfilling its duty under a Directive, however, the case law of the European Court of Justice suggests that certain provisions might automatically become directly applicable without domestic transposition. How does that differ from a Regulation, which leaves no margin for the consideration of national differences and interests? Regulations are directly enforceable as law in the member states and are, for that reason, a less accommodating and more obtrusive form of European Law.[10] The principle of Direct Effect established by *Van Gend en Loos* applies to the primary European treaty norms and secondary norms established by European Regulations. The other forms of secondary law are usually not covered by the principle of Direct Effect.
- *Van Gend en Loos* was a groundbreaking judgment. Germany, along with Belgium and the Netherlands (half of the total number of member states at the time) intervened with strong submissions suggesting that the principle of Direct Effect did not accord with their understanding of the obligations they

12.1 EU Law: Supranational and Supreme

had assumed when they became parties to the Treaty of Rome. These objections were consistent with the traditional view that, while international norms bind states *inter se* in the international community, they typically do not automatically create domestic legal rights and obligations *within* states. This is the "dualist" approach to international law. Insisting (as the European Court of Justice did in *Van Gend en Loos*) that European law has automatic consequence for and within domestic legal systems suggested that the European legal order involves something other than traditional international law. It is a hybrid species, neither fully international nor fully domestic, bearing characteristics of both. European Law, with this unique posture, has been described as "supranational" law or a *sui generis* legal order. In *Van Gend en Loos* the European Court of Justice called it a "new legal order." How does this unique feature – neither international nor domestic – orient European Law as a distinct legal tradition? How are the "attitudes about the nature of law" different when norms originate from a supranational legal system? What institutions or centers of power gain and lose authority with the emergence of a new supranational legal order whose law has direct domestic effect within states?

- In its decision in *Van Gend en Loos* the European Court of Justice reasoned partly by reference to the text of the treaty itself. More markedly, however, the Court relied on the spirit and vision of the kind of legal community that the treaty seemed designed to create. This is a teleological approach to interpretation that involves reading the text of the treaty in such a way as to further the underlying and evolving aims of the European project. Is this closer to the legal style and understanding of the role of judges in the Civil Law tradition or the Common Law tradition?

Two years after *Van Gend en Loos* the European Court of Justice affirmed and further refined its theory of the supranational character and Direct Effect of European Law, spelling out the precise implications for a provision of national law that is found to be in conflict with a provision of European law.

Similar to the principle of Direct Effect, the doctrine of the Supremacy of European Law had no basis in the text of the Treaty of Rome. It was developed by the European Court of Justice in *Costa v. ENEL* (1964) on the basis of its conception of how the "new legal order" should operate.

Judgment of the Court of 15 July 1964
Flaminio Costa v. *ENEL*, Reference for a preliminary ruling: Giudice Conciliatore di Milano
Case 6/64

On the interpretation of Articles 102, 93, 53 and 37 of the said Treaty

THE COURT ... gives the following JUDGMENT ...

By contrast with ordinary international treaties, the EEC Treaty has created its own legal system which, on the entry into force of the Treaty, became an integral part of the legal systems of the member states and which their courts are bound to apply.

By creating a Community of unlimited duration, having its own institutions, its own personality, its own legal capacity and capacity of representation on the international plane and, more particularly, real powers stemming from a limitation of sovereignty or a transfer of powers from the States to the Community, the member states have limited their sovereign rights, albeit within limited fields, and have thus created a body of law which binds both their nationals and themselves.

The integration into the laws of each member state of provisions which derive from the Community, and more generally the terms and the spirit of the Treaty, make it impossible for the States, as a corollary, to accord precedence to a unilateral and subsequent measure over a legal system accepted by them on a basis of reciprocity. Such a measure cannot therefore be inconsistent with that legal system. The executive force of Community law cannot vary from one State to another in deference to subsequent domestic laws, without jeopardizing the attainment of the objectives of the Treaty set out in Article 5 (2) and giving rise to the discrimination prohibited by Article 7.

The obligations undertaken under the Treaty establishing the Community would not be unconditional, but merely contingent, if they could be called in question by subsequent legislative acts of the signatories. [...]

It follows from all these observations that the law stemming from the Treaty, an independent source of law, could not, because of its special and original nature, be overridden by domestic legal provisions, however framed, without being deprived of its character as Community law and without the legal basis of the Community itself being called into question.

The transfer by the States from their domestic legal system to the Community legal system of the rights and obligations arising under the Treaty carries with it a permanent limitation of their sovereign rights, against which a subsequent unilateral act incompatible with the concept of the Community cannot prevail. [...]

* * *

Questions/Comments

- Focusing on the nature of the European legal system, the Court reasoned that the whole of the European project would be at risk if national laws at variance to European Law could retain their force. Doesn't that sound like the reasoning that suggests the supremacy of constitutional law, as discussed in Chapter 8? What was the institutional consequence of attributing supremacy to a constitution? Which legal tradition seems to be aligned with this kind of normative supremacy?
- On the one hand, *Van Gend en Loos* is significant because it demonstrated the power of the European Court of Justice to define – even make – European Law. The Court used that power to articulate the concept of a new European supranational legal order that will shape the future of law in the member states, including Germany. On the other hand, *Costa v. ENEL* established that, also with respect to cases in which Germany is not involved as a party, European Law and the rulings of the European Court of Justice will have an impact on law in Germany. Strange as this might seem from the perspective of international law, this is the nature of the new supranational legal order. Would you have any difficulty imagining, or accepting, European Law as a form of constitutional law – even if it were to supplant your domestic constitutional

12.2 EU Law: Common Market and Neoliberalism

The European Court of Justice

The soaring, golden-hued towers of the European Court of Justice in Luxembourg signal the power and prominence the Court enjoys in the European Union. Through its decisions, that power is projected into the legal systems of the EU member states.

Figure 12.2 The European Court of Justice

law?[11] The potential clash of supremacies this framework raises – between supreme and directly applicable European Law and supreme domestic constitutional law – will be the focus of this chapter's concluding section.

- The European Court of Justice, with its glowing, golden towers based in Luxembourg, can be seen in the photograph presented in Figure 12.2. How has the Court's judicial activism strengthened the European project? In what ways does it weaken it? Is there something about the nature and character of supranational law that preordained the emergence of a strong and active judicial lawmaker like the European Court of Justice? How does the Court's role – as exemplified in *Van Gend en Loos* and *Costa* – differ from the judicial function in the Civil Law tradition? How does it differ from the role of the Federal Constitutional Court, which I have portrayed as an expression of the Common Law tradition?

12.2 A European Legal Tradition: Common Market and a Neoliberal Agenda

European Law is supranational and supreme. Another possible distinguishing characteristic, when conceptualizing it as a "legal tradition" vying for influence in the German legal system, is European Law's supposed neoliberal orientation. Neither the Civil Law tradition nor the Common Law tradition, in their nature, prefer a particular economic order. But the European Union's single market – one of the regime's historical justifications – embraces and promotes market capitalism. This is done chiefly by ensuring the "four freedoms" as laid down in Articles 28 to 66 TFEU: free movement of goods, free movement of capital, free movement of services, and free movement of people. Under Article 34 TFEU, "quantitative restrictions on imports and all measures having equivalent effect (MEQRs) shall be prohibited between member states." There are numerous examples of cases in which the European Court of Justice struck down national rules that directly or indirectly discriminated between domestic goods, on the one hand, and goods imported from elsewhere in the common market, on the other hand.[12] Yet, even if trade rules are found to be discriminatory, they can nevertheless be saved through the application of Article 36 TFEU:

> The provisions of Articles 34 and 35 shall not preclude prohibitions or restrictions on imports, exports or goods in transit justified on grounds of public morality, public policy or public security; the protection of health and life of humans, animals or plants; the protection of national treasures possessing artistic, historic or archaeological value; or the protection of industrial and commercial property. Such prohibitions or restrictions shall not, however, constitute a means of arbitrary discrimination or a disguised restriction on trade between member states.

Germany has regularly sought to justify restrictions on imports under the terms of the predecessor of Article 36 TFEU. In *Rewe-Zentrale AG v. Bundesmonopolverwaltung für Branntwein* (1979), for example, the applicant intended to import the liqueur "Cassis de Dijon" into Germany from France. The German authorities blocked the import because the French drink was not of sufficient alcoholic strength to be marketed as an alcoholic beverage in Germany. Under German law such liqueurs had to have an alcohol content of 25 percent, whereas the French product had an alcohol content of between 15 and 20 percent. The applicant argued that the German rule was a restriction on trade because it prevented the French product from being lawfully sold in Germany.

Judgment of the Court of 20 February 1979
Rewe-Zentral AG v. Bundesmonopolverwaltung für Branntwein
Reference for preliminary ruling: Hessisches Finanzgericht
Case 120/78

THE COURT ... gives the following JUDGMENT ....

In the absence of common rules relating to the production and marketing of alcohol – a proposal for a regulation submitted to the Council by the Commission on 7 December 1976 (Official Journal C 309, p. 2) not yet having received the Council's approval – it is for the member states to regulate all matters relating to the production and marketing of alcohol and alcoholic beverages on their own territory.

12.2 EU Law: Common Market and Neoliberalism

Obstacles to movement within the Community resulting from disparities between the national laws relating to the marketing of the products in question must be accepted in so far as those provisions may be recognized as being necessary in order to satisfy mandatory requirements relating in particular to the effectiveness of fiscal supervision, the protection of public health, the fairness of commercial transactions and the protection of the consumer.

The Government of the Federal Republic of Germany, intervening in the proceedings, put forward various arguments which, in its view, justify the application of provisions relating to the minimum alcohol content of alcoholic beverages, adducing considerations relating on the one hand to the protection of public health and on the other to the protection of the consumer against unfair commercial practices.

As regards the protection of public health the German Government states that the purpose of the fixing of minimum alcohol contents by national legislation is to avoid the proliferation of alcoholic beverages on the national market, in particular alcoholic beverages with a low alcohol content, since, in its view, such products may more easily induce a tolerance towards alcohol than more highly alcoholic beverages.

Such considerations are not decisive since the consumer can obtain on the market an extremely wide range of weakly or moderately alcoholic products and furthermore a large proportion of alcoholic beverages with a high alcohol content freely sold on the German market is generally consumed in a diluted form.

The German Government also claims that the fixing of a lower limit for the alcohol content of certain liqueurs is designed to protect the consumer against unfair practices on the part of producers and distributors of alcoholic beverages.

This argument is based on the consideration that the lowering of the alcohol content secures a competitive advantage in relation to beverages with a higher alcohol content, since alcohol constitutes by far the most expensive constituent of beverages by reason of the high rate of tax to which it is subject.

Furthermore, according to the German Government, to allow alcoholic products into free circulation wherever, as regards their alcohol content, they comply with the rules laid down in the country of production would have the effect of imposing as a common standard within the Community the lowest alcohol content permitted in any of the member states, and even of rendering any requirements in this field inoperative since a lower limit of this nature is foreign to the rules of several member states.

As the Commission rightly observed, the fixing of limits in relation to the alcohol content of beverages may lead to the standardization of products placed on the market and of their designations, in the interests of a greater transparency of commercial transactions and offers for sale to the public.

However, this line of argument cannot be taken so far as to regard the mandatory fixing of minimum alcohol contents as being an essential guarantee of the fairness of commercial transactions, since it is a simple matter to ensure that suitable information is conveyed to the purchaser by requiring the display of an indication of origin and of the alcohol content on the packaging of products.

It is clear from the foregoing that the requirements relating to the minimum alcohol content of alcoholic beverages do not serve a purpose which is in the general interest and such as to take precedence over the requirements of the free movement of goods, which constitutes one of the fundamental rules of the Community.

In practice, the principle effect of requirements of this nature is to promote alcoholic beverages having a high alcohol content by excluding from the national market products of other member states which do not answer that description.

It therefore appears that the unilateral requirement imposed by the rules of a member state of a minimum alcohol content for the purposes of the sale of alcoholic beverages constitutes an obstacle to trade which is incompatible with the provisions of [the current Article 36 TFEU].

There is therefore no valid reason why, provided that they have been lawfully produced and marketed in one of the member states, alcoholic beverages should not be introduced into any other member state; the sale of such products may not be subject to a legal prohibition on the marketing of beverages with an alcohol content lower than the limit set by the national rules. [...]

* * *

Questions/Comments

- The *Cassis de Dijon* case is representative of the neoliberal ambitions of the European project and European law. The aim was to establish a common market amongst the member states and this required the elimination of most domestic commercial limits, restrictions, and regulations that impeded commercial movement from one state to another. This was the core dynamic of a European integration process driven forward by "mainstream neoliberal policies [that] circumvented and eroded those state traditions and national compromises that, in the past" fostered a European Social Model.[13] At least in the initial "common market phase" of the European project this cast into doubt national laws establishing subsidies for market participants, tariffs and import restrictions, labor or environmental standards affecting production, and consumer protection regimes.
- It says something important about German culture that some of the prominent cases involving challenges to European law's liberalizing pressures featured German attempts to protect its domestic alcoholic beverages market. The Case 178/84 *Commission v. Germany* (*German Beer Purity*) (1987) involved the 500-year-old Bavarian *Reinheitsgebot* (Beer Purity Law), a printed version of which is depicted in Figure 12.3. The *Reinheitsgebot*, which had been incorporated into West Germany's post-war federal law regulating the production and taxation of beer, famously limited the ingredients in beer to just three things: water, barley, and hops. At the time the law was promulgated it was not known that beer also contained yeast. This additional ingredient was left out of the law's modern iteration out of respect for the long tradition of German beer purity. Far more than the *Schreber* gardens mentioned at the beginning of this chapter, beer is a distinctly iconic emblem of German life and culture. Think of the *Oktoberfest* clichés that dominate many portrayals of Germany. Beer continues to play an important role in German life. A European intrusion on this sacred sphere was sure to prompt German indignation as an incendiary example of the sometimes tense encounter between European and German law. That encounter came in the form of a challenge, brought by the European Commission, against the

12.2 EU Law: Common Market and Neoliberalism

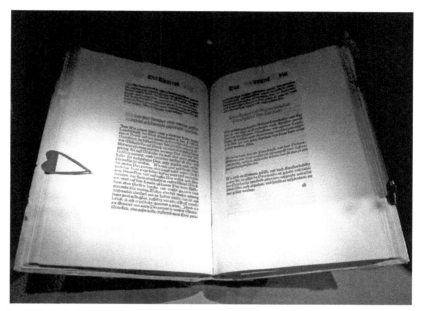

German Beer Purity Law

The German Beer Purity Law recorded in the Bavarian State Regulations from 1516. This copy of the State Regulations is one of only a handful of surviving examples of the code. It was displayed during the State Exhibition held at Aldersbach, Bavaria, as part of the events in 2016 celebrating the 500th anniversary of the *Rheinheitsgebot*. It is still the mandate for all beer brewed in Bavaria.

Figure 12.3 German Beer Purity Law and the European Union

German ban on marketing beer that did not conform to the *Reinheitsgebot*. Many countries saw Germany's contemporary insistence upon the ancient Beer Purity Law as little more than a poorly disguised trade barrier that made it practically impossible for other member states to export their (less pure) beer to Germany. Once again invoking the predecessor of Article 36 TFEU, Germany argued that the *Reinheitsgebot* advanced health concerns over the use of additives and preservatives in beer. Germany also argued that its citizens' disproportionately heavy *per capita* consumption of beer gave it a unique interest in regulating beer at the national level. The European Court of Justice rejected these arguments, striking another blow for supranational European legal supremacy and European law's neoliberal ambitions. It should be noted, however, that the single market in beer can also be counted as a victory for Germans who are now free to sample the brewed wares of their fellow Europeans, from Italy's Birra Peroni to the Swedish Starköl called Norrlands Guld. And, in any case, the German brands still indicate their compliance with the ancient *Reinheitsgebot* on their labels.

- How neoliberal can European legal culture be if it provides an exception to the free market commitment for public health or consumer protection reasons?

In both the *Cassis de Dijon* and *Germany Beer Purity* decisions, Germany's arguments were based in part on its consumer protection laws. In the cases described, European Law undermined those national regulatory limits in pursuit of a more open and free market. Although implicating a relatively lighthearted issue in these cases, this is an example of the tendency in European Law that makes it susceptible to the criticism that it is has an essential neoliberal character. European Law, in the name of the common market, also has superseded national regulations on labor relations and the financial markets.

- Which is more market friendly – Germany's Civil Code with its commitment to *Privatautonomie* seasoned with just a few "drops of social oil," or the European Union with its single market mandate? What term or phrase does the European Court of Justice use in *Cassis de Dijon* as the standard for identifying impermissible, anti-market policies?
- It is remarkable to see a supranational tribunal such as the European Court of Justice undertake its own assessment of the integrity and efficacy of the challenged domestic policy. Showing no deference to German policymakers in these cases, the European Court of Justice evaluated the justifications offered by Germany on its own terms and, in *Cassis de Dijon*, concluded that Germany had "no valid reason" for enacting the alcohol content rule. Is this a standard of review as permissive as the American Supreme Court's "rational basis test" (which requires the court to defer to government policy that is rationally related to a legitimate end) or is it a more robust form of judicial scrutiny? Is supranational judicial scrutiny of a democratically – and domestically – legitimated policy problematic? The European Court's defenders note that the judges were forced into this role by the dysfunctional political apparatus created by the founders of the European project. Deepening integration was stymied, above all, by the need for unanimity among the member states for many policies. How else to achieve the Treaty of Rome's summons to an ever-closer union? Is that goal worth a little (or even a lot of) judicial activism?

12.3 Europeanization of German Law: The Example of Contract Law

As discussed in Chapter 7, since entering into force in 1900, Germany's revered Civil Code hasn't changed much. In particular, the provisions addressing contracts have remained almost unaltered. Major modifications were made to the Civil Code for the first time shortly after its 100th anniversary. The first of these changes was the "contract law reform" of 2001.[14] Simultaneously, a less extensive but equally controversial reform loomed over the Civil Code, triggered by Germany's obligation, as a member of the European Union, to implement four civil rights Directives, including:

- Directive 2000/43/EC of 29 June 2000 ("anti-racism Directive");
- Directive 2000/78/EC of 27 November 2000 ("framework Directive regarding occupation");

12.3 Europeanization of German Contract Law

- Directive 2002/73/EC of 23 September 2002 ("gender Directive regarding access to employment") changing Directive 76/207/EEC, "merged" into the new gender Directive 2006/54/EC; and
- Directive 2004/113/EC of 13 December 2004 ("gender Directive regarding access to goods and services").

Together, these Directives sought to combat various forms of discrimination and unequal treatment, not between the state and the individual (in the vertical dimension), but between individuals in different fields governed by private law (in the horizontal dimension). The Directives would not require sweeping changes, but they represented a clear Europeanization of the member states' labor and private law.

The Directives could be categorized into two groups.[15] Three of them principally referred to nondiscrimination in the employment and occupation field: the "anti-racism Directive," the "framework Directive," and the "new gender Directive." The "anti-racism Directive" also addressed the areas of social security and health services, education, and public services such as housing.[16] In contrast, the "gender Directive regarding access to goods and services" does not concern employment but generally all services provided to individuals and consumers, in particular with respect to private insurance.[17] Therefore, the first three Directives were similar in their wording. They commenced with a statement of their purpose, namely the prohibition of discrimination. The concept "discrimination" was defined in the Directives' first sections followed by a set of exceptions, the demand that the member states take positive action to combat discrimination, and the establishment of legal remedies for violations of the anti-discrimination policy.[18] The broader gender Directive was more extensive in its wording. But all of the anti-discrimination Directives were modeled on Directive 76/207/EC, which was the original gender equality Directive implemented in the 1970s. The Directives gave the member states a deadline for transposing their terms through the enactment of commensurate domestic legislation.

The Directives confronted German law with a new approach to equal treatment. The law of obligations, which is one of the cornerstones of the German Civil Code, was especially affected. After all, "there was [the] widespread perception that [Germany's] existing legal framework [for combating discrimination] was not satisfactory."[19] That was especially true because of the high value the Code placed on *Privatautonomie* (private autonomy). Recall from Chapter 7 that, out of respect for private autonomy, the Civil Code seeks to empower individuals to freely act on their own behalf and in their own interests when interacting with others in economic matters. Despite that commitment, Germany had constitutional safeguards and other legal measures in place to protect the individual against discrimination. But those protections were largely aimed at discrimination perpetrated by the state. The legal situation in Germany before the enactment of the domestic anti-discrimination law transposing the European Directives is summarized in the following excerpts.

Florian Stork
Comments on the Draft of the New German Private Law Anti-Discrimination Act: Implementing Directives 2000/43/EC and 2004/113/EC in German Private Law
6 GERMAN LAW JOURNAL 533, 536–537 (2005)[*]

* * *

According to Art. 3 para 1 of the *Grundgesetz* (German Basic Law, GG), all human beings are equal before the law. Art. 3 para 3 GG prohibits discrimination based on sex, parentage, race, language, homeland and origin, belief, religious or political opinions. The primary aim of Art. 3 para 3 GG is to protect individuals against discrimination by public authorities. It is well established that the fundamental rights in the German Constitution do not apply directly to the private sphere of citizens; they do not have *direkte Drittwirkung* (direct horizontal effect). However, these rights lay down an objective value system, which influences not only legislative, executive and judicial authorities, but also civil law. Therefore, mandatory general provisions such as sections 138, 826 of the *Bürgerliches Gesetzbuch* (German Civil Code, BGB), which constitute part of the *ordre public*, have to be interpreted in light of the objective value system established by the fundamental rights contained in the *Grundgesetz*. Understood like that, they are supposed to be a sufficient base to remedy any grievances in connection with discriminatory practices in civil law, for example, if goods or services are denied because of the ethnic origin of the applicant.

In contrast to many other EU member states such as the UK or the Netherlands, in Germany there still is no act dealing exclusively with non-discrimination. In civil law, there only remain several scattered provisions that may be used to combat severe acts of discrimination. Some have already been mentioned: For example, section 826 BGB stipulates the right to compensation for damage suffered from an intentional, immoral injury. In German Case law, section 826 BGB has already served as a tool for the granting of compensation for discrimination on the grounds of sexual identity. Other general *bona fide* and equity clauses of civil law are also to be interpreted in the light of the constitutional provision of equal treatment. There is, however, very little case law dealing with discrimination in civil law. Explicit regulations providing the right to equal access and treatment can be found in section 611a BGB in terms of sex and section 81 of the *Neuntes Buch Sozialgesetzbuch* (Ninth Book of the Social Act, SGB IX) in terms of disability. Both tackle, however, exclusively discrimination related to employment.

* * *

Eddie Bruce-Jones
Race, Space and the Nation-State: Racial Recognition and the Prospects for Substantive Equality Under Anti-Discrimination Law in France and Germany
39 COLUMBIA HUMAN RIGHTS LAW REVIEW 423, 439–443 (2007)[*]

* * *

German race-based anti-discrimination laws are underinclusive in several ways. First, the German principle of freedom of contract allows private parties the opportunity to racially discriminate. Second, because race (*Rasse*) has been all but removed from popular

---

[*] Excerpt reprinted with permission of the author.
[*] Excerpt reprinted with permission of the author.

language, there are few real legal standards that elaborate direct or pretextual racism. Third, victims of discrimination regime for the private sphere. In the spring of 2005, the German parliament debated broad new anti-discrimination legislation. A German congressman of Indian descent, Sebastian Edathy, testified that he had been hassled in his apartment search because the landlord did not want her apartment building to smell like Indian food. The congressman found this to be a pretext for racial or ethnic discrimination and called for legislation that would make such practice unlawful. Congressional representatives who opposed this view emphasized that the German notion of the freedom of contract is one of the strengths of the German legal institution, and that it should not be compromised, a sentiment shared by many in the Senate and in the business world. Passage of the debated legislation failed, and to date, anti-discrimination legislation does not cover the private sector other than in the realm of employment. The German use of the term "minority group" (*Minderheitsgruppe* or *ethnische Minderheit*) is different from its usage in the United States. Germany has only granted a few "ethnic" groups national minority status. As a result, Germany only recognizes four groups as being covered by the protections of international law: Serbs, Fresians, Sinti and Roma peoples, and Danes. In Germany, the term "ethnic minority" is reserved for these groups. The Turkish minority – by some accounts the largest minority group in Germany – is not protected as a "national minority"; neither are Black Germans. Although such groups do receive constitutional protections, they are not equivalent to those enjoyed by "national minority" groups. Thus, German law explicitly contains a stratification of protection, a hierarchy of insider and outsider group identities.

* * *

This academic commentary confirms that there was protection against discrimination in Germany before the implementation of the European Directives. But, in the case that one individual discriminated against another, there was no direct, binding effect of the Basic Law's equality guarantee. As you learned in Chapter 8, the Basic Law's "objective order of values" only exerts indirect and limited "horizontal" influence over private affairs. The doctrine of *Drittwirkung* requires very unequal relationships between private parties before it will limit the *Privatautonomie* that is codified and celebrated in the German Civil Code. The Basic Law generally does not apply to the mere use of one's superior position in order to gain an advantage from a contract. Therefore, the Civil Code traditionally tolerated a large degree of contractual discretion without much concern for fundamental rights or equality. Cases upholding the denial of employment to a black woman in a luxury hotel in Berlin (resulting in a settlement), or the exclusion of a black customer from a restaurant whom the owner "mistook for a drug dealer," show the limits of the protection against discrimination that existed in Germany prior to the implementation of the European anti-discrimination Directives.[20]

There were several attempts by parties in the German parliament to provide better protection against unequal treatment in the private sector. In 1995 the Party of Democratic Socialism (PDS) issued a first draft of a law against racism, which was then followed by two more drafts of equal treatment laws, one from the Social Democratic Party of Germany (SPD) and the other from the Green Party. These gained little traction and it was only after the SPD/Green center-left government swept to power in 1998 that the German Federal Ministry of Justice issued a viable draft of a law prohibiting discrimination in private matters. This draft was part of an already vigorous discussion, but it acquired importance and momentum due to Germany's duty to transpose the European Directives. Still, the draft law showed considerable deviation from the Directives.[21]

Partly due to scholarly objections, but also because of significant political opposition, attempts to enact anti-discrimination legislation stalled until the European Court of Justice threatened Germany with judicial sanctions pursuant to the current Article 258 TFEU for failing to fulfill its obligation under the European Treaties to transpose a Directive into domestic law. Those proceedings could have resulted in tens of millions of Euros in penalties.[22] After a lively political and scholarly debate the German *Bundestag* passed the "Act for the Implementation of European Directives Regarding the Realization of the Principle of Equal Treatment," which has been in force since 18 August 2006.[23] This Act can be called a "meta-law." It includes only four articles. Two of those articles (Articles 1 and 2) refer to and include two complete and separate federal laws: the Act on Equal Treatment of Female and Male Soldiers; and the General Act on Equal Treatment known in German as the *Allgemeines Gleichbehandlungsgesetz* (AGG).[24]

The AGG largely copies the wording and the provisions of the European Directives with regard to substantive anti-discrimination as well as administrative provisions.

General Act on Equal Treatment[*]

Part 1
General Provisions
§ 1 Purpose

The purpose of this Act is to prevent or to stop discrimination on the grounds of race or ethnic origin, gender, religion or belief, disability, age or sexual orientation.

§ 2 Scope

(1) For the purposes of this Act, any discrimination within the meaning of Section 1 shall be inadmissible in relation to:

1. conditions for access to dependent employment and self-employment, including selection criteria and recruitment conditions, whatever the branch of activity and at all levels of professional hierarchy, including promotion;
2. employment conditions and working conditions, including pay and reasons for dismissal, in particular in contracts between individuals, collective

---

[*] Translation reprinted with permission of the Federal Anti-Discrimination Agency.

bargaining agreements and measures to implement and terminate an employment relationship, as well as for promotion;
3. access to all types and to all levels of vocational guidance, vocational training, advanced vocational training and retraining, including practical work experience;
4. membership of and involvement in an organization of workers or employers or any organization whose members carry on a particular profession, including all benefits provided for by such organizations;
5. social protection, including social security and health care;
6. social advantages;
7. education;
8. access to and supply of goods and services which are available to the public, including housing.

* * *

§ 3 Definitions

(1) Direct discrimination shall be taken to occur where one person is treated less favorably than another is, has been or would be treated in a comparable situation on any of the grounds referred to under Section 1. Direct discrimination on grounds of sex shall also be taken to occur in relation to Section 2(1) Nos 1 to 4 in the event of the less favorable treatment of a woman on account of pregnancy or maternity.

(2) Indirect discrimination shall be taken to occur where an apparently neutral provision, criterion or practice would put persons at a particular disadvantage compared with other persons on any of the grounds referred to under Section 1, unless that provision, criterion or practice is objectively justified by a legitimate aim and the means of achieving that aim are appropriate and necessary....

Questions/Comments

- How does this excerpt from the AGG compare with the Civil Code provisions discussed in earlier chapters?
- The AGG and its drafts stirred an intense discussion focusing on several points. On the critical side, the primary concern was that the Act would destroy the principle of private autonomy that is thought to be so central to the German Civil Code and its provisions relating to contracts. The following essay is representative of the substance and tone of the many critical reactions to the AGG. Professor Ladeur's comments were written when the domestic implementation of the European Directives was still focused on an amendment of the Civil Code. Ultimately, the AGG was enacted as a free-standing corpus of legislation and was not incorporated into the nearly sacred BGB. This means that the European-mandated anti-discrimination measures were

given, as *Nebengesetze* (side laws), a place on the margin of the Civil Code, which remains the central organizing regime of all German private law. This is sure to have implications for the prominence and coherence of the AGG's provisions in the broader German legal culture. Ladeur's arguments, and others like them, tilted against this European "assault" on the Civil Code.

Karl-Heinz Ladeur
The German Proposal of an 'Anti-Discrimination'-Law: Anticonstitutional and Anti-Common Sense. A Response to Nicola Vennemann
3 GERMAN LAW JOURNAL (2002)[*]

* * *

I cannot endorse the positive evaluation of the German Proposal of an Anti-Discrimination Law. On the contrary, I take the view that it is in several respects unconstitutional and incompatible with both common sense and the requirements of the rule of law. (Apart from that it is written in an amateurish non-juridical jargon which in the past was noticeably widespread in sectarian political groups.) That it shall be integrated into the BGB with its clear systematic liberal approach, one of the masterpieces of European legal culture, has to be regarded as an act of legal vandalism.

It is first of all in clear contradiction with the constitutional principle of protection of marriage and family as legal institutions (Art.6 par.1 GG) inasmuch as it does not allow discrimination, for example, in the selection of a tenant by a landlord against persons of minority "sexual identity": If the government has the obligation to protect and support families it cannot be constitutional to impose on private persons a duty not to privilege traditional nuclear families and decide against gays and lesbians. The prohibition to discriminate is only acceptable with respect to single persons. From the point of view of a liberal theory of rights, and privacy in particular, it is not acceptable to force private individuals who disapprove of gays and lesbians to accept such persons as tenants. In a liberal society there should be a difference between prosecution of public discrimination against citizens and public invasion of privacy in order to impose "correct" views on citizens.

While, certainly nobody can be in favour of discrimination. However, in a liberal society there is a legal rationality which is different from morality and which cannot be ignored without provoking serious doctrinal and practical problems: the law wants to sanction bad intentions whereas a liberal legal system is based on the assumption that these can only be the object of legal concern in extreme cases. Neglecting simple rules of legal rationality, the proposal even goes so far as to discriminate against the "majority" and to violate the right to equality itself: As a rule, the "majoritarian" *everybody* has to prove the facts from which he or she derives a favorable legal consequence. Pursuant to the new § 319c BGB a person who is protected by the anti-discrimination law has only to make plausible ("*glaubhaft*") the facts which indicate (*vermuten lassen*) a discrimination. This means that protected persons can by a formal declaration *vis-à-vis* a solicitor etc. (affidavit – *eidesstattliche Versicherung*) provoke the reversal of the normal burden of proof. [A slightly different but in the end corresponding wording is now included in § 22 AGG] This is nothing but a legal presumption against the majoritarian everybody:

---

[*] Excerpt reprinted with permission of the author.

such a reversal of proof is only acceptable if the defendant has some privileged access to facts–this is the case, for example, in environmental law or product liability etc. It might also be acceptable for organized decision-makers but not for the average individual. This is all the more so as it is extremely difficult to prove a "negative" fact–that a decision was not based on discriminatory intentions. To impose such a disadvantage on the average person including the risk of being arbitrarily brought to court is incompatible with the constitutional right to equality, Art. 3 GG.

This is all the more so because many individual contracts are not based on "facts" at all: a landlord may well rent an apartment to persons he just likes without being able or being forced to give reasons–this is the core element of the freedom of contract. The proposal considers this possibility and offers "balancing" (*Güterabwägung*) as a way out and accepts a certain leeway for evaluation. How should one imagine such a balancing procedure in court? Would the judge have a look at the rejected contract partner and decide whether the person could with reason be regarded as "unpleasant", or whether this judgment is simply arbitrary and capricious? Would he decide that the discrimination can only be regarded as racist because the person was in fact "nice"? Control of motives (of individuals–not of organizations which have to standardize contracts) cannot be the legitimate object of a law. Incidentally, the law neglects the difference between substantive and procedural law when it introduces procedural possibilities of proof into civil law: good intentions apparently must not be blocked by formal rules! The law creates a high risk of persons being brought to court arbitrarily.

But there will also be serious problems on the side of the protected groups: how can a man prove that he really is homosexual and not just trying to profit from a privilege? Does he have to tell his potential partners that he is protected as a homosexual? How about discrimination of race or ethnic origin? Do judges define what races are? How about Jews who are in fact not religious–do they have to prove that they are?

This problem will only touch the stupid: for the rest the law creates a strong incentive to avoid any contact with protected people right from the outset because the safe strategy is not to give any possibility for protected persons to bring someone to court. It is easy to use new filters (anonymous advertising, requirement of written application and letters of recommendation etc.). It is also recommendable always to have a third person participating in the bargaining process in order to have a neutral testimony. It is not by chance that good intentions (but bad professional standards) at the end of the day will impose new burdens on protected groups.

The law will also create a lot of problems for owners of discothèques: the authors of the proposal explicitly refer to this case: How can a doorkeeper who rejects a protected person prove that he might be a trouble-maker? Shall a judge decide whether a foreigner is in fact acceptable or not whereas the majoritarian group has to accept arbitrary decisions? The right to get compensation might create the risk of being harassed by criminal gangs.

With respect to organized decision-making (differentiation between groups in insurance tariffs etc.) a new problem comes to the fore. In this case the facts will often be beyond doubt whereas the justification of the difference creates a problem. The authors want to refer this problem to the view of the "average person." But how and why should this kind of judgment be accepted? This is a complex professional problem, and why should a firm be forced to accept the view of the "average person" – which will also be difficult to ascertain. The average person can only be referred to when information or a declaration is addressed to the attention of the public at large. The average person, for example, does not know the rules of statistical decision-making, why then should he be competent to judge tariffs based thereupon? How could he judge the "objectivity" (*Sachlichkeit*) of those rules?

The proposal indicates a general problem of modern (social-) democratic governments: the real problems of society become increasingly intractable and escape the reach of public decision-making. As a consequence we are witnessing more and more symbolic and ideological acts of "solidarity" which seem to be costless and which speculate that hypocrisy will dampen opposition because they offer a lot of possibilities for circumvention and stupid persons should blame themselves. Such laws only function as a trap for inexperienced people. Thus they will probably have no consequences at all. But if they do have consequences they will give good argument to the rising right wing populist parties who try to gather more and more "average people" who do not oppose discriminatory practices because they no longer feel their interests are being taken care of by governments.

* * *

Still, it must be noted that other German scholars passionately advocated for the anti-discrimination law. Professor Susanne Baer, who would later serve as the first openly gay or lesbian justice at the Federal Constitutional Court, was one of them.

Susanne Baer
"The End of Private Autonomy" or Rights-Based Legislation? The Anti-Discrimination Law Debate in Germany
I ANNUAL OF GERMAN & EUROPEAN LAW 323–326, 328–330
(Russell A. Miller & Peer Zumbansen eds., 2003)[*]

The relationship between freedom and equality has been controversial in law ever since these values began to be acknowledged as individual rights in constitutions and human rights catalogues. History shows us that freedom dominates, as a subjective claim to individual autonomy. Equality is taken for granted as a premise, insofar as it refers to the universal validity of norms, which is essential to the rule of law. But beyond this – as equality not only in the formal sense, but as a prohibition of discrimination against individuals by violating their right to respect *qua* human dignity – it must constantly be asserted and struggled for even today.

In Germany, too, the discussion on freedom and equality has long been marked by a debate in which one side – old hat! – proclaims the "death of private autonomy," and thus, rhetorically, the loss of the most personal of all rights and freedoms, while on the other hand the right to equality is strangely underexposed. This clouding of equality is mainly a result of cultural as well as ideological factors. In a society that perceives itself as egalitarian – and especially, in post-war Germany's case, as a welfare state that is neither inhumane nor discriminatory – it is difficult to assert that the constitution establishes the equal importance of freedom and equality, even from an interpretive standpoint. For by calling for equality, one is ultimately pointing out inequality; whereas by refusing to acknowledge that inequality is a fact of daily life, one fails to recognize the continuing relevance of the right to equality.

A timely example of this phenomenon of the neglect of certain basic rights in favor of others is the discussion on changing the BGB (Civil Code) to prohibit discrimination in contract law. This debate has been sparked by a draft law with which the federal

---

[*] Excerpt reprinted with permission of the author.

government, in 2001, hoped to fulfill its obligation to apply two European Directives against discrimination. The draft, which has since been withdrawn [will] be replaced by "less radical" legislation [...] The date set in the existing European Directives for their implementation in the member states has now passed, and the German government must make haste if it is to fulfill its obligations to Europe.

It has been claimed that "the last shreds of self-determination" will be eliminated [by the proposed anti-discrimination legislation]. Participants at the 53rd German Lawyers Congress feared the "end of private autonomy." This is also the concern, especially, of the major state-supported churches. Private tenants' associations have also proclaimed their "fury and horror." All were reacting to a federal draft law [that would] subject the general rules on the content of contracts to a general prohibition on discrimination. [The law] would prohibit discrimination "on the basis of sex, race, ethnic origin, religion or belief, disability, age or sexual identity or for any other reason" in public contracts and contracts involving essential services or membership in professional organizations [...]. Those guilty of differential treatment without justification could be required to conclude a contract, to adjust it, or to pay damages; in any case, they would be expected to cease discriminating [...].

Is this kind of prohibition on discrimination under contract law legally, and above all constitutionally, tenable? Under European law, such a regulation would fulfill Germany's obligations regarding ethnic discrimination, from Directive 2000/43/EC regarding the other discriminatory factors targeted by the EU, Germany would be going beyond the legal minimum required by the European Directives (as Sweden, as well as other European states, have long done). From a constitutional perspective, the protests I have cited against this draft legislation imply that it represents an unjustified interference with the basic right of freedom of contract, an aspect of self-determination that is protected under Article 2 section 1 of the Basic Law. As I will show, however, this is not the case.

The right to freedom is protected in the Basic Law as individual freedom in a comprehensive sense, known to encompass such things as riding in the woods. The right to arrange one's legal relationships according to one's own will is part of the general freedom of action. But the right to arrange legal relationships that have consequences for others is also subject to limitation. A law that limits freedom is an intervention. It is justified if it meets the requirements of Article 2 section 2, especially the principles of practical concordance and proportionality. Simply put, taking advantage of individual freedom may not disproportionately limit the rights of others. A radical concept of unbounded autonomy has thus not been accepted constitutionally. Freedom of contract has limits. The "power of self-determination" [...] is not a power to determine others.

This is expressed in the Europeanized legal order in which we live today. It is true that European law has a markedly liberal and sometimes even neoliberal tendency, but social aspects are not foreign to it [...]. Thus, in many areas, it is not unbridled will which governs – or, as Flume, a major German civil law theorist, put it, self-importance – but legally determined, limited freedom that ensures the common good [...].

The German government's proposal that contracts be tied to a prohibition on discrimination is [...] constitutionally tenable. The Basic Law provides that law, and thus also civil law, should follow a model of liberalism cushioned within the welfare state. Private law makes possible an ordering of the market that works not according to Darwinist principles, but on the basis of justice. The view, advocated not only in the United States, that the market regulates everything is rejected by the Basic Law through the triad of human dignity, freedom and equality and a sophisticated system of checks and balances. The unchecked market can destroy some people.

The functions of law are manifold. Law, for example, establishes burdens of proof, and it guides an objective and just balancing of interests, which includes ensuring the restoration of disrupted contractual parity. This limiting function of civil law is highlighted in labor law. There are no convincing arguments for why it should not be recognized in other contractual relationships. Proximity and dependence for a certain amount of time also affect landlord-tenant relationships and provision of other services. It is thus only logical that private autonomy be controlled in application of general rules of contract, for monopolies, and in other situations of imbalance. It would be logical to adopt basic laws to prevent discrimination for all of contract law [...].

The German debate is, as are debates elsewhere, filled with distortions rather than rational arguments [...]. Up to now, sensational, but hardly illuminating, examples have been constructed that supposedly take the law against discrimination *ad absurdum*; on closer examination, they describe behaviors that are not ultimately problematic, because they involve relevant differential treatment, but not discrimination [...]. It is not compatible with the basic rights, however, when people are excluded from the market because they simply live differently than the majority. Those who use the market must expect to be bound in public by the basic rules of, if one so wishes, tolerant coexistence [...].

With its basic right to dignity and its commands for tolerance, the constitution demands social integration from all citizens, not only immigrants or other "others," who suffer far more from the refusal to accept social integration. As the European Court of Justice has pointed out, such rules work only if they include effective sanctions. Thus, it is logical to legally require conclusion of a contract, in cases where that can reasonably be expected.

Questions/Comments

- The European anti-discrimination Directives, ultimately implemented in Germany as the AGG, contradict the claims that European Law fundamentally seeks to advance a neoliberal agenda. After all, the anti-discrimination Directives imposed limits on market and economic freedom. There are other examples of the European Union using its supranational authority over the European market to pursue regulatory, as opposed to deregulatory, aims. This has been true, in particular, of consumer protection and data privacy issues.[25] If this fact undermines – or at least softens – criticism that the European project is a neoliberal Trojan Horse, then is there another noneconomic criticism that can be leveled against the European Union's jurisprudential meddling in the legal systems of the member states? How does your answer to this question affect your willingness to treat European Law as a distinct "legal tradition"?
- Ladeur concluded that the German Civil Code is "one of the masterpieces of European legal culture," and that the imposition of the European anti-discrimination regime on the Civil Code would constitute an "act of legal vandalism." This is a remarkably colorful example of the high esteem in which the Civil Code is held by German jurists, lawyers, and legal scholars. Is Ladeur's objection partly rooted in the concern that the Europeanization of German private law also involves a shift away from that regime's orientation towards the Civil Law tradition?
- Ladeur reanimates our discussions from earlier in this book about the Civil Law tradition's tendency towards positivism and formalism. He described

12.3 Europeanization of German Contract Law

the "separation thesis" of positivism (mentioned in Chapter 3 in relation to Hans Kelsen) as a "legal rationality which is different from morality." As an example of the legally irrational character of the European-imposed anti-discrimination regime, Ladeur suggested that the German transposition of the regime would lead to discrimination "against the 'majority.'" Is respect for and obsequiousness to the majority a requirement of the rule of law? Is it a natural part of the Civil Law tradition?

- Baer pointed out that contractual freedom never has enjoyed unlimited protection. Under the Basic Law, she explained, "taking advantage of individual freedom may not disproportionately limit the rights of others." You understand, after the exposure you gained in Chapters 7 and 8, that she is referring to the Code's general clauses and the constitutional doctrine of *Drittwirkung*. She also noted that contractual freedom found limits in German private law, including labor law and landlord/tenant law.
- Do Ladeur and Baer, respectively, embody the Civil Law tradition and the Common Law tradition? Does the European anti-discrimination regime advance one or the other legal tradition, or a distinct legal tradition?
- Both Ladeur and Baer seem skeptical (in varying degrees) of the European-imposed anti-discrimination regime. How much blame and/or credit do they direct at Europe? For them, is the German AGG an example of the Europeanization of German legal culture or do they regard it as a strictly domestic legal development, perhaps with a distinctly European hue?
- The harmonization of member states' laws that results from the Europeanization process exemplified by the anti-discrimination Directives poses a distinct challenge to my comparative law commitment to celebrating differences between legal systems. After the anti-discrimination Directives, private law relations in the member states must look more (and not less) similar. Is this another characteristic of European law? Is it assimilationist – or perhaps even imperialist? Pierre Legrand thinks so. You will recall from Chapter 1 that I find inspiration for the commitment to showing respect for law's social and cultural difference in the work of Legrand. He has been an outspoken critic of the Europeanization of law. He was especially bothered by the conceit of those who advocate the harmonization of law under the banner of European unity. And he has argued that harmonization will ultimately fail:

> You see, despite [the best efforts of advocates of legal harmonization in Europe], Europe still has not achieved uniformisation of law. Local legal practices have not, in fact, been abolished. [...] [Harmonization] cannot supply transcultural efficacy, [...] it cannot foreclose the matter of differentiation of laws. [...] [D]o you recall Gunther Teubner's view about EU law generating new, if unintended, differences across and within discursive configurations (including national law) prevailing in the various member states. [...] There was also that professor in the United States claiming that [harmonization] of law was useless anyway. [...] Well, here we are now. [...] There is still this indeterminacy. It is like a massive residue of indeterminacy. [...]

[Harmonization], the written subjugation of life-in-the-law, is, in fact, doomed. The cogitator's formalistic harnessing of legal multiplicity will founder. His homogenised, centralised, and standardised construction will collapse. His doctrinal abstraction and formal logical rationality will fall short. His blind spots will have the better of his gaze. The European [impetus for harmonization] will not generate the *beata vita* that it is meant to create. While on autopilot, [advocates of harmonization] fail to appreciate that systematicity has its limits, that knowledge is inherently centrifugal. [...] The life-world will refuse enclosure, will resist embalming. Indeed, a poet, the Spanish writer Antonio Machado, aptly renders the inevitable point: "All the efforts of human reason tend to the elimination of [the other]. The other does not exist: such is rational faith, the incurable belief of human reason. Identity = reality, as if, in the end, everything must absolutely and necessarily be one and the same. But the other refuses to disappear: it subsists, it persists; it is the hard bone on which reason breaks its teeth. [There is] what might be called the incurable otherness from which oneness must always suffer."[26]

Must a comparative law scholar who is sensitive to law's cultural mooring and meaning also be suspicious of the European project of legal harmonization?

In contrast to the alarmist rhetoric involved in the debate over the AGG's enactment, there was little action under the AGG in its first years in force. Yet, by 2010, litigation was finding its way into the German courts in which plaintiffs sought remedies under the Act for alleged discrimination in employment and private services. How the German courts interpreted and applied the Act – whether in keeping with its progressive spirit or with a formalistic suspicion – would say a great deal about the real extent of the Europeanization of German private law. Already, the successful campaign to preserve and protect the Civil Code from "contamination" signaled the resilience and resistance of German law. The following case excerpt implicates the central elements of the European legal tradition I identified earlier: the Superiority and Direct Effect of supranational European law as managed by the European Court of Justice; and, in a confounding twist, the regulatory (as opposed to the neoliberal) character of this particular European normative agenda.

Labour Court of Stuttgart (17th Chamber)
Minus "Ossi" Case

[Translation by Russell A. Miller]

File No.: 17 Ca 8907/09 (2010)

[In the Name of the People]

[Judgment]

The claim for reimbursement under §§ 1, 15 (2) General Act on Equal Treatment [AGG or *Allgemeines Gleichbehandlungsgesetz*] requires discrimination, among others, based on "ethnic origin." [The term] "Ossi" does not refer to an ethnic group.

12.3 Europeanization of German Contract Law

Tenor

1. The claim is rejected.
2. The plaintiff has to bear the costs of the legal dispute.
3. The value of the claim is set to amount to €5,000.00.

Facts of the case:

The parties dispute damage claims due to discrimination.

The plaintiff was born in 1961 and, in 1988, resettled from the territory of the former GDR [German Democratic Republic or East Germany] to the Federal Republic of Germany where she worked as an accountant for several companies in the area near S. In mid-July 2009 she applied for a position as an accountant with the defendant. With a letter dated 3 August 2009 the defendant, while thanking the plaintiff for her interest in the position, nevertheless returned her application documents as well as the plaintiff's curriculum vitae. On the latter, one of the defendant's employees had made the note "Ossi" with a circled minus symbol next to it and also added the notation "GDR" with regard to the plaintiff's prior employment.

The plaintiff is of the opinion that these notes prove that her employment was only unsuccessful due to her national origin. The plaintiff sought to characterize her national origin as a form of ethnic origin in the sense of the General Act on Equal Treatment. The AGG prohibits discrimination and, under § 15, provides remedies for discrimination. The plaintiff argues that damages are all the more justified because the notes are alleged to have affected her in person in a serious degree.

The plaintiff moves:

The defendant is ordered to pay damages to the plaintiff as well as default interest of 5 percent in addition to the base lending rate since the initiation of the case. The amount of the damages is to be at the discretion of the court but should not be less than €5,000.00 […].

[Extract from grounds]

Under § 1 AGG discrimination, for example, "on the grounds of race or ethnic origin," shall be prevented or stopped. The parties argue about this condition as well as the legal consequence of damages under § 15(2) AGG, while the facts of the case focus on the notes "(–) Ossi" and on two occasions "GDR," […].

According to the prevailing opinion in the scholarly literature, the term "ethnic origin" is to be interpreted in a broad fashion […]. With regard to the interpretation, the term cannot be interpreted independent of the discussion on human rights since 1945. This discussion may suggest an expansive interpretation of the term. It is given its meaning, for example, by Art. 1 and Art. 55 of the Charter of the United Nations 26 June 1945, whereby the main goal shall be "solving international problems of an economic, social, cultural, or humanitarian character, and in promoting and encouraging respect for human rights and for fundamental freedoms for all without distinction as to race, sex, language, or religion." The Universal Declaration of Human Rights of 10 December 1948 [stipulates equal treatment] "without distinction of any kind, such as race, color, sex, language, religion, political or other opinion, national or social origin, property, birth or other status." In a related sense, Art. 14 of the European Convention for the Protection of Human Rights and Fundamental Freedoms of 4 November 1950 stipulates the exclusion of discriminatory treatment, for example, based on "national or social origin, association with a national minority, property, birth or other status." And now the Charter of Fundamental Rights of the European Union and thereafter the Treaty on the Foundation of the European Community in its version of 16 April 2003 prohibit discrimination "on the grounds of ethnic origin."

From this context of international law it becomes clear that the term "ethnic origin" is based on the manifested differences of humankind. Therefore, this term requires further illumination.

If this term is based on the Greek word "ethnos" and the transference of the latter into the German language means "people" or "ethnicity," it becomes clear that "ethnic origin" in the sense of § 1 AGG means more than just one's origin in a local community, a region, a country [or a "*Land*" in the German original] or a common territory. The term ethnicity only carries meaning if it serves to demonstrate a common history and culture, a connection to a certain territory and a feeling of a community based on solidarity for a certain population of people. This might include a common language, traditional customs, or the like.

The term "Ossi" at the center of the dispute may be tied to an element of a "territory" as that is understood for fashioning an ethnicity (in this case the territory of the former GDR/the "New Federal States"). However, it is not linked with a distinct, common language. Many dialects, ranging from Saxon to Low German, are spoken in the East German *Länder*. The history of the term "Ossi," which has developed after 1989, is a much too novel development to describe a distinguishable population. The fact that the former GDR and the Federal Republic of Germany represent different socio-political developments up to 1989 does not mean that the (former) citizens of the two state entities can be described as distinguishable ethnicities of a distinct and separate kind. The common Germany history shared since the abolition of particularism [i.e., the division of the German territory into many small monarchies], the common culture of the last 250 years, and the common language except for dialects, underline that, in the twenty-first century, regional differences do not constitute Swabians, Bavarians, or "Wessis" (those born in West Germany) as distinguishable ethnic groups.

Paragraph 75 of the Works Constitution Act [the antidiscrimination clause of the German *Betriebsverfassungsgesetz* or BetrVG] does not contradict this interpretation of § 1 AGG. It may be that the employer and the works council are required to prevent any discrimination against employees, for example, due to their ethnic origin or "their descent or other origin." This broader prohibition, which does not result in an individual, actionable claim for damages, serves ends with respect to employment that are different from those pursued by § 1 AGG. Paragraph 1 AGG provides sanctions, for example. As regards the Works Constitution Act, differentiation based on regional domestic origin also are prohibited.

The term "Ossi" may be discriminatory (this is disputed by the defendant) because it is associated with a negative judgment (as the plaintiff claims). However, as § 1 AGG does not serve to abolish or prevent every imaginable form of discrimination and even more so because the term cannot be subsumed under the legal prerequisite of "ethnic origin," the claim, if based on § 15(2) AGG, is unfounded. It must be rejected. […]

Questions/Comments

- The term "Ossi" is derived from the word "Ostdeutsche(r)" (East German) and refers to former citizens or inhabitants of the German Democratic Republic. It is paired with "Wessi" for "Westdeutsche(r)," which refers to citizens or inhabitants of West Germany. After reunification, "Ossi" initially had a humorous tone but over the years it developed a pejorative connotation.

- The court refers to other non-ethnic regional identities when dismissing the ethnic character of someone who was raised in the former GDR. Swabians, for example, come from the historic region in southern Germany that today intersects with the states of Baden-Württemberg and Bavaria. The larger portion of Swabia is commonly seen as equivalent to (the former kingdom and then *Land*) Württemberg, which is known for its distinct cultural features and historical rivalry with its neighbour Baden. Bavaria is also known to have distinct cultural features, most of all its dialect, cuisine, and strong regional self-consciousness evident in the fact that it is generally only referred to as the "*Free State* of Bavaria" not merely as the State Bavaria.
- One commentator remarked: "The decision of the Labour Court of Stuttgart probably will be only an intermediate stage. The legal situation is not at all clear. [...] One can therefore remain curious how the case is going to develop. It is possible that there will be a request for a preliminary ruling by the European Court of Justice. It is not likely that the Federal Labour Court will decide the case without such a request – if the case should make it all the way up, at least not after the latest 'reprimand' from Karlsruhe (states case). Under Art. 101 of the Basic Law the last instance is required to request a preliminary ruling from the European Court of Justice under Art. 267 TFEU for the interpretation of European norms, except if the interpretation were to be 'self-evident.'" This comment suggests another remarkable example of the Europeanization of German law. It acknowledges that German courts are now under an obligation to refer unresolved questions arising out of European-oriented norms (either domestic law giving force to European Directives or the direct enforcement of European Treaty norms or Regulations) to the European Court of Justice. This makes the supranational tribunal a last-instance court for the interpretation of European Law to which the German courts owe their fealty. Is this the natural consequence of the European system's supranational and supreme character?
- The documents in the *Minus "Ossi" Case* can be seen in the photograph in Figure 12.4. An appeal in the *Minus "Ossi" Case* to the second-instance labor court was resolved without a decision because the parties settled the dispute out of court.[27]
- Does the enactment of the AGG, and the Stuttgart Court's interpretation of its provisions in the *Minus "Ossi" Case*, suggest the successful Europeanization of German contract law? How directly has European law impacted German law – in this instance taking the form of the European anti-discrimination Directives? What about this encounter between European Law and German law underscores the supranational character of what I've referred to as the European legal tradition and, conversely, the national character of German law? Does this story conform to my claim that one possible characteristic of European law is its neoliberal character?
- Over all, how would you assess the consequences of this encounter between European Law and the German law of obligations? Has German contract law

The Minus "Ossi" Case

The applicant in the *Minus "Ossi" Case* meeting with her attorney. In the foreground, on the left, the application material can be seen with the notes "minus Ossi" handwritten on the form. The German courts approached the case with the positivism and formalism characteristic of the Civil Law tradition. They rejected the complaint under the General Act on Equal Treatment, which transposed the EU Anti-Discrimination Directives. The German courts also did not apply to the European Court of Justice to seek a preliminary reference on the meaning of the European anti-discrimination policy.

Figure 12.4 European Anti-discrimination Law Applied in Germany: The *Minus "Ossi" Case*. Source: Getty Images

been Europeanized? Has the prized Civil Code, with all of its meaning for legal culture in Germany, withstood European legal colonization? Is Legrand right when he said that differences will persist?

12.4 Limits to the Europeanization of German Law

It is one thing that European Law might meddle with German private law. But, sacred as the Civil Code may be, we have seen that the Basic Law – as the Federal Republic's *Grundnorm* – is superior to the Code. So, it would be another thing altogether if the process of the Europeanization of German law also touched German constitutional law. That would involve an impact on the root of German law, not just a branch.

The encounters between European Law and German constitutional law raise questions about the extent, and any possible limits, to Germany's integration into the European Union and its legal order. The difficulty is that the Basic Law itself mandates Germany's participation in the European project. The constitution's preamble calls for Germany to contribute to "world peace as an equal partner in a united Europe." More significantly, Article 23(1) of the Basic Law provides:

12.4 Limits to the Europeanization of German Law

> The Federal Republic of Germany shall participate in the development of the European Union that is committed to democratic, social and federal principles, to the rule of law and to the principle of subsidiarity and that guarantees a level of protection of basic rights essentially comparable to that afforded by this Basic Law. To this end the Federation may transfer sovereign powers by a law with the consent of the *Bundesrat*.

This is part of the German Basic Law's "openness" to international and European law. Yet, the constitutional commitment to openness might conflict with a range of other constitutional mandates. A major concern has been the extent to which, and the terms for managing, Germany's transfer of sovereign governing authority to the European Union pursuant to Article 23. How far can Germany go with the project of European integration? Which German institutions must be involved in that process? What constitutional values should inform the standards used to answer those questions? The German Federal Constitutional Court has charted Germany's path through these demanding and complex issues.

Donald P. Kommers & Russell A. Miller
THE CONSTITUTIONAL JURISPRUDENCE OF THE FEDERAL REPUBLIC OF GERMANY
326–327, 331–334, 338–339, 343–344, 349–352 (3rd ed. 2012)*

* * *

The transfer of sovereign powers to a supranational entity like the European Community and the European Union involves an altogether different – a more complete – openness, necessitating even greater vigilance from the Court in its effort to preserve the sovereignty secured by the Basic Law. In resolving the distinct problems raised by the tension between the supranational and the domestic exercise of authority, the Court has guided Germany's deep integration into European governance while, at the same time, repeatedly insisting on constitutional limits to that process.

[...] Two factors featured prominently in the Constitutional Court's *Solange I Case* (1974), in which it imposed constitutional limits on Germany's integration into the European system. First, the Court expressed concern about the European project's untested novelty and institutional immaturity, both of which were manifested by a "democratic deficit" in European governance. It is common, now, to refer to the European Union as a completely new framework for governance. Europe is neither a nation-state nor a traditional international organization. Thus, in *Solange I*, the Constitutional Court reaffirmed its earlier conclusion that the European Community possesses an "independent system of law flowing from an autonomous legal source [... that is] a '*sui generis* community in the process of progressive integration.'" On this basis it might not be surprising that the Constitutional Court was particularly concerned with Europe's early-stage development and its prominent lack of a "democratically legitimate parliament directly elected by general suffrage."

Second, the Court's reticence in *Solange I* was justified by the high priority the Basic Law sets on protecting and promoting human dignity. The Constitutional Court was determined to ensure that the exercise of sovereign German power respects human dignity and

---

* Excerpt reprinted with permission of Duke University Press.

other basic rights, even if the sovereign power was one that had been transferred to a supranational entity. In *Solange I* the Court noted that the European Community "still lacks [...] a codified catalogue of fundamental rights, the substance of which is reliably and unambiguously fixed for the future in the same way as the substance of the Basic Law. [...]"

Five justices of the Court's Second Senate concluded [in *Solange I*] that Germany's transfer of sovereign power to the European Community knows some outer limit "so long as" (*solange*) the European system lacks adequate democratic legitimacy and fails to more thoroughly protect fundamental rights. In particular, the Court found that the German Constitution has precedence when secondary European Community law conflicts with fundamental rights secured by the Basic Law. This is true, said the Court, despite the fact that Community law emanates from a wholly independent, external political authority that is not responsible to the Basic Law. It is also true, the Court continued, despite the fact that Community law has priority over domestic law. The Court articulated a narrow, sovereigntist vision of constitutional openness in the context of European integration [...].

* * *

The limits on constitutional openness identified by the Court in *Solange I* had the incidental effect of empowering the Constitutional Court, as guardian of the constitution, to enforce the newly articulated restrictions on European integration. The responsibility undertaken by the Constitutional Court in *Solange I* opened an amicable rivalry – some prefer to call it a "cooperative relationship" – between the Constitutional Court and the European Court of Justice. In the litigation leading to the Constitutional Court's *Solange I* decision the European Court of Justice already had issued a preliminary ruling confirming the legality of the challenged Community regulations. The Constitutional Court justified its decision to pursue its own review of the matter, pursuant to a concrete judicial review "referral" from an administrative court, by noting that the "European Court of Justice cannot decide, with binding effect, whether a rule of Community law is compatible with the Basic Law." The interaction between these two respected European courts, sometimes rather tense, is a central feature of the Constitutional Court's European jurisprudence.

Europe took a dynamic turn in the years following the Constitutional Court's *Solange I* decision. The Communities continued to add new members. And efforts to enhance the common market were achieved with the Single European Act, which was announced in 1986 and entered into force in 1987. The European Parliament was given a greater role in Community lawmaking. The Community acquired new competences. The European judicial infrastructure was expanded and refined. The time was ripe for the Constitutional Court to reassess Europe's democratic integrity and respect for fundamental rights, the bases for the Court's earlier reservations about the extent of Germany's European integration.

* * *

[...] In *Solange II* the Constitutional Court found that improvements in the democratic character of the Communities' policy-making and in the Communities' protection of fundamental rights justified the Court's retreat from its frontline patrols along the border between Europe's supranational authority and Germany's constitutional identity. While the Court clearly did not surrender its right to monitor the Basic Law's openness to supranational power – jurisdiction it secured for itself in *Solange I* – it was satisfied that it would not have to exercise its review "so long as" (*solange*) Europe's enhanced democracy and protection of rights remained in force.

* * *

12.4 Limits to the Europeanization of German Law

[...] The German debate over national sovereignty and European integration – positions largely advanced through arguments over how to interpret the Basic Law's openness to the transfer of sovereign power to Europe – was fanned by Europe's evolution from a "community" into an "ever closer union among the peoples of Europe." This was the stated aim of the Treaty on European Union (TEU), signed at Maastricht, the Netherlands, on 7 February 1992. Under the Maastricht Treaty, the member states would weld themselves into a tighter economic and political union. Deeper integration, through a process of economic and monetary union, would culminate in a single European currency superintended by a European Central Bank. Political union, although not an express goal, would be facilitated through several measures every bit as dramatic as the promised common currency. [...] In sum, under the umbrella of the European Union, the Maastricht Treaty called for a further significant transfer of states' governing power and extensive intergovernmental cooperation, involving a breathtaking range of subjects traditionally understood to be at the core of a state's sovereign power.

The *Bundestag* and *Bundesrat* ratified Germany's commitment to the Maastricht Treaty. Simultaneously, in order to remove all constitutional doubts about the treaty, they also amended several articles of the Basic Law. The centerpiece of these amendments was a new Article 23, the so-called Europe Article, which supports the goal of European unity, explicitly authorizes the federation's transfer of sovereign power to the European Union, and enhances the *Bundestag's* right to participate in the national decision-making process concerned with European matters. Beyond this, Article 23 also requires the federation to consider the *Bundesrat's* opinion on European policy when the vital interests of the *Länder* are affected.

Article 23 also establishes that any transfer of sovereign power to the European Union, resulting in any change in the system and principles of government established by the Basic Law, must conform to paragraphs 2 and 3 of Article 79, respectively requiring a formal amendment to the Basic Law (and concomitant *Bundestag* approval) and barring any infringement of its unalterable principles. This constitutional limit on European integration, and the principle it secures, has come to be known as the "political question" on enhanced European integration. As the Constitutional Court has interpreted this doctrine, it limits Germany's participation in the European project to nothing more than the European integration provided in the principal treaties that have benefited from parliamentary ratification. As we will see, expansion of Europe's competences will be subject to challenges before the Constitutional Court to ensure its conformity with this principle. Ultimately, in the *Lisbon Treaty Case* (2009), the Constitutional Court invoked this doctrine as the basis for its insistence that Europe be regarded as an association of sovereign states (*Staatenverbund*) and not an incipient federal state (*Staatsverband* or *Bundesstaat*).

* * *

The Maastricht Treaty did not settle the fundamental political and jurisprudential debate over the proper extent of Germany's integration into Europe, despite the expanded and more detailed commitment to constitutional openness achieved by Article 23 in support of the Maastricht Treaty. The treaty, its ratification by the Parliament, and the attending constitutional amendments, provoked an immediate challenge in the form of constitutional complaints [arguing that the surrender of national authority to the European Union demanded by the Maastricht Treaty] would deprive [Germans] of certain fundamental rights and violate the democratic state principle secured by Articles 21(1) (ensuring a role for political parties in the formation of public opinion) and 38(1) (securing the right to vote in parliamentary elections). They also alleged that the transfer of sovereign national powers to the European Union harmed Germany's constitutional identity in contravention of Article 79(3), which makes the principles of human dignity, federalism, democracy, popular sovereignty, the *Sozialstaat* and the *Rechtsstaat* eternally unamendable.

As for national sovereignty, the complainants argued that the Basic Law permits the transfer of powers to intergovernmental organizations, not to a super-state entity such as the European Union. [...] In the *Maastricht Treaty Case*, the battle between sovereigntism and cosmopolitanism – cast in the distinct mold of the European Union – again was joined before the Constitutional Court.

* * *

[...] In its result, the Court's *Maastricht Treaty* decision was an important victory for European integration. It allowed Germany to participate in the enhanced European Community and the new European Union. There had been some concern that the Court might fundamentally object to Germany's ratification of the Maastricht Treaty, causing this leap toward closer European unity to stumble. [...] [D]espite the general holding of the case, *Maastricht* was a significantly qualified victory for European integration. For example, even the Court's adherence to the relatively pro-European *Solange II* doctrine – which it used to justify the dismissal of the rights-based complaints – had a sharp sovereigntist edge. In *Solange II* the Court ruled that it could review secondary European law to ensure its conformity with the Basic Law's fundamental rights regime. In *Maastricht* the Court saw no reason to revisit this rule despite the fact that the new treaty, at last, formally referred to Europe's commitment to protecting fundamental rights. [...]

The more significant sovereigntist elements of the *Maastricht Treaty Case* involved the democratic state principle, a component of Germany's constitutional identity that ensures that all state power derives from the will of the people. This relates to Article 38(1) of the Basic Law, in particular, because that provision guarantees Germany's representative democracy via "general, direct, free, equal and secret elections." Relying on the democratic state principle, the Court established two new lines of doctrine in the *Maastricht Treaty Case*. First, the Court ruled that it would enforce an absolute limit on the amount of sovereign power Germany can transfer to Europe. This was necessary, the Court explained, because European democracy remained inadequate and could not satisfy the Basic Law's guarantee of popular sovereignty. Describing this part of the Court's decision, Steve Boom said, "Should the *Bundestag* transfer too many of its competences, too much state power would be legitimated only indirectly; as a result, the [democratic state principle] would be violated." Second, the Court ruled that it would closely monitor Europe's exercise of the sovereign powers it had acquired from the member states to ensure that it did not independently expand its range of competences. This concern implicated the democratic state principle because Europe possesses only those competences conferred on it through the democratically legitimated treaty ratification processes that take place in the member states. To acquire power for itself – most troublingly through what the Federal Constitutional Court regarded as the European Court's judicial activism – would circumvent this essential democratic feature of the European integration process. Significantly, unlike the right of review for fundamental rights protection that the Court reaffirmed but simultaneously held in abeyance in *Solange II*, the Court did not say that it would refrain from exercising this new authority to prevent *ultra vires* European acts. Especially the latter of these new doctrines – the Court's new *ultra vires* review – advanced the sovereigntist view that Europe should remain a *Staatenverbund* over which the member states would remain the "masters of the treaties" (*Herren der Verträge*).

* * *

[...] For all its sovereigntist hand-wringing, the Constitutional Court's fundamental decision in *Maastricht*, permitting Germany's participation in the enhanced European

12.4 Limits to the Europeanization of German Law

Community and the new European Union, had let the federalist genie out of the bottle. With the Maastricht Treaty, European integration acquired a powerful, centralizing – and seemingly irreversible – momentum. Perhaps as a concession to this, and with the forces favoring European integration again ascendant in the German debate, the Constitutional Court's subsequent European jurisprudence was more accommodating of European integration.

* * *

[The pro-European mood at the Constitutional Court began to cool once again with the *European Arrest Warrant Case* (2005). A majority of the Constitutional Court's Second Senate ruled that the European Arrest Warrant Act should be declared null and void. The European Arrest Warrant Act had been enacted in response to a European Union "framework decision" (not a Directive) to facilitate judicial cooperation among member states in criminal matters. The majority of the Constitutional Court found that the European Arrest Warrant Act hadn't adequately accounted for constitutional basic rights ensuring access to judicial process. The majority also ruled that the policy lacked the prominence and weight of Union economic initiatives advanced under the authority of primary or secondary Union law. Those formalist distinctions pointed towards new constitutional limits on Germany's integration into the European Union. Integration under the commercial and economic facets of the European project would be given greater respect because only that project had achieved the unique, *sui generis* status of a supranational exercise of member states' sovereign power. Other European initiatives promoting political integration, the majority reasoned, did not aspire to something so comprehensive. The Constitutional Court ruled that the *Bundestag* had neglected these subtle limits on integration when enacting the European Arrest Warrant Act. This suggested that the *Bundestag* would be charged with exercising strict scrutiny when enacting European policy. And it meant, in turn, that the Constitutional Court would monitor closely the *Bundestag's* exercise of that scrutiny.]

[…] In the *European Arrest Warrant Case*, the Court's majority resorted once again to the limits on European integration that, in its jurisprudence on the constitution's openness to Europe, it attributes to the Basic Law's democratic state principle. Europe's authority and development, the argument goes, must be kept squarely within the terms of the treaties. Anything else would avoid the *Bundestag's* right to ratify (or reject) each successive step in Europe's deepening integration and thereby undercut the Basic Law's fundamental decision that all sovereign power derive from the democratically legitimized will of the people. The democratic state principle, the Court has said, constitutes a part of Germany's unamendable constitutional identity that must be protected against the Basic Law's commitment to openness. […]

This state-centric approach to the European project would be harder to defend, however, if Europe were to formally adopt a constitution. Constitutions typically have been political and legal decisions that frame and manage the functioning of a state. A European federal state was the undeniable ambition of the advocates for a European constitution, an old dream that, as it gained significant new momentum with the establishment of the European Union, prompted Federal Constitutional Court Justice Dieter Grimm to famously pose this question: "does Europe need a constitution?" The Constitutional Court's caution towards unfettered European integration gave Grimm's reticence exceptional gravity. In a widely discussed speech delivered at Humboldt University in Berlin in May 2000, German foreign minister Joschka Fischer answered Justice Grimm's question with an authoritative "yes." After cataloguing the difficulties confronting the project of European integration, Fischer explained that the only viable solution would be "the transition from a union of states to full parliamentarization as a European Federation." That remarkable future, Fischer admitted, "will have to be based on a constituent treaty" that "constitutionally enshrines" the principle of subsidiarity. Later, the German philosopher Jürgen Habermas influentially argued that, more than a concrete constitution, Europe needed a formal constitutional process as the way to nurture the constitutional prerequisite of a shared European civic identity.

German theoretical engagement with the question shadowed a roller-coaster ride of political action, including the declaration from the European heads of states and governments in Laaken in 2001 that they would pursue a European constitution; the work of Valéry Giscard d'Estaing's constitutional drafting convention; the triumphal endorsement of the constitutional treaty by European heads of states and governments in Rome in 2004; and the treaty's surprising defeat in ratification referenda in France and the Netherlands in 2005.

Not to be deterred by a popular setback, the European elites pressing for the constitution pleaded for a "period of reflection" that resulted in the Lisbon Reform Treaty that was signed on 13 December 2007. The Lisbon Treaty, although abandoning constitutional pretensions, implemented most of the reform to the substance of European law and to the European Union's infrastructure that had been at the heart of the failed constitution. First, the European Union was given legal personality, which, among other consequences, permits it to accede to the European Convention on Human Rights. Nearly thirty-five years after the Federal Constitutional Court expressed its concern about Europe's inadequate rights protections in *Solange I*, the Lisbon Treaty also gave the Charter of Fundamental Rights legal status. At last, Europe would have a codified catalogue of fundamental rights that is "recognized" by the European Union. [...] Second, the Lisbon Treaty rationalized and streamlined governance for a European Union now consisting of twenty-seven member states. The treaty created a permanent President of the European Council and a High Representative for Foreign and Security Affairs. The Council of the European Union was empowered to act on the basis of a double majority, as opposed to the previous system, which required unanimous or supermajority approval of initiatives. The European Union was given new competences, and some of its existing intergovernmental competences (under the second and third pillars) were given supranational status of the kind accorded to the first pillar. Third, the Lisbon Treaty upgraded European democracy, in part by giving the directly elected European Parliament bicameral legislative status along-side the Council of the European Union when the "ordinary" legislative procedure is used. A "citizens' initiative" was created. The treaty also aimed to formally integrate the member states' democratically legitimate national parliaments into the "good functioning of the Union." The national parliaments were to be given early notice of European legislation to allow them to object on subsidiarity and proportionality grounds by offering a "reasoned opinion" to the European institutions. The national parliaments also were given the authority to bring "subsidiarity actions" before the European Court of Justice. Finally, the national parliaments were given the right to object to exercises of some of the European Union's new capacities to expand its own competences.

Irish voters scuttled the Lisbon reform but eventually were persuaded to ratify the treaty in a second national referendum. Meanwhile, the other member states were ratifying the Lisbon Treaty, including Germany in the spring of 2008, when the *Bundestag* and *Bundesrat* approved the treaty, made necessary amendments to the Basic Law, and enacted legislation that was meant to expand their role (as chambers of the national parliament) in European policy making. Predictably, these acts were challenged before the Federal Constitutional Court [in the seminal *Lisbon Treaty Case* (2009)].

* * *

[...] The Constitutional Court's holding in *Lisbon* was modest. Germany's ratification of the Lisbon Treaty, with its sweeping centralizing reform, had not been called into question. The Court only found fault with the accompanying legislation (*Begleitgesetz*). That was easily corrected. [...] The new law cleared the way for Germany to finalize its ratification on 25 September 2009. The Lisbon Treaty entered into force on 1 December 2009.

The wave of criticism that crashed against the decision was stirred by the 170 pages of dicta-heavy exposition through which the Court waded on the way to its anti-climactic conclusion. The Court discussed extensively the theory of democracy that is to be realized by the Basic Law's democratic state principle, whether it serves to legitimize domestic or supranational governance. Regarding the "political question" on Europe's status, the Court concluded that the Lisbon Treaty unequivocally confirmed that the European Union is a *Staatenverbund* conceived by means of international law treaties. "The Treaty of Lisbon decided against the concept of a European Federal Constitution [and] a new federal people constituted by it," the Court explained. "A will aiming at founding a state cannot be ascertained." These points informed the Court's insistence upon the outer limits of the sovereign power the European Union might exercise, at least in the absence of dramatic constitutional change within Germany. The civil society, or demos, essential to democracy, said the Court, still is centered on the nation-state, framed by a common language, culture, and history.

To protect Germany's constitutional identity, in *Lisbon* the Court also granted itself a new form of review over European sovereign acts – including the decisions of the European Court of Justice. "Identity review," to which the Court already had alluded in *Solange II*, permits the Court to "examine whether, due to the action of European institutions, the principles under Article 1 and Article 20 of the Basic Law, declared inviolable in Article 79(3) of the Basic Law, have been violated. This ensures the primacy of European Union law only by virtue and in the context of the domestic constitutional empowerment that continues in effect." Identity review joined two existing forms of review. The first is the long-dormant (and, after the *Banana Market Regulation Case*, practically foreclosed) authority to review for fundamental rights deficiencies at the European level. The second is the *ultra vires* review announced in the *Maastricht Case*.

All of this prompted one scholar to call the Lisbon Treaty Case "a black day in the history of Europe." This reaction to *Lisbon*, and the many others like it, may have been premature. A year later the Court issued its much-anticipated decision in the *Honeywell Case*, the first-ever exercise of its *ultra vires* review jurisdiction. Following so close on the heels of *Lisbon*, *Honeywell* was the Court's chance to add some bite to its many years of barking over the gradual drift of sovereign powers – through the door created by the Basic Law's openness – to the supranational European Union. Instead, the Court seemed to draw back from the chauvinism many find in the *Lisbon Treaty Case*. [Honeywell involved an *ultra vires* challenge to a decision of the European Court of Justice that settled a German labor contract dispute in conformity with European antidiscrimination policy.]

The Constitutional Court rejected the complaint and, in doing so, significantly narrowed the scope of its *ultra vires* review authority. Above all, the Court insisted that its *ultra vires* review must be exercised within the framework of – and not counter to – the Basic Law's fundamental commitment to an open state and *Europarechtsfreundlichkeit*. To ensure this, the Court said it would find that a European institution had acted *ultra vires* only in cases involving a "sufficiently qualified" breach of European competences [...].

For those favoring integration, the deference to Europe that the Constitutional Court exercised in *Honeywell* took some of the sting out of *Lisbon's* decidedly sovereigntist tone. This, however, should not be interpreted as a dramatic shift in the Court's posture toward Europe. In its rulings concerned with Germany's participation in the European

Union's haphazard and frantic efforts to save the euro from the sovereign debt crisis plaguing a number of euro-zone countries, the Constitutional Court [...] maintained its tradition of cautious acquiescence – accepting evermore Europe but without surrendering Germany's constitutional identity. For example, in its decision in the *Greek Rescue Package Case* (2011) the Court sustained the German law implementing Germany's contributions to the first Greek rescue package (2010) and the first iteration of a broader European rescue package (2010). Several constitutional complaints alleged that the enabling act violated the Basic Law's democratic state principle (rooted in Article 38(1) of the Basic Law and part of Germany's unamendable constitutional identity) because it gave European institutions, and not the democratically elected *Bundestag*, authority over Germany's massive budgetary commitments to the initiatives (at their maximum, the contributions would be Germany's largest budget item). Putting the world's markets at ease – and giving the global economy a momentary reprieve from the persistent fear of a chaotic Greek default – the Court rejected the complaints, thereby allowing Germany's nearly €150 billion mix of payments and credit guarantees to go forward.

But the Second Senate took the opportunity in *Greek Rescue Package* to articulate further constitutional limits on European integration. First, the Court insisted that budgetary matters remain a competence of the *Bundestag*. The Court explained that budgets define a state's functions and the people the state serves must have the authority to take those decisions through their democratically elected representatives. This does not preclude the Parliament from externalizing this authority, as in the case of the new European Financial Stability Facility (the EFSF is the permanent, broader European rescue mechanism), which has the power to make decisions at the European level on the basis of German credit guarantees. The Court concluded, however, that the delegation of budgetary authority to the EFSF was constitutional only because it complied with a number of democratic safeguards. Above all, it did not empower European institutions to make decisions about Germans' tax burden and it did not permit European institutions to automatically avail themselves of the German credit guarantees. Instead, said the Court, the regime affirmed the *Bundestag's* status as the master of such budgetary matters by requiring its continuous and repeated approval of decisions related to the externalization of its competence over the budget. Second, and more fundamentally, the Court declared that the rescue initiatives conformed with Germany's treaty and constitutional commitments to a European Monetary Union that is merely a "stability community" and not a more fully integrated "transfer union." On this point, the Second Senate explicitly excluded the possibility, without reform of the European treaties and the Basic Law, of eurobonds backed by the European Central Bank and the member states of the European Monetary Union.

These cases are representative of the Court's vacillating European jurisprudence. And, if that is thought to be a criticism of the Constitutional Court, then two points must be considered. On the one hand, the Court has not been helped in its work by the inherent tension between sovereignty and openness that was written into the Basic Law. With Europe, as with international law, the Court has sought to reconcile these seemingly irreconcilable commands. Nor has the Court been helped in that effort by the fact that the social and political consensus over full German integration in a united Europe has, over the last generations, begun to weaken. On the other hand, the Court's hesitance toward Europe largely has been a matter of tone and not results. For all the formal authority it has given itself to prevent the erosion of German constitutional sovereignty and identity in the European project, the Court has not rushed to take up that role. Its detailed European doctrine seems more instructive than actionable. Instead, with each dramatic development in Europe's integration, the Court has given priority to the Basic Law's preambular summons to a Germany that serves as an "equal partner in a united Europe."

* * *

[The] clear lesson of the Court's jurisprudence is that there are limits to the state's openness. [...] The Court has narrowed the prescribed openness out of respect for the sovereign state, consisting of an unamendable core identity that is established by the Basic Law. It may not easily fit with the constitution's openness, but the Court has sought to safeguard state sovereignty as an essential framework for the democratic state principle that also is prescribed by the Basic Law.

Negotiating these opposing demands with respect to the Basic Law's nexus with international law and European law will remain the heroic, if often messy, work of the Constitutional Court.

* * *

Questions/Comments

- Can you name the major Constitutional Court decisions that have framed the scope of Germany's integration into the European project? What are the terms and limits they set out for German participation in that project? Which German institutions are called upon to manage the constitutionally tolerable move towards integration? What are the constitutional elements that inform the limits on Germany's integration into the European Union?
- Do the limits on European integration carved out by the Constitutional Court involve sacrosanct topics and competences reserved exclusively for German governance? Or, is everything fair game, so long as European governance is exercised in conformity with constitutional commitments?
- In the *Lisbon Treaty Case* the Constitutional Court identified a range of governing competences that, at least under the existing constitutional framework in Germany, may never be assigned to the European Union. These involve government policies affecting "the political formation of the economic, cultural and social circumstances of life."[28] To be more concrete, the Court identified the following subjects as the culturally and historically sensitive subjects that form the "core functions" of a state: citizenship policy; the monopoly on the use of force, both domestically and for military defense; taxation, budget policy, and expenditure of public revenue; the protection of fundamental rights, especially as they touch on the enforcement of criminal law; cultural issues concerning language, education, and family policy; and the protection of fundamental rights with respect to freedom of opinion, a free press, freedom of association, and freedom of religion.[29] Does that strike you as the most reasonable or logical catalogue of sacred state prerogatives? What else would you include in a list of inalienable core state functions, while nonetheless accepting that you are constitutionally obliged to transfer some sovereign power in order to facilitate supranational cooperation?
- What are the three forms of review the Constitutional Court has established to allow it to oversee Germany's participation in European integration?

12.5 Conclusion

From lawnmowers to beer and beyond, European law has come crashing into the German legal system. This is no less true for constitutional law, where the German Constitutional Court has developed a complex and dynamic jurisprudence seeking to both foster Germany's participation in a united Europe while preserving Germany's constitutional identity and core functions as a state.

European Law exhibits characteristics that are meaningfully distinct from a domestic legal system – and the German legal system in particular. Not the least among these differences are European Law's supranational character and neoliberal orientation. But, are those differences enough to qualify European Law as yet another "legal tradition" woven into the fabric of the German legal system? In any case, imagining European Law as another legal tradition enriches and enlivens this book's insistence upon a more pluralistic portrayal of German law and legal culture.

Further Reading

- *Constitutional Identity in a Europe of Multilevel Constitutionalism* (Christian Calliess & Gerhard van der Schyff eds.) (Cambridge University Press) (2021)
- Robert Schütze, *An Introduction to European Law* (Oxford University Press) (3rd ed. 2020)
- Damian Chalmers *et al.*, *European Union Law* (Cambridge University Press) (4th ed. 2019)
- Jule Mulder, *EU Non-discrimination Law in the Courts: Approaches to Sex and Sexualities Discrimination in EU Law* (Bloomsbury) (2017)
- Bill Davies, *Resisting the European Court of Justice: West Germany's Confrontation with European Law, 1949–1979* (Cambridge University Press) (2012)
- Giuseppe Martinico & Oreste Pollicino, *The Interaction between Europe's Legal Systems: Judicial Dialogue and the Creation of Supranational Laws* (Edward Elgar) (2012)
- Alexander Somek, *Engineering Equality: An Essay on European Anti-Discrimination Law* (Oxford University Press) (2011)

NOTES

1 Kevin Vallier, *Neoliberalism*, in THE STANFORD ENCYCLOPEDIA OF PHILOSOPHY (Edward N. Zalta ed., 2021), https://plato.stanford.edu/archives/sum2021/entries/neoliberalism/.

2 Diane Fromage & Bruno de Witte, *Guest Editors' Introduction National Constitutional Identity Ten Years On: State of Play and Future Perspectives*, 27 EUROPEAN PUBLIC LAW 411 (2021).

3 Marac Lehmann, *Neue EU-Vorschriften regelt das Rasenmähen*, WELT-ONLINE (Apr. 15, 2008), www.welt.de/finanzen/article1904560/Neue_EU_Vorschrift_regelt_das_Rasenmaehen.html (Russell A. Miller trans.).

4 Notoriously, the EU sought to strictly regulate the size and shape of produce. *See* Stephen Castle, *EU Relents and Lets a Banana Be a Banana*, N.Y. TIMES (Nov. 12, 2008), www.nytimes.com/2008/11/12/world/europe/12iht-food.4.17771299.html#:~:text=Commission%20Regulation%20(EC)%202257%2F,a%20preoccupation%20of%20European%20officials.

5 *See, e.g.*, DESMOND DINAN, ORIGINS AND EVOLUTION OF THE EUROPEAN UNION (2nd ed. 2014); THE INSTITUTIONS OF THE EUROPEAN UNION (Dermot Hodson et al. eds., 5th ed. 2022); SIMON BULMER & WILLIAM E. PATERSON, GERMANY AND THE EUROPEAN UNION: EUROPE'S RELUCTANT HEGEMON? (2019); JOHN MCCORMICK, UNDERSTANDING THE EUROPEAN UNION: A CONCISE INTRODUCTION (8th ed. 2020); JOHN PINDER & SIMON USHERWOOD, EUROPEAN UNION: A VERY SHORT INTRODUCTION (4th ed. 2018); DAMIAN CHALMERS ET AL., EUROPEAN UNION LAW (4th ed. 2019); ROBERT SCHÜTZE, AN INTRODUCTION TO EUROPEAN LAW (3rd ed. 2020); ANTHONY ARNULL, EUROPEAN UNION LAW: A VERY SHORT INTRODUCTION (2018).

6 *See, e.g.*, JACOBS, WHITE AND OVEY – THE EUROPEAN CONVENTION ON HUMAN RIGHTS (Bernadette Rainey et al. eds, 7th ed. 2017).

7 H. PATRICK GLENN, LEGAL TRADITIONS OF THE WORLD (5th ed. 2014)

8 JOHN HENRY MERRYMAN & ROGELIO PÉREZ-PERDOMO, THE CIVIL LAW TRADITION 2 (4th ed. 2019).

9 Thomas M.J. Mollers, *European Directives on Civil Law – Shaping a New German Civil Code*, 18 TUL. EUR. & CIV. L.F. 1 (2003).

10 *Legal Instruments*, EU MONITOR, www.eumonitor.eu/9353000/1/j9vvik7m1c3gyxp/vh75mdhkg4s0.

11 *See* Armin von Bogdandy & Jürgen Bast, *The Constitutional Approach to EU Law – From Taming Intergovernmental Relationships to Framing Political Processes*, in PRINCIPLES OF EUROPEAN CONSTITUTIONAL LAW 1 (Armin von Bogdandy & Jürgen Bas eds., 2nd ed. 2010); Armin von Bogdandy, *Founding Principles*, in PRINCIPLES OF EUROPEAN CONSTITUTIONAL LAW 11 (Armin von Bogdandy & Jürgen Bas eds., 2nd ed. 2010).

12 *See, e.g.*, Case C-170/04, Rosengren and Others v. Riksåklagaren, 2007 E.C.R. I-4071; Case C-28/09 European Commission v. Republic of Austria, 2011 E.C.R. I-13525; Case C-492/14, Essent Belgium NV v. Vlaams Gewest, ECLI:EU:C:2016:732 (Sept. 29, 2016).

13 Christoph Hermann, *Neoliberalism in the European Union*, 79 STUD. POL. ECON. 61 (2007); *see* RESILIENT LIBERALISM IN EUROPE'S POLITICAL ECONOMY (Vivien A. Schmidt & Mark Thatcher eds., 2013); JULIEN MERCILLE & ENDA MURPHY, DEEPENING NEOLIBERALISM, AUSTERITY, AND CRISIS EUROPE'S TREASURE IRELAND (2015); CONTRADICTIONS AND LIMITS OF NEOLIBERAL EUROPEAN GOVERNANCE: FROM LISBON TO LISBON (Bastiaan van Apeldoorn et al. eds., 2009).

14 *See* Mathias Reimann, *The Good, The Bad, and The Ugly: The Reform of the German Law of Obligations*, 83 TUL. L. REV. 877 (2009).

15 *See* JOBST-JUBERTUS BAUER ET AL., ALLGEMEINES GLEICHBEHANDLUNGSGESETZ, KOMMENTAR (2nd ed. 2009).

16 *Id.*

17 *Id.*

18 *See* Joachim Wiemann, *Obligation to Contract and the German General Act on Equal Treatment* (Allgemeines Gleichbehandlungsgesetz), 11 GER. L. J. 1131 (2010), www.germanlawjournal.com/pdfs/Vol11-No10/PDF_Vol_11_No_10_1131-1146_DAAD_Wiemann%20FINAL.pdf.

19 Matthias Mahlmann, *Legal Parameters of European Anti-Discrimination Law*, in I ANNUAL OF GERMAN & EUROPEAN LAW 334, 335 (Russell A. Miller & Peer Zumbansen eds., 2004).

20 For these cases, *see* Rainer Nickel, *Widening the Scope: Anti-Discrimination Law, Social Equality, and the Right to Equal Treatment*, in I ANNUAL OF GERMAN & EUROPEAN LAW 353, 357 (Russell A. Miller & Peer Zumbansen eds., 2004).

21 *See* Mahlmann, *supra* note 19, at 336–337.

22 *See* BAUER ET AL., *supra* note 15.

23 Gesetz zur Umsetzung europäischer Richtlinien zur Verwirklichung des Grundsatzes der Gleichbehandlung, 17 August 2006, BGBl. I:1897.

24 The former law was also a reaction to intervention by the European Court of Justice. *See* Karen Raible, *Compulsory Military Service and Equal Treatment of Men and Women – Recent Decisions of the Federal Constitutional Court and the European Court of Justice* (Alexander Dory v. Germany), 4 GER. L. J. 299 (2003), www.germanlawjournal.com/pdfs/Vol04No04/PDF_vol_04_no_04_299-308_public_Raible.pdf.

25 *See, e.g.,* ANU BRADFORD, THE BRUSSELS EFFECT: HOW THE EUROPEAN UNION RULES THE WORLD (2020).

26 Pierre Legrand, *Antivonbar*, 1 J. COMPAR. L. 13 (2006).

27 *"Ossi-Fall" endet mit Vergleich – Keine Entscheidung in der Sache*, KOSTENLOSE URTEILE (Dec. 29, 2010), available at www.kostenlose-urteile.de/LAG-Baden-Wuerttemberg_8-Sa-3110_Ossi-Fall-endet-mit-Vergleich.news10806.htm

28 Armin Steinbach, *The Lisbon Judgement of the German Federal Constitutional Court – New Guidance on the Limits of European Integration?*, 11 GER. L. J. 367, 374 (2010).

29 *See* Lisbon Treaty Case, 123 BVerfGE 267, 358 (2009); *see also* Steinbach, *supra* note 31, at 375.

13

Epilogue
Germany's German Law

Now, suddenly, you find yourself at the end of this book and your journey into the strange new world of German law. Even if our work together cannot go on and on, I hope this encounter has fostered the values of curiosity and wonder that will compel you to return to the study of foreign law – whether for a deeper dive into German law and legal culture, or to destinations beyond. Nurturing those broad, cosmopolitan impulses were always the first aim of this book. I remain convinced that those intellectual traits will serve you well in the law, and in life.

Still, along the way you encountered and worked to understand quite a lot of German law. You now know a fair amount about the history of German law. You studied the foundations of the German legal system, covering a wide range of institutions, traditions, and practices. And you had first contact with several prominent fields of German law, including *Privatrecht* (private law), *Öffentliches Recht* (public law, covering constitutional and administrative law), *Strafrecht* (criminal law), *Prozessrecht* (procedural law), and the omnipresent *Europäisches Recht* (European Union law). It was just enough to have learned some of the important concepts and to begin to see a faint sketch of the values and doctrine in each of those fields. All of this positions you to engage confidently with professional colleagues from Germany and it serves as a useful prompt for more work with, and a more thorough study of, German law. Here at the end, you see, it is only the beginning. There is an old German saying: *Nach dem Spiel ist vor dem Spiel!* (After the football match is only before the next football match!).

But you know, by now, that those practical achievements were secondary to the hope that I might persuade you to imagine that German law and legal culture are something more than merely a one-dimensional example of the Civil Law family. Traditional introductions to German law might have settled for that. But the reality is far richer than that common depiction. I've tried to show you that the German legal system is a meeting point for a variety of legal traditions. They are woven together, some more prominently than others, but all constituting the fabric of a dynamic and pluralistic "law world." Germanic tribal custom interacted with Roman Law and Canon Law. The Civil Law tradition ascended with the codification of private law and criminal law in the central European realm that was at last unified as Germany. But it carried with it the

DNA of the Roman Law and Canon Law. The Common Law tradition, especially expressed through Germany's stumbling experience with constitutionalism, arrived and receded until the Basic Law could secure a foothold in the ruins of post-war Germany. Administrative law has particularly been a point of negotiation between these prominent legal traditions. Inquisitorial procedure, rooted in the Civil Law tradition, is in dialogue with the adversarialism typical of the Common Law tradition. Faint but unmistakable threads representing Socialist Law and Islamic Law are there, too. And now, the supranational and neoliberal law of the *sui generis* European Union has arrived to reframe law in Germany.

That colorful and textured depiction of German legal culture (and any other legal culture you might encounter) is so important to me, that I want to take the opportunity presented by this epilogue to make a final case for it. The following excerpt comes from an article in which I sought to apply these principles in the search for a more nuanced and complex understanding of German constitutional law. According to H. Patrick Glenn, we should see dynamism and diversity in the German constitutional regime, which may incline towards the Common Law tradition while nevertheless featuring other threads and other voices. That's exactly what I found. Read the following for what it says about German constitutional law. But more importantly, read it as my closing argument for the "multivalent" way in which I hope you will see the broader German legal culture.

Russell A. Miller
Germany's German Constitutional Law
57 Virginia Journal of International Law 95, 96–97, 99–101, 112–115, 118–128 (2017)[*]

Introduction

Not long ago I visited the German Federal Constitutional Court (*Bundesverfassungsgericht*) with a group of my American law students. When our tour of the Court reached the luminous, wood-and-glass hearing chamber, our guide triumphantly declared: "Welcome to the only common law court in Germany!"

It would have pleased the legendary comparative law scholar H. Patrick Glenn to hear it. In his seminal work, *Legal Traditions of the World*, he argues that legal systems such as Germany's cannot be categorically classified as emblematic of a single legal tradition. Glenn contends that state legal systems are the sites of encounters between the world's complex, commensurable, and interdependent legal traditions. He uses words such as "bridging," "dialogue," and "interchange" to describe this unavoidable dynamic, which he imagined to be something similar to Russian nesting dolls, with lateral traditions and subtraditions supporting and complementing a system's leading or primary tradition. The tour guide at the Constitutional Court seemed to have all of this in mind, implying that German constitutional law (embodied by the Constitutional Court) represents the

[*] Excerpt reprinted with permission of the author and the *Virginia Journal of International Law*.

subaltern common law tradition asserting itself in the German legal culture, which is predominantly shaped by the continental or civil law tradition.

* * *

Yet, although there is considerable evidence of constitutional common law's ascendance in contemporary German legal culture, Glenn understood that the encounters between legal traditions within a particular system are reciprocal affairs. The post-war constitutional regime profoundly introduced elements of the common law tradition into the German legal culture. But the old, predominant civilian legal tradition in Germany has influenced German constitutional law, too. Glenn suggests that the interaction of these legal traditions would "blur the distinction between the two" and that both traditions would become subject to "multivalent, bridging, complexity" involving "rejection, limitation, accommodation or even adoption." It is on this unremarked dynamic – the civil law tradition's influence on Germany's constitutional law – that I want to focus in this article. [...] There is evidence of this influence in the character of the constitutional text, in some constitutional theory, in the lingering priority given to the legislature (as opposed to the judiciary) to develop and refine the constitutional framework [...] and in the Constitutional Court's civilian decisional style.

My analysis is significant for comparative lawyers' work because it suggests that German constitutional law – if it is to be studied and understood at all – must be taken on its own complex, multivalent terms. Of course, the common law/civil law interdependence I describe here is just one such distinctly contextual facet of German constitutional law. There are other influences – ranging from the expansive sweep of political history to the contributions made by discrete individuals – that make equally important explanatory and determinative contributions to the tapestry of contemporary German constitutional law. As comparative lawyers we ignore this thick web of meaning at the risk of engaging with nothing more than a chimera of German constitutional law. The object of comparative lawyers' study cannot be an abstract classification or taxonomic archetype of constitutional law, at least not if we want to be saying anything about something. As this study demonstrates, the Basic Law anchors a highly contingent and contextually determined constitutional regime that features a unique mix of distinct kinds of common law and civil law traditions and much, much more: it is Germany's German constitutional law.

* * *

Half the Story: German Constitutional Law as the Triumph of the Common Law Tradition over the Civil Law Tradition

There is an almost messianic narrative about post-war German law that suggests that the Basic Law has vanquished the formalistic and positivistic impulses in the German legal culture that are the residue of the civil law tradition's historical predominance in Germany. This myth depends on four premises. The first is that German legal culture is steeped in the civil law tradition's statutory formalism and positivism. The second is that constitutional law, with its focus on judicial interpretation and case-by-case decision-making, resembles the common law. The third is that the German Constitutional Court, as the guardian of the constitution (and, thereby, the prophet of the common law tradition in Germany's civilian desert), has had to struggle against the enduring dominance of the civil law in post-war Germany. The fourth is that the German Constitutional Court has triumphed in this struggle, ushering in an era of previously unattainable constitutional law and justice – of *Rechtsstaatlichkeit*. Each of these premises has a basis in truth [...].

* * *

The Post-War Civil Law/Common Law Clash in the German Legal Culture

[…] The third premise of this prevalent narrative is that the civil law and the common law traditions have found themselves in conflict with one another, vying for the soul of the German jurist.

In fact, that tension is on spectacular display in Karlsruhe, Germany. On the northern edge of this charming little city known as the *Hauptstadt des Rechts* ("Capital of Justice"), the "new" Constitutional Court serves as the "protector of the *Grundgesetz*" from its sleek, modern, Bauhaus-influenced building. But the Constitutional Court has had to carve out a place for itself alongside the revered Federal Court of Justice (*Bundesgerichtshof*). From its baroque residence in a leafy neighborhood in the southwest corner of Karlsruhe, the Federal Court of Justice, a most civilian institution, presides as the last-instance jurisdiction over Germany's four great codifications, including the Civil Code. The Federal Court of Justice, in particular, is seen as a bastion of civilian formalism and positivism in Germany. Its judgments have been described as formulaic, abstract, "highly conceptual, even metaphysical," and containing "detailed consideration of the views of contemporary (and past) academic writers." That is classic civilian jurisprudence.

Knut Wolfgang Nörr characterizes this clash of cultures as a struggle between codification and the constitution.

* * *

The Myth of German Constitutional Law's Triumph over Civilian Formalism and Positivism

According to the myth, the result of this culture clash has been constitutional law's victory over the civil law tradition. But constitutional law's triumph in Germany is just another way of saying that the common law tradition now plays a prominent role in the German legal culture where it is in dialogue with the still-predominant formalism and positivism of the civil law tradition.

* * *

Germany's Civilian Constitution

The encounter between the civil law tradition and the common law tradition in the German legal system has not been a one-way street. It is not just Germany's old civilian approach to the law that has been touched by the common law tradition; the civil law tradition has also had an influence on German constitutional law. The gravitational pull of the civil law tradition in Germany is simply too strong for it to have been otherwise.

The evidence of the persistent civilian orientation of German law – even German constitutional law – can be seen, *inter alia*, in the code-like text of the Basic Law, in some theories about constitutional law in Germany […] and in the Constitutional Court's judicial style.

The Basic Law as Code

In many places the text of the Basic Law has the characteristics of a civilian code. Some provisions are famously short and open-textured, such as the terse promise in Article 1 that "human dignity shall be inviolable." These provisions naturally demand a rambling, unfettered interpretive role from the Constitutional Court. And in those places, German constitutional law lurches decisively in the direction of the common law tradition with its confidence in the judiciary. But many other provisions in the Basic Law are long, detailed, and systematic, exceeding even the depth and scope of many paragraphs of the

Civil Code. These provisions, in their precision, seem designed to prescribe a very specific constitutional result rather than map the stars of constitutional values. These code-like constitutional provisions necessarily limit the Constitutional Court's interpretive room to maneuver.

* * *

Several basic rights provisions [...] contain nearly definitive detail. Article 7, for example, addresses the "school system" in six subparagraphs and more than 250 words. Article 12a, speaking to "compulsory military service," involves six subparagraphs and 500 words. Article 13, which provides constitutional protection for the "inviolability of the home," consists of seven subparagraphs and more than 400 words. It is a detailed text that very clearly aspires to a systematic and comprehensive solution to the issues involved. Article 13 is patently deductive in its content and structure. It begins with the broad principle that the home is sacrosanct. It then descends through a series of ever-more-precise exceptions and their accompanying procedural requirements.

American constitutional law may offer similar protection for the sanctity of the home, but it does not build from a similarly concrete textual commitment. [...]

* * *

Constitutional Theory and Constitutional Codification

Theorists in Germany have embraced this codified understanding of the constitution. Peter Unruh has explained that some constitutional theory in Germany, under the influence of the civil law tradition, has sought to treat the Basic Law as part of the civil law tradition. This theoretical approach accepts that constitutions are not a classical example of codification. But it insists that there is no reason why constitutions must be treated as antithetical to civilian codification. In particular, Unruh notes, the Basic Law creates a closed constitutional system that is similar to the comprehensive and complete order framed by the Civil Code. On the one hand, the Basic Law requires that all constitutional change occurs through constitutional amendment. On the other hand, the Basic Law prohibits some constitutional changes. The result of this arrangement is the suggestion that there is no constitutional law beyond the written text of the Basic Law. This is not a place for judicially-conceived penumbras.

A constitution can claim to be a comprehensive and systematic regime addressing the state's organization as well as the relation between the citizen and the state. A constitution can be civilian. [...]

* * *

[...] [Consequently, the Basic Law] is often treated as a codification in German jurisprudence. This also involves the approach scholars take toward constitutional law. Similar to the way the other codes are studied, German constitutional law scholars write commentaries on the Basic Law. These commentaries pursue a systematic exegesis of each article in the constitution. This tradition, a distinct part of the civil law culture, has no equivalent in the United States' common law-oriented constitutional scholarship and practice. Of course, casebooks are almost unknown in Germany.

Werner Heun explains that, in technical terms, constitutional law in Germany has been treated as if it were codified civil law. Constitutional law, Heun notes, is assessed in almost complete accordance with the conditions of the dogmatic science that dominates the practice and study of the codes. This can be seen in several ways. First, "the Constitution is regarded as a predetermined normative decision, which is beyond criticism within the system." Second, constitutional analysis aims for the "systematization of all written and unwritten rules, their interpretation and development." Third, "the interpretation of the Basic Law essentially follows the commonly accepted classical rules and methods that were established already by Friedrich Carl von Savigny in the early nineteenth century." This interpretive canon, similar to civilian statutory interpretation, gives priority to text, system, structure, and teleology. Heun explains that original intent, with its practice of divining meaning from the ether of history and far afield from the constitutional code, "plays only a minor role." Finally, Heun notes that the "Constitutional Court, affirmed by the overwhelming majority of scholars, has always stressed the 'objective meaning' of a provision." This, of course, is the abstract and conceptual approach taken to interpreting comprehensive codes.

The Basic Law's Deference to Statutory Law

The Basic Law's civilian orientation is also evident in its preference for legislative resolution of its interpretive ambiguities. Especially with respect to the protection of basic rights, where the constitutional text might never have achieved code-like detail and precision, the Basic Law often assigns the task of rounding out the meaning of the enumerated rights to the legislature. The common law solution to these uncertainties is to entrust the matter to the courts. The approach adopted by the Basic Law, however, denies the Constitutional Court the fullest possible authority over the Basic Law's meaning. The civil law's confidence in legislation – and its distrust for the judiciary – is unmistakable in this arrangement.

The Constitutional Court is not troubled by its subordination: "The Court has […] stated on numerous occasions that it will not substitute its judgment of sound or wise public policy for that of the legislature." Thus, the Court exercises significant restraint when reviewing legislation that is enacted pursuant to the legislature's authority to define and limit constitutional law, despite the fact that the legislation directly touches upon the enjoyment of a basic right. […] In terms that simply radiate with the residual ethos of the civil law tradition, Hans Jarass explains that, "for the exercise of basic rights, fundamental questions must be settled by the parliament." […]

* * *

The Constitutional Court's Civilian Decisional Style

The Constitutional Court's decisional style also suggests the strong influence the civil law tradition maintains over German constitutional law. Maybe this should not be surprising. After all, the Federal Constitutional Court Act (*Bundesverfassungsgerichtsgesetz*) provides that eight of the Court's justices must have served as judges at the federal high courts, such as the Federal Court of Justice. These federal high courts sit as the last instance of review in disputes arising out of distinct code regimes, including the Civil Code. Judges reach these prestigious ranks of the judiciary by having demonstrated mastery over the civilian application and interpretation of codified law.

The Constitutional Court's decisions unwaveringly hew to a formulaic structure that seems to yearn for the systematic and orderly nature of the civil law, even in the midst of the chaos and liberty that judges confront in the constitutional common law. Every one of the Constitutional Court's judgments follows the same pattern: In Section A., the Court provides an objective presentation of the relevant law, facts, and procedural background, as well as the arguments of complainants. In Section B., the Court provides an objective presentation of the respondents' arguments and the presentations made at a hearing (if one was held), including the contributions to the proceeding from experts in the relevant facts and law. In Section C., the Court announces and justifies its decisions regarding admissibility and the merits of the case. Anyone familiar with the rambling, unsystematic, facts-heavy judicial style of the United States Supreme Court's judgments is immediately struck by the systematic, abstract, and rational structure of the Constitutional Court's decisions.

The following practices also confirm the Constitutional Court's civilian understanding of constitutional law because they reinforce the law's abstract or conceptual nature.

First, the Court almost always reaches its decisions by unanimous judgments. This helps to avoid the impression that constitutional decision-making is a matter of the justices' personal or political preferences. Constitutional law is presented as a coherent and objective normative framework. It does not appear, as is often the case in the judgments of the United States Supreme Court, as a pluralistic and disputed enterprise that lurches toward results only through sometimes-fragile majorities of the justices. The Constitutional Court justices have had a right to publish dissenting opinions since the early 1970s, but, in keeping with the civil law's principled conceptualism, they rarely do so.

Second, the Court has developed highly systematized approaches to its practice in the areas of constitutional interpretation that otherwise would have demanded the greatest discretion and flexibility. In this way, the Court has sought to limit and restrain its role in ways that resonate with the civil law tradition's suspicion of judicial power.

The Court invariably approaches the review of alleged basic rights violations by resorting to a formula prominently promoted by the scholars Bodo Pieroth and Bernhard Schlink (now joined by Thorsten Kingreen and Ralf Poscher). Adjudicating the constitution's basic rights might have involved a nearly unbounded jurisprudential practice, especially when one considers that the broad textual framing rights, such as dignity, personality, and equality must be given. But the Court has yoked itself to a three-part formula that gives its work in this context the feeling of objectivity and scientific inquiry. […]

* * *

Conclusion

My American law students were relieved to hear the tour guide's claim that the German Constitutional Court was the country's common law tribunal. Implied in the claim was the idea that the entire German legal culture was now keyed to the common law. After all, whatever else the American students might have understood about their visit to the Court in Karlsruhe, they knew that the Constitutional Court is Germany's most powerful and important judicial organ. The common law – the tour guide wanted them to believe – now radiates across all German law. This put the young American jurists on stable and familiar ground. It was a different country and a different legal tradition, the sentiment ran, but at least when it comes to constitutional law we speak the same (common law) language. It must have been the familiarity that the tour guide sought to engender with her remark that emboldened that group of too-often-reluctant students to join the discussion about the Court with real interest and vigor. The questions they raised quickly exposed the problems with the tour guide's claim about the Constitutional Court's common law orientation. "Who is the best known justice?" one of the students asked. The tour guide explained that the Court's President often has a significant public profile. But she noted that the Constitutional Court's justices, mostly working anonymously and unanimously, do not enjoy anything like the celebrity of the United States Supreme Court justices. "What was her favorite dissenting opinion?" another student asked. The justices of the Constitutional Court are rarely divided in their votes, the tour guide explained. And when they are, it is even rarer for the dissenters to write a separate opinion. "What is the Court's process for deciding which cases it will consider?" a third student asked. The tour guide explained that the Constitutional Court doesn't select the cases on its docket, but must decide all admissible cases. Another student asked, "What are the standards the Court follows if it wants to abandon its own precedent?" The tour guide explained that the Constitutional Court does not follow the common law doctrine of *stare decisis*. The magic of the earlier moment, stirred when the tour guide declared the Court to be Germany's only common law tribunal, was waning. Maybe it was the bank of clouds that had crept in front of the sun and muted the glow of the Constitutional Court's hearing chamber. But one of my students put it more bluntly. "Well," she said, "this doesn't sound like any common law court I'm familiar with."

Constitutional law has not only been the vehicle for the common law's triumph over civilian formalism and positivism in the post-War German legal culture as the prevailing myth would suggest. German constitutional law has also been colored by the still-predominant civil law tradition. In fact, German constitutional law is distinctly and significantly civilian in character and style. This is nothing more than the symbiotic interchange between legal traditions that H. Patrick Glenn envisioned. The continuously evolving mix of these traditions – as well as of history, and politics, and culture – leaves us undeniably with Germany's uniquely German constitutional law. It suggests that any credible study of German constitutional law must account for the German constitutional regime's civilian orientation and a potentially infinite array of other "traces." […]

Questions/Comments

- I encouraged you earlier in this book to imagine which varied legal traditions might be a part of the chorus that makes up your primary or "national" legal system. Now that you've practiced recognizing diverse traditions in the context of the German legal system (and again, more narrowly, in German constitutional law in the excerpted article), let me urge you to do that again: What legal traditions are present – "bridging," "dialoguing," and "interchanging" – in the legal culture you call home?
- From this excerpt – and from your work with this book – are you able to succinctly state the characteristics of the Civil Law tradition and the Common Law tradition? Could you do that for the other legal traditions that have been mentioned in this book? What would you look for if you wanted to claim that you had identified a new thread, an unremarked or neglected legal tradition, in a particular legal system?
- In this excerpt I argue that a more "complex and multivalent" portrayal of German constitutional law (and, I would insist, law more generally) is necessary to have an encounter with something more than a "chimera" of constitutional law, to be "saying anything about something." Do you agree? Could you thoughtfully engage with German constitutional law if you simply embraced the common law myth about the regime? What if the Germans themselves (as seemed to be the case with the tour guide at the Constitutional Court) don't bother with the composite picture I paint in the article?
- Elements of the myth of the ascendance of constitutional common law in Germany should have been familiar to you from your exposure to these

themes elsewhere in this book. Or, were there new elements, new tones, and new emphases in that story as it was presented in this article?
- Have you ever imagined the constitution of your primary or "national" legal system to be something like a Civil Law codification, a formal, positivist, and systematic rulebook? Were you convinced by the arguments in the article that German constitutional law has Civil Law characteristics? What is it about the Constitutional Court's "decisional style," for example, that suggests the lingering influence of the Civil Law tradition in German constitutional law?

At the very least, this final demonstration might persuade you of the value of pushing past accepted classifications and boundaries in order to see more in the new worlds you encounter. That is a deeply ethical posture, committed to openness and infused with respect and tolerance. More specifically, it might convince you – or confirm for you – that the German legal system, however characterized, consists of much much more than the Civil Law tradition (and the private law regime embodying that tradition). If so, then, alongside everything else you have learned from this book, you will have acquired something marvelous, something grand. As Johann Wolfgang von Goethe, Germany's canonical literary figure, might have put it, you will have encountered a version of Germany's German law that is "an instance worth a thousand ... bearing all within itself."

Index

Alliance for German Law (*Bündnis für das deutsche Recht*), 38

Baer, Susanne, 33, 440
   '*The End of Private Autonomy' or Rights-based Legislation?*, 440
Basic Law (*Grundgesetz*), 63, 67, 87, 104, 114–115, 125, 151–152, 195, 242, 244, 248, 286–289, 297, 302–304, 309–310, 326, 336–337, 357, 386, 416, 434, 464
BGB, values and style, 209
   continuity, historical, 210
   legal science, highly developed, 212
   long shelf life, 212
   nationalism, (German), 212
   process, thorough drafting, 212
   tension, subjective/objective, 210
Bill of Fundamental Rights (*Grundrechte*), 87
Bruce-Jones, Eddie, 434
   Race, Space and the Nation-State, 434
Bündnis 90/Die Grünen (Greens), 134–135, 139
bureaucracy, German, 140, 293, 314

Case, Frankfurt Police Torture, 342, 359, 361, 368, 370, 377, 422
   defense of a third party, 363
   factors, mitigating, 332, 365–366
   Gäfgen Case, 359
   ground, supra-statutory, 365
   human dignity, respect for, 364, 413
   kidnappers, 359
   necessity, 355, 363–364
   relationship, special legal, 365, 379
   torture, 100–101, 181, 252, 361–362, 368–370, 382
Chief Justice Marshall, 256
Christian Democratic Union, 134, 146, 330
Christian Social Union, 134, 146
Civil Law tradition, the central elements of the, 44

   authority, "higher instance" of, 46
   codification effect, 55–56
   enactments, legislative, 50, 55
   Enlightenment, 38, 45, 47–49, 51–53, 56, 92, 107, 110, 142, 156, 196, 246, 341–342, 380, 404
   norm, general universal legal, 48
   objectivity, 18, 27–28, 50, 54, 64, 73, 77–79, 108, 191, 246, 350, 355, 369, 375, 412, 439, 467
   truth, absolute, 48
   written law, judicial applications of the, 47
Code, French, 55, 110, 200, 209, 211–214, 400
Code, Prussian, 199–200, 213
codification, constitutional, 465
constitutionalism, German, 70, 111, 114–115, 117, 232, 237, 244–245, 248, 252–253, 270, 274, 286, 294
   Basic Law's supremacy, 249, 253
   Bill of Rights, 112–113, 249–250, 252
   human dignity, prioritization of, 252
   "new constitutionalism," 248, 253
   rights, conditional, 250
   "supra-positive" norms, 251, 253
   value, objective, 251, 434
constitutionalization, 96
controlling opinion (*herrschende Meinung*), 197, 231
Court, Hamburg Regional, 87, 232, 236
Court, Moabit, 149–150
crime novel (*der Krimi*), 376
Crucifix Case, 148, 152
Curran, Vivian Grosswald, 32–33, 45, 92, 110, 239
   Romantic Common Law, Enlightened Civil Law, 45
Currie, David P., 288–289, 311

David, René, 10, 34, 38, 189, 195, 335
democracy, parliamentary, 117, 251

Index

democracy, representative, 135, 452
detective novel (*der Detektivroman*), 376
deterrence, general, 413
deterrence, specific, 413
Deutsche Telekom, 392–394, 396
Die Welt (*The World*), 419, 421
Dieselgate scandal, 396, 398–399
   collective redress, 396–397
   corporatism, 397–398
   Eurolegalism, 396, 398
   legal proceedings, marketisation of, 397
   model declaratory proceedings (*Musterfeststellungsklage*), 397
   protection, consumer, 392, 396–399, 430–432, 442
difference, cultural, 26, 32, 232, 462
difference engineers, 26
differencing, 28–29, 31, 175, 247, 390
dispute, a suretyship contract, 223
   accessoriness (*Akzessorietät*), 230
distancing, 28–29, 31, 175, 390
diversity-deficit, 191
Dubber, Markus Dirk, 343, 377
   The Promise of German Criminal Law, 343

East German Disbarment Case, 181
   assessment, proportionality, 184
   commissions, review, 182
   crossings, illegal border, 185
   Ministry for State Security (*Stasi*), 181–182, 185
economic criminal law (*Wirtschaftsstrafrecht*), 406
effect, horizontal, 67, 92, 243–244, 272, 274, 276, 284–285, 434
Eser, Albin, 351
   justification and excuse, 351
European legal tradition, Free Trade and a Neoliberal Agenda, 427
   Beer Purity Law, 430–431
   capitalism, market, 428
   Cassis de Dijon, 428, 430, 432
   market, common, 2, 423, 428, 430, 450
   Rewe-Zentrale AG v. Bundesmonopolverwaltung für Branntwein, 428
European legal tradition, supranational and supreme, 422
   character, supranational, 425, 447, 458
   Costa v. ENEL, 425–426
   direct effect, 418, 422, 424–425
   European law, Supremacy of, 418, 425
   Van Gend en Loos, 422, 424–427

Europeanization of German law, contract law, 418, 432, 448
   Art. 3 para 3 GG, 434
   Directives, antidiscrimination, 433–435, 442–443, 447
   freedom and equality, 328, 440–441
   General Act on Equal Treatment (*Allgemeines Gleichbehandlungsgesetz*), 239, 418–419, 436, 444–445, 448, 460
   "legal vandalism," 438, 442
   Minus "Ossi" Case, 444, 447–448
   private parties, 272, 276, 434–435
Europeanization of German law, limits to the, 448
   Article 23, 419, 448–449, 451
   deficit, democratic, 449
   European Arrest Warrant Case, 453
   Greek Rescue Package, 456
   Honeywell Case, 455
   limits, constitutional, 308, 449, 453, 456
   Lisbon Treaty, 378, 451, 454–455, 457, 460
   Lisbon Treaty Case, 378, 451, 454–455, 457, 460
   Maastricht Treaty, 451–453
   Maastricht Treaty Case, 452
   openness, constitutional, 450–451
   "political question," 451, 455
   principle, democratic state, 451–453, 455–457
   review, identity, 455
   Solange I Case, 449
   Solange II, 450, 452, 455
ex officio, 173, 400, 408, 411, 413
executive power, German, 136
   administration, public, 91, 136, 139, 161, 306
   chancellor's democracy (*Kanzlerdemokratie*), 124, 136
   Chancellor's Office (*Bundeskanzleramt*), 137
   Federal President (*Bundespräsident*), 136, 141, 152, 180, 259, 264–265, 316
   state governors (*Ministerpräsidenten*), 136, 258
   vote-of-confidence, 124, 137, 152

families, legal, 10–16, 18, 32, 38, 69–70, 238
family, the Civil Law, 39, 69–70, 461
family, the Common Law, 70
Federal Council of States (*Bundesrat*), 130, 257, 259, 264–265
   interests of the states (Länder), 132
   veto power, 112, 133, 310–311
the Federal Government (*Bundesregierung*), 130, 264–265

Federal Lawyer's Act
  (*Bundesrechtsanwaltsordnung*), 155, 190
Federal Minister of Justice, 1, 38, 146
Federal Parliament (*Bundestag*), 123, 130, 137,
  141, 255, 257, 259, 264–267, 308, 368
  cabinet ministers, 123–124, 132, 138, 141
  Chancellor, Federal, 132
  institution, popularly elected, 130
  political party (Fraktionen), 131
federalism, cooperative, 123
federalism, dual sovereignty, 123
federalism, German, 123, 128–130, 142,
  309–310
  federalism, cooperative, 129–130, 140,
    142–144, 291
feudalism, 41
formalism, legal, 67, 93
France, xxiii, xxiv, 19, 38, 41–43, 47–48, 50, 58,
  96, 112, 126, 136, 214, 240, 316, 338, 422,
  428, 434, 454
  law, French, 20, 22–23, 42, 50, 103, 199,
    209–210
  Napoleon, 42, 62, 103–104, 111, 273
Frankenberg, Günter, 27, 33, 289
Frankfurt, University of, 78, 171
Free Democratic Party, 134
Freund, Ernst, 204, 215, 239
  The Proposed German Civil Code, 215, 239
functionality, principle of, 23
fundamentalists, Islamic, 330–331

GDR Criminal Court Judge II Case, 185
  trials, political, 185
Gerber, David J., 106–107
  idea-systems in law, 107
German administrative law, qualities of, 294
  Administrative Procedure Act
    (*Verwaltungsverfahrensgesetz*), 291–292,
    295–297, 306, 336
  administrative regulations (*allgemeine
    Verwaltungsvorschriften*), 261, 296, 314
  codification, patch-work, 295
  constitutional law, expression of, 294
  mandate, statutory, 256, 291, 296
  statutory instruments
    (*Rechtsverordnungen*), 296, 314
German administrative law–substance, 299
  administration, legality of, 305
  Bundesrat approval, 132–133, 311–312
  discretion, administrative, 304–305, 309
  equality, principle of, 243, 291, 303–304
  federal law, state enforcement of, 312

federalism, administrative, 123–124, 295,
  307, 310, 312–314
formal Rechtsstaat, 249, 302
review, *ex post* judicial, 293, 300, 310, 334
review, substantive judicial, 305, 309, 327, 334
rights, procedural, 304
substantive Rechtsstaat, 302
German Civil Code (*Bürgerliches Gesetzbuch*),
  63, 95, 108, 111, 196–198, 204–205, 209,
  214, 227, 240–241, 386, 434
German Civil Code, regulatory technique
  of the, 214
  brackets principle (*Klammerprinzip*), 218
  family law, 215, 296
  general part, 196, 215, 296, 340–341,
    344–345, 351
  The Law of Obligations, 215
  Law of Succession, 215
  The Law of Things, 215
  legal scholars, the commentary of, 219
German Civil Code and the Civil Law
  tradition, 199
  codification dispute (*Kodifikationsstreit*),
    106, 203
  legitimacy, superior, 204
  nation building, 204
  Section 138, BGB, 208, 282, 382
  Section 242, BGB, 208–209
  system, organized, 58, 200, 203
German Criminal Code (*Strafgesetzbuch*), 144,
  340–341
  general part (*Allgemeine Teil*), 341
  special part (*Besonderer Teil*), 341
German criminal law, theory and logic of, 343
  achievement, scientific, 345
  analysis, tripartite, 345, 351, 359, 363, 367, 377
  blameworthiness (*Schuld*), 172, 340, 343–344,
    351–352, 354–355, 365, 367–369, 376, 407
  criminal offense system (*Straftatsystem*),
    340, 343–344, 356
  elements of the crime
    (*Tatbestandsmäßigkeit*), 367
  formalism, taxonomical, 347
  law, substantive criminal, 347
  necessity, excusing, 351, 354–355
  necessity, justifying, 351, 353–355
  principle of blameworthiness
    (*Schuldprinzip*), 342, 358
  professoriate, 344–347
German law, alternative histories of, 117
  jurists, Jewish, 117, 119, 121
  tradition, Jewish legal, 118

Index

German legal culture, tapestry of, 7, 32, 39, 56, 92, 189, 237, 244, 286, 293, 328
Germany's German constitutional law, 7, 462–463
Glenn, H. Patrick, 10–12, 34, 38, 40, 65, 245, 287–288, 459, 462, 468
   Comparative Legal Families and Comparative Legal Traditions, 12, 34, 288
   Legal Traditions of the World, 11, 35, 40, 65, 287, 459, 462
Goethe, Johann Wolfgang von, 156, 193, 469
   Faust, 156–157, 193

Halberstam, Michael, 392, 416
   The American Advantage in Civil Procedure, 392
Harlan, Veit, 87–88, 276, 285
Heun, Werner, 106, 111–112, 121, 465
   The Constitution of Germany, 112, 121
history, new German legal, 106
   German Basic Law of 1949, 90, 114
   German Civil Code, the creation of the, 108
   German Reich in 1871, 108
   idea-systems, 107
   monarchs, 103, 112, 301
   period, German Romantic, 107–108
   unification, national, 108–109, 248
   Weimar Constitution, 104, 113–114, 118, 132, 145, 248, 255, 303
history, old German legal, 97
   Charlemagne, 42, 99–100, 104
   Church, Catholic, 99–100, 102–103
   Digest, 40, 98–100, 273
   feud or vendetta, 98–99
   glossators, 58, 99
   humanism, juristic, 102
   Justinian, 37, 40, 44, 62, 96, 98, 199
   Law, Canon, 96, 99–103, 105, 117, 120, 461
   law, Roman-Canon (*ius commune*), 100–101, 103
   norms, customary, 98, 101, 103–104, 106
   Revolution, The French, 103
   tribes, Germanic, 98
Hoffmann-Riem, Wolfgang, 270, 289
   Two Hundred Years of Marbury v. Madison, 270, 289
horizontal effect (*Drittwirkung*), 272, 289
   Suretyship Case, 276–277, 283–285
Human Rights, European Court of, 359, 368–369, 377, 422
Hungary, 187, 195

Imperial Parliament (*Reichstag*), 116, 204, 206, 212
integration, European, 160, 163, 242, 419, 421, 430, 449–453, 456–457
Italy, xxiv, 41–42, 47, 431

John, Michael, 107–108
judges, East German, 175–178, 180–181, 183, 188
   disputes, social context of, 177
   hours, legal consultation, 177
   justice, substantive, 178, 302, 305
   pedagogic dictatorship (*eine Erziehungsdiktatur*), 177
   solutions, politically correct, 177
judicial review, the Federal Constitutional Court, 256
   complaints, constitutional, 91, 145, 259–260, 271, 277, 279–280, 322
   conflicts, federal-state, 259
   First Senate, 90, 257, 322
   Organstreit proceedings, 259
   political parties, unconstitutionality of, 264
   posture, passive, 218, 260
   proportionality analysis, 172, 243, 268–270, 275, 285, 291, 307, 321, 326, 334
   review, abstract judicial, 259, 265
   review, concrete judicial, 259, 266–267
   Scheffler, Erna, 258
   Second Senate, 257, 450, 453, 456
   selection, judicial, 258
judicial system, German, 142–144, 146, 148–149, 307
   Courts Constitution Act (*Gerichtsverfassungsgesetz*), 141–142, 144, 152
   decentralization, 126, 142–144, 146, 148
   Federal Court of Justice (*Bundesgerichtshof*), 142, 145, 230, 272, 278, 348, 357, 393, 417, 464
   first-instance courts (*Amtsgerichte* and *Landgerichte*), 143, 149, 307
   intermediate appellate courts (*Oberlandesgerichte*), 143
   judiciary, independence of the, 142
   jurisdictions, specialized subject matter, 143, 385
   specialization, 142–145, 148, 154, 157, 180
   supreme federal courts (*Bundesgerichte*), 143, 145
jurisprudence, paper, 73–74

Kagan, Robert, 383
  Adversarial Legalism, 383–384, 396, 415
Kantorowicz, Hermann, 67–68, 71, 94, 144
  The Battle for Legal Science, 71, 74, 94
  Flavius, Ganeus, 71
Karlsruhe, 145, 243, 261–262, 289, 308, 349, 447, 464, 467
Kelsen, Hans, 67, 76–77, 94, 118, 121, 443
  Judicial Formalism and Pure Jurisprudence, 76
killings, honor, 330, 332
Kommers, Donald P., 194, 248, 257, 288, 449
Korioth, Stefan, 157
  Legal Education in Germany Today, 157
Kubler, Friedrich, 55

Ladeur, Karl-Heinz, 438
  The German Proposal of an 'Anti-Discrimination'-Law, 438
Langbein, John H., 387, 400
  The German Advantage in Civil Procedure, 387, 393
  Land without Plea Bargaining, 400
Langenbacher, Eric, 125, 131, 151
  The German Polity, 125, 131, 151
law, chthonic, 41–42
law, customary, 41, 44, 96, 101, 103, 105, 204, 211, 237
Law, Islamic, 11, 70, 292–293, 314, 316, 318, 328–329, 334, 339, 462
law, moral, 79
law, natural, 67, 93
law, pure theory of, 67, 77–78, 85
  positive law, theory of, 77
Law, Socialist, 11, 189, 462
law, substantive, 1, 41–43, 46, 81, 166, 169, 172, 257, 273, 381–382, 385
law, Swiss, 41
Law, Western, 11, 38
lawlessness, statutory, 82–83, 175
lawyers, East German, 176, 178–182, 187
  educators, 177, 180
  Gysi, Gregor, 179–180, 184
  journal *Neue Justiz*, 179
  legality, socialist, 178
  process, ideological cleansing, 176
  specialists, 25, 176, 178, 214
learning, the dialectic of, 28
legal education, German, 7, 148, 154–157, 161–164, 167, 176, 194, 399
  attorneys at law (*Rechtsanwälte*), 155, 157
  classes, private repetition, 159
  complete jurist (*Einheitsjurist*), 154, 157, 160–163, 193
  compulsory subjects (*Pflichtfächer*), 158
  elective subject (*Schwerpunktbereich*), 158
  examination, state, 157–159
  first examination, 159–160
  formally admitted to the bar (*Assessoren*), 157
  legal studies at university, 157–158
  practical training (*Referendarzeit*), 4, 154, 157, 159–161, 163–164
  second state examination, 160
  students in practical training (*Referendare*), 159–160
  young lawyer (*Assessor*), 157
legal science (*Rechtswissenschaft*), 5, 37, 57, 71, 78, 144, 194–195, 212, 336
  expansion, logical, 60, 71
  lacunae, 49, 60, 75, 218
  method, scientific, 17, 59, 61
  Pandectists, 61
  professors, law, 58, 61–62, 109, 176, 346
  scholar, the civil law, 58
  scientists, legal, 60, 62, 78, 346
Legrand, Pierre, 18–21, 32–33, 35, 44, 54–55, 65, 78, 94, 443, 460
  difference, comparative law of, 26
  The Impossibility of 'Legal Transplants', 18, 21, 24, 94
  Negative Comparative Law, 18, 20, 23, 54
  The Same and the Different, 18–19, 23, 56
Lehmann, Marc, 419
  new EU-directive regulates lawnmowing, 419
Leipzig, 145, 156, 201, 308, 349, 420
liberalism, 76, 108–109, 196, 207, 237, 255, 380, 441
Life Imprisonment Case, 412–413, 417
Limbach, Jutta, 47, 191, 195, 258
Lindseth, Peter L., 309, 336
  Review Essay–Comparing Administrative States, 309
Lüth, Erich, 87
Lüth Case, 89–90, 92–93, 95, 115, 274–275, 285, 289
  human dignity, respect for, 88
  opinion, freedom of, 88–89, 91–92, 243, 353, 457
  values, objective order of, 70, 88–90, 92, 171, 251, 274, 276–277, 285, 435
macro-comparison, 10

Markovits, Inga, 175–176, 195
  Children of a Lesser God, 176, 195
Marx, 33, 171, 335–336
Mattei, Ugo, 15, 19, 35
Merryman and Pérez-Perdomo, 14, 56, 57, 62, 64, 188, 198
  the Civil Law tradition, 57
method, criminal law, 172
method, German legal, 168–169, 188
  approach, methodological, 164
  basis, hypothetical legal, 165, 168
  claim, enforceability of the, 166
  claim, object of the, 165
  dichotomy, private/public, 170
  facts of a problem, 164
  judgment style (*Urteilsstil*), 167
  language, legal, 166
  legal opinion style (*Gutachtenstil*), 167
  preconditions, 164–166, 168, 399
  private lecturers (*Repetitoren*), 164
  problem-solving, efficient, 167
  relationships, claim, 154, 164–165, 167, 172
  solve (*lösen*), 169
method of statutory interpretation, 173
  plain-meaning, 173
  teleology, 35, 173
methods, public law, 171
  claim, admissibility of a, 171
  Code of Administrative Court Procedure (*Verwaltungsgerichtsordnung*), 171, 386
  Federal Constitutional Court Act (*Bundesverfassungsgerichtsgesetz*), 171, 244, 257, 263, 271, 326, 386, 466
  proportionality principle (*Verhältnismäßigkeitsgrundsatz*), 172, 243, 268, 270, 291, 297, 326
micro-comparison, 10
Movement, Free Law, 67, 71, 74–76, 79, 94
  gaps in the code, 72, 75
  philosophy, natural law, 75
  realism, American legal, 71
myth, 463–464, 468

Nolte, Georg, 300, 335
  General Principles of German and European Administrative Law, 300, 336
Nörr, Knut Wolfgang, 272, 464
  From Codification to Constitution, 272

object, mere, 252, 364, 412
object formula (*Objektformel*), 252
ownership, 19, 40–41, 215, 221

Palandt, 231–232
Party, Communist, 175, 181, 183–184, 189
party democracy (*Parteiendemokratie*), 124, 134
patriotism, constitutional, 286–287
people's parties (*Volksparteien*), 134, 137
Plea Bargains Case, 410, 412–413
  Plea Bargaining Act, 410–412
Poland, xxiv, 187, 195
police law (*Polizeirecht*), 297, 405
positivism, legal, 67, 93
post-war Germany, 92, 130, 137–138, 440, 462–463
powers, separation of, 58, 103, 117, 145, 243, 249, 256, 260, 291, 294, 297, 407
Printz v. United States, 151, 313, 337
private autonomy (*Privatautonomie*), 170, 196, 210, 277, 380, 389, 392, 395–396, 404, 433, 435
procedural law, German, 101, 105, 173, 190, 376, 382, 385–387, 398, 414
  civil procedure, German, 380–382, 385, 387, 389–394, 396, 399, 404
  discovery, lack of, 393
  individual autonomy (*Privatautonomie*), 170, 358, 369, 375, 377, 389, 404, 440
  lawyer, modest role of the, 391
  parties' authority over the process (*Dispositionsmaxime*), 380, 389–390
  parties' responsibility for the facts of the case (*Verhandlungsmaxime*), 380, 389–390
procedure, adversarial, 380, 398, 401, 421
  advocacy, legal, 384
  class action, 381, 392, 394–399
  "discovering" evidence, 392
  groups, interest, 212, 384, 397–398
  justice, adversarial, 383, 385, 389, 399
  party influence, 384
procedure, German criminal, 306, 381, 399–400, 403–407, 413
  agreement (*Absprache*), 406–407
  Code of Criminal Procedure (*Strafprozessordnung*), 63, 103, 144, 372, 381, 386, 400, 402, 407–409, 416
  compulsory prosecution (*Legalitätsprinzip*), 402–403
  confession, 401
  discretionary non-prosecution (*Opportunitätsprinzip*), 402
  the dossier, 388, 401
  innocence, presumption of, 403, 413
  right to remain silent, 359, 401, 403
  system, inquisitorial, 100, 385, 391, 400, 408

procedure, inquisitorial, 101, 105, 380
  authority, hierarchical, 383
  justice, inquisitorial, 383, 385, 387
  legalism, inquisitorial, 383
  process, bureaucratic, 383, 386
process, inquisitorial, 100, 349, 367, 398
public law (Öffentliches Recht), 294
punishing state (strafende Staat), 170

racism, 163, 432–433, 435
Radbruch, Gustav, 67–68, 74, 79–80, 94, 302
  Statutory Lawlessness and Supra-Statutory Law, 79–80
Radbruch Formula, 67, 84–85
ratification, 113, 215, 237, 368, 451–452, 454–455
realism, legal, 75–76, 93–94
realists, legal, 75
reasoning, deductive, 37
reasoning, inductive, 37
Reimann, Mathias, 12, 34–35, 93, 194, 205, 211–212, 240, 288, 290, 337, 377, 459
  The Good, the Bad, and the Ugly, 212
religion, 25, 29, 102, 128, 191, 243, 247, 249, 251, 253, 292, 320, 323–325, 327–328, 338, 418, 436, 441, 445, 457
Ritual Slaughter Cases, 318
  animals, protection of, 299, 323, 325
  freedom, occupational, 299, 322–324, 327
  freedom, religious, 117, 320, 323, 328, 331, 334
  restrictions, halal dietary, 321
  Sunni Islam, 321–322, 325, 328
Robbers, Gerhard, 65, 85–86, 94, 120, 195, 379, 415
Romanticism, 45–51, 65, 92, 142, 156, 246
Rome, 39–40, 100, 107, 350, 422–423, 425, 432, 454
  Empire, Roman, 42
Rose-Ackerman, Susan, 292, 300, 309, 336

sameness, 19–20, 23, 56
Schirach, Ferdinand von, 370–371
Schorling, Felix, 97–98, 120
  A Deeper History of German Law, 98, 120
Schultz, Ulrike, 149, 153
Schuster, Ernest J., 199, 240
  The German Civil Code, 199, 206, 227, 239–241, 341
seisin (saisine, gewehr), 41
separation thesis, 78, 84, 329, 443
similarity, presumption of, 23
Social Democratic Party of Germany, 130, 134, 435

social oil, drops of, 232, 237, 277, 432
sovereignty, dual, 142
sovereignty, popular, 112–113, 117, 245, 249, 452
Spain, 41, 332, 341
Stork, Florian, 434
  Comments on the Draft of the New German Private Law, 434
Strasbourg, 156, 422
studies, comparative legal, 2–3, 8, 11, 16–17, 19–20, 23, 25, 27, 38, 314
  law, macro-comparative, 10–12, 14–17, 32, 38, 69–70
  legal origins, 54, 238–239
subjectivity, 17–18, 27–30, 32, 78–79, 252
system, codified legal, 38, 69
system, German legal, 1, 4–7, 10–11, 15, 17, 30–31, 38, 69–70, 86–87, 97, 115, 125, 145, 155, 161, 174–175, 178, 180, 187–189, 192, 197–198, 206, 208–210, 244, 247, 270, 272–274, 294, 333, 383, 385, 399–400, 414, 421, 428, 458, 461, 464, 468–469
  procedural law, adversarial tradition of, 6
  tradition, Islamic Legal, 6, 16, 292, 328, 333, 421
  tradition, Socialist Legal, 6, 155, 189, 328
  tradition, *sui generis* European Legal, 6, 418, 425, 449, 453, 462
system, "national" legal, 1, 4, 8, 25, 30, 53, 68, 106, 148, 162, 180, 205, 231, 236, 247, 263, 285, 333, 349, 358, 375, 384, 468

Terror, 369–371, 375–376
  aircraft, hijacked, 372
  terrorists, 370, 374
third-effect (*Drittwirkung*), 67, 92, 243–245, 272–273, 276–277, 284–285, 434–435, 443

ultra vires, 301, 418, 452, 455

Valcke, Catherine, 209, 240
  Comparative History and the Internal View of French, German, and English Private Law, 209, 240
values, objective order of, 67, 87–88, 243, 251

Watson, Alan, 19, 24, 33, 35
  legal transplants, 24
Weimar Republic, 113, 126, 131–132, 135, 145, 301–302, 304
Whitman, James, 107–108
will, free, 73, 196, 358, 380
Wolff, Lutz-Christian, 164
  Structured Problem Solving, 164